Praise for Gruber's SAT® prep system . . .*

Students often ask, "How can I raise my SAT score?" My advice is to buy Dr. Gruber's book.
—*Mathematics Teacher, official journal of the National Council of Teachers of Mathematics*

The most scholarly, useful, and complete work of its kind now on the market.—*Henry Lewenberg, Chairman, English Department, Channel Island High School, Oxnard, California*

The best book I've seen in ages. It not only helps you learn the material but also teaches you what you did wrong. It gives you so many different tips on how to approach different types of problem questions. It raised my score from an 890 to a 1410. Thank you Gruber—this is the best!—*Amazon customer review*

A teacher who recommends an SAT preparation book should do so only if the book follows the actual exam closely in regard to format, question types, and level of difficulty. Gruber's SAT is such a book.—*Robert Frankel, Math Department Chairman, Tottenville High School, Staten Island, New York*

Very comprehensive. The kid is learning!—*Amazon customer review*

Best SAT prep book. Period. Gruber's is by far the best SAT prep book around. I am a mathematics tutor (K through calculus, 25+ years), and this is the only SAT prep book I recommend to my SAT prep students, as well as to my own children, when they are preparing for the SAT! This book is well worth the minor cost, and more effective than any SAT course my students have attended. . . . Two of my children increased their scores by 100 points per section—300 points total—just by using this book.—*Amazon customer review*

I was able to solve questions three to five times faster with your methods. As soon as you gave me a strategy, it clicked and I was just tickled that somebody finally exposed the code to efficient thinking.—*Dr. Larry Weitz, Psychologist, WLAC Radio, Nashville, Tennessee*

I only wish he'd written this book when I took the SAT.—*Peter Cleaveland, ABC Network News*

"Excellent-plus" for the Math Refresher section and for the explanatory answers to the questions in the Practice Tests.—*John J. Bailey, Math Department Supervisor, Kingston City Schools, Kingston, New York*

The Gruber program contains strategies that teachers can teach their students to use to achieve better scores on the SAT and other standardized tests. They also help students improve and refine their basic thinking and reasoning skills. Dr. Gruber's methods emphasize skills and strategies that lead to correct answers rather than reliance on rote memorization.—*Dana McDougald, School Library Journal*

I thank you and my 15-year-old son (high school jr.) thanks you.—*Ted Koppel*

The explanatory answers for the practice tests are superlative.—*Bob Ingalls, English Chairman, Mount Vernon High School, Alexandria, Virginia*

Truly the best SAT preparation book out there. . . . This book does not focus on drill, drill, drill, but instead on enhancing Critical Thinking Skills and teaching the Strategies needed to succeed on the SAT. The Strategies and Critical Thinking Skills in this book reflect those of the test-makers themselves and are a sure thing for SAT success! I would highly recommend it to anyone taking the SAT. The methods in this book will last a lifetime!—*Amazon customer review*

By learning Dr. Gruber's strategies, a student can do well on *any* exam, not just the SAT.—Teen *magazine*

This book is full of excellent strategies for how to take tests. I would recommend this book for any kid starting high school! Really, the people who tend to do best on tests are those who understand the process . . . not those who regurgitate information. When kids learn strategies, their scores will naturally rise even if they do not know all the answers. Glad I bought this, and will be using it for my kids in high school as well as the one entering in a few years!—*Amazon customer review*

Gruber's book is no "quick" fix—instead it's a sure way. That's what I think is important—a sure way, more than a trick or something that might get you the answer.—*Amazon customer review*

As the name says, indeed this book is a *complete* SAT guide. In this book you can find all grammar required for the SAT writing test in one place . . . as well as vocabulary. . . . The Math Refresher covers all math concepts needed for the SAT. Students who are self-motivated, focused, and hardworking can use this book and achieve great scores, and can save a lot of time and money not having to go to an SAT test prep center.—*Amazon customer review*

As a college admissions consultant, SAT tutor, and Harvard alumnus, I highly recommend Gruber as a terrific guide and superb tool to help students prepare for the SAT test. Gruber provides detailed explanations. . . . His overview of math, grammar, vocabulary, critical reading and writing is outstanding. He is simply the best!—*Amazon customer review*

What distinguishes this SAT review book from the others on the market is the emphasis on thinking rather than drill.—English Journal, *official magazine of the National Council of Teachers of English*

This is simply a great book. It is organized into clear, concise strategies. After reading this book, I can safely say that I am confident in my math abilities. If you don't understand it, you're probably just skimming through it. Don't do that. Absorb it all, because each and every word is important. —*Amazon customer review*

We've used the Gruber text in our community SAT prep programs for over five years with excellent results. A student using this inexpensive book is getting an experience comparable to any $1000 course. Gruber's book is excellent.—*Amazon customer review*

The Best Book on the SAT.—*CBS Radio*

What Dr. Gruber is giving the student is an increase in intelligence. . . . Gruber offers students preparation in test-taking strategies designed to save time in the testing room by zeroing in on a fast, logical way to answer a problem. . . . Get what you've missed out of four years of high school. —*Valerie Sullivan, United Press International*

With the use of Gruber's special techniques, students can raise their test scores significantly and increase their general learning ability.—Courier Journal, *Louisville, Kentucky*

Your approach to using the test as a vehicle for developing critical thinking skills is clear, practical, and very positive. Your regard for the test experience as a way for students to participate in the inherent joy of problem solving . . . was made "alive" for us by your obvious enthusiasm for [meeting] the kinds of challenges presented by the SAT/PSAT.—*Laura Alvarenga, Assistant Superintendent, San Francisco Unified School District*

Top rating for the book in the areas of readability, vocabulary, critical thinking skills, and practice tests —with a special star for the explanatory answers.—*Paulette Dewey, English Department Chairperson, Robert S. Rogers High School, Toledo, Ohio*

This is the man who knows the ins and outs of testing.—*Bob Lee,* Bob Lee Magazine, *KSL Radio, Salt Lake City, Utah*

[Dr. Gruber's book] is the only commercial book that I've seen that would actually help a test-taker.—*David Owen,* Washington Post

Dr. Gruber is recognized as the leading expert on standardized tests. His results have been lauded throughout the country. His personal presentation spreads "contagious enthusiasm" like an epidemic with his audiences.—*Public Broadcasting Service*

Gary Gruber is the Guru of College Testing Programs.—The Light, *San Antonio Texas*

Register Your Book!

It's quick and easy, and it connects you to Dr. Gruber, study alerts, continuing advice, bonus features, and premium content. Most important, registration will make your experience with The Gruber Method personal. Just go to DaviesPublishing.com/Gruber/SAT/book-registration and follow the instructions. It will be helpful to have your book's ISBN at hand. Thank you!

Established in 1981, Davies Publishing Inc. has a long history of publishing landmark works in medicine, surgery, and diagnostic imaging. It is currently a leader in education, test preparation, and continuing education in diagnostic medical sonography. Now we are excited to be extending our reach to students bound for college and graduate programs. We never forget that it is a privilege to help our customers succeed in both learning and life.

---

*This book is a brand-new edition specifically tuned for the New SAT® exam by Dr. Gruber personally. The praise for Dr. Gruber's previous editions quoted here is documented.

GRUBER'S
COMPLETE
NEW SAT® GUIDE 2018

20th Edition

Gary R. Gruber, Ph.D.

The City College of New York (B.S., Physics)
Columbia University (M.A., Physics)
Yeshiva University (Ph.D., Astrophysics)

Davies Publishing, Inc.
Los Angeles

*To the millions of students who have successfully used my
books to markedly increase their scores and get into the
college of their choice.*

*And to all of the students who seek to achieve and excel in
both school and life, and to the parents and teachers who
encourage their children in the path of curiosity, critical
thinking, and joyful passion for life and learning.*

Gary R. Gruber, Ph.D.

Published by Davies Publishing, Inc.
Education | Test Prep | Continuing Education

32 South Raymond Avenue
Suites 4 and 5
Pasadena, California 91105-1961
Tel: (626) 792-3046
Fax: (626) 792-5308
www.DaviesPublishing.com

Michael P. Davies
President and Publisher

Charlene Locke, Director of Book Design and Production
Christina J. Moose, Editorial Director
Janet Heard, Operations Manager
Bill Murawski, cover concept

Printed and bound in the United States of America.

978-0-941022-37-8

Davies Publishing books are available at special quantity discounts to use for sales promotions, employee premiums,
or educational purposes. Dr. Gruber is available for speaking engagements and Skype conferences with schools and
student groups. For more information or to purchase books, please call Davies Publishing at 877-792-0005 (toll-free
in the continental U.S.) or 626-792-3046.

Recent Study Aids from Dr. Gary Gruber Include

Gruber's Complete ACT® Guide 2018, 7th Edition

Gruber's Complete GRE® Guide 2018, 6th Edition

Forthcoming Study Aids from Dr. Gary Gruber Include

Gruber's Essential Strategies for Common Core Success: Level 1

Gruber's Essential Strategies for Common Core Success: Level 2

Gruber's World's Most Interesting Brainteasers

Gruber's Word Master for Standardized Tests

DaviesPublishing.com/Gruber

CONTENTS

Part 7: Vocabulary Building That Is Guaranteed to Raise Your SAT Score   305

Part 8: Grammar and Usage Refresher   325

ACKNOWLEDGMENTS

The author gratefully acknowledges sources for reading and English passages quoted or adapted within. All original sources have been attributed wherever determinable. Readers who identify additional sources are invited to contact the publisher at info@daviespublishing.com or the address below so that additional sources may be acknowledged in future printings:

Davies Publishing, Inc.
32 South Raymond Avenue, Suites 4 and 5
Pasadena, California 91105-1961

The following passages are reprinted with permission:

Pages 127–128: Arthur Whimbey, "Teaching Sequential Thought: The Cognitive-Skills Approach." *The Phi Delta Kappan* 59, no. 4 (December 1977), pp 255–259. Reprinted with permission of Phi Delta Kappa International, www.pdkintl.org. All rights reserved.

Pages 139–140: Milton Lomask, "When Congress Tried to Rule." *American Heritage* 11, no. 1 (December 1959). Reprinted by permission.

Pages 418–419: Paul Bogard, "Let There Be Dark." *Los Angeles Times*, December 21, 2012. Reprinted by permission of the author.

Pages 444–445: Christopher Lehmann-Haupt, "Books of the Times." *The New York Times*, May 29, 1974. Reprinted by permission.

Pages 522–523: John McDermott, "Technology: The Opiate of the Intellectuals." *The New York Review of Books*, July 31, 1969. Copyright © 1969 by John McDermott. Reprinted by permission.

Page 528: H. L. Mencken, "The Relation of Artists to Their Society." *The Baltimore Evening Sun*, April 7, 1924. Reprinted by permission from *The Baltimore Sun*.

Introduction

IMPORTANT NOTE ABOUT THIS BOOK AND ITS AUTHOR

This book is the most up-to-date and complete guide to the current SAT. Each practice exam is patterned after the SAT, and *all* the strategies and techniques deal with the SAT. The Gruber Critical-Thinking Strategies are useful for every SAT exam.

This book was written by Dr. Gary Gruber, the leading authority on the SAT, who knows more than anyone else in the test-prep field exactly what is being tested on the SAT. In fact, the procedures to answer the SAT questions rely more heavily on the Gruber Critical-Thinking Strategies than ever before, and this is the only book that has the exact thinking strategies you need to use to maximize your SAT score. Gruber's SAT books are used by the nation's school districts more than any other books and are proven to get the highest documented school district SAT scores.

Dr. Gruber has published more than 40 books with major publishers on test-taking and critical-thinking methods, with more than 7 million copies sold. He has also authored more than 1,000 articles on his work in scholarly journals and nationally syndicated newspapers, has appeared on numerous television and radio shows, and has been interviewed by hundreds of magazines and newspapers. He has developed major programs for school districts and for city and state educational agencies for improving and restructuring curriculum, increasing learning ability and test scores, increasing motivation, developing a passion for learning and problem solving, and decreasing the student dropout rate. For example, PBS (the Public Broadcasting Service) chose Dr. Gruber to train the nation's teachers on how to prepare students for the SAT through a national satellite teleconference and video. His results have been lauded by people throughout the country from all walks of life.

Dr. Gruber is recognized nationally as the leading expert on standardized tests. It is said that no one in the nation is better at assessing the thinking patterns behind the way a person answers questions and providing the mechanisms to improve faulty thinking.

Gruber's unique methods have been and are being used by the nation's learning centers, by international publications, textbooks, and teaching aids, by school districts throughout the country, in homes and workplaces across the nation, and by a host of other entities.

His goal and mission is to get people's potential realized and the nation impassioned with learning and problem solving, so that they don't merely try to get a fast, uncritical answer, but actually enjoy and look forward to solving problems and learning.

For more information on Gruber courses and additional Gruber products, visit www.drgarygruber.com.

Important: Many books do not reflect the SAT questions. Don't practice with questions that misrepresent the actual questions on the SAT. For example, the math questions created by the test makers are oriented toward allowing you to solve many problems without a calculator as fast as you could with one, and some can be solved faster without a calculator. The strategies contained in this book are exactly those needed to be used on the SAT. It is said that only Dr. Gruber has the expertise and ability to provide you with the tools needed for success on the exam far better than any competitor! Don't trust your future with less than the best material.

KEY POINTS YOU SHOULD KNOW
ABOUT THE NEW SAT

Many students ask what the New SAT is about. On the New SAT:

1. Some questions may be tedious and memory oriented but you still need strategies and critical-thinking skills to answer them.

2. *Important Note:* On the actual SAT there will be only 4 choices. For all instructional material in this book I have used 5 choices. The two Practice Tests at the end of the book, however, use the 4 choices you will find on the actual SAT.

3. You will have grammar questions based on reading passages, so you need to concentrate not only on grammar but also on the meaning of the reading passage.

4. On the New SAT, questions in reading ask which part of the passage enables you to get your answer.

5. I advised the College Board to have separate calculator and noncalculator sections, and they took my advice. On the New SAT, there is a math section where you can use a calculator and a math section where you cannot. However, they ultimately did this superficially. Many of the questions in the calculator section do not require the use of a calculator, while many of the questions in the noncalculator section do not challenge the test taker since they are easily answered without a calculator. Nevertheless, in the calculator section you should be able to determine when to use a calculator if you learn the right strategies. For example in this question: What is the value of

$$\frac{2}{3} \times \frac{3}{4} \times \frac{4}{5} \times \frac{5}{6} \times \frac{6}{7}$$

you should realize that if you canceled like numerators and denominators, you would get $\frac{2}{7}$ as an

answer almost immediately. You can imagine how much longer it would take you if you used a calculator for this particular question.

6. On the New SAT, many of the items in the Math, Reading, and Writing/Language sections will test data analysis through graphs, charts, and tables. This is useful in the real world.

7. The New SAT contains questions on trigonometry and imaginary numbers.

The key element is to learn the strategies and basic skills and when tackling a question on the New SAT try to extract something from the question, maybe even something that is *curious, that will lead you to the next step without getting fixated on just getting an answer.* Be *active* in your reading of the questions. For example, if a Reading passage states something like "Half a thousand years ago," figure out what that would translate to—"500 years ago." So you've figured the time period to be about "1500." This tells you what period of time you are in and psychologically motivates your interest in reading the rest of the passage. If in a math question you see it says "whole numbers" make sure you use that information actively in the problem.

Specific strategies let you answer a question without racking your brain, and even though you can do the problem almost mechanically, without anxiety, you still get the excitement of solving it. Here is an example: What percent of 20 is 200? By translating "what" to x, "of" to $\times$ (times), "is" to $=$, and "percent" to $\frac{}{100}$, you can almost solve the problem immediately and mechanically, and without any anxiety or probability of making a mistake.

THE AUTHOR HAS SOMETHING IMPORTANT TO TELL YOU ABOUT HOW TO RAISE YOUR SAT SCORE

What Are Critical-Thinking Skills?

First of all, I believe that intelligence can be taught. Intelligence, simply defined, is the ability to reason things out. I am convinced that *you can learn to think logically* and figure things out better and faster, *particularly in regard to SAT Math and Verbal problems.* But someone must give you the tools. Let us call these tools *strategies.* And that's what Critical-Thinking Skills are all about—*strategies.*

Learn the Strategies to Get More Points

The Strategy Section (beginning on page 63) will sharpen your reasoning ability so that you can increase your score dramatically on each part of the SAT.

These Critical-Thinking Skills—5 General Strategies, 19 Math Strategies, and 13 Verbal Strategies—course right through this book. The Explanatory Answers for the 2 Practice Tests in the book direct you to those strategies that may be used to answer specific types of SAT questions. The strategies in Part 4 of this book are usable for more than 90 percent of the questions that will appear on your SAT. *Each additional correct answer you get gives you approximately 10 more points.* It is obvious, then, that your *learning* and *using* the 37 easy-to-understand strategies in this book will very likely raise your SAT score substantially.

Are the Practice Tests in This Book Like an Actual SAT?

If you compare the 2 Practice Tests in this book with an actual SAT, you will find the Practice Tests very much like the *actual* test in regard to *format, question types,* and *level of difficulty.* Compare these Practice Tests with one of the official tests published by the College Board!

Building Your Vocabulary Can Make a Big Difference on Your Test

Knowing how to figure out the meanings of words in the Reading and Writing/Language sections is important. Instead of bogging you down with a 3,400-word list I used to publish in my books, I have created four compact tools to give you the meanings of more than 150,000 words:

1. 3 Vocabulary Strategies (page 148)
2. The Gruber Prefix-Root-Suffix List (page 309)
3. Hot Prefixes and Roots (Appendix A, page 627)
4. The 250 Most Common SAT Vocabulary Words (page 315)

QUESTIONS ASKED ABOUT THE NEW SAT

What Is the New SAT Like?

The new SAT relies more heavily on "process" thinking—that is, how you are approaching a question. You will need to get involved with the best "process" for the problem rather than just relying on getting a quick answer. Of course this is what I advocate in all my books.

What Sections Are on the New SAT?

There is one Reading section, one Writing and Language section, and two Math sections (one where you can use a calculator and one where you cannot). Finally, there is an optional Essay section. If you opt to take the Essay exam, the test will be 3 hours and 50 minutes.

If you opt *not* to take the essay portion of the test, there will be a 20-minute Experimental section for pretesting items. This section will not count in your score. When taken with the Experimental section, the test will last 3 hours and 20 minutes.

SAT vs. ACT: How Should I Decide Which Test to Take?

College applicants are often required to take either the SAT or the ACT, depending on the college to which they apply. Check first with the schools you are applying to and find out which test they prefer.

Depending on the school, you may have a choice in whether to take the ACT or the SAT. The correlation between the questions on the SAT and those on the ACT happens to be very high—if you score well on one, you will likely score about as well on the other. They cover a lot of the same material. Both exams test grammar, math, and critical reading skills. However, the ACT includes a whole section on scientific data interpretation (the SAT has a few similar questions in its Math section); fortunately, you don't have to have a scientific background to excel on the ACT.

The ACT is more *memory*-oriented, while the SAT is more *strategy*-oriented. If you memorize quickly and retain facts well under pressure, I recommend the ACT. If you are more prone to strategizing or you like puzzles, I would take the SAT.

What Is the Format of the New SAT?

The New SAT has two Verbal sections—"Evidence-Based Reading" and "Writing and Language" (scored from 200 to 800) and a Math section (scored from 200 to 800)—along with an optional Essay section. The New SAT is scored from 400 to 1,600.

Reading

Time: 65 minutes
Total Number of Questions: 52
Passage Word Count: 3,250 words in 4 single passages and one double passage. 500–750 words per passage or double passage

Type of Question	Number of Questions
Words in Context	10
Command of Evidence	10
Analysis in History/Social Studies and in Science	32

Subjects of Passages

U.S. or World Literature	10–11
History (primary documents)	10–11
Science	20
Social Studies	10–11

(4 passages and one double passage)

Graphics

1 or more graphics in 1 or more sets of questions

Text Types

Information and Ideas
Rhetoric
Synthesis

Writing and Language

Time: 35 minutes
Total Number of Questions: 44
Passage Word Count: 1,700 words in 4 passages.
400–450 words per passage

Type of Question	Number of Questions
Expression of Ideas	24
Standard English Conventions	20
Subjects of Passages	
Careers	11 (1 passage)
History/Social Studies	11 (1 passage)
Humanities	11 (1 passage)
Science	11 (1 passage)
Graphics	
1 or more graphics in 1 or more sets of questions	
Text Types	
Argumentative	1–2 passages
Informative/Explanatory	1–2 passages
Nonfiction Narrative	1 passage

Math

Total Time: 80 minutes
Calculator Section: 55 minutes (38 questions)
Noncalculator Section: 25 minutes (20 questions)
Total Number of Questions: 58

Type of Question	Number of Questions
Multiple Choice (4 choices)	45
Grid-Type	12
Extended Thinking, Grid-Type	1
Categories	
Heart of Algebra	21
Problem Solving and Data Analysis	14
Passport to Advanced Math	16
Additional Topics*	7

*These do not contribute to a subscore but do contribute to total Math score.

What Will Be Tested on the New SAT?

Vocabulary Words

Students are tested for their understanding of vocabulary words they can expect to use in life; these appear in the context of a reading passage on which the questions are based. There are no "sentence completions" on the New SAT, so the new test tends to omit more esoteric, uncommon, and difficult words.

Reading

1. Passages will deal with "evidence-based readings" that test your ability to comprehend and combine many sources of evidence to answer the questions.

2. Various forms of evidence will be provided in passages and in graphics such as tables, charts, and graphs.

3. At least one question in a passage will require you to choose a quotation in the passage that supports your answer to a previous question.

4. One of the passages will be taken from the text of a U.S. founding document or a text from the Great Global Conversation (a famous or noteworthy text that shaped world affairs).

Writing and Language

1. The Writing and Language test will measure your skills in revising and editing passages, as outlined in the table in column 1 on this page.

2. The questions focus on one of two categories, "Expression of Ideas" (topic development, organization of ideas, and word choice) or "Standard English Conventions" (sentence structure, grammar, usage, punctuation).

3. Some passages will include tables, graphs, or charts supporting points made in the text. A question may ask you to correct an error in the text using a graphic, or replace the passage's vague description with a more precise one.

Math

The Math section will include questions on

1. **Problem Solving and Data Analysis,** including ratios, percentages, and proportions. These questions will test your ability to create and analyze relationships using ratios, proportions, percentages,

and units; describe relationships shown graphically; and summarize qualitative and quantitative data.

2. **Heart of Algebra,** including use of linear equations to aid in the interpretation of more abstract concepts and problems. These questions will test your ability to analyze and solve equations; create expressions, equations, and inequalities to represent relationships between quantities and to solve problems; rearrange and interpret formulas.

3. **Passport to Advanced Math,** where you will need to use and manipulate more complex equations. These questions will test your ability to rewrite expressions using their structure; create, analyze, and solve quadratic and higher-order equations; and manipulate polynomials to solve problems.

4. **Additional Topics.** These questions test your ability to make area and volume calculations; analyze lines, angles, triangles, and circles; and use trigonometric functions and complex numbers.

Essay

1. The Essay test is optional but may be required by some colleges. (Check with the schools to which you are applying.)

2. The SAT Essay is based on a passage. It measures your reading skills (comprehension, use of textual evidence), your analytical skills (developing your claims based on the passage's evidence, style, and persuasive techniques), and your writing skills (focusing, organizing, and precisely conveying your claims using the conventions of standard written English).

3. You will have 50 minutes to complete the essay.

4. You will read a passage, explain how the author persuades the audience, and use evidence from the passage to support your explanation.

5. The essay prompt will be the same for many test dates and you will be able to view the prompt before the test.

6. Although the prompt may be the same as in a previous test, the passage on which your essay is based will change every time. This passage will be provided, and you must use it to draw evidence for your essay.

7. The passage will include all the information you need for your essay; you will not be required to refer to your personal experience or to agree or disagree with a position.

Should I Take an Administered Actual SAT for Practice?

Yes, but only if you will learn from your mistakes by recognizing the strategies you should have used on your exam. Taking the SAT merely for its own sake is a waste of time and may in fact reinforce bad methods and habits. Note that the SAT is released to students on the Question-and-Answer Service three times a year, in October, March, and May. It includes a booklet copy of the SAT questions, a report including your answers, the correct answers, and information about the test questions' type and difficulty. It is available worldwide only in May. It is wise to take the exam in one of these months if you wish to see your mistakes and correct them. You can register for the Question-and-Answer service at https://collegereadiness.collegeboard.org/sat/scores/verifying-scores.

What about the PSAT?

For students who elect to take the PSAT (preliminary SAT) to prepare for the actual SAT, it's important to note that the PSAT is a different test. The differences are described in the shaded box below. (The PSAT is given 2 times each year in the month of October.)

Note: Multiple-choice questions will have 4 choices, with no penalty for incorrect answers.

Math	
Time	70 minutes total, 47 questions, 2 sections: 1 with calculator, 1 noncalculator
Content	Multiple-Choice Items, Student-Produced Responses (grid-type questions), Measuring: Numbers and Operations, Algebra I and Functions, Geometry and Measurement; Statistics, Probability, and Data Analysis, Trigonometry
Score	200–800

(table continues . . .)

(continued from page xxiii)

Reading

Time	60 minutes, 47 questions, 1 section
Content	Critical Reading: Short and Long Reading Passages, with one Double Passage, Graphs included in some passages
Score	Score will be combined with Writing and Language and shown as 200–800

Writing and Language

Time	35 minutes, 44 questions, 1 section
Content	Identifying Errors, Improving Sentences and Paragraphs: Test will contain passages where corrections or additions need to be made. Measuring: Grammar, Usage, Word Choice, Passage Construction
Score	Score will be combined with Reading and shown as 200–800

What Percentage of SAT Study Time Should I Spend Learning Vocabulary Words?

A student should not spend too much time on this—perhaps 4 hours at most. To build your word recognition quickly, learn the "Hot Prefixes and Roots" list in Appendix A, as well as the 3 Vocabulary Strategies (page 148).

Vocabulary will be tested in context on the New SAT. Although straight vocabulary will not be tested as in the previous exam's sentence completion questions, don't think that vocabulary won't be tested as much in the reading passages! Now more than ever, you need to know prefixes and roots, along with the specific vocabulary strategies in this book, which work better than ever. Luckily you don't have to memorize a set of 3,400 words anymore. Here are some of the words used in just one New SAT passage; understanding their meanings is necessary to understand the passage:

inquisitor	diminution
hyperbole	jurisdiction
subversion	misdemeanors
astute	indignation
maladministration	ratification

All the meanings of these words can be derived using the vocabulary sections in this book.

Here are the sections:

(1) 3 Vocabulary Strategies (page 148)

(2) The Gruber Prefix-Root-Suffix List That Gives You the Meanings of More than 150,000 Words (page 309)

(3) 250 Most Common SAT Vocabulary Words (page 315)

(4) The Most Important/Frequently Used SAT Words and Their Opposites (page 319)

(5) Hot Prefixes and Roots (page 627)

(6) Words Commonly Mistaken for Each Other (page 633)

Should I Be Familiar with the Directions for Answering the Various Items on the SAT before Taking the SAT?

Make sure you are completely familiar with the directions to each of the item types on the SAT—the directions for answering the Reading, Writing/Language, and Math questions, especially the Grid-Type questions (see General Strategy 2, page 64, and the directions that go with each of the Practice Tests—Reading, Writing/Language, Math, and the optional Essay—in Part 10).

What Should I Do to Prepare on Friday Night? Cram? Watch TV? Relax?

The SAT is typically administered on Saturdays. On Friday night, just refresh your knowledge of the structure of the test, some strategies, and some basic skills (verbal or math). You want to do this to keep the thinking going so that it is continual right up to the exam. Don't overdo it; just do enough so that it's somewhat continuous—this will also relieve some anxiety, so that you won't feel you are forgetting things before the exam.

What Should I Bring to the Exam on the Test Date?

You should bring the following items with you to the test, and nothing else:

- a few sharpened #2 pencils with erasers
- a valid ID such as a driver license or school ID
- a calculator

Can I Use a Calculator on the Math Portion of the Test?

Students may use a calculator on a designated calculator math section of the test. Be aware that every math question on the SAT can be solved without a calculator. For many questions, it's actually easier *not* to use one. At the same time, it is recommended that you use a calculator if you don't immediately see a faster way to solve the problem without one.

- *Acceptable calculators:* Graphing calculators, scientific calculators, and four-function calculators (the last is not recommended) are all permitted during testing. If you have a calculator with characters that are one inch or higher, or if your calculator has a raised display that might be visible to other test takers, you will be seated at the discretion of the test supervisor.

- *Unacceptable calculators:* Laptops, smartphones, and portable/handheld computers; calculators that have a QWERTY keyboard, make noise, use an electrical outlet, or have a paper tape; electronic writing pads or stylus-driven devices; pocket organizers; and cell phone calculators will not be allowed during the test.

Should I Guess on the New SAT?

There is no penalty for guessing, so if you cannot answer a question, you should certainly guess. Do not leave any answer blank. You have a 25% chance of getting the answer just from guessing. And in this book I will show you how to make very wise guesses if you can't figure out how to solve the problem.

How Should I Pace Myself on the Exam? How Much Time Should I Spend on Each Question?

Calculate the time allowed for the particular section—for example, 25 minutes. Divide by the number of questions—for example, 20. That gives you an average of 1.25 minutes to spend on each question in this example. Spend less than a minute on the first set of questions and perhaps more than a minute on the last set. With the reading passages you should give yourself only about 30 seconds per question and spend the extra time on the other reading questions. Also, more difficult questions may take more time.

The Test Is Given in One Booklet. Can I Skip Between Sections?

No—you cannot skip between the sections. You have to work on the particular section until time is called to move on to the next section. If you get caught skipping sections or going back to earlier sections, you risk being asked to leave the exam.

Should I Answer All Easy Questions First and Save Difficult Ones for Last?

The easy questions used to appear at the beginning of the section, the medium-difficulty ones in the middle, and the hard ones toward the end. That is no longer the case. So I would answer the questions as they are presented to you, and if you find you are spending more than 30 seconds on a question and not getting anywhere, go to the next question. You may, however, find that the more difficult questions are actually easy for you because you have learned the strategies in this book.

Should I Use Scrap Paper to Write on and to Do Calculations?

Always use your test booklet (not your answer sheet) to draw on. Many of my strategies expect you to label diagrams, draw and extend lines, circle important words and sentences, etc., so feel free to write anything in your booklet. The booklets aren't graded—just the answer sheets (see General Strategy 4, page 65).

What Is the Most Challenging Type of Question on the Exam and How Does One Attack It?

Many questions on the test can be challenging. You should always attack challenging questions by using a specific strategy or strategies and common sense.

What Are the Most Crucial Strategies for Students?

All specific Verbal (Reading Comprehension and Vocabulary) and Math Strategies are crucial, including the general test-taking strategies (described starting on page 64): guessing, writing and drawing in your test booklet, and being familiar with question-type directions. The key Reading Strategy is to know the four general types of questions that are asked in reading—

main idea, inference, specific details, and tone or mood (page 132). In math (starting on page 72), it's the translations strategy (Strategy #2) along with several others that are marked "Very Important Strategy." Also make sure you know the basic math skills cold (see pages 153–162 for these rules—*make sure you know them*).

How Is the Exam Scored? Are Some Questions Worth More Points?

Each question is worth the same number of points. After getting a raw score—the number of questions right—this is equated to a "scaled" score from 400 to 1600. The Math section is scored 200–800, and the combined Reading and Writing/Language sections are scored from 200 to 800. A scaled score of 500 in each part is considered average.

Can I Get Back the SAT with My Answers and the Correct Ones After I Take It? How Can I Make Use of This Service?

The disclosed SAT is sent back to the student upon request with a payment. You can also order a copy of your answer sheet for an additional fee. Very few people take advantage of this fact or use the disclosed SAT to see what mistakes they've made and what strategies they could have used on the questions.

Check in your SAT information bulletin or log on to www.collegeboard.org for the dates this Question-and-Answer Service is available.

Can I Take the Test More than Once, and If So, How Will the Scores Be Reported to the Schools of My Choice? Will All Scores Be Reported to the Schools, and How Will They Be Used?

Check with the schools to which you are applying to see how they use the reported scores, e.g., whether they average them or whether they take the highest. Ask the schools whether they see unreported scores; if they do, find out how the individual school deals with single and multiple unreported scores.

What Is the Recommended Course of Study for Those Retaking the Exam?

Try to get a copy of the exam that you took if it was a disclosed one—the disclosed ones, which you have to send a payment for, are usually given in October, March, and May. Try to learn from your mistakes by seeing what strategies you could have used to get questions right. Certainly learn the specific strategies for taking your next exam.

Can I Use the Strategies and Examples in This Book for the GRE and the ACT?

Most other exams are modeled after the SAT, so the strategies presented here are definitely useful when taking them. For example, the questions on the GRE (Graduate Record Examinations, for entrance into graduate school) benefit from identical strategies used for the SAT. The questions are just worded at a slightly higher level. The ACT (American College Testing) examination, another college entrance exam, reflects more than ever strategies that are used on the SAT. For the ACT, you can get *Gruber's Complete ACT® Guide 2018*. For the GRE, you can get *Gruber's Complete GRE® Guide 2018*.

How Does the Gruber Preparation Method Differ from Other Programs and SAT Books?

Many other SAT programs try to use "quick-fix" methods or subscribe to memorization. So-called quick-fix methods can be detrimental to effective preparation because the SAT people constantly change questions to prevent "gimmick" approaches. Rote memorization methods do not enable you to answer a variety of questions that appear in the SAT exam. In more than thirty years of experience writing preparation books for the SAT, Dr. Gruber has developed and honed the Critical-Thinking Skills and Strategies that are based on all standardized tests' construction. So, while his method immediately improves your performance on the SAT, it also provides you with the confidence to tackle problems in all areas of study for the rest of your life. He remarkably enables you to look at a problem or question without panic, extract something curious or useful from the problem, and move on to the next step and finally to a solution, without rushing into a wrong answer or getting lured into a wrong choice. It has been said that test taking through his methodology becomes enjoyable rather than painful.

THE INSIDE TRACK ON HOW SAT QUESTIONS ARE DEVELOPED AND HOW THEY <u>VARY FROM TEST TO TEST</u>

When SAT questions are developed, they are based on a set of criteria and guidelines. Knowing how these guidelines work should demystify the test-making process and explain why the strategies in this book are so critical to getting a high score.

Inherent in the SAT questions are Critical-Thinking Skills, which embrace strategies that enable you to solve a question by the quickest method with the least amount of panic and brain-racking, and describe an elegance and excitement in problem solving. Adhering to and using the strategies (which the test makers use to develop the questions) will let you sail through the SAT. This is summed up in the following statement:

Show me the solution to a problem, and I'll solve that problem. Show me a Gruber strategy for solving the problem, and I'll solve hundreds of problems.

Here's a sample of a set of guidelines presented for making up an SAT-type question in the math area:

The test maker is to create a hard problem in the regular math multiple-choice area, which involves

(A) algebra
(B) two or more equations
(C) two or more ways to solve: one way being standard substitution; the other, faster way using the *strategy* of merely *adding* or *subtracting* equations.*

Previous examples given to the test maker for reference:

1. If $x + y = 3$, $y + z = 4$, and $z + x = 5$, find the value of $x + y + z$.

    (A) 4
    (B) 5
    (C) 6
    (D) 7

Solution: **Add** equations and get $2x + 2y + 2z = 12$; divide both sides of the equation by 2 and we get $x + y + z = 6$. (Answer is C)

2. If $2x + y = 8$ and $x + 2y = 4$, find the value of $x - y$.

    (A) 3
    (B) 4
    (C) 5
    (D) 6

Solution: **Subtract** equations and get $x - y = 4$. (Answer is B)

Here's an example from a recent SAT.

If $y - x = 5$ and $2y + z = 11$, find the value of $x + y + z$.

    (A) 3
    (B) 6
    (C) 8
    (D) 16

Solution: **Subtract** equation $y - x = 5$ from $2y + z = 11$.
We get $2y - y + z - (-x) = 11 - 5$.
So, $y + z + x = 6$. (Answer is B)

Note: See Math Strategy #13 on page 102.

WHAT ARE
CRITICAL-THINKING SKILLS?

Critical-Thinking Skills, a current buzz phrase, are generic skills for finding the most creative and effective way of solving a problem or evaluating a situation. The most effective way of solving a problem is to extract some piece of information or observe something curious from the problem and then use one or more of the specific strategies or Critical-Thinking Skills (together with basic skills or information you already know) to get to the next step in the problem. This next step will catapult you toward a solution with further use of the specific strategies or thinking skills.

1. ***Extract or observe something curious.***

2. ***Use specific strategies together with basic skills.***

These specific strategies will enable you to "process" think rather than just be concerned with the end result; the latter usually gets you to a fast, rushed, and wrong answer. The Gruber strategies have been shown to make test takers more comfortable with problem solving and to make the process enjoyable. The skills will last a lifetime, and you will develop a passion for problem solving. These Critical-Thinking Skills show that conventional "drill and practice" is a waste of time unless the practice is based on these generic thinking skills.

Here's a simple example of how these Critical-Thinking Skills can be used in a math problem:

Which is greater, $7\frac{1}{7} \times 8\frac{1}{8} \times 6\frac{1}{6}$ or $8\frac{1}{8} \times 6\frac{1}{6} \times 7$?

Long and tedious way: Multiply $7\frac{1}{7} \times 8\frac{1}{8} \times 6\frac{1}{6}$ and compare it with $8\frac{1}{8} \times 6\frac{1}{6} \times 7$.

Error in doing the problem the "long way": You don't have to *calculate;* you just have to *compare,* so you need a *strategy* for *comparing* two quantities.

Critical-Thinking way:

1. *Observe:* Each expression contains $8\frac{1}{8}$ and $6\frac{1}{6}$.

2. *Use strategy:* Since both $8\frac{1}{8}$ and $6\frac{1}{6}$ are just weighting factors, like the same quantities on both sides of a balance scale, just *cancel* them from both multiplied quantities above.

You are then left comparing $7\frac{1}{7}$ with 7, so the first quantity, $7\frac{1}{7}$, is greater. Thus $7\frac{1}{7} \times 8\frac{1}{8} \times 6\frac{1}{6}$ is greater than $8\frac{1}{8} \times 6\frac{1}{6} \times 7$.

Here's a simple example of how Critical-Thinking Skills can be used for a verbal problem:

If you see a word such as *delude* in a sentence or in a reading passage, you can assume that the word *delude* is negative and probably means "taking away from something" or "distracting," since the prefix *de-* means "away from" and thus has a negative connotation. Although you may not get the exact meaning of the word (in this case the meaning is to "deceive" or "mislead"), you can see how the word may be used in the context of the sentence in which it appears, and thus get the flavor or feeling of the sentence or paragraph. I have researched and developed more than 50 prefixes and roots (included in Appendix A to this book) that let you make use of this context strategy.

Notice that the Critical-Thinking approach gives you a fail-safe and exact path to the solution without requiring you to try to solve the problem superficially or merely guess at it. This book contains all the Critical-Thinking Strategies you need to know for the SAT test, allowing you to solve hundreds of problems.

I have researched hundreds of SAT tests, including many of the New SAT tests (thousands of SAT questions), and documented 37 Critical-Thinking Strategies (all found in this book) common to every test. These strategies can be used for any Math or Verbal problem.

In short, you can learn how to solve a specific problem and thus find how to answer that specific problem, or you can learn a powerful logical-thinking strategy that will enable you to answer hundreds of problems.

MULTILEVEL APPROACHES
TO THE SOLUTION OF PROBLEMS

How a student answers a question is more important than the answer given by the student. For example, the student may have randomly guessed, the student may have used a rote and unimaginative method for reaching a solution, or the student may have used a very creative method. It seems that one should judge the student by the way he or she answers the question and not just by whether that student gets the correct answer to the question.

Example:

Question: **Without using a calculator, which is greater:**

$$355 \times 356 \quad \text{or} \quad 354 \times 357?$$

Case 1: **Rote Memory Approach** (a completely mechanical approach that does not take into account the possibility of a faster method based on patterns or connections of the numbers in the question): The student multiplies 355×356, gets 126,380, and then multiplies 354×357 and gets 126,378.

Case 2: **The Observer's Rote Approach** (an approach that makes use of a mathematical strategy that can be memorized and tried for various problems): The student does the following:

He or she divides both quantities by 354.

He or she then gets $\dfrac{355 \times 356}{354}$ compared with $\dfrac{354 \times 357}{354}$.

He or she then divides these quantities by 356 and gets $\dfrac{355}{354}$ compared with $\dfrac{357}{356}$.

Now he or she realizes that $\dfrac{355}{354} = 1\dfrac{1}{354}$; $\dfrac{357}{356} = 1\dfrac{1}{356}$.

He or she then reasons that since the left side, $1\dfrac{1}{354}$, is greater than the right side, $1\dfrac{1}{356}$, the left side of the original quantities, 355×356, is greater than the right side of the original quantities, 354×357.

Case 3: **The Pattern Seeker's Method** (the most mathematically creative method—an approach in which the student looks for a pattern or sequence in the numbers and then is astute enough to represent the pattern or sequence in more general algebraic language to see the pattern or sequence more clearly):

Look for a pattern. Represent 355×356 and 354×357 by symbols.

Let $x = 354$.

Then $355 = x + 1$; $356 = x + 2$; $357 = x + 3$.

So $355 \times 356 = (x + 1)(x + 2)$ and $354 \times 357 = x(x + 3)$.

Multiplying the factors, we get

$355 \times 356 = x^2 + 3x + 2$ and $354 \times 357 = x^2 + 3x$.

The difference is $355 \times 356 - 354 \times 357 = x^2 + 3x + 2 - x^2 - 3x$, which is just 2.

So 355×356 is greater than 354×357 by 2.

Note: You could have also represented 355 by x. Then $356 = x + 1$; $354 = x - 1$; $357 = x + 2$. We would then get $355 \times 356 = (x)(x + 1)$ and $354 \times 357 = (x - 1)(x + 2)$. Then we would use the method above to compare the quantities.

—OR—

You could have written 354 as a and 357 as b. Then $355 = a + 1$ and $356 = b - 1$. So $355 \times 356 = (a + 1)(b - 1)$ and $354 \times 357 = ab$.

Let's see what $(355 \times 356) - (354 \times 357)$ is. This is the same as $(a + 1)(b - 1) - ab$, which is $(ab + b - a - 1) - ab$, which is in turn $b - a - 1$. Since $b - a - 1 = 357 - 354 - 1 = 2$, the quantity $355 \times 356 - 354 \times 357 = 2$, so 355×356 is greater than 354×357 by 2.

Case 4: **The Astute Observer's Approach** (the simplest approach—an approach that attempts to figure out a connection between the numbers and uses that connection to figure out the solution):

$355 \times 356 = (354 + 1) \times 356 = (354 \times 356) + 356$ and

$354 \times 357 = 354 \times (356 + 1) = (354 \times 356) + 354$

One can see that the difference is just 2.

Case 5: **The Observer's Common Relation Approach** (the approach that people use when they want to connect two items to a third to see how the two items are related):

355×356 is greater than 354×356 by 356.

354×357 is greater than 354×356 by 354.

So this means that 355×356 is greater than 354×357.

Case 6: **Scientific, Creative, and Observational Generalization Method** (a highly creative method and the most scientific method, as it spots a critical and curious aspect of the sums being equal and provides for a generalization to other problems of that nature):

Represent $354 = a$, $357 = b$, $355 = c$, and $356 = d$

We have now that (1) $a + b = c + d$
$\qquad\qquad$ (2) $|b - a| > |d - c|$

We want to prove: $ab < dc$

Proof:

Square inequality (2): $(b - a)^2 > (d - c)^2$

Therefore: (3) $b^2 - 2ab + a^2 > d^2 - 2dc + c^2$

Multiply (3) by -1, and this reverses the inequality sign:

$-(b^2 - 2ab + a^2) < -(d^2 - 2dc + c^2)$

or

(4) $-b^2 + 2ab - a^2 < -d^2 + 2dc - c^2$

Now square (1): $(a + b) = (c + d)$ and we get:

(5) $a^2 + 2ab + b^2 = c^2 + 2dc + d^2$

Add inequality (4) to equality (5) and we get:

$4ab < 4dc$

Divide by 4 and we get:

$ab < dc$

The generalization is that for any positive numbers a, b, c, d, when $|b - a| > |d - c|$ and $a + b = c + d$, then $ab < dc$.

This also generalizes in a geometrical setting where for two rectangles whose perimeters are the same $(2a + 2b = 2c + 2d)$, the rectangle whose absolute difference in sides $|d - c|$ is *least* has the *greatest* area.

Case 7: **Geometric and Visual Approach*** (the approach used by visual people or people who have a curious geometric bent and possess "out-of-the-box" insights):

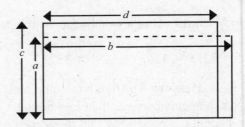

Where $a = 354$, $b = 357$, $c = 355$, and $d = 356$, we have two rectangles where the first one's length is d and width is c, and the second one's length is b (dotted line) and width is a.

Now the area of the first rectangle (dc) is equal to the area of the second (ab) minus the area of the rectangular slab, which is $(b - d)a$, plus the area of the rectangular slab $(c - a)d$. So we get: $cd = ab - (b - d)a + (c - a)d$. Since $b - d = c - a$, we get $cd = ab - (c - a)a + (c - a)d = ab + (d - a)(c - a)$.

Since $d > a$ and $c > a$, $cd > ab$. So $355 \times 356 > 354 \times 357$.

---

*This method of solution was developed by and sent to the author from Dr. Eric Cornell, a Nobel laureate in Physics.

Note: Many people have thought that by multiplying units digits from one quantity and comparing that with the product of the units digits from the other quantity, they would get the answer. For example, they would multiply $5 \times 6 = 30$ from 355×356, then multiply $4 \times 7 = 28$ from 354×357, and then say that 355×356 is greater than 354×357 because $5 \times 6 > 4 \times 7$. They would be lucky. That works if the sum of units digits of the first quantity is the same as or greater than the sum of units digits of the second quantity. However, if we want to compare something like $354 \times 356 = 126{,}024$ with $352 \times 359 = 126{,}368$, that method would not work.

A 4-HOUR STUDY PROGRAM
FOR THE SAT

For those who have only a few hours to spend in SAT preparation, I have worked out a *minimum* study program to get you by. It tells you what basic math skills you need to know, what vocabulary practice you need, and the most important strategies to focus on, from the 37 in this book.

General

Study General Strategies, pages 64–65.

Reading

Study the following Verbal Strategies beginning on page 123 (first three questions for each strategy):

Vocabulary Strategies 1, 2, and 3, pages 148–152

Reading Comprehension Strategies 1, 2, 9, and 10, pages 132–136 and 144–147

Also study the Most Important/Frequently Used SAT Words and Their Opposites, page 319.

Writing and Language

Look through the material in Part 8, "Grammar and Usage Refresher," starting on page 325.

Math

Study the Mini Math Refresher beginning on page 153.

Study the following Math Strategies (first three questions for each strategy):

Strategy 2, page 74

Strategy 4, page 83

Strategy 8, page 93

Strategy 12, page 101

Strategy 13, page 102

Strategy 14, page 105

Strategy 17, page 114

Strategy 18, page 117

If you have time, take Practice Test 1, starting on page 432. Do sections 1–10. Check your answers with the explanatory answers starting on page 478, and look again at the strategies and basic skills that apply to the questions you missed.

LONGER-RANGE STUDY PROGRAM AND HELPFUL STEPS FOR USING THIS BOOK

1. Learn the 5 General Strategies for test taking on pages 64–65.

2. Take the Strategy Diagnostic Test for the New SAT on page 1 and follow the directions for diagnosis on page 16.

3. Take the SAT Practice Test 1 starting on page 432 and score yourself according to the instructions.

4. For those problems or questions that you answered incorrectly or were uncertain of, see the explanatory answers, beginning on page 478, and make sure that you learn the strategies keyed to the questions. For complete strategy development, it is a good idea to study *all* the strategies beginning on page 63 (in the Strategy Section), and learn how to do all the problems within each strategy.

5. If you are weak in basic math skills, answer "The 101 Most Important Math Questions You Need to Know How to Solve" beginning on page 35 and follow the directions for diagnosis.

6. To see if you are making use of the strategies you've learned, you should take "The World's Shortest New SAT Practice Test" beginning on page 21 and follow the directions for diagnosis.

For Vocabulary Building

7. Learn "The Gruber Prefix-Root-Suffix List" beginning on page 309. This will significantly build your vocabulary. You may also want to study the "Hot Prefixes and Roots" in Appendix A beginning on page 627.

For Math-Area Basic Skills Help

8. For the basic math skills keyed to the questions, study the "Complete SAT Math Refresher" beginning on page 163, or for a quicker review, look at the "Mini Math Refresher" beginning on page 153.

For Writing Help

9. Refresh your grammar ability by looking through the "Grammar and Usage Refresher" starting on page 325.

Now

10. Take the SAT Practice Test 2 beginning on page 513, score yourself, and compare your answers with the explanatory answers. Always refer to the associated strategies and basic skills for questions you answered incorrectly or were not sure how to do.

QUESTIONS RECENTLY ASKED OF
DR. GRUBER IN INTERVIEWS

How Did You Get Started in Test Prep? Do You Still Personally Train Students?

When I was in fifth grade, I scored 90 (below average) on an IQ test. My father, who was a high school teacher at the time, was concerned, so he was able to get me an IQ test, hoping I could study it and increase my score. However, when I looked at the test, I was so fascinated with what the questions were trying to assess, I started to figure out what strategies and thinking could have been used for the questions and saw interesting patterns for what the test maker was trying to test.

I increased my IQ to 126 and then to 150. The initial experience of scoring so low on my first IQ test and being branded as "dull minded" actually sparked my fascination and research with standardized tests. I was determined to help all other students obtain my knowledge and experience so they would be able to reach their full potential, as I had. So I constantly write books, newspaper and magazine articles and columns, and software, and I personally teach students and teachers.

What Is the "Gruber Method" and How Does It Differ from Other Test Prep Methods?

The unique aspect of my method is that I provide a mechanism and process whereby students internalize the use of the strategies and thinking skills I've developed and honed over thirty years. The method reinforces those strategies and skills so that students can answer questions on the SAT or ACT without panic or brain-racking. This is actually a fun process. The Gruber Method focuses on the students' patterns of thinking and how each student should best answer the questions. I have even developed a nationally syndicated test—the only one of its kind—that actually tracks a student's thinking approach to the SAT (and ACT) and directs the student to the exact strategies

necessary for him or her to learn. Instead of just learning how to solve one problem at a time, if you learn a Gruber strategy you can use it to solve thousands of problems.

How Do You Ensure That the Practice Tests in Your Books Are Accurate Reflections of What Students Will See on the Actual Tests?

There are two processes for this. First, I am constantly critically reviewing and analyzing all the current questions and patterns on the actual tests. The second process is that I am directly in touch with the research development teams for any new items or methods used in the questions on any upcoming tests, so I am probably the only one besides the actual SAT or ACT staff who knows exactly what is being tested and why it is being tested on current and upcoming exams.

What Percentage of Test Prep Study Time Should Students Spend Learning Vocabulary Words?

Students should not spend too much time on this— perhaps 4 hours at most. The rest of the time should be invested in learning the "Hot Prefixes and Roots" list (page 627).

What Advice Can You Give to Students Suffering from Test Anxiety?

I find that when students learn specific strategies, they see how a strategy can be used for a multitude of questions. And when they see a question on an actual SAT that uses the strategy, it reinforces their self-confidence and reduces their sense of panic. Students can also treat the SAT as a game by using my strategic approaches, and this also reduces panic.

SAT vs. ACT: How Should Students Decide Which Test to Take?

The correlation happens to be very high for both tests, so if you score well on one, you will score equivalently on the other. The material is about the same; for example, there is grammar on both tests. Math is about the same, except the ACT is less strategically oriented. There is reading on both tests, and those sections test about the same things. However, on the ACT there is a whole section on scientific data interpretation (the SAT has some questions on this topic in the Math section). And the ACT is more memory-oriented than the SAT. If you are more prone to using memory, I would take the ACT. If you are more prone to strategizing or if you like puzzles, I would take the SAT. In any event, I would check with the schools to which you're applying to find out which test they prefer.

What Is the Single Most Important Piece of Advice You Can Give to Students Taking the SAT or ACT?

Learn some specific strategies, which can be found in my books. This will let you think mechanically without racking your brain. When answering the questions, don't concentrate on or panic about finding the answer. Try to extract something in the question that is curious and/or will lead you to the next step in the question. Through this, you will process the question, enabling you to reach an answer.

What Is the Single Most Important Piece of Advice You Can Give to Tutors Teaching the SAT or ACT?

Make sure you learn the strategies. Teach students those strategies by using many different questions that employ each strategy, so students will see variations on how each particular strategy is used.

What Recommendations Can You Give to Tutors Who Want to Use Your Books in Their Test Prep Programs?

The sections "A 4-Hour Study Program for the SAT" (page xxvi) and "Longer-Range Study Program and Helpful Steps for Using This Book" (page xxvii) present a condensed and a more comprehensive approach to studying for the SAT. You can use this information to create a program for teaching the student. Always try to reinforce the strategic approach, where the student can focus on and internalize strategies so he or she can use them for multitudes of questions.

Apparently, Very Few People Know the Answer to This Important Question: When Should Students Take the SAT or ACT?

Students should find out from the school to which they are applying the preferred test dates for the SAT or ACT that they need to register for. However, if a student wants to take an SAT or ACT for practice, he or she should take it only on the test dates that are earmarked for later test disclosure, which means that the test answers and the students' answers are given back to them. For the SAT, check the College Board's website at www.collegeboard.org and https://collegereadiness.collegeboard.org/pdf/sat-answer-verification-service-order-form.pdf, and for the ACT, check www.actstudent.org. After getting the test and the results for each question back, students can learn from their mistakes by going through the questions they got wrong and then working on the strategies and basic skills they could have used to solve those questions.

WHAT YOU CAN DO AS A PARENT TO HELP YOUR CHILD

First, you should be aware of what the SAT tests and why it is important.

What Is the Importance of the SAT and What Background Is Required to Do Well on It?

A good score on the SAT is needed to get into a good college. Your child will need to have taken courses in geometry and algebra (elementary and intermediate). Some topics in advanced algebra are good to know, but trigonometry is not needed. Your child should know writing skills and grammar, and know how to understand what he or she is reading.

What Should My Child Know Before Taking or Practicing SAT Tests?

It is important for your child to develop a way of answering questions on the test without panic and without tediously racking his or her brain. In order to answer questions in the most efficient manner, your child needs to be sure of basic skills, including math, the meaning of certain vocabulary words, the best ways to understand a passage in reading, and grammar rules. Then he or she must learn specific strategies in the math and reading areas.

What Does My Child Need for the Test?

Your child should have an approved calculator (calculators are discussed in detail on page xxii). He or she should also have a watch to keep track of time, two sharpened #2 pencils with erasers, and also a valid ID such as a driver license or school ID.

Very Important: When Should My Child Take the SAT If He or She Takes It for Practice?

Your child should take the SAT for practice in January, May, or October, and you should make sure you subscribe to the College Board's Question-and-Answer Service (see www.collegeboard.org and https://collegereadiness.collegeboard.org/pdf/sat-answer-verification-service-order-form.pdf) so you can get the test and your child's answers back for those dates.

How Should My Child Study for the Test?

Depending on when he or she will take the test, your child should brush up on basic skills (math, vocabulary, writing, and reading) and learn specific strategies. Then your child should take some practice tests. It is important that you tell your child that quality, not quantity, is important. So if your child can spend two hours a day learning some strategies and taking only two sections of the test and effectively learning from his or her mistakes, that is much better than learning all the strategies or taking a whole test and superficially learning from his or her mistakes. The best way is to do a little each day, so that the strategies and methods are internalized.

How Can I Work with My Child?

You can go over some of the strategies with your child and some practice questions. You may enjoy the strategies and questions and even learn something yourself. You may want to try to answer some of the questions and see how your child does with the same questions. And then both of you should figure out the best approach or strategies for the questions. Many parents have commented to me that they never realized there were such powerful strategies for the math and verbal skills and that they wished they had learned these strategies when they were in high school.

PART 1

Strategy Diagnostic Test for the New SAT

Take This Test to Find Out What Strategies You Don't Know

The purpose of this test is to find out *how* you approach SAT problems of different types and to reveal your understanding and command of the various strategies and Critical-Thinking Skills. After checking your answers in the table at the end of the test, you will have a profile of your performance. You will know exactly what strategies you must master and where you may learn them.

Important Note: On the actual SAT there will be only 4 choices. For instructional purposes, in this and other diagnostic tests I have used 5 choices. The two Practice Tests at the end of the book, however, use the 4 choices you will find on the actual SAT.

DIRECTIONS

For each odd-numbered question (1, 3, 5, 7, etc.), choose the best answer. In the even-numbered questions (2, 4, 6, 8, etc.), you will be asked how you solved the preceding odd-numbered question. Make sure that you answer the even-numbered questions carefully, as your answers will determine whether or not you used the right strategy. Be completely honest in your answers to the even-numbered questions, since you do want an accurate assessment in order to be helped. *Note*: Only the odd-numbered questions are SAT-type questions that would appear on the actual exam. The even-numbered questions are for self-diagnosis purposes only.

Example:

1. The value of $17 \times 98 + 17 \times 2 =$

   (A) 1,550
   (B) 1,600
   (C) 1,700
   (D) 1,800
   (E) 1,850

   (The correct answer is Choice C.)

2. How did you get your answer?

   (A) I multiplied 17×98 and added that to 17×2.
   (B) I approximated and found the closest match in the choices.
   (C) I factored out the 17 to get $17(98 + 2)$.
   (D) I guessed.
   (E) By none of the above methods.

In question 2:

- If you chose A, you did the problem the long way unless you used a calculator.
- If you chose B, you probably approximated 98 by 100 and got 1,700.
- If you chose C, you factored out the 17 to get $17(98 + 2) = 17(100) = 1,700$. This was the best strategy to use.
- If you chose D, you probably didn't know how to solve the problem and just guessed.
- If you chose E, you did not use any of the methods above but used your own different method.

Note: In the even-numbered questions, you may have used a different approach from what will be described in the answer to that question. It is, however, a good idea to see if the alternate approach is described, as you may want to use that approach for solving other questions. Now turn to the next page to take the test.

ANSWER SHEET

It is recommended that you use a No. 2 pencil. It is very important that you fill in the entire circle darkly and completely. If you change your response, erase as completely as possible. Incomplete marks or erasures may affect your score.

Complete Mark ● **Examples of Incomplete Marks** ⊙ ⊗ ⊖ ◐ ◑ ◔ ● ◕

SECTION 1: VERBAL ABILITY

	A B C D E		A B C D E		A B C D E		A B C D E		A B C D E
1	○ ○ ○ ○ ○	10	○ ○ ○ ○ ○	19	○ ○ ○ ○ ○	28	○ ○ ○ ○ ○	37	○ ○ ○ ○ ○
2	○ ○ ○ ○ ○	11	○ ○ ○ ○ ○	20	○ ○ ○ ○ ○	29	○ ○ ○ ○ ○	38	○ ○ ○ ○ ○
3	○ ○ ○ ○ ○	12	○ ○ ○ ○ ○	21	○ ○ ○ ○ ○	30	○ ○ ○ ○ ○	39	○ ○ ○ ○ ○
4	○ ○ ○ ○ ○	13	○ ○ ○ ○ ○	22	○ ○ ○ ○ ○	31	○ ○ ○ ○ ○	40	○ ○ ○ ○ ○
5	○ ○ ○ ○ ○	14	○ ○ ○ ○ ○	23	○ ○ ○ ○ ○	32	○ ○ ○ ○ ○	41	○ ○ ○ ○ ○
6	○ ○ ○ ○ ○	15	○ ○ ○ ○ ○	24	○ ○ ○ ○ ○	33	○ ○ ○ ○ ○	42	○ ○ ○ ○ ○
7	○ ○ ○ ○ ○	16	○ ○ ○ ○ ○	25	○ ○ ○ ○ ○	34	○ ○ ○ ○ ○	43	○ ○ ○ ○ ○
8	○ ○ ○ ○ ○	17	○ ○ ○ ○ ○	26	○ ○ ○ ○ ○	35	○ ○ ○ ○ ○	44	○ ○ ○ ○ ○
9	○ ○ ○ ○ ○	18	○ ○ ○ ○ ○	27	○ ○ ○ ○ ○	36	○ ○ ○ ○ ○		

SECTION 2: MATH ABILITY

	A B C D E		A B C D E		A B C D E		A B C D E		A B C D E
1	○ ○ ○ ○ ○	9	○ ○ ○ ○ ○	17	○ ○ ○ ○ ○	25	○ ○ ○ ○ ○	33	○ ○ ○ ○ ○
2	○ ○ ○ ○ ○	10	○ ○ ○ ○ ○	18	○ ○ ○ ○ ○	26	○ ○ ○ ○ ○	34	○ ○ ○ ○ ○
3	○ ○ ○ ○ ○	11	○ ○ ○ ○ ○	19	○ ○ ○ ○ ○	27	○ ○ ○ ○ ○	35	○ ○ ○ ○ ○
4	○ ○ ○ ○ ○	12	○ ○ ○ ○ ○	20	○ ○ ○ ○ ○	28	○ ○ ○ ○ ○	36	○ ○ ○ ○ ○
5	○ ○ ○ ○ ○	13	○ ○ ○ ○ ○	21	○ ○ ○ ○ ○	29	○ ○ ○ ○ ○		
6	○ ○ ○ ○ ○	14	○ ○ ○ ○ ○	22	○ ○ ○ ○ ○	30	○ ○ ○ ○ ○		
7	○ ○ ○ ○ ○	15	○ ○ ○ ○ ○	23	○ ○ ○ ○ ○	31	○ ○ ○ ○ ○		
8	○ ○ ○ ○ ○	16	○ ○ ○ ○ ○	24	○ ○ ○ ○ ○	32	○ ○ ○ ○ ○		

SECTION 1: VERBAL ABILITY

Vocabulary

Directions

Each of the following questions consists of a word in capital letters, followed by five lettered words or phrases. Choose the word or phrase that is most nearly *opposite* in meaning to the word in capital letters. Since some of the questions require you to distinguish fine shades of meaning, consider all the choices before deciding which is best.

Example:

GOOD:

   (A) sour
   (B) bad
   (C) red
   (D) hot
   (E) ugly

   A B C D E
   ○ ● ○ ○ ○

Note: Although antonyms are no longer a part of the SAT, we are still testing vocabulary through antonyms on this particular test, since it is important for you to develop vocabulary strategies for the Reading Comprehension parts of the SAT.

1. TENACIOUS:

   (A) changing
   (B) stupid
   (C) unconscious
   (D) poor
   (E) antagonistic

2. How did you get your answer?

   (A) I knew the meaning of the word *tenacious*.
   (B) I knew what the root *ten* meant and looked for the opposite of that root.
   (C) I did not know what *tenacious* meant but knew a word that sounded like *tenacious*.

   (D) I guessed.
   (E) none of these

3. PROFICIENT:

   (A) antiseptic
   (B) unwilling
   (C) incompetent
   (D) antagonistic
   (E) awkward

4. How did you get your answer?

   (A) I knew what the prefix *pro-* meant and used it to figure out the capitalized word, but I didn't use any root of *proficient*.
   (B) I used the meaning of the prefix *pro-* and the meaning of the root *fic* to figure out the meaning of the word *proficient*.
   (C) I knew from memory what the word *proficient* meant.
   (D) I guessed.
   (E) none of these

5. DELUDE:

   (A) include
   (B) guide
   (C) reply
   (D) upgrade
   (E) welcome

6. How did you get your answer?

   (A) I knew what the prefix *de-* meant and used it to figure out the meaning of the word *delude*, but I didn't use any root of *delude*.
   (B) I used the meaning of the prefix *de-* and the meaning of the root *lud* to figure out the meaning of the word *delude*.
   (C) I knew from memory what the word *delude* meant.
   (D) I guessed.
   (E) none of these

7. POTENT:
  (A) imposing
  (B) pertinent
  (C) feeble
  (D) comparable
  (E) frantic

8. How did you get your answer?
  (A) I knew what the capitalized word meant.
  (B) I knew a word or part of a word that sounded the same as *potent* or had a close association with the word *potent*.
  (C) I knew a prefix or root of the capitalized word, which gave me a clue to the meaning of the word.
  (D) I knew from a part of the capitalized word that the word had a negative or positive association. Thus, I selected a choice that was opposite in flavor (positive or negative).
  (E) none of these

9. RECEDE:
  (A) accede
  (B) settle
  (C) surrender
  (D) advance
  (E) reform

10. How did you get your answer?
  (A) I found a word opposite in meaning to the word *recede*, *without* looking at the choices. Then I matched my word with the choices.
  (B) I used prefixes and/or roots to get the meaning of the word *recede*.
  (C) I looked at the choices to see which word was opposite to *recede*. I *did not* try first to get my own word that was opposite to the meaning of *recede*, as in Choice A.
  (D) I guessed.
  (E) none of these

11. THERMAL:
  (A) improving
  (B) possible
  (C) beginning
  (D) reduced
  (E) frigid

12. How did you get your answer?
  (A) I knew what the capitalized word meant.
  (B) I knew a word or part of a word that sounded the same as *thermal* or had a close association with the word *thermal*.
  (C) I knew a prefix or root of the capitalized word, which gave me a clue to the meaning of the word.
  (D) I knew from a part of the capitalized word that the word had a negative or positive association. Thus, I selected a choice that was opposite in flavor (positive or negative).
  (E) none of these

13. SLOTHFUL:
  (A) permanent
  (B) ambitious
  (C) average
  (D) truthful
  (E) plentiful

14. How did you get your answer?
  (A) I knew what the capitalized word meant.
  (B) I knew a word or part of a word that sounded the same as *sloth* or had a close association with the word *sloth*.
  (C) I knew a prefix or root of the capitalized word, which gave me a clue to the meaning of the word.
  (D) I knew from a part of the capitalized word that the word had a negative or positive association. Thus, I selected a choice that was opposite in flavor (positive or negative).
  (E) none of these

15. MUNIFICENCE:
  (A) disloyalty
  (B) stinginess
  (C) dispersion
  (D) simplicity
  (E) vehemence

16. How did you get your answer?
  (A) I knew what the capitalized word meant.
  (B) I knew a word or part of a word that sounded the same as *munificence* or had a close association with the word *munificence*.
  (C) I knew a prefix or root of the capitalized word, which gave me a clue to the meaning of the word.

(D) I knew from a part of the capitalized word that the word had a negative or positive association. Thus, I selected a choice that was opposite in flavor (positive or negative).

(E) none of these

17. FORTITUDE:

(A) timidity
(B) conservatism
(C) placidity
(D) laxness
(E) ambition

18. How did you get your answer?

(A) I knew what the capitalized word meant.
(B) I knew a word or part of a word that sounded the same as *fortitude* or had a close association with the word *fortitude*.
(C) I knew a prefix or root of the capitalized word, which gave me a clue to the meaning of the word.
(D) I knew from a part of the capitalized word that the word had a negative or positive association. Thus, I selected a choice that was opposite in flavor (positive or negative).
(E) none of these

19. DETRIMENT:

(A) recurrence
(B) disclosure
(C) resemblance
(D) enhancement
(E) postponement

20. How did you get your answer?

(A) I knew what the capitalized word meant.
(B) I knew a word or part of a word that sounded the same as *detriment* or had a close association with the word *detriment*.
(C) I knew a prefix or root of the capitalized word, which gave me a clue to the meaning of the word.
(D) I knew from a part of the capitalized word that the word had a negative or positive association. Thus, I selected a choice that was opposite in flavor (positive or negative).
(E) none of these

21. CIRCUMSPECT:

(A) suspicious
(B) overbearing
(C) listless
(D) determined
(E) careless

22. How did you get your answer?

(A) I knew what the capitalized word meant.
(B) I knew a word or part of a word that sounded the same as *circumspect* or had a close association with the word *circumspect*.
(C) I knew a prefix or root of the capitalized word, which gave me a clue to the meaning of the word.
(D) I knew from a part of the capitalized word that the word had a negative or positive association. Thus, I selected a choice that was opposite in flavor (positive or negative).
(E) none of these

23. LUCID:

(A) underlying
(B) complex
(C) luxurious
(D) tight
(E) general

24. How did you get your answer?

(A) I knew what the capitalized word meant.
(B) I knew a word or part of a word that sounded the same as *lucid* or had a close association with the word *lucid*.
(C) I knew a prefix or root of the capitalized word, which gave me a clue to the meaning of the word.
(D) I knew from a part of the capitalized word that the word had a negative or positive association. Thus, I selected a choice that was opposite in flavor (positive or negative).
(E) none of these

Reading Passages

Directions

Each of the following passages is followed by questions based on its content. Answer all questions following a passage on the basis of what is *stated* or *implied* in that passage.

Questions 25–30 are based on the following passage.

She walked along the river until a policeman stopped her. It was one o'clock, he said. Not the best time to be walking alone by the side of a half-frozen river. He smiled at her, then offered to walk her home. It was the

5 first day of the new year, 1946, eight and a half months after the British tanks had rumbled into Bergen-Belsen.

That February, my mother turned twenty-six. It was difficult for strangers to believe that she had ever been a concentration camp inmate. Her face was smooth and

10 round. She wore lipstick and applied mascara to her large dark eyes. She dressed fashionably. But when she looked into the mirror in the mornings before leaving for work, my mother saw a shell, a mannequin who moved and spoke but who bore only a superficial

15 resemblance to her real self. The people closest to her had vanished. She had no proof that they were truly dead. No eyewitnesses had survived to vouch for her husband's death. There was no one living who had seen her parents die. The lack of confirmation haunted her.

20 At night before she went to sleep and during the day as she stood pinning dresses she wondered if, by some chance, her parents had gotten past the Germans or had crawled out of the mass grave into which they had been shot and were living, old and helpless, somewhere in

25 Poland. What if only one of them had died? What if they had survived and had died of cold or hunger after she had been liberated, while she was in Celle* dancing with British officers?

She did not talk to anyone about these things. No

30 one, she thought, wanted to hear them. She woke up in the morning, went to work, bought groceries, went to the Jewish Community Center and to the housing office like a robot.

---
*Celle is a small town in Germany.

Questions

25. The policeman stopped the author's mother from walking along the river because

    (A) the river was dangerous
    (B) it was the wrong time of day
    (C) it was still wartime
    (D) it was too cold
    (E) she looked suspicious

26. Which part of the passage gives you the best clue for getting the right answer?

    (A) Line 2: "It was one o'clock, he said."
    (B) Lines 2–3: "It was one o'clock, he said. Not the best time to be walking alone. . . ."
    (C) Lines 2–3: "It was one o'clock, he said. Not the best time to be walking alone by the side of a half-frozen river."
    (D) none of these
    (E) I don't know.

27. The author states that his mother thought about her parents when she

    (A) walked along the river
    (B) thought about death
    (C) danced with the officers
    (D) arose in the morning
    (E) was at work

28. Which part of the passage gives you the best clue for getting the right answer?

    (A) Line 20: "At night before she went to sleep. . . ."
    (B) Lines 20–21: ". . . and during the day as she stood pinning dresses she wondered. . . ."
    (C) Lines 11–12: "But when she looked into the mirror in the mornings. . . ."
    (D) Lines 25–28: "What if they had survived and died of cold . . . while she was . . . dancing with British officers?"
    (E) I don't know.

29. When the author mentions his mother's dancing with the British officers, he implies that his mother

    (A) compared her dancing to the suffering of her parents
    (B) had clearly put her troubles behind her

(C) felt it was her duty to dance with them

(D) felt guilty about dancing

(E) regained the self-confidence she once had

30. Which words expressed in the passage lead us to the right answer?

(A) Line 26: "had survived"

(B) Line 26: "had died of cold or hunger"

(C) Line 22: "gotten past the Germans"

(D) Line 33: "like a robot"

(E) I don't know.

Questions 31–36 are based on the following passage.

This passage is adapted from Claude M. Fuess, "The Retreat from Excellence," Saturday Review, *March 26, 1960, p. 21.*

That one citizen is as good as another is a favorite American axiom, supposed to express the very essence of our Constitution and way of life. But just what do we mean when we utter that platitude? One surgeon
5 is not as good as another. One plumber is not as good as another. We soon become aware of this when we require the attention of either. Yet in political and economic matters we appear to have reached a point where knowledge and specialized training count for very
10 little. A newspaper reporter is sent out on the street to collect the views of various passersby on such a question as "Should the United States defend Afghanistan?" The answer of the barfly who doesn't even know where the country is located, or that it is a country, is quoted
15 in the next edition just as solemnly as that of the college teacher of history. With the basic tenets of democracy— that all people are born free and equal and are entitled to life, liberty, and the pursuit of happiness—no decent American can possibly take issue. But that the opinion
20 of one citizen on a technical subject is just as authoritative as that of another is manifestly absurd. And to accept the opinions of all comers as having the same value is surely to encourage a cult of mediocrity.

Questions

31. Which phrase best expresses the main idea of this passage?

(A) the myth of equality

(B) a distinction about equality

(C) the essence of the Constitution

(D) a technical subject

(E) knowledge and specialized training

32. Which is the best title for this passage?

(A) "Equality—for Everyone, for Every Situation?"

(B) "Dangers of Opinion and Knowledge"

(C) "The American Syndrome"

(D) "Freedom and Equality"

(E) I don't know.

33. The author most probably included the example of the question on Afghanistan (line 12) in order to

(A) move the reader to rage

(B) show that he is opposed to opinion sampling

(C) show that he has thoroughly researched his project

(D) explain the kind of opinion sampling he objects to

(E) provide a humorous but temporary diversion from his main point

34. The distinction between a "barfly" and a college teacher (lines 12–16) is that

(A) one is stupid, the other is not

(B) one is learned, the other is not

(C) one is anti-American, the other is not

(D) one is pro-Afghani, the other is not

(E) I don't know.

35. The author would be most likely to agree that

(A) some men are born to be masters; others are born to be servants

(B) the Constitution has little relevance for today's world

(C) one should never express an opinion on a specialized subject unless he is an expert in that subject

(D) every opinion should be treated equally

(E) all opinions should not be given equal weight

36. Which lines give the best clue to the answer to this question?

(A) Lines 3–6

(B) Lines 4–6

(C) Lines 14–18

(D) Lines 19–23

(E) I don't know.

Questions 37–44 are based on the following passage.

This passage is attributed to D. G. Schueler.

Mist continues to obscure the horizon, but above us the sky is suddenly awash with lavender light. At once the geese respond. Now, as well as their cries, a beating roar rolls across the water as if five thousand house-
5 wives have taken it into their heads to shake out blankets all at one time. Ten thousand housewives. It keeps up—the invisible rhythmic beating of all those goose wings—for what seems a long time. Even Lonnie is held motionless with suspense.
10   Then the geese begin to rise. One, two, three hundred—then a thousand at a time—in long horizontal lines that unfurl like pennants across the sky. The horizon actually darkens as they pass. It goes on and on like that, flock after flock, for three or four minutes,
15 each new contingent announcing its ascent with an accelerating roar of cries and wingbeats. Then gradually the intervals between flights become longer. I think the spectacle is over, until yet another flock lifts up, following the others in a gradual turn toward the north-
20 eastern quadrant of the refuge.
   Finally the sun emerges from the mist; the mist itself thins a little, uncovering the black line of willows on the other side of the wildlife preserve. I remember to close my mouth—which has been open for some
25 time—and inadvertently shut two or three mosquitoes inside. Only a few straggling geese oar their way across the sun's red surface. Lonnie wears an exasperated, proprietary expression, as if he had produced and directed the show himself and had just received a bad
30 review. "It would have been better with more light," he says; "I can't always guarantee just when they'll start moving." I assure him I thought it was a fantastic sight. "Well," he rumbles, "I guess it wasn't too bad."

Questions

37. In the descriptive phrase "shake out blankets all at one time" (lines 5–6), the author is appealing chiefly to the reader's
    (A) background
    (B) sight
    (C) emotions
    (D) thoughts
    (E) hearing

38. Which words preceding the descriptive phrase "shake out blankets all at one time" (lines 5–6) give us a clue to the correct answer to the previous question (question 37)?
    (A) "into their heads"
    (B) "lavender light"
    (C) "across the water"
    (D) "a beating roar"
    (E) I don't know.

39. The mood created by the author is one of
    (A) tranquility
    (B) excitement
    (C) sadness
    (D) bewilderment
    (E) unconcern

40. Which word in the passage is most closely associated with the correct answer?
    (A) mist
    (B) spectacle
    (C) geese
    (D) refuge
    (E) I don't know.

41. The main idea expressed by the author about the geese is that they
    (A) are spectacular to watch
    (B) are unpredictable
    (C) disturb the environment
    (D) produce a lot of noise
    (E) fly in large flocks

42. Which line or lines give us a clue to the answer?
    (A) Line 1
    (B) Lines 17–18
    (C) Line 21
    (D) Line 33
    (E) I don't know.

43. Judging from the passage, the reader can conclude that
    (A) the speaker dislikes nature's inconveniences
    (B) the geese's timing is predictable
    (C) Lonnie has had the experience before
    (D) both observers are hunters
    (E) the author and Lonnie are the same person

44. Which gives us a clue to the right answer?
    (A) Lines 10–11
    (B) Line 21
    (C) Lines 23–25
    (D) Lines 31–32
    (E) I don't know.

SECTION 2: MATH ABILITY

Directions

For this section, solve each problem and decide which is the best of the choices given. Fill in the corresponding circle on the answer sheet. You may use any available space for scratch work.

Notes

1. The use of a calculator is permitted.
2. All numbers used are real numbers.
3. Figures that accompany problems in this test are intended to provide information useful in solving the problems. They are drawn as accurately as possible EXCEPT when it is stated in a specific problem that the figure is not drawn to scale. All figures lie in a plane unless otherwise indicated.
4. Unless otherwise specified, the domain of any function f is assumed to be the set of all real numbers x for which $f(x)$ is a real number.

Geometry Reference

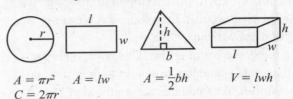

$A = \pi r^2$ $A = lw$ $A = \frac{1}{2}bh$ $V = lwh$
$C = 2\pi r$

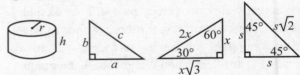

$V = \pi r^2 h$ $c^2 = a^2 + b^2$ *Special Right Triangles*

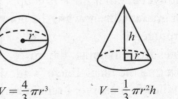

$V = \frac{4}{3}\pi r^3$ $V = \frac{1}{3}\pi r^2 h$ $V = \frac{1}{3}lwh$

The number of degrees of arc in a circle is 360. The sum of the measures in degrees of the angles of a triangle is 180.

Mathematical Symbols

· multiplication dot; as in $x \cdot y$
( ) parentheses; used to group expressions
% percent
÷ division
: ratio
= equals
≠ does not equal
< less than
> greater than
≤ less than or equal to
≥ greater than or equal to
√ square root

π pi, the ratio of the circumference of a circle to its diameter, which is approximately equal to $\frac{22}{7}$ or 3.14.
∠ angle
‖ is parallel to
⊥ is perpendicular to
∧ and
∨ or
~ is similar to, or approximately
→ implies
∈ belongs to
⊂ is a subset of

1. If $P \times \frac{11}{14} = \frac{11}{14} \times \frac{8}{9}$, then $P =$

(A) $\frac{8}{9}$

(B) $\frac{9}{8}$

(C) 8

(D) 11

(E) 14

2. How did you get your answer?

(A) I multiplied $\frac{11}{14}$ by $\frac{8}{9}$, reducing first.

(B) I multiplied 11×8 and then divided the product by 14×9.

(C) I canceled $\frac{11}{14}$ from both sides of the equals sign.

(D) I guessed.

(E) none of these

3. Sarah is twice as old as John. Six years ago, Sarah was 4 times as old as John was then. How old is John now?

(A) 3

(B) 9

(C) 18

(D) 20

(E) cannot be determined

4. How did you get your answer?

(A) I substituted S for *Sarah*, $=$ for *is*, and J for *John* in the first sentence of the problem. Then I translated the second sentence into mathematical terms also.

(B) I tried specific numbers for *Sarah* and/or *John*.

(C) I racked my brain to figure out the ages but didn't write any equations down.

(D) I guessed.

(E) none of these

5. 200 is what percent of 20?

(A) $\frac{1}{10}$

(B) 10

(C) 100

(D) 1,000

(E) 10,000

6. How did you get your answer?

(A) I translated *is* to $=$, *what* to a variable, *of* to $\times$, etc. Then I was able to set up an equation.

(B) I just divided the two numbers and multiplied by 100 to get the percentage.

(C) I tried to remember how to work with *is-of* problems, putting the *of* over *is* or the *is* over *of*.

(D) I guessed.

(E) none of these

7. In the diagram below, $\triangle XYZ$ has been inscribed in a circle. If the circle encloses an area of 64, and the area of $\triangle XYZ$ is 15, then what is the area of the shaded region?

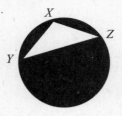

(A) 25

(B) 36

(C) 49

(D) 79

(E) cannot be determined

8. How did you get your answer?

(A) I tried to calculate the area of the circle and the area of the triangle.

(B) I used a special triangle or tried different triangles whose area was 15.

(C) I subtracted 15 from 64.

(D) I guessed.

(E) none of these

9. $66^2 + 2(34)(66) + 34^2 =$

(A) 4,730

(B) 5,000

(C) 9,860

(D) 9,950

(E) 10,000

10. How did you get your answer?

    (A) I multiplied 66×66, $2 \times 34 \times 66$, and 34×34 and added the results.
    (B) I approximated a solution.
    (C) I noticed that $66^2 + 2(34)(66) + 34^2$ had the form of $a^2 + 2ab + b^2$ and set the form equal to $(a + b)^2$.
    (D) I guessed.
    (E) none of these

11. The average height of three students is 68 inches. If two of the students have heights of 70 inches and 72 inches respectively, then what is the height (in inches) of the third student?

    (A) 60
    (B) 62
    (C) 64
    (D) 65
    (E) 66

12. How did you get your answer?

    (A) I used the following equation:

    $$(68 + 2) + (68 + 4) + x = 68 + 68 + 68$$

    Then I got:
    $68 + 68 + (x + 6) = 68 + 68 + 68$, and crossed off the two 68s on both sides of the equation to come up with $x + 6 = 68$.
    (B) I was able to eliminate the incorrect choices without figuring out a complete solution.
    (C) I got the equation $\dfrac{(70 + 72 + x)}{3} = 68$, then solved for x.
    (D) I guessed.
    (E) none of these

13. If $0 < x < 1$, then which of the following must be true?

    I. $2x < 2$
    II. $x - 1 < 0$
    III. $x^2 < x$

    (A) I only
    (B) II only
    (C) I and II only
    (D) II and III only
    (E) I, II, and III

14. How did you get your answer?

    (A) I plugged in only one number for x in I, II, and III.
    (B) I plugged in more than one number for x and tried I, II, and III using each set of numbers.
    (C) I used the fact that $0 < x$ and $x < 1$ and manipulated those inequalities in I, II, and III.
    (D) I guessed.
    (E) none of these

15. The sum of the cubes of any two consecutive positive integers is always

    (A) an odd integer
    (B) an even integer
    (C) the cube of an integer
    (D) the square of an integer
    (E) the product of an integer and 3

16. How did you get your answer?

    (A) I translated the statement into the form $x^3 + (x + 1)^3 = $ _____ and tried to see what I would get.
    (B) I tried numbers like 1 and 2 for the consecutive integers. Then I calculated the sum of the cubes of those numbers. I was able to eliminate some choices and then tried some other numbers for the consecutive integers to eliminate more choices.
    (C) I said, of two consecutive positive integers, one is even and therefore its cube is even. The other integer is odd; therefore its cube is odd. An odd + an even is an odd.
    (D) I guessed.
    (E) none of these

17. If p is a positive integer, which *could* be an odd integer?

    (A) $2p + 2$
    (B) $p^3 - p$
    (C) $p^2 + p$
    (D) $p^2 - p$
    (E) $7p - 3$

18. How did you get your answer?

(A) I plugged in a number or numbers for p and started testing all the choices, *starting with Choice A.*

(B) I plugged in a number or numbers for p in each of the choices, *starting with Choice E.*

(C) I looked at Choice E first to see if $7p - 3$ had the form of an even or odd integer.

(D) I guessed.

(E) none of these

19. In this figure,

A
•━━━━━━━━━ l

two points, B and C, are placed to the right of point A such that $4AB = 3AC$. The value of $\dfrac{BC}{AB}$

(A) equals $\dfrac{1}{3}$

(B) equals $\dfrac{2}{3}$

(C) equals $\dfrac{3}{2}$

(D) equals 3

(E) cannot be determined

20. How did you get your answer?

(A) I drew points B and C on the line and labeled AB as a and BC as b and then worked with a and b.

(B) I substituted numbers for AB and AC.

(C) I drew points B and C on the line and worked with equations involving BC and AB.

(D) I guessed.

(E) none of these

21. A man rode a bicycle a straight distance at a speed of 10 miles per hour. He came back the same way, traveling the same distance at a speed of 20 miles per hour. What was the man's total number of miles for the trip back and forth if his total traveling time was one hour?

(A) 15

(B) $13\dfrac{1}{3}$

(C) $7\dfrac{1}{2}$

(D) $6\dfrac{2}{3}$

(E) $6\dfrac{1}{3}$

22. How did you answer this question?

(A) I used Rate × Time = Distance and plugged in my own numbers.

(B) I averaged 10 and 20 and worked from there.

(C) I called the times going back and forth by two different unknown variables but noted that the sum of these times was 1 hour.

(D) I guessed.

(E) none of these

23. If the symbol ϕ is defined by the equation

$$a \phi b = a - b - ab$$

for all a and b, then $\left(-\dfrac{1}{3}\right) \phi (-3) =$

(A) $\dfrac{5}{3}$

(B) $\dfrac{11}{3}$

(C) $-\dfrac{13}{5}$

(D) -4

(E) -5

24. How did you get your answer?

(A) I played around with the numbers $-\dfrac{1}{3}$ and -3 to get my answer. I didn't use any substitution method.

(B) I substituted in $a \phi b = a - b - ab$, $\left(-\dfrac{1}{3}\right)$ for a and -3 for b.

(C) I worked backward.

(D) I guessed.

(E) none of these

25. If $y^8 = 4$ and $y^7 = \dfrac{3}{x}$, what is the value of y in terms of x?

(A) $\dfrac{4x}{3}$

(B) $\dfrac{3x}{4}$

(C) $\dfrac{4}{x}$

(D) $\dfrac{x}{4}$

(E) $\dfrac{12}{x}$

26. How did you get your answer?

   (A) I solved for the value of y from $y^8 = 4$. Then I substituted that value of y in $y^7 = \dfrac{3}{x}$.

   (B) I took the seventh root of y in the second equation.

   (C) I divided the first equation by the second equation to get y alone in terms of x.

   (D) I guessed.

   (E) none of these

27. If $4x + 5y = 10$ and $x + 3y = 8$, then $\dfrac{5x + 8y}{3} =$

   (A) 18

   (B) 15

   (C) 12

   (D) 9

   (E) 6

28. How did you get your answer?

   (A) I solved both simultaneous equations for x and for y, then substituted the values of x and y into $\dfrac{(5x + 8y)}{3}$.

   (B) I tried numbers for x and for y that would satisfy the first two equations.

   (C) I added both equations to get $5x + 8y$. Then I divided my result by 3.

   (D) I guessed.

   (E) none of these

29. The circle with center A and radius AB is inscribed in the square here. AB is extended to C. What is the ratio of AB to AC?

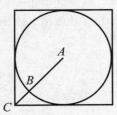

   (A) $\sqrt{2}$

   (B) $\dfrac{\sqrt{2}}{4}$

   (C) $\dfrac{\sqrt{2} - 1}{2}$

   (D) $\dfrac{\sqrt{2}}{2}$

   (E) none of these

30. How did you get your answer?

   (A) I approximated the solution. I looked to see what the ratio of AB to AC might be from the diagram. Then I looked through the choices to see which choice was reasonable or to eliminate incorrect choices.

   (B) I saw a relationship between AB and AC but didn't draw any other lines.

   (C) I dropped a perpendicular from A to one of the sides of the square, then worked with the isosceles right triangle. I also labeled length AB by a single letter, and BC by another single letter.

   (D) I guessed.

   (E) none of these

31. In the accompanying figure, BD is a straight line. What is the value of a?

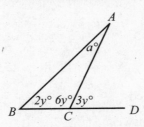

   (*Note*: Figure is not drawn to scale.)

   (A) 15

   (B) 17

   (C) 20

   (D) 24

   (E) 30

32. How did you get your answer?

   (A) I *first* said that $2y + 6y + a = 180$.

   (B) I *first* said that $6y + 3y = 180$, then solved for y.

   (C) I *first* said $3y = 2y + a$.

   (D) I guessed.

   (E) none of these

33. What is the perimeter of the accompanying figure if *B* and *C* are right angles?

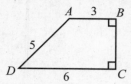

(*Note*: Figure is not drawn to scale.)

(A) 14
(B) 16
(C) 18
(D) 20
(E) cannot be determined

34. How did you get your answer?

(A) I tried to first find angles *A* and *D*.
(B) I drew a perpendicular from *A* to *DC* and labeled *BC* as an unknown (*x* or *y*, etc.).
(C) I labeled *BC* as an unknown (*x* or *y*, etc.) but *did not* draw a perpendicular line from *A* to *DC*.
(D) I guessed.
(E) none of these

35. Which of the angles below has a degree measure that can be determined?

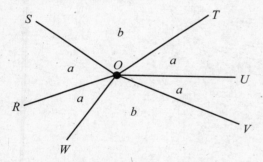

(*Note*: Figure is not drawn to scale.)

(A) ∠*WOS*
(B) ∠*SOU*
(C) ∠*WOT*
(D) ∠*ROV*
(E) ∠*WOV*

36. How did you get your answer?

(A) I first said that $4a + 2b = 360$, got $2a + b = 180$, and then looked through the choices.
(B) I looked through the choices first.
(C) I knew that the sum of the angles added up to 360° but didn't know where to go from there.
(D) I guessed.
(E) none of these

This is the end of the Strategy Diagnostic Test for the New SAT. You've answered the questions in both the Verbal and Math sections, and you've recorded how you arrived at each answer.

Now you're ready to find out how you did. Go right to the table that follows for answer checking, diagnosis, and prescription.

Remember, the questions are in pairs: the odd-numbered ones are the questions themselves; the even-numbered ones, the approach you used to solve the questions. If either or both of your answers—solution and/or approach—fail to correspond to the answers given in the table, you should study the strategy for that pair.

The table also gives the SAT score increase that's possible if you master that strategy. The approximate time it should take to answer a particular question is also supplied. By using the best strategies throughout the actual SAT, you should increase accuracy, make the best use of your time, and thus improve your score dramatically.

Note: If the even-numbered answer (for questions 2, 4, 6, etc.) does not match with your answer, you may want to look at the approach described in the answer, as you may be able to use that approach with other questions.

ANSWER AND DIAGNOSTIC TABLE

SECTION 1: VERBAL ABILITY

Question number	Answer	*If either or both of your answers do not match the answers to the left, then refer to this strategy	Possible score increase if strategy is learned	Estimated time to solve each odd-numbered question (in seconds)
1	A			
2	B	Vocabulary 1, pp. 148–149	60	20
3	C			
4	B	Vocabulary 1, pp. 148–149	60	20
5	B			
6	B	Vocabulary 1, pp. 148–149	60	20
7	C			
8	B	Vocabulary 3, pp. 151–152	30	20
9	D			
10	B	Vocabulary 1, pp. 148–149	60	20
11	E			
12	B	Vocabulary 3, pp. 151–152	30	20
13	B			
14	B	Vocabulary 2, pp. 150–151	30	20
15	B			
16	B, C	Vocabulary 2, pp. 150–151	30	20
17	A			
18	B	Vocabulary 3, pp. 151–152	30	20
19	D			
20	B, C, D	Vocabulary 2, pp. 150–151	30	20
21	E			
22	B	Vocabulary 1, pp. 148–149	60	30
23	B			
24	B	Vocabulary 3, pp. 151–152	30	20

*Note: The solution to the odd-numbered question appears in the strategy section listed.

ANSWER AND DIAGNOSTIC TABLE (CONTINUED)

SECTION 1: VERBAL ABILITY

Question number	Answer	*If either or both of your answers do not match the answers to the left, then refer to this strategy	Possible score increase if strategy is learned	Estimated time to solve each odd-numbered question (in seconds)
25	B	Reading Comprehension 1, 2, pp. 132–136		
26	B		200	15
27	E	Reading Comprehension 1, 2, pp. 132–136		
28	B		200	20
29	D	Reading Comprehension 1, 2, pp. 132–136		
30	B		200	20
31	B	Reading Comprehension 1, 2, pp. 132–136		
32	B		200	20
33	D	Reading Comprehension 1, 2, pp. 132–136		
34	B		200	30
35	E	Reading Comprehension 1, 2, pp. 132–136		
36	D		200	30
37	E	Reading Comprehension 1, 2, pp. 132–136		
38	D		200	20
39	B	Reading Comprehension 1, 2, pp. 132–136		
40	B		200	20
41	A	Reading Comprehension 1, 2, pp. 132–136		
42	B		200	20
43	C	Reading Comprehension 1, 2, pp. 132–136		
44	D		200	30

*Note: The solution to the odd-numbered question appears in the strategy section listed.

ANSWER AND DIAGNOSTIC TABLE (CONTINUED)

SECTION 2: MATH ABILITY

Question number	Answer	*If either or both of your answers do not match the answers to the left, then refer to this strategy	Possible score increase if strategy is learned	Estimated time to solve each odd-numbered question (in seconds)
1	A			
2	C	Math 1, pp. 72–73	20	10
3	B			
4	A	Math 2, pp. 74–80	60	40
5	D			
6	A	Math 2, pp. 74–80	60	30
7	C			
8	C	Math 3, pp. 80–82	10	20
9	E			
10	C	Math 4, pp. 83–86	20	40
11	B			
12	C	Math 5, pp. 86–89	20	40
13	E			
14	C	Math 6, pp. 89–91	140	50
15	A			
16	B or C	Math 7, pp. 91–93	30	40
17	E			
18	B or C	Math 8, pp. 93–95	20	30

*Note: The solution to the odd-numbered question appears in the strategy section listed.

ANSWER AND DIAGNOSTIC TABLE *(CONTINUED)*

SECTION 2: MATH ABILITY

Question number	Answer	*If either or both of your answers do not match the answers to the left, then refer to this strategy	Possible score increase if strategy is learned	Estimated time to solve each odd-numbered question (in seconds)
19	A			
20	A	Math 14, pp. 105–111	50	40
21	B			
22	C	Math 9, pp. 95–97	10	60
23	A			
24	B	Math 11, pp. 99–101	30	50
25	A			
26	C	Math 12 or 13, pp. 101–105	50	30
27	E			
28	C	Math 13, pp. 102–105	20	20
29	D			
30	C	Math 14, 18, pp. 105–111, 117–121	80	50
31	C			
32	B	Math 17, 18, pp. 114–121	160	40
33	C			
34	B	Math 14, 18, pp. 105–111, 117–121	80	30
35	C			
36	A	Math 17, pp. 114–117	140	40

*Note: The solution to the odd-numbered question appears in the strategy section listed.

PART 2

The World's Shortest New SAT Practice Test

20 Questions to Approximate Your New SAT Score

And the Exact Strategies You Need to Improve Your Score

Although it shouldn't take you more than approximately 40 seconds to answer each Verbal (Reading and Writing) question and 1 minute to answer each Math question, you may take this test untimed and still get a fairly accurate prediction of your SAT score.

Notes: The PSAT score is approximately calculated by dividing the SAT score by 10 and is used for National Merit Scholarships.

Top schools expect SAT scores in the 75th percentile or higher. Following is a test that can determine if you have the goods—and it won't take you more than 28 minutes.

ANSWER SHEET

Complete Mark ●   **Examples of Incomplete Marks** ⦿ ⊗ ⊖ ◑ ⊘ ◔ ◕ ●

READING

	A	B	C	D			A	B	C	D
1	○	○	○	○		4	○	○	○	○
2	○	○	○	○		5	○	○	○	○
3	○	○	○	○						

WRITING AND LANGUAGE

	A	B	C	D			A	B	C	D
1	○	○	○	○		4	○	○	○	○
2	○	○	○	○		5	○	○	○	○
3	○	○	○	○						

MATH

	A	B	C	D			A	B	C	D
1	○	○	○	○		6	○	○	○	○
2	○	○	○	○		7	○	○	○	○
3	○	○	○	○		8	○	○	○	○
4	○	○	○	○		9	○	○	○	○
5	○	○	○	○		10	○	○	○	○

This is a 20-question test—28 minutes—that I developed. Although my test has appeared in many newspapers and magazines (*Washington Post, St. Louis Post-Dispatch, Business Insider*, etc.) I wanted to make sure you have it here.

This is the shortest test which will provide you with an approximate score you would expect to receive from the New SAT, which was first given in March 2016. It provides you with explanatory answers and strategies for solving the questions as well as what score increase you might receive if you learn the strategies.

Here is the test.

READING TEST

8 Minutes

Questions 1–5 are based on the following passage.

Classical music is termed "classical" because it can be heard over and over again without the listener tiring of the music. A symphony of Brahms can be heard and heard again with the same or even heightened enjoy-
5 ment a few months later. It is unfortunate that the sales of classical music are dismal compared to other types of music. Perhaps this is because many people in our generation were not exposed to classical music at an early age and therefore did not get to know the music.
10   In contrast to classical music, contemporary non-classical music has a high impact on the listener but unfortunately is not evergreen. Its enjoyment lasts only as long as there is current interest in the topic or emotion that the music portrays, and that only lasts for
15 three months or so until other music replaces it, espe-cially when another best-selling song comes out. The reason that the impact of this type of music is not as great when it first comes out is thought to be because technically the intricacy of the music is not high and
20 not sophisticated, although many critics believe it is because the music elicits a particular emotional feeling that gradually becomes worn out in time.

Questions

1. According to the passage, it can be assumed that the majority of younger people do not like classical music because they:
   (A) buy only the best-selling songs
   (B) do not have the sophistication of a true music lover
   (C) grow tired of classical music
   (D) did not hear that type of music in their youth

2. A particular piece of contemporary music may not be enjoyed as long as a piece of classical music because of the:
   (A) emotion of a person, which is thought to change in time
   (B) high sophistication of the classical music and its technical intricacy
   (C) fact that there is always another piece of contemporary music that replaces the one before it
   (D) economy and marketing of the songs

3. Which choice provides the best evidence for the answer to the previous question?
   (A) Lines 7–9: "Perhaps . . . music."
   (B) Lines 10–12: "In contrast . . . evergreen."
   (C) Lines 16–19: "The reason . . . high. . . ."
   (D) Lines 21–22: "because . . . time."

4. The graph below illustrates the number of listeners of a particular type of music per day in a metro-politan area.

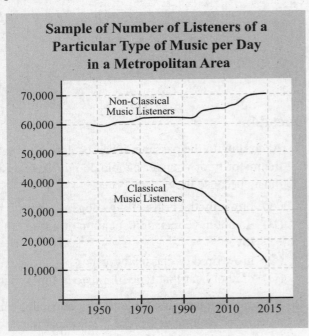

Sample of Number of Listeners of a Particular Type of Music per Day in a Metropolitan Area

According to the graph,

(A) the number of those who listen to classical music and non-classical music is steadily declining

(B) the gap between the listeners of classical music and non-classical music steadily increased through the years 1970–2015

(C) the number of listeners of classical music was at some time as large as the listeners of non-classical music

(D) it can be assumed that the number of classical music listeners will exceed the number of listeners of non-classical music at some point in time

5. The term *evergreen* at the beginning of the second paragraph most nearly means:

(A) colorful

(B) lasting

(C) current

(D) encompassing

WRITING AND LANGUAGE TEST

5 Minutes

Directions

Some questions will direct you to an underlined portion of the passage. Other questions will direct you to a location in the passage. After reading the passage, choose the answer to each question that most effectively improves the quality of writing or that makes the passage conform to the conventions of standard written English. Some questions include a "NO CHANGE" option. Choose that option if you think the best choice is to leave the relevant portion of the passage as it is.

Questions 1–5 are based on the following passage.

This passage is from Rachel Carson's The Sea Around Us, *1950.*

(1) Sometimes the meaning of the glowing water is ominous. (2) <u>On</u> the Pacific Coast of North America, it may mean that the sea is filled with . . . a minute plant that contains a poison of strange and terrible virulence (3) <u>about four days</u> after this minute plant comes to dominate the coastal plankton, some of the fishes and shellfish in the vicinity become toxic. (4) This is because in (5) <u>their</u> normal feeding, they have strained the poisonous plankton out of the water.

Questions

1. Which sentence could appear as the sentence preceding the first sentence of this passage?

   (A) The sea has many interesting attributes.
   (B) The Pacific Coastline is frightening.
   (C) Ships sometimes take Southern routes to avoid bad weather conditions.
   (D) There are strange plants in the sea.

2. (A) NO CHANGE
   (B) Off
   (C) Apart from
   (D) Not from

3. (A) NO CHANGE
   (B) . About four days
   (C) ; about four days
   (D) , about four days

4. At this point the author is considering adding the following true statement right before the last sentence: "The fishes and shellfish die soon after." Should the author make this addition here?

   (A) No, because this destroys the connection between the last sentence and the initial preceding one.
   (B) No, because there is too much of a leap from "toxicity" to "death."
   (C) Yes, because it follows that if fish are toxic they will soon die.
   (D) Yes, because this qualifies the last sentence and puts it in its right place.

5. (A) NO CHANGE
   (B) they're
   (C) its
   (D) it's

MATH TEST

15 Minutes

Questions 1–3 (calculator allowed)

1. In a college biology class, 60 students are chosen to study microorganisms. The study groups have been divided into 18 sections and each section will have 3 or 6 students. How many of the sections will have exactly 3 students?

   (A) 2
   (B) 4
   (C) 12
   (D) 16

2. If $-\dfrac{5}{4} < -2p + 3 < -1$, what is one possible value of $6p - 9$?

   (A) 2
   (B) $2\dfrac{1}{2}$
   (C) 3
   (D) $3\dfrac{1}{2}$

3. There are 180 tennis players competing in a tournament. The tennis players are separated into three levels of ability: **A** (high), **B** (middle), and **C** (low), with the number of players in each category shown in the table below.

Level	Number of Players
A	30
B	60
C	90

   The tennis committee has 54 prizes and will award them proportionately to the number of players at each level. How many prizes will be awarded to players in level A?

   (A) 6
   (B) 7
   (C) 8
   (D) 9

Questions 4–10 (no calculator allowed)

4. If $x - 4$ is a factor of $x^2 - ax + a$, what is the value of a if a is a constant?

   (A) $\dfrac{16}{3}$
   (B) $\dfrac{8}{3}$
   (C) $-\dfrac{8}{3}$
   (D) $-\dfrac{16}{3}$

5. In triangle AEF, $AE = AF$ and $EF = 24$. $\angle EBD$ and $\angle DCF = 90°$. The ratio of BD to CD is 4:6. What is the length of ED?

   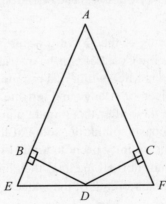

   (Note: Triangle is not drawn to scale.)

   (A) $\dfrac{48}{5}$
   (B) $\dfrac{44}{5}$
   (C) $\dfrac{42}{5}$
   (D) 8

6. If $8x - 2y = 6y + 14$ and $4x + 16y = 9$, what is the value of xy?

(A) $\dfrac{7}{40}$

(B) $\dfrac{9}{50}$

(C) $\dfrac{37}{200}$

(D) $\dfrac{19}{100}$

7. Mr. Martinez's tenth-grade class took a survey to see what activities each student engages in one hour before bed. When the survey was complete, 5 students selected "Play video games" and "Watch TV." 14 students selected "Watch TV," and 8 students selected "Play video games." How many students are in Mr. Martinez's class? (Assume that every student in the class watches TV only, plays video games only, or does both.)

(A) 11
(B) 17
(C) 22
(D) 25

8. A band wants to produce CDs from their music. They have an original CD but need to duplicate the CD to sell to the public. The band buys a CD burning machine for $169.99. Each blank CD they use will cost $1.50. What is the total production cost for making x CDs from their original CD?

(A) $168.49
(B) $169.99 + 1.50x$
(C) 169.99x$ + $1.50
(D) $171.49

9. In the following figure, adjacent sides meet at right angles. What is the perimeter of the figure?

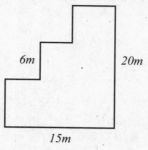

(A) 35 m
(B) 70 m
(C) 140 m
(D) 160 m

10. A ladder (represented by the hypotenuse of the triangle below) is set up against the wall as shown below. The bottom of the ladder is 6 feet from the wall. Which is true of the angle the ladder makes with the ground if the ladder is 10 feet in length?

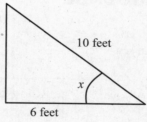

(A) $\sin x^\circ = \dfrac{4}{5}$

(B) $\cos x^\circ = \dfrac{4}{5}$

(C) $\cot x^\circ = \dfrac{4}{3}$

(D) $\tan x^\circ = \dfrac{3}{4}$

ANSWER AND DIAGNOSTIC TABLES

READING

Question number	Correct answer	Strategies found in this book	Score increase if you learn strategies shown in answers for either test
1	D	Readings 1, 2	50
2	A	Readings 1, 2	50
3	D	Readings 1, 2	50
4	B	Readings 1, 10	40
5	B	Reading 5	40

WRITING AND LANGUAGE

Question number	Correct answer	Strategies found in this book	Score increase if you learn strategies shown in answers for either test
1	A	Know how to connect sentences in a passage	30
2	B	Know how to use appropriate words to describe something	30
3	B	Know how to use punctuation to link parts of the passage	30
4	A	Know when and how to make connections by using another sentence	40
5	A	Know what to use when we are talking about quantity	30

ANSWER AND DIAGNOSTIC TABLES (CONTINUED)

MATH

Question number	Correct answer	Strategies found in this book	Score increase if you learn strategies shown in answers for either test
1	D	2, 13	60, 30
2	D	13	30
3	D	17	70
4	A	2, 4	60, 20
5	A	2, 14	60, 50
6	C	17, 13	70, 30
7	B	Know how to use Venn diagrams	20
8	B	2	60
9	B	14	50
10	A	17	70

Here's the table to calculate your score and thus your approximate actual NEW SAT score.

READING AND WRITING
(Reading Questions 1–5; Writing Questions 1–5)

Questions right	New SAT score
10	800
9	780
8	700
7	630
6	540
5	500
4	430
3	320
2	250
1	210

MATH
(Questions 1–10)

Questions right	New SAT score
10	800
9	780
8	700
7	650
6	550
5	500
4	450
3	350
2	250
1	220

EXPLANATORY ANSWERS

With Important Strategies

Reading Test Answers

1. Choice D is correct. See lines where it states that many people in our generation were not exposed to classical music. Don't be lured to the distractor Choice A, even though there was mention of sales.

   Strategy: Determine the Type of Question: Main Idea, Detecting Details, Inference, or Tone/Mood.

   Strategy: Underline Key Parts of Passage.

2. Choice A is correct. See lines where it mentions that the emotional feeling gradually wears out in time.

   Strategy: Determine the Type of Question: Main Idea, Detecting Details, Inference, or Tone/Mood.

   Strategy: Underline Key Parts of Passage.

3. Choice D is correct. The phrase "although many critics believe it is because the music elicits a particular emotional feeling that gradually becomes worn out in time."

   Strategy: Determine the Type of Question: Main Idea, Detecting Details, Inference, or Tone/Mood.

   Strategy: Underline Key Parts of Passage.

4. Choice B is correct. You can see that the difference (gap) between the number of classical music lovers and non-classical music lovers gets greater as time goes on. Choice A is incorrect: The number of listeners of non-classical music was not steadily declining. Choice C is incorrect: The number of listeners of classical music was always less than the listeners of non-classical music. Choice D is incorrect: It seems that the number of classical music lovers is diminishing in time while the number of non-classical music lovers is increasing or remaining steady.

   Strategy: Determine the Type of Question: Main Idea, Detecting Details, Inference, or Tone/Mood.

   Strategy: Know How to Work with Graphs.

5. Choice B is correct. Since the sentence after the one with "evergreen" indicates that the enjoyment lasts only for a short time, "lasting" would be an appropriate definition of "evergreen" in this context. Be careful of the distractor choice "colorful."

   Strategy: Get Meanings of Words Using Context Method.

Writing and Language Test Answers

1. Choice A is correct. In a passage, we start generally, then discuss specifics. Choice B is incorrect. We are discussing the sea, not the Pacific Coastline. Choice C is incorrect. There is no direct connection between this sentence and the first sentence in the passage. Choice D is incorrect. Plants are discussed later in the passage, so the first sentence about plants would not be appropriate here.

   Strategy: Know How to Connect Sentences in a Passage.

2. Choice B is correct. We are talking about something away from, or "off," the Pacific Coast. Choice A is incorrect. We are not talking about something on the coast—we are talking about something in the water *off* the coast. Choice C is incorrect. We are not contrasting the coast and the sea, so we do not use the word *apart*. Choice D is incorrect. "Not from" does not make sense here, since we eventually talk about the sea.

   Strategy: Know How to Use Appropriate Words to Describe Something.

3. Choice B is correct. We need a new sentence here, because something new is discussed. Choice A is incorrect. The dash is not appropriate since the part is not directly linked to the preceding part—a new idea is discussed. Choice C is incorrect. The semicolon is not appropriate since a new idea is discussed here. Choice D is incorrect. The comma would create a run-on sentence.

Strategy: Know How to Use Punctuation to Link Parts of the Passage.

4. Choice A is correct. We need to maintain a connection here—when it says the fish become toxic, we need another sentence immediately following this one explaining why they become toxic. Choice B is incorrect. There is not too much of a leap from "toxicity" to "death." Choice C is incorrect. This may be so, but inserting the sentence would destroy a connection, as described before. Choice D is incorrect. This is not true since a connection would be destroyed between the last sentence and the one preceding initially.

Strategy: Know When and How to Make Connections by Using Another Sentence.

5. Choice A is correct. Since we mean more than one, we use *their*. Choice B is incorrect. *They're* means "they are," which does not make sense. Choice C is incorrect. Since we are referring to more than one, we do not use *its*. Choice D is incorrect. *It's* means "It is," which does not make sense.

Strategy: Know What to Use When We Are Talking about Quantity.

Math Test Answers

1. Choice D is correct.

Strategy: Translate Words into Math.

Let the number of sections with 3 students be denoted as x and the number of sections with 6 students be denoted as y.

Then $\boxed{1}$, $3x + 6y = 60$ (the total number of students),

And $\boxed{2}$, $x + y = 18$ (the number of sections).

Now use a strategy of simplifying the equations.

Simplify Equation $\boxed{1}$ by dividing both sides by 3:

Equation $\boxed{1}$ becomes: $x + 2y = 20$.

But we have $\boxed{2}$: $x + y = 18$.

Now use a strategy of subtracting Equation $\boxed{2}$ from Equation $\boxed{1}$. We get:

$$y = 2$$

Now substitute $y = 2$ into Equation $\boxed{2}$ and we get:

$$x = 16$$

2. Choice D is correct.

Anything less than $\frac{15}{4}$ or greater than $+3$.

Look at $\boxed{1}$: $-\frac{5}{4} < -2p + 3$

Use the strategy of representing $6p - 9$ in a form you already have:

$(-2p + 3)(-3) = 6p - 9$

So multiply inequality $\boxed{1}$ by (-3).

You need to use the basic skill: You reverse the inequality when you multiply by a negative number.

So $\left(-\frac{5}{4}\right)(-3) > (-2p + 3)(-3)$

or

$\frac{15}{4} > 6p - 9$

Now look at the given $-2p + 3 < -1$

Multiply this by (-3):

You again have to reverse the inequality sign and get:

$(-2p + 3)(-3) > (-3)(-1)$

or

$6p - 9 > 3$

So the value of $6p - 9$ is such that

$\frac{15}{4} > 6p - 9 > 3$

or

$3\frac{3}{4} > 6p - 9 > 3$

Thus one value of $6p - 9$ can be $3\frac{1}{2}$.

3. Choice D is correct.

Strategy: Use Given Information Effectively.

The phrase "proportionately . . . in each category" means that

$$\frac{number\ of\ tennis\ players\ in\ Category\ A}{total\ number\ of\ tennis\ players}$$

$$= \frac{number\ of\ prizes\ awarded\ in\ Category\ A}{total\ number\ of\ prizes}$$

So, where x is the number of prizes awarded in Category A:

$$\frac{30}{180} = \frac{x}{54}$$

$$\frac{1}{6} = \frac{x}{54}$$

$$x = \frac{54}{6} = 9$$

4. Choice A is correct.

Strategy: Translate Words into Math.

$(x - 4)$ is a factor of $x^2 - ax + a$ means that there is another factor

$(x + b)$ of $x^2 - ax + a$ such that
$(x - 4)(x + b) = x^2 - ax + a$.

Now use the strategy of writing $(x - 4)(x + b)$ in another form to get more information.

Multiply out:
$(x - 4)(x + b) = x^2 - 4x + bx - 4b$ which is equal to $x^2 - ax + a$.

From this we get:
$-4x + bx - 4b = -ax + a$

Now think of the possibilities. If $x = 0$, then
1 $-4b = a$

But if $-4b = a$, then $-4x + bx = -ax$ for all x and if $x = 1$, then
2 $-4 + b = -a$

or

3 $b = -a + 4$

Substituting b in 3 into b in 1, we get:
4 $-4(-a + 4) = a$ or $4a - 16 = a$ and get

$3a = 16, a = \frac{16}{3}$

5. Choice A is correct.

Strategy: Translate Words into Math.

The ratio of BD to CD is 4:6 means $BD = 4x$ and $CD = 6x$. Since the triangle is isosceles, that is, $AE = AF$, then $\angle E = \angle F$.

Also since $\angle EBD = \angle DCF = 90°$, triangles BED and CDF are similar so corresponding sides are in proportion.

Now use the strategy of labeling sides.
Call $ED = y$. Then $DF = 24 - y$ since $EF = 24$.

So since sides are in proportion,

$$\frac{BD}{CD} = \frac{4x}{6x} = \frac{ED}{DF} = \frac{y}{(24 - y)}$$

$$\frac{4}{6} = \frac{y}{(24 - y)}$$

Cross multiply: $(24 - y)4 = 6y$
$$96 - 4y = 6y$$
$$96 = 10y$$
$$\frac{96}{10} = y$$
$$\frac{48}{5} = y$$

6. Choice C is correct.

Strategy: First Get All Variables on One Side of the Equation.

1 $8x - 2y = 6y + 14$ becomes
1 $8x - 8y = 14$

Now divide Equation 1 by 8 to make it simpler:

1 $x - y = \frac{14}{8} = \frac{7}{4}$

Also divide the second equation by 4 to make it simpler:

2 $4x + 16y = 9$ becomes

2 $x + 4y = \frac{9}{4}$

Now use the strategy of subtracting equations.

Subtract Equation 1 from Equation 2:

$$x + 4y = \frac{9}{4}$$
$$- \quad \left(x - y = \frac{7}{4} \right)$$
_____
$$x - x + 4y + y = \frac{9}{4} - \frac{7}{4}$$

We get: $5y = \dfrac{9}{4} - \dfrac{7}{4} = \dfrac{2}{4} = \dfrac{1}{2}$

$$y = \dfrac{1}{10}$$

Now substitute $y = \dfrac{1}{10}$ into Equation $\boxed{1}$:

$$x - \dfrac{1}{10} = \dfrac{7}{4}$$

$$x = \dfrac{7}{4} + \dfrac{1}{10} = \dfrac{74}{40} = \dfrac{37}{20}$$

Thus, $xy = \dfrac{37}{20} \times \dfrac{1}{10} = \dfrac{37}{200}$

7. Choice B is correct.

Draw two intersecting circles.

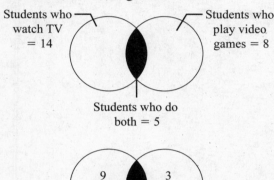

Students who watch TV = 14

Students who play video games = 8

Students who do both = 5

Above, subtracting: all students who watch TV (14) − students who watch TV *and* also play video games (5), we get 9.

Above, subtracting: all students who play video games (8) − students who watch TV *and* also play video games (5), we get 3.

So the total number of students is $9 + 5 + 3 = 17$.

8. Choice B is correct.

Strategy: Translate words into mathematical expressions.

The total cost of production equals the cost of the machine ($169.99) plus the cost of the CDs: (cost of 1 CD) × (number of CDs produced). Since we know that 1 CD costs $1.50 and we're producing x CDs, the total cost is:

$169.99 + $1.50x$

9. Choice B is correct.

Strategy: Label Sides.

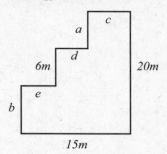

Label the sides of the figure, adding variables where no number is given. You can see that for the vertical sides of the figure:

$a + 6m + b = 20m$

While for the horizontal sides:

$c + d + e = 15m$

The perimeter equals:

$b + e + 6m + d + a + c + 20m + 15m$

$= (a + 6m + b) + (c + d + e) + 20m + 15m$

$= (20m) + (15m) + 20m + 15m = 70m$

10. Choice A is correct.

Strategy: Use Given Information Effectively.

First, find the height of the ladder on the wall. Remember a 3-4-5 right triangle. There is also a 6-8-10 right triangle. So the height is 8 feet.

$\sin x^{\circ} = \text{opposite/hypotenuse} = \dfrac{8}{10} = \dfrac{4}{5}$

Note:

Choice B: $\cos x^{\circ} = \dfrac{6}{10} = \dfrac{3}{5}$

Choice C: $\cot x^{\circ} = \dfrac{6}{8} = \dfrac{3}{4}$

Choice D: $\tan x^{\circ} = \dfrac{8}{6} = \dfrac{4}{3}$

PART 3

The 101 Most Important Math Questions You Need to Know How to Solve

Take This Test to Determine Your Basic (as Contrasted with Strategic) Math Weaknesses (Diagnosis and Corrective Measures Follow Test)

ANSWER SHEET

A. Fractions

1. _____
2. _____
3. _____
4. _____
5. _____

B. Even–Odd Relationships

6. _____
7. _____
8. _____
9. _____
10. _____
11. _____
12. _____

C. Factors

13. _____
14. _____
15. _____
16. _____
17. _____
18. _____
19. _____
20. _____
21. _____

D. Exponents

22. _____
23. _____
24. _____
25. _____
26. _____
27. _____
28. _____
29. _____
30. _____
31. _____
32. _____

E. Percentages

33. _____
34. _____
35. _____

F. Equations

36. _____
37. _____
38. _____
39. _____
40. _____

G. Angles

41. _____
42. _____
43. _____
44. _____

H. Parallel Lines

45. _____

46. _____

47. _____

48. _____

49. _____

50. _____

51. _____

I. Triangles

52. _____

53. _____

54. _____

55. _____

56. _____

57. _____

58. _____

59. _____

60. _____

61. _____

62. _____

63. _____

64. _____

65. _____

J. Circles

66. _____

67. _____

68. _____

69. _____

70. _____

K. Other Figures

71. _____

72. _____

73. _____

74. _____

75. _____

76. _____

77. _____

78. _____

79. _____

80. _____

L. Number Lines

81. _____

82. _____

M. Coordinates

83. _____

84. _____

85. _____

86. _____

N. Inequalities

87. _____

88. _____

89. _____

90. _____

91. _____

92. _____

O. Averages

93. _____

94. _____

P. Shortcuts

95. _____

96. _____

97. _____

98. _____

99. _____

100. _____

101. _____

101 MATH QUESTIONS TEST

Following are the 101 most important math questions you should know how to solve. After you take the test, check to see whether your answers are the same as those described, and whether or not you answered the question in the way described. After a solution, there is usually (where appropriate) a rule or generalization of the math concept just used in the solution to the particular problem. Make sure that you understand this generalization or rule, as it will apply to many other questions. Remember that these are the most important basic math questions you need to know how to solve. Make sure that you understand *all of them* before taking any standardized math test such as the SAT.

IN THIS DIAGNOSTIC TEST, DO NOT GUESS AT ANY ANSWER! IF YOU DON'T KNOW THE ANSWER LEAVE IT BLANK.

A. Fractions

1. $\dfrac{\dfrac{a}{b}}{c} =$

   (A) $\dfrac{ab}{c}$

   (B) $\dfrac{ac}{b}$

   (C) $\dfrac{a}{bc}$

   (D) abc

   (E) none of these

2. $\dfrac{1}{\dfrac{1}{y}} =$

   (A) y

   (B) y^2

   (C) $\dfrac{1}{y}$

   (D) infinity

   (E) none of these

3. $\dfrac{a}{\dfrac{b}{c}} =$

   (A) $\dfrac{a}{bc}$

   (B) $\dfrac{ac}{b}$

   (C) $\dfrac{ab}{c}$

   (D) abc

   (E) none of these

4. $\dfrac{1}{\dfrac{x}{y}} =$

   (A) xy

   (B) $\dfrac{x}{y}$

   (C) $\dfrac{y}{x}$

   (D) $\left(\dfrac{x}{y}\right)^2$

   (E) none of these

5. $\dfrac{\dfrac{a}{b}}{\dfrac{b}{a}} =$

   (A) $\dfrac{b^2}{a^2}$

   (B) $\dfrac{a^2}{b^2}$

   (C) 1

   (D) $\dfrac{a}{b}$

   (E) none of these

B. Even–Odd Relationships

6. ODD INTEGER × ODD INTEGER =

   (A) odd integer only
   (B) even integer only
   (C) even or odd integer

7. ODD INTEGER + or − ODD INTEGER =

   (A) odd integer only
   (B) even integer only
   (C) even or odd integer

8. EVEN INTEGER × EVEN INTEGER =

   (A) odd integer only
   (B) even integer only
   (C) even or odd integer

9. EVEN INTEGER + or − EVEN INTEGER =

   (A) odd integer only
   (B) even integer only
   (C) even or odd integer

10. (ODD INTEGER)$^{\text{ODD POWER}}$ =

    (A) odd integer only
    (B) even integer only
    (C) even or odd integer

11. (EVEN INTEGER)$^{\text{EVEN POWER}}$ =

    (A) odd integer only
    (B) even integer only
    (C) even or odd integer

12. (EVEN INTEGER)$^{\text{ODD POWER}}$ =

    (A) odd integer only
    (B) even integer only
    (C) even or odd integer

C. Factors

13. $(x + 3)(x + 2) =$

    (A) $x^2 + 5x + 6$
    (B) $x^2 + 6x + 5$
    (C) $x^2 + x + 6$
    (D) $2x + 5$
    (E) none of these

14. $(x + 3)(x - 2) =$

    (A) $x^2 - x + 6$
    (B) $x^2 + x + 5$
    (C) $x^2 + x - 6$
    (D) $2x + 1$
    (E) none of these

15. $(x - 3)(y - 2) =$

    (A) $xy - 5y + 6$
    (B) $xy - 2x - 3y + 6$
    (C) $x + y + 6$
    (D) $xy - 3y + 2x + 6$
    (E) none of these

16. $(a + b)(b + c) =$

    (A) $ab + b^2 + bc$
    (B) $a + b^2 + c$
    (C) $a^2 + b^2 + ca$
    (D) $ab + ac + b^2 + bc$
    (E) none of these

17. $(a + b)(a - b) =$

    (A) $a^2 + 2ba - b^2$
    (B) $a^2 - 2ba - b^2$
    (C) $a^2 - b^2$
    (D) 0
    (E) none of these

18. $(a + b)^2 =$

    (A) $a^2 + 2ab + b^2$
    (B) $a^2 + b^2$
    (C) $a^2 + b^2 + ab$
    (D) $2a + 2b$
    (E) none of these

19. $-(a - b) =$

    (A) $a - b$
    (B) $-a - b$
    (C) $a + b$
    (D) $b - a$
    (E) none of these

20. $a(b + c) =$

    (A) $ab + ac$
    (B) $ab + c$
    (C) abc
    (D) $ab + bc$
    (E) none of these

21. $-a(b - c) =$

    (A) $ab - ac$
    (B) $-ab - ac$
    (C) $ac - ab$
    (D) $ab + ac$
    (E) none of these

D. Exponents

22. $10^5 =$

    (A) 1,000
    (B) 10,000
    (C) 100,000
    (D) 1,000,000
    (E) none of these

23. $107076.5 = 1.070765 \times$

    (A) 10^4
    (B) 10^5
    (C) 10^6
    (D) 10^7
    (E) none of these

24. $a^2 \times a^5 =$

    (A) a^{10}
    (B) a^7
    (C) a^3
    (D) $(2a)^{10}$
    (E) none of these

25. $(ab)^7 =$

    (A) ab^7
    (B) a^7b
    (C) a^7b^7
    (D) $a^{14}b^{14}$
    (E) none of these

26. $\left(\dfrac{a}{c}\right)^8 =$

    (A) $\dfrac{a^8}{c^8}$

    (B) $\dfrac{a^8}{c}$

    (C) $\dfrac{a}{c^8}$

    (D) $\dfrac{a^7}{c}$

    (E) none of these

27. $a^4 \times b^4 =$

    (A) $(ab)^4$
    (B) $(ab)^8$
    (C) $(ab)^{16}$
    (D) $(ab)^{12}$
    (E) none of these

28. $a^{-3} \times b^5 =$

    (A) $\dfrac{b^5}{a^3}$

    (B) $(ab)^2$

(C) $(ab)^{-15}$

(D) $\dfrac{a^3}{b^5}$

(E) none of these

29. $(a^3)^5 =$

    (A) a^8
    (B) a^2
    (C) a^{15}
    (D) a^{243}
    (E) none of these

30. $2a^{-3} =$

    (A) $\dfrac{2}{a^3}$

    (B) $2a^3$
    (C) $2\sqrt[3]{a}$
    (D) a^{-6}
    (E) none of these

31. $2a^m \times \dfrac{1}{3}a^{-n} =$

    (A) $\dfrac{2}{3}a^{m+n}$

    (B) $\dfrac{2a^m}{3a^n}$

    (C) $\dfrac{2}{3}a^{-mn}$

    (D) $-\dfrac{2}{3}a^{-mn}$

    (E) none of these

32. $3^2 + 3^{-2} + 4^1 + 6^0 =$

    (A) $8\dfrac{1}{9}$

    (B) $12\dfrac{1}{9}$

    (C) $13\dfrac{1}{9}$

    (D) $14\dfrac{1}{9}$

    (E) none of these

E. Percentages

33. 15% of 200 =

    (A) 3
    (B) 30
    (C) 300
    (D) 3,000
    (E) none of these

34. What is 3% of 5?

    (A) $\frac{5}{3}$

    (B) 15

    (C) $\frac{3}{20}$

    (D) $\frac{3}{5}$

    (E) none of these

35. What percent of 3 is 6?

    (A) 50

    (B) 20

    (C) 200

    (D) $\frac{1}{2}$

    (E) none of these

F. Equations

36. If $y^2 = 16$, then $y =$

    (A) +4 only

    (B) −4 only

    (C) ±4

    (D) ±8

    (E) none of these

37. If $x - y = 10$, then $y =$

    (A) $x - 10$

    (B) $10 + x$

    (C) $10 - x$

    (D) 10

    (E) none of these

38. What is the value of x if $x + 4y = 7$ and $x - 4y = 8$?

    (A) 15

    (B) $\frac{15}{2}$

    (C) 7

    (D) $\frac{7}{2}$

    (E) none of these

39. What is the value of x and y if $x - 2y = 2$ and $2x + y = 4$?

    (A) $x = 2, y = 0$

    (B) $x = 0, y = -2$

    (C) $x = -1, y = 2$

    (D) $x = 0, y = 2$

    (E) none of these

40. If $\frac{x}{5} = \frac{7}{12}$, then $x =$

    (A) $2\frac{11}{12}$

    (B) $\frac{12}{35}$

    (C) $\frac{7}{60}$

    (D) $\frac{60}{7}$

    (E) none of these

G. Angles

Questions 41–42 refer to the diagram below:

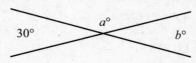

41. $a =$

    (A) 30

    (B) 150

    (C) 45

    (D) 90

    (E) none of these

42. $b =$

    (A) 30

    (B) 150

    (C) 45

    (D) 90

    (E) none of these

Question 43 refers to the diagram below:

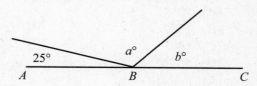

ABC is a straight angle.

43. $a + b =$

    (A) 155

    (B) 165

    (C) 180

    (D) 145

    (E) none of these

44. What is the value of $a + b + c + d + e + f + g + h$ in this diagram?

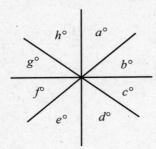

(A) 180
(B) 240
(C) 360
(D) 540
(E) none of these

H. Parallel Lines

Questions 45–51 refer to the diagram below:

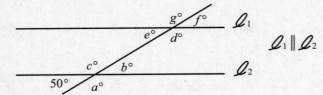

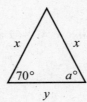

$\ell_1 \| \ell_2$

45. $a =$
(A) 50
(B) 130
(C) 100
(D) 40
(E) none of these

46. $b =$
(A) 50
(B) 130
(C) 100
(D) 40
(E) none of these

47. $c =$
(A) 50
(B) 130
(C) 100
(D) 40
(E) none of these

48. $d =$
(A) 50
(B) 130
(C) 100
(D) 40
(E) none of these

49. $e =$
(A) 50
(B) 130
(C) 100
(D) 40
(E) none of these

50. $f =$
(A) 50
(B) 130
(C) 100
(D) 40
(E) none of these

51. $g =$
(A) 50
(B) 130
(C) 100
(D) 40
(E) none of these

I. Triangles

(*Note*: Figures are not drawn to scale.)

52. $a =$

(A) 70°
(B) 40°
(C) $\dfrac{xy}{70°}$
(D) cannot be determined
(E) none of these

53. $x =$

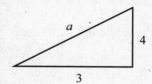

(A) 3

(B) $\dfrac{50}{3}$

(C) $3\sqrt{2}$

(D) cannot be determined

(E) none of these

54. Which is a possible value for a?

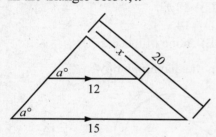

(A) 1

(B) 6

(C) 10

(D) 7

(E) 8

55. In the triangle below, $x =$

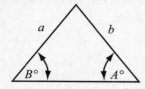

(A) 12

(B) 16

(C) 15

(D) 10

(E) none of these

56. In the triangle below, if $B > A$, then

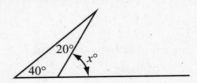

(A) $b = a$

(B) $b > a$

(C) $b < a$

(D) a relation between b and a cannot be determined

(E) none of these

57. In the triangle below, if $b < a$, then

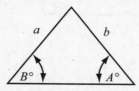

(A) $B > A$

(B) $B = A$

(C) $B < A$

(D) a relation between B and A cannot be determined

(E) none of these

58. In the triangle below, $x =$

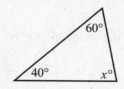

(A) 100

(B) 80

(C) 90

(D) 45

(E) none of these

59. In the triangle below, $x =$

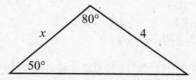

(A) $4\sqrt{2}$

(B) 8

(C) 4

(D) a number between 1 and 4

(E) none of these

60. In the diagram below, $x =$

(A) 40

(B) 20

(C) 60

(D) 80

(E) none of these

61. In the right triangle below, $x =$

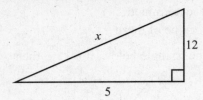

(A) 17
(B) 13
(C) 15
(D) $12\sqrt{2}$
(E) none of these

Questions 62–63 refer to the diagram below:

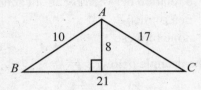

62. The perimeter of the triangle ABC is

(A) 16
(B) 48
(C) 168
(D) 84
(E) none of these

63. The area of triangle ABC is

(A) 170
(B) 85
(C) 168
(D) 84
(E) none of these

Questions 64–65 refer to the diagram below:

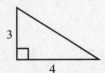

64. The area of the triangle is

(A) 6
(B) 7
(C) 12
(D) any number between 5 and 7
(E) none of these

65. The perimeter of the triangle is

(A) 7
(B) 12
(C) 15
(D) any number between 7 and 12
(E) none of these

J. Circles

Questions 66–67 refer to the diagram below:

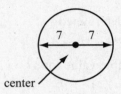

66. The area of the circle is

(A) 49
(B) 49π
(C) 14π
(D) 196π
(E) none of these

67. The circumference of the circle is

(A) 14π
(B) 7π
(C) 49π
(D) 14
(E) none of these

68. In the diagram below, $x =$

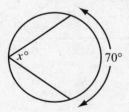

(A) 70°
(B) 35°
(C) 90°
(D) a number that cannot be determined
(E) none of these

69. In the diagram below, $x =$

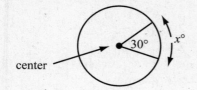

(A) 30°
(B) 60°
(C) 90°
(D) a number that cannot be determined
(E) none of these

70. In the diagram below, $y =$

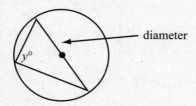

(A) 145°
(B) 60°
(C) 90°
(D) a number that cannot be determined
(E) none of these

K. Other Figures

(*Note*: Figures are not drawn to scale.)

Questions 71–72 refer to the diagram below:

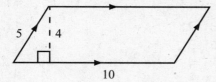

71. The area of the figure is

(A) 15
(B) 20
(C) 40
(D) 50
(E) none of these

72. The perimeter of the figure is

(A) 15
(B) 30
(C) 40
(D) 50
(E) none of these

Questions 73–75 refer to the figure below:

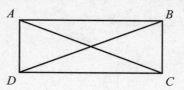

ABCD is a rectangle.

73. What is *BC* if *AD* = 6?

(A) 4
(B) 6
(C) 8
(D) 10
(E) 12

74. What is *DC* if *AB* = 8?

(A) 4
(B) 6
(C) 8
(D) 10
(E) 12

75. What is *DB* if *AC* = 10?

(A) 4
(B) 6
(C) 8
(D) 10
(E) 12

Questions 76–77 refer to the diagram below:

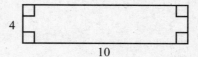

76. The area of the figure is

(A) 14
(B) 40
(C) 80
(D) 28
(E) none of these

77. The perimeter of the figure is

(A) 14
(B) 28
(C) 36
(D) 40
(E) none of these

Questions 78–79 refer to the figure below:

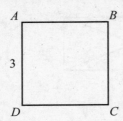

ABCD is a square; *AD* = 3.

78. What is the area of the square?

(A) 9
(B) 12
(C) 16
(D) 20
(E) none of these

79. What is the perimeter of the square?

(A) 9
(B) 12
(C) 16
(D) 20
(E) none of these

80. The volume of the rectangular solid below is

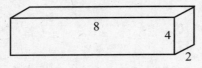

(A) 48
(B) 64
(C) 128
(D) 72
(E) none of these

L. Number Lines

Questions 81–82 refer to the diagram below:

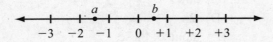

81. Which best defines the range in values of *b*?

(A) $-2 < b < 1$
(B) $0 < b < 2$
(C) $0 < b < 1$
(D) $-3 < b < 3$
(E) $0 < b$

82. Which best defines the range in values of *a*?

(A) $-2 < a$
(B) $-2 < a < -1$
(C) $-2 < a < 0$
(D) $a < -1$
(E) $-3 < a < 0$

M. Coordinates

Questions 83–85 refer to the diagram below:

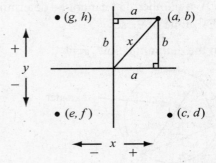

83. How many of the variables *a*, *b*, *c*, *d*, *e*, *f*, *g*, *h* are positive?

(A) 1
(B) 2
(C) 3
(D) 4
(E) 5

84. How many of the variables *a*, *b*, *c*, *d*, *e*, *f*, *g*, *h* are negative?

(A) 1
(B) 2
(C) 3
(D) 4
(E) 5

85. If *a* = 3, *b* = 4, what is *x*?

(A) 3
(B) 4
(C) 5
(D) 6
(E) none of these

86. What is the slope of the line below?

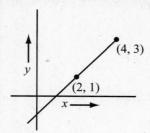

(A) −1
(B) 0
(C) +1
(D) +2
(E) +3

N. Inequalities

Note: Any variable can be positive or negative or 0.

87. If $x > y$, then $4x > 4y$

(A) always
(B) sometimes
(C) never

88. If $x + y > z$, then $y > z − x$

(A) always
(B) sometimes
(C) never

89. If $−4 < −x$, then $+4 > +x$

(A) always
(B) sometimes
(C) never

90. If $m > n,$ where q is any number, then $qm > qn$

(A) always
(B) sometimes
(C) never

91. If $x > y$ and $p > q$, then $x + p > y + q$

(A) always
(B) sometimes
(C) never

92. If $x > y$ and $p > q,$ then $xp > qy$

(A) always
(B) sometimes
(C) never

O. Averages

93. What is the average of 30, 40, and 80?

(A) 150
(B) 75
(C) 50
(D) 45
(E) none of these

94. What is the average speed in mph of a car traveling 40 miles in 4 hours?

(A) 160
(B) 10
(C) 120
(D) 30
(E) none of these

P. Shortcuts

95. Which is greater?
(*Don't calculate a common denominator!*)

$$\frac{7}{16} \text{ or } \frac{3}{7}$$

(A) $\frac{7}{16}$

(B) $\frac{3}{7}$

(C) They are equal.
(D) A relationship cannot be determined.

96. $\frac{7}{12} + \frac{3}{5} =$

(A) $1\frac{11}{60}$

(B) $1\frac{13}{60}$

(C) $1\frac{15}{60}$

(D) $\frac{10}{17}$

(E) none of these

97. $\frac{7}{12} − \frac{3}{5} =$

(A) $−\frac{1}{60}$

(B) $−\frac{3}{60}$

(C) $−1\frac{11}{60}$

(D) $\frac{4}{7}$

(E) none of these

98. $\dfrac{4}{250} =$

    (*Don't divide 250 into 4!*)

    (A) 0.016
    (B) 0.04
    (C) 0.004
    (D) 0.025
    (E) none of these

99. What is c if

    $200 = \dfrac{a + b + c}{2}$ and $80 = \dfrac{a + b}{3}$?

    (A) 160
    (B) 140
    (C) 120
    (D) 100
    (E) none of these

100. What is the value of $95 \times 75 - 95 \times 74$?
     (*Don't multiply* 95×75 *or* $95 \times 74!$)

     (A) 65
     (B) 75
     (C) 85
     (D) 95
     (E) none of these

101. Find the value of

     $\dfrac{140 \times 15}{5 \times 7}$

     (*Don't multiply* $140 \times 15!$)

     (A) 20
     (B) 40
     (C) 60
     (D) 90
     (E) none of these

ANSWERS, DIAGNOSIS, SOLUTIONS, GENERALIZATIONS, AND RULES

Answers

A. Fractions
1. B
2. A
3. A
4. C
5. B

B. Even–Odd Relationships
6. A
7. B
8. B
9. B
10. A
11. B
12. B

C. Factors
13. A
14. C
15. B
16. D
17. C
18. A
19. D
20. A
21. C

D. Exponents
22. C
23. B
24. B
25. C
26. A
27. A
28. A
29. C
30. A
31. B
32. D

E. Percentages
33. B
34. C
35. C

F. Equations
36. C
37. A
38. B
39. A
40. A

G. Angles
41. B
42. A
43. A
44. C

H. Parallel Lines
45. B
46. A
47. B
48. B
49. A
50. A
51. B

I. Triangles
52. A
53. A
54. B
55. B
56. B
57. C
58. B
59. C
60. C
61. B
62. B
63. D
64. A
65. B

J. Circles
66. B
67. A
68. B
69. A
70. C

K. Other Figures
71. C
72. B
73. B
74. C
75. D
76. B
77. B
78. A
79. B
80. B

L. Number Lines
81. C
82. B

M. Coordinates
83. D
84. D
85. C
86. C

N. Inequalities
87. A
88. A
89. A
90. B
91. A
92. B

O. Averages
93. C
94. B

P. Shortcuts
95. A
96. A
97. A
98. A
99. A
100. D
101. C

Basic Math Skills Diagnosis

Math Area	Total Questions	Study These Answers (see answer key, p. 49)	Pages in Text for Review	Complete Math Refresher Numbers (starting on p. 163)
A. Fractions	5	1–5	38, 51	101–112, 123–129
B. Even–Odd Relationships	7	6–12	39, 51	603–606
C. Factors	9	13–21	39, 51–52	409
D. Exponents	11	22–32	40, 52	429–430
E. Percentages	3	33–35	40–41, 53	106, 107, 114
F. Equations	5	36–40	41, 53	406–409
G. Angles	4	41–44	41–42, 54	500–503
H. Parallel Lines	7	45–51	42, 54	504
I. Triangles	14	52–65	42–44, 54–57	306–308, 505–516
J. Circles	5	66–70	44–45, 57	310–311, 524–529
K. Other Figures	10	71–80	45–46, 58	303–305, 309, 312–316, 517–523
L. Number Lines	2	81–82	46, 59	410a
M. Coordinates	4	83–86	46–47, 59	410b–418
N. Inequalities	6	87–92	47, 59–60	419–428
O. Averages	2	93–94	47, 60	601
P. Shortcuts	7	95–101	47–48, 60–61	128, 609

Solutions, Generalizations, and Rules

A. Fractions

1. (B)

$$\frac{\dfrac{a}{b}}{c} = a \times \frac{c}{b} = \boxed{\frac{ac}{b}}$$

Invert to multiply

Alternate way:

$$\frac{\dfrac{a}{b}}{c} = \frac{\dfrac{a}{b}}{c} \times \frac{c}{c} = \frac{ac}{\dfrac{b}{\cancel{c}} \times \cancel{c}} = \boxed{\frac{ac}{b}}$$

2. (A)

$$\frac{1}{\dfrac{1}{y}} = 1 \times \frac{y}{1} = \boxed{y}$$

Invert to multiply

3. (A)

$$\frac{\dfrac{a}{b}}{c} = \frac{\dfrac{a}{b}}{c} \times \frac{b}{b} = \frac{a}{cb} = \boxed{\frac{a}{bc}}$$

Multiply by $\frac{b}{b}$

4. (C)

$$\frac{1}{\dfrac{x}{y}} = 1 \times \frac{y}{x} = \boxed{\frac{y}{x}}$$

Invert to multiply

5. (B)

$$\frac{\dfrac{a}{b}}{\dfrac{b}{a}} = \frac{a}{b} \times \frac{a}{b} = \boxed{\frac{a^2}{b^2}}$$

Invert to multiply

Alternate way:

$$\frac{\dfrac{a}{b}}{\dfrac{b}{a}} = \frac{\dfrac{a}{b} \times a}{\dfrac{b}{a} \times a} = \frac{\dfrac{a^2}{b}}{\dfrac{b}{\cancel{a}}\cancel{a}} = \frac{\dfrac{a^2}{b}}{b} = \frac{\dfrac{a^2}{\cancel{b}} \times \cancel{b}}{b \times b} = \boxed{\frac{a^2}{b^2}}$$

B. Even–Odd Relationships

6. (A) ODD × ODD = $\boxed{\text{ODD ONLY}}$

   $3 \times 3 = 9$; $5 \times 5 = 25$

7. (B) ODD + or − ODD = $\boxed{\text{EVEN ONLY}}$

   $5 + 3 = 8$; $5 - 3 = 2$

8. (B) EVEN × EVEN = $\boxed{\text{EVEN ONLY}}$

   $2 \times 2 = 4$; $4 \times 2 = 8$

9. (B) EVEN + or − EVEN = $\boxed{\text{EVEN ONLY}}$

   $6 + 2 = 8$; $10 - 4 = 6$

10. (A) (ODD)^{ODD} = $\boxed{\text{ODD ONLY}}$

    $3^3 = 3 \times 3 \times 3 = 27$ (odd)

    $1^{27} = 1$ (odd)

11. (B) (EVEN)^{EVEN} = $\boxed{\text{EVEN ONLY}}$

    $2^2 = 4$ (even); $4^2 = 16$ (even)

12. (B) (EVEN)^{ODD} = $\boxed{\text{EVEN ONLY}}$

    $2^3 = 2 \times 2 \times 2 = 8$ (even)

    $4^1 = 4$ (even)

C. Factors

13. (A) $(x + 3)(x + 2) = x^2 \ldots$

    $(x + 3)(x + 2) = x^2 + 2x + 3x \ldots$

    $(x + 3)(x + 2) = x^2 + 2x + 3x + 6$

    $(x + 3)(x + 2) = \boxed{x^2 + 5x + 6}$

14. (C) $(x + 3)(x - 2) = x^2 \ldots$

    $(x + 3)(x - 2) = x^2 - 2x + 3x \ldots$

    $(x + 3)(x - 2) = x^2 - 2x + 3x - 6$

    $(x + 3)(x - 2) = \boxed{x^2 + x - 6}$

15. (B) $(x - 3)(y - 2) = xy \ldots$

$(x - 3)(y - 2) = xy - 2x - 3y \ldots$

$(x - 3)(y - 2) = \boxed{xy - 2x - 3y + 6}$

16. (D) $(a + b)(b + c) = ab \ldots$

$(a + b)(b + c) = ab + ac + b^2 \ldots$

$(a + b)(b + c) = \boxed{ab + ac + b^2 + bc}$

17. (C) $(a + b)(a - b) =$

$(a + b)(a - b) = a^2 \ldots$

$(a + b)(a - b) = a^2 - ab + ba \ldots$

$(a + b)(a - b) = a^2 - ab + ba - b^2$

$(a + b)(a - b) = a^2 - ab + ba - b^2$

$(a + b)(a - b) = \boxed{a^2 - b^2}$ ***Memorize***

18. (A) $(a + b)^2 = (a + b)(a + b)$

$(a + b)(a + b) = a^2 \ldots$

$(a + b)(a + b) = a^2 + ab + ba \ldots$

$(a + b)(a + b) = a^2 + ab + ba + b^2$

$(a + b)^2 = \boxed{a^2 + 2ab + b^2}$ ***Memorize***

19. (D) $-(a - b) = -a - (-b)$

$-(a - b) = -a + b$

$-(a - b) = \boxed{b - a}$ ***Memorize***

20. (A) $a(b + c) =$

$a(b + c) = \boxed{ab + ac}$

21. (C) $-a(b - c) =$

$-a(b - c) = -ab - a(-c)$

$= -ab + ac = \boxed{ac - ab}$

D. Exponents

22. (C) $10^5 = \boxed{100,000}$

    ⎿ 5 zeros

23. (B) $107076.5 = 1\,0\,7\,0\,7\,6\,.\,5$

    $\quad\quad\quad\quad\quad\quad\quad\quad\quad\quad 5\;4\;3\;2\;1$

    $= 1.070765 \times \boxed{10^5}$

24. (B) $a^2 \times a^5 = \boxed{a^7}$

    Add exponents

    $a^m \times a^n = a^{m+n}$

25. (C) $(ab)^7 = \boxed{a^7 b^7}$

    $(ab)^m = a^m b^m$

26. (A) $\left(\dfrac{a}{c}\right)^8 = \boxed{\dfrac{a^8}{c^8}}$

    $\left(\dfrac{a}{c}\right)^m = \dfrac{a^m}{c^m}$

27. (A) $a^4 \times b^4 = \boxed{(ab)^4}$

    $a^m \times b^m = (ab)^m$

28. (A) $a^{-3} \times b^5 = \boxed{\dfrac{b^5}{a^3}}$

    $a^{-m} \times b^n = \dfrac{b^n}{a^m}$

29. (C) $(a^3)^5 = \boxed{a^{15}}$

    Multiply exponents

    $(a^m)^n = a^{mn}$

30. (A) $2a^{-3} = \boxed{\dfrac{2}{a^3}}$

    $ax^{-b} = \dfrac{a}{x^b}$

    since $a^{-n} = \dfrac{1}{a^n}$

31. (B) $2a^m \times \dfrac{1}{3}a^{-n} = \dfrac{2}{3}a^m a^{-n}$

    $\quad\quad\quad\quad\quad = \dfrac{2}{3}a^{m-n}$ or $\boxed{\dfrac{2a^m}{3a^n}}$

32. (D) $3^2 + 3^{-2} + 4^1 + 6^0 =$

    $3^2 = 3 \times 3 = 9$

    $3^{-2} = \dfrac{1}{3^2} = \dfrac{1}{9}$

    $4^1 = 4$ (any number to 1 power = that number)

    $6^0 = 1$ (any number to 0 power = 1)

    $3^2 + 3^{-2} + 4^1 + 6^0 = 9 + \dfrac{1}{9} + 4 + 1 = \boxed{14\dfrac{1}{9}}$

E. Percentages

Translate: is → =

of → × (times)

percent (%) → $\dfrac{}{100}$

what → x (or y, etc.)

33. (B) 15 % of 200 =

↓ ↓ ↓ ↓ ↓

$15\dfrac{}{100} \times 200 =$

$\dfrac{15}{100} \times 200 =$

$\dfrac{15}{100} \times 200 = \boxed{30}$

34. (C) What is 3 % of 5?

↓ ↓ ↓ ↓ ↓ ↓

$x = 3\dfrac{}{100} \times 5$

$x = \dfrac{3}{100} \times 5$

$x = \dfrac{15}{100} = \boxed{\dfrac{3}{20}}$

35. (C) What percent of 3 is 6?

↓ ↓ ↓ ↓ ↓

$x \quad \dfrac{}{100} \quad \times 3 = 6$

$\dfrac{x}{100} \times 3 = 6$

$\dfrac{3x}{100} = 6$

$3x = 600$

$x = \boxed{200}$

F. Equations

36. (C) $y^2 = 16$

$\sqrt{y^2} = \pm\sqrt{16}$

$y = \boxed{\pm 4}$

37. (A) $x - y = 10$

Add y:

$x - y + y = 10 + y$

$x = 10 + y$

Subtract 10:

$x - 10 = 10 - 10 + y$

$\boxed{x - 10} = y$

38. (B) Add equations:

$x + 4y = 7$

$\underline{x - 4y = 8}$

$2x + 4y - 4y = 15$

$2x = 15$

$x = \boxed{\dfrac{15}{2}}$

39. (A) $x - 2y = 2$ **1**

$2x + y = 4$ **2**

Multiply **1** by 2:

$2(x - 2y) = 2(2)$

We get:

$2x - 4y = 4$ **3**

Subtract **2** from **3**:

$2x - 4y = 4$

$\underline{- (2x + \ y = 4)}$

$0 - 5y = 0$

$\boxed{y = 0}$ **4**

Substitute **4** into either **1** or **2**:

In **1**:

$x - 2y = 2$

$x - 2(0) = 2$

$\boxed{x = 2}$

40. (A) $\dfrac{x}{5} = \dfrac{7}{12}$

Here's how to find x:

Cross-multiply x:

$\left(\dfrac{x}{5} = \dfrac{7}{12} \right)$

$12x = 35$

Divide by 12:

$\dfrac{12x}{12} = \dfrac{35}{12}$

$x = \dfrac{35}{12} = \boxed{2\dfrac{11}{12}}$

G. Angles

Questions 41–42 refer to the diagram.

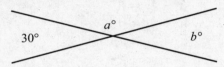

41. (B) $a°$ and 30° are *supplementary* angles (they add up to 180°).
    So $a + 30 = 180$; $a = \boxed{150}$.

42. (A) $b°$ and 30° are *vertical* angles (vertical angles are equal).
    So $b = \boxed{30}$.

43. (A) $a°$, $b°$, and 25° make up a *straight* angle, which is 180°.

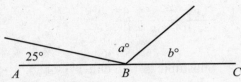

ABC is a straight angle.

$a + b + 25 = 180$
$a + b = 180 - 25$
$a + b = \boxed{155}$

44. (C) The sum of the angles in the diagram is $\boxed{360°}$, the number of degrees around the circumference of a circle.

H. Parallel Lines

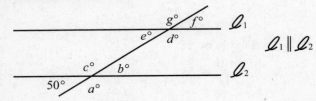

45. (B) $a + 50 = 180$
    $a = \boxed{130}$

46. (A) $b = \boxed{50}$ (vertical angles)

47. (B) $c = a$ (vertical angles)
    $= \boxed{130}$

48. (B) $d = c$ (alternate interior angles are equal)
    $= \boxed{130}$

49. (A) $e = b$ (alternate interior angles)
    $= \boxed{50}$

50. (A) $f = e$ (vertical angles)
    $= \boxed{50}$

51. (B) $g = d$ (vertical angles)
    $= \boxed{130}$

I. Triangles

(*Note*: Figures are not drawn to scale.)

52. (A)

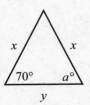

If two sides are equal, base angles are equal. Thus a = $\boxed{70°}$.

53. (A)

If base angles are equal, then sides are equal, so $\boxed{x = 3}$.

54. (B)

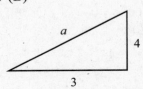

The sum of two sides must be *greater* than the third side. Try choices:

(A) $1 + 3 = 4$: (A) is not possible.
(B) $3 + 4 > \boxed{6}$; $\boxed{6} + 3 > 4$;
     $4 + \boxed{6} > 3$: OK.
(C) $3 + 4 \ngtr 10$: (C) is not possible.
(D) $3 + 4 = 7$: (D) is not possible.
(E) $3 + 4 \ngtr 8$: (E) is not possible.

55. (B) Using similar triangles, write a *proportion* with x.

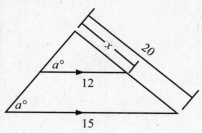

$$\frac{x}{20} = \frac{12}{15}$$

$$15x = 12 \times 20$$

$$x = \frac{12 \times 20}{15}$$

$$x = \frac{4 \times 3 \times 5 \times 4}{5 \times 3}$$

$$x = \frac{4 \times \cancel{3} \times \cancel{5} \times 4}{\cancel{5} \times \cancel{3}} = \boxed{16}$$

In general:

$$\frac{m}{n} = \frac{q}{p} = \frac{r}{r+s}$$

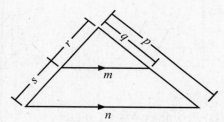

56. (B) The greater angle lies opposite the greater side and vice versa.

If $B > A$, $\boxed{b > a}$

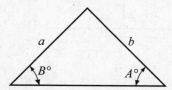

57. (C) The greater side lies opposite the greater angle and vice versa.

If $b < a$, then $\boxed{B < A}$

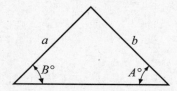

58. (B) Sum of angles of triangle $= 180°$.

So $40 + 60 + x = 180$

$$100 + x = 180$$

$$x = \boxed{80}$$

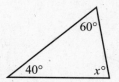

59. (C)

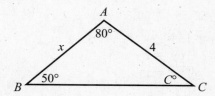

First calculate $\angle C$. Call it y.

$80 + 50 + y = 180$ (sum of angles $= 180°$)

$y = 50$

Since $\angle C = y = 50$ and $\angle B = 50$, side $AB =$ side AC.

$AB = x = \boxed{4}$

60. (C) $x° = 20° + 40°$ (sum of *remote* interior angles $=$ exterior angle).

$x = \boxed{60}$

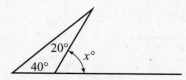

In general,

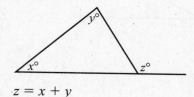

$z = x + y$

61. (B)

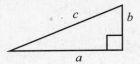

In right Δ, $a^2 + b^2 = c^2$
So for

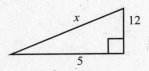

$5^2 + 12^2 = x^2$
$25 + 144 = x^2$
$169 = x^2$
$\sqrt{169} = x$
$\boxed{13} = x$

Note: Specific right triangles you should memorize; use multiples to generate other triangles.

Example of multiples:

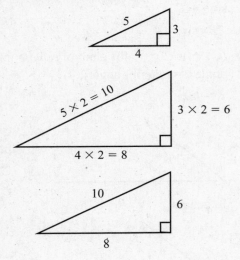

Memorize the following standard triangles (not drawn to scale):

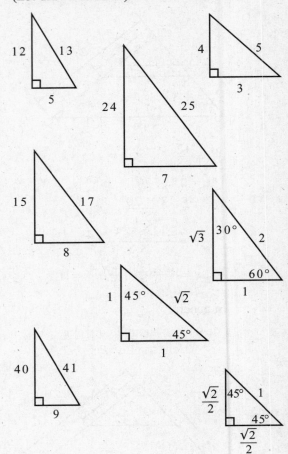

62. (B) Perimeter = sum of sides

$10 + 17 + 21 = \boxed{48}$

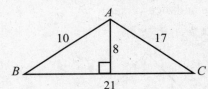

63. (D)

Area of $\Delta = \frac{1}{2}bh$

Area of $\Delta = \frac{1}{2}(21)(8) = \boxed{84}$

64. (A) Area of any triangle $= \frac{1}{2}$base $\times$ height

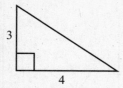

Here 4 is base and 3 is height.

So area $= \frac{1}{2}(4 \times 3) = \frac{1}{2}(12) = \boxed{6}$.

65. (B)

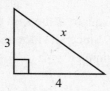

To find perimeter, we need to find the sum of the sides. The sum of the sides is $3 + 4 + x$.

We need to find x. From the solution in Question 61, we should realize that we have a 3–4–5 right triangle, so $x = 5$.

The perimeter is then $3 + 4 + 5 = \boxed{12}$.

Note that you could have found x by using the Pythagorean theorem:

$3^2 + 4^2 = x^2$; $9 + 16 = x^2$; $25 = x^2$; $\sqrt{25} = x$; $5 = x$

J. Circles

Questions 66–67 refer to the figure below.

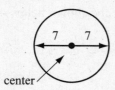

66. (B) Area $= \pi r^2 = \pi(7)^2$
$\qquad\qquad = \boxed{49\pi}$

67. (A) Circumference $= 2\pi r = 2\pi(7)$
$\qquad\qquad\qquad\quad = \boxed{14\pi}$

68. (B) Inscribed angle $= \frac{1}{2}$arc

$x° = \frac{1}{2}(70°)$

$\quad = \boxed{35°}$

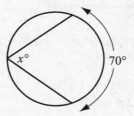

69. (A) Central angle $=$ arc
$\boxed{30°} = x°$

Note: The *total* number of degrees around the circumference is 360°. So a central angle of 30°, like the one below, cuts $\frac{30}{360} = \frac{1}{12}$ the circumference.

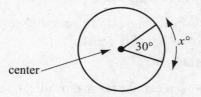

70. (C) The diameter cuts a 180° arc on the circle,

so an inscribed angle $y = \frac{1}{2}$arc $= \frac{1}{2}(180°) = \boxed{90°}$.

Here is a good thing to remember: Any inscribed angle whose triangle base is a diameter is 90°.

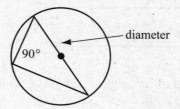

K. Other Figures

Questions 71–72 refer to the figure below.

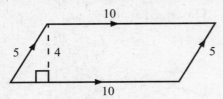

71. (C) Area of parallelogram = base × height = (10)(4) = $\boxed{40}$

72. (B) Perimeter = sum of sides = 5 + 5 + 10 + 10 = $\boxed{30}$

Questions 73–75 refer to the figure below.

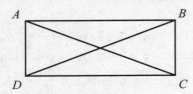

ABCD is a rectangle.

73. (B) In a rectangle (as in a parallelogram), opposite sides are equal.
    So $AD = BC = \boxed{6}$.

74. (C) In a rectangle (as in a parallelogram), opposite sides are equal.
    So $DC = AB = \boxed{8}$.

75. (D) In a rectangle (but not in a parallelogram), the diagonals are equal.
    So $DB = AC = \boxed{10}$.

Questions 76–77 refer to the figure below.

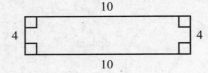

76. (B) Area of rectangle = length × width = 4 × 10 = $\boxed{40}$.

77. (B) Perimeter = sum of sides = 4 + 4 + 10 + 10 = $\boxed{28}$.

Questions 78–79 refer to the figure below.

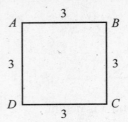

78. (A) Area of a square with side x is x^2. (All sides of a square are equal.) So length = width. Since $x = 3$, $x^2 = \boxed{9}$.

79. (B) Perimeter of a square is the sum of all sides of the square. Since all sides are equal, if one side is x, perimeter = $4x$.
    $x = 3$, so $4x = \boxed{12}$.

80. (B) Volume of rectangular solid shown below = $a \times b \times c$

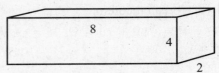

So for:

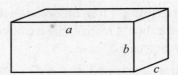

$a = 8$, $b = 4$, $c = 2$
and $a \times b \times c = 8 \times 4 \times 2 = \boxed{64}$.

Note: Volume of cube shown below = $a \times a \times a = a^3$

L. Number Lines

Questions 80–81 refer to the diagram below.

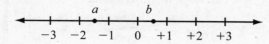

81. (C) b is between 0 and $+1$

so $0 < b < 1$.

82. (B) a is between -2 and -1

so $-2 < a < -1$.

M. Coordinates

Questions 83–85 refer to the diagram below.

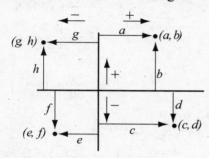

Horizontal right $= +$
Horizontal left $\ = -$
Vertical up $\qquad = +$
Vertical down $\ = -$

83. (D) a, b, c, h positive (4 letters)

84. (D) d, e, f, g negative (4 letters)

85. (C)

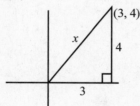

Remember the 3–4–5 right triangle. $x = 5$
You can also use the Pythagorean theorem:
$3^2 + 4^2 = x^2$; $9 + 16 = x^2$; $x^2 = 25$; $x = 5$

86. (C)

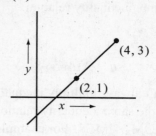

The slope of a line $y = mx + b$ is m. If two points (x_1, y_1) and (x_2, y_2) are on the line, then the slope is

$$\frac{y_2 - y_1}{x_2 - x_1} = m.$$

Here $x_1 = 2, y_1 = 1, x_2 = 4, y_2 = 3$.

So $\dfrac{y_2 - y_1}{x_2 - x_1} = \dfrac{3 - 1}{4 - 2} = \dfrac{2}{2} = 1$.

N. Inequalities

87. (A) You can multiply an inequality by a positive number and retain the same inequality:

$x > y$

$4x > 4y$ ALWAYS

88. (A) You can subtract the same number from both sides of an inequality and retain the same inequality:

$$x + y > z$$
$$x + y - x > z - x$$
$$y > z - x \quad \text{ALWAYS}$$

89. (A) If you multiply an inequality by -1, you *reverse* the original inequality sign:

$$-4 < -x$$
$$-(-4 < -x)$$
$$+4 > +x \quad \text{ALWAYS}$$

90. (B) If $m > n$,

$qm > qn$ if q is *positive*
$qm < qn$ if q is *negative*
$qm = qn$ if q is *zero*

So, $qm > qn$ SOMETIMES

91. (A) You can always add inequality relations to get the same inequality relation:

$$x > y$$
$$+ p > q$$
$$\overline{x + p > y + q} \quad \boxed{\text{ALWAYS}}$$

92. (B) You can't always multiply inequality relations to get the same inequality relation. The answer is $\boxed{\text{SOMETIMES}}$. For example:

$$3 > 2 \qquad\qquad 3 > 2$$
$$\times -2 > -3 \qquad \times 2 > 1$$
$$\overline{-6 \not> -6} \qquad\qquad \overline{6 > 2}$$

However, if x, y, p, q are positive, then if $x > y$ and $p > q$, $xp > yq$.

O. Averages

93. (C) Average of 30, 40, and 80 =

$$\frac{30 + 40 + 80}{3} = \boxed{50}$$

Average of $x + y + z + t + \ldots$

$$= \frac{x + y + z + t + \ldots}{number\ of\ items}$$

94. (B) Average speed $= \dfrac{\text{total distance}}{\text{total time}}$

Distance = 40 miles, Time = 4 hours

Average speed $= \dfrac{40 \text{ miles}}{4 \text{ hours}}$

$= \boxed{10 \text{ miles per hour}}$

P. Shortcuts

95. (A) Don't get a common denominator if you can do something easier:

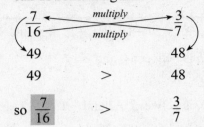

$$49 \quad > \quad 48$$

so $\boxed{\dfrac{7}{16}} \quad > \quad \dfrac{3}{7}$

96. (A)

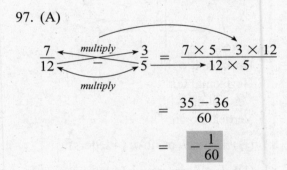

$$= \frac{35 + 36}{60}$$

$$= \frac{71}{60} = \boxed{1\frac{11}{60}}$$

97. (A)

$$\frac{7}{12} \xleftarrow{multiply} \frac{3}{5} = \frac{7 \times 5 - 3 \times 12}{12 \times 5}$$

$$= \frac{35 - 36}{60}$$

$$= \boxed{-\frac{1}{60}}$$

98. (A) Don't divide by 250! Multiply both numerator and denominator by 4:

$$\frac{4}{250} \times \frac{4}{4} = \frac{16}{1,000} = \boxed{0.016}$$

99. (A) Get rid of denominators!

$$200 = \frac{a + b + c}{2} \qquad \boxed{1}$$

Multiply $\boxed{1}$ by 2:
$$200 \times 2 = a + b + c \qquad \boxed{2}$$

$$80 = \frac{a + b}{3} \qquad \boxed{3}$$

Multiply $\boxed{3}$ by 3:
$$80 \times 3 = a + b \qquad \boxed{4}$$

Now subtract $\boxed{4}$ from $\boxed{2}$:
$$200 \times 2 - 80 \times 3 = a + b + c - (a + b)$$
$$= \cancel{a} + \cancel{b} + c - \cancel{a} - \cancel{b}$$
$$400 - 240 = c$$
$$\boxed{160} = c$$

100. (D) Don't multiply 95×75 or 95×74!

Factor *common* 95:

$$95 \times 75 - 95 \times 74 = 95(75 - 74)$$
$$= 95(1)$$
$$= \boxed{95}$$

101. (C) $\dfrac{140 \times 15}{5 \times 7}$

Don't multiply 140×15 if you can first *reduce*.

$$\frac{\overset{20}{\cancel{140}} \times 15}{5 \times \underset{1}{\cancel{7}}} = \frac{20 \times 15}{5}$$

Further reduce:

$$\frac{20 \times \overset{3}{\cancel{15}}}{\underset{1}{\cancel{5}}} = \boxed{60}$$

PART 4

Strategy Section

Using Critical-Thinking Skills to Score High on the SAT

5 GENERAL STRATEGIES

General Strategies for Taking the SAT Examination

Before studying the 32 specific strategies for the Math and Verbal questions, you will find it useful to review the following 5 General Strategies for taking the SAT examination.

<table>
<tr><td>General Strategy</td><td>1</td></tr>
</table>

Don't Rush into Getting an Answer without Thinking

Beware of Choice A if You Get the Answer Fast or without Really Thinking

Everybody panics when taking an exam like the SAT. And what happens is that they rush into getting answers. That's okay, except that you have to think carefully. If a problem looks too easy, beware! Especially beware of the Choice A answer. It's usually a "lure" choice for those who rush into getting an answer without critically thinking about it. Here's an example:

Below is a picture of a digital clock. The clock shows that the time is 6:06. Consider all the times on the clock where the hour is the same as the minute, as in the clock shown below. Another such "double" time would be 8:08 or 9:09. What is the smallest time period between any two such doubles?

6:06

(A) 61 minutes
(B) 60 minutes
(C) 58 minutes
(D) 50 minutes
(E) 49 minutes

Did you subtract 7:07 from 8:08 and get 1 hour and 1 minute (61 minutes)? If you did you probably chose Choice A: the *lure choice*. Think—do you really believe that the test maker would give you such an easy question? The fact that you figured it out so easily and saw that Choice A was your answer should make you think twice. The thing you have to realize is that there is another possibility: 12:12 to 1:01 gives 49 minutes, and so Choice E is correct.

So, in summary, if you get the answer fast and without doing much thinking, and it's a Choice A answer, think again. You may have fallen for the Choice A lure.

Note: Choice A is often a "lure choice" for those who quickly get an answer without doing any real thinking. However, you should certainly realize that Choice A answers can occur, especially if there is no "lure choice."

<table>
<tr><td>General Strategy</td><td>2</td></tr>
</table>

Know and Learn the Directions to the Question Types before You Take the Actual Test

Never Spend Time Reading Directions during the Test or Doing Sample Questions That Don't Count

All SAT exams are standardized. For example, all the Regular Math questions have the same directions from test to test, as do the Writing Questions, etc. So it's a good idea to learn these sets of directions and familiarize yourself with the types of questions early in the game before you take your actual SAT.

Here's an example of a set of SAT directions for the Writing Questions.

Directions:

Each passage below is accompanied by a number of questions. For some questions, you will consider how the passage might be revised to improve the expression of ideas. For other questions, you will consider how the passage might be edited to correct errors in sentence structure, usage, or punctuation. A passage or a question may be accompanied by one or more graphics (such as a table or graph) that you will consider as you make revising and editing decisions.

Some questions will direct you to an underlined portion of a passage. Other questions will direct you to a location in a passage or ask you to think about the passage as a whole.

After reading each passage, choose the answer to each question that most effectively improves the quality of writing in the passage or that makes the passage conform to the conventions of standard written English. Many questions include a "NO CHANGE" option. Choose that option if you think the best choice is to leave the relevant portion of the passage as it is.

If on your actual test you spend time reading these directions, you will waste valuable time.

As you go through this book, you will become familiar with all the question types so that you won't have to read their directions on the actual test.

General Strategy 3

Answer Every Multiple Choice Question

There Is No Penalty for Guessing

Of course you should answer every question. Just try not to get "lured into" the wrong answer.

General Strategy 4

Write As Much As You Want in Your Test Booklet

Test Booklets Aren't Graded—So Use Them as You Would Scrap Paper

Many students are afraid to mark up their test booklets. But the booklets are not graded! Make any marks you want. In fact, some of the strategies demand that you extend or draw lines in geometry questions or label diagrams, circle incorrect answers, etc. That's why when I see computer programs that show only the questions on a screen and prevent the student from marking a diagram or circling an answer, I realize that such programs prevent the student from using many powerful strategies. *So write all you want in your test booklet—use your test paper as you would scrap paper*.

General Strategy 5

Use Your Own Coding System to Tell You Which Questions to Return To

If You Have Extra Time after Completing a Test Section, You'll Know Exactly Which Questions Need More Attention

When you are sure that you have answered a question correctly, mark your question paper with ✓. For questions you are not sure of but for which you have eliminated some of the choices, use **?**. For questions that you're not sure of at all or for which you have not been able to eliminate any choices, use **??**. This will give you a bird's-eye view of what questions you should return to if you have time left after completing a particular test section.

32 EASY-TO-LEARN STRATEGIES

19 Math Strategies + 13 Verbal (Reading) Strategies

Critical thinking is the ability to think clearly in order to solve problems and answer questions of all types— for example, SAT questions, both Math and Verbal.

Educators who are deeply involved in research on Critical-Thinking Skills tell us that such skills are straightforward, practical, teachable, and learnable.

The 19 Math Strategies and 13 Verbal Strategies in this section are Critical-Thinking Skills. These strategies have the potential to raise your SAT scores dramatically. Since each correct SAT question gives you an additional 10 points on average, it is reasonable to assume that if you can learn and then use these valuable SAT strategies, you can boost your SAT scores phenomenally!

Be sure to learn and use the strategies that follow!

How to Learn the Strategies

1. For each strategy, look at the heading describing the strategy.

2. Try to answer the first example without looking at the explanatory answer.

3. Then look at the explanatory answer and, if you got the right answer, see if the method described will enable you to solve the question in a better way with a faster approach.

4. Then try each of the next examples without looking at the explanatory answer.

5. Use the same procedure as in (3) for each of the examples.

The Math Strategies start on page 72, and the Verbal Strategies start on page 123. However, before you start the Math Strategies, it would be wise for you to look at the "Important Note on the Allowed Use of Calculators on the SAT," following; the "Important Note on Math Questions on the SAT," page 67; "The Grid-Type Math Questions," page 68; and "Use of a Calculator in the Grid-Type Questions," page 71.

Important Note on the Allowed Use of Calculators on the SAT

Although the use of calculators on the SAT will be allowed, using a calculator may be sometimes more tedious, when in fact you can use another problem-solving method or shortcut. So you must be selective on when and when not to use a calculator on the test.

Here's an example of when a calculator should *not* be used:

$$\frac{2}{5} \times \frac{5}{6} \times \frac{6}{7} \times \frac{7}{8} \times \frac{8}{9} \times \frac{9}{10} \times \frac{10}{11} =$$

(A) $\dfrac{9}{11}$

(B) $\dfrac{2}{11}$

(C) $\dfrac{11}{36}$

(D) $\dfrac{10}{21}$

Here the use of a calculator may take some time. However, if you use the strategy of canceling numerators and denominators (Math Strategy 1, Example 3 on page 73) as shown,

Cancel numerators/denominators:

$$\frac{2}{5} \times \frac{5}{6} \times \frac{6}{7} \times \frac{7}{8} \times \frac{8}{9} \times \frac{9}{10} \times \frac{10}{11} = \frac{2}{11}$$

you can see that the answer comes easily as $\dfrac{2}{11}$.

Later I will show you an example in the *grid-type* question whose problem's solution would take you longer using a calculator than it does using my strategy. Here's an example of when using a calculator may get you the solution *as fast as* using a strategy without the calculator:

25 percent of 16 is equivalent to $\frac{1}{2}$ of what number?

- (A) 2
- (B) 4
- (C) 8
- (D) 16

Using a calculator, you'd use Math Strategy 2 (page 74) (translating *of* to *times* and *is* to *equals*), first calculating 25 percent of 16 to get 4. Then you'd say 4 = half of what number and you'd find that number to be 8.

Without using a calculator, you'd still use Math Strategy 2 (the translation strategy), but you could write 25 percent as $\frac{1}{4}$, so you'd figure out that $\frac{1}{4} \times 16$ is 4.

Then you'd call the number you want to find x, and say $4 = \frac{1}{2}(x)$. You'd find $x = 8$.

Note that for these examples both methods, with and without a calculator, are about equally efficient; however, the technique in the second method can be used for many more problems and hones more thinking skills.

Important Note on Math Questions on the SAT

There are two types of math questions on the SAT.

1. The Regular Math Questions (total of 45 counted questions), which have 4 choices. The strategies for these start on page 72.

2. The Grid-Type Math Questions (total of 12 counted questions) are described below.

   Note: The grid-type questions can be solved using the Regular Math Strategies.

The Grid-Type Math Questions

There will be 13 questions on the SAT where you will have to "grid in" your answer rather than choose from a set of four choices. These are known as Student-Produced Response questions. Here are the directions for answering grid-type questions. Make sure that you understand these directions completely before you answer any of the grid-type questions. Here is some practice with grids.

Directions: For grid-type questions 1–15, use the grids on the following page.

Each of the remaining questions requires you to solve the problem and enter your answer by marking the circles in the special grid, as shown in the examples here. You may use any available space for scratchwork.

- Mark no more than one oval in any column.

- Because the answer sheet will be machine-scored, **you will receive credit only if the ovals are filled in correctly.**

- Although not required, it is suggested that you write your answer in the boxes at the top of the columns to help you fill in the ovals accurately.

- Some problems may have more than one correct answer. In such cases, grid only one answer.

- No question has a negative answer.

- **Mixed numbers** such as $2\frac{1}{2}$ must be gridded as 2.5 or 5/2.

  (If $\boxed{2\,1\,/\,2}$ is gridded, it will be interpreted as $\frac{21}{2}$, not $2\frac{1}{2}$.)

- **Decimal accuracy:** If you obtain a decimal answer, **enter the most accurate value the grid will accommodate.** For example, if you obtain an answer such as 0.6666 . . . , you should record the result as .666 or .667. **Less accurate values such as .66 or .67 are not acceptable.**

Answer: $\frac{7}{12}$ Answer: 2.5

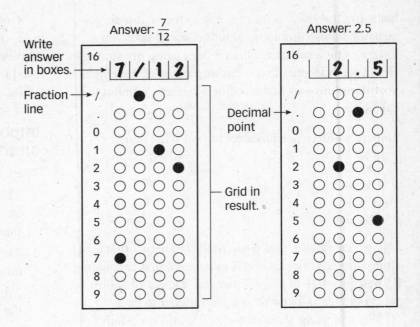

Write answer in boxes. →   Fraction line →   Decimal point →   Grid in result.

Acceptable ways to grid $\frac{2}{3}$ = .6666 . . . are:

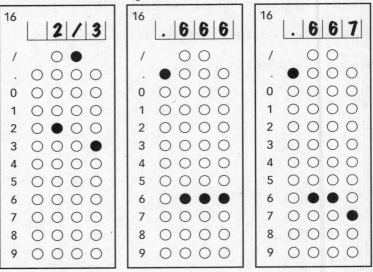

Answer: 201 – Either position is correct.

NOTE: You may start your answers in any column, space permitting. Columns you don't need to use should be left blank.

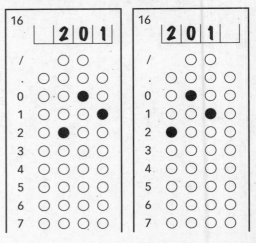

Practice with Grids

According to the directions on the previous page, grid the following values in the grids 1–15:

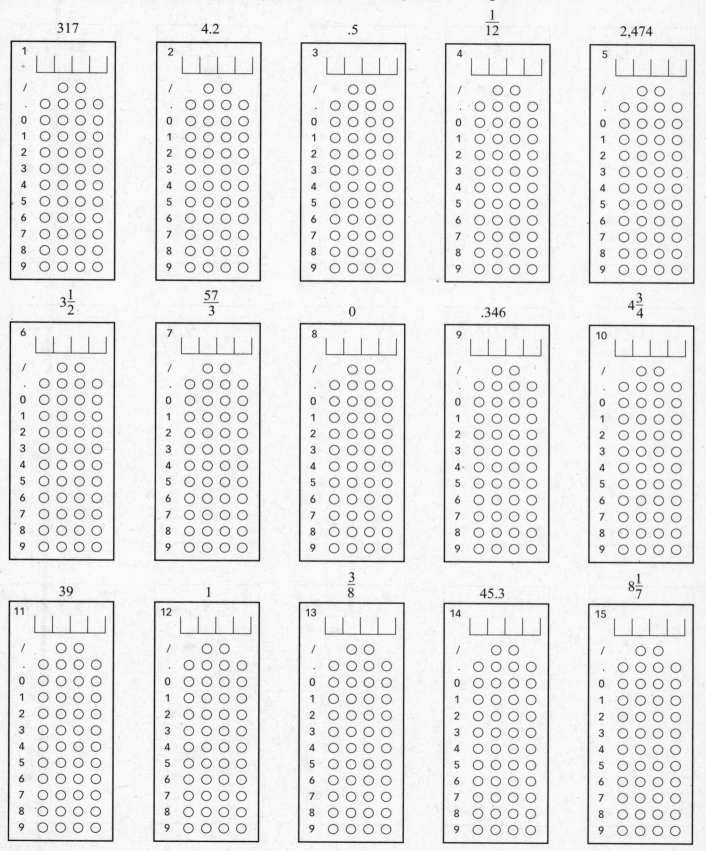

Answers

The answers are displayed on grid-in answer sheets:

1. 317
2. 4.2
3. .5
4. $\frac{1}{12}$ (1/12)
5. 2,474
6. $3\frac{1}{2}$ (7/2)
7. $\frac{57}{3}$ (57/3)
8. 0
9. .346
10. $4\frac{3}{4}$ (19/4)
11. 39
12. 1
13. $\frac{3}{8}$ (3/8)
14. 45.3
15. $8\frac{1}{7}$ (57/7)

Use of a Calculator in the Grid-Type Questions

In the following example, you can either use a calculator or not. However, the use of a calculator will require a different gridding.

Example:

If $\frac{2}{7} < x < \frac{3}{7}$ find one value of x.

Solution *without* a calculator:

Get some value between $\frac{2}{7}$ and $\frac{3}{7}$. Write $\frac{2}{7} = \frac{4}{14}$ and $\frac{3}{7} = \frac{6}{14}$.

So we have $\frac{4}{14} < x < \frac{6}{14}$ and x can be $\frac{5}{14}$.

The grid will look like this:

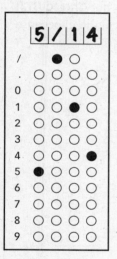

Solution *with* a calculator:

Calculate on a calculator:

$$\frac{3}{7} = .4285714\ldots$$

$$\frac{2}{7} = .2857142\ldots$$

So $.2857142 < x < .4285714$.

You could have the grid as follows:

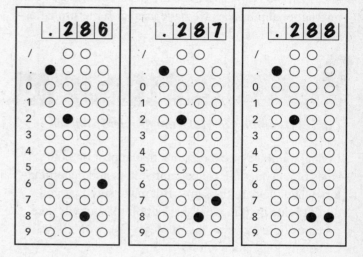

all the way to

19 MATH STRATEGIES

Using Critical-Thinking Skills in Math Questions

Note: On the New SAT there are only 4 choices. For instructional purposes we have used 5 in the strategies sections.

Math Strategy   1

Cancel Quantities to Make the Problem Simpler

Cancel numbers or expressions that appear on both sides of an equation; cancel numerators and denominators when they are the same. But make sure that you don't divide by 0 in what you're doing! You will save precious time by using this strategy. You won't have to make any long calculations.

Example 1

If $P \times \dfrac{11}{14} = \dfrac{11}{14} \times \dfrac{8}{9}$, then $P =$

(A) $\dfrac{8}{9}$

(B) $\dfrac{9}{8}$

(C) 8

(D) 11

(E) 14

Choice A is correct. Do not multiply $\dfrac{11}{14} \times \dfrac{8}{9}$!

Cancel the common $\dfrac{11}{14}$:

$$P \times \dfrac{\cancel{11}}{\cancel{14}} = \dfrac{\cancel{11}}{\cancel{14}} \times \dfrac{8}{9}$$

$$P = \dfrac{8}{9} \text{ (Answer)}$$

Note: You can cancel the $\dfrac{11}{14}$ because you are *dividing* both sides by the same nonzero number. Suppose you had a problem like the following:

If $R \times a = a \times \dfrac{4}{5}$, then $R =$

(A) $\dfrac{2}{3}$

(B) $\dfrac{4}{5}$

(C) 1

(D) $\dfrac{5}{4}$

(E) cannot be determined

What do you think the answer is? It's not Choice B! It is Choice E, because you cannot cancel the a, because a may be 0 and you cannot divide by 0. So if $a = 0$, R can be *any* number.

Example 2

If $y + \dfrac{7}{13} + \dfrac{6}{19} = \dfrac{3}{5} + \dfrac{7}{13} + \dfrac{6}{19}$, then $y =$

(A) $\dfrac{6}{19}$

(B) $\dfrac{13}{32}$

(C) $\dfrac{7}{13}$

(D) $\dfrac{3}{5}$

(E) $\dfrac{211}{247}$

Choice D is correct. *Do not add the fractions!*

Don't add $\dfrac{3}{5} + \dfrac{7}{13} + \dfrac{6}{19}$! You waste a lot of time!

There is a much shorter way to do the problem. Cancel $\dfrac{7}{13} + \dfrac{6}{19}$ from both sides of the equation. Thus,

$$y + \dfrac{\cancel{7}}{\cancel{13}} + \dfrac{\cancel{6}}{\cancel{19}} = \dfrac{3}{5} + \dfrac{\cancel{7}}{\cancel{13}} + \dfrac{\cancel{6}}{\cancel{19}}$$

$$y = \dfrac{3}{5} \text{ (Answer)}$$

Example 3

$$\frac{2}{5} \times \frac{5}{6} \times \frac{6}{7} \times \frac{7}{8} \times \frac{8}{9} \times \frac{9}{10} \times \frac{10}{11} =$$

(A) $\frac{9}{11}$

(B) $\frac{2}{11}$

(C) $\frac{11}{36}$

(D) $\frac{10}{21}$

(E) $\frac{244}{360}$

Choice B is correct.

Cancel numerators/denominators:

$$\frac{2}{5} \times \frac{\cancel{5}}{\cancel{6}} \times \frac{\cancel{6}}{\cancel{7}} \times \frac{\cancel{7}}{\cancel{8}} \times \frac{\cancel{8}}{\cancel{9}} \times \frac{\cancel{9}}{\cancel{10}} \times \frac{\cancel{10}}{11} = \frac{2}{11}$$

Example 4

If $a + b > a - b$, which must follow?

(A) $a < 0$
(B) $b < 0$
(C) $a > b$
(D) $b > a$
(E) $b > 0$

Choice E is correct.

$a + b > a - b$

Cancel common a's:

$$\cancel{a} + b > \cancel{a} - b$$
$$b > -b$$
$$\text{Add } b: b + b > b - b$$
$$2b > 0$$
$$b > 0$$

Example 5

If $7\frac{2}{9} = 6 + \frac{y}{27}$, then $y =$

(A) 8
(B) 30
(C) 35
(D) 37
(E) 33

Choice E is correct.

Subtract 6 from both sides:

$$7\frac{2}{9} - 6 = 6 + \frac{y}{27} - 6$$
$$1\frac{2}{9} = \frac{y}{27}$$
$$\frac{11}{9} = \frac{y}{27}$$
$$\frac{33}{27} = \frac{y}{27}$$
$$y = 33$$

Math Strategy   2

Very Important Strategy:

Translate English Words into Mathematical Expressions

Many of the SAT problems are word problems. Being able to translate word problems from English into mathematical expressions or equations will help you to score high on the test. The following table translates some commonly used words into their mathematical equivalents.

By knowing this table, you will find word problems much easier to do.

TRANSLATION TABLE

Words	Math Way to Say It
is, was, has, cost	= (equals)
of	× (times)
percent	$\frac{}{100}$ (the percent number over 100)
x percent	$\frac{x}{100}$
which, what	x (or any other variable)
x and y	$x + y$
the sum of x and y	$x + y$
the difference between x and y	$x - y$
x more than y	$x + y$
x less than y	$y - x$
the product of x and y	xy
the square of x	x^2
x is greater than y	$x > y$ (or $y < x$)
x is less than y	$x < y$ (or $y > x$)
y years ago	$- y$
y years from now	$+ y$
c times as old as John	$c \times$ (John's age)
x older than y	$x + y$
x younger than y	$y - x$
the increase from x to y	$y - x$
the decrease from x to y	$x - y$
the percent increase from x to y ($y > x$)	$\left(\frac{y - x}{x}\right)100$
the percent decrease from x to y ($y < x$)	$\left(\frac{x - y}{x}\right)100$
the percent of increase	$\left(\frac{\text{amount of increase}}{\text{original amount}}\right) \times 100$
the percent of decrease	$\left(\frac{\text{amount of decrease}}{\text{original amount}}\right) \times 100$
n percent greater than x	$x + \left(\frac{n}{100}\right)x$
n percent less than x	$x - \left(\frac{n}{100}\right)x$

Optional Quiz on Translation Table

Take this quiz to see if you understand the translation table before attempting the problems in Strategy 2 that follow.

1. **Mila is five years older than Juan** translates to:

(A) $J = 5 + M$
(B) $M + J = 5$
(C) $M > 5 + J$
(D) $M = 5 + J$
(E) none of these

Answer

(D) Translate: **Mila** to M; **Juan** to J; **is** to $=$; **older than** to $+$

So **Mila is five years older than Juan** becomes:

$$M = 5 \quad + \quad J$$

2. **3 percent of 5** translates to:

(A) $\dfrac{3}{5}$
(B) $\dfrac{3}{100} \div 5$
(C) $\left(\dfrac{3}{100}\right) \times 5$
(D) $3 \times 100 \times 5$
(E) none of these

Answer

(C) percent or $\% = \dfrac{}{100}$; of $= \times$; so

3% of 5 translates to:

$$\dfrac{3}{100} \times 5$$

3. **What percent of 3** translates to:

(A) $x(100) \times 3$
(B) $\left(\dfrac{x}{100}\right) \times 3$
(C) $\left(\dfrac{x}{100}\right) \div 3$
(D) $\left(\dfrac{3}{100}\right)x$
(E) none of these

Answer

(B) Translate: **what** to x; **percent** to $\dfrac{}{100}$. Thus **What percent of 3** becomes:

$$x \quad \dfrac{}{100} \times 3$$

4. **Six years ago, Sophia was 4 times as old as Jacob was then** translates to:

(A) $S - 6 = 4J$
(B) $6 - S = 4J$
(C) $6 - S = 4(J - 6)$
(D) $S - 6 = 4(J - 6)$
(E) none of these

Answer

(D) **Six years ago, Sophia was** translates to $S - 6$. **4 times as old as Jacob is** would be $4J$. However, **4 times as old as Jacob was then** translates to $4(J - 6)$. Thus **six years ago, Sophia was 4 times as old as Jacob was then** translates to:

$$S - 6 = 4 \times (J - 6)$$

5. **The percent increase from 5 to 10** is

(A) $\left[\dfrac{(10 - 5)}{5}\right] \times 100$
(B) $\left[\dfrac{(5 - 10)}{5}\right] \times 100$
(C) $\left[\dfrac{(10 - 5)}{10}\right] \times 100$
(D) $\left[\dfrac{(5 - 10)}{10}\right] \times 100$
(E) none of these

Answer

(A) Percent increase from a to b is $\left[\dfrac{(b - a)}{a}\right] \times 100$.

So **the percent increase from 5 to 10** would be $\left[\dfrac{(10 - 5)}{5}\right] \times 100$

6. **Hudson is older than John and John is older than Madison** translates to:

(A) $H > J > M$
(B) $H > J < M$
(C) $H > M > J$
(D) $M > H > J$
(E) none of these

Answer

(A) **Hudson is older than John** translates to: $H > J$. **John is older than Madison** translates to $J > M$. So we have $H > J$ and $J > M$, which, consolidated, becomes $H > J > M$.

7. **Even after Phil gives Sam 6 DVDs, he still has 16 more DVDs than Sam has** translates to:

   (A) $P - 6 = 16 + S$
   (B) $P - 6 = 16 + S + 6$
   (C) $P + 6 = 16 + S + 6$
   (D) $P + 6 + 16 + S$
   (E) none of these

   Answer
   (B) **Even after Phil gives Sam 6 DVDs** translates to:

   $P - 6$ 1

   He still has 16 more DVDs than Sam has translates to:

   $= 16 + S + 6$ 2

   since Sam has gotten 6 additional DVDs. Thus, combining 1 and 2, we get:
   $P - 6 = 16 + S + 6$.

8. **q is 10% greater than p** translates to:

   (A) $q = \left(\dfrac{10}{100}\right)q + p$

   (B) $q > \left(\dfrac{10}{100}\right)p$

   (C) $q = \left(\dfrac{10}{100}\right)p + p$

   (D) $q = \left(\dfrac{10}{100}\right) + p$

   (E) none of these

   Answer
   (C) **q is** translates to $q =$ 1

   10% greater than p translates to   2

   $\left(\dfrac{10}{100}\right)p + p$ so

   q is 10% greater than p
   translates to:
   $q = \left(\dfrac{10}{100}\right)p + p$

9. **200 is what percent of 20** translates to:

   (A) $200 = x \times 100 \times 20$

   (B) $200 = \left(\dfrac{x}{100}\right) \div 20$

   (C) $200 = \left(\dfrac{x}{100}\right) \times 20$

   (D) $200 = x \times 20$

   (E) none of these

   Answer
   (C) Translate **is** to $=$; **what** to x; **percent** to $\dfrac{1}{100}$; **of** to $\times$ so we get that:

   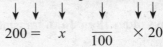

   200 is what percent of 20 translates to:

   $200 = \quad x \quad \dfrac{1}{100} \quad \times 20$

10. **The product of the sums of x and y and y and z is 5** translates to:

   (A) $xy + yz = 5$
   (B) $x + y + y + z = 5$
   (C) $(x + y)(yz) = 5$
   (D) $(x + y)(y + z) = 5$
   (E) none of these

   Answer
   (D) **The sum of x and y** is $x + y$. **The sum of y and z** is $y + z$. So the **product of those sums** is $(x + y)(y + z)$.

   Thus **The product of the sums of x and y and y and z is 5** translates to:
   $(x + y)(y + z) = 5$

Math Strategy 2: Examples

Example 1

Sarah is twice as old as John. Six years ago, Sarah was 4 times as old as John was then. How old is John now?

   (A) 3
   (B) 9
   (C) 18
   (D) 20
   (E) impossible to determine

Choice B is correct. Translate:

   Sarah is twice as old as John.

   $S = 2 \times J$

   $S = 2J$ 1

Six years ago Sarah was 4 times as old as John was then

   $-6 \qquad S = 4 \times (J - 6)$

   This becomes $S - 6 = 4(J - 6)$ 2

Substituting 1 into 2:

$$2J - 6 = 4(J - 6)$$
$$2J - 6 = 4J - 24$$
$$18 = 2J$$
$$9 = J \ (\textit{Answer})$$

Example 2

200 is what percent of 20?

(A) $\frac{1}{10}$

(B) 10

(C) 100

(D) 1,000

(E) 10,000

Choice D is correct. Translate:

200 is what percent of 20
↓ ↓ ↓ ↓ ↓ ↓
$200 = x \quad \overline{100} \quad \times 20$

$$200 = \frac{x}{100}(20)$$

Divide by 20: $10 = \frac{x}{100}$

Multiply by 100: $1,000 = x$ (*Answer*)

Example 3

An ice cream store sells ice cream cones for $2.50 each and ice cream pops for $1.50 each. The revenue for selling a total of 210 ice cream cones and pops was $405. How many ice cream pops were sold?

(A) 90

(B) 120

(C) 130

(D) 140

(E) 160

Choice B is correct. Translate words to math: Number of cones sold = c. Number of pops sold = p.

The statement **210 ice cream cones and pops were sold for $405** actually translates to two equations:

$$210 = c + p \qquad \boxed{1}$$

(since the total number of cones and pops was 210)

$$2.50c + 1.50p = 405 \qquad \boxed{2}$$

(since each cone sold for $2.50 and each pop sold for $1.50 and the total revenue was $405).

The easiest way to solve these equations is to multiply Equation $\boxed{1}$ by 2.5. We get:

$$210(2.5) = 2.5c + 2.5p \qquad \boxed{3}$$

Now we can subtract Equation $\boxed{2}$ from Equation $\boxed{3}$ and get:

$$
\begin{aligned}
210(2.5) &= 2.5c + 2.5p \\
- \quad 405 &= 2.5c + 1.5p \\
\hline
525 - 405 = \quad 0 &+ 1p \\
120 &= p
\end{aligned}
$$

Example 4

Peter is a biologist who is studying two different species of spiders. He noticed that spiders of species A produced 25% more offspring than spiders of species B. If spiders of species A produced 120 offspring, how many offspring did spiders of species B produce?

(A) 94

(B) 96

(C) 98

(D) 100

(E) 102

Choice B is correct. Translate from verbal to math. Let the number of offspring species A produces be denoted as A, and the number of offspring species B produces be denoted as B. The statement **Spiders of species A produced 25% more offspring than spiders of species B** translates to:

$$A = \left(\frac{25}{100}\right)B + B$$

$$A = \left(\frac{25}{100}\right)B + \frac{100B}{100} = \left(\frac{25}{100}\right)B.$$

But species A produced 120 offspring. So substituting 120 for A, we get:

$$120 = \frac{125B}{100}$$

$$\frac{12,000}{125} = B \text{ and } B = 96.$$

Example 5

If A is 250 percent of B, what percent of A is B?

(A) 125%

(B) $\frac{1}{250}$%

(C) 50%

(D) 40%

(E) 400%

Choice D is correct.

If *A* is 250 percent of *B* becomes:

$$A = 250 \quad \frac{}{100} \quad \times B$$

What percent of *A* is *B*? becomes:

$$x \quad \frac{}{100} \quad \times A = B$$

Set up the equations:

$$A = \frac{250}{100}B \qquad \boxed{1}$$

$$\frac{x}{100}A = B \qquad \boxed{2}$$

Divide Equation $\boxed{1}$ by Equation $\boxed{2}$:

$$\frac{A}{\frac{x}{100}A} = \frac{\frac{250}{100}B}{B}$$

We get:

$$\frac{1}{\frac{x}{100}} = \frac{250}{100}$$

Inverting, we get:

$$\frac{x}{100} = \frac{100}{250}$$

$$x = \frac{10,000}{250}$$

To simplify, multiply both numerator and denominator by 4:

$$x = \frac{10,000 \times 4}{250 \times 4} = 40$$

$$x = \frac{40,000}{1,000} = 40$$

Alternate way:

Let *B* = 100 (choose any number for *B*).
We get (after translation):

$$A = \left(\frac{250}{100}\right)100 \qquad \boxed{1}$$

$$\left(\frac{x}{100}\right)A = 100 \qquad \boxed{2}$$

From $\boxed{1}$,

$$A = 250 \qquad \boxed{3}$$

Substituting $\boxed{3}$ into $\boxed{2}$, we get:

$$\left(\frac{x}{100}\right)250 = 100 \qquad \boxed{4}$$

Multiplying both sides of $\boxed{4}$ by 100,

$$(x)(250) = (100)(100)$$

Dividing by 250:

$$x = \frac{100 \times 100}{250}$$

Simplify by multiplying numerator and denominator by 4:

$$x = \frac{100 \times 100 \times 4}{250 \times 4} = \frac{40,000}{1,000}$$

$$= 40$$

Example 6

John is now *m* years old and Sally is 4 years older than John. Which represents Sally's age 6 years ago?

   (A) $m + 10$
   (B) $m - 10$
   (C) $m - 2$
   (D) $m - 4$
   (E) $4m - 6$

Choice C is correct.

Translate:

John is now *m* years old

$$J = m$$

Sally is 4 years older than John

$$S = 4 + J$$

Sally's age 6 years ago

$$S - 6$$

So we get: $J = m$

$$S = 4 + J$$

and find: $S - 6 = 4 + J - 6$

$$S - 6 = J - 2$$

$$S - 6 = m - 2 \text{ (substituting } m \text{ for } J\text{)}$$

See Math Strategy 7, Example 2 (page 91) for an alternate approach to solving this problem, using a different strategy: ***Use Specific Numerical Examples to Prove or Disprove Your Guess.***

Example 7

Phil has three times as many DVDs as Sam has. Even after Phil gives Sam 6 DVDs, he still has 16 more DVDs than Sam has. What was the original number of DVDs that Phil had?

   (A) 20
   (B) 24
   (C) 28
   (D) 33
   (E) 42

Choice E is correct.

Translate:

Phil has three times as many DVDs as Sam has

$$P \quad = \quad 3 \quad \times \quad\quad\quad\quad\quad\quad S$$

Even after Phil gives Sam 6 DVDs, he still has 16

$$P \quad - \quad 6 \quad\quad\quad\quad\quad = 16$$

more DVDs than Sam has

$$+ \quad\quad\quad S + 6$$

Sam now has $S + 6$ DVDs because Phil gave Sam 6 DVDs. So we end up with the equations:

$$P = 3S$$
$$P - 6 = 16 + S + 6$$

Find P; get rid of S:

$$P = 3S; \frac{P}{3} = S$$

$$P - 6 = 16 + \frac{P}{3} + 6$$

$$P - 6 = \frac{48 + P + 18}{3}$$

$$3P - 18 = 48 + P + 18$$

$$2P = 84$$

$$P = 42$$

Example 8

If q is 10% greater than p and r is 10% greater than y, qr is what percent greater than py?

   (A) 1%
   (B) 20%
   (C) 21%
   (D) 30%
   (E) 100%

Choice C is correct.

Translate:

If q is 10% greater than p

$$q = \quad \frac{10}{100}p + p$$

and r is 10% greater than y

$$r = \quad \frac{10}{100}y + y$$

qr is what percent greater than py?

$$qr = \quad\quad \frac{x}{100}py + py$$

So we have three equations:

$$q = \frac{10}{100}p + p = \left(\frac{10}{100} + 1\right)p \quad\quad \boxed{1}$$

$$r = \frac{10}{100}y + y = \left(\frac{10}{100} + 1\right)y \quad\quad \boxed{2}$$

$$qr = \frac{x}{100}py + py = \left(\frac{x}{100} + 1\right)py \quad\quad \boxed{3}$$

Multiply $\boxed{1}$ and $\boxed{2}$:

$$qr = \left(\frac{10}{100} + 1\right)^2 py \quad\quad \boxed{4}$$

Now equate $\boxed{4}$ with $\boxed{3}$:

$$qr = \left(\frac{x}{100} + 1\right)py = \left(\frac{10}{100} + 1\right)^2 py$$

You can see that $\left(\frac{10}{100} + 1\right)^2 = \frac{x}{100} + 1$, canceling py.

So, $\left(\frac{10}{100} + 1\right)^2 = \frac{100}{10,000} + 2\left(\frac{10}{100}\right) + 1 = \frac{x}{100} + 1$

$$\frac{100}{10,000} + \frac{20}{100} = \frac{21}{100} = \frac{x}{100}$$

$$21 = x$$

The answer is $x = 21$.

Alternate approach:

Choose numbers for p and for y:

Let $p = 10$ and $y = 20$

Then, since q is 10% greater than p:

$$q = 10\% \text{ greater than } 10$$

$$q = \left(\frac{10}{100}\right)10 + 10 = 11$$

Next, r is 10% greater than y:

$$r = 10\% \text{ greater than } 20$$

Or, $r = \frac{10}{100}(20) + 20 = 22$

Then:

$$qr = 11 \times 22$$
$$\text{and } py = 20 \times 10$$

So, to find what percent qr is greater than py, you would need to find:

$$\frac{qr - py}{py} \times 100 \text{ or}$$

$$\frac{11 \times 22 - 20 \times 10}{20 \times 10} \times 100$$

This is:

$$\frac{42}{200} \times 100 = 21$$

Example 9

Sales of Item X Jan–Jun 2016	
Month	**Sales ($)**
Jan	800
Feb	1,000
Mar	1,200
Apr	1,300
May	1,600
Jun	1,800

According to the table above, the monthly percent increase in sales was greatest for which of the following periods?

(A) Jan–Feb
(B) Feb–Mar
(C) Mar–Apr
(D) Apr–May
(E) May–Jun

Choice A is correct.

The percent increase from Month A to Month B =

$$\frac{\text{sales (month B)} - \text{sales (month A)}}{\text{sales (month A)}} \times 100$$

You can see that $\frac{200}{800} \times 100$ (Jan–Feb) is the greatest.

Month	Sales ($)	Period	% Increase in Sales
Jan	800	Jan–Feb	$\frac{1,000 - 800}{800} \times 100 = \frac{200}{800} \times 100$
Feb	1,000	Feb–Mar	$\frac{1,200 - 1,000}{1,000} \times 100 = \frac{200}{1,000} \times 100$
Mar	1,200	Mar–Apr	$\frac{1,300 - 1,200}{1,200} \times 100 = \frac{100}{1,200} \times 100$
Apr	1,300	Apr–May	$\frac{1,600 - 1,300}{1,300} \times 100 = \frac{300}{1,300} \times 100$
May	1,600	May–Jun	$\frac{1,800 - 1,600}{1,600} \times 100 = \frac{200}{1,600} \times 100$
Jun	1,800		

Math Strategy   3

Know How to Find Unknown Quantities (Areas, Lengths, Arc and Angle Measurements) from Known Quantities (The Whole Equals the Sum of Its Parts)

When asked to find a particular area or length, instead of trying to calculate it directly, find it by subtracting two other areas or lengths—a method based on the fact that the whole minus a part equals the remaining part.

This strategy is very helpful in many types of geometry problems. A very important equation to remember is

The whole = the sum of its parts   **1**

Equation **1** is often disguised in many forms, as seen in the following examples:

Example 1

In the diagram below, $\triangle XYZ$ has been inscribed in a circle. If the circle encloses an area of 64, and the area of $\triangle XYZ$ is 15, then what is the area of the shaded region?

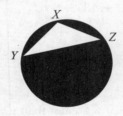

(A) 25
(B) 36
(C) 49
(D) 79
(E) It cannot be determined from the information given.

Choice C is correct. Use Equation **1**. Here, the whole refers to the area within the circle, and the parts refer to the areas of the shaded region and the triangle. Thus,

Area within circle =
Area of shaded region +
Area of $\triangle XYZ$

64 = Area of shaded region + 15

or Area of shaded region = 64 − 15 = 49 (*Answer*)

Example 2

In the diagram below, $\overline{AE}$ is a straight line, and F is a point on $\overline{AE}$. Find an expression for $m\angle DFE$.

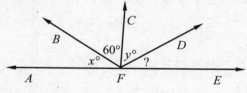

(A) $x + y - 60$
(B) $x + y + 60$
(C) $90 - x - y$
(D) $120 - x - y$
(E) $180 - x - y$

Choice D is correct. Use Equation 1. Here, the whole refers to the straight angle, $\angle AFE$, and its parts refer to $\angle AFB$, $\angle BFC$, $\angle CFD$, and $\angle DFE$. Thus,

$$m\angle AFE = m\angle AFB + m\angle BFC +$$
$$m\angle CFD + m\angle DFE$$
$$180 = x + 60 + y + m\angle DFE$$
$$\text{or}\quad m\angle DFE = 180 - x - 60 - y$$
$$m\angle DFE = 120 - x - y \,(Answer)$$

Example 3

In the diagram below, $AB = m$, $BC = n$, and $AD = 10$. Find an expression for CD.

(*Note*: Diagram represents a straight line.)

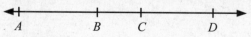

(A) $10 - mn$
(B) $10 - m - n$
(C) $m - n + 10$
(D) $m + n - 10$
(E) $m + n + 10$

Choice B is correct. Use Equation 1. Here, the whole refers to AD, and its parts refer to AB, BC, and CD. Thus,

$$AD = AB + BC + CD$$
$$10 = m + n + CD$$
$$\text{or}\quad CD = 10 - m - n \,(Answer)$$

Example 4

The area of triangle $ACE = 64$. The sum of the areas of the shaded triangles ABF and FDE is 39. What is the side of square $BFDC$?

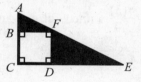

(A) 5
(B) 4
(C) $\sqrt{5}$
(D) $\sqrt{44}$
(E) cannot be determined

Choice A is correct.

Since we are dealing with areas, let's establish the area of the square $BFDC$, which will then enable us to get its side (the positive square root of its area).

Now, the area of square $BFDC$ = area of triangle ACE − (area of triangles $ABF + FDE$)

Area of square $BFDC = 64 - 39$
$$= 25$$

Therefore, the side of square $BFDC$ = the square root of 25 = 5.

Example 5

In the figure below, O is the center of the circle. Triangle AOB has side 3 and angle $AOB = 90°$. What is the area of the shaded region?

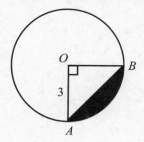

(A) $9\left(\dfrac{\pi}{4} - \dfrac{1}{2}\right)$

(B) $9\left(\dfrac{\pi}{2} - 1\right)$

(C) $9(\pi - 1)$

(D) $9\left(\dfrac{\pi}{4} - \dfrac{1}{4}\right)$

(E) cannot be determined

Choice A is correct.

Subtract knowns from knowns:

Area of shaded region = area of quarter circle AOB − area of triangle AOB

Area of quarter circle $AOB = \dfrac{\pi(3)^2}{4}$ (since $OA = 3$ and

area of a quarter of a circle $= \dfrac{1}{4} \times \pi \times \text{radius}^2$)

Area of triangle $AOB = \dfrac{3 \times 3}{2}$ (since $OB = 3$ and area

of a triangle $= \dfrac{1}{2}$ base × height)

Thus, area of shaded region $= \dfrac{9\pi}{4} - \dfrac{9}{2} = 9\left(\dfrac{\pi}{4} - \dfrac{1}{2}\right)$

Example 6

The sides in the square below are each divided into five equal segments. What is the value of

$$\dfrac{\text{area of square}}{\text{area of shaded region}}?$$

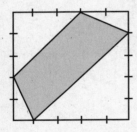

(A) $\dfrac{50}{29}$

(B) $\dfrac{50}{21}$

(C) $\dfrac{25}{4}$

(D) $\dfrac{29}{25}$

(E) none of these

Choice B is correct.

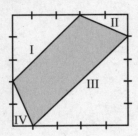

Subtract knowns from knowns:

Area of square = $5 \times 5 = 25$

Area of shaded region = area of square − area of I − area of II − area of III − area of IV

$$\text{Area of I} = \dfrac{3 \times 3}{2} = \dfrac{9}{2}$$

$$\text{Area of II} = \dfrac{2 \times 1}{2} = 1$$

$$\text{Area of III} = \dfrac{4 \times 4}{2} = 8$$

$$\text{Area of IV} = \dfrac{2 \times 1}{2} = 1$$

Area of shaded region $= 25 - \dfrac{9}{2} - 1 - 8 - 1 = \dfrac{21}{2}$

$$\dfrac{\text{area of square}}{\text{area of shaded region}} = \dfrac{25}{\dfrac{21}{2}} = 25 \times \dfrac{2}{21} = \dfrac{50}{21}$$

Example 7

Two concentric circles are shown below with inner radius of m and outer radius of n. What is the area of the shaded region?

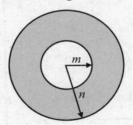

(A) $\pi(n - m)^2$
(B) $\pi(n^2 + m^2)$
(C) $\pi(n^2 - m^2)$
(D) $2\pi(n - m)$
(E) $2\pi(n + m)$

Choice C is correct.

Subtract knowns from knowns:

Area of shaded region = area of circle of radius n − area of circle of radius m

Area of circle of radius $n = \pi n^2$

Area of circle of radius $m = \pi m^2$

Area of shaded region $= \pi n^2 - \pi m^2$
$$= \pi(n^2 - m^2)$$

Math Strategy   4

Very Important Strategy:

Remember Classic Expressions Such as

$$x^2 - y^2, x^2 + 2xy + y^2, x^2 - 2xy + y^2, \frac{x+y}{xy}$$

Memorize the following factorizations and expressions:

$x^2 - y^2 = (x + y)(x - y)$	Equation 1
$x^2 + 2xy + y^2 = (x + y)(x + y) = (x + y)^2$	Equation 2
$x^2 - 2xy + y^2 = (x - y)(x - y) = (x - y)^2$	Equation 3
$\frac{x+y}{xy} = \frac{1}{x} + \frac{1}{y}$ $x, y \neq 0$	Equation 4
$\frac{x-y}{xy} = \frac{1}{y} - \frac{1}{x}$ $x, y \neq 0$	Equation 4A
$xy + xz = x(y + z)$	Equation 5
$xy - xz = x(y - z)$	Equation 5A

Examples 1, 3, and 11 can also be solved with the aid of a calculator and some with the aid of a calculator allowing for exponential calculations. However, to illustrate the effectiveness of Math Strategy 4, we did not use the calculator method of solution for these examples.

Use algebra to see patterns.

Example 1

$66^2 + 2(34)(66) + 34^2 =$

(A) 4,730
(B) 5,000
(C) 9,860
(D) 9,950
(E) 10,000

Choice E is correct. Notice that there is a 34 and 66 running through the left side of the equality. To see a pattern, *use algebra*. Substitute *a* for 66 and *b* for 34. You get:

$$66^2 + 2(34)(66) + 34^2 =$$
$$a^2 + 2(b)(a) + b^2$$

But from Equation 2,

$$a^2 + 2ab + b^2 = \qquad \boxed{1}$$
$$(a + b)(a + b) =$$
$$(a + b)^2$$

Now substitute the numbers 34 and 66 *back into* $\boxed{1}$ to get:

$$66^2 + 2(34)(66) + 34^2 =$$
$$(66 + 34)(66 + 34) =$$
$$100 \times 100 =$$
$$10,000 \quad (Answer)$$

Example 2

If $(x + y) = 9$ and $xy = 14$, find $\frac{1}{x} + \frac{1}{y}$.

(*Note: x, y > 0*)

(A) $\frac{1}{9}$

(B) $\frac{2}{7}$

(C) $\frac{9}{14}$

(D) 5

(E) 9

Choice C is correct. We are given:

$$(x + y) = 9 \qquad \boxed{1}$$
$$xy = 14 \qquad \boxed{2}$$
$$x, y > 0 \qquad \boxed{3}$$

I hope that you did not solve $\boxed{2}$ for *x* (or *y*), and then substitute it into $\boxed{1}$. If you did, you obtained a quadratic equation.

Here is the FAST method. Use Equation 4:

$$\frac{1}{x} + \frac{1}{y} = \frac{x+y}{xy} \qquad \boxed{4}$$

From $\boxed{1}$ and $\boxed{2}$, we find that $\boxed{4}$ becomes

$$\frac{1}{x} + \frac{1}{y} = \frac{9}{14} \ (Answer)$$

Example 3

The value of $100 \times 100 - 99 \times 99 =$

(A) 1
(B) 2
(C) 99
(D) 199
(E) 299

Choice D is correct.

Write a for 100 and b for 99 to see a pattern:

$100 \times 100 - 99 \times 99$

$a \times a - b \times b = a^2 - b^2$. Use Equation 1:
Use the fact that $a^2 - b^2 = (a + b)(a - b)$ **1**

Put back 100 for a and 99 for b in **1**:

$a^2 - b^2 = 100^2 - 99^2 = (100 + 99)(100 - 99) = 199$

Example 4

Use factoring to make problems simpler.

$$\frac{8^7 - 8^6}{7} =$$

(A) $\dfrac{8}{7}$

(B) 8^7

(C) 8^6

(D) 8^5

(E) 8^4

Choice C is correct.

Factor: $8^7 - 8^6 = 8^6(8^1 - 1)$ Equation 5A

$\qquad\qquad\quad = 8^6(8 - 1)$

$\qquad\qquad\quad = 8^6(7)$

So $\dfrac{8^7 - 8^6}{7} = \dfrac{8^6(7)}{7} = \dfrac{8^6(\cancel{7})}{\cancel{7}} = 8^6$

Represented algebraically, the problem would look like this.

Where $a \neq 1$,

$$\frac{a^7 - a^6}{a - 1} =$$

(A) $\dfrac{a}{a - 1}$

(B) $\dfrac{1}{a - 1}$

(C) $a^6 - a^5$

(D) a^5

(E) a^6

Choice E is correct.

Factor: $a^7 - a^6 = a^6(a - 1)$ Equation 5A

The expression

$$\frac{a^7 - a^6}{a - 1}$$

becomes

$$\frac{a^6(a - 1)}{a - 1}$$

Since $a \neq 1$, this becomes a^6

Example 5

Use factoring to make problems simpler.

$\sqrt{(88)^2 + (88)^2(3)} =$

(A) 88

(B) 176

(C) 348

(D) 350

(E) 352

Choice B is correct. Factor:

$(88)^2 + (88)^2(3) = 88^2(1 + 3) = 88^2(4)$ Equation 5

So:

$\sqrt{(88)^2 + (88)^2(3)} = \sqrt{88^2(4)}$

$\qquad\qquad\qquad\quad = \sqrt{88^2} \times \sqrt{4}$

$\qquad\qquad\qquad\quad = 88 \times 2$

$\qquad\qquad\qquad\quad = 176$

Example 6

If $y + \dfrac{1}{y} = 9$, then $y^2 + \dfrac{1}{y^2} =$

(A) 76

(B) 77

(C) 78

(D) 79

(E) 81

Choice D is correct.

Square $\left(y + \dfrac{1}{y}\right) = 9$

Substituting y for x and $\dfrac{1}{y}$ for y in Equation 2, we get:

$$\left(y + \frac{1}{y}\right)^2 = 81 = y^2 + 2(y)\left(\frac{1}{y}\right) + \left(\frac{1}{y}\right)^2$$

$$= y^2 + 2 + \left(\frac{1}{y}\right)^2$$

$$= y^2 + 2 + \frac{1}{y^2}$$

$$79 = y^2 + \frac{1}{y^2}$$

Example 7

If $a - b = 4$ and $a + b = 7$, then $a^2 - b^2 =$

(A) $5\dfrac{1}{2}$

(B) 11

(C) 28

(D) 29

(E) 56

Choice C is correct.

Use $(a - b)(a + b) = a^2 - b^2$ **Equation 1**

$$a - b = 4$$
$$a + b = 7$$
$$(a - b)(a + b) = 28 = a^2 - b^2$$

Example 8

If $x^2 - y^2 = 66$ and $x + y = 6$, what is the value of x?

(A) 11

(B) $\dfrac{21}{2}$

(C) $\dfrac{17}{2}$

(D) $\dfrac{13}{2}$

(E) $\dfrac{11}{2}$

Choice C is correct. Use

$$x^2 - y^2 = (x + y)(x - y) \quad \text{**Equation 1**}$$
$$(x + y)(x - y) = 66$$

But we already know $x + y = 6$, so

$$6(x - y) = 66$$
$$x - y = 11$$

Now compare your two equations:

$$x + y = 6$$
$$x - y = 11$$

Adding these equations (see Strategy 13) gets you

$$2x = 17$$
$$x = \frac{17}{2}$$

Example 9

What is the least possible value of $\dfrac{x + y}{xy}$ if $2 \le x < y \le 11$ and x and y are integers?

(A) $\dfrac{22}{121}$

(B) $\dfrac{5}{6}$

(C) $\dfrac{21}{110}$

(D) $\dfrac{13}{22}$

(E) 1

Choice C is correct.

Use $\dfrac{x + y}{xy} = \dfrac{1}{x} + \dfrac{1}{y}$ **Equation 4**

$\dfrac{1}{x} + \dfrac{1}{y}$ is *least* when x is *greatest* and y is *greatest*.

Since it was given that x and y are integers and that $2 \le x < y \le 11$, the greatest value of x is 10 and the greatest value of y is 11.

So the *least* value of $\dfrac{1}{x} + \dfrac{1}{y} = \dfrac{x + y}{xy} = \dfrac{10 + 11}{10 \times 11} = \dfrac{21}{110}$.

Example 10

If $(a + b)^2 = 20$ and $ab = -3$, then $a^2 + b^2 =$

(A) 14
(B) 20
(C) 26
(D) 32
(E) 38

Choice C is correct.

Use $(a + b)^2 = a^2 + 2ab + b^2 = 20$ **Equation 2**

$ab = -3$

So, $2ab = -6$

Substitute $2ab = -6$ in:

$a^2 + 2ab + b^2 = 20$

We get:

$$a^2 - 6 + b^2 = 20$$
$$a^2 + b^2 = 26$$

Example 11

If $998 \times 1{,}002 > 10^6 - x$, x could be

(A) 4 but not 3
(B) 4 but not 5
(C) 5 but not 4
(D) 3 but not 4
(E) 3, 4, or 5

Choice C is correct.

Use $(a + b)(a - b) = a^2 - b^2$ Equation 1

$$998 \times 1{,}002 = (1{,}000 - 2)(1{,}000 + 2) > 10^6 - x$$
$$= 1{,}000^2 - 4 > 10^6 - x$$
$$= (10^3)^2 - 4 > 10^6 - x$$
$$= 10^6 - 4 > 10^6 - x$$

Multiply by -1; *reverse inequality sign*:

$$-1(-4 > -x)$$
$$+4 < +x$$

Example 12

If $x^2 + y^2 = 2xy$ and $x > 0$ and $y > 0$, then

  (A) $x = 0$ only
  (B) $y = 0$ only
  (C) $x = 1, y = 1$, only
  (D) $x > y > 0$
  (E) $x = y$

Choice E is correct. In the given equation $x^2 + y^2 = 2xy$, subtract $2xy$ from both sides to get it to look like what you have in Equation 3.

$$x^2 + y^2 - 2xy = 2xy - 2xy = 0$$
$$\text{so } x^2 - 2xy + y^2 = 0$$

We have:

$$x^2 - 2xy + y^2 = (x - y)^2 = 0 \quad \text{Equation 3}$$
$$x - y = 0, \text{ and thus } x = y$$

Example 13

If $x + y = 7$ and $xy = 4$, then $x^2 + y^2 =$

  (A)   16
  (B)   28
  (C)   41
  (D)   49
  (E)   65

Choice C is correct. Since we are trying to find $x^2 + y^2$, square $x + y = 7$ to get:

$$(x + y)^2 = 49$$

Use Equation 2 to get:

$$x^2 + 2xy + y^2 = 49$$

Since $xy = 4$, substitute that quantity into the expanded equation.

We get:

$$x^2 + 8 + y^2 = 49$$
$$x^2 + y^2 = 41$$

Math Strategy 5

Know How to Manipulate Averages

Almost all problems involving averages can be solved by remembering that

$$\text{Average} = \frac{\text{sum of the individual quantities or measurements}}{\text{number of quantities or measurements}}$$

(*Note*: Average is also called Arithmetic Mean.)

Example 1

The average height of three students is 68 inches. If two of the students have heights of 70 inches and 72 inches respectively, then what is the height (in inches) of the third student?

  (A)   60
  (B)   62
  (C)   64
  (D)   65
  (E)   66

Choice B is correct. Recall that

$$\text{Average} = \frac{\text{sum of the individual measurements}}{\text{number of measurements}}$$

Let x = height (in inches) of the third student. Thus,

$$68 = \frac{70 + 72 + x}{3}$$

Multiplying by 3,

$$204 = 70 + 72 + x$$
$$204 = 142 + x$$
$$x = 62 \text{ inches}$$

Example 2

The average of 30 numbers is 65. If one of these numbers is 65, the sum of the remaining numbers is

(A) 65×64
(B) 30×64
(C) 29×30
(D) 29×64
(E) 29×65

Choice E is correct.

$$\text{Average} = \frac{\text{sum of numbers}}{30}$$

Call the numbers $a, b, c, d,$ etc.

$$\text{So } 65 = \frac{a + b + c + d + \dots}{30}$$

Now immediately get rid of the fractional part: Multiply by 30 to get: $65 \times 30 = a + b + c + d + \dots$

Since we were told *one of the numbers is 65,* let $a = 65$:

$65 \times 30 = 65 + b + c + d + \dots$
So $65 \times 30 - 65 = b + c + d + \dots$
$b + c + d + \dots = $ sum of remaining numbers

Factor:

$65 \times 30 - 65 = 65(30 - 1) = $ sum of remaining numbers
$65 \times 29 = $ sum of remaining numbers

Example 3

The average length of 6 objects is 25 cm. If 5 objects are each 20 cm in length, what is the length of the sixth object in cm?

(A) 55
(B) 50
(C) 45
(D) 40
(E) 35

Choice B is correct.

Use the formula:

$$\text{Average} = \frac{\text{sum of the individual items}}{\text{number of items}}$$

Now call the length of the sixth item, x. Then:

$$25 = \frac{20 + 20 + 20 + 20 + 20 + x}{6}$$

$$\text{or } \quad 25 = \frac{20 \times 5 + x}{6}$$

Multiply by 6:

$$25 \times 6 = 20 \times 5 + x$$
$$150 = 100 + x$$
$$50 = x$$

Example 4

Scores on five tests range from 0 to 100 inclusive. If Don gets 70 on the first test, 76 on the second, and 75 on the third, what is the minimum score Don may get on the fourth test to average 80 on all five tests?

(A) 76
(B) 79
(C) 82
(D) 89
(E) 99

Choice B is correct.

Use the formula:

$$\text{Average} = \frac{\text{sum of scores on tests}}{\text{number of tests}}$$

Let x be the score on the fourth test and y be the score on the fifth test.

Then:

$$80 = \text{Average} = \frac{70 + 76 + 75 + x + y}{5}$$

The minimum score x Don can get is the *lowest* score he can get. The higher the score y is, the lower the score x can be. The greatest value of y can be 100. So:

$$80 = \frac{70 + 76 + 75 + x + 100}{5}$$
$$80 = \frac{321 + x}{5}$$

Multiply by 5:

$$400 = 321 + x$$
$$79 = x$$

Example 5

Eighteen students attained an average score of 70 on a test, and 12 students on the same test scored an average of 90. What is the average score for all 30 students on the test?

(A) 78
(B) 80
(C) 82
(D) 85
(E) cannot be determined

Choice A is correct.

Use the formula:

$$\text{Average} = \frac{\text{sum of scores}}{\text{number of students}}$$

"Eighteen students attained an average of 70 on a test" translates mathematically to:

$$70 = \frac{\text{sum of scores of 18 students}}{18} \qquad \boxed{1}$$

"Twelve students on the same test scored an average of 90" translates to:

$$90 = \frac{\text{sum of scores of other 12 students}}{12} \qquad \boxed{2}$$

Now what you are looking for is the *average score of all 30 students*. That is, you are looking for:

$$\frac{\text{Average of}}{\text{30 students}} = \frac{\text{sum of scores of all 30 students}}{30} \qquad \boxed{3}$$

So, if you can find the *sum of scores of all 30 students*, you can find the required average.

Now, the sum of all 30 students = sum of scores of 18 students + sum of scores of other 12 students.

And this can be gotten from $\boxed{1}$ and $\boxed{2}$:

From $\boxed{1}$: $70 \times 18 = $ sum of scores of 18 students

From $\boxed{2}$: $90 \times 12 = $ sum of scores of other 12 students

So adding:

$70 \times 18 + 90 \times 12 = $ sum of scores of 18 students + sum of scores of other 12 students = sum of scores of 30 students

Put all this in $\boxed{3}$:

$$\text{Average of 30 students} = \frac{70 \times 18 + 90 \times 12}{30}$$
$$= \frac{7\cancel{0} \times 18 + 9\cancel{0} \times 12}{3\cancel{0}}$$
$$= \frac{7 \times 18 + 9 \times 12}{3}$$
$$= \frac{7 \times \overset{6}{\cancel{18}} + \overset{3}{\cancel{9}} \times 12}{\cancel{3}}$$
$$= 42 + 36 = 78$$

Example 6

The average length of 10 objects is 25 inches. If the average length of 2 of these objects is 20 inches, what is the average length of the remaining 8 objects?

(A) $22\frac{1}{2}$ inches

(B) 24 inches

(C) $26\frac{1}{4}$ inches

(D) 28 inches

(E) cannot be determined

Choice C is correct.

Denote the lengths of the objects by *a, b, c, d*, etc. Since the average length of 10 objects is given to be 25 inches, establish an equation for the average length:

$$\text{Average length} = 25 = \frac{\overset{\text{sum of 10 lengths}}{\downarrow}a + b + c + d + \ldots + j}{\underset{\uparrow}{10}} \qquad \boxed{1}$$

number of objects

The question also says that the average length of 2 of these objects is 20. Let the lengths of two we choose be *a* and *b*. So,

$$\text{Average length of } a \text{ and } b = 20 = \frac{\overset{\text{lengths of 2 objects}}{\downarrow}a + b}{\underset{\uparrow}{2}} \qquad \boxed{2}$$

number of objects

Now we want to find the average length of the *remaining* objects. There are 8 remaining objects of lengths *c, d, e, . . . j*. Call the average of these lengths *x*, which is what we want to find.

$$\text{Average length} = x = \frac{\overset{\substack{\text{sum of lengths of remaining objects}\\(a + b \text{ are not present because only}\\c + d + \ldots + j \text{ remain})}}{\downarrow}c + d + e + \ldots + j}{\underset{\uparrow}{8}}$$

number of remaining objects

Use Equations $\boxed{1}$ and $\boxed{2}$:

$$25 = \frac{a + b + c + \ldots + j}{10} \qquad \boxed{1}$$

$$20 = \frac{a + b}{2} \qquad \boxed{2}$$

Now, remember, we want to find the value of *x*:

$$x = \frac{c + d + e + \ldots + j}{8}$$

Multiply Equation 1 by 10 to get rid of the denominator. We get:

$$25 \times 10 = 250 = a + b + c + \ldots + j$$

Now multiply Equation 2 by 2 to get rid of the denominator:

$$20 \times 2 = 40 \doteq a + b$$

Subtract these two new equations:

$$250 = a + b + c + \ldots + j$$
$$- [40 = a + b]$$

You get:
$$210 = c + d + \ldots + j$$

Now you just have to divide by 8 to get:

$$\frac{210}{8} = \frac{c + d + \ldots + j}{8} = x$$

$$= 26\frac{1}{4}$$

Math Strategy   6

Know How to Manipulate Inequalities

Most problems involving inequalities can be solved by remembering one of the following statements.

If $x > y$, then $x + z > y + z$	Statement 1
If $x > y$ and $w > z$, then $x + w > y + z$	Statement 2

(Note that Statement 1 and Statement 2 are also true if all the $>$ signs are changed to $<$ signs.)

If $w > 0$ and $x > y$, then $wx > wy$	Statement 3
If $w < 0$ and $x > y$, then $wx < wy$	Statement 4
If $x > y$ and $y > z$, then $x > z$	Statement 5
$x > y$ is the same as $y < x$	Statement 6
$a < x < b$ is the same as both $a < x$ and $x < b$	Statement 7
If $x > y > 0$ and $w > z > 0$, then $xw > yz$	Statement 8
If $x > 0$ and $z = x + y$, then $z > y$	Statement 9
If $x < 0$, then $\begin{cases} x^n < 0 \text{ if } n \text{ is odd} \\ x^n > 0 \text{ if } n \text{ is even} \end{cases}$	Statement 10 Statement 11
If $xy > 0$, then $x > 0$ and $y > 0$ or $x < 0$ and $y < 0$	Statement 12
If $xy < 0$, then $x > 0$ and $y < 0$ or $x < 0$ and $y > 0$	Statement 13

Example 1

If $0 < x < 1$, then which of the following must be true?

   I. $2x < 2$
  II. $x - 1 < 0$
 III. $x^2 < x$

(A) I only
(B) II only
(C) I and II only
(D) II and III only
(E) I, II, and III

Choice E is correct. We are told that $0 < x < 1$. Using Statement 7, we have

$$0 < x \qquad \boxed{1}$$
$$x < 1 \qquad \boxed{2}$$

For Item I, we multiply 2 by 2.

See Statement 3

$$2x < 2$$

Thus, Item I is true.

For Item II, we add -1 to both sides of 2.

See Statement 1 to get

$$x - 1 < 0$$

Thus, Item II is true.

For Item III, we multiply 2 by x.

See Statement 3 to get

$$x^2 < x$$

Thus, Item III is true.

All items are true, so Choice E is correct.

Example 2

Given that $\frac{a}{b}$ is less than 1, $a > 0$, $b > 0$. Which of the following must be greater than 1?

(A) $\dfrac{a}{2b}$

(B) $\dfrac{b}{2a}$

(C) $\dfrac{\sqrt{b}}{a}$

(D) $\dfrac{b}{a}$

(E) $\left(\dfrac{a}{b}\right)^2$

Choice D is correct.

Given:

$$\frac{a}{b} < 1 \qquad \boxed{1}$$

$$a > 0 \qquad \boxed{2}$$

$$b > 0 \qquad \boxed{3}$$

See Statement $\boxed{3}$: Multiply $\boxed{1}$ by b. We get:

$$\cancel{b}\left(\frac{a}{\cancel{b}}\right) < b\,(1)$$

$$a < b \qquad \boxed{4}$$

Use Statement $\boxed{3}$ where $w = \dfrac{1}{a}$. Divide $\boxed{4}$ by a. We get:

$$\frac{a}{a} < \frac{b}{a}$$

$$1 < \frac{b}{a}$$

$$\text{or} \quad \frac{b}{a} > 1$$

Example 3

Which combination of the following statements can be used to demonstrate that x is positive?

   I. $x > y$

  II. $1 < y$

(A) I alone but not II

(B) II alone but not I

(C) I and II taken together but neither taken alone

(D) Both I alone and II alone

(E) Neither I nor II nor both

Choice C is correct. We want to know which of the following

$$x > y \qquad \boxed{1}$$

$$1 < y \qquad \boxed{2}$$

is enough information to conclude that

$$x > 0 \qquad \boxed{3}$$

$\boxed{1}$ alone is not enough to determine $\boxed{3}$ because $0 > x > y$ could be true. (*Note*: x is greater than y, but they both could be negative.)

$\boxed{2}$ alone is not enough to determine $\boxed{3}$ because we don't know whether x is greater than, less than, or equal to y.

However, if we use $\boxed{1}$ and $\boxed{2}$ together, we can compare the two:

$$1 < y \text{ is the same as } y > 1.$$

Therefore, $x > y$ with $y > 1$ yields   Statement 5

$$x > 1. \qquad \boxed{4}$$

Since $1 > 0$ is always true, then from $\boxed{4}$

$$x > 0 \text{ is always true.}$$

Example 4

What are all values of x such that $(x - 7)(x + 3)$ is positive?

(A) $x > 7$

(B) $-7 < x < 3$

(C) $-3 < x < 7$

(D) $x > 7$ or $x < -3$

(E) $x > 3$ or $x < -7$

Choice D is correct.

$$(x - 7)(x + 3) > 0 \text{ when}$$

$$x - 7 > 0 \text{ and } x + 3 > 0 \qquad \boxed{1}$$

$$\text{or} \quad x - 7 < 0 \text{ and } x + 3 < 0 \qquad \boxed{2}$$

Statement 12

From $\boxed{1}$ we have $x > 7$ and $x > -3$ $\boxed{3}$

Thus $x > 7$ $\boxed{4}$

From $\boxed{2}$, we have $x < 7$ and $x < -3$ $\boxed{5}$

Thus $x < -3$ $\boxed{6}$

Example 5

If p and q are nonzero real numbers and if $p^2 + q^3 < 0$ and if $p^3 + q^5 > 0$, which of the following number lines shows the relative positions of p, q, and 0?

Choice B is correct.

Method I:

$$\text{Given: } p^2 + q^3 < 0 \qquad \boxed{1}$$

$$p^3 + q^5 > 0 \qquad \boxed{2}$$

Subtracting p^2 from $\boxed{1}$ and q^5 from $\boxed{2}$, we have

$$q^3 < -p^2 \qquad \boxed{3}$$

$$p^3 > -q^5 \qquad \boxed{4}$$

Since the square of any real number is greater than 0, $p^2 > 0$ and $-p^2 < 0$. $\boxed{5}$

Using Statement $\boxed{5}$, combining $\boxed{3}$ and $\boxed{5}$ we get:

$$q^3 < -p^2 < 0 \qquad \boxed{6}$$

$$\text{and get: } q^3 < 0. \qquad \boxed{7}$$

$$\text{Thus,} \quad q < 0. \qquad \boxed{8}$$

From 8, we can say $q^5 < 0$ or $-q^5 > 0$. 9

Using Statement 5, combining 4 and 9,

$p^3 > -q^5 > 0$ and $p^3 > 0$. Thus $p > 0$. 10

Using 8 and 10, it is easily seen that Choice B is correct.

Method II:

Use Strategy 6: **Know How to Manipulate Inequalities**

$$\text{Given: } p^2 + q^3 < 0 \qquad 1$$
$$p^3 + q^5 > 0 \qquad 2$$

Since p^2 is always > 0, using this with 1, we know that

$$q^3 < 0 \text{ and, therefore, } q < 0. \qquad 3$$

If $q^3 < 0$ then $q^5 < 0$. 4

Using 4 and 2, we know that

$$p^3 > 0, \text{ and therefore } p > 0 \qquad 5$$

Using 3 and 5, only Choice B is correct.

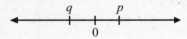

Example 6

Janie is older than Tammy, but she is younger than Lori. Let j, t, and l be the ages in years of Janie, Tammy, and Lori, respectively. Which of the following is true?

   (A) $j < t < l$
   (B) $t < j < l$
   (C) $t < l < j$
   (D) $l < j < t$
   (E) $l < t < j$

Choice B is correct.

First, use Strategy 2: **Translate English Words into Mathematical Expressions**

"Janie is older than Tammy, but she is younger than Lori" translates to:

   Janie's age > Tammy's age 1
   Janie's age < Lori's age 2

   Given: Janie's age $= j$ 3
            Tammy's age $= t$ 4
            Lori's age $= l$ 5

Substituting 3, 4, and 5 into 1 and 2, we get:

$$j > t \qquad 6$$
$$j < l \qquad 7$$

Use Statement 5. Reversing 6, we get:

$$t < j \qquad 8$$

Combining 8 and 7, we get:

$$t < j < l$$

Math Strategy   7

Use Specific Numerical Examples to Prove or Disprove Your Guess

When you do not want to do a lot of algebra, or when you are unable to prove what you think is the answer, you may want to substitute numbers.

Example 1

The sum of the cubes of any two consecutive positive integers is always

   (A) an odd integer
   (B) an even integer
   (C) the cube of an integer
   (D) the square of an integer
   (E) the product of an integer and 3

Choice A is correct. *Try specific numbers.* Call consecutive positive integers 1 and 2.

Sum of cubes:

$$1^3 + 2^3 = 1 + 8 = 9$$

You have now eliminated Choices B and C. You are left with Choices A, D, and E.

Now try two other consecutive integers: 2 and 3.

$$2^3 + 3^3 = 8 + 27 = 35$$

Choice A is acceptable. Choice D is false. Choice E is false.

Thus, Choice A is the only choice remaining.

Example 2

Jason is now m years old, and Serena is 4 years older than Jason. Which represents Serena's age 6 years ago?

   (A) $m + 10$
   (B) $m - 10$
   (C) $m - 2$
   (D) $m - 4$
   (E) $4m - 6$

Choice C is correct.

Try a specific number.

Let $m = 10$

Jason is 10 years old. Serena is 4 years older than Jason, so Serena is 14 years old. Serena's age 6 years ago was 8 years.

Now look for the choice that gives you 8 with $m = 10$.

(A) $m + 10 = 10 + 10 = 20$
(B) $m - 10 = 10 - 10 = 0$
(C) $m - 2 = 10 - 2 = 8$—that's the one

See Math Strategy 2, Example 4 (page 77) for an alternate approach to solving this problem, using a different strategy: *Translate English Words into Mathematical Expressions*.

Example 3

If $x \neq 0$, then $\dfrac{(-3x)^3}{-3x^3} =$

(A) -9
(B) -1
(C) 1
(D) 3
(E) 9

Choice E is correct.

Try a specific number.

Let $x = 1$. Then:

$$\frac{(-3x)^3}{-3x^3} = \frac{[-3(1)]^3}{-3(1^3)} = \frac{(-3)^3}{-3} = 9$$

Example 4

If $a = 4b$, then the average of a and b is

(A) $\frac{1}{2}b$
(B) $\frac{3}{2}b$
(C) $\frac{5}{2}b$
(D) $\frac{7}{2}b$
(E) $\frac{9}{2}b$

Choice C is correct.

Try a specific number.

Let $b = 1$. Then $a = 4b = 4$. So the average $=$

$$\frac{1 + 4}{2} = \frac{5}{2}.$$

Look at choices where $b = 1$. The only choice that gives $\frac{5}{2}$ is Choice C.

Example 5

The sum of three consecutive even integers is P. Find the sum of the next three consecutive *odd* integers that follow the greatest of the three even integers.

(A) $P + 9$
(B) $P + 15$
(C) $P + 12$
(D) $P + 20$
(E) none of these

Choice B is correct.

Try specific numbers.

Let the three consecutive even integers be 2, 4, 6.

$$\text{So, } 2 + 4 + 6 = P = 12.$$

The next three consecutive odd integers that follow 6 are:

$$7, 9, 11$$

So the sum of

$$7 + 9 + 11 = 27.$$

Now, where $P = 12$, look for a choice that gives you 27:

(A) $P + 9 = 12 + 9 = 21$—NO
(B) $P + 15 = 12 + 15 = 27$—YES

Example 6

If $3 > a$, which of the following is *not* true?

(A) $3 - 3 > a - 3$
(B) $3 + 3 > a + 3$
(C) $3(3) > a(3)$
(D) $3 - 3 > 3 - a$
(E) $\frac{3}{3} > \frac{a}{3}$

Choice D is correct.

Try specific numbers.

Work backward from Choice E if you wish.

Let $a = 1$.

Choice E:

$$\frac{3}{3} > \frac{a}{3} = \frac{1}{3} \qquad \text{TRUE STATEMENT}$$

Choice D:

$3 - 3 > 3 - a = 3 - 1$, or $0 > 2$ FALSE STATEMENT

Example 7

In the figure of intersecting lines below, which of the following is equal to $180 - a$?

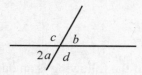

(A) $a + d$
(B) $a + 2d$
(C) $c + b$
(D) $b + 2a$
(E) $c + d$

Choice A is correct.

Try a specific number.

Let $a = 20°$

Then $2a = 40°$

Be careful now—all of the other angles are now determined, so don't choose any more.

Because vertical angles are equal, $2a = b$, so

$$b = 40°.$$

Now $c + b = 180°$, so $c + 40 = 180$ and

$$c = 140°.$$

Thus, $d = 140°$ (vertical angles are equal).

Now look at the question:

$$180 - a = 180 - 20 = 160$$

Which is the correct choice?

(A) $a + d = 20 + 140 = 160$—that's the one!

See Math Strategy 17, Example 2 (page 114) for an alternate approach to solving this problem, using a different strategy: ***Use the Given Information Effectively (and Ignore Irrelevant Information).***

Math Strategy　　　　8

Very Important Strategy:

When Each Choice Must Be Tested, Start with the Last Choice and Work Backward

If you must check each choice for the correct answer, start with the last choice (whether D or E) and work backward. The reason for this is that the test maker of a question *in which each choice must be tested* often puts the correct answer as Choice D or E. The careless student will start testing with Choice A and work

downward to the last choice, wasting time. So if you're trying all the choices, start with the last choice, then the next to last choice, etc. See Example 9 for an example of when this strategy should *not* be used.

Example 1

$$\frac{3y - 2}{y + 4}$$

is equivalent to

(A) $\dfrac{3 - 2}{4}$

(B) $3 - \dfrac{1}{2}$

(C) $3 - \dfrac{2}{y - 8}$

(D) $3 - \dfrac{2}{y + 4}$

(E) $3 - \dfrac{14}{y + 4}$

Choice E is correct. To see which fraction the quantity stated is equivalent to, you would want to test out the choices. But always when you test choices, start with the last choice and work backward. The test maker usually puts the correct choice in a case like this at the end of the choices, usually E or D because he or she expects you to test the choices from A downward. So starting with choice E, we find what $3 - \dfrac{14}{y + 4}$ is.

$$3 - \frac{14}{y + 4} = \frac{3(y + 4)}{y + 4} - \frac{14}{y + 4} = \frac{3y + 12 - 14}{y + 4}$$

$$= \frac{3y - 2}{y + 4}$$

Example 2

If p is a positive integer, which *could* be an odd integer?

(A) $2p + 2$
(B) $p^3 - p$
(C) $p^2 + p$
(D) $p^2 - p$
(E) $7p - 3$

Choice E is correct. Start with Choice E first, since you have to *test* the choices.

Method I:

Try a number for p. Let $p = 1$. Then (starting with Choice E), $7p - 3 = 7(1) - 3 = 4$. 4 is even, so try another number for p to see whether $7p - 3$ is odd. Let $p = 2$. $7p - 3 = 7(2) - 3 = 11$. 11 is odd. Therefore, Choice E is correct.

Method II:

Look at Choice E. $7p$ could be even or odd, depending on what p is. If p is even, $7p$ is even. If p is odd, $7p$ is odd. Accordingly, $7p - 3$ is either even or odd. Thus, Choice E is correct.

Note: When using either Method I or Method II, you have eliminated the need to test the other choices.

Example 3

If $y = x^2 + 3$, then for which value of x is y divisible by 7?

    (A) 10
    (B) 8
    (C) 7
    (D) 6
    (E) 5

Choice E is correct. Since you must check all of the choices, start with Choice E:

$$y = 5^2 + 3 = 25 + 3 = 28$$
$$28 \text{ is divisible by } 7$$

If you had started with Choice A, you would have had to test four choices instead of one choice before finding the correct answer.

Example 4

Which fraction is greater than $\frac{1}{2}$?

    (A) $\frac{4}{9}$

    (B) $\frac{17}{35}$

    (C) $\frac{6}{13}$

    (D) $\frac{12}{25}$

    (E) $\frac{8}{15}$

Choice E is correct.

Look at Choice E first.

$$\text{Is } \frac{8}{15} > \frac{1}{2}?$$

Use the cross-multiplication method.

$$\frac{1}{2} \quad \frac{8}{15}$$
$$15 \qquad 16$$
$$15 \ < \ 16$$

So, $\frac{1}{2} < \frac{8}{15}$.

You also could have looked at Choice E and said $\frac{8}{16} = \frac{1}{2}$ and realized that $\frac{8}{15} > \frac{1}{2}$ because $\frac{8}{15}$ has a smaller denominator than $\frac{8}{16}$.

Example 5

If n is an even integer, which of the following is an odd integer?

    (A) $n^2 - 2$
    (B) $n - 4$
    (C) $(n - 4)^2$
    (D) n^3
    (E) $n^2 - n - 1$

Choice E is correct.

Look at Choice E first.

$$n^2 - n - 1$$
$$\text{If } n \text{ is even}$$
$$n^2 \text{ is even}$$
$$n \text{ is even}$$
$$1 \text{ is odd}$$

So, $n^2 - n - 1 = \text{even} - \text{even} - \text{odd} = \text{odd}$.

Example 6

Which of the following is an odd number?

    (A) 7×22
    (B) $59 - 15$
    (C) $55 + 35$
    (D) $75 \div 15$
    (E) 4^7

Choice D is correct.

Look at Choice E first.

4^7 is even because all positive integral powers of an even number are even.

So now look at Choice D: $\frac{75}{15} = 5$, which is odd.

Example 7

$$\begin{array}{r} 3\,\#\,2 \\ \times \quad 8 \\ \hline 28 \star 6 \end{array}$$

If # and $\star$ are different digits in the correctly calculated multiplication problem above, then # could be

    (A) 1
    (B) 2

(C) 3
(D) 4
(E) 6

Choice E is correct.
Try Choice E first.

$$3 \; \# \; 2 \qquad 3 \; \textcircled{6} \; 2$$
$$\times \quad 8 \qquad \times \quad 8$$
$$\overline{28 \; \star \; 6} \qquad \overline{28 \; \textcircled{9} \; 6}$$

9 and 6 are different numbers, so Choice E is correct.

Example 8

Which choice describes a pair of numbers that are *unequal*?

(A) $\dfrac{1}{6}, \dfrac{11}{66}$

(B) $3.4, \dfrac{34}{10}$

(C) $\dfrac{15}{75}, \dfrac{1}{5}$

(D) $\dfrac{3}{8}, 0.375$

(E) $\dfrac{86}{24}, \dfrac{42}{10}$

Choice E is correct.
Look at Choice E first.

$$\frac{86}{24} \qquad ? \qquad \frac{42}{10}$$

Cross multiply:

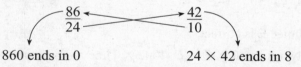

860 ends in 0 $\qquad\qquad$ 24 × 42 ends in 8

Thus, the numbers must be *different* and *unequal*.

When *Not* to Use This Strategy:

If you can spot something in the question that shows you how to solve the problem readily without having to test each choice, there's no need to go through every answer by working backward.

Example 9

If $|6 - 5y| > 20$, which of the following is a possible value of y?

(A) −3
(B) −1
(C) 1

(D) 3
(E) 5

Choice A is correct.

Instead of plugging in values for y, starting with Choice E, you should realize there will only be one answer listed for which $6 - 5y > 20$. So which choice gives you the largest product for $-5y$? Start by checking the *most negative* choice, or $y = -3$.

This gives you $|6 - 5(-3)| = |6 + 15| = |21|$, which is greater than 20.

Know How to Solve Problems Using the Formula $R \times T = D$

Almost every problem involving motion can be solved using the formula

$$R \times T = D$$
$$\text{or}$$
$$\text{rate} \times \text{elapsed time} = \text{distance}$$

Example 1

The diagram below shows two paths: Path 1 is 10 miles long, and Path 2 is 12 miles long. If Person X runs along Path 1 at 5 miles per hour and Person Y runs along Path 2 at y miles per hour, and if it takes exactly the same amount of time for both runners to run their whole path, then what is the value of y?

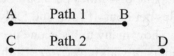

(A) 2
(B) $4\dfrac{1}{6}$
(C) 6
(D) 20
(E) 24

Choice C is correct. Let T = Time (in hours) for either runner to run the whole path.

Using $R \times T = D$, for Person X, we have

$$\left(\frac{5 \text{ mi}}{\text{hr}}\right)(T \text{ hours}) = 10 \text{ miles}$$

$$\text{or} \quad 5T = 10$$

$$\text{or} \quad T = 2$$

1

For Person Y, we have

$$\left(\frac{y \text{ mi}}{\text{hr}}\right)(T \text{ hours}) = 12 \text{ miles}$$

$$\text{or} \quad yT = 12$$

Using $\boxed{1}$ $y(2) = 12$ or $y = 6$.

Example 2

A car traveling at 50 miles per hour for 2 hours travels the same distance as a car traveling at 20 miles per hour for x hours. What is x?

(A) $\dfrac{4}{5}$

(B) $\dfrac{5}{4}$

(C) 5

(D) 2

(E) $\dfrac{1}{2}$

Choice C is correct.

Use $R \times T = D$.

Call the distance both cars travel D (since distance is the same for both cars).

So we get:

$$50 \times 2 = D = 100 \qquad \boxed{1}$$
$$20 \times x = D = 100 \qquad \boxed{2}$$

Solving $\boxed{2}$ you can see that $x = 5$.

Example 3

John walks at a rate of 4 miles per hour. Sally walks at a rate of 5 miles per hour. If John and Sally both start at the same point, how many miles is one person from the other after t hours of walking? (*Note*: Both are walking on the same road in the same direction.)

(A) $\dfrac{t}{2}$

(B) t

(C) $2t$

(D) $\dfrac{4}{5}t$

(E) $\dfrac{5}{4}t$

Choice B is correct.

Draw a diagram:

John (4 mph)

Sally (5 mph)

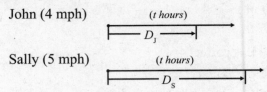

Let D_J be the distance that John walks in t hours. Let D_S be the distance that Sally walks in t hours. Then, using $R \times t = D$,

for John: $4 \times t = D_J$
for Sally: $5 \times t = D_S$

The distance between Sally and John after t hours of walking is:

$$D_S - D_J = 5t - 4t = t$$

Example 4

A man rode a bicycle a straight distance at a speed of 10 miles per hour and came back the same distance at a speed of 20 miles per hour. What was the man's total number of miles for the trip back and forth, if his total traveling time was 1 hour?

(A) 15

(B) $7\dfrac{1}{2}$

(C) $6\dfrac{1}{3}$

(D) $6\dfrac{2}{3}$

(E) $13\dfrac{1}{3}$

Choice E is correct.

Always use $R \times T = D$ (Rate $\times$ Time = Distance) in problems like this. Call the first distance D and the time for the first part T_1. Since he rode at 10 mph:

$$10 \times T_1 = D \qquad \boxed{1}$$

Now for the trip back. He rode at 20 mph. Call the time it took to go back T_2. Since he came back the *same* distance, we can call that distance D also. So for the trip back using $R \times T = D$, we get:

$$20 \times T_2 = D \qquad \boxed{2}$$

Since it was given that the total traveling time was 1 hour, the total traveling time is:

$$T_1 + T_2 = 1$$

Now here's the trick: Let's make use of the fact that $T_1 + T_2 = 1$. Dividing Equation **1** by 10, we get:

$$T_1 = \frac{D}{10}$$

Dividing **2** by 20, we get:

$$T_2 = \frac{D}{20}$$

Now add $T_1 + T_2$ and we get:

$$T_1 + T_2 = 1 = \frac{D}{10} + \frac{D}{20}$$

Factor D:

$$1 = D\left(\frac{1}{10} + \frac{1}{20}\right)$$

Add $\frac{1}{10} + \frac{1}{20}$. Remember the fast way of adding fractions?

$$\frac{1}{10} \underset{+}{\overset{}{\rightleftarrows}} \frac{1}{20} = \frac{20 + 10}{20 \times 10} = \frac{30}{200}$$

So:

$$1 = (D)\frac{30}{200}$$

Multiply by 200 and divide by 30 and we get:

$$\frac{200}{30} = D; D = 6\frac{2}{3}$$

Don't forget, we're looking for $2D$: $2D = 13\frac{1}{3}$

Example 5

What is the average rate of a bicycle traveling at 10 mph a distance of 5 miles and at 20 mph the same distance?

- (A) 15 mph
- (B) 20 mph
- (C) $12\frac{1}{2}$ mph
- (D) $13\frac{1}{3}$ mph
- (E) 16 mph

Choice D is correct.

Ask yourself, what does *average rate* mean? It *does not* mean the average of the rates! If you thought it did, you would have selected Choice A as the answer (averaging 10 and 20 to get 15)—the "lure" choice.

Average is a word that *modifies* the word *rate* in this case. So you must define the word *rate* first, before you do anything with averaging.

Since rate $\times$ time $=$ distance,

$$\text{rate} = \frac{\text{distance}}{\text{time}}$$

Then *average* rate must be:

$$\text{Average rate} = \frac{\text{total distance}}{\text{total time}}$$

The *total distance* is the distance covered on the whole trip, which is $5 + 5 = 10$ miles.

The *total time* is the time traveled the first 5 miles at 10 mph added to the time the bicycle traveled the next 5 miles at 20 mph.

Let t_1 be the time the bicycle traveled the first 5 miles.

Let t_2 be the time the bicycle traveled the next 5 miles.

Then the *total time* $= t_1 + t_2$.

Since $R \times T = D$,

for the first 5 miles: $10 \times t_1 = 5$
for the next 5 miles: $20 \times t_2 = 5$

Finding t_1: $t_1 = \frac{5}{10}$

Finding t_2: $t_2 = \frac{5}{20}$

So, $t_1 + t_2 = \frac{5}{10} + \frac{5}{20}$

$$= \frac{1}{2} + \frac{1}{4} \quad \textit{(remembering how to quickly add fractions)}$$

$$= \frac{4 + 2}{8}$$

$$= \frac{6}{8} = \frac{3}{4}$$

$$\text{Average rate} = \frac{\text{total distance}}{\text{total time}}$$

$$= \frac{5 + 5}{\frac{3}{4}}$$

$$= (5 + 5) \times \frac{4}{3}$$

$$= 10 \times \frac{4}{3} = \frac{40}{3} = 13\frac{1}{3} \text{ (Answer)}$$

Here's a formula you can memorize:

If a vehicle travels a certain distance at a mph and travels the same distance at b mph, the *average rate* is

$$\frac{2ab}{a + b}$$

Try doing the problem using this formula:

$$\frac{2ab}{a + b} = \frac{2 \times 10 \times 20}{10 + 20} = \frac{400}{30} = 13\frac{1}{3}$$

Caution: Use this formula only when you are looking for *average* rate, and when the distance is the same for both speeds.

Math Strategy 10

Know How to Use Units of Time, Distance, Area, or Volume to Find or Check Your Answer

By knowing what the units in your answer must be, you will often have an easier time finding or checking your answer. A very helpful thing to do is to treat the units of time or space as variables (like x or y). Thus, you should substitute, multiply, or divide these units as if they were ordinary variables. The following examples illustrate this idea.

Example 1

What is the distance in miles covered by a car that traveled at 50 miles per hour for 5 hours?

(A) 10
(B) 45
(C) 55
(D) 200
(E) 250

Choice E is correct. Although this is an easy $R \times T = D$ problem, it illustrates this strategy very well.

Recall that

$$\text{rate} \times \text{time} = \text{distance}$$
$$\left(\frac{50 \text{ mi}}{\text{hr}}\right)(5 \text{ hours}) = \text{distance}$$

Notice that when I substituted into $R \times T = D$, *I kept the units of rate and time* (miles/hour and hours). Now I will *treat these units as if they were ordinary variables.* Thus,

$$\text{distance} = \left(\frac{50 \text{ mi}}{\text{hr}}\right)(5 \text{ hours})$$

I have canceled the variable "hour(s)" from the numerator and denominator of the right side of the equation. Hence,

$$\text{distance} = 250 \text{ miles}$$

The distance has units of "miles," as I would expect. In fact, if the units in my answer had been "miles/hour" or "hours," then I would have been in error.

Thus, *the general procedure* for problems using this strategy is:

Step 1. *Keep the units given in the question.*
Step 2. *Treat the units as ordinary variables.*
Step 3. *Make sure the answer has units that you would expect.*

Example 2

How many inches are equivalent to 2 yards, 2 feet, and 7 inches?

(A) 11
(B) 37
(C) 55
(D) 81
(E) 103

Choice E is correct.

Remember that

$$1 \text{ yard} = 3 \text{ feet} \qquad \boxed{1}$$
$$1 \text{ foot} = 12 \text{ inches} \qquad \boxed{2}$$

Treat the units of length as variables! Divide $\boxed{1}$ by 1 yard, and $\boxed{2}$ by 1 foot, to get

$$1 = \frac{3 \text{ feet}}{1 \text{ yard}} \qquad \boxed{3}$$
$$1 = \frac{12 \text{ inches}}{1 \text{ foot}} \qquad \boxed{4}$$

We can multiply any expression by 1 and get the same value. Thus, 2 yards + 2 feet + 7 inches =

$$(2 \text{ yards})(1)(1) + (2 \text{ feet})(1) + 7 \text{ inches} \qquad \boxed{5}$$

Substituting $\boxed{3}$ and $\boxed{4}$ into $\boxed{5}$, 2 yards + 2 feet + 7 inches

$$= 2 \text{ yards}\left(\frac{3 \text{ feet}}{\text{yard}}\right)\left(\frac{12 \text{ inches}}{\text{foot}}\right) + 2 \text{ feet}\left(\frac{12 \text{ inches}}{\text{foot}}\right) + 7 \text{ inches}$$
$$= 72 \text{ inches} + 24 \text{ inches} + 7 \text{ inches}$$
$$= 103 \text{ inches}$$

Notice that the answer is in "inches," as I expected. If the answer had come out in "yards" or "feet," then I would have been in error.

Example 3

A car wash cleans x cars per hour, for y hours, at z dollars per car. How much money in *cents* does the car wash receive?

(A) $\dfrac{xy}{100z}$

(B) $\dfrac{xyz}{100}$

(C) $100xyz$

(D) $\dfrac{100x}{yz}$

(E) $\dfrac{yz}{100x}$

Choice C is correct.

Use units:

$$\left(\frac{x \text{ cars}}{\text{hour}}\right)(y \text{ hours})\left(\frac{z \text{ dollar}}{\text{car}}\right) = xyz \text{ dollars} \quad \boxed{1}$$

Since there are 100 cents to a dollar, we multiply $\boxed{1}$ by 100. We get $100xyz$ cents.

Example 4

There are 3 feet in a yard and 12 inches in a foot. How many yards are there altogether in 1 yard, 1 foot, and 1 inch?

(A) $1\dfrac{1}{3}$

(B) $1\dfrac{13}{36}$

(C) $1\dfrac{11}{18}$

(D) $2\dfrac{5}{12}$

(E) $4\dfrac{1}{12}$

Choice B is correct. ***Know how to work with units.***

$$\text{Given: } 3 \text{ feet} = 1 \text{ yard}$$
$$12 \text{ inches} = 1 \text{ foot}$$

Thus,

$$1 \text{ yard} + 1 \text{ foot} + 1 \text{ inch} =$$

$$1 \text{ yard} + 1 \text{ foot}\left(\frac{1 \text{ yard}}{3 \text{ feet}}\right) + 1 \text{ inch}\left(\frac{1 \text{ foot}}{12 \text{ inches}}\right) \times \left(\frac{1 \text{ yard}}{3 \text{ feet}}\right)$$

$$= \left(1 + \frac{1}{3} + \frac{1}{36}\right) \text{ yards}$$

$$= \left(1 + \frac{12}{36} + \frac{1}{36}\right) \text{ yards}$$

$$= 1\frac{13}{36} \text{ yards}$$

Math Strategy 11

Use New Definitions and Functions Carefully

Some SAT questions use new symbols, functions, or definitions that were created in the question. At first glance, these questions may seem difficult because you are not familiar with the new symbol, function, or definition. *However, most of these questions can be solved through simple substitution or application of a simple definition.*

Example 1

If the symbol ϕ is defined by the equation
$$a \phi b = a - b - ab$$
for all a and b, then $\left(-\dfrac{1}{3}\right) \phi (-3) =$

(A) $\dfrac{5}{3}$

(B) $\dfrac{11}{3}$

(C) $-\dfrac{13}{3}$

(D) -4

(E) -5

Choice A is correct. All that is required is substitution:

$$a \phi b = a - b - ab$$
$$\left(-\frac{1}{3}\right) \phi (-3)$$

Substitute $-\dfrac{1}{3}$ for a and -3 for b in $a - b - ab$:

$$\left(-\frac{1}{3}\right) \phi (-3) = -\frac{1}{3} - (-3) - \left(-\frac{1}{3}\right)(-3)$$

$$= -\frac{1}{3} + 3 - 1$$

$$= 2 - \frac{1}{3}$$

$$= \frac{5}{3} \text{ (Answer)}$$

Example 2

Let $x = \begin{cases} \dfrac{5}{2}(x+1) & \text{if } x \text{ is an odd integer} \\ \dfrac{5}{2}x & \text{if } x \text{ is an even integer} \end{cases}$

Find $2y$, where y is an integer.

(A) $\dfrac{5}{2}y$

(B) $5y$

(C) $\dfrac{5}{2}y + 1$

(D) $5y + \dfrac{5}{2}$

(E) $5y + 5$

Choice B is correct. All we have to do is substitute $2y$ into the definition of x. In order to know which definition of x to use, we want to know if $2y$ is even. Since y is an integer, then $2y$ is an even integer. Thus,

$$2y = \frac{5}{2}(2y)$$

$$\text{or} \quad 2y = 5y \text{ (Answer)}$$

Example 3

As in Example 1, ϕ is defined as

$$a \phi b = a - b - ab.$$

If $a \phi 3 = 6$, $a =$

(A) $\dfrac{9}{2}$

(B) $\dfrac{9}{4}$

(C) $-\dfrac{9}{4}$

(D) $-\dfrac{4}{9}$

(E) $-\dfrac{9}{2}$

Choice E is correct.

$$a \phi b = a - b - ab$$
$$a \phi 3 = 6$$

Substitute a for a, 3 for b:

$$a \phi 3 = a - 3 - a(3) = 6$$
$$= a - 3 - 3a = 6$$
$$= -2a - 3 = 6$$
$$2a = -9$$
$$a = -\dfrac{9}{2}$$

Example 4

The symbol $\left(\; x \;\right)$ is defined as the greatest integer less than or equal to x.

$$\left(-3.4\right) + \left(21\right) =$$

(A) 16
(B) 16.6
(C) 17
(D) 17.6
(E) 18

Choice C is correct.

$\left(-3.4\right)$ is defined as the *greatest integer less than or equal to* -3.4. This is -4, since $-4 < -3.4$.

$\left(21\right)$ is defined as the *greatest integer less than or equal to* 21. That is just 21, since $21 = 21$.

Thus, $-4 + 21 = 17$. (*Answer*)

Example 5

 is defined as $xz - yt$

$$\begin{pmatrix} 2 & 1 \\ 1 & 1 \end{pmatrix} =$$

(A) $\begin{pmatrix} 1 & 1 \\ 1 & 1 \end{pmatrix}$

(B) $\begin{pmatrix} 3 & 2 \\ 2 & 1 \end{pmatrix}$

(C) $\begin{pmatrix} 4 & 3 \\ 2 & 1 \end{pmatrix}$

(D) $\begin{pmatrix} 5 & 4 \\ 4 & 2 \end{pmatrix}$

(E) $\begin{pmatrix} 3 & 1 \\ 1 & 2 \end{pmatrix}$

Choice E is correct.

$$\begin{pmatrix} x & y \\ z & t \end{pmatrix} = xz - yt; \quad \begin{pmatrix} 2 & 1 \\ 1 & 1 \end{pmatrix} = ?$$

Substituting 2 for x, 1 for z, 1 for y, and 1 for t,

$$\begin{pmatrix} 2 & 1 \\ 1 & 1 \end{pmatrix} = (2)(1) - (1)(1)$$
$$= 1$$

Now work from Choice E:

(E) $\begin{pmatrix} 3 & 1 \\ 1 & 2 \end{pmatrix} = xz - yt = (3)(1) - (1)(2)$
$$= 3 - 2 = 1$$

Example 6

If for all numbers a, b, c, the operation ● is defined as

$$a \bullet b = ab - a$$

then

$$a \bullet (b \bullet c) =$$

(A) $a(bc - b - 1)$
(B) $a(bc + b + 1)$
(C) $a(bc - c - b - 1)$
(D) $a(bc - b + 1)$
(E) $a(b - a + c)$

Choice A is correct.

$$a \bullet b = ab - a$$
$$a \bullet (b \bullet c) = ?$$

Find $(b \bullet c)$ first. *Use substitution:*

$$a \bullet b = ab - a$$
$$\uparrow \quad \uparrow$$
$$b \bullet c$$

Substitute b for a and c for b:

$$b \bullet c = b(c) - b$$

Now, $a \bullet (b \bullet c) = a \bullet (bc - b)$

Use definition $a \bullet b = ab - a$

Substitute a for a and $bc - b$ for b:

$$a \bullet b = ab - a$$
$$\uparrow \quad \nwarrow$$

$$a \bullet (bc - b) = a(bc - b) - a$$
$$= abc - ab - a$$
$$= a(bc - b - 1)$$

Math Strategy — 12

Very Important Strategy:

Try Not to Make Tedious Calculations, Since There Is Usually an Easier Way

In many of the examples given in these strategies, it has been explicitly stated that one should not calculate complicated quantities. In some of the examples, we have demonstrated a fast and a slow way of solving the same problem. On the actual exam, if you find that your solution to a problem involves a tedious and complicated method, then you are probably doing the problem in a long, hard way. Many times, you can DIVIDE, MULTIPLY, ADD, SUBTRACT, or FACTOR to simplify. Almost always, there will be an easier way.

Examples 5 and 6 can also be solved with the aid of a calculator and some with the aid of a calculator allowing for exponential calculations. However, to illustrate the effectiveness of Math Strategy 12, we did not use the calculator method of solving these examples.

Example 1

What is the value of
$2^1 + 2^2 + 2^3 + 2^4 + 2^5 + 2^6 + 2^7 + 2^8 + 2^9$?

(A) $2^{11} - 2$
(B) 2^{10}
(C) $2^{10} - 2$
(D) $2^{10} - 4$
(E) $2^{10} - 8$

Choice C is correct.

Let $x = 2^1 + 2^2 + 2^3 + 2^4 + 2^5 + 2^6 + 2^7 + 2^8 + 2^9$ **1**

Now multiply **1** by 2:

$$2x = 2(2^1 + 2^2 + 2^3 + 2^4 + 2^5 + 2^6 + 2^7 + 2^8 + 2^9)$$

Thus,

$$2x = 2^2 + 2^3 + 2^4 + 2^5 + 2^6 + 2^7 + 2^8 + 2^9 + 2^{10} \quad \boxed{2}$$

Subtracting **1** from **2**, we get:

$$2x - x = x = 2^{10} - 2^1 = 2^{10} - 2$$

Example 2

If $16r - 24q = 2$, then $2r - 3q =$

(A) $\dfrac{1}{8}$

(B) $\dfrac{1}{4}$

(C) $\dfrac{1}{2}$

(D) 2

(E) 4

Choice B is correct.
Divide by 8:

$$\frac{16r - 24q}{8} = \frac{2}{8}$$

$$2r - 3q = \frac{1}{4}$$

Example 3

If $(a^2 + a)^3 = x(a + 1)^3$, where $a + 1 \neq 0$, then $x =$

(A) a
(B) a^2
(C) a^3
(D) $\dfrac{a + 1}{a}$
(E) $\dfrac{a}{a + 1}$

Choice C is correct.

Isolate x first:

$$x = \frac{(a^2 + a)^3}{(a + 1)^3}$$

Now use the fact that $\left(\dfrac{x^3}{y^3}\right) = \left(\dfrac{x}{y}\right)^3$:

$$\frac{(a^2 + a)^3}{(a + 1)^3} = \left(\frac{a^2 + a}{a + 1}\right)^3$$

Now *factor* $a^2 + a = a(a + 1)$

So:

$$\left(\frac{a^2 + a}{a + 1}\right)^3 = \left[\frac{a(a + 1)}{a + 1}\right]^3$$

$$= \left[\frac{a\cancel{(a + 1)}}{\cancel{a + 1}}\right]^3$$

$$= a^3$$

Example 4

If $\frac{p + 1}{r + 1} = 1$ and p, r are nonzero, and p is not equal to -1, and r is not equal to -1, then

(A) $2 > \frac{p}{r} > 1$ always

(B) $\frac{p}{r} < 1$ always

(C) $\frac{p}{r} = 1$ always

(D) $\frac{p}{r}$ can be greater than 2

(E) $\frac{p}{r} = 2$ always

Choice C is correct.

Get rid of the fraction. *Multiply* both sides of the equation

$$\frac{p + 1}{r + 1} = 1 \text{ by } r + 1$$

$$\left(\frac{p + 1}{\cancel{r + 1}}\right)\cancel{r + 1} = r + 1$$

$$p + 1 = r + 1$$

Cancel the 1s:

$$p = r$$

So:

$$\frac{p}{r} = 1$$

Example 5

$$\frac{4}{250} =$$

(A) 0.16
(B) 0.016
(C) 0.0016
(D) 0.00125
(E) 0.000125

Choice B is correct.

Don't divide 4 into 250! *Multiply:*

$$\frac{4}{250} = \frac{4}{4} = \frac{16}{1,000}$$

Now $\frac{16}{100} = 0.16$, so $\frac{16}{1,000} = 0.016$.

Example 6

$(3 \times 4^{14}) - 4^{13} =$

(A) 4
(B) 12
(C) 2×4^{13}
(D) 3×4^{13}
(E) 11×4^{13}

Choice E is correct.

Factor 4^{13} from

$(3 \times 4^{14}) - 4^{13}$

We get: $4^{13}[(3 \times 4^1) - 1]$

or $4^{13}(12 - 1) = 4^{13}(11)$

You will see more of the technique of dividing, multiplying, adding, and subtracting in the next strategy, Math Strategy 13.

Math Strategy　　　**13**

Very Important Strategy:

Know How to Find Unknown Expressions by Adding, Subtracting, Multiplying, or Dividing Equations or Expressions

When you want to calculate composite quantities like $x + 3y$ or $m - n$, often you can do it by adding, subtracting, multiplying, or dividing the right equations or expressions.

Example 1

If $4x + 5y = 10$ and $x + 3y = 8$, then $\frac{5x + 8y}{3} =$

(A) 18
(B) 15
(C) 12
(D) 9
(E) 6

Choice E is correct. Don't solve for x, then for y.

Try to get the quantity $\dfrac{5x + 8y}{3}$ by adding or subtracting the equations. In this case, *add* equations.

$$4x + 5y = 10$$
$$+ \quad x + 3y = \ \ 8$$
$$\overline{5x + 8y = 18}$$

Now divide by 3:

$$\frac{5x + 8y}{3} = \frac{18}{3} = 6 \ (Answer)$$

Example 2

If $25x + 8y = 149$ and $16x + 3y = 89$, then $\dfrac{9x + 5y}{5} =$

(A) 12
(B) 15
(C) 30
(D) 45
(E) 60

Choice A is correct. We are told

$$25x + 8y = 149 \qquad \boxed{1}$$
$$16x + 3y = \ \ 89 \qquad \boxed{2}$$

The long way to do this problem is to solve $\boxed{1}$ and $\boxed{2}$ for x and y, and then substitute these values into $\dfrac{9x + 5y}{5}$.

The fast way to do this problem is to *subtract* $\boxed{2}$ from $\boxed{1}$ and get

$$9x + 5y = 60 \qquad \boxed{3}$$

Now all we have to do is to divide $\boxed{3}$ by 5:

$$\frac{9x + 5y}{5} = 12 \ (Answer)$$

Example 3

If $21x + 39y = 18$, then $7x + 13y =$

(A) 3
(B) 6
(C) 7
(D) 9
(E) It cannot be determined from the information given.

Choice B is correct. We are given

$$21x + 39y = 18 \qquad \boxed{1}$$

Divide $\boxed{1}$ by 3:

$$7x + 13y = 6 \ (Answer)$$

Example 4

If $x + 2y = 4$, then $5x + 10y - 8 =$

(A) 10
(B) 12
(C) −10
(D) −12
(E) 0

Choice B is correct.

Multiply $x + 2y = 4$ by 5 to get:

$$5x + 10y = 20$$

Now subtract 8:

$$5x + 10y - 8 = 20 - 8$$
$$= 12$$

Example 5

If $6x^5 = y^2$ and $x = \dfrac{1}{y}$, then $y =$

(A) x^6
(B) $\dfrac{x^5}{6}$
(C) $6x^6$
(D) $\dfrac{6x^5}{5}$
(E) $\dfrac{x^5}{5}$

Choice C is correct.

Multiply $6x^5 = y^2$ by $x = \dfrac{1}{y}$ to get:

$$6x^6 = y^2\left(\frac{1}{y}\right) = y$$

Example 6

If $y^8 = 4$ and $y^7 = \dfrac{3}{x}$, what is the value of y in terms of x?

(A) $\dfrac{4x}{3}$
(B) $\dfrac{3x}{4}$
(C) $\dfrac{4}{x}$
(D) $\dfrac{x}{4}$
(E) $\dfrac{12}{x}$

Choice A is correct.

Don't solve for the *value* of y first, by finding $y = 4^{\frac{1}{8}}$.

Just divide the two equations:

$y^8 = 4$ by $y^7 = \dfrac{3}{x}$

We get:

$$\dfrac{y^8}{y^7} = \dfrac{4}{\left(\dfrac{3}{x}\right)}$$

So $y = \dfrac{4}{\left(\dfrac{3}{x}\right)}$

and so $y = \dfrac{4x}{3}$ (*Answer*)

Example 7

If $x > 0$, $y > 0$ and $x^2 = 27$ and $y^2 = 3$, then $\dfrac{x^3}{y^3} =$

    (A) 9
    (B) 27
    (C) 36
    (D) 48
    (E) 54

Choice B is correct.

Divide: $\dfrac{x^2}{y^2} = \dfrac{27}{3} = 9$

Take square root: $\dfrac{x}{y} = 3$

So $\left(\dfrac{x}{y}\right)^3 = \dfrac{x^3}{y^3} = 3^3 = 27$

Example 8

If $\dfrac{m}{n} = \dfrac{3}{8}$ and $\dfrac{m}{q} = \dfrac{4}{7}$, then $\dfrac{n}{q} =$

    (A) $\dfrac{12}{15}$

    (B) $\dfrac{12}{56}$

    (C) $\dfrac{56}{12}$

    (D) $\dfrac{32}{21}$

    (E) $\dfrac{21}{32}$

Choice D is correct.

First get rid of fractions!

Cross-multiply $\dfrac{m}{n} = \dfrac{3}{8}$ to get $8m = 3n$.   **1**

Now cross-multiply $\dfrac{m}{q} = \dfrac{4}{7}$ to get $7m = 4q$.   **2**

Now divide Equations **1** and **2**:

$$\dfrac{8m}{7m} = \dfrac{3n}{4q}$$ **3**

The m's cancel and we get:

$$\dfrac{8}{7} = \dfrac{3n}{4q}$$ **4**

Multiply Equation **4** by 4 and divide by 3 to get

$$\dfrac{8 \times 4}{7 \times 3} = \dfrac{n}{q}$$

Thus $\dfrac{n}{q} = \dfrac{32}{21}$.

Example 9

If $\dfrac{a + b + c + d}{4} = 20$

And $\dfrac{b + c + d}{3} = 10$

Then $a =$

    (A) 50
    (B) 60
    (C) 70
    (D) 80
    (E) 90

Choice A is correct.

We have

$$\dfrac{a + b + c + d}{4} = 20$$ **1**

$$\dfrac{b + c + d}{3} = 10$$ **2**

Multiply Equation **1** by 4:

We get: $a + b + c + d = 80$ **3**

Now *multiply* Equation **2** by 3:

We get: $b + c + d = 30$ **4**

Now *subtract* Equation **4** from Equation **3**:

$$a + b + c + d = 80 \qquad \textbf{3}$$
$$- \quad (b + c + d = 30) \qquad \textbf{4}$$
$$\overline{\text{We get: } a = 50.}$$

Example 10

If $y + 2q = 15$, $q + 2p = 5$, and $p + 2y = 7$, then $p + q + y =$

- (A) 81
- (B) 45
- (C) 27
- (D) 18
- (E) 9

Choice E is correct.

There's no need to solve for each variable. Just *add* the equations and divide by 3! To do this, write one equation below the other. Be sure to line up the common variables.

$$
\begin{array}{r}
y + 2q = 15 \\
+ q + 2p = 5 \\
+ 2y + p = 7 \\
\hline
3y + 3q + 3p = 27
\end{array}
$$

$$y + 2q + q + 2p + p + 2y = 27$$
$$3y + 3q + 3p = 27$$

Factor by 3:

$$3(y + q + p) = 27$$

So

$$p + q + y = 9$$

Example 11

If $x > 0$, $xy = 2$, $yz = 5$, and $xz = 10$, then $xyz =$

- (A) 10
- (B) 17
- (C) 50
- (D) 100
- (E) 200

Choice A is correct. Since we are dealing with multiplication in all of the equations, *multiply* the expressions xy, yz, and xz.

We get:

$$(xy)(yz)(xz) = 2 \times 5 \times 10 = 100$$

This becomes

$$x^2y^2z^2 = 100$$

This is the same as

$$(xyz)^2 = 100$$

Take the square root of both sides to get

$$xyz = 10$$

Math Strategy 14

Very Important Strategy:

Draw or Extend Lines in a Diagram to Make a Problem Easier; Label Unknown Quantities

Remember when you took geometry in your early years in high school and the teacher drew a perpendicular line from the top of the triangle to the base of the triangle to prove that "if two sides of a triangle are equal, the base angles are equal"? By drawing this line, the teacher was able to prove the theorem.

Unfortunately, the teacher did not say that whenever you draw a line in a diagram, you usually get more information to work with. If the teacher had said this, you would then use the strategy of drawing lines in diagrams to get more information and results. This strategy is a very powerful one and is used in many questions on tests and in figuring out many geometric problems.

When you see a diagram, be curious as to what lines you can draw to get more information to solve a problem. Also, label lines, angles, etc.

Example 1

The circle with center A and radius AB is inscribed in the square below. AB is extended to C. What is the ratio of AB to AC?

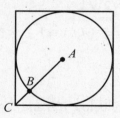

- (A) $\sqrt{2}$
- (B) $\dfrac{\sqrt{2}}{4}$
- (C) $\dfrac{\sqrt{2} - 1}{2}$
- (D) $\dfrac{\sqrt{2}}{2}$
- (E) none of these

Choice D is correct. Always draw or extend lines to get more information. Also label unknown lengths, angles, or arcs with letters.

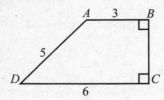

Label $AB = a$ and $BC = b$.

Draw perpendicular AD. Note it is just the radius, a.

CD also $= a$, because each side of the square is length $2a$ (the diameter) and CD is $\frac{1}{2}$ the side of the square.

We want to find $\dfrac{AB}{AC} = \dfrac{a}{a+b}$

Now $\triangle ADC$ is an isosceles right triangle, so $AD = CD = a$.

By the Pythagorean theorem, $a^2 + a^2 = (a+b)^2$ where $a+b$ is the hypotenuse of a right triangle.

We get: $2a^2 = (a+b)^2$

Divide by $(a+b)^2$:

$$\frac{2a^2}{(a+b)^2} = 1$$

Divide by 2:

$$\frac{a^2}{(a+b)^2} = \frac{1}{2}$$

Take square roots of both sides:

$$\frac{a}{(a+b)} = \frac{1}{\sqrt{2}}$$
$$= \frac{1}{\sqrt{2}}\left(\frac{\sqrt{2}}{\sqrt{2}}\right)$$
$$= \frac{\sqrt{2}}{2} \ (Answer)$$

Example 2

What is the perimeter of the figure below if B and C are right angles?

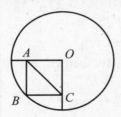

(A) 14
(B) 16
(C) 18
(D) 20
(E) cannot be determined

Choice C is correct.

Draw perpendicular AE. Label side $BC = h$. You can see that $AE = h$.

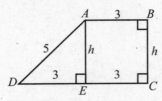

$ABCE$ is a rectangle, so $CE = 3$. This makes $ED = 3$ since the whole $DC = 6$.

Now use the Pythagorean theorem for triangle AED:

$$h^2 + 3^2 = 5^2$$
$$h^2 = 5^2 - 3^2$$
$$h^2 = 25 - 9$$
$$h^2 = 16$$
$$h = 4$$

So the perimeter is
$3 + h + 6 + 5 = 3 + 4 + 6 + 5 = 18$. (*Answer*)

Example 3

In the figure below, O is the center of a circle with a radius of 6, and $AOCB$ is a square. If point B is on the circumference of the circle, the length of $AC =$

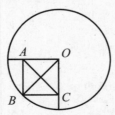

(A) $6\sqrt{2}$
(B) $3\sqrt{2}$
(C) 3
(D) 6
(E) $6\sqrt{3}$

Choice D is correct.

This is tricky if not impossible if you don't draw OB.
So draw OB:

Since $AOCB$ is a square, $OB = AC$; and since $OB =$ radius $= 6$, $AC = 6$.

Example 4

In the figure below, lines ℓ_1 and ℓ_2 are parallel.

$$AB = \frac{1}{3}AC$$

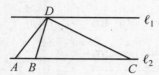

$$\frac{\text{area of triangle } ABD}{\text{area of triangle } DBC} =$$

(A) $\frac{1}{4}$

(B) $\frac{1}{3}$

(C) $\frac{3}{8}$

(D) $\frac{1}{2}$

(E) cannot be determined

Choice D is correct.

$$AB = \frac{1}{3}AC$$

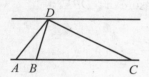

Ask yourself, what is the area of a triangle? It is $\frac{1}{2}$ (height $\times$ base). So let's get the heights and the bases of the triangles ABD and DBC. First *draw the altitude* (call it h).

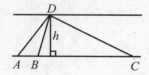

Now label $AB = \frac{1}{3}AC$ (given).

This makes $BC = \frac{2}{3}AC$, since $AB + BC = AC$

Thus the area of $\triangle ABD = \frac{1}{2}h(AB) = \frac{1}{2}h\left(\frac{1}{3}AC\right)$

Area of $\triangle DBC = \frac{1}{2}h(BC) = \frac{1}{2}h\left(\frac{2}{3}AC\right)$

$$\frac{\text{Area of } ABD}{\text{Area of } DBC} = \frac{\frac{1}{2}h\left(\frac{1}{3}AC\right)}{\frac{1}{2}h\left(\frac{2}{3}AC\right)}$$

$$= \frac{\frac{1}{3}}{\frac{2}{3}} = \frac{1}{3} \times \frac{3}{2} = \frac{1}{2}$$

Example 5

The area of the figure $ABCD$

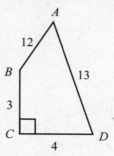

(*Note*: Figure is not drawn to scale.)

(A) is 36
(B) is 108
(C) is 156
(D) is 1,872
(E) cannot be determined

Choice A is correct.

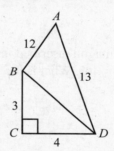

Draw BD. BCD is a 3–4–5 right triangle, so $BD = 5$. Now remember that a 5–12–13 triangle is also a right triangle, so angle ABD is a right angle. The area of triangle BCD is $\frac{(3 \times 4)}{2} = 6$ and the area of triangle BAD is $\frac{(5 \times 12)}{2} = 30$, so the total area is 36.

Example 6

In the figure, two points, B and C, are placed to the right of point A such that $4AB = 3AC$. The value of $\frac{BC}{AB}$

$$\underset{A}{\bullet\!\!\rule{2cm}{0.4pt}}\quad \ell$$

(A) equals $\frac{1}{3}$

(B) equals $\frac{2}{3}$

(C) equals $\frac{3}{2}$

(D) equals 3

(E) cannot be determined

Choice A is correct.

Place B and C to the right of A:

$$\overset{\bullet\quad\bullet\quad\bullet\quad\quad}{\underset{A\quad\;\; B\quad\;\; C}{\rule{3cm}{0.4pt}}}\ell$$

Now label $AB = a$ and $BC = b$:

$$\overset{\quad\; a\quad\; b\quad\quad}{\overset{\bullet\quad\bullet\quad\bullet\quad\quad}{\underset{A\quad\;\; B\quad\;\; C}{\rule{3cm}{0.4pt}}}}\ell$$

$\dfrac{BC}{AB} = \dfrac{b}{a}\left(\dfrac{b}{a}\text{ is what we want to find}\right)$

We are given $4AB = 3AC$.

So, $4a = 3(a + b)$

Expand: $4a = 3a + 3b$

Subtract $3a$: $a = 3b$

Divide by 3 and a: $\dfrac{1}{3} = \dfrac{b}{a}$

But remember $\dfrac{BC}{AB} = \dfrac{b}{a}$, so $\dfrac{BC}{AB} = \dfrac{1}{3}$

Example 7

In the figure below, $ABCDE$ is a pentagon inscribed in the circle with center at O. $\angle DOC = 40°$. What is the value of $x + y$?

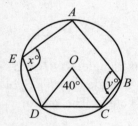

(A) 80
(B) 100
(C) 180
(D) 200
(E) cannot be determined

Choice D is correct.

Label degrees in each arc.

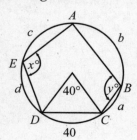

$\angle x$ is measured by $\dfrac{1}{2}$ the arc it cuts.

So, $x = \dfrac{1}{2}(b + a + 40)$

Likewise, $y = \dfrac{1}{2}(c + d + 40)$

You want to find $x + y$, so add:

$$x = \dfrac{1}{2}(b + a + 40)$$
$$+\; y = \dfrac{1}{2}(c + d + 40)$$
$$\overline{}$$
$$x + y = \dfrac{1}{2}(b + a + 40 + c + d + 40)$$

But what is $a + b + c + d + 40$? It is the total number of degrees around the circumference, which is 360.

So, $x + y = \dfrac{1}{2}\underbrace{(b + a + c + d + 40} + 40)$

$$= \dfrac{1}{2}(360 + 40)$$

$$= \dfrac{1}{2}(400) = 200$$

Example 8

In the figure below, if $\angle ABE = 40°$, $\angle DBC = 60°$, and $\angle ABC = 90°$, what is the measure of $\angle DBE$?

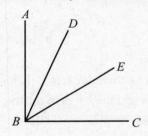

(A) 10°
(B) 20°
(C) 40°
(D) 100°
(E) cannot be determined

Choice A is correct.

Label angles first.

Now $\angle ABE = 40$, so $a + b = 40$
$\angle DBC = 60$, so $b + c = 60$
$\angle ABC = 90$, so $a + b + c = 90$

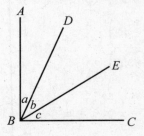

You want to find $\angle DBE$. $\angle DBE = b$, and you want to get the value of b from:

$$a + b = 40 \qquad \boxed{1}$$
$$b + c = 60 \qquad \boxed{2}$$
$$a + b + c = 90 \qquad \boxed{3}$$

Add $\boxed{1}$ and $\boxed{2}$:
$$\begin{array}{r} a + b = 40 \\ + \ b + c = 60 \\ \hline a + 2b + c = 100 \end{array}$$

Subtract $\boxed{3}$:
$$\begin{array}{r} -(a + b + c = 90) \\ \hline b = 10 \end{array}$$

Example 9

In the figure below, three lines intersect at the points shown. What is the value of $A + B + C + D + E + F$?

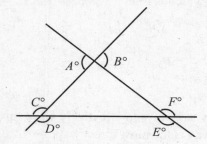

(A) 1,080
(B) 720
(C) 540
(D) 360
(E) cannot be determined

Choice B is correct.

Relabel, using the fact that *vertical angles are equal*.

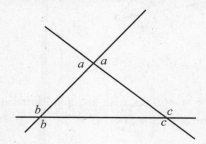

Now use the fact that a straight angle has $180°$ in it:

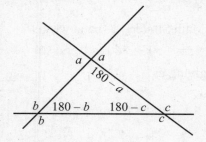

Now use the fact that the sum of the angles of a triangle $= 180°$:

$$180 - a + 180 - b + 180 - c = 180$$
$$540 - a - b - c = 180$$
$$540 - 180 = a + b + c$$
$$360 = a + b + c$$

Now remember what we are looking to find (the sum):

$$a + a + b + b + c + c = 2a + 2b + 2c$$

But this is just $2(a + b + c) = 2(360) = 720$.

Example 10

In the figure below, lines l and q are shown to be perpendicular on a coordinate plane. If line l contains the points $(0,0)$ and $(2,1)$, and line q contains the points $(2,1)$ and $(0,t)$, what is the value of t?

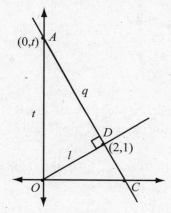

(A) -3
(B) -2
(C) 2
(D) 3
(E) 5

Choice E is correct. You want to find the value of t.

Start by drawing line DE, the altitude of $\triangle DOC$. Then label $EC = x$.

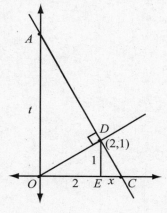

Because the altitude drawn to the hypotenuse of a right triangle forms two similar triangles, $\triangle AOC \sim \triangle DOC \sim \triangle OED$.

This gives $\dfrac{t}{(2+x)} = \dfrac{2}{1}$ **1**

We need to find the value of x in order to find the value of t.

Look at other similar triangles that involve just the variable x:

$\triangle DEC$ and $\triangle OED$

This gives: $\dfrac{2}{1} = \dfrac{1}{x}$

So, we get: $x = \dfrac{1}{2}$

Plug $x = \dfrac{1}{2}$ into Equation **1** and we get:

$$\frac{t}{\frac{5}{2}} = \frac{2}{1}$$
$$t = 5$$

Alternate way:

If the lines are perpendicular, the slope of one line is the negative reciprocal of the other line. (See Math Refresher 416.)

Line l contains the points $(0,0)$ and $(2,1)$, so the slope is $\dfrac{(y_2 - y_1)}{(x_2 - x_1)} = \dfrac{(1 - 0)}{(2 - 0)} = \dfrac{1}{2}$.

The slope of line q is $\dfrac{(y_2 - y_1)}{(x_2 - x_1)} = \dfrac{(t - 1)}{(0 - 2)} = \dfrac{(t - 1)}{-2}$.

The slope of line $l = \dfrac{1}{2}$. Since lines l and q are perpendicular, the slope of line q is the negative reciprocal of line l.

$$\frac{t - 1}{-2} = -2$$
$$t - 1 = -2(-2)$$
$$t - 1 = 4$$
$$t = 5$$

Example 11

Here's an example where only a handful of students got the right answer. However, by using one or two powerful strategies, we can solve it.

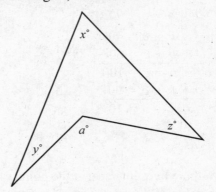

In the figure above, which is true?

  (A) $x + y + z = 180 - a$
  (B) $2x + y + z = a$
  (C) $x - y + x - z = a$
  (D) $x + y + z + a = 270$
  (E) $x + y + z = a$

There are essentially two ways to effectively solve this problem. The first way is the most direct way:

Label the unmarked angle t (Math Strategy 14).

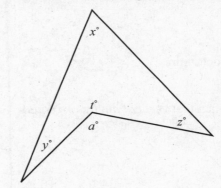

Then
  (1) $x + y + t + z = 360$ because in a quadrilateral, the sum of the angles is 360°.

But
  (2) $a + t = 360$ since the sum of the angles around a circle is 360.

Subtract equations (Math Strategy 13) and we get:

$x + y + t + z - a - t = 360 - 360 = 0$ and so

$x + y + z - a = 0$ giving us

$x + y + z = a$ *(Answer)*

Although the second method is a little longer and uses a different version of one of the strategies, I like this second method because it reinforces the use of the "drawing lines" strategy.

The first is to **draw lines to extend a diagram and label parts (Math Strategy 14).** Draw line *BC* and label the extra angles, *b* and *c*. We get:

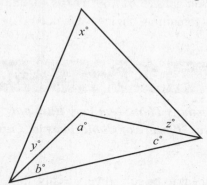

Now use the fact that the sum of the interior angles of any triangle equals 180°. We get:

$x + y + b + z + c = 180$ for the larger triangle   **1**

and $a + b + c = 180$ for the smaller triangle   **2**

Now use the second powerful strategy: **Don't just solve for variables, especially when you have many of them. Just add or subtract equations (Math Strategy 13).**

In this case we would subtract equations to reduce the amount of variables.

Subtracting Equation **2** from Equation **1**, we get:
$x + y + b + z + c - a - b - c = 180 - 180 = 0$

We end up with: $x + y + z - a = 0$ or

$x + y + z = a$ (*Answer*).

Math Strategy   15

Know How to Eliminate Certain Choices

Instead of working out a lot of algebra, you may be able to eliminate several of the choices at first glance. In this way you can save yourself a lot of work. The key is to remember to use pieces of the given information to eliminate several of the choices at once.

Example 1

The sum of the digits of a three-digit number is 15. If this number is not divisible by 2 but is divisible by 5, which of the following is the number?

  (A) 384
  (B) 465
  (C) 635
  (D) 681
  (E) 780

Choice B is correct. Use pieces of the given information to eliminate several of the choices.

Which numbers are divisible by 2? Choices A and E are divisible by 2 and, thus, can be eliminated. Of Choices B, C, and D, which are *not* divisible by 5? Choice D can be eliminated because the units digit of the number must be 0 or 5 for the number to be divisible by 5. We are left with Choices B and C.

Only Choice B (465) has the sum of its digits equal to 15. Thus, 465 is the only number that satisfies all the pieces of the given information.

If you learn to use this method well, you can save loads of time.

Example 2

Which of the following numbers is divisible by 5 and 9, but not by 2?

  (A) 625
  (B) 639
  (C) 650
  (D) 655
  (E) 675

Choice E is correct. Clearly, a number is divisible by 5 if, and only if, its last digit is either 0 or 5. A number is also divisible by 2 if, and only if, its last digit is divisible by 2. *Certain choices are easily eliminated.* Thus we can *eliminate* Choices B and C.

Method I:

To eliminate some more choices, remember that a number is divisible by 9 if, and only if, the sum of its digits is divisible by 9. Thus, Choice E is the only correct answer.

Method II:

If you did not know the test for divisibility by 9, divide the numbers in Choices A, D, and E by 9 to find the answer.

Example 3

If the last digit and the first digit are interchanged in each of the numbers below, which will result in the number with the *largest* value?

(A) 5,243
(B) 4,352
(C) 4,235
(D) 2,534
(E) 2,345

Choice E is correct.

Certain choices are easily eliminated.

One of the numbers with the largest last digit (the *units* digit) will be the answer. **1**

Using **1**, we see that Choices C and E each end in 5. All others end in digits less than 5 and may be eliminated. Starting with Choice E (see Strategy 8),

Choice E, 2,345, becomes 5,342. **2**

Choice C, 4,235, becomes 5,234. **3**

2 is larger than **3**.

Example 4

Which of the following could be the value of 3^x where x is an integer?

(A) 339,066
(B) 376,853
(C) 411,282
(D) 422,928
(E) 531,441

Choice E is correct. Let's look at what 3^x looks like for integral values of x:

$3^1 = 3$
$3^2 = 9$
$3^3 = 27$
$3^4 = 81$
$3^5 = 243$
$3^6 = \ldots 9$
$3^7 = \ldots 7$
$3^8 = \ldots 1$

Note that 3^x always has the *units* digit of 3, 9, 7, or 1. So we can eliminate Choices A, C, and D, since those choices end in numbers other than 3, 9, 7, or 1. We are left with Choices B and E. The number in the correct choice must be exactly divisible by 3, since it is of the form 3^x ($= 3 \times 3 \times 3 \ldots$) where x is an integer. This is a good time to use your calculator. Divide the number in Choice B by 3: You get 125,617.66. That's *not* an integer. So the only remaining choice is Choice E.

Math Strategy   16

Watch Out for Questions That Seem Very Easy but That Can Be Tricky—Beware of Choice A as a "Lure Choice"

When questions appear to be solved very easily, think again! Watch out especially for the "lure," Choice A.

Example 1*

The diagram below shows a 12-hour digital clock whose hours value is the same as the minutes value. Consider each time when the same number appears for both the hour and the minutes as a "double time" situation. What is the shortest elapsed time period between the appearance of one double time and an immediately succeeding double time?

6:06

(A) 61 minutes
(B) 60 minutes
(C) 58 minutes
(D) 50 minutes
(E) 49 minutes

Choice E is correct. Did you think that just by subtracting something like 8:08 from 9:09 you would get the answer (1 hour and 1 minute = 61 minutes)? That's Choice A, which is wrong. So beware, because your answer came too easily for a test like the SAT. You must realize that there is another possibility of "double time" occurrence—12:12 and 1:01, whose difference is 49 minutes. This is Choice E, the correct answer.

---

*This problem also appears in Strategy 1 of the 5 General Strategies on page 64.

Example 2

The letters d and m are integral digits in a certain number system. If $0 \leq d \leq m$, how many different possible values are there for d?

(A) m
(B) $m - 1$
(C) $m - 2$
(D) $m + 1$
(E) $m + 2$

Choice D is correct. Did you think that the answer was m? Do not be careless! The list 1, 2, 3, . . ., m contains m elements. If 0 is included in the list, then there are $m + 1$ elements. Hence, if $0 \leq d \leq m$ where d is integral, then d can have $m + 1$ different values.

Example 3

There are some flags hanging in a horizontal row. Starting at one end of the row, the U.S. flag is 25th. Starting at the other end of the row, the U.S. flag is 13th. How many flags are in the row?

(A) 36
(B) 37
(C) 38
(D) 39
(E) 40

Choice B is correct. **The obvious may be tricky!**

Method I:

Given:

The U.S. flag is 25th from one end. 1
The U.S. flag is 13th from the other end. 2

At first glance it may appear that adding 1 and 2, $25 + 13 = 38$, will be the correct answer. This is WRONG!

If you add $25 + 13$ you are counting the U.S. flag twice: once as the 25th and again as the 13th from the other end. The correct answer is

$$25 + 13 - 1 = 37$$

Method II:

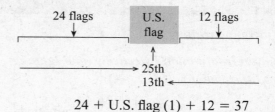

$$24 + \text{U.S. flag } (1) + 12 = 37$$

Example 4

$OR = RQ$ in the figure below. If the coordinates of Q are $(5,m)$, find the value of m.

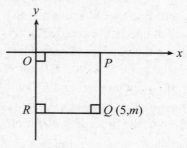

(A) -5
(B) $-\sqrt{5}$
(C) 0
(D) $\sqrt{5}$
(E) 5

Choice A is correct.

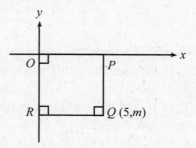

Given: $OR = RQ$ 1
Coordinates of $Q = (5,m)$ 2
From 2, we get: $RQ = 5$ 3
Substitute 3 into 1. We get:

$$OR = 5$$

The obvious may be tricky! Since Q is below the x-axis, its y-coordinate is negative. Thus $m = -5$.

Math Strategy 17

Very Important Strategy:

Use the Given Information Effectively (and Ignore Irrelevant Information)

You should always first use the piece of information that tells you the most, gives you a useful idea, or brings you closest to the answer.

Example 1

Mary is a computer expert. Each week she is handed a number of computers that need to be fixed. The following equation represents the number of computers at the end of the day that need to be fixed: $C = 16 - 2D$, where C is the number of computers left and D is the number of days Mary has worked that week. What is the meaning of the number 16 in the preceding equation?

(A) Mary will finish fixing all the computers in 16 days.
(B) Mary fixes the computers at the rate of 16 per hour.
(C) Mary fixes the computers at the rate of 16 per day.
(D) Mary starts each week with 16 computers to fix.
(E) none of these

Choice D is correct. What do you look for to get a grip on this question? You look for something that will give you some kind of result. In the equation $C = 16 - 2D$, if you let $D = 0$, then $C = 16$ and this would mean that when Mary starts (no days spent, where $D = 0$) the number of C computers to be fixed is 16. This corresponds to Choice D.

Example 2

In the figure below, *BD* is a straight line. What is the value of *a*?

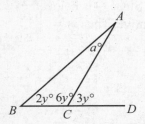

(*Note*: Figure is not drawn to scale.)

(A) 15
(B) 17
(C) 20
(D) 24
(E) 30

Choice C is correct.

Use the piece of information that will give you something definite. You might at first think of using the fact that the sum of the angles of a triangle = 180°. However, that will give you

$$a + 2y + 6y = 180$$

That's not very useful. But if you use the fact that the sum of the angles in a straight angle is 180, we get:

$$6y + 3y = 180$$

and we get: $9y = 180$

$$y = 20$$

Now we have something useful. At this point, we can apply the fact that the sum of the angles in a triangle is 180.

$$a + 2y + 6y = 180$$

Substituting 20 for *y*, we get:

$$a + 2(20) + 6(20) = 180$$

$$a = 20 \ (Answer)$$

Example 3

Avriel, Braden, and Carlos will be seated at random in three chairs, each denoted by X below. What is the probability that Avriel will be seated next to Carlos?

X   X   X

(A) $\frac{1}{8}$

(B) $\frac{1}{3}$

(C) $\frac{3}{8}$

(D) $\frac{5}{8}$

(E) $\frac{2}{3}$

Represent the students as A, B, and C respectively. However, don't make the mistake of representing the students in an unorganized or random fashion, such as ABC, BAC, CAB, and then try to get all the other possibilities.

Represent the students systematically. Start with A at the extreme left, B at the extreme left, and then C at the extreme left.

Like this:

ABC
ACB   only two possibilities
BAC
BCA   only two possibilities
CAB
CBA   again only two possibilities

Thus, there are 6 total possibilities: ABC, ACB, BAC, BCA, CAB, CBA.

Probability is defined as the favorable number of ways divided by the total number of ways.

The favorable number of ways is the number of ways where Avriel is seated next to Carlos. This is:

ACB, BAC, BCA, and CAB—4 ways.

Thus, the probability is $\frac{4}{6}$, or $\frac{2}{3}$.

Note that by organizing the information like this, we get all the possibilities in a systemized manner.

Example 4

In the figure of intersecting lines below, which of the following is equal to $180 - a$?

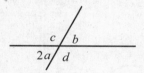

(A) $a + d$
(B) $a + 2d$
(C) $c + b$
(D) $b + 2a$
(E) $c + d$

Choice A is correct. Try to get something you can work with. From the diagram,

$$2a + d = 180.$$

So, to find $180 - a$, just subtract a from both sides of the equation above.

$$2a + d - a = 180 - a.$$

You get:

$$a + d = 180 - a.$$

See Math Strategy 7, Example 7 (page 93) for an alternate approach to solving this problem, using a different strategy: **Use Specific Numerical Examples to Prove or Disprove Your Guess.**

Example 5

Which of the angles in the figure below has a degree measure that can be determined?

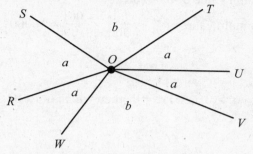

(*Note*: Figure is not drawn to scale.)

(A) $\angle WOS$
(B) $\angle SOU$
(C) $\angle WOT$
(D) $\angle ROV$
(E) $\angle WOV$

Choice C is correct.

Use information that will get you something useful.

$$4a + 2b = 360 \text{ (sum of all angles } = 360°)$$

Divide by 2 to simplify:

$$2a + b = 180$$

Now try all the choices. You could work backward from Choice E, but we'll start with Choice A:

(A) $\angle WOS = 2a$. You know that $2a + b = 180$ but don't know the value of $2a$.
(B) $\angle SOU = b + a$. You know $2a + b = 180$ but don't know the value of $b + a$.
(C) $\angle WOT = b + 2a$. You know that $2a + b = 180$, so you know the value of $b + 2a$.

Example 6

If a ranges in value from 0.003 to 0.3 and b ranges in value from 3.0 to 300.0, then the minimum value of $\frac{a}{b}$ is:

(A) 0.1
(B) 0.01
(C) 0.001
(D) 0.0001
(E) 0.00001

Choice E is correct.

Start by using the definitions of *minimum* and *maximum*.

The minimum value of $\frac{a}{b}$ is when a is *minimum* and b is *maximum*.

The minimum value of $a = .003$

The maximum value of $b = 300$

So the minimum value of $\frac{a}{b} = \frac{.003}{300} = \frac{.001}{100} = .00001$.

Example 7

If $xry = 0$, $yst = 0$, and $rxt = 1$, then which must be 0?

(A) r
(B) s
(C) t
(D) x
(E) y

Choice E is correct.

Use information that will give you something to work with.

$rxt = 1$ tells you that $r \neq 0$, $x \neq 0$, and $t \neq 0$.

So if $xry = 0$ then y must be 0.

Example 8

On a street with 25 houses, 10 houses have *fewer than 6 rooms,* 10 houses have *more than 7 rooms,* and 4 houses have *more than 8 rooms.* What is the total number of houses on the street that are either 6-, 7-, or 8-room houses?

(A) 5
(B) 9
(C) 11
(D) 14
(E) 15

Choice C is correct.

There are three possible situations:

(a) Houses that have *fewer than 6 rooms* (call the number a)
(b) Houses that have *6, 7, or 8 rooms* (call the number b)
(c) Houses that have *more than 8 rooms* (call the number c)

$a + b + c$ must total 25 (given). |1|

a is 10 (given). |2|

c is 4 (given). |3|

Substituting 2 and 3 in 1, we get: $10 + b + 4 = 25$. Therefore b must be 11.

Example 9

Mr. Martinez's tenth-grade class took a survey to see what activities each student engages in one hour before bed. When the survey was complete, 5 students selected "Play video games" and "Watch TV," 14 students selected "Watch TV," and 8 students selected "Play video games." How many students are in Mr. Martinez's class? (Assume that every student in the class watches TV only, plays video games only, or does both.)

(A) 11
(B) 17
(C) 22
(D) 25
(E) 27

Choice B is correct.

Method I:

Draw two intersecting circles.

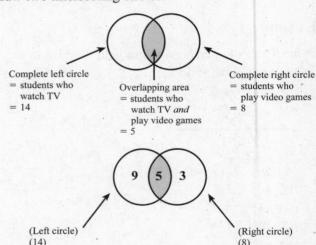

Above, subtracting: all students who watch TV (14) − students who watch TV *and* also play video games (5), we get 9.

Above, subtracting: all students who play video games (8) − students who watch TV *and* also play video games (5), we get 3.

So the total number of students is $9 + 5 + 3 = 17$.

Method II:

Total number of students are:

(a) students who only watch TV
(b) students who only play video games
(c) students who watch TV *and* also play video games

(a) There are 14 students who watch TV and 5 students who watch TV *and* play video games, so subtracting, *there are 9 students who watch TV only*.

(b) There are 8 students who play video games and 5 students who watch TV *and* also play video games, so subtracting, *there are 3 students who play video games only*.

(c) The number of students who watch TV *and* also play video games is 5 (given).

Adding the number of students in (a), (b), and (c) we get: $9 + 3 + 5 = 17$.

Example 10

Points A, B, and X do not all lie on the same line. Point X is 5 units from A and 3 units from B. How many other points in the same plane as A, B, and X are also 5 units from A and 3 units from B?

(A) 0
(B) 1
(C) 2
(D) 4
(E) more than 4

Choice B is correct.

First let's draw the points, making sure A, B, and X do not all lie on the same line.

What do we do next? Consider all possibilities. Consider all points that are 5 units from A. They would be all points on the circumference of a circle whose radius is 5 units.

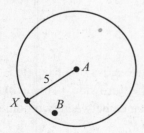

Consider all points that are 3 units from B. They would be all points on the circumference of a circle whose radius is 3 units.

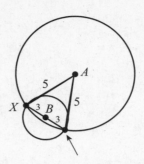

Notice that the two circles intersect at Point X and *only one* other point. That point is both 5 units from A and 3 units from B.

Very Important Strategy:

Know and Use Facts about Triangles

By remembering the following facts about triangles, you can often save yourself a lot of time and trouble.

Statements about Triangles

I.

If $a = b$, then $x = y$.

The base angles of an isosceles triangle are equal.

If $x = y$, then $a = b$.

If the base angles of a triangle are equal, the triangle is isosceles.

II.

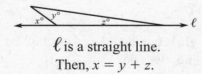

ℓ is a straight line.
Then, $x = y + z$.

The measure of an exterior angle is equal to the sum of the measures of the remote interior angles.

III.

If $a < b$, then $y < x$.

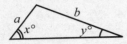

If $y < x$, then $a < b$.

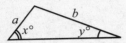

In a triangle, the greater angle lies opposite the greater side.

IV.

Similar Triangles

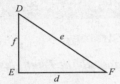

If $\triangle ABC \sim \triangle DEF$, then
$$m\angle A = m\angle D$$
$$m\angle B = m\angle E$$
$$m\angle C = m\angle F$$
and $\dfrac{a}{d} = \dfrac{b}{e} = \dfrac{c}{f}$

V.

$$m\angle A + m\angle B + m\angle C = 180°$$

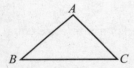

The sum of the interior angles of a triangle is 180°.

VI.

Area of $\triangle ABC = \dfrac{AD \times BC}{2}$

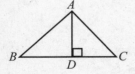

The area of a triangle is one-half the product of the altitude to a side times the side.

Note: If $m\angle A = 90°$, area also $= \dfrac{AD \times BC}{2}$.

VII.

In a right triangle, $c^2 = a^2 + b^2$ and $x° + y° = 90°$.

VIII. Memorize the following standard triangles:

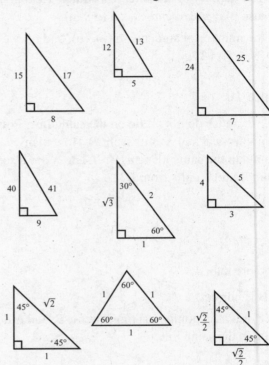

IX.

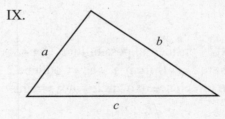

$a + b > c$
$a + c > b$
$b + c > a$

The sum of the lengths of two sides of a triangle is greater than the length of the third side. (This is like saying that the shortest distance between two points is a straight line.)

Example 1

In the diagram below, what is the value of x?

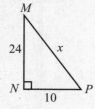

(A) 20
(B) 25
(C) 26
(D) 45
(E) 48

Choice C is correct.

Method I:

Use Statement VII. Then,

$$x^2 = 24^2 + 10^2$$
$$= 576 + 100$$
$$= 676$$

Thus, $x = 26$ (*Answer*)

Method II:

Look at Statement VIII. Notice that $\triangle MNP$ is similar to one of the standard triangles:

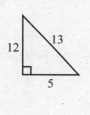 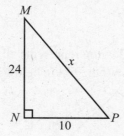

This is true because

$$\frac{12}{24} = \frac{5}{10} \text{ (Look at Statement IV)}$$

Hence, $\dfrac{12}{24} = \dfrac{13}{x} =$ or $x = 26$ (*Answer*)

Example 2

If Masonville is 50 kilometers due north of Adamston and Elvira is 120 kilometers due east of Adamston, then the minimum distance between Masonville and Elvira is

(A) 125 kilometers
(B) 130 kilometers
(C) 145 kilometers
(D) 160 kilometers
(E) 170 kilometers

Choice B is correct. *Draw a diagram first.*

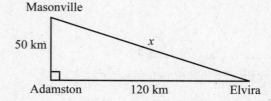

The given information translates into the diagram above. Note Statement VIII. The triangle above is a multiple of the special 5–12–13 right triangle.

$$50 = 10(5)$$
$$120 = 10(12)$$
$$\text{Thus, } x = 10(13) = 130 \text{ kilometers}$$

(*Note*: The Pythagorean theorem could also have been used: $50^2 + 120^2 = x^2$.)

Example 3

In triangle ABC, if $a > c$, which of the following is true?

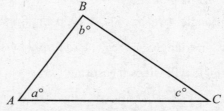

(*Note*: Figure is not drawn to scale.)

(A) $BC = AC$
(B) $AB > BC$
(C) $AC > AB$
(D) $BC > AB$
(E) $BC > AC$

Choice D is correct. *(Remember triangle inequality facts.)* From basic geometry, Statement III, we know that, since $m\angle BAC$ is greater than $m\angle BCA$, the leg opposite $\angle BAC$ is greater than the leg opposite $\angle BCA$, or

$$BC > AB$$

Example 4

In the triangle below, side $BC = 10$, angle $B = 45°$, and angle $A = 90°$.

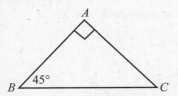

(*Note*: Figure is not drawn to scale.)

The area of the triangle

   (A) is 15
   (B) is 20
   (C) is 25
   (D) is 30
   (E) cannot be determined

Choice C is correct.

First find angle C using Statement V.

$$90° + 45° + m\angle C = 180°$$
$$\text{so } m\angle C = 45°.$$

Using Statement I, we find $AB = AC$, since

$$m\angle B = m\angle C = 45°.$$

Since our right triangle ABC has $BC = 10$, using Statement VIII (the right triangle $\frac{\sqrt{2}}{2}, \frac{\sqrt{2}}{2}, 1$), multiply by 10 to get a right triangle with sides measuring:

$$\frac{10\sqrt{2}}{2}, \frac{10\sqrt{2}}{2}, 10$$

Thus side $AB = \frac{10\sqrt{2}}{2} = 5\sqrt{2}$

$$\text{side } AC = \frac{10\sqrt{2}}{2} = 5\sqrt{2}$$

Now the area of triangle ABC, according to Statement VI, is

$$\frac{5\sqrt{2} \times 5\sqrt{2}}{2} = \frac{25 \times 2}{2} = 25$$

Example 5

In the figure below, what is the value of x?

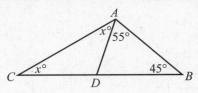

   (A) 30
   (B) 40
   (C) 50
   (D) 80
   (E) 100

Choice B is correct.

Remember triangle facts. Use Statement II.

$\angle ADB$ is an exterior angle of $\triangle ACD$, so

$$m\angle ADB = x + x = 2x \qquad \boxed{1}$$

In $\triangle ADB$, the sum of its angles $= 180$ (Statement V), so

$$m\angle ADB + 55 + 45 = 180$$
$$\text{or} \quad m\angle ADB + 100 = 180$$
$$\text{or} \quad m\angle ADB = 80 \qquad \boxed{2}$$

Equating $\boxed{1}$ and $\boxed{2}$ we have

$$2x = 80$$
$$x = 40 \text{ (\textit{Answer})}$$

Example 6

Which of the following represents all of the possibilities for the value of a in the figure below?

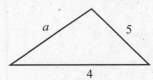

(*Note*: Figure is not drawn to scale.)

   (A) $1 < a < 9$
   (B) $4 < a < 5$
   (C) $0 < a < 9$
   (D) $4 < a < 9$
   (E) $5 < a < 9$

Choice A is correct. From Statement IX, since the sum of the lengths of two sides of a triangle is greater than the length of the third side, we have:

$$a + 5 > 4 \qquad \boxed{1}$$
$$a + 4 > 5 \qquad \boxed{2}$$
$$5 + 4 > a \qquad \boxed{3}$$

From 2 we get:

$$a > 1$$

From 3 we get:

$$9 > a$$

This means that

$$9 > a > 1, \text{ or } 1 < a < 9$$

Math Strategy   19

When Calculating Answers, Never Multiply and/or Do Long Division If You Can Reduce First

On the SAT exam, because calculators are permitted, you may do the following problems with a calculator also. But it would be wise for you to see the other approach too—how the problem can be solved *without* the use of a calculator.

Example 1

If $w = \dfrac{81 \times 150}{45 \times 40}$, then $w =$

(A) 3

(B) $6\dfrac{3}{4}$

(C) $7\dfrac{1}{4}$

(D) 9

(E) $20\dfrac{1}{4}$

Choice B is correct.

Do *not* multiply 81×150 and 45×40 to get:

$$\frac{12,150}{1,800}$$

Factor first:

$$\frac{\overbrace{9 \times 9}^{81} \times \overbrace{15 \times 10}^{150}}{\underbrace{9 \times 5}_{45} \times \underbrace{4 \times 10}_{40}}$$

Then cancel like factors in numerator and denominator:

$$\frac{\cancel{9} \times 9 \times 15 \times \cancel{10}}{\cancel{9} \times 5 \times 4 \times \cancel{10}}$$

Reduce further:

$$\frac{9 \times \cancel{5} \times 3}{\cancel{5} \times 4}$$

Then simplify:

$$\frac{27}{4} = 6\frac{3}{4} \ (Answer)$$

Example 2

$$\frac{4^2 + 4^2 + 4^2}{3^3 + 3^3 + 3^3} =$$

(A) $\dfrac{16}{27}$

(B) $\dfrac{8}{9}$

(C) $\dfrac{4}{3}$

(D) $\dfrac{64}{27}$

(E) $\dfrac{512}{81}$

Choice A is correct.

$$\frac{4^2 + 4^2 + 4^2}{3^3 + 3^3 + 3^3} =$$

Factor and reduce:

$$\frac{\cancel{3}(4^2)}{\cancel{3}(3^3)} = \frac{16}{27}$$

Example 3

If $6 \times 7 \times 8 \times 9 = \dfrac{12 \times 14 \times 18}{x}$, then $x =$

(A) $\dfrac{1}{2}$

(B) 1

(C) 4

(D) 8

(E) 12

Choice B is correct.

Given: $6 \times 7 \times 8 \times 9 = \dfrac{12 \times 14 \times 18}{x}$ 1

so that $x = \dfrac{12 \times 14 \times 18}{6 \times 7 \times 8 \times 9}$ 2

Do *not* multiply the numbers out in the numerator and denominator of 2! It is too much work! Rewrite 2.

Factor and reduce:

$x =$

$$\frac{12 \times 14 \times 18}{6 \times 7 \times 8 \times 9} = \frac{2 \times \cancel{6} \times 2 \times \cancel{7} \times 2 \times \cancel{9}}{\cancel{6} \times \cancel{7} \times 8 \times \cancel{9}}$$

$$= \frac{2 \times 2 \times 2}{8} = \frac{\cancel{8}}{\cancel{8}} = 1 \ (Answer)$$

Example 4

If $\dfrac{81 \times y}{27} = 21$, then $y =$

(A) $\dfrac{1}{21}$

(B) $\dfrac{1}{7}$

(C) 3

(D) 7

(E) 21

Choice D is correct.

$$Given: \dfrac{81 \times y}{27} = 21$$

Multiply both sides by 27 to get $81 \times y = 21 \times 27$.

$$y = \dfrac{21 \times 27}{81}$$

Factor and reduce:

$$y = \dfrac{3 \cdot 7 \times 3 \cdot \cancel{9}}{9 \cdot \cancel{9}}$$

$$= \dfrac{\cancel{3} \cdot 7 \times \cancel{3}}{\cancel{3} \cdot \cancel{3}}$$

$$y = 7 \ (Answer)$$

Example 5

Find the value of $\dfrac{y^2 - 7y + 10}{y - 2}$ rounded to the nearest whole number if $y = 8.000001$.

(A) 2

(B) 3

(C) 5

(D) 6

(E) 16

Choice B is correct.

$$Given: \dfrac{y^2 - 7y + 10}{y - 2} \qquad \boxed{1}$$

Factor and reduce:

Factor the numerator of $\boxed{1}$. We get:

$$\dfrac{(y - 5)\cancel{(y - 2)}}{\cancel{y - 2}} = y - 5 \qquad \boxed{2}$$

Substitute 8.000001 in $\boxed{2}$. We have:

$$8.000001 - 5 =$$

$$3.000001 \approx 3 \ (Answer)$$

13 VERBAL STRATEGIES

Using Critical-Thinking Skills in Verbal Questions for the SAT Reading Section

Note: There are only 4 choices for the questions on the actual SAT. For instructional purposes in this strategy section we have used 5.

Introduction to Passage Reading

Before getting into the detailed strategies, I want to say that the most important way to really understand what you're reading is to *get involved* with the passage—as if a friend of yours were reading the passage to you and you wanted to be interested so you wouldn't hurt your friend's feelings. When you see the passage on paper it is also a good idea to *underline* important parts of the passage, which we'll also go over later in one of the strategies.

So many students ask, How do I answer reading comprehension questions? How do I read the passage effectively? Do I look at the questions before reading the passage? Do I underline things in the passage? Do I have to memorize details and dates? How do I get interested and involved in the passage?

All of these are good questions. They will be answered carefully and in the right sequence.

What Reading Comprehension Questions Ask

First of all, it is important to know that most reading comprehension questions ask about one of four things:

1. The MAIN IDEA of the passage.

2. INFORMATION SPECIFICALLY MEN-TIONED in the passage.

3. INFORMATION IMPLIED (not directly stated) in the passage.

4. The TONE or MOOD of the passage.

For example, following are some typical question stems. Each lets you immediately know which of the above is being asked about.

1. It can be inferred from the passage that . . . (IMPLIED INFORMATION)

2. According to the author . . . (MAIN IDEA)

3. The passage is primarily concerned with . . . (MAIN IDEA)

4. The author's statement that . . . (SPECIFIC INFORMATION)

5. Which of the following describes the mood of the passage? (TONE or MOOD)

6. The author implies that . . . (IMPLIED INFORMATION)

7. The use of paper is described in lines 14–16 . . . (SPECIFIC INFORMATION)

8. The main purpose of the passage . . . (MAIN IDEA)

9. The author's tone is best described as . . . (TONE or MOOD)

10. One could easily see the author as . . . (IMPLIED INFORMATION)

Getting Involved with the Passage

Now, let's first answer the burning question: Should I read the questions first before reading the passage? The answer is NO! If you have in mind the four main question types given above, you will not likely be in for any big surprises. Many questions, when you get to them, will be reassuringly familiar in the way they're framed and in their intent. You can best answer them by reading the passage first, allowing yourself to become involved with it.

To give you an idea of what I mean, look over the following passage. When you have finished, I'll show you how you might read it so as to get involved with it and with the author's intent.

Introductory Passage 1*

Yesterday, December 7, 1941—a date which will live in infamy—the United States of America was suddenly and deliberately attacked by naval and air forces of the Empire of Japan.

The United States was at peace with that nation, and, at the solicitation of Japan, was still in conversation with its government and its Emperor looking toward the maintenance of peace in the Pacific.

Indeed, one hour after Japanese air squadrons had commenced bombing in the American island of Oahu, the Japanese Ambassador to the United States and his colleague delivered to our Secretary of State a formal reply to a recent American message. And, while this reply stated that it seemed useless to continue the existing diplomatic negotiations, it contained no threat or hint of war or of armed attack.

It will be recorded that the distance of Hawaii from Japan makes it obvious that the attack was deliberately planned many days or even weeks ago. During the intervening time the Japanese Government has deliberately sought to deceive the United States by false statements and expressions of hope for continued peace.

The attack yesterday on the Hawaiian Islands has caused severe damage to American naval and military forces. I regret to tell you that very many American lives have been lost. In addition, American ships have been reported torpedoed on the high seas between San Francisco and Honolulu.

Yesterday the Japanese Government also launched an attack against Malaya.

Last night Japanese forces attacked Hong Kong.

Last night Japanese forces attacked Guam.

Last night Japanese forces attacked the Philippine Islands.

Last night the Japanese attacked Wake Island.

And this morning the Japanese attacked Midway Island.

Japan has therefore undertaken a surprise offensive extending throughout the Pacific area. The facts of yesterday and today speak for themselves. The people of the United States have already formed their opinions and well understand the implications to the very life and safety of our nation.

As Commander-in-Chief of the Army and Navy I have directed that all measures be taken for our defense, that always will our whole nation remember the character of the onslaught against us.

No matter how long it may take us to overcome this premeditated invasion, the American people, in their righteous might, will win through to absolute victory.

I believe that I interpret the will of the Congress and of the people when I assert that we will not only defend ourselves to the uttermost but will make it very certain that this form of treachery shall never again endanger us.

Hostilities exist. There is no blinking at the fact that our people, our territory and our interests are in grave danger.

With confidence in our armed forces, with the unbounding determination of our people, we will gain the inevitable triumph, so help us God.

I ask that the Congress declare that since the unprovoked and dastardly attack by Japan on Sunday, December 7, 1941, a state of war has existed between the United States and the Japanese Empire.

---

*From President Franklin Delano Roosevelt's address to the U.S. Congress on December 8, 1941.

Breakdown and Underlining of the Passage

Before going over the passage with you, I want to suggest some underlining you might want to make and show what different parts of the passage refer to.

Yesterday, December 7, 1941—<u>a date which will live in infamy</u>—the United States of America was suddenly and deliberately attacked by naval and air forces of the Empire of Japan.

The United States <u>was at peace with that nation</u>, and, at the solicitation of Japan, was still in conversation with its government and its Emperor looking toward the maintenance of peace in the Pacific.

→ *Sets the stage.*

Indeed, one hour after Japanese air squadrons had commenced bombing in the American island of Oahu, the Japanese Ambassador to the United States and his colleague delivered to our Secretary of State a formal reply to a recent American message. And, while this reply stated that it seemed useless to continue the existing diplomatic negotiations, it contained <u>no threat or hint of war or of armed attack</u>.

It will be recorded that the distance of Hawaii from Japan makes it obvious that the attack was deliberately planned many days or even weeks ago. During the intervening time the Japanese Government has deliberately sought to deceive the United States by false statements and expressions of hope for continued peace.

The attack yesterday on the Hawaiian Islands has caused <u>severe damage to American naval and military forces</u>. I regret to tell you that very many American lives have been lost. In addition, American ships have been reported torpedoed on the high seas between San Francisco and Honolulu.

→ *This should interest and surprise you.*

Yesterday the Japanese Government <u>also launched an attack</u> against Malaya.
Last night Japanese forces attacked Hong Kong.
Last night Japanese forces attacked Guam.
Last night Japanese forces attacked the Philippine Islands.
Last night the Japanese attacked Wake Island.
And this morning the Japanese attacked Midway Island.

→ *Examples of hostility.*

Japan has therefore undertaken a surprise offensive extending throughout the Pacific area. The facts of yesterday and today speak for themselves. The people of the United States have already formed their opinions and <u>well understand the implications</u> to the very life and safety of our nation.

As Commander-in-Chief of the Army and Navy I have directed that all measures be taken for our defense, that always will our whole nation remember the character of the onslaught against us.

No matter how long it may take us to overcome this premeditated invasion, the American people, in their righteous might, will <u>win through to absolute victory</u>.

I believe that I interpret the will of the Congress and of the people when I assert that we will not only defend ourselves to the uttermost but will make it very certain that <u>this form of treachery shall never again endanger us</u>.

→ *Leading to a conclusion.*

Hostilities exist. There is no blinking at the fact that our people, our territory and our interests are in <u>grave danger</u>.

With confidence in our armed forces, with the unbounding determination of our people, we will gain the <u>inevitable triumph</u>, so help us God.

I ask that the Congress declare that since the unprovoked and dastardly attack by Japan on Sunday, December 7, 1941, a state of war has existed between the United States and the Japanese Empire.

Now I'll go over the passage with you, showing you what might go through your mind as you read. This will let you see how to get involved with the passage and how this involvement facilitates answering the questions that follow the passage. In many cases, you'll actually be able to anticipate the questions. Of course, when you are preparing for the SAT, you'll have to develop this skill so that you do it rapidly and almost automatically.

Let's look at the first sentence:

Yesterday, December 7, 1941—a date which will live in infamy—the United States of America was suddenly and deliberately attacked by naval and air forces of the Empire of Japan.

Immediately you should say to yourself, "Something catastrophic has happened—what is the president going to do about it?" Read on:

The United States was at peace with that nation, and, at the solicitation of Japan, was still in conversation with its government and its Emperor looking toward the maintenance of peace in the Pacific.

Now you might say to yourself, "Why did they attack? Was it a mistake or did they trick us deliberately?" Read on:

Indeed, one hour after Japanese air squadrons had commenced bombing in the American island of Oahu, the Japanese Ambassador to the United States and his colleague delivered to our Secretary of State a formal reply to a recent American message. . . . it contained no threat or hint of war or of armed attack.

You are now probably saying to yourself, "Hmmm, this sounds bad if the attack occurred only an hour after that benign, neutral message. What is the president about to suggest?" Read on:

The attack yesterday on the Hawaiian Islands has caused severe damage to American naval and military forces. I regret to tell you that very many American lives have been lost. . . . Yesterday the Japanese Government also launched an attack against. . . .

Now you are probably both sad and angered by the news of the losses. And the list of other nations Japan has attacked at the same time probably has you saying to yourself, "We must do something—what are we going to do?!" Read on:

As Commander-in-Chief of the Army and Navy I have directed that all measures be taken for our defense, that

always will our whole nation remember the character of the onslaught against us.

This has probably boosted your confidence in the president's leadership, but you are also worried: Will I or a member of my family be fighting in a war? What will happen to us? Can we win? Read on:

. . . the American people, in their righteous might, will win through to absolute victory.
. . . we . . . will make it very certain that this form of treachery shall never again endanger us.
. . . There is no blinking at the fact that our people, our territory and our interests are in grave danger.
. . . we will gain the inevitable triumph, so help us God.

Now you are probably saying to yourself, "We are going to war. We must go to war not only to defend ourselves now but to make the world safe for our future." You should easily anticipate the conclusion that the president has prepared you for:

I ask that the Congress declare that since the unprovoked and dastardly attack by Japan on Sunday, December 7, 1941, a state of war has existed between the United States and the Japanese Empire.

How to Answer Reading Comprehension Questions Most Effectively

Before we start to answer the questions, let me tell you the best and most effective way of answering passage questions. You should read the question and proceed to look at the choices in the order of Choice A, Choice B, etc. If a choice (such as Choice A) doesn't give you the definite feeling that it is correct, don't try to analyze it further. Go on to Choice B, and so forth. Read all of the choices and choose the best one.

Suppose you have gone through all five choices, and you don't see any one that stands out as obviously being correct. Then quickly guess or leave the question blank and go on to the next question. You can go back after you have answered the other questions relating to the passage. But remember, when you return to the questions you weren't sure of, don't spend too much time on them. Try to forge ahead on the test.

Let's proceed to answer the questions now. Look at the first question:

1. This passage assumes the desirability of
   (A) maintaining peace at any price
   (B) instigating war before the enemy does
   (C) defending against unprovoked aggression

(D) conducting diplomacy when attacked

(E) declaring war on Japan

Choice A is incorrect, because the president is recommending a declaration of war because of the attack. Choice B is incorrect because the president is declaring war after the attack. Choice D is incorrect because the suggested response to the bombing of U.S. ships and the loss of American lives is war, not a delegation of diplomats. Choice E might be seen as correct, but the passage does not support the desirability of declaring war on Japan, in and of itself. Choice C is correct: The president begins by telling Americans that the attack was a surprise and unprovoked—"The United States was at peace with that nation"—and emphasizes that the purpose of the declaration of war against Japan is self-defense: "all measures be taken for our defense" and "we will . . . defend ourselves to the uttermost."

Let's look at Question 2:

2. According to this passage, the Japanese government probably instigated the surprise attack

(A) by mistake

(B) after being forced to do so

(C) because it wanted to increase its territory

(D) deliberately to provoke a war with the United States

(E) to avenge past offenses

Choice D, according to the passage, is the best answer: ". . . the distance of Hawaii from Japan makes it obvious that the attack was deliberately planned many days or even weeks ago. During the intervening time the Japanese Government has deliberately sought to deceive the United States by . . . expressions of hope for continued peace." Choices A, B, C, and E are not supported by the passage. While the Japanese may in fact have wanted to increase their territory (Choice C), nowhere in his speech does the president suggest that as a motivation for their attack.

Let's look at Question 3:

3. The passage indicates that the U.S. president can declare war

(A) by making an announcement to the American people

(B) when provoked by foreign aggression

(C) only with the approval of Congress

(D) when there is a threat to the mainland

(E) as soon as we are attacked

Choice C is correct: At the end of the passage the president asks Congress to declare that a state of war

exists between Japan and the United States. The other choices may be reasons for war, but only Congress can declare war.

Let's look at Question 4:

4. The purpose of the president's address was to

(A) explain why the United States was going to war

(B) justify U.S. aggression against Japan

(C) announce the loss of American lives

(D) prepare Americans for a justifiable war

(E) encourage Americans to distrust Japanese people

The best answer is Choice D. The structure of the speech makes this clear: First the president announces the atrocity against Americans in detail ("lives lost" etc.), next he lists other nations Japan simultaneously attacked, and finally he asserts that Americans will not stand for the aggression and will defend themselves "to the uttermost" to make certain that "this form of treachery shall never again endanger us." Choice A is incorrect because the speech requests a declaration of war from Congress. Choice B is incorrect because no U.S. aggression against Japan is indicated. Choice C is incorrect; the loss of American lives is announced, but the purpose of the speech is not to stop with that. Choice E is clearly incorrect—although some Americans may have formed anti-Japanese prejudice as a result of the aggression, that is not the purpose of the speech.

Introductory Passage 2*

Some scraps of evidence bear out those who hold a very high opinion of the average level of culture among the Athenians of the great age. The funeral speech of Pericles is the most famous indication from Athenian literature that its level was indeed high. Pericles was, however, a politician, and he may have been flattering his audience. We know that thousands of Athenians sat hour after hour in the theater listening to the plays of the great Greek dramatists. These plays, especially the tragedies, are at a very high intellectual level throughout. There are no letdowns, no concessions to the lowbrows or to the demands of "realism," such as the scene of the gravediggers in *Hamlet*. The music and dancing woven into these plays were almost certainly at an equally high level. Our opera—not Italian opera, not even Wagner, but the restrained, difficult opera of

*From Arthur Whimbey, "Teaching Sequential Thought: The Cognitive-Skills Approach," *The Phi Delta Kappan* vol. 59, no. 4 (December 1977), pp. 255–259.

the 18th century—is probably the best modern parallel. The comparison is no doubt dangerous, but can you imagine almost the entire population of an American city (in suitable installments, of course) sitting through performances of Mozart's *Don Giovanni* or Gluck's *Orpheus*? Perhaps the Athenian masses went to these plays because of a lack of other amusements. They could at least understand something of what went on, since the subjects were part of their folklore. For the American people, the subjects of grand opera are not part of their folklore.

Let's start reading the passage:

Some scraps of evidence bear out those who hold a very high opinion of the average level of culture among the Athenians of the great age.

Now this tells you that the author is going to talk about the culture of the Athenians. Thus the stage is set. Go on reading now:

The funeral speech of Pericles is the most famous indication from Athenian literature that its level was indeed high.

At this point you should say to yourself, "That's interesting, and there was an example of the high level of culture." Read on:

Pericles was, however, a politician, and he may have been flattering his audience.

Now you can say, "So that's why those people were so attentive in listening—they were being flattered." Read on:

We know that thousands of Athenians sat hour after hour in the theater listening to the plays of the great Greek dramatists. These plays, especially the tragedies, are at a very high intellectual level throughout. There are no letdowns, no concessions to the lowbrows or to the demands of "realism"...

At this point you should say to yourself, "That's strange—it could not have been just flattery that kept them listening hour after hour. How is this possible?" You can almost anticipate that the author will now give examples and contrast what he is saying to our plays and our audiences. Read on:

The music and dancing woven into these plays were almost certainly at an equally high level. Our opera—not Italian opera... is probably the best modern parallel. The comparison is no doubt dangerous, but can you

imagine almost the entire population of an American city... sitting through performances of...

Your feeling at this point should be, "No, I cannot imagine that. Why is that so?" So you should certainly be interested to find out. Read on:

Perhaps the Athenian masses went to these plays because of a lack of other amusements. They could at least understand something of what went on, since the subjects were part of their folklore.

Now you can say, "So that's why those people were able to listen hour after hour—the material was all part of their folklore!" Read on:

For the American people, the subjects... are not part of their folklore.

Now you can conclude, "So that's why the Americans cannot sit through these plays and perhaps cannot understand them—they were not part of their folklore!"

Here are the questions that follow the passage:

1. The author seems to question the sincerity of

    (A) politicians
    (B) playwrights
    (C) operagoers
    (D) lowbrows
    (E) gravediggers

2. The author implies that the average American

    (A) enjoys *Hamlet*
    (B) loves folklore
    (C) does not understand grand opera
    (D) seeks a high cultural level
    (E) lacks entertainment

3. The author's attitude toward Greek plays is one of

    (A) qualified approval
    (B) grudging admiration
    (C) studied indifference
    (D) partial hostility
    (E) great respect

4. The author suggests that Greek plays

    (A) made great demands upon their actors
    (B) flattered their audiences
    (C) were written for a limited audience
    (D) were dominated by music and dancing
    (E) stimulated their audiences

Let's try to answer them.

Question 1:

Remember the statement about Pericles? This statement was almost unrelated to the passage since it was not discussed or referred to again. And here we have a question about it. Usually, if you see something that you think is irrelevant in a passage you may be pretty sure that a question will be based on that irrelevancy. It is apparent that the author seems to question the sincerity of politicians (*not* playwrights), since Pericles was a politician. Therefore Choice A is correct.

Question 2:

We know that it was implied that the average American does not understand grand opera. Therefore Choice C is correct.

Question 3:

From the passage, we see that the author is very positive about the Greek plays. Thus the author must have great respect for the plays. Note that the author may not have respect for Pericles, but Pericles was not a playwright; he was a politician. Therefore Choice E (not Choice A) is correct.

Question 4:

It is certainly true that the author suggests that the Greek plays stimulated their audiences. They didn't necessarily flatter their audiences—there was only one indication of flattery, and that was by Pericles, who was not a playwright, but a politician. Therefore Choice E (not Choice B) is correct.

Example of Underlinings

Some scraps of evidence bear out those who hold a very high opinion of the average level of culture among the Athenians of the great age. → *Sets stage.*

The funeral speech of Pericles is the most famous indication from Athenian literature that its level was indeed high. Pericles was, however, a politician, and he may have been flattering his audience. → *Example.*

We know that thousands of Athenians sat hour after hour in the theater listening to the plays of the great Greek dramatists. These plays, especially the tragedies, are at a very high intellectual level throughout. → *Qualification.*

There are no letdowns, no concessions to the lowbrows or to the demands of "realism," such as the scene of the gravediggers in *Hamlet*. The music and dancing woven into these plays were almost certainly at an equally high level. Our opera—not Italian opera, not even Wagner, but the restrained, difficult opera of → *Further examples.*

the 18th century—is probably the best modern parallel. → *Comparison.*

The comparison is no doubt dangerous, but can you imagine almost the entire population of an American city (in suitable installments, of course) sitting through performances of Mozart's *Don Giovanni* or Gluck's *Orpheus*? Perhaps the Athenian masses went to these plays because of a lack of other amusements. They could at least understand something of what went on, since the subjects were part of their folklore. For the American people, the subjects of grand opera are not part of their folklore. → *Explanation of previous statements.*

Now the whole purpose of analyzing this passage the way I did was to show you that if you get involved and interested in the passage, you will not only anticipate many of the questions, but when you answer them you will be able to zero in on the right question choice without having to necessarily analyze or eliminate the wrong choices first. That's a great time-saver on a standardized test such as the SAT.

Now here's a short passage from which four questions were derived. Let's see if you can answer them after you've read the passage.

Introductory Passage 3*

Sometimes the meaning of the glowing water is ominous. Off the Pacific Coast of North America, it may mean that the sea is filled with . . . a minute plant that contains a poison of strange and terrible virulence.
5 About four days after this minute plant comes to dominate the coastal plankton, some of the fishes and shellfish in the vicinity become toxic. This is because in their normal feeding, they have strained the poisonous plankton out of the water.

1. Fish and shellfish become toxic when they

   (A) swim in poisonous water
   (B) feed on poisonous plants
   (C) change their feeding habits
   (D) give off a strange glow
   (E) take strychnine into their systems

2. One can most reasonably conclude that plankton are

   (A) minute organisms
   (B) mussels
   (C) poisonous fish
   (D) shellfish
   (E) fluids

3. In the context of the passage, the word *virulence* in line 4 means

   (A) strangeness
   (B) color
   (C) calamity
   (D) toxicity
   (E) powerful odor

4. The paragraph preceding this one most probably discussed

   (A) phenomena of the Pacific coastline
   (B) poisons that affect man
   (C) the culture of the early Indians
   (D) characteristics of plankton
   (E) phenomena of the sea

Explanatory Answers

1. Choice B is correct. See the last three sentences. Fish become toxic when they feed on poisonous plants. Don't be fooled into using the first sentence, which seemingly leads to Choice A.

2. Choice A is correct. Since we are talking about *minute* plants (second sentence), it is reasonable to assume that plankton are *minute* organisms.

3. Choice D is correct. We understand that the poison is very strong and noxious. Thus it is "toxic," virulent.

4. Choice E is correct. Since the second and not the first sentence was about the Pacific Coast, the paragraph preceding this one probably didn't discuss the phenomena of the Pacific coastline. It might have, if the first sentence—the sentence that links the ideas in the preceding paragraph—were about the Pacific coastline. Now, since we are talking about glowing water being ominous (first sentence), the paragraph preceding the passage is probably about the sea or the phenomena of the sea.

---

*This example also appears in Part 2, "The World's Shortest New SAT Practice Test," on page 25. From Rachel Carson, *The Sea Around Us*, 1950.

Summary

So in summary:

1. Make sure that you get involved with the passage. You may even want to select first the passage that interests you most. For example, if you're interested in science, you may want to choose the science passage first. Just make sure that you make some notation so that you don't mismark your answer sheet by putting the answers in the wrong answer boxes.

2. Pay attention to material that seems unrelated in the passage—there will probably be a question or two based on that material.

3. Pay attention to the mood created in the passage or the tone of the passage. Here again, especially if the mood is striking, there will probably be a question relating to mood.

4. Don't waste valuable time looking at the questions before reading the passage.

5. When attempting to answer the questions (after reading the passage) it is sometimes wise to try to figure out the answer before going through the choices. This will enable you to zero in on the correct answer without wasting time with all of the choices.

6. You may want to underline any information in the passages involving dates, specific names, etc., on your test to have as a ready reference when you come to the questions.

7. Always try to see the overall attempt of the author of the passage or try to get the main gist of why the passage was being written. Try to get involved by asking yourself if you agree or disagree with the author, etc.

The 10 Reading Comprehension Strategies begin on page 132.

About the Double-Reading Passages

On your SAT, you will be given a "double passage" (two separate passages) with about 11 questions. Some of the questions will be based on *only* the first passage, some will be based on *only* the second passage, and some will be based on *both* passages. Although you may want to read both passages first, then answer all the questions, some of you may find it less anxiety-inducing to **read the first passage, answer those questions relating to the first passage, then read the second passage and answer those questions relating to the second passage, and then finally answer the remaining questions relating to both passages.** By using this approach, since you are reading one passage at a time, the time you would have spent on the second passage could be spent on answering the first set of questions relating to the first passage. This approach helps you to avoid running out of time by reading both passages. The other advantage of this approach is that you do not have to keep both passages in mind at all times when answering the questions. That is, the only time you have to be aware of the content of both passages is when answering only those few questions related to both passages.

10 READING COMPREHENSION STRATEGIES

This section of Reading Comprehension Strategies includes several passages. These passages, though somewhat shorter than the passages that appear on the actual SAT and in the 2 SAT Practice Tests in this book, illustrate the general nature of the "real" SAT reading passages.

Each of the 10 Reading Comprehension Strategies that follow is accompanied by at least two different passages followed by questions and explanatory answers in order to explain how the strategy is used.

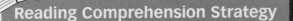

Reading Comprehension Strategy   1

Very Important Strategy:

As You Read Each Question, Determine the Type: Main Idea, Detecting Details, Inferential Reasoning, or Tone/Mood

Here are the four major abilities tested in Reading Comprehension questions:

1. **Main Idea**: The main idea of a passage is the central topic of the passage. As you are reading the passage, try to understand the general point of what the author is trying to convey. Try to ascertain the purpose and feel of the piece. The main idea will summarize the complete passage in a short and succinct way.

2. **Detecting Details**: To detect the details of a passage, pay close attention to the specific references of the piece. Curious statements such as "Einstein doesn't believe that nature plays dice with the universe" are clues to the details in the passage. When you see a curious statement, underline that statement so you can reference it again easily. Pay close attention when the author describes a specific example.

3. **Inferential Reasoning**: You must be able to ascertain what the author is trying to convey through the passage. For example, in the quote, "Einstein doesn't believe that nature plays dice with the universe," you will have to infer what the author means by this statement. You'll need to detect the author's viewpoint via the passage.

4. **Tone or Mood**: The tone or mood of a passage can be found by determining how the author or narrator *feels* in the passage. Is the passage angry or light, happy or melancholy, humorous or frightening? What feeling do you get from the passage? Knowing this will also give you insight as you are reading the passage, and offer psychological insight into the passage.

Example 1*

The fight crowd is a beast that lurks in the darkness behind the fringe of white light shed over the first six rows by the incandescents atop the ring, and is not to be trusted with pop bottles or other hardware.

5　People who go to prize fights are sadistic.

When two prominent pugilists are scheduled to pummel one another in public on a summer's evening, men and women file into the stadium in the guise of human beings, and thereafter become a part of a gray thing that
10　squats in the dark until, at the conclusion of the bloodletting, they may be seen leaving the arena in the same guise they wore when they entered.

As a rule, the mob that gathers to see men fight is unjust, vindictive, swept by intense, unreasoning
15　hatreds, and proud of its swift recognition of what it believes to be sportsmanship. It is quick to greet the purely phony move of the boxer who extends his gloves to his rival who has slipped or been pushed to the floor, and to reward this stimulating but still balo-
20　ney gesture with a pattering of hands that indicates the following: "You are a good sport. We recognize that you are a good sport, and we know a sporting gesture when we see one. Therefore we are all good sports too. Hurrah for us!"

25　The same crowd doesn't see the same boxer stick his thumb in his opponent's eye or try to cut him with the laces of his glove, butt him or dig him a low one when the referee isn't in a position to see. It roots consistently for the smaller man, and never for a moment
30　considers the desperate psychological dilemma of the larger of the two. It howls with glee at a good finisher making his kill. The Roman hordes were more civilized. Their gladiators asked them whether the final blow should be administered or not. The main attraction

---

*Adapted from Paul Gallico.

35 at the modern prize fight is the spectacle of a man club-
bing a helpless and vanquished opponent into complete
insensibility. The referee who stops a bout to save a
slugged and punch-drunken man from the final igno-
miny is hissed by the assembled sportsmen.

Questions

1. The tone of the passage is chiefly
   (A) disgusted
   (B) jovial
   (C) matter-of-fact
   (D) satiric
   (E) devil-may-care

2. Which group of words from the passage best indi-
   cates the author's opinion?
   (A) referee, opponent, finisher
   (B) gladiators, slugged, sporting gesture
   (C) stimulating, hissing, pattering
   (D) beast, lurks, gray thing
   (E) dilemma, hordes, spectacle

3. Apparently, the author believes that boxing crowds
   find the referee both
   (A) gentlemanly and boring
   (B) entertaining and essential
   (C) blind and careless
   (D) humorous and threatening
   (E) necessary and bothersome

Explanatory Answers

1. Choice A is correct. The author is obviously much
   offended (disgusted) by the inhuman attitude of the
   crowd watching the boxing match. For example, see
   these lines:

   Line 1: "The fight crowd is a beast. . . ."
   Line 5: "People who go to prize fights are sadistic."
   Lines 13–15: ". . . the mob that gathers to see men
   fight is unjust, vindictive, swept by
   intense . . . hatreds. . . ."
   Lines 32–33: "The Roman hordes were more
   civilized."

   To answer this question, you must be able to determine
   the tone that is dominant in the passage. Accordingly,
   this is a TONE/MOOD type of question.

2. Choice D is correct. The author's opinion is clearly
   one of disgust and discouragement because of the
   behavior of the fight crowd. Accordingly, you would
   expect the author to use words that were condemna-
   tory, like *beast*, and gloom-filled words like *lurks*
   and *gray thing*. To answer this question, you must
   see relationships between words and feelings. So,
   we have here an INFERENTIAL REASONING
   question type.

3. Choice E is correct. Lines 25–28 show that the
   referee is *necessary:* "The same crowd doesn't see
   the same boxer stick his thumb into his opponent's
   eye . . . when the referee isn't in a position to see."
   Lines 37–39 show that the referee is *bothersome*:
   "The referee who stops a bout . . . is hissed by the
   assembled sportsmen." To answer this question, you
   must have the ability to understand the writer's specific statements. Accordingly, this is a DETECTING
   DETAILS type of question.

Example 2*

Mist continues to obscure the horizon, but above us the
sky is suddenly awash with lavender light. At once the
geese respond. Now, as well as their cries, a beating
roar rolls across the water as if five thousand house-
5 wives have taken it into their heads to shake out blankets all at one time. Ten thousand housewives. It keeps
up—the invisible rhythmic beating of all those goose
wings—for what seems a long time. Even Lonnie is
held motionless with suspense.
10 Then the geese begin to rise. One, two, three hundred—then a thousand at a time—in long horizontal
lines that unfurl like pennants across the sky. The horizon actually darkens as they pass. It goes on and on like
that, flock after flock, for three or four minutes, each
15 new contingent announcing its ascent with an accelerating roar of cries and wingbeats. Then gradually the
intervals between flights become longer. I think the
spectacle is over, until yet another flock lifts up, following the others in a gradual turn toward the northeastern
20 quadrant of the refuge.
Finally the sun emerges from the mist; the mist
itself thins a little, uncovering the black line of willows
on the other side of the wildlife preserve. I remember

---

*This passage, from D. G. Schueler, also appears in Part 1, Strategy
Diagnostic Test for the New SAT, page 9.

to close my mouth—which has been open for some
25 time—and inadvertently shut two or three mosquitoes inside. Only a few straggling geese oar their way
across the sun's red surface. Lonnie wears an exasperated, proprietary expression, as if he had produced and
directed the show himself and had just received a bad
30 review. "It would have been better with more light,"
he says; "I can't always guarantee just when they'll
start moving." I assure him I thought it was a fantastic
sight. "Well," he rumbles, "I guess it wasn't too bad."

Questions

1. In the descriptive phrase "shake out blankets all at
   one time" (lines 5–6), the author is appealing chiefly
   to the reader's
   (A) background
   (B) sight
   (C) emotions
   (D) thoughts
   (E) hearing

2. The mood created by the author is one of
   (A) tranquility
   (B) excitement
   (C) sadness
   (D) bewilderment
   (E) unconcern

3. The main idea expressed by the author about the
   geese is that they
   (A) are spectacular to watch
   (B) are unpredictable
   (C) disturb the environment
   (D) produce a lot of noise
   (E) fly in large flocks

4. Judging from the passage, the reader can conclude
   that
   (A) the speaker dislikes nature's inconveniences
   (B) the geese's timing is predictable
   (C) Lonnie has had the experience before
   (D) both observers are hunters
   (E) the author and Lonnie are the same person

Explanatory Answers

1. Choice E is correct. See lines 3–6: ". . . a beating
   roar rolls across the water . . . shake out blankets
   all at one time." The author, with these words, is no
   doubt appealing to the reader's hearing. To answer
   this question, the reader has to identify those words
   dealing with sound and noise. Therefore, we have
   here a DETECTING DETAILS type of question.
   It is also an INFERENTIAL REASONING question type in that the "sound" words such as *beating*
   and *roar* lead the reader to infer that the author is
   appealing to the auditory (hearing) sense.

2. Choice B is correct. Excitement courses right
   through this passage. Here are examples:

   Lines 7–8: ". . . the invisible rhythmic beating of all
   those goose wings. . . ."

   Lines 8–9: "Even Lonnie is held motionless with
   suspense."

   Lines 10–11: "Then the geese begin to rise . . . a
   thousand at a time. . . ."

   Lines 14–16: ". . . flock after flock . . . roar of cries
   and wingbeats."

   To answer this question, you must determine the
   dominant tone in this passage. Therefore, we have
   here a TONE/MOOD question type.

3. Choice A is correct. The word *spectacular* means
   "dramatic," "thrilling," or "impressive." There is
   considerable action expressed throughout the passage. Sometimes there is a lull—then the action
   begins again. See lines 17–19: "I think the spectacle
   is over, until yet another flock lifts up, following the
   others. . . ." To answer this question, you must have
   the ability to judge the general significance of the
   passage. Accordingly, we have here a MAIN IDEA
   type of question.

4. Choice C is correct. See lines 27–32: "Lonnie wears
   an exasperated, proprietary expression . . . when
   they'll start moving.'" To answer this question, you
   must be able to draw a correct inference. Therefore,
   we have here an INFERENTIAL REASONING type
   of question.

Reading Comprehension Strategy 2

Very Important Strategy:

Underline the Key Parts of the Reading Passage*

The underlinings will help you to answer questions. Again, practically every question will ask you to detect the following:

(a) the main idea
   or
(b) information that is specifically mentioned in the passage
   or
(c) information that is implied (not directly stated) in the passage
   or
(d) the tone or mood of the passage.

If you find out quickly what the question is aiming for, you will more easily arrive at the correct answer by referring to your underlinings in the passage.

Example 1**

That one citizen is as good as another is a favorite American axiom, supposed to express the very essence of our Constitution and way of life. But just what do we mean when we utter that platitude? One surgeon
5 is not as good as another. One plumber is not as good as another. We soon become aware of this when we require the attention of either. Yet in political and economic matters we appear to have reached a point where knowledge and specialized training count for very little.
10 A newspaper reporter is sent out on the street to collect the views of various passers-by on such a question as "Should the United States defend Formosa?" The answer of the bar-fly who doesn't even know where the island is located, or that it is a island, is quoted in
15 the next edition just as solemnly as that of the college teacher of history. With the basic tenets of democracy—that all men are born free and equal and are

entitled to life, liberty, and the pursuit of happiness—no decent American can possibly take issue. But that
20 the opinion of one citizen on a technical subject is just as authoritative as that of another is manifestly absurd. And to accept the opinions of all comers as having the same value is surely to encourage a cult of mediocrity.

Questions

1. Which phrase best expresses the main idea of this passage?
   (A) the myth of equality
   (B) a distinction about equality
   (C) the essence of the Constitution
   (D) a technical subject
   (E) knowledge and specialized training

2. The author most probably included the example of the question on Formosa (lines 12–16) in order to
   (A) move the reader to rage
   (B) show that he is opposed to opinion sampling
   (C) show that he has thoroughly researched his project
   (D) explain the kind of opinion sampling he objects to
   (E) provide a humorous but temporary diversion from his main point

3. The author would be most likely to agree that
   (A) some men are born to be masters; others are born to be servants
   (B) the Constitution has little relevance for today's world
   (C) one should never express an opinion on a specialized subject unless he is an expert in that subject
   (D) every opinion should be treated equally
   (E) all opinions should not be given equal weight

Explanatory Answers

1. Choice B is correct. See lines 1–7: "That one citizen . . . attention of either." These lines indicate that there is quite a distinction about equality when we are dealing with all the American people.

2. Choice D is correct. See lines 10–16: "A newspaper reporter . . . college teacher of history." These lines show that the author probably included the example of the question of Formosa in order to explain the kind of opinion sampling he objects to.

---

*Strategy 2 is considered the Master Reading Comprehension Strategy because it can be used effectively in every Reading Comprehension question. However, it is important that you learn the other Reading Comprehension Strategies because you may need to use them in conjunction with this strategy to find the answer efficiently.

**This example also appears in Part 1, Strategy Diagnostic Test for the New SAT, page 8. From Claude M. Fuess, "The Retreat from Excellence," *Saturday Review*, March 26, 1960, p 21.

3. Choice E is correct. See lines 19–23: "But that the opinion . . . to encourage a cult of mediocrity." Accordingly, the author would be most likely to agree that all opinions should *not* be given equal weight.

Example 2

She walked along the river until a policeman stopped her. It was one o'clock, he said. Not the best time to be walking alone by the side of a half-frozen river. He smiled at her, then offered to walk her home. It was the
5   first day of the new year, 1946, eight and a half months after the British tanks had rumbled into Bergen-Belsen.
    That February, my mother turned twenty-six. It was difficult for strangers to believe that she had ever been a concentration-camp inmate. Her face was smooth and
10 round. She wore lipstick and applied mascara to her large, dark eyes. She dressed fashionably. But when she looked into the mirror in the mornings before leaving for work, my mother saw a shell, a mannequin who moved and spoke but who bore only a superficial
15 resemblance to her real self. The people closest to her had vanished. She had no proof that they were truly dead. No eyewitnesses had survived to vouch for her husband's death. There was no one living who had seen her parents die. The lack of confirmation haunted her. At
20 night before she went to sleep and during the day as she stood pinning dresses, she wondered if, by some chance, her parents had gotten past the Germans or had crawled out of the mass grave into which they had been shot and were living, old and helpless, somewhere in Poland.
25 What if only one of them had died? What if they had survived and had died of cold or hunger after she had been liberated, while she was in Celle* dancing with British officers?
    She did not talk to anyone about these things. No one,
30 she thought, wanted to hear them. She woke up in the mornings, went to work, bought groceries, went to the Jewish Community Center and to the housing office like a robot.

---

*Celle is a small town in Germany.

Questions

1. The policeman stopped the author's mother from walking along the river because

    (A) the river was dangerous
    (B) it was the wrong time of day
    (C) it was still wartime
    (D) it was so cold
    (E) she looked suspicious

2. The author states that his mother thought about her parents when she

    (A) walked along the river
    (B) thought about death
    (C) danced with officers
    (D) arose in the morning
    (E) was at work

3. When the author mentions his mother's dancing with the British officers, he implies that his mother

    (A) compared her dancing to the suffering of her parents
    (B) had clearly put her troubles behind her
    (C) felt it was her duty to dance with them
    (D) felt guilty about dancing
    (E) regained the self-confidence she once had

Explanatory Answers

1. Choice B is correct. See lines 1–4: "She walked along . . . offered to walk her home." The policeman's telling her that it was not the best time to be walking alone indicates clearly that "it was the wrong time of day."

2. Choice E is correct. Refer to lines 20–21: ". . . and during the day as she stood pinning dresses, she wondered. . . ."

3. Choice D is correct. See lines 25–28: "What if they had survived . . . dancing with British officers?"

Reading Comprehension Strategy 3

Look Back at the Passage When in Doubt

Sometimes while you are answering a question, you are not quite sure whether you have chosen the correct answer. Often, the underlinings that you have made in the reading passage will help you to determine whether a certain choice is the only correct choice.

Example 1

All museum adepts are familiar with examples of *ostrakoi*, the oystershells used in balloting. As a matter of fact, these "oystershells" are usually shards of pot-tery, conveniently glazed to enable the voter to express
5 his wishes in writing. In the Agora, a great number of these have come to light, bearing the thrilling name Themistocles. Into rival jars were dropped the ballots for or against his banishment. On account of the huge vote taken on that memorable date, it was to be expected
10 that many ostrakoi would be found, but the interest of this collection is that a number of these ballots are inscribed in an *identical* handwriting. There is nothing mysterious about it! The Boss was on the job, then as now. He prepared these ballots and voters cast them—
15 no doubt for the consideration of an obol or two. *The ballot box was stuffed.*

How is the glory of the American boss diminished! A vile imitation, he. His methods as old as Time!

Question

1. The title that best expresses the ideas of this passage is

    (A) An Odd Method of Voting
    (B) Themistocles, an Early Dictator
    (C) Democracy in the Past
    (D) Political Trickery—Past and Present
    (E) The Diminishing American Politician

Explanatory Answer

1. Choice D is correct. Important ideas that you might have underlined are expressed in lines 13–18: "The Boss was on the job, then as now. . . . His methods as old as Time!"

    These underlinings reveal that stuffing the ballot box is a time-honored tradition.

Example 2

But the weather predictions that an almanac always contains are, we believe, mostly wasted on the farmer. He can take a squint at the moon before turning in. He can "smell" snow or tell if the wind is shifting danger-
5 ously east. He can register forebodingly an extra twinge in a rheumatic shoulder. With any of these to go by, he can be reasonably sure of tomorrow's weather. He can return the almanac to the nail behind the door and put a last stick of wood in the stove. For an almanac, a zero
10 night or a morning's drifted road—none of these has changed much since Poor Richard wrote his stuff and barns were built along the Delaware.

Question

1. The author implies that, in predicting weather, there is considerable value in

    (A) reading the almanac
    (B) placing the last stick of wood in the stove
    (C) sleeping with one eye on the moon
    (D) keeping an almanac behind the door
    (E) noting rheumatic pains

Explanatory Answer

1. Choice E is correct. Important ideas that you might have underlined are the following:

    Line 3: "He can take a squint at the moon. . . ."
    Lines 3–4: "He can 'smell' snow. . . ."
    Lines 5–6: "He can register forebodingly an extra twinge in a rheumatic shoulder."

    These underlinings will reveal the quote, in lines 5–6, that gives you the correct answer.

Reading Comprehension Strategy 4

Before You Start Answering the Questions, Read the Passage Carefully

A great advantage of careful reading of the passage is that you will, thereby, get a very good idea of what the passage is about. If a particular sentence is not clear to you as you read, then reread that sentence to get a bet-ter idea of what the author is trying to say.

Example 1

Underlining important ideas as you are reading this passage is strongly urged:

The American Revolution is the only one in modern history which, rather than devouring the intellectuals who prepared it, carried them to power. Most of the signatories of the Declaration of Independence were
5 intellectuals. This tradition is ingrained in America, whose greatest statesmen have been intellectuals— Jefferson and Lincoln, for example. These statesmen performed their political function, but at the same time they felt a more universal responsibility, and they
10 actively defined this responsibility. Thanks to them there is in America a living school of political science. In fact, it is at the moment the only one perfectly adapted to the emergencies of the contemporary world, and one that can be victoriously opposed to commu-
15 nism. A European who follows American politics will be struck by the constant reference in the press and from the platform to this political philosophy, to the historical events through which it was best expressed, to the great statesmen who were its best representatives.

Questions

1. The title that best expresses the ideas of this passage is

   (A) Fathers of the American Revolution
   (B) Jefferson and Lincoln—Ideal Statesmen
   (C) The Basis of American Political Philosophy
   (D) Democracy vs. Communism
   (E) The Responsibilities of Statesmen

2. According to the passage, intellectuals who pave the way for revolutions are usually

   (A) honored
   (B) misunderstood
   (C) destroyed
   (D) forgotten
   (E) elected to office

3. Which statement is true according to the passage?

   (A) America is a land of intellectuals.
   (B) The signers of the Declaration of Independence were well educated.
   (C) Jefferson and Lincoln were revolutionaries.
   (D) Adaptability is a characteristic of American political science.
   (E) Europeans are confused by American politics.

Explanatory Answers

1. Choice C is correct. Throughout this passage, the author speaks about the basis of American political philosophy. For example, see lines 5–11: "This tradition is ingrained in America, . . . a living school of political science."

2. Choice C is correct. See lines 1–3: "The American Revolution is the only one . . . carried them to power." These lines may be interpreted to mean that intellectuals who pave the way for revolutions— other than the American Revolution—are usually destroyed (devoured).

3. Choice D is correct. The word *adaptability* means "the ability to adapt"—to adjust to a specified use or situation. Now see lines 11–15: ". . . there is in America . . . opposed to communism."

Example 2*

Underlining important ideas as you are reading this passage is strongly urged:

The activities of the microscopic vegetables of the sea, of which the diatoms are most important, make the mineral wealth of the water available to the animals. Feeding directly on the diatoms and other groups of minute uni-
5 cellular algae are the marine protozoa, many crustaceans, the young of crabs, barnacles, sea worms, and fishes. Hordes of small carnivores, the first link in the chain of flesh eaters, move among these peaceful grazers. There are fierce little dragons half an inch long, the sharp-
10 jawed arrow-worms. There are gooseberrylike comb jellies, armed with grasping tentacles, and there are the shrimplike euphausiids that strain food from the water with their bristly appendages. Since they drift where the currents carry them, with no power or will to oppose
15 that of the sea, this strange community of creatures and the marine plants that sustain them are called *plankton*, a word derived from the Greek, meaning "wandering."

Questions

1. According to the passage, diatoms are a kind of

   (A) mineral
   (B) alga
   (C) crustacean
   (D) protozoan
   (E) fish

*From Rachel Carson, *The Sea Around Us*, 1950.

2. Which characteristic of diatoms does the passage emphasize?

   (A) size
   (B) feeding habits
   (C) activeness
   (D) numerousness
   (E) cellular structure

Explanatory Answers

1. Choice B is correct. See lines 3–5: "Feeding directly on the diatoms . . . minute unicellular algae are the marine protozoa. . . ." These lines indicate that diatoms are a kind of alga.

2. Choice A is correct. See lines 1–5: "The activities of the microscopic vegetables of the sea . . . minute unicellular algae. . . ." In these lines, the words *microscopic* and *minute* emphasize the small size of the diatoms.

Reading Comprehension Strategy 5

Get the Meanings of "Tough" Words by Using the Context Method

Suppose you don't know the meaning of a certain word in a passage. Then try to determine the meaning of that word from the context—that is, from the words that are close in position to that word whose meaning you don't know. Knowing the meanings of difficult words in the passage will help you to better understand the passage as a whole.

Example 1

Like all insects, it wears its skeleton on the outside—a marvelous chemical compound called *chitin* which sheathes the whole of its body. This flexible armor is tremendously tough, light, shatterproof, and resistant
5 to alkali and acid compounds that would eat the clothing, flesh, and bones of man. To it are attached muscles so arranged around catapult-like hind legs as to enable the hopper to hop, if so diminutive a term can describe so prodigious a leap as ten or twelve feet—about 150
10 times the length of the one-or-so-inch-long insect. The equivalent feat for a man would be a casual jump, from a standing position, over the Washington Monument.

Questions

1. The word *sheathes* (line 3) means

   (A) strips
   (B) provides
   (C) exposes
   (D) encases
   (E) excites

2. The word *prodigious* (line 9) means

   (A) productive
   (B) frightening
   (C) criminal
   (D) enjoyable
   (E) enormous

Explanatory Answers

1. Choice D is correct. The words in line 1, "it wears its skeleton on the outside," give us the idea that *sheathes* probably means "covers" or "encases."

2. Choice E is correct. See the surrounding words in lines 7–10: "enable the hopper to hop . . . so prodigious a leap as ten or twelve feet—about 150 times the length of the one-or-so-inch-long insect." We may easily infer that the word *prodigious* means "great in size" or "enormous."

Example 2*

Since the days when the thirteen colonies, each so jealous of its sovereignty, got together to fight the lobsterbacks, the American people have exhibited a tendency—a genius—to maintain widely divergent viewpoints in
5 normal times, but to unite and agree in times of stress. One reason the federal system has survived is that it has demonstrated this same tendency. Most of the time the three coequal divisions of the general government tend to compete. In crises they tend to cooperate. And
10 not only during war. A singular instance of cooperation took place in the opening days of the first administration of Franklin D. Roosevelt, when the harmonious efforts of the executive and the legislature to arrest the havoc of depression brought the term *rubber-stamp*
15 *Congress* into the headlines. On the other hand, when in 1937 Roosevelt attempted to bend the judiciary to the will of the executive by "packing" the Supreme

---

*From Milton Lomask, "When Congress Tried to Rule." *American Heritage* vol. 11, no. 1 (December 1959).

Court, Congress rebelled. This frequently proved flexibility—this capacity of both people and government to
20 shift from competition to cooperation and back again as
circumstances warrant—suggests that the federal system will be found equal to the very real dangers of the
present world situation.

Questions

1. The word *havoc* (line 14) means

    (A) possession
    (B) benefit
    (C) destruction
    (D) symptom
    (E) enjoyment

2. The word *divergent* (line 4) means

    (A) interesting
    (B) discussed
    (C) flexible
    (D) differing
    (E) appreciated

Explanatory Answers

1. Choice C is correct. The prepositional phrase "of
   depression," which modifies "havoc," should indicate that this word has an unfavorable meaning.
   The only choice that has an unfavorable meaning is
   Choice C—"destruction."

2. Choice D is correct. See lines 3–5: ". . . the American people . . . widely divergent viewpoints . . . but
   to unite and agree in times of stress." The word *but*
   in this sentence is an *opposition indicator*. We may,
   therefore, assume that a "divergent viewpoint" is a
   "differing" one from the idea expressed in the words
   "to unite and agree in times of stress."

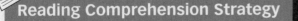

Reading Comprehension Strategy   6

Circle Transitional Words in the Passage

There are certain transitional words—also called
"bridge" or "key" words—that will help you to discover logical connections in a reading passage. *Circling*
these transitional words will help you to get a better
understanding of the passage.

Here are examples of commonly used transitional
words and what these words may indicate.

Transitional Word	Indicating
although	OPPOSITION
however	
in spite of	
rather than	
nevertheless	
on the other hand	
but	
moreover	SUPPORT
besides	
additionally	
furthermore	
in fact	
therefore	RESULT
consequently	
accordingly	
because	
when	
so	

Example 1

Somewhere between 1860 and 1890, the dominant
emphasis in American literature was radically changed.
But it is obvious that this change was not necessarily a
matter of conscious concern to all writers. In fact, many
5 writers may seem to have been actually unaware of the
shifting emphasis. Moreover, it is not possible to trace
the steady march of the realistic emphasis from its first
feeble notes to its dominant trumpet-note of unques-
tioned leadership. The progress of realism is to change
10 the figure to that of a small stream, receiving acces-
sions from its tributaries at unequal points along its
course, its progress now and then balked by the sand-
bars of opposition or the diffusing marshes of error and
compromise. Again, it is apparent that any attempt to
15 classify rigidly, as romanticists or realists, the writers of
this period is doomed to failure, since it is not by virtue
of the writer's conscious espousal of the romantic or
realistic creed that he does much of his best work, but
by virtue of that writer's sincere surrender to the atmo-
20 sphere of the subject.

Questions

1. The title that best expresses the ideas of this passage is
   (A) Classifying American Writers
   (B) Leaders in American Fiction
   (C) The Sincerity of Writers
   (D) The Values of Realism
   (E) The Rise of Realism

2. Which characteristic of writers does the author praise?
   (A) their ability to compromise
   (B) their allegiance to a "school"
   (C) their opposition to change
   (D) their awareness of literary trends
   (E) their intellectual honesty

Explanatory Answers

1. Choice E is correct. Note some of the transitional words that help you to interpret the passage and see why a title of "The Rise of Realism" would be warranted. In line 6, "Moreover" is a key word that is connected to "realistic emphasis" in line 7. This idea is also connected to the sentence involving the "progress of realism" in line 9. The word *again* in line 14 is also connected with this rise in realism.

2. Choice E is correct. See lines 16–20: ". . . since it is not by virtue of . . . but by virtue of that writer's sincere . . . of the subject." The transitional word *but* helps us to arrive at the correct answer, which is "their intellectual honesty."

Example 2*

A humorous remark or situation is, furthermore, always a pleasure. We can go back to it and laugh at it again and again. One does not tire of the *Pickwick Papers,* or of the humor of Mark Twain, any more than the child

5 tires of a nursery tale that he knows by heart. Humor is a feeling, and feelings can be revived. But wit, being an intellectual and not an emotional impression, suffers by repetition. A witticism is really an item of knowledge. Wit, again, is distinctly a gregarious quality, whereas

10 humor may abide in the breast of a hermit. Those who live by themselves almost always have a dry humor.

*From "Wit and Humor," *The Atlantic Monthly: A Magazine of Literature, Science, Art, and Politics, Volume C*. Boston, Houghton Mifflin, 1907, p 427.

Wit is a city, humor a country, product. Wit is the accomplishment of persons who are busy with ideas; it is the fruit of intellectual cultivation and abounds

15 in coffeehouses, in salons, and in literary clubs. But humor is the gift of those who are concerned with persons rather than ideas, and it flourishes chiefly in the middle and lower classes.

Question

1. It is probable that the paragraph preceding this one discussed the
   (A) *Pickwick Papers*
   (B) characteristics of literature
   (C) characteristics of human nature
   (D) characteristics of humor
   (E) nature of human feelings

Explanatory Answer

1. Choice D is correct. See lines 1–2: "A humorous remark or situation is, furthermore, always a pleasure." The transitional word *furthermore* means "in addition." We may, therefore, assume that something dealing with humor has been discussed in the previous paragraph.

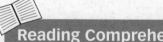

Reading Comprehension Strategy 7

Don't Answer a Question on the Basis of Your Own Opinion

Answer each question on the basis of the information given or suggested in the passage itself. Your own views or judgments may sometimes conflict with what the author of the passage is expressing. Answer the question according to what the author believes.

Example 1

The drama critic, on the other hand, has no such advantages. He cannot be selective; he must cover everything that is offered for public scrutiny in the principal playhouses of the city where he works.

5 The column space that seemed, yesterday, so pitifully inadequate to contain his comments on *Long Day's Journey into Night* is roughly the same as that which yawns today for his verdict on some inane comedy that has chanced to find for itself a numskull

10 backer with five hundred thousand dollars to lose.
This state of affairs may help to explain why the New
York theater reviewers are so often, and so unjustly,
stigmatized as baleful and destructive fiends. They
spend most of their professional lives attempting to
15 pronounce intelligent judgments on plays that have no
aspiration to intelligence. It is hardly surprising that
they lash out occasionally; in fact, what amazes me
about them is that they do not lash out more violently
and more frequently. As Shaw said of his fellow-critics
20 in the 1890s, they are "a culpably indulgent body of
men." Imagine the verbal excoriations that would
be inflicted if Lionel Trilling, or someone of comparable eminence, were called on to review five books
a month of which three were novelettes composed
25 of criminal confessions. The butchers of Broadway
would seem lambs by comparison.

Questions

1. In writing this passage, the author's purpose seems
   to have been to
   (A) comment on the poor quality of our plays
   (B) show why book reviewing is easier than play
       reviewing
   (C) point out the opinions of Shaw
   (D) show new trends in literary criticism
   (E) defend the work of the play critic

2. The passage suggests that, as a play, *Long Day's
   Journey into Night* was
   (A) inconsequential
   (B) worthwhile
   (C) poorly written
   (D) much too long
   (E) much too short

Explanatory Answers

1. Choice E is correct. Throughout the passage, the
   author is defending the work of the play critic. See,
   for example, lines 11–16: "This state of affairs . . .
   plays that have no aspiration to intelligence." Be
   sure that you do not answer a question on the basis
   of your own views. You yourself may believe that
   the plays presented on the stage today are of poor
   quality (Choice A) generally. The question, however, asks about the *author's opinion*—not yours.

2. Choice B is correct. See lines 5–10: "The column
   space . . . dollars to lose." *Long Day's Journey into
   Night* is contrasted here with an inane comedy.
   This implies that *Long Day's Journey into Night* is
   a worthwhile play. You yourself may believe that it
   is a bad or underwhelming play (Choice A or C or
   D or E). But remember—the author's opinion, not
   yours, is asked for.

Example 2

History has long made a point of the fact that the mag-
nificent flowering of ancient civilization rested upon
the institution of slavery, which released opportunity
at the top of the art and literature that became the
5 glory of antiquity. In a way, the mechanization of the
present-day world produces the condition of the ancient
in that the enormous development of labor-saving
devices and of contrivances that amplify the capacities
of mankind affords the base for the leisure necessary
10 for widespread cultural pursuits. Mechanization is the
present-day slave power, with the difference that in the
mechanized society there is no group of the community
that does not share in the benefits of its inventions.

Question

1. The author's attitude toward mechanization is one of
   (A) awe
   (B) acceptance
   (C) distrust
   (D) fear
   (E) devotion

Explanatory Answer

1. Choice B is correct. Throughout the passage, the
   author's attitude toward mechanization is one of
   acceptance. Such acceptance on the part of the
   author is indicated particularly in lines 10–13:
   "Mechanization is . . . the benefits of its inventions."
   You yourself may have a feeling of distrust (Choice
   C) or fear (Choice D) toward mechanization. But
   the author does not have such feelings.

Reading Comprehension Strategy 8

After Reading the Passage, Read Each Question Carefully

Be sure that you read *with care* not only the stem (beginning) of a question but also *each* of the choices. Some students select a choice just because it is a true statement—or because it answers part of a question. This can get you into trouble.

Example 1

The modern biographer's task becomes one of discovering the "dynamics" of the personality he is studying rather than allowing the reader to deduce that personality from documents. If he achieves a reasonable like-
5 ness, he need not fear too much that the unearthing of still more material will alter the picture he has drawn; it should add dimension to it, but not change its lineaments appreciably. After all, he has had more than enough material to permit him to reach conclusions and
10 to paint his portrait. With this abundance of material he can select moments of high drama and find episodes to illustrate character and make for vividness. In any event, biographers, I think, must recognize that the writing of a life may not be as "scientific" or as "defini-
15 tive" as we have pretended. Biography partakes of a large part of the subjective side of man; and we must remember that those who walked abroad in our time may have one appearance for us—but will seem quite different to posterity.

Question

1. According to the author, which is the real task of the modern biographer?

 (A) interpreting the character revealed to him by study of the presently available data
 (B) viewing the life of the subject in the biographer's own image
 (C) leaving to the reader the task of interpreting the character from contradictory evidence
 (D) collecting facts and setting them down in chronological order
 (E) being willing to wait until all the facts on his subject have been uncovered

Explanatory Answer

1. Choice A is correct. See lines 1–8: "The modern biographer's task . . . but not change its lineaments appreciably." The word *dynamics* is used here to refer to the physical and moral forces that exerted influence on the main character of the biography. The lines quoted indicate that the author believes that the real task of the biographer is to study the *presently available data*. Choice D may also appear to be a correct choice since a biographer is likely to consider his job to be collecting facts and setting them down in chronological order. But the passage does not directly state that a biographer has such a procedure.

Example 2

Although patience is the most important quality a trea-sure hunter can have, the trade demands a certain amount of courage too. I have my share of guts, but make no boast about ignoring the hazards of diving. As all good
5 divers know, the business of plunging into an alien world with an artificial air supply as your only link to the world above can be as dangerous as stepping into a den of lions. Most of the danger rests within the diver himself.
  The devil-may-care diver who shows great bravado
10 underwater is the worst risk of all. He may lose his bearings in the glimmering dim light that penetrates the sea and become separated from his diving companions. He may dive too deep, too long and suffer painful, sometimes fatal, bends.

Question

1. According to the author, an underwater treasure hunter needs above all to be

 (A) self-reliant
 (B) adventuresome
 (C) mentally alert
 (D) patient
 (E) physically fit

Explanatory Answer

1. Choice D is correct. See lines 1–3: "Although patience is the most important . . . courage too." Choice E ("physically fit") may also appear to be a correct choice, since an underwater diver certainly has to be physically fit. Nevertheless, the passage nowhere states this directly.

Reading Comprehension Strategy 9

Very Important Strategy:

Increase Your Vocabulary to Boost Your Reading Comprehension Score

1. You can increase your vocabulary tremendously by learning Latin and Greek roots, prefixes, and suffixes. Knowing the meanings of difficult words will thereby help you to understand a passage better.

   Sixty percent of all the words in our English language are derived from Latin and Greek. By learning certain Latin and Greek roots, prefixes, and suffixes, you will be able to understand the meanings of more than 150,000 additional English words. See "The Gruber Prefix-Root-Suffix List" beginning on page 309.

2. Learn the vocabulary strategies on pages 148–152. There are other steps—in addition to these two steps—to increase your vocabulary. Here they are:

3. Read as widely as possible—novels, nonfiction, newspapers, magazines.

4. Listen to people who speak well. Many TV programs have very fine speakers. You can pick up many new words listening to such programs.

5. Get into the habit of using a dictionary often. You can get a dictionary app for your phone or look up words online.

6. Play word games—crossword puzzles will really build up your vocabulary.

Example 1

Acting, like much writing, is probably a compensation for and release from the strain of some profound maladjustment of the psyche. The actor lives most intensely by proxy. He has to be somebody else to be himself.
5 But it is all done openly and for our delight. The dangerous man, the enemy of nonattachment or any other wise way of life, is the born actor who has never found his way into the Theater, who never uses a stage door, who does not take a call and then wipe the paint off his
10 face. It is the intrusion of this temperament into political life, in which at this day it most emphatically does not belong, that works half the mischief in the world. In every country you may see them rise, the actors who will not use the Theater, and always they bring down
15 disaster from the angry gods who like to see mountebanks in their proper place.

Questions

1. The meaning of *maladjustment* (lines 2–3) is a
   (A) replacement of one thing with another
   (B) profitable experience in business
   (C) consideration for the feelings of others
   (D) disregard of advice offered by others
   (E) poor relationship with one's environment

2. The meaning of *psyche* (line 3) is
   (A) person
   (B) mind
   (C) personality
   (D) psychology
   (E) physique

3. The meaning of *intrusion* (line 10) is
   (A) entering without being welcome
   (B) acceptance after considering the facts
   (C) interest that has developed after a period of time
   (D) fear as the result of imagination
   (E) refusing to obey a command

4. The meaning of *mountebanks* (lines 15–16) is
   (A) mountain climbers
   (B) cashiers
   (C) high peaks
   (D) fakers
   (E) mortals

Explanatory Answers

1. Choice E is correct. The prefix *mal-* means "bad." Obviously a maladjustment is a bad adjustment—that is, a poor relationship with one's environment.

2. Choice B is correct. The root *psyche* means "the mind" functioning as the center of thought, feeling, and behavior.

3. Choice A is correct. The prefix *in-* means "into" in this case. The root *trud* or *trus* means "pushing into"—or entering without being welcome.

4. Choice D is correct. The root *mont* means "to climb." The root *banc* means a "bench." A mountebank means literally "one who climbs on a bench." The actual meaning of *mountebank* is a "quack" (faker) who sells useless medicines from a platform in a public place.

Example 2

The American Museum of Natural History has long portrayed various aspects of man. Primitive cultures have been shown through habitat groups and displays of man's tools, utensils, and art. In more recent years,
5 there has been a tendency to delineate man's place in nature, displaying his destructive and constructive activities on the earth he inhabits. Now, for the first time, the Museum has taken man apart, enlarged the delicate mechanisms that make him run, and examined
10 him as a biological phenomenon.

In the new Hall of the Biology of Man, Museum technicians have created a series of displays that are instructive to a degree never before achieved in an exhibit hall. Using new techniques and new materials,
15 they have been able to produce movement as well as form and color. It is a human belief that beauty is only skin deep. But nature has proved to be a master designer, not only in the matter of man's bilateral symmetry but also in the marvelous packaging job
20 that has arranged all man's organs and systems within his skin-covered case. When these are taken out of the case, greatly enlarged, and given color, they reveal form and design that give the lie to that old saw. Visitors will be surprised to discover that man's insides,
25 too, are beautiful.

Questions

1. The meaning of *bilateral* (line 18) is
   (A) biological
   (B) two-sided
   (C) natural
   (D) harmonious
   (E) technical

2. The meaning of *symmetry* (line 19) is
   (A) simplicity
   (B) obstinacy
   (C) sincerity
   (D) appearance
   (E) proportion

Explanatory Answers

1. Choice B is correct. The prefix *bi-* means "two." The root *latus* means "side." Therefore, *bilateral* means "two-sided."

2. Choice E is correct. The prefix *sym-* means "together." The root *metr* means "measure." The word *symmetry*, therefore, means "proportion," "harmonious relation of parts," "balance."

Reading Comprehension Strategy   10

Very Important Strategy:

Know How to Answer Questions That Deal with Graphs, Charts, etc. Look for a Trend, Something Curious in the Graph, Chart, or Table or Things That Look Significant in the Data Presented and Described

Some reading passages will contain data in graphs, charts, tables, etc. You have to interpret the data in order to answer the data-related questions. You can also find practice questions on this strategy in "Math Refresher Session 7—Tables, Charts, and Graphs," on pages 285–293.

Here are three SAT-type questions that you will find dealing with data interpretation in the reading passages.

1. Based on the data, the world population has grown by about 1 billion people approximately every

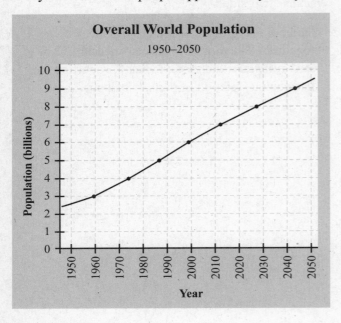

Overall World Population

1950–2050

(A) 5–7 years
(B) 7–9 years
(C) 9–11 years
(D) 11–15 years

2. Which of the following is true according to the graph below?

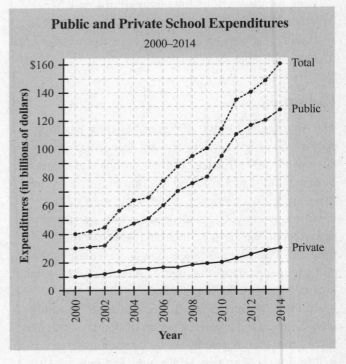

Public and Private School Expenditures

2000–2014

(A) The difference between the total number of expenditures and the public school expenditures during the years 2000–2014 remained constant.
(B) The total expenditures increased the most in 2011 from the year before.
(C) The public school expenditures increased at the same rate as the private school expenditures from 2000 to 2014.
(D) The greatest difference between the total and public school expenditures occurred in 2010.

3. From 2001 to 2017 where is there a projected increase in the number of workers?

Distribution of Workforce by Occupational Category for Region in 2001 and Projected for 2017

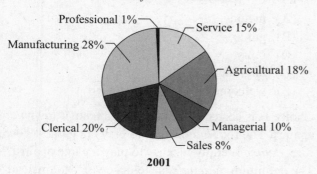

Total workforce: 150 million

Professional 1%
Service 15%
Manufacturing 28%
Agricultural 18%
Clerical 20%
Managerial 10%
Sales 8%

2001

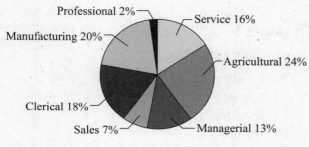

Total workforce: 175 million

Professional 2%
Service 16%
Manufacturing 20%
Agricultural 24%
Clerical 18%
Sales 7%
Managerial 13%

2017 (Projected)

  I. Sales
 II. Service
III. Clerical

(A) I only
(B) II only
(C) III only
(D) I, II, and III

Explanatory Answers

1. Choice D is correct. The 6 billion mark is left of (before) the 2000 mark and 7 billion occurs right of (after) the 2010 mark, meaning there are more than 10 years between each billion (eliminating Choices A and B). The distance between 8 and 9 billion (or 3 and 4 billion) appears to be even greater than the distance between 6 and 7 billion, suggesting a range of 11–15 years.

2. Choice B is correct. Look for something that stands out. You can see that for Total Expenditures the slope of the graph is greatest between 2010 and 2011. That's where the greatest increase would be.

3. Choice D is correct. Look at each category in the choices. For Sales, you might think that because it goes from 8% in 2001 to 7% in 2017, there is no increase. However, you have to take 8% of 150 million to get the number of workers in Sales in 2001. That is 12 million. Now in 2017, you take 7% of 175 million, which is 12.25%. So there was a projected increase in Sales. Let's look at Service. Service increases from 15% to 16% and the total workforce is greater in 2017. Thus there is a definite increase in the number of workers in Service. No need to calculate. Look at Clerical. Although Clerical decreases from 20% to 18%, you still have to calculate the number of workers in 2001 and in 2017. In 2001 there were 20% × 150 million workers or 30 million workers. In 2017 there would be 18% × 175 million workers or 31.5 million workers. Thus Choice D is correct.

3 VOCABULARY STRATEGIES

Introduction

Although *antonyms* (words with opposite meanings) are not on the SAT, it is still important for you to know vocabulary and the strategies to figure out the meanings of words, since there are many questions involving difficult words in all the sections on the Verbal part of the SAT.

Vocabulary Strategy 1

Use Roots, Prefixes, and Suffixes to Get the Meanings of Words

You can increase your vocabulary tremendously by learning Latin and Greek roots, prefixes, and suffixes. Sixty percent of all the words in our English language are derived from Latin and Greek. By learning certain Latin and Greek roots, prefixes, and suffixes, you will be able to understand the meanings of more than 150,000 additional English words. See "The Gruber Prefix-Root-Suffix List" beginning on page 309 and "Hot Prefixes and Roots" in Appendix A beginning on page 627.

Example 1

Opposite of PROFICIENT:

- (A) antiseptic
- (B) unwilling
- (C) inconsiderate
- (D) neglectful
- (E) incompetent

Choice E is correct. The prefix *pro-* means "forward," or "for the purpose of ." The root *fic* means "to make" or "to do." Therefore, *proficient* literally means "doing something in a forward way." The definition of *proficient* is "skillful," "adept," "capable." The antonym of *proficient* is, accordingly, "incompetent."

Example 2

Opposite of DELUDE:

- (A) include
- (B) guide
- (C) reply
- (D) upgrade
- (E) welcome

Choice B is correct. The prefix *de-* means "downward," against. The root *lud* means "to play" (a game). Therefore, *delude* literally means "to play a game against." The definition of *delude* is "to deceive," "to mislead." The antonym of *delude* is, accordingly, "to guide."

Example 3

Opposite of LAUDATORY:

- (A) vacating
- (B) satisfactory
- (C) revoking
- (D) faultfinding
- (E) silent

Choice D is correct. The root *laud* means *praise*. The suffix *-ory* means "a tendency toward." Therefore, *laudatory* means "having a tendency toward praising someone." The definition of *laudatory* is "praising." The antonym of *laudatory* is, accordingly, *faultfinding*.

Example 4

Opposite of SUBSTANTIATE:

- (A) reveal
- (B) intimidate
- (C) disprove
- (D) integrate
- (E) assist

Choice C is correct. The prefix *sub-* means "under." The root *sta* means "to stand." The suffix *-ate* is a verb form indicating "the act of." Therefore, *substantiate* literally means "to perform the act of standing under." The definition of *substantiate* is "to support" with proof or evidence. The antonym is, accordingly, *disprove*.

Example 5

Opposite of TENACIOUS:

- (A) changing
- (B) stupid
- (C) unconscious
- (D) poor
- (E) antagonistic

Choice A is correct.
ten = to hold; *tenacious* = holding
OPPOSITE = *changing*

Example 6

Opposite of RECEDE:

- (A) accede
- (B) settle
- (C) surrender
- (D) advance
- (E) reform

Choice D is correct.
re- = back; *ced* = to go; *recede* = to go back
OPPOSITE = *advance*

Example 7

Opposite of CIRCUMSPECT:

- (A) suspicious
- (B) overbearing
- (C) listless
- (D) determined
- (E) careless

Choice E is correct.
circum- = around; *spect* = to look or see; *circumspect* = seeing all around, careful
OPPOSITE = *careless*

Example 8

Opposite of MALEDICTION:

- (A) sloppiness
- (B) praise
- (C) health
- (D) religiousness
- (E) proof

Choice B is correct.
mal = bad; *dict* = to speak; *malediction* = bad speaking, a curse
OPPOSITE = *praise*

Example 9

Opposite of PRECURSORY:

- (A) succeeding
- (B) flamboyant
- (C) cautious
- (D) simple
- (E) cheap

Choice A is correct.
pre- = before; *curs* = to run; *precursory* = running before
OPPOSITE = *succeeding*

Example 10

Opposite of CIRCUMVENT:

- (A) to go the straight route
- (B) alleviate
- (C) to prey on one's emotions
- (D) scintillate
- (E) perceive correctly

Choice A is correct.
circum- = around (like a circle); *vent* = to come; *circumvent* = to come around
OPPOSITE = *to go the straight route*

Vocabulary Strategy 2

Pay Attention to the Sound or Feeling of the Word—Whether Positive or Negative, Harsh or Mild, Big or Little, Etc.

If the word sounds harsh or terrible, such as "obstreperous," the meaning probably is something harsh or terrible. If you're looking for a word opposite in meaning to *obstreperous*, look for a word or words that have a softer sound, such as *docile*. The sense of *obstreperous* can also seem to be negative—so if you're looking for a synonym, look for a negative word. If you're looking for an opposite (antonym), look for a positive word.

Example 1

Opposite of BELLIGERENCY:

- (A) pain
- (B) silence
- (C) homeliness
- (D) elegance
- (E) peacefulness

Choice E is correct. The word *belligerency* imparts a tone of forcefulness or confusion and means "warlike." The opposite would be calmness or peacefulness. The closest choices are B or E, with E a little closer to the opposite in tone for the capitalized word. Of course, if you knew the root *belli* means "war," you could see the opposite as (E) peacefulness.

Example 2

Opposite of DEGRADE:

- (A) startle
- (B) elevate
- (C) encircle
- (D) replace
- (E) inspire

Choice B is correct. Here you can think of the *de-* in *degrade* as a prefix that is negative (bad) and means "down," and in fact *degrade* does mean "to debase" or "lower." So you should look for an opposite that would be a word with a positive (good) meaning. The best word from the choices is (B) elevate.

Example 3

Opposite of OBFUSCATION:

- (A) illumination
- (B) irritation
- (C) conviction
- (D) minor offense
- (E) stable environment

Choice A is correct. The prefix *ob-* is usually negative, as in obstacle or obliterate, and in fact *obfuscate* means "darken" or "obscure." So since we are looking for an opposite, you would look for a positive word. Choices A and E are positive, and you should go for the more positive of the two, which is Choice A.

Example 4

Opposite of MUNIFICENCE:

- (A) disloyalty
- (B) stinginess
- (C) dispersion
- (D) simplicity
- (E) vehemence

Choice B is correct because *munificence* means "generosity." Many of the words ending in *-ence*, like *opulence*, *effervescence*, *luminescence*, *quintessence*, etc., represent or describe something big or bright. So the opposite of one of these words would denote something small or dark.

You can associate the prefix *muni-* with money, so the word *munificence* must deal with money and in a big way. The opposite deals with money in a small way. Choice B fits the bill.

Example 5

Opposite of DETRIMENT:

- (A) recurrence
- (B) disclosure
- (C) resemblance
- (D) enhancement
- (E) postponement

Choice D is correct. The prefix *de-* can also mean "against" and is negative, and *detriment* means "something that causes damage or loss." So you should look for a positive word. The only one is D, enhancement.

Example 6

Opposite of UNDERSTATE:

- (A) embroider
- (B) initiate
- (C) distort
- (D) pacify
- (E) violate

Choice A is correct. *Understate* means "to express something in a restrained or downplayed manner." You see "under" in *understate*, so look for a choice that gives you the impression of something that is "over," as in "overstated." The only choice is A, embroider, which means "to embellish."

Example 7

Opposite of DISHEARTEN:

- (A) engage
- (B) encourage
- (C) predict
- (D) dismember
- (E) misinform

Choice B is correct. You see *heart* in *dishearten*. The *dis-* is negative and means "not to," or "not to have heart," and *dishearten* does mean "to discourage." So you want to look for a positive word. Choice B, encourage, fits the bill.

Example 8

Opposite of FIREBRAND:

- (A) an intellect
- (B) one who is charitable
- (C) one who makes peace
- (D) a philanthropist
- (E) one who is dishonest

Choice C is correct. You see *fire* in *firebrand*. So think of something fiery or dangerous. The opposite of *firebrand* must be something that's calm or safe. The best choice is Choice C.

Vocabulary Strategy 3

Use Word Associations to Determine Word Meanings and Their Opposites

Looking at the root or part of any capitalized word may suggest an association with another word that looks similar and whose meaning you know. This new word's meaning may give you a clue as to the meaning of the original word or the opposite in meaning to the original word if you need an opposite. For example, *extricate* reminds us of the word *extract*, the opposite of which is "to put together."

Example 1

Opposite of STASIS:

- (A) stoppage
- (B) reduction
- (C) depletion
- (D) fluctuation
- (E) completion

Choice D is correct. Think of *static* or *stationary*. The opposite would be *moving* or *fluctuating* since *stasis* means "stopping" or "retarding movement."

Example 2

Opposite of APPEASE:

- (A) criticize
- (B) analyze
- (C) correct
- (D) incense
- (E) develop

Choice D is correct. *Appease* means "to placate." Think of *peace* in *appease*. The opposite would be "to enrage" or "incense."

Example 3

Opposite of COMMISERATION:

- (A) undeserved reward
- (B) lack of sympathy
- (C) unexpected success
- (D) absence of talent
- (E) inexplicable danger

Choice B is correct. Think of *misery* in the word *commiseration. Co-* refers to sharing, as in "cooperate." *Commiseration* means "the sharing of misery." Choice B is the only appropriate choice.

Example 4

Opposite of JOCULAR:

- (A) unintentional
- (B) exotic
- (C) muscular
- (D) exaggerated
- (E) serious

Choice E is correct. Think of *joke* in the word *jocular,* which means "given to joking." The opposite would be *serious.*

Example 5

Opposite of ELONGATE:

- (A) melt
- (B) wind
- (C) confuse
- (D) smooth
- (E) shorten

Choice E is correct. Think of the word *long* in *elongate,* which means "to lengthen." The opposite would be short or *shorten.*

Example 6

Opposite of SLOTHFUL:

- (A) permanent
- (B) industrious
- (C) average
- (D) truthful
- (E) plentiful

Choice B is correct. Think of *sloth*, a very, very slow animal. So *slothful*, which means "lazy" or "sluggish," must be slow and unambitious. The opposite would be *industrious.*

Example 7

Opposite of FORTITUDE:

- (A) timidity
- (B) conservatism
- (C) placidity
- (D) laxness
- (E) ambition

Choice A is correct. *Fortitude* means "strength in the face of adversity"; you should think of *fort* or *fortify* as something strong. The opposite would be weakness or *timidity.*

Example 8

Opposite of LUCID:

- (A) underlying
- (B) abstruse
- (C) luxurious
- (D) tight
- (E) general

Choice B is correct. *Lucid* means "easily understood" or "clear"; you should think of lucite, a clear plastic. The opposite of *clear* is "hard to see through" or *abstruse. Note*: The *ab-* in *abstruse* makes Choice B the only negative choice, which is the opposite of the positive word *lucid.*

Example 9

Opposite of POTENT:

- (A) imposing
- (B) pertinent
- (C) feeble
- (D) comparable
- (E) frantic

Choice C is correct. Think of the word *potential* or *powerful.* To have potential is to have the ability or power to be able to do something. So the opposite would be *feeble.* You could also have thought of *potent* as a positive word. The opposite would be a negative word. The only two choices that are negative are Choices C and E.

PART 5

Mini Math Refresher

The Most Important Basic Math Rules and Concepts You Need to Know

Make sure that you understand each of the following math rules and concepts. It is a good idea to memorize them all. Refer to the section of the Complete SAT Math Refresher (Part 6 starting on page 163) shown in parentheses, e.g., (409), for a complete explanation of each.

ALGEBRA AND ARITHMETIC

Percentage Problems

(107)

Percentage

$x\% = \dfrac{x}{100}$

Example:

$5\% = \dfrac{5}{100}$

(107)

RULE:

"What" becomes x

"percent" becomes $\dfrac{x}{100}$

"of" becomes $\times$ (times)

"is" becomes $=$ (equals)

Examples:

(1) What percent of 5 is 2?

$\dfrac{x}{100}$ $\times 5 = 2$

or

$\left(\dfrac{x}{100}\right)(5) = 2$

$\dfrac{5x}{100} = 2$

$5x = 200$

$x = 40$

Answer = 40%

(2) 6 is what percent of 24?

$6 = \dfrac{x}{100}$ $\times 24$

$6 = \dfrac{24x}{100}$

$600 = 24x$

$100 = 4x$ (dividing both sides by 6)

$25 = x$

Answer = 25%

Equations

(407)

Example:

$x + y = 1$; $x - y = 2$. Solve for x and y.

Procedure:

Add equations:

$x + y = 1$
$\underline{x - y = 2}$
$2x + 0 = 3$

Therefore $2x = 3$ and $x = \dfrac{3}{2}$

Substitute $x = \dfrac{3}{2}$ back into one of the equations:

$x + y = 1$

$\dfrac{3}{2} + y = 1$

$y = -\dfrac{1}{2}$

Factoring

(409)

Example:
$x^2 - 2x + 1 = 0$. Solve for x.

Note that in general:
$(mx + b)(nx + c) = mnx^2 + bnx + mxc + bc$

Procedure:
Factor: $(x - 1)(x - 1) = 0$
$$x - 1 = 0$$
$$x = 1$$

In the example $x^2 - 2x + 1 = 0$, $m = 1, n = 1, b = -1, c = -1$, so
$(x - 1)(x - 1) = (1)(1)x^2 + (-1)(1)x + (1)x(-1) + (-1)(-1)$
$$= x^2 + -x + -x + 1$$
$$= x^2 - 2x + 1$$

(409)

$(a + b)(c + d) = ac + ad + bc + bd$

Example:
$(2 + 3)(4 - 6) = (2)(4) + (2)(-6) + (3)(4) + (3)(-6)$
$$= 8 - 12 + 12 - 18$$
$$= -10$$

(409)

$a(b + c) = ab + ac$

Example:
$5(4 + 5) = 5(4) + 5(5)$
$$= 20 + 25$$
$$= 45$$

(409)

$(a + b)^2 = a^2 + 2ab + b^2$

Example:
$(9 + 1)^2 = 9^2 + 2(9)(1) + 1^2$
$$= 81 + 18 + 1$$
$$= 100$$

(409)

$(a - b)^2 = a^2 - 2ab + b^2$

Example:
$(9 - 1)^2 = 9^2 - 2(9)(1) + 1^2$
$$= 81 - 18 + 1$$
$$= 64$$

(409)

$(a + b)(a - b) = a^2 - b^2$

Example:
$(10 + 9)(10 - 9)$
$$= (10)(10) - (9)(9)$$
$100 - 81 = 19$

(409)

$-(a - b) = b - a$

Example:
$-(5 - 4) = 4 - 5 = -1$

Exponents and Roots

(429)

$a^2 = (a)(a)$

Examples:

$2^2 = (2)(2) = 4$

$a^3 = (a)(a)(a)$

(429)

$a^x a^y = a^{x+y}$

Examples:

$a^2 \times a^3 = a^5$

$2^2 \times 2^3 = 2^5 = 32$

(429)

$(a^x)^y = a^{xy}$

Examples:

$(a^3)^5 = a^{15}$

$(2^3)^5 = 2^{15}$

(429)

$(ab)^x = a^x b^x$

Examples:

$(2 \times 3)^3 = 2^3 \times 3^3$

$(ab)^2 = a^2 b^2$

(429)

$a^{-y} = \dfrac{1}{a^y}$

Example:

$2^{-3} = \dfrac{1}{2^3} = \dfrac{1}{8}$

(429)

$a^0 = 1$

$10^0 = 1$

$10^1 = 10$

$10^2 = 100$

$10^3 = 1,000$, etc.

Example:

$8.6 \times 10^4 = 8.6\,0\,0\,0\,.\,0$

Move decimal 4   1 2 3 4
places to the right

The end result is 86,000.

(429)

$\dfrac{a^x}{a^y} = a^{x-y}$

Examples:

$\dfrac{a^3}{a^2} = a^{3-2} = a$

$\dfrac{2^3}{2^2} = 2^{3-2} = 2$

(430)

If $y^2 = x$, then $y = \pm\sqrt{x}$.

Example:

If $y^2 = 4$, then $y = \pm\sqrt{4} = \pm 2$.

Equalities

(402)

$$
\begin{array}{ll}
a + b = c & 3 + 4 = 7 \\
\underline{+ d = d} & \underline{+ 2 = 2} \\
a + b + d = c + d & 3 + 4 + 2 = 7 + 2
\end{array}
$$

Inequalities

(419–425)

$>$ means "greater than," $<$ means "less than," $\geq$ means "greater than or equal to," $\leq$ means "less than or equal to."

$$
\begin{array}{lll}
b > c & 4 > 3 & 4 > 3 \\
\underline{+\ d > e} & \underline{+\ 7 > 6} & \underline{+\ {-6} > -7} \\
b + d > c + e & 11 > 9 & -2 > -4
\end{array}
$$

Note: Multiplying both sides of an inequality by -1 reverses the order of the inequality.

$$
\begin{array}{l|l}
5 > 4 & -5 < -4 \\
(6)5 > (6)4 & -(-5) > -(-4) \\
\text{Thus} & \text{Thus} \\
30 > 24 & 5 > 4
\end{array}
$$

If $-2 < x < +2$ then $+2 > -x > -2$

If $a > b > 0$ then $a^2 > b^2$

GEOMETRY

Angles

(501)

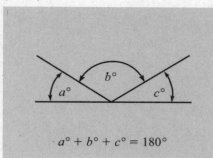

$$a° + b° + c° = 180°$$

(504)

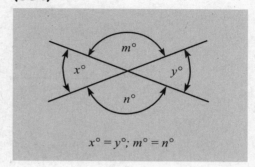

$$x° = y°; m° = n°$$

(504)

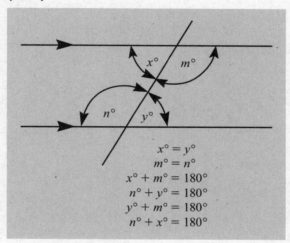

$$x° = y°$$
$$m° = n°$$
$$x° + m° = 180°$$
$$n° + y° = 180°$$
$$y° + m° = 180°$$
$$n° + x° = 180°$$

Triangles

(501)

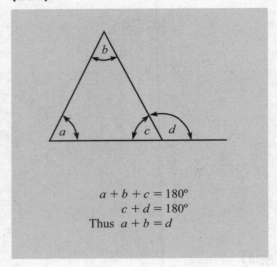

$$a + b + c = 180°$$
$$c + d = 180°$$
Thus $a + b = d$

(506)

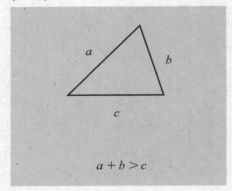

$$a + b > c$$

(506)

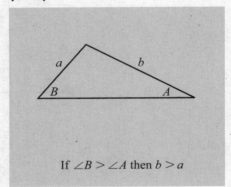

If $\angle B > \angle A$ then $b > a$

(507)

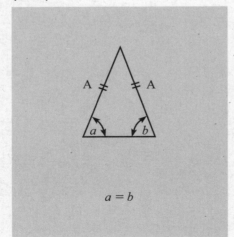

$$a = b$$

(510)

Similar Triangles

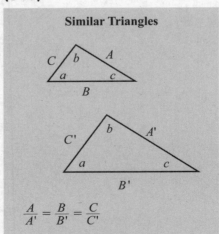

$$\frac{A}{A'} = \frac{B}{B'} = \frac{C}{C'}$$

Triangles—Pythagorean Theorem
Note: Figures not drawn to scale.

(509)

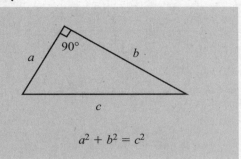

$$a^2 + b^2 = c^2$$

(509)

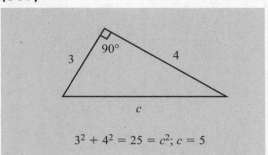

$$3^2 + 4^2 = 25 = c^2; c = 5$$

(509)

Important Right Triangle Relations

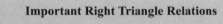

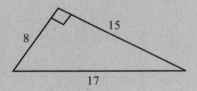

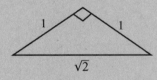

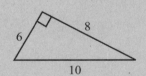

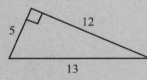

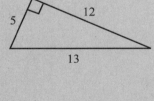

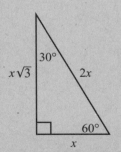

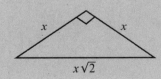

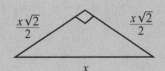

Areas and Perimeters

(304)

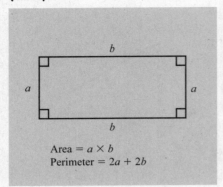

Area = $a \times b$
Perimeter = $2a + 2b$

(305)

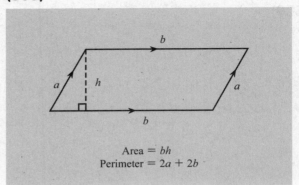

Area = bh
Perimeter = $2a + 2b$

(306)

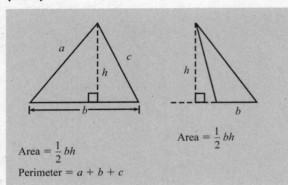

Area = $\frac{1}{2}bh$

Area = $\frac{1}{2}bh$
Perimeter = $a + b + c$

(310)

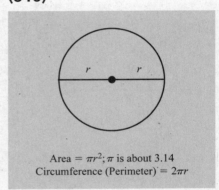

Area = πr^2; π is about 3.14
Circumference (Perimeter) = $2\pi r$

Circles

(526–527)

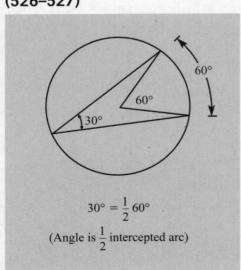

$30° = \frac{1}{2} 60°$

(Angle is $\frac{1}{2}$ intercepted arc)

(527)

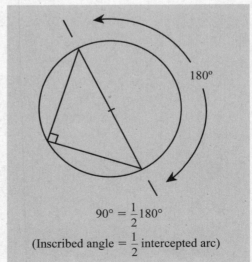

$90° = \frac{1}{2} 180°$

(Inscribed angle = $\frac{1}{2}$ intercepted arc)

Coordinate Geometry

(410a)

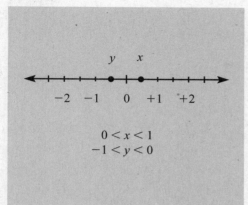

$$0 < x < 1$$
$$-1 < y < 0$$

(410b)

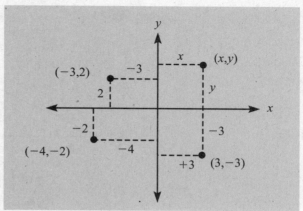

(411)

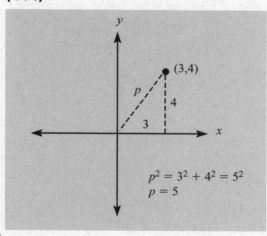

$$p^2 = 3^2 + 4^2 = 5^2$$
$$p = 5$$

(416)

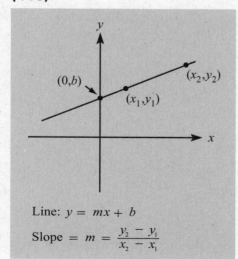

Line: $y = mx + b$

Slope $= m = \dfrac{y_2 - y_1}{x_2 - x_1}$

(416)

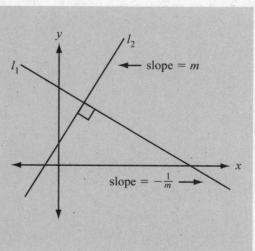

slope $= m$

slope $= -\dfrac{1}{m}$

TRIGONOMETRY

(901)

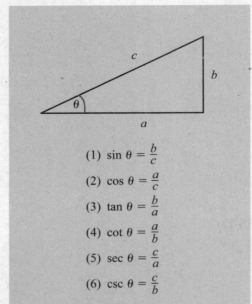

(1) $\sin \theta = \dfrac{b}{c}$

(2) $\cos \theta = \dfrac{a}{c}$

(3) $\tan \theta = \dfrac{b}{a}$

(4) $\cot \theta = \dfrac{a}{b}$

(5) $\sec \theta = \dfrac{c}{a}$

(6) $\csc \theta = \dfrac{c}{b}$

PART 6

Complete SAT Math Refresher

There are many SAT exam takers whose math backgrounds are not quite up to par—probably because their basic math skills are rusty or because they never did do well in their math classes. For these math-troubled students, this Math Refresher section will be "manna from heaven." The pages that follow constitute a complete basic math course that will help students greatly in preparing for the math part of the SAT. *Note*: Many of the examples or methods can be done with a calculator, but it is wise for students to know how to solve problems without a calculator.

This Math Refresher offers the following:

1. a systematic review of every math area covered by the questions in the math part of the SAT

   and

2. short review tests throughout the Refresher to check whether the student has grasped the math principles that he or she has just studied.

The review tests will also provide students with valuable reinforcement so that they will remember how to go about solving math problems they would otherwise have difficulty with on the actual SAT.

Each of the 9 "Sessions" in this Math Refresher has a section of math principles, numbered "Refreshers," followed by a review test or "Practice Test." Almost every review test has 50 questions followed by 50 detailed solutions. All of the solutions for the 9 review tests include a number (or numbers) in parentheses *after each solution*. These numbers refer back to one or more of that Session's Refreshers, which explain, clearly and simply, the rules and principles pertaining to the question.

There is another very important purpose that this Math Refresher serves. You will find, after every solution in the math sections of the 2 SAT Practice Tests in this book, a key to the mathematical principles of this Math Refresher. For example, a solution may direct you to Math Refresher 202, which deals with distance and time problems. If you happen to be weak in this mathematical operation, the Math Refresher 202 explanation will immediately clarify for you how to do distance and time problems. In other words, for those who are weak in any area of Basic Math, this invaluable keying system will help you get the right answer to your SAT math question—and thereby increase your SAT score.

Mathematical Symbols

·	multiplication dot; as in $x \cdot y$	π	pi, the ratio of the circumference of a circle to its diameter, which is approximately equal to $\frac{22}{7}$ or 3.14.
( )	parentheses; used to group expressions		
%	percent		
÷	division	$\angle$	angle
:	ratio	$\parallel$	is parallel to
=	equals	$\perp$	is perpendicular to
≠	does not equal	$\wedge$	and
<	less than	$\vee$	or
>	greater than	~	is similar to, or approximately
≤	less than or equal to	→	implies
≥	greater than or equal to	$\in$	belongs to
$\sqrt{\ }$	square root	$\subset$	is a subset of

MATH REFRESHER SESSION 1

Fractions, Decimals, Percentages, Deviations, Ratios and Proportions, Variations, and Comparison of Fractions

Fractions, Decimals, Percentages

These problems involve the ability to perform numerical operations quickly and correctly. It is essential that you learn the arithmetical procedures outlined in this section.

101. Four different ways to write "a divided by b" are

$$a \div b, \frac{a}{b}, a : b, b\overline{)a}.$$

Example: 7 divided by 15 is

$$7 \div 15 = \frac{7}{15} = 7 : 15 = 15\overline{)7}.$$

102. The numerator of a fraction is the upper number and the denominator is the lower number.

Example: In the fraction $\frac{8}{13}$, the numerator is 8 and the denominator is 13.

103. Moving a decimal point one place to the right multiplies the value of a number by 10, whereas moving the decimal point one place to the left divides a number by 10. Likewise, moving a decimal point two places to the right multiplies the value of a number by 100, whereas moving the decimal point two places to the left divides a number by 100.

Example: $24.35 \times 10 = 243.5$
(decimal point moved to *right*)
$24.35 \div 10 = 2.435$
(decimal point moved to *left*)

104. To change a fraction to a decimal, divide the numerator of the fraction by its denominator.

Example: Express $\frac{5}{6}$ as a decimal. We divide 5 by 6, obtaining 0.83.

$$\frac{5}{6} = 5 \div 6 = 0.833 \ldots$$

105. To convert a decimal to a fraction, delete the decimal point and divide by whatever unit of 10 the number of decimal places represents.

Example: Convert 0.83 to a fraction. First, delete the decimal point. Second, two decimal places represent hundredths, so divide 83 by 100: $\frac{83}{100}$.

$$0.83 = \frac{83}{100}$$

106. To change a fraction to a percent, find its decimal form, multiply by 100, and add a percent sign.

Example: Express $\frac{3}{8}$ as a percent. To convert $\frac{3}{8}$ to a decimal, divide 3 by 8, which gives us 0.375. Multiplying 0.375 by 100 gives us 37.5%.

107. To change a percent to a fraction, drop the percent sign and divide the number by 100.

Example: Express 17% as a fraction. Dropping the % sign gives us 17, and dividing by 100 gives us $\frac{17}{100}$.

108. To *reduce* a fraction, divide the numerator and denominator by the largest number that divides them both evenly.

Example: Reduce $\frac{10}{15}$. Dividing both the numerator and denominator by 5 gives us $\frac{2}{3}$.

Example: Reduce $\frac{12}{36}$. The largest number that divides into both 12 and 36 is 12. Reducing the fraction, we have

$$\frac{\overset{1}{\cancel{12}}}{\underset{3}{\cancel{36}}} = \frac{1}{3}.$$

Note: In both examples, the reduced fraction is exactly equal to the original fraction:

$$\frac{2}{3} = \frac{10}{15} \text{ and } \frac{12}{36} = \frac{1}{3}.$$

109. To add fractions with like denominators, add the numerators of the fractions, keeping the same denominator.

Example: $\frac{1}{7} + \frac{2}{7} + \frac{3}{7} = \frac{6}{7}$.

110. To add fractions with different denominators, you must first change all of the fractions to *equivalent fractions* with the same denominator.

Step 1. Find the *lowest (or least) common denominator*, the smallest number divisible by all of the denominators.

Example: If the fractions to be added are $\frac{1}{3}$, $\frac{1}{4}$, and $\frac{5}{6}$, then the lowest common denominator is 12, because 12 is the smallest number that is divisible by 3, 4, and 6.

Step 2. Convert all of the fractions to *equivalent fractions*, each having the lowest common denominator as its denominator. To do this, multiply the numerator of each fraction by the number of times that its denominator goes into the lowest common denominator. The product of this multiplication will be the *new numerator*. The denominator of the equivalent fractions will be the lowest common denominator. (See Step 1 above.)

Example: The lowest common denominator of $\frac{1}{3}$, $\frac{1}{4}$, and $\frac{5}{6}$ is 12. Thus, $\frac{1}{3} = \frac{4}{12}$, because 12 divided by 3 is 4, and 4 times $1 = 4$. $\frac{1}{4} = \frac{3}{12}$, because 12 divided by 4 is 3, and 3 times $1 = 3$. $\frac{5}{6} = \frac{10}{12}$, because 12 divided by 6 is 2, and 2 times $5 = 10$.

Step 3. Now add all of the equivalent fractions by adding the numerators.

Example: $\frac{4}{12} + \frac{3}{12} + \frac{10}{12} = \frac{17}{12}$

Step 4. Reduce the fraction if possible, as shown in Section 108.

Example: Add $\frac{4}{5}$, $\frac{2}{3}$, and $\frac{8}{15}$. The lowest common denominator is 15, because 15 is the smallest number that is divisible by 5, 3, and 15. Then, $\frac{4}{5}$ is equivalent to $\frac{12}{15}$; $\frac{2}{3}$ is equivalent to $\frac{10}{15}$; and $\frac{8}{15}$ remains as $\frac{8}{15}$. Adding these numbers gives us

$\frac{12}{15} + \frac{10}{15} + \frac{8}{15} = \frac{30}{15}$. Both 30 and 15 are divisible by 15, giving us $\frac{2}{1}$, or 2.

111. To *multiply fractions,* follow this procedure:

Step 1. To find the numerator of the product, multiply all the numerators of the fractions being multiplied.

Step 2. To find the denominator of the product, multiply all of the denominators of the fractions being multiplied.

Step 3. Reduce the product.

Example: $\frac{5}{7} \times \frac{2}{15} = \frac{\overset{1}{\cancel{5}}}{7} \times \frac{2}{\underset{3}{\cancel{15}}} = \frac{2}{21}$.

We reduced by dividing both the numerator and denominator by 5, the common factor.

112. To *divide fractions,* follow this procedure:

Step 1. Invert the divisor. That is, switch the positions of the numerator and denominator in the fraction you are dividing *by.*

Step 2. Replace the division sign with a multiplication sign.

Step 3. Carry out the multiplication indicated.

Step 4. Reduce the product.

Example: Find $\frac{3}{4} \div \frac{7}{8}$. Inverting $\frac{7}{8}$, the divisor, gives us $\frac{8}{7}$. Replacing the division sign with a multiplication sign gives us $\frac{3}{4} \times \frac{8}{7}$. Carrying out the multiplication gives us $\frac{3}{4} \times \frac{8}{7} = \frac{24}{28}$. The fraction $\frac{24}{28}$ may then be reduced to $\frac{6}{7}$ by dividing both the numerator and the denominator by 4.

113. To *multiply decimals*, follow this procedure:

Step 1. Disregard the decimal point. Multiply the factors (the numbers being multiplied) as if they were whole numbers.

Step 2. In each factor, count the number of digits to the *right* of the decimal point. Find the total number of these digits in all the factors. In the product, start at the right and count to the left this (total) number of places. Put the decimal point there.

Example: Multiply 3.8×4.01. First, multiply 38 and 401, getting 15,238. There is a total of 3 digits to the right of the decimal points in the factors. Therefore, the decimal point in the product is placed 3 units to the left of the digit farthest to the right (8).

$$3.8 \times 4.01 = 15.238$$

Example: 0.025×3.6. First, multiply 25×36, getting 900. In the factors, there is a total of 4 digits to the right of the decimal points; therefore, in the product, we place the decimal point 4 units to the left of the digit farthest to the right in 900. However, there are only 3 digits in the product, so we add a 0 to the left of the 9, getting 0900. This makes it possible to place the decimal point correctly, thus: 0.0900, or 0.09. From this example, we can derive the rule that in the product we add as many zeros as are needed to provide the proper number of digits to the left of the digit farthest to the right.

114. To find a percent of a given quantity:

Step 1. Replace the word "of" with a multiplication sign.

Step 2. Convert the percent to a decimal: drop the percent sign and divide the number by 100. This is done by moving the decimal point two places to the left, adding zeros where necessary.

Examples:
$30\% = 0.30$ $2.1\% = 0.021$ $78\% = 0.78$

Step 3. Multiply the given quantity by the decimal.

Example: Find 30% of 200.

30% of $200 = 30\% \times 200 = 0.30 \times 200 = 60.00$

Deviations

Estimation problems arise when dealing with approximations, that is, numbers that are not mathematically precise. The error, or *deviation*, in an approximation is a measure of the closeness of that approximation.

115. *Absolute error*, or *absolute deviation*, is the difference between the estimated value and the real value (or between the approximate value and the exact value).

Example: If the actual value of a measurement is 60.2 and we estimate it as 60, then the absolute deviation (absolute error) is $60.2 - 60 = 0.2$.

116. *Fractional error*, or *fractional deviation*, is the ratio of the absolute error to the exact value of the quantity being measured.

Example: If the exact value is 60.2 and the estimated value is 60, then the fractional error is

$$\frac{60.2 - 60}{60.2} = \frac{0.2}{60.2} = \frac{0.2 \times 5}{60.2 \times 5} = \frac{1}{301}$$

117. *Percent error,* or *percent deviation,* is the fractional error expressed as a percent. (See Section 106 on page 165 for the method of converting fractions to percents.)

118. Many business problems, including the calculation of loss, profit, interest, and so forth, are treated as deviation problems. Generally, these problems concern the difference between the original value of a quantity and some new value after taxes, after interest, etc. The following chart shows the relationship between business and estimation problems.

Business Problems	Estimation Problems
original value	= exact value
new value	= approximate value
net profit net loss net interest	= absolute error
fractional profit fractional loss fractional interest	= fractional error
percent profit percent loss percent interest	= percent error

Example: An item that originally cost $50 is resold for $56.

Thus the *net profit* is $56 - 50 = 6$.

The *fractional profit* is $\dfrac{\$56 - \$50}{\$50} = \dfrac{\$6}{\$50} = \dfrac{3}{25}$.

The *percent profit* is equal to the percent equivalent of $\dfrac{3}{25}$, which is 12%. (See Section 106 for converting fractions to percents.)

119. When there are two or more *consecutive changes in value,* remember that the new value of the first change becomes the original value of the second; consequently, successive fractional or percent changes may not be added directly.

Example: Suppose that a $100 item is reduced by 10% and then by 20%. The first reduction puts the price at $90 (10% of $100 = $10; $100 − $10 = $90). Then, reducing the $90 (the new original value) by 20% gives us $72 (20% of $90 = $18; $90 − $18 = $72). Therefore, it is *not* correct to simply add 10% and 20% and then take 30% of $100.

Ratios and Proportions

120. A *proportion* is an equation stating that two ratios are equal. For example, $3 : 2 = 9 : x$ and $7 : 4 = a : 15$ are proportions. To solve for a variable in a proportion:

Step 1. First change the ratios to fractions. To do this, remember that $a : b$ is the same as $\frac{a}{b}$, or $1 : 2$ is equivalent to $\frac{1}{2}$, or $7 : 4 = a : 15$ is the same as $\frac{7}{4} = \frac{a}{15}$.

Step 2. Now cross-multiply. That is, multiply the numerator of the first fraction by the denominator of the second fraction. Also multiply the denominator of the first fraction by the numerator of the second fraction. Set the first product equal to the second. This rule is sometimes stated as "The product of the means equals the product of the extremes."

Example: When cross-multiplying in the equation $\frac{3}{2} = \frac{9}{y}$, we get $3 \times y = 2 \times 9$, or $3y = 18$. Dividing by 3, we get $y = 6$.

When we cross-multiply in the equation $\frac{a}{2} = \frac{4}{8}$, we get $8a = 8$, and by dividing each side of the equation by 8 to reduce, $a = 1$.

Step 3. Solve the resulting equation. This is done algebraically.

Example: Solve for a in the proportion $7 : a = 6 : 18$.

Change the ratios to the fractional relation $\frac{7}{a} = \frac{6}{18}$. Cross-multiply: $7 \times 18 = 6 \times a$, or $126 = 6a$.

Solving for a gives us $a = 21$.

121. In solving proportions that have units of measurement (feet, seconds, miles, etc.), each ratio must have the same units. For example, if we have the ratio 5 inches : 3 feet, we must convert the 3 feet to 36 inches and then set up the ratio 5 inches : 36 inches, or 5 : 36. We might wish to convert inches to feet. Noting that 1 inch = $\frac{1}{12}$ foot, we get 5 inches : 3 feet = $5\left(\frac{1}{12}\right)$ feet: 3 feet = $\frac{5}{12}$ feet : 3 feet.

Example: On a blueprint, a rectangle measures 6 inches in width and 9 inches in length. If the actual width of the rectangle is 16 inches, how many feet are there in the length?

Solution: We set up the proportions, 6 inches : 9 inches = 16 inches : x feet. Since x feet is equal to $12x$ inches, we substitute this value in the proportion. Thus, 6 inches : 9 inches = 16 inches : $12x$ inches. Since all of the units are now the same, we may work with the numbers alone. In fractional terms we have $\frac{6}{9} = \frac{16}{12x}$. Cross-multiplication gives us $72x = 144$, and solving for x gives us $x = 2$. The rectangle is 2 feet long.

Variations

122. In a *variation* problem, you are given a relationship between certain variables. The problem is to determine the change in one variable when one or more of the other variables change.

Direct Variation (Direct Proportion)

If x varies directly with y, this means that $\frac{x}{y} = k$ (or $x = ky$) where k is a constant.

Example: If the cost of a piece of glass varies directly with the area of the glass, and a piece of glass of 5 square feet costs $20, then how much does a piece of glass of 15 square feet cost?

Represent the cost of the glass as c and the area of the piece of glass as A. Then we have $\frac{c}{A} = k$.

Now since we are given that a piece of glass of 5 square feet costs \$20, we can write $\frac{20}{5} = k$, and we find $k = 4$.

Let's say a piece of glass of 15 square feet costs \$$x$. Then we can write $\frac{x}{15} = k$. But we found $k = 4$, so $\frac{x}{15} = 4$ and $x = 60$. \$60 is then the answer.

Inverse Variation (Inverse Proportion)

If x varies inversely with y, this means that $xy = k$ where k is a constant.

Example: If a varies inversely with b, and when $a = 5$, $b = 6$, then what is b when $a = 10$?

We have $ab = k$. Since $a = 5$ and $b = 6$, $5 \times 6 = k = 30$. So if $a = 10$, $10 \times b = k = 30$ and $b = 3$.

Other Variations

Example: In the formula $A = bh$, if b doubles and h triples, what happens to the value of A?

Step 1. Express the new values of the variables in terms of their original values, that is, $b' = 2b$ and $h' = 3h$.

Step 2. Substitute these values in the formula and solve for the desired variable: $A' = b'h' = (2b)(3h) = 6bh$.

Step 3. Express this answer in terms of the original value of the variable, that is, since the new value of A is $6bh$, and the old value of A was bh, we can express this as $A_{new} = 6A_{old}$. The new value of the variable is expressed with a prime mark and the old value of the variable is left as it was. In this problem, the new value of A would be expressed as A' and the old value as A. $A' = 6A$.

Example: If $V = e^3$ and e is doubled, what happens to the value of V?

Solution: Replace e with $2e$. The new value of V is $(2e)^3$. Since this is a new value, V becomes V'. Thus $V' = (2e)^3$, or $8e^3$. Remember, from the original statement of the problem, that $V = e^3$. Using this, we may substitute V for e^3 found in the equation $V' = 8e^3$. The new equation is $V' = 8V$. Therefore, the new value of V is 8 times the old value.

Comparison of Fractions

In *fraction comparison* problems, you are given two or more fractions and are asked to arrange them in increasing or decreasing order, or to select the larger or the smaller. The following rules and suggestions will be very helpful in determining which of two fractions is greater.

123. If fractions A and B have the same denominator, and A has a larger numerator, then fraction A is larger. (We are assuming here, and for the rest of this Refresher Session, that numerators and denominators are positive.)

   Example: $\frac{56}{271}$ is greater than $\frac{53}{271}$ because the numerator of the first fraction is greater than the numerator of the second.

124. If fractions A and B have the same numerator, and A has a larger denominator, then fraction A is smaller.

   Example: $\frac{37}{256}$ is smaller than $\frac{37}{254}$.

125. If fraction A has a larger numerator and a smaller denominator than fraction B, then fraction A is larger than B.

   Example: $\frac{6}{11}$ is larger than $\frac{4}{13}$. (If this does not seem obvious, compare both fractions with $\frac{6}{13}$.)

126. Another method is to convert all of the fractions to equivalent fractions. To do this follow these steps:

   Step 1. First find the *lowest common denominator* of the fractions. This is the smallest number that is divisible by all of the denominators of the original fractions. See Section 110 for the method of finding lowest common denominators.

   Step 2. The fraction with the greatest numerator is the largest fraction.

127. Still another method is the *conversion to approximating decimals*.

   Example: To compare $\frac{5}{9}$ and $\frac{7}{11}$, we might express both as decimals to a few places of accuracy: $\frac{5}{9}$ is approximately equal to 0.555, while $\frac{7}{11}$ is approximately equal to 0.636, so $\frac{7}{11}$ is obviously greater.

   To express a fraction as a decimal, divide the numerator by the denominator.

128. If all of the fractions being compared are very close in value to some easy-to-work-with number, such as $\frac{1}{2}$ or 5, you may subtract this number from each of the fractions without changing this order.

Example: To compare $\frac{151}{75}$ with $\frac{328}{163}$, we notice that both of these fractions are approximately equal to 2. If we subtract 2 (that is, $\frac{150}{75}$ and $\frac{326}{163}$, respectively) from each, we get $\frac{1}{75}$ and $\frac{2}{163}$, respectively. Since $\frac{1}{75}$ (or $\frac{2}{150}$) exceeds $\frac{2}{163}$, we see that $\frac{151}{75}$ must also exceed $\frac{328}{163}$.

An alternative method of comparing fractions is to change the fractions to their decimal equivalents and then compare the decimals. (See Sections 104 and 127.) You should weigh the relative amount of work and difficulty involved in each method when you face each problem.

129. The following is a quick way of comparing fractions.

Example: Which is greater, $\frac{3}{8}$ or $\frac{7}{18}$?

Procedure:

$$\frac{3}{8} \underset{multiply}{\overset{multiply}{\rlap{\hspace{2em}}\times}} \frac{7}{18}$$

Multiply the 18 by the 3. We get 54. Put the 54 on the *left* side.

    54

Now *multiply* the 8 by the 7. We get 56. Put the 56 on the *right* side.

    54   56

Since $56 > 54$ and 56 is on the *right* side, the fraction $\frac{7}{18}$ (which was also originally on the *right* side) is *greater* than the fraction $\frac{3}{8}$ (which was originally on the *left* side).

Example: If $y > x$, which is greater, $\frac{1}{x}$ or $\frac{1}{y}$? (x and y are positive numbers.)

Procedure:

$$\frac{1}{x} \underset{multiply}{\overset{multiply}{\rlap{\hspace{2em}}\times}} \frac{1}{y}$$

Multiply y by 1. We get y. Put y on the left side:

    y

Multiply x by 1. We get x. Put x on the right side:

    y x

Since $y > x$ (given), $\frac{1}{x}$ (which was originally on the left) is greater than $\frac{1}{y}$ (which was originally on the right).

Example: Which is greater?

$$\frac{7}{9} \qquad or \qquad \frac{3}{4}$$

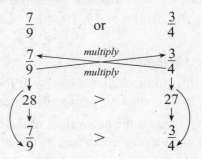

SESSION 1 PRACTICE TEST

Fractions, Decimals, Percentages, Deviations, Ratios and Proportions, Variations, and Comparison of Fractions

Correct answers and solutions follow this test.

1. Which of the following answers is the sum of the following numbers:

$$2\frac{1}{2}, \frac{21}{4}, 3.350, \frac{1}{8}?$$

(A) 8.225
(B) 9.825
(C) 10.825
(D) 11.225
(E) 12.350

A B C D E
○ ○ ○ ○ ○

2. A chemist was preparing a solution that should have included 35 milligrams of a chemical. If she actually used 36.4 milligrams, what was her percentage error (to the nearest 0.01%)?

(A) 0.04%
(B) 0.05%
(C) 1.40%
(D) 3.85%
(E) 4.00%

A B C D E
○ ○ ○ ○ ○

3. A retailer buys a popular brand of athletic shoe from the wholesaler for $75. He then marks up the price by $\frac{1}{3}$ and sells each pair at a discount of 20%.

What profit does the retailer make on each pair of athletic shoes?

(A) $5.00
(B) $6.67
(C) $7.50
(D) $10.00
(E) $13.33

A B C D E
○ ○ ○ ○ ○

4. On a blueprint, $\frac{1}{4}$ inch represents 1 foot. If a window is supposed to be 56 inches wide, how wide would its representation be on the blueprint?

(A) $1\frac{1}{6}$ inches
(B) $4\frac{2}{3}$ inches
(C) $9\frac{1}{3}$ inches
(D) 14 inches
(E) $18\frac{2}{3}$ inches

A B C D E
○ ○ ○ ○ ○

5. If the radius of a circle is increased by 50%, what will be the percent increase in the circumference of the circle? (Circumference $= 2\pi r$)

(A) 25%
(B) 50%
(C) 100%
(D) 150%
(E) 225%

A B C D E
○ ○ ○ ○ ○

6. Which of the following fractions is the greatest?

(A) $\frac{403}{134}$
(B) $\frac{79}{26}$
(C) $\frac{527}{176}$
(D) $\frac{221}{73}$
(E) $\frac{99}{34}$

A B C D E
○ ○ ○ ○ ○

7. A store usually sells a certain item at a 40% profit. One week the store has a sale, during which the item is sold for 10% less than the usual price. During the sale, what is the percent profit the store makes on each of these items?

(A) 4%
(B) 14%
(C) 26%
(D) 30%
(E) 36%

A B C D E
○ ○ ○ ○ ○

8. What is 0.05 percent of 6.5?

(A) 0.00325
(B) 0.013
(C) 0.325
(D) 1.30
(E) 130.0

A B C D E
○ ○ ○ ○ ○

9. What is the value of $\dfrac{\left(3\frac{1}{2} + 3\frac{1}{4} + 3\frac{1}{4} + 3\frac{1}{2}\right)}{4\frac{1}{2}}$?

(A) $1\frac{1}{2}$

(B) $2\frac{1}{4}$

(C) 3

(D) $3\frac{1}{4}$

(E) $3\frac{3}{8}$

A B C D E
○ ○ ○ ○ ○

10. If 8 loggers can chop down 28 trees in one day, how many trees can 20 loggers chop down in one day?

(A) 28 trees
(B) 160 trees
(C) 70 trees
(D) 100 trees
(E) 80 trees

A B C D E
○ ○ ○ ○ ○

11. What is the product of the following fractions: $\dfrac{3}{100}$, $\dfrac{15}{49}$, $\dfrac{7}{9}$?

(A) $\dfrac{215}{44,100}$

(B) $\dfrac{1}{140}$

(C) $\dfrac{1}{196}$

(D) $\dfrac{25}{158}$

(E) $\dfrac{3}{427}$

A B C D E
○ ○ ○ ○ ○

12. In calculating the height of an object, Mrs. Downs mistakenly observed the height to be 72 cm instead of 77 cm. What was her percentage error (to the nearest hundredth of a percent)?

(A) 6.49%
(B) 6.69%
(C) 6.89%
(D) 7.09%
(E) 7.19%

A B C D E
○ ○ ○ ○ ○

13. A retailer buys 1,440 dozen pens at $2.50 a dozen and then sells them at a price of 25¢ apiece. What is the total profit after the retailer sells all the pens?

(A) $60.00
(B) $72.00
(C) $720.00
(D) $874.00
(E) $8,740.00

A B C D E
○ ○ ○ ○ ○

14. On a map, 1 inch represents 1,000 miles. If the area of a country is actually 16 million square miles, what is the area of the country's representation on the map?

(A) 4 square inches
(B) 16 square inches
(C) 4,000 square inches
(D) 16,000 square inches
(E) 4,000,000 square inches

A B C D E
○ ○ ○ ○ ○

15. The formula for the volume of a cone is $V = \frac{1}{3}\pi r^2 h$.

    If the radius (r) is doubled and the height (h) is divided by 3, what will be the ratio of the new volume to the original volume?

    (A) 2 : 3
    (B) 3 : 2
    (C) 4 : 3
    (D) 3 : 4
    (E) none of these

    A B C D E
    ○ ○ ○ ○ ○

16. Which of the following fractions has the smallest value?

    (A) $\frac{34.7}{163}$

    (B) $\frac{125}{501}$

    (C) $\frac{173}{700}$

    (D) $\frac{10.9}{42.7}$

    (E) $\frac{907}{3,715}$

    A B C D E
    ○ ○ ○ ○ ○

17. Mr. Cutler usually makes a 45% profit on every flat-screen TV he sells. During a sale, he reduces his margin of profit to 40%, while his sales increase by 10%. What is the ratio of his new total profit to the original profit?

    (A) 1 : 1
    (B) 9 : 8
    (C) 9 : 10
    (D) 11 : 10
    (E) 44 : 45

    A B C D E
    ○ ○ ○ ○ ○

18. What is 1.3 percent of 0.26?

    (A) 0.00338
    (B) 0.00500
    (C) 0.200
    (D) 0.338
    (E) 0.500

    A B C D E
    ○ ○ ○ ○ ○

19. What is the average of the following numbers: $3.2, \frac{47}{12}, \frac{10}{3}$?

    (A) 3.55

    (B) $\frac{10}{3}$

    (C) $\frac{103}{30}$

    (D) $\frac{209}{60}$

    (E) $\frac{1,254}{120}$

    A B C D E
    ○ ○ ○ ○ ○

20. If it takes 16 faucets 10 hours to fill 8 tubs, how long will it take 12 faucets to fill 9 tubs?

    (A) 10 hours
    (B) 12 hours
    (C) 13 hours
    (D) 14 hours
    (E) 15 hours

    A B C D E
    ○ ○ ○ ○ ○

21. If the 8% tax on a sale amounts to 96¢, what is the final price (tax included) of the item?

    (A) $1.20
    (B) $2.16
    (C) $6.36
    (D) $12.00
    (E) $12.96

    A B C D E
    ○ ○ ○ ○ ○

22. In a certain class, 40% of the students are girls, and 20% of the girls wear glasses. What percent of the children in the class are girls who wear glasses?

    (A) 6%
    (B) 8%
    (C) 20%
    (D) 60%
    (E) 80%

    A B C D E
    ○ ○ ○ ○ ○

23. What is 1.2% of 0.5?

    (A) 0.0006
    (B) 0.006
    (C) 0.06
    (D) 0.6
    (E) 6.0

    A B C D E
    ○ ○ ○ ○ ○

24. Which of the following quantities is the largest?

    (A) $\frac{275}{369}$

    (B) $\frac{134}{179}$

    (C) $\frac{107}{144}$

    (D) $\frac{355}{476}$

    (E) $\frac{265}{352}$

    A B C D E
    ○ ○ ○ ○ ○

25. If the length of a rectangle is increased by 120%, and its width is decreased by 20%, what happens to the area of the rectangle?

    (A) It decreases by 4%.
    (B) It remains the same.
    (C) It increases by 24%.
    (D) It increases by 76%.
    (E) It increases by 100%.

    A B C D E
    ○ ○ ○ ○ ○

26. A merchant buys an old carpet for $25.00. He spends $15.00 to have it restored to good condition and then sells the rug for $50.00. What is the percent profit on his total investment?

    (A) 20%
    (B) 25%
    (C) 40%
    (D) $66\frac{2}{3}$%
    (E) 100%

    A B C D E
    ○ ○ ○ ○ ○

27. Of the following sets of fractions, which one is arranged in *decreasing* order?

    (A) $\frac{5}{9}, \frac{7}{11}, \frac{3}{5}, \frac{2}{3}, \frac{10}{13}$

    (B) $\frac{2}{3}, \frac{3}{5}, \frac{7}{11}, \frac{5}{9}, \frac{10}{13}$

    (C) $\frac{3}{5}, \frac{5}{9}, \frac{7}{11}, \frac{10}{13}, \frac{2}{3}$

    (D) $\frac{10}{13}, \frac{2}{3}, \frac{7}{11}, \frac{3}{5}, \frac{5}{9}$

    (E) none of these

    A B C D E
    ○ ○ ○ ○ ○

28. If the diameter of a circle doubles, the circumference of the larger circle is how many times the circumference of the original circle? (Circumference $= \pi d$)

    (A) π
    (B) 2π
    (C) 1
    (D) 2
    (E) 4

    A B C D E
    ○ ○ ○ ○ ○

29. The scale on a set of plans is 1 : 8. If a man reads a certain measurement on the plans as 5.6″ instead of 6.0″, what will be the resulting approximate percent error on the full-size model?

    (A) 6.7%
    (B) 7.1%
    (C) 12.5%
    (D) 53.6%
    (E) 56.8%

    A B C D E
    ○ ○ ○ ○ ○

30. G&R Electronics bought 2 dozen megapixel digital cameras for $300 each. The company sold two-thirds of them at a 25% profit but was forced to take a 30% loss on the rest. What was the total profit (or loss) on the digital cameras?

    (A) a loss of $200
    (B) a loss of $15
    (C) no profit or loss
    (D) a profit of $20
    (E) a profit of $480

    A B C D E
    ○ ○ ○ ○ ○

31. The sum of $\frac{1}{2}, \frac{1}{3}, \frac{1}{8}, \frac{1}{15}$ is:

(A) $\frac{9}{8}$

(B) $\frac{16}{15}$

(C) $\frac{41}{40}$

(D) $\frac{65}{64}$

(E) $\frac{121}{120}$

A B C D E
○ ○ ○ ○ ○

32. What is $\frac{2}{3}$% of 90?

(A) 0.006
(B) 0.06
(C) 0.6
(D) 6.0
(E) 60

A B C D E
○ ○ ○ ○ ○

33. Lucas borrows $360. If he pays it back in 12 monthly installments of $31.50, what is the interest rate?

(A) 1.5%
(B) 4.5%
(C) 10%
(D) 5%
(E) 7.5%

A B C D E
○ ○ ○ ○ ○

34. A merchant marks up a certain lighting fixture 30% above original cost. Then the merchant gives a customer a loyalty discount of 15%. If the final selling price for the lighting fixture was $86.19, what was the original cost?

(A) $66.30
(B) $73.26
(C) $78.00
(D) $99.12
(E) $101.40

A B C D E
○ ○ ○ ○ ○

35. In a certain recipe, $2\frac{1}{4}$ cups of flour are called for to make a cake that serves 6. If Mrs. Jenkins wants to use the same recipe to make a cake for 8, how many cups of flour must she use?

(A) $2\frac{1}{3}$ cups

(B) $2\frac{3}{4}$ cups

(C) 3 cups

(D) $3\frac{3}{8}$ cups

(E) 4 cups

A B C D E
○ ○ ○ ○ ○

36. If 10 people can survive for 24 days on 15 cans of rations, how many cans will be needed for 8 people to survive for 36 days?

(A) 15 cans
(B) 16 cans
(C) 17 cans
(D) 18 cans
(E) 19 cans

A B C D E
○ ○ ○ ○ ○

37. If, on a map, $\frac{1}{2}$ inch represents 1 mile, how long is a border whose representation is $1\frac{1}{15}$ feet long?

(A) $2\frac{1}{30}$ miles

(B) $5\frac{1}{15}$ miles

(C) $12\frac{4}{5}$ miles

(D) $25\frac{3}{5}$ miles

(E) $51\frac{1}{5}$ miles

A B C D E
○ ○ ○ ○ ○

38. In the formula $e = hf$, if e is doubled and f is halved, what happens to the value of h?

    (A) h remains the same.
    (B) h is doubled.
    (C) h is divided by 4.
    (D) h is multiplied by 4.
    (E) h is halved.

    A B C D E
    ○ ○ ○ ○ ○

39. Which of the following expresses the ratio of 3 inches to 2 yards?

    (A) 3 : 2
    (B) 3 : 9
    (C) 3 : 12
    (D) 3 : 24
    (E) 3 : 72

    A B C D E
    ○ ○ ○ ○ ○

40. If it takes Mark twice as long to earn $6.00 as it takes Carl to earn $4.00, what is the ratio of Mark's pay per hour to Carl's pay per hour?

    (A) 2 : 1
    (B) 3 : 1
    (C) 3 : 2
    (D) 3 : 4
    (E) 4 : 3

    A B C D E
    ○ ○ ○ ○ ○

41. What is the lowest common denominator of the following set of fractions:
$$\frac{1}{6}, \frac{13}{27}, \frac{4}{5}, \frac{3}{10}, \frac{2}{15}?$$

    (A) 27
    (B) 54
    (C) 135
    (D) 270
    (E) none of these

    A B C D E
    ○ ○ ○ ○ ○

42. The average grade on a certain examination was 85. Raul scored 90 on the same examination. What was Raul's *percent* deviation from the average score (to the nearest tenth of a percent)?

    (A) 5.0%
    (B) 5.4%
    (C) 5.5%
    (D) 5.8%
    (E) 5.9%

    A B C D E
    ○ ○ ○ ○ ○

43. Successive discounts of 20% and 12% are equivalent to a single discount of:

    (A) 16.0%
    (B) 29.6%
    (C) 31.4%
    (D) 32.0%
    (E) 33.7%

    A B C D E
    ○ ○ ○ ○ ○

44. On a blueprint of a park, 1 foot represents $\frac{1}{2}$ mile. If an error of $\frac{1}{2}$ inch is made in reading the blueprint, what will be the corresponding error on the actual park?

    (A) 110 feet
    (B) 220 feet
    (C) 330 feet
    (D) 440 feet
    (E) none of these

    A B C D E
    ○ ○ ○ ○ ○

45. If the two sides of a rectangle change in such a manner that the rectangle's area remains constant, and one side increases by 25%, what must happen to the other side?

    (A) It decreases by 20%.
    (B) It decreases by 25%.
    (C) It decreases by $33\frac{1}{3}$%.
    (D) It decreases by 50%.
    (E) none of these

    A B C D E
    ○ ○ ○ ○ ○

46. Which of the following fractions has the smallest value?

(A) $\dfrac{6,043}{2,071}$

(B) $\dfrac{4,290}{1,463}$

(C) $\dfrac{5,107}{1,772}$

(D) $\dfrac{8,935}{2,963}$

(E) $\dfrac{8,016}{2,631}$

A B C D E
○ ○ ○ ○ ○

47. A certain company increased its prices by 30% during 2016. Then, in 2017, it was forced to cut back its prices by 20%. What was the net change in price?

(A) −4%

(B) −2%

(C) +2%

(D) +4%

(E) 0%

A B C D E
○ ○ ○ ○ ○

48. What is 0.04%, expressed as a fraction?

(A) $\dfrac{2}{5}$

(B) $\dfrac{1}{25}$

(C) $\dfrac{4}{25}$

(D) $\dfrac{1}{250}$

(E) $\dfrac{1}{2,500}$

A B C D E
○ ○ ○ ○ ○

49. What is the value of the fraction

$$\dfrac{16 + 12 + 88 + 34 + 66 + 21 + 79 + 11 + 89}{25}$$

(A) 15.04

(B) 15.44

(C) 16.24

(D) 16.64

(E) none of these

A B C D E
○ ○ ○ ○ ○

50. If coconuts are twice as expensive as bananas, and bananas are one-third as expensive as grapefruits, what is the ratio of the price of one coconut to one grapefruit?

(A) 2 : 3

(B) 3 : 2

(C) 6 : 1

(D) 1 : 6

(E) none of these

A B C D E
○ ○ ○ ○ ○

Answer Key for Session 1 Practice Test

1. D	14. B	27. D	39. E
2. E	15. C	28. D	40. D
3. A	16. A	29. A	41. D
4. A	17. E	30. E	42. E
5. B	18. A	31. C	43. B
6. B	19. D	32. C	44. A
7. C	20. E	33. D	45. A
8. A	21. E	34. C	46. C
9. C	22. B	35. C	47. D
10. C	23. B	36. D	48. E
11. B	24. E	37. D	49. D
12. A	25. D	38. D	50. A
13. C	26. B		

Answers and Solutions for Session 1 Practice Test

1. Choice D is correct. First, convert the fractions to decimals, as the final answer must be expressed in decimals: $2.500 + 5.250 + 3.350 + 0.125 = 11.225$. (Refreshers 104, 127, 128)

2. Choice E is correct. This is an estimation problem. Note that the correct value was 35, not 36.4. Thus the *real* value is 35 mg and the *estimated* value is 36.4 mg. Thus, percent error is equal to $(36.4 - 35) \div 35$, or 0.04, expressed as a percent, which is 4%. (Refreshers 115, 116, 117)

3. Choice A is correct. This is a business problem. First, the retailer marks up the wholesale price by $\frac{1}{3}$, so the marked-up price equals $75(1 + \frac{1}{3})$, or $100; then it is reduced 20% from the $100 price, leaving a final price of $80. Thus, the net profit on each pair of athletic shoes is $5.00. (Refresher 118)

4. Choice A is correct. Here we have a proportion problem: length on blueprint : actual length $= \frac{1}{4}$ inch : 1 foot. The second ratio is the same as 1 : 48, because 1 foot = 12 inches. In the problem the actual length is 56 inches, so that if the length on the blueprint equals x, we have the proportion $x : 56 = 1 : 48; \frac{x}{56} = \frac{1}{48}. 48x = 56;$ so $x = \frac{56}{48}$, or $1\frac{1}{6}$ inches. (Refresher 120)

5. Choice B is correct. $C = 2\pi r$ (where r is the radius of the circle, and C is its circumference). The new value of r, r', is $(1.5)r$ since r is increased by 50%. Using this value of r', we get the new C, $C' = 2\pi r' = 2\pi(1.5)r = (1.5)2\pi r$. Remembering that $C = 2\pi r$, we get that $C' = (1.5)C$. Since the new circumference is 1.5 times the original, there is an increase of 50%. (Refresher 122)

6. Choice B is correct. In this numerical comparison problem, it is helpful to realize that all of these fractions are approximately equal to 3. If we subtract 3 from each of the fractions, we get $\frac{1}{134}, \frac{1}{26}$, $-\frac{1}{176}, \frac{2}{73}$, and $-\frac{3}{34}$, respectively. Clearly, the greatest of these is $\frac{1}{26}$, which therefore shows the greatest of the five given fractions. Another method of solving this type of numerical comparison problem is to convert the fractions to decimals by dividing the numerator by the denominator. (Refreshers 127, 128)

7. Choice C is correct. This is another business problem, this time asking for percentage profit. Let the original price be P. A 40% profit means that the store will sell the item for $100\%P + 40\%P$, which is equal to $140\%P$, which in turn is equal to $\left(\frac{140}{100}\right)P = 1.4P$. Then the marked-up price will be $1.4(P)$. Ten percent is taken off this price, to yield a final price of $(0.90)(1.40)(P)$, or $(1.26)(P)$. Thus, the fractional increase was 0.26, so the percent increase was 26%. (Refresher 118)

8. Choice A is correct. Remember that in the phrase "percent of," the "of" may be replaced by a multiplication sign. Thus, $0.05\% \times 6.5 = 0.0005 \times 6.5$, so the answer is 0.00325. (Refresher 114)

9. Choice C is correct. First, add the fractions in the numerator to obtain $13\frac{1}{2}$. Then divide $13\frac{1}{2}$ by $4\frac{1}{2}$. If you cannot see immediately that the answer is 3, you can convert the halves to decimals and divide, or you can express the fractions in terms of their common denominator, thus: $13\frac{1}{2} = \frac{27}{2}; 4\frac{1}{2} = \frac{9}{2};$ $\frac{27}{2} \div \frac{9}{2} = \frac{27}{2} \times \frac{2}{9} = \frac{54}{18} = 3$. (Refreshers 110, 112)

10. Choice C is correct. This is a proportion problem. If x is the number of loggers needed to chop down 20 trees, then we form the proportion 8 loggers : 28 trees = 20 loggers : x trees, or $\frac{8}{28} = \frac{20}{x}$. Solving for x, we get $x = \frac{(28)(20)}{8}$, or $x = 70$.

(Refresher 120)

11. Choice B is correct. $\frac{3}{100} \times \frac{15}{49} \times \frac{7}{9} = \frac{3 \times 15 \times 7}{100 \times 49 \times 9}$. Canceling 7 out of the numerator and denominator gives us $\frac{3 \times 15}{100 \times 7 \times 9}$. Canceling 5 out of the numerator and denominator gives us $\frac{3 \times 3}{20 \times 7 \times 9}$. Finally, canceling 9 out of both numerator and denominator gives us $\frac{1}{20 \times 7}$, or $\frac{1}{140}$.

(Refresher 111)

12. Choice A is correct. Percent error = (absolute error) ÷ (correct measurement) = 5 ÷ 77 = 0.0649 (approximately) × 100 = 6.49%.

(Refreshers 115, 116, 117)

13. Choice C is correct. Profit on each dozen pens = selling price − cost = 12(25¢) − $2.50 = $3.00 − $2.50 = 50¢ profit per dozen. Total profit = profit per dozen × number of dozens = 50¢ × 1,440 = $720.00.

(Refresher 118)

14. Choice B is correct. If 1 inch represents 1,000 miles, then 1 square inch represents 1,000 miles squared, or 1,000,000 square miles. Thus, the area would be represented by 16 squares of this size, or 16 square inches.

(Refresher 120)

15. Choice C is correct. Let V' equal the new volume. Then if $r' = 2r$ is the new radius, and $h' = \frac{h}{3}$ is the new height, $V' = \frac{1}{3}\pi(r')^2(h') = \frac{1}{3}\pi(2r)^2\left(\frac{h}{3}\right) = \frac{4}{9}\pi r^2 h = \frac{4}{3}V$, so the ratio $V' : V$ is equal to 4 : 3.

(Refresher 122)

16. Choice A is correct. Using a calculator, we get: $\frac{34.7}{163} = 0.2128$ for Choice A; $\frac{125}{501} = 0.2495$ for Choice B; $\frac{173}{700} = 0.2471$ for Choice C; $\frac{10.9}{42.7} = 0.2552$ for Choice D; and $\frac{907}{3,715} = 0.2441$ for Choice E. Choice A is the smallest value.

(Refreshers 104, 127)

17. Choice E is correct. Let N = the original cost of a flat-screen TV. Then, original profit = 45% × N. New profit = 40% × 110%N = 44% × N. Thus, the ratio of new profit to original profit is 44 : 45.

(Refresher 118)

18. Choice A is correct.
1.3% × 0.26 = 0.013 × 0.26 = 0.00338.

(Refresher 114)

19. Choice D is correct. Average = $\frac{1}{3}\left(3.2 + \frac{47}{12} + \frac{10}{3}\right)$. The decimal 3.2 = $\frac{320}{100} = \frac{16}{5}$, and the lowest common denominator of the three fractions is 60, so $\frac{16}{5} = \frac{192}{60}, \frac{47}{12} = \frac{235}{60}$, and $\frac{10}{3} = \frac{200}{60}$. Then, $\frac{1}{3}\left(\frac{192}{60} + \frac{235}{60} + \frac{200}{60}\right) = \frac{1}{3}\left(\frac{627}{60}\right) = \frac{209}{60}$.

(Refreshers 101, 105, 109)

20. Choice E is correct. This is an inverse proportion. If it takes 16 faucets 10 hours to fill 8 tubs, then it takes 1 faucet 160 hours to fill 8 tubs (16 faucets : 1 faucet = x hours : 10 hours; $\frac{16}{1} = \frac{x}{10}$; $x = 160$). If it takes 1 faucet 160 hours to fill 8 tubs, then (dividing by 8) it takes 1 faucet 20 hours to fill 1 tub. If it takes 1 faucet 20 hours to fill 1 tub, then it takes 1 faucet 180 hours (9 × 20 hours) to fill 9 tubs. If it takes 1 faucet 180 hours to fill 9 tubs, then it takes 12 faucets $\frac{180}{12}$, or 15 hours, to fill 9 tubs.

(Refresher 120)

21. Choice E is correct. Let P be the original price. Then 0.08P = 96¢, so that 8P = $96, or P = $12. Adding the tax, which equals 96¢, we obtain our final price of $12.96.

(Refresher 118)

22. Choice B is correct. The number of girls who wear glasses is 20% of 40% of the children in the class. Thus, the indicated operation is multiplication; 20% × 40% = 0.20 × 0.40 = 0.08 = 8%.

(Refresher 114)

23. Choice B is correct.
1.2% × 0.5 = 0.012 × 0.5 = 0.006.

(Refresher 114)

24. Choice E is correct. Using a calculator to find the answer to three decimal places, we get: $\frac{275}{369} = 0.745$ for Choice A; $\frac{134}{179} = 0.749$ for Choice B; $\frac{107}{144} = 0.743$ for Choice C; $\frac{355}{476} = 0.746$ for Choice D;

$\frac{265}{352} = 0.753$ for Choice E. Choice E is the largest value. (Refreshers 104, 127)

25. Choice D is correct. Area = length × width. The new area will be equal to the new length × the new width. The new length = (100% + 120%) × old length = 220% × old length = $\frac{220}{100}$ × old length = 2.2 × old length. The new width = (100% − 20%) × old width = 80% × old width = $\frac{80}{100}$ × old width = 0.8 × old width. The new area = new width × new length = 2.2 × 0.8 × old length × old width. So the new area = 1.76 × old area, which is 176% of the old area. This is an increase of 76% from the original area. (Refresher 122)

26. Choice B is correct. Total cost to merchant = $25.00 + $15.00 = $40.00.
Profit = selling price − cost = $50 − $40 = $10.
Percent profit = profit ÷ cost = $10 ÷ $40 = 25%. (Refresher 118)

27. Choice D is correct. We can convert the fractions to decimals or to fractions with a lowest common denominator. Inspection will show that all sets of fractions contain the same members; therefore, if we convert one set to decimals or find the lowest common denominator for one set, we can use our results for all sets. Converting a fraction to a decimal involves only one operation, a single division, whereas converting to the lowest common denominator involves a multiplication, which must be followed by a division and a multiplication to change each fraction to one with the lowest common denominator. Thus, conversion to decimals is often the simpler method: $\frac{10}{13} = 0.769; \frac{2}{3} = 0.666;$ $\frac{7}{11} = 0.636; \frac{3}{5} = 0.600; \frac{5}{9} = 0.555.$

However, in this case there is an even simpler method. Convert two of the fractions to equivalent fractions: $\frac{3}{5} = \frac{6}{10}$ and $\frac{2}{3} = \frac{8}{12}$. We now have $\frac{5}{9}$, $\frac{6}{10}, \frac{7}{11}, \frac{8}{12}$, and $\frac{10}{13}$. Remember this rule: When the numerator and denominator of a fraction are both positive, adding 1 to both will bring the value of the fraction closer to 1. (For example, $\frac{3}{4} = \frac{2+1}{3+1}$, so $\frac{3}{4}$ is closer to 1 than $\frac{2}{3}$ and is therefore the

greater fraction.) Thus we see that $\frac{5}{9}$ is less than $\frac{6}{10}$, which is less than $\frac{7}{11}$, which is less than $\frac{8}{12}$, which is less than $\frac{9}{13} \cdot \frac{9}{13}$ is obviously less than $\frac{10}{13}$, so $\frac{10}{13}$ must be the greatest fraction. Thus, in decreasing order, the fractions are $\frac{10}{13}, \frac{2}{3}, \frac{7}{11}, \frac{3}{5}$, and $\frac{5}{9}$. This method is a great time-saver once you become accustomed to it. (Refresher 104)

28. Choice D is correct. The formula governing this situation is $C = \pi d$, where C = circumference and d = diameter. Thus, if the new diameter is $d' = 2d$, then the new circumference is $C' = \pi d' = 2\pi d = 2C$. Thus, the new, larger circle has a circumference twice that of the original circle. (Refresher 122)

29. Choice A is correct. The most important feature of this problem is recognizing that the scale does not affect percent (or fractional) error, since it simply results in multiplying the numerator and denominator of a fraction by the same factor. Thus, we need only calculate the original percent error. Although it would not be incorrect to calculate the full-scale percent error, it would be time-consuming and might result in unnecessary errors. Absolute error = 0.4″. Actual measurement = 6.0″. Therefore, percent error = (absolute error ÷ actual measurement) × 100% = $\frac{0.4}{6.0}$ × 100%, which equals 6.7% (approximately). (Refresher 117)

30. Choice E is correct. Total cost = number of cameras × cost of each = 24 × $300 = $7,200.
Revenue = (number sold at 25% profit × price at 25% profit) + (number sold at 30% loss × price at 30% loss)
= (16 × $375) + (8 × $210) = $6,000 + $1,680 = $7,680.
Profit = revenue − cost = $7,680 − $7,200 = $480. (Refresher 118)

31. Choice C is correct. $\frac{1}{2} + \frac{1}{3} + \frac{1}{8} + \frac{1}{15} = \frac{60}{120} + \frac{40}{120}$ $+ \frac{15}{120} + \frac{8}{120} = \frac{123}{120} = \frac{41}{40}.$ (Refresher 110)

32. Choice C is correct. $\frac{2}{3}\% \times 90 = \frac{2}{300} \times 90 = \frac{180}{300}$ $= \frac{6}{10} = 0.6.$ (Refresher 114)

33. Choice D is correct. If Lucas makes 12 payments of $31.50, he pays back a total of $378.00. Since the loan is for $360.00, his net interest is $18.00. Therefore, the rate of interest is $\frac{\$18.00}{\$360.00}$, which can be reduced to 0.05, or 5%. (Refresher 118)

34. Choice C is correct. Final selling price = 85% × 130% × cost = 1.105 × cost. Thus, $86.19 = 1.105C, where C = cost. C = $86.19 ÷ 1.105 = $78.00 (exactly). (Refresher 118)

35. Choice C is correct. If x is the amount of flour needed for 8 people, then we can set up the proportion $2\frac{1}{4}$ cups : 6 people = x : 8 people. Solving for x gives us $x = \frac{8}{6} \times 2\frac{1}{4}$ or $\frac{8}{6} \times \frac{9}{4} = 3$. (Refresher 120)

36. Choice D is correct. If 10 people can survive for 24 days on 15 cans, then 1 person can survive for 240 days on 15 cans. If 1 person can survive for 240 days on 15 cans, then 1 person can survive for $\frac{240}{15}$, or 16 days, on 1 can. If 1 person can survive for 16 days on 1 can, then 8 people can survive for $\frac{16}{8}$, or 2 days, on 1 can. If 8 people can survive for 2 days on 1 can, then for 36 days 8 people need $\frac{36}{2}$, or 18 cans, to survive. (Refresher 120)

37. Choice D is correct. $1\frac{1}{15}$ feet = $1\frac{1}{15} \times 12$ inches = $\frac{16}{15} \times 12$ inches = 12.8 inches. So we have a proportion, $\frac{\frac{1}{2} \text{ inch}}{1 \text{ mile}} = \frac{12.8 \text{ inches}}{x \text{ miles}}$. Cross-multiplying, we get $\frac{1}{2}x = 12.8$, so $x = 25.6 = 25\frac{3}{5}$. (Refresher 120)

38. Choice D is correct. If e = hf, then $h = \frac{e}{f}$. If e is doubled and f is halved, then the new value of h, $h' = \left(\frac{2e}{\frac{1}{2}f}\right)$. Multiplying the numerator and denominator by 2 gives us $h' = \frac{4e}{f}$. Since $h = \frac{e}{f}$ and $h' = \frac{4e}{f}$ we see that $h' = 4h$. This is the same as saying that h is multiplied by 4. (Refresher 122)

39. Choice E is correct. 3 inches : 2 yards = 3 inches : 72 inches = 3 : 72. (Refresher 121)

40. Choice D is correct. If Carl and Mark work for the same length of time, then Carl will earn $8.00 for every $6.00 Mark earns (since in the time Mark can earn one $6.00 wage, Carl can earn *two* $4.00 wages). Thus, their hourly wage rates are in the ratio $6.00 (Mark) : $8.00 (Carl) = 3 : 4. (Refresher 120)

41. Choice D is correct. The lowest common denominator is the smallest number that is divisible by all of the denominators. Thus we are looking for the smallest number that is divisible by 6, 27, 5, 10, and 15. The smallest number that is divisible by 6 and 27 is 54. The smallest number that is divisible by 54 and 5 is 270. Since 270 is divisible by 10 and 15 also, it is the lowest common denominator. (Refreshers 110, 126)

42. Choice E is correct.
Percent deviation = $\frac{\text{absolute deviation}}{\text{average score}} \times 100\%$.
Absolute deviation = Raul's score − average score = 90 − 85 = 5.
Percent deviation = $\frac{5}{85} \times 100\% = 500\% \div 85 = 5.88\%$ (approximately).
5.88% is closer to 5.9% than to 5.8%, so 5.9% is correct. (Refresher 117)

43. Choice B is correct. If we discount 20% and then 12%, we are, in effect, taking 88% of 80% of the original price. Since "of" represents multiplication, when we deal with percent we can multiply 88% × 80% = 70.4%. This is a deduction of 29.6% from the original price. (Refreshers 119, 114)

44. Choice A is correct.
This is a simple proportion: $\frac{1 \text{ foot}}{\frac{1}{2} \text{ mile}} = \frac{\frac{1}{2} \text{ inch}}{x}$.
Our first step must be to convert all these measurements to one unit. The most logical unit is the one our answer will take—feet. Thus, $\frac{1 \text{ foot}}{2,640 \text{ feet}} = \frac{\frac{1}{24} \text{ foot}}{x}$. (1 mile equals 5,280 feet.) Solving for x, we find $x = \frac{2,640}{24}$ feet = 110 feet. (Refreshers 120, 121)

45. Choice A is correct. Let the two original sides of the rectangle be a and b and the new sides be a' and b'. Let side a increase by 25%. Then

$$a' = (100 + 25)\%a = 125\%a = \frac{125}{100}a = 1.25a$$

$= \frac{5a}{4}$. We also have that $ab = a'b'$. Substituting $a' = \frac{5a}{4}$, we get $ab = \frac{5a}{4}b'$. The a's cancel and we get $b = \frac{5}{4}b'$. So $b' = \frac{4}{5}b$, a decrease of $\frac{1}{5}$, or 20%.

(Refresher 122)

46. Choice C is correct. Using a calculator, we get: $\frac{6,043}{2,071} = 2.9179$ for Choice A; $\frac{4,290}{1,463} = 2.9323$ for Choice B; $\frac{5,107}{1,772} = 2.8820$ for Choice C; $\frac{8,935}{2,963} = 3.0155$ for Choice D; and $\frac{8,016}{2,631} = 3.0467$ for Choice E. Choice C has the smallest value.

(Refreshers 104, 127)

47. Choice D is correct. Let's say that the price was $100 during 2016. 30% of $100 = $30, so the new price in 2016 was $130. In 2017, the company cut back its prices 20%, so the new price in 2017 =

$$\$130 - \left(\frac{20}{100}\right)\$130 =$$

$$\$130 - \left(\frac{1}{5}\right)\$130 =$$

$130 - $26 = $104.
The net change is $104 - $100 = $4.

$\frac{\$4}{\$100} = 4\%$ increase. (Refresher 118)

48. Choice E is correct. $0.04\% = \frac{0.04}{100} = \frac{4}{10,000} = \frac{1}{2,500}$. (Refresher 107)

49. Choice D is correct. Before adding you should examine the numbers to be added. They form pairs, like this: $16 + (12 + 88) + (34 + 66) + (21 + 79) + (11 + 89)$, which equals $16 + 100 + 100 + 100 + 100 = 416$. Dividing 416 by 25, we obtain $16\frac{16}{25}$, which equals 16.64. (Refresher 112)

50. Choice A is correct. We can set up a proportion as follows:

$\frac{1 \text{ coconut}}{1 \text{ banana}} = \frac{2}{1}, \frac{1 \text{ banana}}{1 \text{ grapefruit}} = \frac{1}{3}$, so by multiplying the two equations together

$\left(\frac{1 \text{ coconut}}{1 \text{ banana}} \times \frac{1 \text{ banana}}{1 \text{ grapefruit}} = \frac{2}{1} \times \frac{1}{3}\right)$ and canceling the bananas and the 1's in the numerators and denominators, we get: $\frac{1 \text{ coconut}}{1 \text{ grapefruit}} = \frac{2}{3}$, which can be written as 2 : 3. (Refresher 120)

MATH REFRESHER SESSION 2

Rate Problems: Distance and Time, Work, Mixture, and Cost

Word Problem Setup

200. Some problems require translation of words into algebraic expressions or equations. For example: 8 more than 7 times a number is 22. Find the number. Let n = the number. We have

$$7n + 8 = 22 \qquad 7n = 14 \qquad n = 2$$

Another example: There are 3 times as many boys as girls in a class. What is the ratio of boys to the total number of students? Let n = number of girls. Then

$$3n = \text{number of boys}$$
$$4n = \text{total number of students}$$
$$\frac{\text{number of boys}}{\text{total students}} = \frac{3n}{4n} = \frac{3}{4}$$

201. Rate problems concern a special type of relationship that is very common: rate × input = output. This results from the definition of *rate* as *the ratio between output and input*. In these problems, input may represent any type of "investment," but the most frequent quantities used as inputs are time, work, and money. Output is usually distance traveled, work done, or money spent.

Note that the word *per*, as used in rates, signifies a ratio. Thus a rate of 25 miles per hour signifies the ratio between an output of 25 miles and an input of 1 hour.

Frequently, the word *per* will be represented by the fraction sign, thus $\frac{25 \text{ miles}}{1 \text{ hour}}$.

Example: Peter can walk a mile in 10 minutes. He can travel a mile on his bicycle in 2 minutes. How far away is his uncle's house if Peter can walk there and bicycle back in 1 hour exactly?

To solve a rate problem such as the one above, follow these steps:

Step 1. Determine the names of the quantities that represent input, output, and rate in the problem you are doing. In the example, Peter's input is *time*, and his output is *distance*. His rate will be *distance per unit of time*, which is commonly called *speed*.

Step 2. Write down the fundamental relationship in terms of the quantities mentioned, making each the heading of a column. In the example, set up the table like this:

$$\text{speed} \times \text{time} = \text{distance}$$

Step 3. Directly below the name of each quantity, write the unit of measurement in terms of the answer you want. Your choice of unit should be the most convenient one, but remember, once you have chosen a unit, you must convert all quantities to that unit.

We must select a unit of time. Since a *minute* was the unit used in the problem, it is the most logical choice. Similarly, we will choose a *mile* for our unit of distance. *Speed* (which is the ratio of distance to time) will therefore be expressed in *miles per minute*, usually abbreviated as *mi/min*. Thus, our chart now looks like this:

speed	×	time	=	distance
mi/min		*minutes*		*miles*

Step 4. The problem will mention various situations in which some quantity of input is used to get a certain quantity of output. Represent each of these situations on a different line of the table, leaving blanks for unknown quantities.

In the sample problem, four situations are mentioned: Peter can walk a mile in 10 minutes; he can bicycle a mile in 2 minutes; he walks to his uncle's house; and he bicycles home. On the diagram, with the appropriate boxes filled, the problem will look like this:

	speed	× time	= distance
	mi/min	*minutes*	*miles*
1. walking		10	1
2. bicycling		2	1
3. walking			
4. bicycling			

Step 5. From the chart and from the relationship at the top of the chart, quantities for filling some of the empty spaces may become obvious. Fill in these values directly.

In the example, on the first line of the chart, we see that the walking speed × 10 equals 1.

Thus, the walking *speed* is 0.1 mi/min

(mi/min × 10 = 1 mi; mi/min = $\frac{1 \text{ mi}}{10 \text{ min}}$ = 0.1).

Similarly, on the second line we see that the bicycle speed equals 0.5 mi/min. Furthermore, his walking speed shown on line 3 will be 0.1, the same speed as on line 1; and his bicycling speed shown on line 4 will equal the speed (0.5) shown on line 2. Adding this information to our table, we get:

	speed	× time	= distance
	mi/min	*minutes*	*miles*
1. walking	0.1	10	1
2. bicycling	0.5	2	1
3. walking	0.1		
4. bicycling	0.5		

Step 6. Next, fill in the blanks with algebraic expressions to represent the quantities indicated, being careful to take advantage of simple relationships stated in the problem or appearing in the chart.

Continuing the example, we represent the time spent traveling shown on line 3 by x. According to the fundamental relationship, the distance traveled on this trip must be $(0.1)x$. Similarly, if y represents the time shown on line 4, the distance traveled is $(0.5)y$. Thus our chart now looks like this:

	speed	× time	= distance
	mi/min	*minutes*	*miles*
1. walking	0.1	10	1
2. bicycling	0.5	2	1
3. walking	0.1	x	$(0.1)x$
4. bicycling	0.5	y	$(0.5)y$

Step 7. Now, from the statement of the problem, you should be able to set up enough equations to solve for all the unknowns. In the example, there are two facts that we have not used yet. First, since Peter is going to his uncle's house and back, it is assumed that the distances covered on the two trips are equal. Thus we get the equation $(0.1)x = (0.5)y$. We are told that the total time to and from his uncle's house is one hour. Since we are using minutes as our unit of time, we convert the one hour to 60 minutes. Thus we get the equation: $x + y = 60$. Solving these two equations $(0.1x = 0.5y$ and $x + y = 60)$ algebraically, we find that $x = 50$ and $y = 10$. (See Section 407 for the solution of simultaneous equations.)

Step 8. Now that you have all the information necessary, you can calculate the answer required. In the sample problem, we are required to determine the distance to the uncle's house, which is $(0.1)x$ or $(0.5)y$. Using $x = 50$ or $y = 10$ gives us the distance as 5 miles.

Now that we have shown the fundamental steps in solving a rate problem, we shall discuss various types of rate problems.

Distance and Time

202. In *distance and time problems* the fundamental relationship that we use is *speed × time = distance*. Speed is the rate, time is the input, and distance is the output. The example in Section 201 is this type of problem.

Example: In a sports-car race, Danica gives Pablo a head start of 10 miles. Danica's car goes 80 miles per hour and Pablo's car goes 60 miles per hour. How long should it take Danica to catch up to Pablo if they both leave their starting marks at the same time?

Step 1. Here the fundamental quantities are *speed*, *time*, and *distance*.

Step 2. The fundamental relationship is speed × time = distance. Write this at the top of the chart.

Step 3. The unit for *distance* in this problem will be a *mile*. The unit for *speed* will be *miles per hour*. Since the speed is in miles per hour, our *time* will be in *hours*. Now our chart looks like this:

speed	×	time	=	distance
mi/hr		hours		miles

Step 4. The problem offers us certain information that we can add to the chart. First we must make two horizontal rows, one for Pablo and one for Danica. We know that Pablo's speed is 60 miles per hour and that Danica's speed is 80 miles per hour.

Step 5. In this case, none of the information in the chart can be used to calculate other information in the chart.

Step 6. Now we must use algebraic expressions to represent the unknowns. We know that both Pablo and Danica travel for the same amount of time, but we do not know for how much time, so we will place an x in the space for each driver's time. Now from the relationship of speed × time = distance, we can calculate Pablo's distance as $60x$ and Danica's distance as $80x$. Now the chart looks like this:

	speed	×	time	=	distance
	mi/hr		hours		miles
Pablo	60		x		$60x$
Danica	80		x		$80x$

Step 7. From the statement of the problem we know that Danica gave Pablo a 10-mile head start. In other words, Danica's distance is 10 more miles than Pablo's distance. This can be stated algebraically as $60x + 10 = 80x$. That is,

Pablo's distance + 10 miles = Danica's distance. Solving for x gives us $x = \frac{1}{2}$.

Step 8. The question asks how much time is required for Danica to catch up to Pablo. If we look at the chart, we see that this time is x, and x has already been calculated as $\frac{1}{2}$, so the answer is $\frac{1}{2}$ hour.

Work

203. In *work problems* the input is time and the output is the amount of work done. The rate is the work per unit of time.

Example: Jack can chop down 20 trees in 1 hour, whereas it takes Ted $1\frac{1}{2}$ hours to chop down 18 trees. If the two of them work together, how long will it take them to chop down 48 trees?

Solution: By the end of Step 5 your chart should look like this:

	rate	×	time	=	work
	trees/hr		hours		trees
1. Jack	20		1		20
2. Ted	12		$1\frac{1}{2}$		18
3. Jack	20				
4. Ted	12				

In Step 6, we represent the time that it takes Jack by x in line 3. Since we have the relationship that rate × time = work, we see that in line 3 the work is $20x$. Since the two boys work together (therefore, for the same amount of time), the time in line 4 must be x, and the work must be $12x$. Now, in Step 7, we see that the total work is 48 trees. From lines 3 and 4, then, $20x + 12x = 48$. Solving for x gives us $x = 1\frac{1}{2}$. We are asked to find the number of hours needed by the boys to chop down the 48 trees together, and we see that this time is x, or $1\frac{1}{2}$ hours.

Mixture

204. In *mixture problems* you are given a percent or a fractional composition of a substance, and you are asked questions about the weights and compositions of the substance. The basic relationship here is that the percentage of a certain substance in a mixture × the amount of the mixture = the amount of substance.

Note that it is often better to change percentages to decimals because it makes it easier to avoid errors.

Example: A chemist has two quarts of 25% acid solution and one quart of 40% acid solution. If he mixes these, what will be the concentration of the mixture?

Solution: Let x = concentration of the mixture. At the end of Step 6, our table will look like this:

	concentration ×	amount of sol	= amount of acid
	$\dfrac{qt\ (acid)}{qt\ (sol)}$	qts (sol)	qts (acid)
25% solution	0.25	2	0.50
40% solution	0.40	1	0.40
mixture	x	3	$3x$

We now have one additional bit of information: The amount of acid in the mixture must be equal to the total amount of acid in each of the two parts, so $3x = 0.50 + 0.40$. Therefore x is equal to 0.30, which is the same as a 30% concentration of the acid in the mixture.

Cost

205. In *cost problems* the rate is the *price per item*, the input is the *number of items*, and the output is the *value* of the items considered. When you are dealing with dollars and cents, you must be very careful to use the decimal point correctly.

Example: Jim has $3.00 in nickels and dimes in his pocket. If he has twice as many nickels as he has dimes, how many coins does he have altogether?

Solution: After Step 6, our chart should look like this (where c is the number of dimes Jim has):

	rate ×	number =	value
	cents/coin	*coins*	*cents*
nickels	5	$2c$	$10c$
dimes	10	c	$10c$

Now we recall the additional bit of information that the total value of the nickels and dimes is $3.00, or 300 cents. Thus, $5(2c) + 10c = 300$; $20c = 300$; so $c = 15$, the number of dimes. Jim has twice as many nickels, so $2c = 30$.

The total number of coins is $c + 2c = 3c = 45$.

The following table will serve as review for this Refresher Session.

Type of Problem	Fundamental Relationship
distance	speed × time = distance
work	rate × time = work done
mixture	concentration × amount of solution = amount of ingredient
cost	rate × number of items = cost

SESSION 2 PRACTICE TEST

Rate Problems: Distance and Time, Work, Mixture, and Cost

Correct answers and solutions follow this test.

1. A person rowed 3 miles upstream (against the current) in 90 minutes. If the river flowed with a current of 2 miles per hour, how long did the person's return trip take?

   (A) 20 minutes
   (B) 30 minutes
   (C) 45 minutes
   (D) 60 minutes
   (E) 80 minutes

   A B C D E
   ○ ○ ○ ○ ○

2. Aaron can do a job in 1 hour, Camilla can do the same job in 2 hours, and Bob can do the job in 3 hours. How long does it take them to do the job working together?

   (A) $\frac{6}{11}$ hour

   (B) $\frac{1}{2}$ hour

   (C) 6 hours

   (D) $\frac{1}{3}$ hour

   (E) $\frac{1}{6}$ hour

   A B C D E
   ○ ○ ○ ○ ○

3. Mr. Cheung had $2,000 to invest. He invested part of it at 5% per year and the remainder at 4% per year. After one year, his investment grew to $2,095. How much of the original investment was at the 5% rate?

   (A) $500
   (B) $750
   (C) $1,000
   (D) $1,250
   (E) $1,500

   A B C D E
   ○ ○ ○ ○ ○

4. Gabriel walks down the road for half an hour at an average speed of 3 miles per hour. He waits 10 minutes for a bus, which brings him back to his starting point at 3:15. If Gabriel began his walk at 2:25 the same afternoon, what was the average speed of the bus?

   (A) 1.5 miles per hour
   (B) 3 miles per hour
   (C) 4.5 miles per hour
   (D) 6 miles per hour
   (E) 9 miles per hour

   A B C D E
   ○ ○ ○ ○ ○

5. Faucet A lets water flow into a 5-gallon tub at a rate of 1.5 gallons per minute. Faucet B lets water flow into the same tub at a rate of 1.0 gallon per minute. Faucet A runs alone for 100 seconds; then the two of them together finish filling up the tub. How long does the whole operation take?

   (A) 120 seconds
   (B) 150 seconds
   (C) 160 seconds
   (D) 180 seconds
   (E) 190 seconds

   A B C D E
   ○ ○ ○ ○ ○

6. Coffee A normally costs 75¢ per pound. It is mixed with Coffee B, which normally costs 80¢ per pound, to form a mixture that costs 78¢ per pound.

If there are 10 pounds of the mix, how many pounds of Coffee A were used in the mix?

(A) 3
(B) 4
(C) 4.5
(D) 5
(E) 6

A B C D E
○ ○ ○ ○ ○

7. If an athlete can run p miles in x minutes, how long will it take her to run q miles at the same rate?

(A) $\dfrac{pq}{x}$ minutes

(B) $\dfrac{px}{q}$ minutes

(C) $\dfrac{q}{px}$ minutes

(D) $\dfrac{qx}{p}$ minutes

(E) $\dfrac{x}{pq}$ minutes

A B C D E
○ ○ ○ ○ ○

8. A train went 300 miles from City X to City Y at an average rate of 80 mph. At what speed did it travel on the way back if its average speed for the whole trip was 100 mph?

(A) 120 mph
(B) 125 mph
(C) $133\frac{1}{3}$ mph
(D) $137\frac{1}{2}$ mph
(E) 150 mph

A B C D E
○ ○ ○ ○ ○

9. Kaylee spent exactly $2.50 on 3¢, 6¢, and 10¢ stamps. If she bought ten 3¢ stamps and twice as many 6¢ stamps as 10¢ stamps, how many 10¢ stamps did she buy?

(A) 5
(B) 10
(C) 12
(D) 15
(E) 20

A B C D E
○ ○ ○ ○ ○

10. If 6 workers can complete 9 identical jobs in 3 days, how long will it take 4 workers to complete 10 such jobs?

(A) 3 days
(B) 4 days
(C) 5 days
(D) 6 days
(E) more than 6 days

A B C D E
○ ○ ○ ○ ○

11. A barge travels twice as fast when it is empty as when it is full. If it travels 20 miles north with a cargo, spends 20 minutes unloading, and returns to its original port empty, taking 8 hours to complete the entire trip, what is the speed of the barge when it is empty?

(A) less than 3 mph
(B) less than 4 mph but not less than 3 mph
(C) less than 6 mph but not less than 4 mph
(D) less than 8 mph but not less than 6 mph
(E) 8 mph or more

A B C D E
○ ○ ○ ○ ○

12. Liam can hammer 20 nails in 6 minutes. Jordan can do the same job in only 5 minutes. How long will it take them to finish if Liam hammers the first 5 nails, then Jordan hammers for 3 minutes, then Liam finishes the job?

(A) 4.6 minutes
(B) 5.0 minutes
(C) 5.4 minutes
(D) 5.8 minutes
(E) 6.0 minutes

A B C D E
○ ○ ○ ○ ○

13. Jessica has 2 quarts of a 30% acid solution and 3 pints of a 20% solution. If she mixes them, what will be the concentration (to the nearest percent) of the resulting solution? (1 quart = 2 pints.)

(A) 22%
(B) 23%
(C) 24%
(D) 25%
(E) 26%

A B C D E
○ ○ ○ ○ ○

14. Luiz has 12 coins totaling $1.45. None of his coins is larger than a quarter. Which of the following *cannot* be the number of quarters he has?

(A) 1
(B) 2
(C) 3
(D) 4
(E) 5

A B C D E
◯ ◯ ◯ ◯ ◯

15. Olivia's allowance is $1.20 per week. Colton's is 25¢ per day. If they save both their allowances together, how long will they have to save before they can get a model car set that costs $23.60?

(A) 6 weeks
(B) 8 weeks
(C) 10 weeks
(D) 13 weeks
(E) 16 weeks

A B C D E
◯ ◯ ◯ ◯ ◯

16. Matt can earn money at the following schedule: $2.00 for the first hour, $2.50 an hour for the next two hours, and $3.00 an hour after that. He also has the opportunity to take a different job that pays $2.75 an hour. He wants to work until he has earned $15.00. Which of the following is true?

(A) The first job will take him longer by 15 minutes or more.
(B) The first job will take him longer by less than 15 minutes.
(C) The two jobs will take the same length of time.
(D) The second job will take him longer by 30 minutes or more.
(E) The second job will take him longer by less than 10 minutes.

A B C D E
◯ ◯ ◯ ◯ ◯

17. If Robert can seal 40 envelopes in one minute, and Paul can do the same job in 80 seconds, how many minutes (to the nearest minute) will it take the two of them, working together, to seal 350 envelopes?

(A) 4 minutes
(B) 5 minutes

(C) 6 minutes
(D) 7 minutes
(E) 8 minutes

A B C D E
◯ ◯ ◯ ◯ ◯

18. Towns A and B are 400 miles apart. If a train leaves A in the direction of B at 50 miles per hour, how long will it take before that train meets another train, going from B to A, at a speed of 30 miles per hour? (*Note*: The train that leaves B departs at the same time as the train that leaves A.)

(A) 4 hours
(B) $4\frac{1}{3}$ hours
(C) 5 hours
(D) $5\frac{2}{3}$ hours
(E) $6\frac{2}{3}$ hours

A B C D E
◯ ◯ ◯ ◯ ◯

19. A rectangular tub has internal measurements of 2 feet × 2 feet × 5 feet. If two faucets, each with an output of 2 cubic feet of water per minute, pour water into the tub simultaneously, how many minutes does it take to fill the tub completely?

(A) less than 3 minutes
(B) less than 4 minutes, but not less than 3
(C) less than 5 minutes, but not less than 4
(D) less than 6 minutes, but not less than 5
(E) 6 minutes or more

A B C D E
◯ ◯ ◯ ◯ ◯

20. A 30% solution of barium chloride is mixed with 10 grams of water to form a 20% solution. How many grams were in the original solution?

(A) 10
(B) 15
(C) 20
(D) 25
(E) 30

A B C D E
◯ ◯ ◯ ◯ ◯

21. Mr. Chan had a coin collection including only nickels, dimes, and quarters. He had twice as many dimes as he had nickels, and half as many quarters as he had nickels. If the total face value of his collection was $300.00, how many quarters did the collection contain?

(A) 75
(B) 100
(C) 250
(D) 400
(E) 800

A B C D E
○ ○ ○ ○ ○

22. Pullig's Office Supply Store stocks a higher-priced pen and a lower-priced pen. If the store sells the higher-priced pens, which yield a profit of $1.20 per pen sold, it can sell 30 in a month. If the store sells the lower-priced pens, making a profit of 15¢ per pen sold, it can sell 250 pens in a month. Which type of pen will yield more profit per month, and by how much?

(A) The cheaper pen will yield a greater profit, by $1.50.
(B) The more expensive pen will yield a greater profit, by $1.50.
(C) The cheaper pen will yield a greater profit, by 15¢.
(D) The more expensive pen will yield a greater profit, by 15¢.
(E) Both pens will yield exactly the same profit.

A B C D E
○ ○ ○ ○ ○

23. At a cost of $2.50 per square yard, what would be the price of carpeting a rectangular floor, 18 feet × 24 feet?

(A) $120
(B) $360
(C) $750
(D) $1,000
(E) $1,080

A B C D E
○ ○ ○ ○ ○

24. Sarita and Elizabeth agreed to race across a 50-foot pool and back again. They started together, but Sarita finished 10 feet ahead of Elizabeth. If their rates were constant, and Sarita finished the race in 27 seconds, how long did it take Elizabeth to finish?

(A) 28 seconds
(B) 30 seconds
(C) $33\frac{1}{3}$ seconds
(D) 35 seconds
(E) 37 seconds

A B C D E
○ ○ ○ ○ ○

25. If four campers need $24.00 worth of food for a three-day camping trip, how much will two campers need for a two-week trip?

(A) $12.00
(B) $24.00
(C) $28.00
(D) $42.00
(E) $56.00

A B C D E
○ ○ ○ ○ ○

26. Wilson walks 15 blocks to work every morning at a rate of 2 miles per hour. If there are 20 blocks in a mile, how long does it take him to walk to work?

(A) $12\frac{1}{2}$ minutes
(B) 15 minutes
(C) $22\frac{1}{2}$ minutes
(D) $37\frac{1}{2}$ minutes
(E) 45 minutes

A B C D E
○ ○ ○ ○ ○

27. Logan River has a current of 3 miles per hour. A boat takes twice as long to travel upstream between two points as it does to travel downstream between the same two points. What is the speed of the boat in still water?

(A) 3 miles per hour
(B) 6 miles per hour

(C) 9 miles per hour
(D) 12 miles per hour
(E) The speed cannot be determined from the given information.

A B C D E
○ ○ ○ ○ ○

28. Raj can run 10 miles per hour, whereas Sheldon can run only 8 miles per hour. If they start at the same time from the same point and run in opposite directions, how far apart (to the nearest mile) will they be after 10 minutes?

(A) 1 mile
(B) 2 miles
(C) 3 miles
(D) 4 miles
(E) 5 miles

A B C D E
○ ○ ○ ○ ○

29. Machine A can produce 40 bolts per minute, whereas Machine B can produce only 30 per minute. Machine A begins alone to make bolts, but it breaks down after $1\frac{1}{2}$ minutes, and Machine B must complete the job. If the job requires 300 bolts, how long does the whole operation take?

(A) $7\frac{1}{2}$ minutes
(B) 8 minutes
(C) $8\frac{1}{2}$ minutes
(D) 9 minutes
(E) $9\frac{1}{2}$ minutes

A B C D E
○ ○ ○ ○ ○

30. Ten pints of 15% salt solution are mixed with 15 pints of 10% salt solution. What is the concentration of the resulting solution?

(A) 10%
(B) 12%
(C) 12.5%
(D) 13%
(E) 15%

A B C D E
○ ○ ○ ○ ○

31. Jeff makes $50 every day, from which he must spend $30 a day for various expenses. Pete makes $100 a day but has to spend $70 each day for expenses. If the two of them save together, how long will it take before they can buy a $1,500 used car?

(A) 10 days
(B) 15 days
(C) 30 days
(D) 50 days
(E) 75 days

A B C D E
○ ○ ○ ○ ○

32. Two cities are 800 miles apart. At 3:00 P.M., Plane A leaves one city, traveling toward the other city at a speed of 600 miles per hour. At 4:00 the same afternoon, Plane B leaves the first city, traveling in the same direction at a rate of 800 miles per hour. Which of the following answers represents the actual result?

(A) Plane A arrives first, by an hour or more.
(B) Plane A arrives first, by less than an hour.
(C) The two planes arrive at exactly the same time.
(D) Plane A arrives after Plane B, by less than an hour.
(E) Plane A arrives after Plane B, by an hour or more.

A B C D E
○ ○ ○ ○ ○

33. Sanjay has as many nickels as Doug has dimes; Doug has twice as many nickels as Sanjay has dimes. If together they have $2.50 in nickels and dimes, how many nickels does Sanjay have?

(A) 1 nickel
(B) 4 nickels
(C) 7 nickels
(D) 10 nickels
(E) The answer cannot be determined from the given information.

A B C D E
○ ○ ○ ○ ○

34. A delivery truck can travel 120 miles in either of two ways. It can travel at a constant rate of 40 miles per hour, or it can travel halfway at 50 miles

per hour, then slow down to 30 miles per hour for the second 60 miles. Which way is faster, and by how much?

(A) The constant rate is faster by 10 minutes or more.
(B) The constant rate is faster by less than 10 minutes.
(C) Neither way is faster; the two ways take exactly the same time.
(D) The changing rate is faster by less than 20 minutes.
(E) The changing rate is faster by 10 minutes or more.

A B C D E
○ ○ ○ ○ ○

35. John walks 10 miles at an average rate of 2 miles per hour and returns on a bicycle at an average rate of 10 miles per hour. How long (to the nearest hour) does the entire trip take him?

(A) 3 hours
(B) 4 hours
(C) 5 hours
(D) 6 hours
(E) 7 hours

A B C D E
○ ○ ○ ○ ○

36. If a plane can travel P miles in Q hours, how long will it take to travel R miles?

(A) $\dfrac{PQ}{R}$ hours

(B) $\dfrac{P}{QR}$ hours

(C) $\dfrac{QR}{P}$ hours

(D) $\dfrac{Q}{PR}$ hours

(E) $\dfrac{PR}{Q}$ hours

A B C D E
○ ○ ○ ○ ○

37. Alison can swim 75 feet in 12 seconds. What is her rate to the nearest mile per hour?

(A) 1 mph
(B) 2 mph

(C) 3 mph
(D) 4 mph
(E) 5 mph

A B C D E
○ ○ ○ ○ ○

38. How many pounds of a $1.20-per-pound nut mixture must be mixed with two pounds of a 90¢-per-pound mixture to produce a mixture that sells for $1.00 per pound?

(A) 0.5
(B) 1.0
(C) 1.5
(D) 2.0
(E) 2.5

A B C D E
○ ○ ○ ○ ○

39. A broken clock is set correctly at 12:00 noon. However, it registers only 20 minutes for each hour. In how many hours will it again register the correct time?

(A) 12
(B) 18
(C) 24
(D) 30
(E) 36

A B C D E
○ ○ ○ ○ ○

40. If a man travels p hours at an average rate of q miles per hour, and then r hours at an average rate of s miles per hour, what is his overall average rate of speed?

(A) $\dfrac{pq + rs}{p + r}$

(B) $\dfrac{q + s}{2}$

(C) $\dfrac{q + s}{p + r}$

(D) $\dfrac{p}{q} + \dfrac{r}{s}$

(E) $\dfrac{p}{s} + \dfrac{r}{q}$

A B C D E
○ ○ ○ ○ ○

41. If Lily can paint 25 feet of fence in an hour, and Samantha can paint 35 feet in an hour, how many minutes will it take them to paint a 150-foot fence, if they work together?

    (A) 150
    (B) 200
    (C) 240
    (D) 480
    (E) 500

    A B C D E
    ◯ ◯ ◯ ◯ ◯

42. If an athlete travels for a half hour at a rate of 20 miles per hour, and for another half hour at a rate of 30 miles per hour, what is the athlete's average speed?

    (A) 24 miles per hour
    (B) 25 miles per hour
    (C) 26 miles per hour
    (D) 26.5 miles per hour
    (E) The answer cannot be determined from the given information.

    A B C D E
    ◯ ◯ ◯ ◯ ◯

43. New York is 3,000 miles from Los Angeles. Sol leaves New York aboard a plane heading toward Los Angeles at the same time that Robert leaves Los Angeles aboard a plane heading toward New York. If Sol is moving at 200 miles per hour and Robert is moving at 400 miles per hour, how soon will one plane pass the other?

    (A) 2 hours
    (B) $22\frac{1}{2}$ hours
    (C) 5 hours
    (D) 4 hours
    (E) 12 hours

    A B C D E
    ◯ ◯ ◯ ◯ ◯

44. A tourist exchanged a dollar bill for change and received 7 coins, none of which was a half dollar. How many of these coins were dimes?

    (A) 0
    (B) 1

(C) 4
(D) 5
(E) The answer cannot be determined from the information given.

A B C D E
◯ ◯ ◯ ◯ ◯

45. A chemist adds two quarts of pure alcohol to a 30% solution of alcohol in water. If the new concentration is 40%, how many quarts of the original solution were there?

    (A) 12
    (B) 15
    (C) 18
    (D) 20
    (E) 24

    A B C D E
    ◯ ◯ ◯ ◯ ◯

46. The Energy Value Power Company charges 8¢ per kilowatt-hour for the first 1,000 kilowatt-hours, and 6¢ per kilowatt-hour after that. If a man uses a 900-watt toaster for 5 hours, a 100-watt lamp for 25 hours, and a 5-watt clock for 400 hours, how much is he charged for the power he uses? (1 kilowatt = 1,000 watts.)

    (A) 56¢
    (B) 64¢
    (C) 72¢
    (D) $560.00
    (E) $720.00

    A B C D E
    ◯ ◯ ◯ ◯ ◯

47. At 30¢ per yard, what is the price of 96 inches of ribbon?

    (A) 72¢
    (B) 75¢
    (C) 80¢
    (D) 84¢
    (E) 90¢

    A B C D E
    ◯ ◯ ◯ ◯ ◯

48. Maya travels for 6 hours at a rate of 50 miles per hour. Her return trip takes her $7\frac{1}{2}$ hours. What is her average speed for the whole trip?

    (A) 44.4 miles per hour
    (B) 45.0 miles per hour
    (C) 46.8 miles per hour
    (D) 48.2 miles per hour
    (E) 50.0 miles per hour

    A B C D E
    ○ ○ ○ ○ ○

49. Lucas puts $100 in the bank for two years at 5% interest compounded annually. At the end of the two years, what is his balance? (Interest = principal × rate × time)

    (A) $100.00
    (B) $105.00
    (C) $105.25
    (D) $110.00
    (E) $110.25

    A B C D E
    ○ ○ ○ ○ ○

50. A 12-gallon tub has a faucet that lets water in at a rate of 3 gallons per minute, and a drain that lets water out at a rate of 1.5 gallons per minute. If you start with 3 gallons of water in the tub, how long will it take to fill the tub completely? (Note that the faucet is on and the drain is open.)

    (A) 3 minutes
    (B) 4 minutes
    (C) 6 minutes
    (D) 7.5 minutes
    (E) 8 minutes

    A B C D E
    ○ ○ ○ ○ ○

Answer Key for Session 2 Practice Test

1. B	14. A	27. C	39. B
2. A	15. B	28. C	40. A
3. E	16. B	29. E	41. A
4. E	17. B	30. B	42. B
5. C	18. C	31. C	43. C
6. B	19. D	32. B	44. E
7. D	20. C	33. E	45. A
8. C	21. D	34. A	46. C
9. B	22. A	35. D	47. C
10. C	23. A	36. C	48. A
11. D	24. B	37. D	49. E
12. C	25. E	38. B	50. C
13. E	26. C		

Answers and Solutions for Session 2 Practice Test

1. Choice B is correct. The fundamental relationship here is: rate × time = distance. The easiest units to work with are miles per hour for the rate, hours for time, and miles for distance. Note that the word *per* indicates division, because when calculating a rate, we *divide* the number of miles (distance units) by the number of hours (time units).

We can set up our chart with the information given.

We know that the upstream trip took $1\frac{1}{2}$ hours (90 minutes) and that the distance was 3 miles. Thus the upstream rate was 2 miles per hour. The downstream distance was also 3 miles, but we use t for the time, which is unknown. Thus the downstream rate was $\frac{3}{t}$. Our chart looks like this:

	rate ×	time =	distance
	miles/hour	*hours*	*miles*
upstream	2	$1\frac{1}{2}$	3
downstream	$\frac{3}{t}$	t	3

We use the rest of the information to solve for t. We know that the speed of the current is 2 miles per hour. We assume the boat to be in still water and assign it a speed, s; then the upstream (against the current) speed of the boat is $s - 2$ miles per hour. Since $s - 2 = 2$, $s = 4$.

Now the speed of the boat downstream (with the current) is $s + 2$, or 6 miles per hour. This is equal to $\frac{3}{t}$, and we get the equation $\frac{3}{t} = 6$, so $t = \frac{1}{2}$ hour. We must be careful with our units because the answer must be in minutes. We can convert $\frac{1}{2}$ hour to 30 minutes to get the final answer.

(Refreshers 201, 202)

2. Choice A is correct.

	rate ×	time =	work
	jobs/hour	*hours*	*jobs*
Aaron	1	1	1
Camilla	$\frac{1}{2}$	2	1
Bob	$\frac{1}{3}$	3	1
together	r	t	1

Let r = rate together and t = time together.

Now, $r = 1 + \frac{1}{2} + \frac{1}{3} = \frac{11}{6}$ because *whenever two or more people are working together, their joint rate is the sum of their individual rates*. This is not necessarily true of the time or the work done. In this case, we know that $r \times t = 1$ and $r = \frac{11}{6}$, so $t = \frac{6}{11}$. (Refreshers 201, 203)

3. Choice E is correct.

	rate ×	principal =	interest
	$/$	*$*	*$*
5%	0.05	x	0.05x
4%	0.04	y	0.04y

Let x = the part of the $2,000 invested at 5%. Let y = the part of $2,000 invested at 4%. We know that since the whole $2,000 was invested, $x + y$ must equal $2,000. Furthermore, we know that the sum of the interests on both investments equaled $95, so $0.05x + 0.04y = 95$. Since we have to solve only for x, we can express this as $0.01x + 0.04x + 0.04y = 95$. Then we factor out 0.04. Thus $0.01x + 0.04(x + y) = 95$. Since we know that $x + y = 2,000$, we have $0.01x + 0.04(2,000) = 95$; $0.01x + 80 = 95$; and $x = 1,500$. Thus, $1,500 was invested at 5%.

(Refreshers 201, 205)

4. Choice E is correct.

	rate $\times$	time $=$	distance
	miles/min	*minutes*	*miles*
walk	$\frac{1}{20}$	30	a
wait	0	10	0
bus	r	t	a

Let a = distance Gabriel walks. Since Gabriel walks at 3 miles per hour, he walks at $\frac{3 \text{ mi}}{60 \text{ min}}$ or $\frac{1 \text{ mi}}{20 \text{ min}}$.

From this we can find $a = \frac{1 \text{ mi}}{20 \text{ min}} \times 30 \text{ min} = 1\frac{1}{2}$ miles. The total time he spent was 50 minutes (the difference between 3:15 and 2:25), and $30 + 10 + t = 50$, so t must be equal to 10 minutes. This reduces our problem to the simple equation $10r = 1\frac{1}{2}$ (where r = rate of the bus), and, on solving, $r = 0.15$ mile per minute. But the required answer is in miles per hour. In one hour, or 60 minutes, the bus can travel 60 times as far as the 0.15 mile it travels in one minute, so the bus travels $60 \times 0.15 = 9$ miles per hour.

(Refreshers 201, 202)

5. Choice C is correct.

	rate $\times$	time $=$	water
	gallons/min	*minutes*	*gallons*
A only	1.5	$\frac{5}{3}$*	2.5
B only	1.0	0	0
A and B	2.5	t	x

*$\frac{5}{3}$ min = 100 sec.

Let t = time faucets A and B run together.

Let x = amount of water delivered when A and B run together.

We know that the total number of gallons is 5, and A alone delivers 2.5 gallons (1.5 gal/min $\times \frac{5}{3}$ min $= 2.5$ gal), so x equals 2.5. This leads us to the simple equation $2.5t = 2.5$, so $t = 1$ minute, or 60 seconds. Thus, the whole operation takes $\frac{5}{3} + t$ minutes, or $100 + 60$ seconds, totaling 160 seconds.

(Refreshers 201, 203)

6. Choice B is correct.

	rate $\times$	amount $=$	cost
	¢/lb	*lb*	*¢*
Coffee A	75	x	$75x$
Coffee B	80	y	$80y$
mix	78	10	780

Let x = weight of Coffee A in the mix.

Let y = weight of Coffee B in the mix.

We know that the weight of the mix is equal to the sum of the weights of its components. Thus, $x + y = 10$. Similarly, the cost of the mix is equal to the sum of the costs of the components. Thus, $75x + 80y = 780$. So we have $x + y = 10$ and $75x + 80y = 780$. Now $y = 10 - x$, so substituting $y = 10 - x$ in the second equation, we get

$$75x + 80(10 - x) = 780$$
$$75x + 800 - 80x = 780$$
$$800 - 5x = 780$$
$$20 = 5x$$
$$4 = x$$

Thus 4 pounds of Coffee A were used.

(Refreshers 201, 204, 407)

7. Choice D is correct.

	rate $\times$	time $=$	distance
	miles/min	*minutes*	*miles*
first run	r	x	p
second run	r	t	q

Let r = rate of the athlete.

Let t = time it takes her to run q miles.

From the first line, we know that $rx = p$, then $r = \frac{p}{x}$. Substituting this in the second line, we get $\left(\frac{p}{x}\right)t = q$, so $t = q\left(\frac{x}{p}\right)$, or $\frac{qx}{p}$ minutes.

(Refreshers 201, 202)

8. Choice C is correct.

	rate $\times$	time $=$	distance
	miles/hour	hours	miles
X to Y	80	t	300
Y to X	r	s	300
whole trip	100	$s + t$	600

Let t = time from city X to city Y.

Let s = time from city Y to city X.

Let r = rate of the train from Y to X.

We know that $80t = 300$, so $t = \dfrac{300}{80}$, or $\dfrac{15}{4}$. Also, $100(s + t) = 600$, so $s + t = 6$. This and the last equation lead us to the conclusion that $s = 6 - \dfrac{15}{4}$, or $\dfrac{9}{4}$. Now, from the middle line, we have $r\left(\dfrac{9}{4}\right) = 300$, so $r = \dfrac{400}{3}$, or $133\dfrac{1}{3}$ miles per hour.

(Note that the reason we chose the equations in this particular order was that it is easiest to concentrate first on those with the most data already given.)
(Refreshers 201, 202)

9. Choice B is correct.

	rate $\times$	number $=$	cost
	¢/stamp	stamps	¢
3¢ stamps	3	10	30
10¢ stamps	10	x	$10x$
6¢ stamps	6	$2x$	$12x$

Let x = the number of 10¢ stamps bought.

We know that the total cost is 250¢, so $30 + 10x + 12x = 250$. This is the same as $22x = 220$, so $x = 10$. Therefore, she bought ten 10¢ stamps.
(Refreshers 201, 205)

10. Choice C is correct.

	rate $\times$	time $=$	work
	jobs/day	days	jobs
6 workers	$6r$	3	9
4 workers	$4r$	t	10

Let r = rate of one worker.

Let t = time for 4 workers to do 10 jobs.

From the first line, we have $18r = 9$, so $r = \dfrac{1}{2}$.

Substituting this in the second line, $4r = 2$, so $2t = 10$. Therefore $t = 5$. The workers will take 5 days.
(Refreshers 201, 203)

11. Choice D is correct.

	rate $\times$	time $=$	distance
	miles/hour	hours	miles
north	r	$\frac{20}{r}$	20
unload	0	$\frac{1}{3}$	0
return	$2r$	$\frac{10}{r}$	20

Let r = loaded rate; then
$$2r = \text{empty rate}$$
Total time $= \dfrac{20}{r} + \dfrac{1}{3} + \dfrac{10}{r} = 8$ hours.

Multiplying by $3r$ on both sides, we get $90 = 23r$, so $r = 90 \div 23$, or about 3.9 miles per hour. However, the problem asks for the speed *when empty*, which is $2r$, or 7.8. This is less than 8 mph, but not less than 6 mph. (Refreshers 201, 202)

12. Choice C is correct.

	rate $\times$	time $=$	work
	nails/min	minutes	nails
Liam	r	6	20
Jordan	s	5	20
Liam	r	$\frac{5}{r}$	5
Jordan	s	3	$3s$
Liam	r	$\frac{x}{r}$	x

Let r = Liam's rate.

Let s = Jordan's rate.

x = number of nails left after Jordan takes her turn.

$6r = 20$, so $r = 3\frac{1}{3}$.

$5s = 20$, so $s = 4$.

Total work $= 5 + 3s + x = 20 = 5 + 12 + x = 20$,

so $x = 3$. Thus $\frac{x}{r} = 0.9$.

Total time $= \frac{5}{r} + 3 + \frac{x}{r}$

$= \dfrac{5}{\left(\dfrac{10}{3}\right)} + 3 + 0.9$

$= \dfrac{15}{10} + 3 + 0.9$

$= 1.5 + 3 + 0.9$

$= 5.4$ \hspace{1em} (Refreshers 201, 203)

13. Choice E is correct.

	concentration × volume =		amount of acid
	% acid	pts	pts
old solution	30%	4	1.2
	20%	3	0.6
new solution	x%	7	1.8

(2 qts = 4 pts)

Let x% = concentration of new solution.

4 pts of 30% + 3 pts of 20% = 7 pts of x%

1.2 pts + 0.6 pt = 1.8 pts

$(x\%)(7) = 1.8$, so $x = 180 \div 7 = 25.7$ (approximately), which is closest to 26%.

(Refreshers 201, 204)

14. Choice A is correct.

	coin × number =		total value
	¢/coin	coins	¢
pennies	1	p	p
nickels	5	n	$5n$
dimes	10	d	$10d$
quarters	25	q	$25q$

Let p = number of pennies
n = number of nickels
d = number of dimes
q = number of quarters

Total number of coins $= p + n + d + q = 12$.

Total value $= p + 5n + 10d + 25q = 145$.

Now, if $q = 1$, then $p + n + d = 11$, $p + 5n + 10d = 120$. But in this case, the greatest possible value of the other eleven coins would be the value of eleven dimes, or 110 cents, which falls short of the amount necessary to give a total of 145 cents for the twelve coins put together. Therefore, Luiz cannot have only one quarter.

(Refreshers 201, 205)

15. Choice B is correct.

	rate ×	time =	money
	¢/week	weeks	¢
Olivia	120	w	$120w$
Colton	175	w	$175w$
together	295	w	$295w$

(25¢/day = $1.75/week)

Let w = the number of weeks they save.

Total money $= 295w = 2,360$.

Therefore, $w = 2,360 \div 295 = 8$.

So, they must save for 8 weeks.

(Refreshers 201, 205)

16. Choice B is correct.

	rate ×	time =	pay
	¢/hour	hours	¢
first job	200	1	200
	250	2	500
	300	x	$300x$
second job	275	y	$275y$

Let x = hours at $3.00.

Let y = hours at $2.75.

Total pay, first job $= 200 + 500 + 300x = 1,500$,

so $x = 2\frac{2}{3}$.

Total time, first job $= 1 + 2 + 2\frac{2}{3} = 5\frac{2}{3}$.

Total pay, second job $= 275y = 1,500$, so $y = 5\frac{5}{11}$.

Total time, second job $= 5\frac{5}{11}$.

$\frac{2}{3}$ hour = 40 minutes

$\frac{5}{11}$ hour = 27.2727 minutes (less than $\frac{2}{3}$ hour).

Thus, the first job will take him longer by less than 15 minutes. \hspace{1em} (Refreshers 201, 203)

17. Choice B is correct.

	rate ×	time =	work
	envelopes/min	min	envelopes
Robert	40	t	40t
Paul	30	t	30t
together	70	t	70t

Let t = time to seal 350 envelopes.

Paul's rate is 30 envelopes/minute, as shown by the proportion:

$$\text{rate} = \frac{40 \text{ envelopes}}{80 \text{ seconds}} = \frac{30 \text{ envelopes}}{60 \text{ seconds}}$$

Total work = $70t = 350$, so $t = 5$ minutes.

(Refreshers 201, 203)

18. Choice C is correct.

	rate ×	time =	distance
	miles/hour	hours	miles
A to B	50	t	50t
B to A	30	t	30t

Let t = time to meet.

Total distance traveled by two trains together equals $50t + 30t = 80t = 400$ miles, so $t = 5$ hrs.

(Refreshers 201, 202)

19. Choice D is correct.

	rate ×	time =	amount of water
	cu ft/min	minutes	cu ft
2 faucets	4	t	20

Let t = time to fill the tub.

Volume of tub = 2 ft × 2 ft × 5 ft = 20 cu ft

Rate = 2 × rate of each faucet

$$= 2 \times \frac{2 \text{ cu ft}}{\text{min}} = \frac{4 \text{ cu ft}}{\text{min}}$$

Therefore, $t = 5$ minutes.   (Refreshers 201, 203)

20. Choice C is correct.

	concentration ×	weight =	amount of barium chloride
	%	grams	grams
original	30%	x	0.30x
water	0%	10	0
new	20%	10 + x	0.30x

Let x = number of grams of original solution.

Total weight and amounts of barium chloride may be added by column.

$(20\%) \times (10 + x) = 0.30x$, so $10 + x = 1.50x$, $x = 20$.   (Refreshers 201, 204)

21. Choice D is correct.

	coin ×	number =	value
	¢/coin	coins	¢
nickels	5	n	5n
dimes	10	2n	20n
quarters	25	$\frac{n}{2}$	$\frac{25n}{2}$

Let n = number of nickels.

Total value = $5n + 20n + \frac{25n}{2} = \left(37\frac{1}{2}\right)n = 30{,}000$.

Thus, $n = 30{,}000 \div 37\frac{1}{2} = 800$.

The number of quarters is then $\frac{n}{2} = \frac{800}{2} = 400$.

(Refreshers 201, 205)

22. Choice A is correct.

	rate ×	number =	profit
	¢/pen	pens	¢
high-price	120	30	3,600
low-price	15	250	3,750

Subtracting 3,600¢ from 3,750¢, we get 150¢.

Thus, the cheaper pen yields a profit of 150¢, or $1.50, more per month than the more expensive one.

(Refreshers 201, 205)

23. Choice A is correct.

price	×	area	=	cost
$/sq yd		sq yd		$
2.50		48		120

Area must be expressed in square yards; 18 ft = 6 yd, and 24 ft = 8 yd, so 18 ft × 24 ft = 6 yd × 8 yd = 48 sq yd. The cost would then be $2.50 × 48 = $120.00.   (Refreshers 201, 205)

24. Choice B is correct.

	rate ×	time =	distance
	feet/sec	sec	feet
Sarita	r	27	100
Elizabeth	s	27	90
Elizabeth	s	t	100

Let r = Sarita's rate.

Let s = Elizabeth's rate.

Let t = Elizabeth's time to finish the race.

$27s = 90$, so $s = \dfrac{90}{27} = \dfrac{10}{3}$;

$st = 100$, and $s = \dfrac{10}{3}$, so $\dfrac{10t}{3} = 100$; thus $t = 30$.
          (Refreshers 201, 202)

25. Choice E is correct. This is a rate problem in which the fundamental relationship is rate × time × number of campers = cost. The rate is in $\dfrac{\text{dollars}}{\text{camper-days}}$.

Thus, our chart looks like this:

	rate ×	time ×	number =	cost
	$/camper-days	days	campers	$
1st trip	r	3	4	$12r$
2nd trip	r	14	2	$28r$

The cost of the first trip is $24, so $12r = 24$ and $r = 2$.

The cost of the second trip is $28r$, or $56.
          (Refreshers 201, 205)

26. Choice C is correct.

rate ×	time =	distance
blocks/min	minutes	blocks
$\frac{2}{3}$	t	15

Let t = time to walk to work.

$$\frac{2 \text{ miles}}{\text{hr}} = 2\frac{(20 \text{ blocks})}{(60 \text{ min})} = \frac{\frac{2}{3} \text{ blocks}}{\text{min}}.$$

$t = 15 \div \dfrac{2}{3} = 22\dfrac{1}{2}$ minutes.
          (Refreshers 201, 202)

27. Choice C is correct.

	rate ×	time =	distance
	miles/hour	hours	miles
down	$r + 3$	h	$h(r + 3)$
up	$r - 3$	$2h$	$2h(r - 3)$

Let h = time to travel downstream.

Let r = speed of the boat in still water.

Since the two trips cover the same distance, we can write the equation: $h(r + 3) = 2h(r - 3)$. Dividing by h, $r + 3 = 2r - 6$, so $r = 9$.
          (Refreshers 201, 202)

28. Choice C is correct. We could treat this as a regular distance problem and make up a table that would solve it, but there is an easier way here, if we consider the quantity representing the distance between the boys. This distance starts at zero and increases at the rate of 18 miles per hour. Thus, in 10 minutes, or $\dfrac{1}{6}$ hour, they will be 3 miles apart. ($\dfrac{1}{6}$ hr × $18\dfrac{\text{mi}}{\text{hr}} = 3$ mi).   (Refreshers 201, 202)

29. Choice E is correct.

	rate ×	time =	work
	bolts/min	minutes	bolts
A	40	$1\frac{1}{2}$	60
B	30	t	240

Let t = time B works.

Since A produces only 60 out of 300 that must be produced, B must produce 240; then, $30t = 240$, so $t = 8$.

Total time $= t + 1\frac{1}{2} = 8 + 1\frac{1}{2} = 9\frac{1}{2}$.

(Refreshers 201, 203)

30. Choice B is correct.

concentration	× volume	= amount of salt
%	pints	pints of salt
15% 15	10	1.5
10% 10	15	1.5
total x	25	3.0

Let $x =$ concentration of resulting solution.

$(x\%)(25) = 3.0$, so $x = 300 \div 25 = 12$.

(Refreshers 201, 204)

31. Choice C is correct.

	rate ×	time =	pay (net)
	$/day	days	$
Jeff	20	d	20d
Pete	30	d	30d
total	50	d	50d

(Net pay = pay − expenses.)

Let $d =$ the number of days it takes to save.

Total net pay $= \$1,500$, so $1,500 = 50d$, thus $d = 30$.

Do not make the mistake of using 50 and 100 as the rates!   (Refreshers 201, 205)

32. Choice B is correct.

	rate ×	time =	distance
	miles/hour	hours	miles
plane A	600	h	800
plane B	0	1	0
plane B	800	t	800

Let $h =$ time for trip at 600 mph.

Let $t =$ time for trip at 800 mph.

Plane A: $600h = 800$, so $h = \frac{800}{600} = 1\frac{1}{3}$ hours $= 1$ hour, 20 minutes.

Plane B: $800t = 800$, so $t = 1$.

Total time for plane A = 1 hour, 20 minutes.

Total time for plane B = 1 hour + 1 hour = 2 hours.

Thus, plane A arrives before plane B by 40 minutes (less than an hour).   (Refreshers 201, 202)

33. Choice E is correct.

	coin ×	number =	value
	¢/coin	coins	¢
Sanjay	5	n	5n
Sanjay	10	d	10d
Doug	5	2d	10d
Doug	10	n	10n

Let $n =$ number of Sanjay's nickels.
Let $d =$ number of Sanjay's dimes.

Total value of coins $= 5n + 10d + 10d + 10n = 15n + 20d$.

Thus, $15n + 20d = 250$. This has many different solutions, each of which is possible (e.g., $n = 2$, $d = 11$, or $n = 6$, $d = 8$, etc.).

(Refreshers 201, 205)

34. Choice A is correct.

	rate ×	time =	distance
	miles/hour	hours	miles
constant rate	40	h	120
two rates	50	m	60
	30	n	60

Let $h =$ time to travel 120 miles at the constant rate.
Let $m =$ time to travel 60 miles at 50 mi/hr.
Let $n =$ time to travel 60 miles at 30 mi/hr.

Forming the equations for h, m, and n, and solving, we get:

$$40h = 120;\ h = \frac{120}{40};\ h = 3$$

$$50m = 60;\ m = \frac{60}{50};\ m = 1.2$$

$$30n = 60;\ n = \frac{60}{30};\ n = 2$$

Total time with constant rate $= h = 3$ hours.
Total time with changing rate $= m + n = 3.2$ hours.

Thus, the constant rate is faster by 0.2 hour, or 12 minutes.   (Refreshers 201, 202)

35. Choice D is correct.

	rate	×	time	=	distance
	miles/hour		hours		miles
walking	2		h		10
bicycling	10		t		10

Let h = time to walk.

Let t = time to bicycle.

Forming equations: $2h = 10$, so $h = 5$; and $10t = 10$, so $t = 1$.

Total time = $h + t = 5 + 1 = 6$.

(Refreshers 201, 202)

36. Choice C is correct.

rate	×	time	=	distance
miles/hour		hours		miles
x		Q		P
x		y		R

Let x = rate at which the airplane travels.

Let y = time to travel R miles.

$Qx = P$, so $x = \dfrac{P}{Q}$.

$xy = \left(\dfrac{P}{Q}\right)y = R$, so $y = \dfrac{QR}{P}$ hours = time to travel R miles. (Refreshers 201, 202)

37. Choice D is correct.

rate	×	time	=	distance
miles/hour		hours		miles
r		$\frac{1}{300}$		$\frac{75}{5,280}$

Let r = rate of swimming.

75 feet = $75\left(\dfrac{1}{5,280} \text{ mile}\right) = \dfrac{75}{5,280}$ mile

12 seconds = $12\left(\dfrac{1}{3,600} \text{ hour}\right) = \dfrac{1}{300}$ hour

$r = \dfrac{75}{5,280} \div \dfrac{1}{300} = \dfrac{22,500}{5,280}$

  = 4.3 (approximately)

  = 4 mi/hr (approximately).

(Refreshers 201, 202)

38. Choice B is correct.

	price	×	amount	=	value
	¢/lb		lbs		¢
$1.20 nuts	120		x		$120x$
$0.90 nuts	90		2		180
mixture	100		$x + 2$		$180 \times 120x$

Let x = pounds of $1.20 mixture.

Total value of mixture = $100(x + 2) = 180 + 120x$.
$100x + 200 = 180 + 120x$, so $x = 1$ pound.

(Refreshers 201, 204)

39. Choice B is correct.

rate	×	time	=	loss
hours/hour		hours		hours
$\frac{2}{3}$		t		12

(Loss is the amount by which the clock time differs from real time.)

Let t = hours to register the correct time.

If the clock registers only 20 minutes each hour, it loses 40 minutes, or $\dfrac{2}{3}$ hour each hour. The clock will register the correct time only if it has lost some multiple of 12 hours. The first time this can occur is after it has lost 12 hours. $\left(\dfrac{2}{3}\right)t = 12$, so $t = 18$ hours. (Refresher 201)

40. Choice A is correct.

	rate	×	time	=	distance
	miles/hour		hours		miles
	q		p		pq
	s		r		rs
total	x		$p + r$		$pq + rs$

Let x = average speed.

We may add times of travel at the two rates, and also add the distances. Then, $x(p + r) = pq + rs$; thus,

$x = \dfrac{pq + rs}{p + r}$. (Refreshers 201, 202)

41. Choice A is correct.

	rate $\times$	time $=$	work
	feet/hour	hours	feet
Samantha	35	x	$35x$
Lily	25	x	$25x$
both	60	x	$60x$

Let $x =$ the time the job takes.

Since they are working together, we add their rates and the amount of work they do. Thus, $60x = 150$, so $x = 2.5$ (hours) $= 150$ minutes.

(Refreshers 201, 203)

42. Choice B is correct.

	rate $\times$	time $=$	distance
	miles/hour	hours	miles
first $\frac{1}{2}$ hour	20	$\frac{1}{2}$	10
second $\frac{1}{2}$ hour	30	$\frac{1}{2}$	15
total	x	1	25

Let $x =$ average speed.

We add the times and distances; then, using the rate formula, $(x)(1) = 25$, so $x = 25$ mi/hr.

(Refreshers 201, 202)

43. Choice C is correct.

	rate $\times$	time $=$	distance
	miles/hour	hours	miles
Sol	200	t	$200t$
Robert	400	t	$400t$

Let $t =$ time from simultaneous departure to meeting.

Sol's time is equal to Robert's time because they leave at the same time and then they meet. Their combined distance is 3,000 miles, so $200t + 400t = 3,000$, or $t = 5$ hours. (Refreshers 201, 202)

44. Choice E is correct.

	coin $\times$	number $=$	value
	¢/coin	coins	¢
pennies	1	p	p
nickels	5	n	$5n$
dimes	10	d	$10d$
quarters	25	q	$25q$

Let $p =$ number of pennies.

Let $n =$ number of nickels.

Let $d =$ number of dimes.

Let $q =$ number of quarters.

Adding the numbers of coins and their values, we get $p + n + d + q = 7$, and $p + 5n + 10d + 25q = 100$. These equations are satisfied by several values of p, n, d, and q. For example, $p = 0$, $n = 0$, $d = 5$, $q = 2$ satisfies the equation, as does $p = 0$, $n = 3$, $d = 1$, $q = 3$, and other combinations.

Thus, the number of dimes cannot be determined.

(Refreshers 201, 205)

45. Choice A is correct.

	concentration $\times$	amount of solution $=$	amount of alcohol
	%	quarts	quarts
pure alcohol	100%	2	2
solution	30%	x	$0.30x$
mixture	40%	$2 + x$	$2 + 0.30x$

Let $x =$ quarts of original solution.

Amounts of solution and of alcohol may be added. $(40\%)(2 + x) = 2 + 0.30x$; so $0.8 + 0.4x = 2.0 + 0.30x$; thus, $x = 12$.　　(Refreshers 201, 204)

46. Choice C is correct.

	rate $\times$	time $=$	cost
	¢/kWh	kWh	¢
first 1,000 kWh	8	t	$8t$

(time expressed in kilowatt-hours, or kWh)

Let t = number of kWh.

This problem must be broken up into two different parts: (1) finding the total power or the total number of kilowatt-hours (kWh) used, and (2) calculating the charge for that amount. (1) Total power used, $t = (900w)(5 \text{ hr}) + (100w)(25 \text{ hr}) + (5w)(400 \text{ hr})$ $= (4,500 + 2,500 + 2,000)$ watt-hours $= 9,000$ watt-hours. (2) 1,000 watt-hours $= 1$ kilowatt-hour. Thus, $t = 9$ kilowatt-hours, so that the charge is $(8¢)(9) = 72¢$. (Refreshers 201, 205)

47. Choice C is correct.

	rate $\times$	amount $=$	cost
	¢/inch	inches	¢
1 yard	r	36	30
96 inches	r	96	$96r$

Let r = cost per inch of ribbon.

From the table, $r \times 36 \text{ in} = 30¢$; $r = \dfrac{30¢}{36 \text{ in.}} = \dfrac{5¢}{6 \text{ in.}}$.

Thus, $96r = 96\left(\dfrac{5}{6}\right) = 80¢$. (Refreshers 201, 205)

48. Choice A is correct.

	rate $\times$	time $=$	distance
	miles/hour	hours	miles
trip	50	6	300
return	r	$7\frac{1}{2}$	300
total	s	$13\frac{1}{2}$	600

Let r = rate for return.

Let s = average overall rate.

$(13\frac{1}{2})(s) = 600$; thus, $s = 600 \div 13\frac{1}{2} = 44.4$

(approximately). (Refreshers 201, 202)

49. Choice E is correct.

	rate $\times$	principal $=$	interest
	%/year	$	$/year
first year	5	100	5
second year	5	105	5.25

Interest first year equals rate $\times$ principal = 5% $\times$ \$100 = \$5.

New principal = \$105.00.

Interest second year = rate $\times$ new principal = 5% $\times$ \$105 = \$5.25.

Final principal = \$105.00 + \$5.25 = \$110.25.

(Refreshers 201, 205)

50. Choice C is correct.

	rate $\times$	time $=$	amount
	gallons/min	minutes	gallons
in	3	x	$3x$
out	$1\frac{1}{2}$	x	$1\frac{1}{2}x$
net	$1\frac{1}{2}$	x	$1\frac{1}{2}x$

(Net = in − out.)

Let x = time to fill the tub completely.

Since only 9 gallons are needed (there are already 3 in the tub), we have $1\frac{1}{2}x = 9$, so $x = 6$.

(Refresher 201)

MATH REFRESHER SESSION 3

Area, Perimeter, and Volume Problems

301. *Formula Problems.* Here, you are given certain data about one or more geometric figures, and you are asked to supply some missing information. To solve this type of problem, follow this procedure:

Step 1. If you are not given a diagram, draw your own; this may make the answer readily apparent or may suggest the best way to solve the problem. You should try to make your diagram as accurate as possible, but *do not waste time perfecting your diagram*.

Step 2. Determine the formula that relates to the quantities involved in your problem. In many cases it will be helpful to set up tables containing the various data. (See Sections 303−317.)

Step 3. Substitute the given information for the unknown quantities in your formulas to get the desired answer.

When doing volume, area, and perimeter problems, keep this hint in mind: Often the solutions to such problems can be expressed as the sum of the areas *or* volumes *or* perimeters of simpler figures. In such cases, do not hesitate to break down your original figure into simpler parts.

> *In doing problems involving the following figures, these approximations and facts will be useful:*
>
> $\sqrt{2}$ is approximately 1.4.
>
> $\sqrt{3}$ is approximately 1.7.
>
> $\sqrt{10}$ is approximately 3.16.
>
> π is approximately $\frac{22}{7}$ or 3.14.
>
> $\sin 30° = \frac{1}{2}$
>
> $\sin 45° = \frac{\sqrt{2}}{2}$, which is approximately 0.71.
>
> $\sin 60° = \frac{\sqrt{3}}{2}$, which is approximately 0.87.

Example: The following figure contains a square, a right triangle, and a semicircle. If $ED = CD$ and the length of CD is 1 unit, find the area of the entire figure.

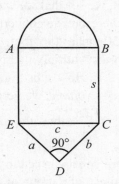

Solution: To calculate the area of the entire figure, we calculate the areas of the triangle, square, and semicircle and then add these together. In a right triangle, the area is $\frac{1}{2}ab$ where a and b are the sides of the triangle. In this case we will call side ED, a, and side CD, b. $ED = CD = 1$, so the area of the triangle is $\frac{1}{2}(1)(1)$, or $\frac{1}{2}$.

The area of a square is s^2, where s is a side. We see that the side EC of the square is the hypotenuse of the right triangle. We can calculate this length by using the formula $c^2 = a^2 + b^2$. Where $a = b = 1$, then $c = \sqrt{2}$. Thus, in this case, $s = \sqrt{2}$ so the area of the square is $(\sqrt{2})^2 = 2$.

AB is the diameter of the semicircle, so $\frac{1}{2}AB$ is the radius. Since all sides of a square are equal, $AB = \sqrt{2}$, and the radius is $\frac{1}{2}\sqrt{2}$. Further, the area of a semicircle is $\frac{1}{2}\pi r^2$, where r is the radius, so the area of this semicircle is $\frac{1}{2}\pi\left(\frac{1}{2}\sqrt{2}\right)^2 = \frac{1}{4}\pi$.

The total area of the whole figure is equal to the area of the triangle plus the area of the square plus the area of the semicircle $= \frac{1}{2} + 2 + \frac{1}{4}\pi = 2\frac{1}{2} + \frac{1}{4}\pi$.

Example: If water flows into a rectangular tank with dimensions of 12 inches, 18 inches, and 30 inches at the rate of 0.25 cubic foot per minute, how long will it take to fill the tank?

Solution: This problem is really a combination of a rate problem and a volume problem. First we must calculate the volume, and then we must substitute in a rate equation to get our final answer. The formula for the volume of a rectangular solid is $V = lwh$, where l, w, and h are the length, width, and height, respectively. We must multiply the three dimensions of the tank to get the volume. However, if we look ahead to the second part of the problem, we see that we want the volume in cubic *feet;* therefore we convert 12 inches, 18 inches, and 30 inches to 1 foot, 1.5 feet, and 2.5 feet, respectively. Multiplying gives us a volume of 3.75 cubic feet. Now substituting in the equation *rate × time = volume*, we get $0.25 \times time = 3.75$; $time = \dfrac{3.75}{0.25}$; thus, the time is 15 minutes.

302. *Comparison problems.* Here you are asked to identify the largest, or smallest, of a group of figures, or to place them in ascending or descending order of size. The following procedure is the most efficient one:

Step 1. Always diagram each figure before you come to any conclusions. Whenever possible, try to include two or more of the figures in the same diagram, so that their relative sizes are most readily apparent.

Step 2. If you have not already determined the correct answer, then (and only then) determine the size of the figures (as you would have done in Section 301) and compare the results. (Note that even if Step 2 is necessary, Step 1 should eliminate most of the possible choices, leaving only a few formula calculations to be done.)

Example: Which of the following is the greatest in length?

(A) The perimeter of a square with a side of 4 inches.

(B) The perimeter of an isosceles right triangle whose equal sides are 8 inches each.

(C) The circumference of a circle with a diameter of $4\sqrt{2}$ inches.

(D) The perimeter of a pentagon whose sides are all equal to 3 inches.

(E) The perimeter of a semicircle with a radius of 5 inches.

Solution: Diagramming the five figures mentioned, we obtain the following illustration:

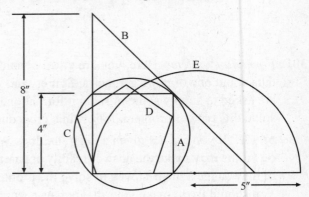

From the diagram, it is apparent that the square and the pentagon are both smaller than the circle. Further observation should show that the circle is smaller than the triangle. Thus we need only to see which is larger—the semicircle or the triangle. The perimeter of the semicircle is found by the formula $P = 2r + \pi r$ (the sum of the diameter and the semicircular arc, where r is the radius). Since r in this case is 5 inches, the perimeter is approximately $10 + (3.14)5$, or 25.7 inches. The formula for the perimeter of a triangle is the sum of the sides. In this case, two of the sides are 8 inches and the third side can be found by using the relationship $c^2 = a^2 + b^2$, where a and b are the sides of a right triangle and c is the hypotenuse. Since in our problem $a = b = 8$ inches, $c = \sqrt{8^2 + 8^2} = \sqrt{128} = \sqrt{2(64)} = 8\sqrt{2}$, which is the third side of the triangle. The perimeter is $8 + 8 + 8\sqrt{2}$, which is $16 + 8\sqrt{2}$. This is approximately equal to $16 + 8(1.4)$, or 27.2, so the triangle is the largest of the figures.

Formulas Used in Area, Perimeter, and Volume Problems

It is important that you know as many of these formulas as possible. Problems using these formulas appear frequently on tests of all kinds. You should not need to refer to the tables that follow when you do problems. Learn these formulas before you go any further.

303. *Square.* The area of a square is the square of one of its sides. Thus, if A represents the area and s represents the length of a side, $A = s^2$. The area of a square is also one-half of the square of its diagonal and may be written as $A = \frac{1}{2}d^2$, where d represents the length of a diagonal. The perimeter of a square is 4 times the length of one of its sides, or $4s$.

Square	
quantity	*formula*
area	$A = s^2$
	$A = \frac{1}{2}d^2$
perimeter	$P = 4s$

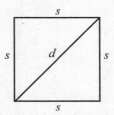

304. *Rectangle.* Let a and b represent the lengths of two adjacent sides of a rectangle, and let A represent the area. Then the area of a rectangle is the product of the two adjacent sides: $A = ab$. The perimeter, P, is the sum of twice one side and twice the adjacent side: $P = 2a + 2b$.

Rectangle	
quantity	*formula*
area	$A = ab$
perimeter	$P = 2a + 2b$

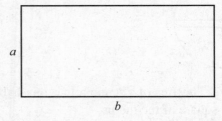

305. *Parallelogram.* The area of a parallelogram is the product of a side and the altitude, h, to that side. $A = bh$ (in this case the altitude to side b). Let a and b represent the length of 2 adjacent sides of a parallelogram. Then, C is the included angle. The area can also be expressed as the product of two

adjacent sides and the sine of the included angle: $A = ab \sin C$, where C is the angle included between side a and side b. The perimeter is the sum of twice one side and twice the adjacent side. $P = 2a + 2b$. A represents its area, P its perimeter, and h the altitude to one of its sides.

Parallelogram	
quantity	*formula*
area	$A = bh$
	$A = ab \sin C$
perimeter	$P = 2a + 2b$

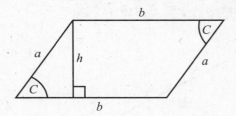

306. *Triangle.* The area of any triangle is one-half of the product of any side and the altitude to that side. $A = \frac{1}{2}bh$, where b is a side and h the altitude to that side. The area may be written also as one-half of the product of any two adjacent sides and the sine of the included angle. $A = \frac{1}{2}ab \sin C$, where A is the area, a and b are two adjacent sides, and C is the included angle. The perimeter of a triangle is the sum of the sides of the triangle. $P = a + b + c$, where P is the perimeter and c is the third side.

Triangle	
quantity	*formula*
area	$A = \frac{1}{2}bh$
	$A = \frac{1}{2}ab \sin C$
perimeter	$P = a + b + c$

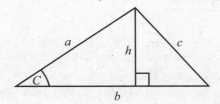

307. *Right triangle.* The area of a right triangle is one-half of the product of the two sides adjacent to the right angle. $A = \frac{1}{2}ab$, where A is the area and a and b are the adjacent sides. The perimeter is the sum of the sides. $P = a + b + c$, where c is the third side, or hypotenuse.

Right Triangle	
quantity	*formula*
area	$A = \frac{1}{2}ab$
perimeter	$P = a + b + c$
hypotenuse	$c^2 = a^2 + b^2$

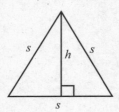

308. *Equilateral triangle.* The area of an equilateral triangle is one-fourth the product of a side squared and $\sqrt{3}$. $A = \frac{1}{4}s^2\sqrt{3}$, where A is the area and s is one of the equal sides. The perimeter of an equilateral triangle is 3 times one side, $P = 3s$, where P is the perimeter.

Equilateral Triangle	
quantity	*formula*
area	$A = \frac{1}{4}s^2\sqrt{3}$
perimeter	$P = 3s$
altitude	$h = \frac{1}{2}s\sqrt{3}$

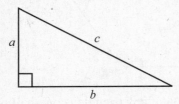

Note: *The equilateral triangle and the right triangle are special cases of the triangle, and any law that applies to the triangle applies to both the right triangle and the equilateral triangle.*

309. *Trapezoid.* The area of a trapezoid is one-half of the product of the altitude and the sum of the bases. $A = \frac{1}{2}h(B + b)$, where A is the area, B and b are the bases, and h is their altitude. The perimeter is the sum of the 4 sides. $P = B + b + c + d$, where P is the perimeter, and c and d are the other 2 sides.

Trapezoid	
quantity	*formula*
area	$A = \frac{1}{2}h(B + b)$
perimeter	$P = B + b + c + d$

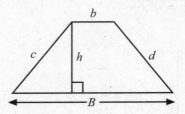

310. *Circle.* The area of a circle is π (pi) times the square of the radius, $A = \pi r^2$, where A is the area and r is the radius. The circumference is pi times the diameter, or pi times twice the radius. $C = \pi d = 2\pi r$, where C is the circumference, d is the diameter, and r is the radius.

Circle	
quantity	*formula*
area	$A = \pi r^2$
circumference	$C = \pi d = 2\pi r$

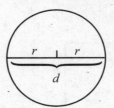

311. *Semicircle.* The area of a semicircle is one-half pi times the square of the radius.

$A = \frac{1}{2}\pi r^2$, where A is the area and r is the radius. The length of the curved portion of the semicircle is one-half pi times the diameter, or pi times the radius. $C = \frac{1}{2}\pi d = \pi r$, where C is the circumference, d is the diameter, and r is the radius. The perimeter of a semicircle is equal to the circumference plus the length of the diameter. $P = C + d = \frac{1}{2}\pi d + d$, where P is the perimeter.

Semicircle	
quantity	*formula*
area	$A = \frac{1}{2}\pi r^2$
circumference	$C = \frac{1}{2}\pi d = \pi r$
perimeter	$P = d\left(\frac{1}{2}\pi + 1\right)$

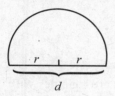

312. *Rectangular solid.* The volume of a rectangular solid is the product of the length, width, and height. $V = lwh$, where V is the volume, l is the length, w is the width, and h is the height. The volume is also the product of the area of one side and the altitude to that side. $V = Bh$, where B is the area of its base and h the altitude to that side. The surface area is the sum of the area of the six faces. $S = 2wh + 2hl + 2wl$, where S is the surface area.

Rectangular Solid	
quantity	*formula*
volume	$V = lwh$
	$V = Bh$
surface area	$S = 2wh + 2hl + 2wl$

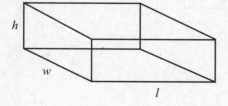

313. *Cube.* The volume of a cube is its edge cubed. $V = e^3$, where V is the volume and e is an edge. The surface area is the sum of the areas of the six faces. $S = 6e^2$, where S is the surface area.

Cube	
quantity	*formula*
volume	$V = e^3$
surface area	$S = 6e^2$

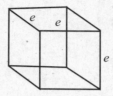

314. *Cylinder.* The volume of a cylinder is the area of the base times the height. $V = Bh$, where V is the volume, B is the area of the base, and h is the height. Note that the area of the base is the area of the circle $= \pi r^2$, where r is the radius of a base. The surface area not including the bases is the circumference of the base times the height. $S_1 = Ch = 2\pi rh$, where S_1 is the surface area without the bases, C is the circumference, and h is the height. The area of the bases $= 2\pi r^2$. Thus, the area of the cylinder, including the bases, is $S_2 = 2\pi rh + 2\pi r^2 = 2\pi r(h + r)$.

Cylinder	
quantity	*formula*
volume	$V = Bh$
	$V = \pi r^2 h$
surface area	$S_1 = 2\pi rh$ (without bases)
	$S_2 = 2\pi r(h + r)$ (with bases)

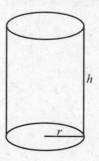

315. *Sphere.* The volume of a sphere is four-thirds π times the cube of the radius. $V = \frac{4}{3}\pi r^3$, where V is the volume and r is the radius. The surface area is 4π times the square of the radius. $S = 4\pi r^2$, where S is the surface area.

Sphere	
quantity	*formula*
volume	$V = \frac{4}{3}\pi r^3$
surface area	$S = 4\pi r^2$

316. *Hemisphere.* The volume of a hemisphere is two-thirds π times the cube of the radius. $V = \frac{2}{3}\pi r^3$, where V is the volume and r is the radius. The surface area not including the area of the base is 2π times the square of the radius. $S_1 = 2\pi r^2$, where S_1 is the surface area without the base. The total surface area, including the base, is equal to the surface area without the base plus the area of the base. $S_2 = 2\pi r^2 + \pi r^2 = 3\pi r^2$, where S_2 is the surface area including the base.

Hemisphere	
quantity	*formula*
volume	$V = \frac{2}{3}\pi r^3$
surface area	$S_1 = 2\pi r^2$ (without base)
	$S_2 = 3\pi r^2$ (with base)

317. *Pythagorean theorem.* The Pythagorean theorem states a very important geometrical relationship. It states that in a right triangle, if c is the hypotenuse (the side opposite the right angle), and a and b are the sides adjacent to the right angle, then $c^2 = a^2 + b^2$.

Pythagorean Theorem	
quantity	*formula*
square of hypotenuse	$c^2 = a^2 + b^2$
length of hypotenuse	$c = \sqrt{a^2 + b^2}$

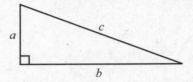

Examples of right triangles are triangles with sides of 3, 4, and 5, or 5, 12, and 13. Any multiples of these numbers also form right triangles—for example, 6, 8, and 10, or 30, 40, and 50.

Using the Pythagorean theorem to find the diagonal of a square, we get $d^2 = s^2 + s^2$ or $d^2 = 2s^2$, where d is the diagonal and s is a side. Therefore, $d = s\sqrt{2}$, or the diagonal of a square is $\sqrt{2}$ times the side.

Square	
quantity	*formula*
diagonal	$d = s\sqrt{2}$

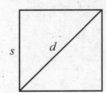

318. Another important fact to remember in doing area problems is that areas of two similar figures (figures having the same shape) are in the same ratio as the squares of corresponding parts of the figures.

Example: Triangles P and Q are similar. Side p of triangle P is 2 inches, the area of triangle P is 3 square inches, and corresponding side q of triangle Q is 4 inches. What is the area of triangle Q?

 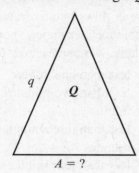

$A = 3$ sq in

$A = ?$

Solution: The square of side p is to the square of side q as the area of P is to the area of Q. If we call x the area of triangle Q, then we get the following relationship: The square of side p is to the square of side q as the area of P is to the area of Q, or

$$\frac{2^2}{4^2} = \frac{3}{x} \text{ or } \frac{4}{16} = \frac{3}{x}$$

Therefore, $x = 12$ square inches.

SESSION 3 PRACTICE TEST

Area, Perimeter, and Volume Problems

Correct answers and solutions follow this test.

1. Which of the following figures has the largest area?

   (A) a square with a perimeter of 12 inches

   (B) a circle with a radius of 3 inches

   (C) a right triangle with sides of 3, 4, and 5 inches

   (D) a rectangle with a diagonal of 5 inches and sides of 3 and 4 inches

   (E) a regular hexagon with a perimeter of 18 inches

   A B C D E
   ○ ○ ○ ○ ○
   ─────────

2. If the area of the base of a rectangular solid is tripled, what is the percent increase in its volume?

   (A) 200%

   (B) 300%

   (C) 600%

   (D) 800%

   (E) 900%

   A B C D E
   ○ ○ ○ ○ ○
   ─────────

3. How many yards of carpeting that is 26 inches wide will be needed to cover a floor that is 12 feet by 13 feet?

   (A) 22 yards

   (B) 24 yards

   (C) 27 yards

   (D) 36 yards

   (E) 46 yards

   A B C D E
   ○ ○ ○ ○ ○
   ─────────

4. If water flows into a rectangular tank at the rate of 6 cubic feet per minute, how long will it take to fill the tank, which measures 18″ × 32″ × 27″?

   (A) less than one minute

   (B) less than two minutes, but not less than one minute

   (C) less than three minutes, but not less than two minutes

   (D) less than four minutes, but not less than three minutes

   (E) four minutes or more

   A B C D E
   ○ ○ ○ ○ ○
   ─────────

5. The ratio of the area of a circle to the radius of the circle is

   (A) π

   (B) 2π

   (C) π^2

   (D) $4\pi^2$

   (E) not determinable

   A B C D E
   ○ ○ ○ ○ ○
   ─────────

6. Which of the following figures has the smallest perimeter or circumference?

   (A) a circle with a diameter of 2 feet

   (B) a square with a diagonal of 2 feet

   (C) a rectangle with sides of 6 inches and 4 feet

   (D) a pentagon with each side equal to 16 inches

   (E) a hexagon with each side equal to 14 inches

   A B C D E
   ○ ○ ○ ○ ○
   ─────────

7. In the figure shown, *DE* is parallel to *BC*. If the area of triangle *ADE* is half that of trapezoid *DECB*, what is the ratio of *AE* to *AC*?

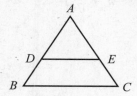

(A) 1 : 2
(B) 1 : √2
(C) 1 : 3
(D) 1 : √3
(E) 1 : √3 − 1

A B C D E
○ ○ ○ ○ ○

8. At a speed of 22 revolutions per minute, how long will it take a wheel of radius 10 inches, rolling on its edge, to travel 10 feet? (Assume π equals $\frac{22}{7}$, and express answer to nearest 0.1 second.)

(A) 0.2 second
(B) 0.4 second
(C) 5.2 seconds
(D) 6.3 seconds
(E) 7.4 seconds

A B C D E
○ ○ ○ ○ ○

9. If the diagonal of a square is 16 inches long, what is the area of the square?

(A) 64 square inches
(B) 64√2 square inches
(C) 128 square inches
(D) 128√2 square inches
(E) 256 square inches

A B C D E
○ ○ ○ ○ ○

10. In the diagram shown, *ACDF* is a rectangle, and *GBHE* is a circle. If *CD* = 4 inches and *AC* = 6 inches, what is the number of square inches in the shaded area?

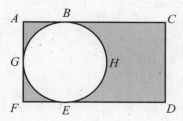

(A) 16 − 4π square inches
(B) 24 − 4π square inches
(C) 24 − 16π square inches
(D) 16 − 2π square inches
(E) 24 − 2π square inches

A B C D E
○ ○ ○ ○ ○

11. What is the area of an equilateral triangle with a side of 1 inch?

(A) 1 square inch
(B) $\frac{\sqrt{3}}{2}$ square inch
(C) $\frac{1}{2}$ square inch
(D) $\frac{\sqrt{3}}{4}$ square inch
(E) $\frac{1}{3}$ square inch

A B C D E
○ ○ ○ ○ ○

12. The measurements of a rectangle are 12 feet by 16 feet. What is the area of the smallest *circle* that can cover this rectangle entirely (so that no part of the rectangle is outside the circle)?

(A) 192 square feet
(B) 384 square feet
(C) 100π square feet
(D) 128π square feet
(E) 400π square feet

A B C D E
○ ○ ○ ○ ○

13. A couple wishes to cover their floor with tiles, each one measuring $\frac{3}{4}$ inch by 2 inches. If the room is a rectangle, measuring 12 feet by 18 feet, how many such tiles will they need?

    (A) 144
    (B) 1,152
    (C) 1,728
    (D) 9,216
    (E) 20,736

    A B C D E
    ○ ○ ○ ○ ○

14. The volume of a sphere is equal to the volume of a cylinder. If the radius of the sphere is 4 meters and the radius of the cylinder is 8 meters, what is the height of the cylinder?

    (A) 8 meters
    (B) $\frac{4}{3}$ meters
    (C) 4 meters
    (D) $\frac{16}{3}$ meters
    (E) 1 meter

    A B C D E
    ○ ○ ○ ○ ○

15. A wheel travels 33 yards in 15 revolutions. What is its diameter? (Assume $\pi = \frac{22}{7}$.)

    (A) 0.35 foot
    (B) 0.70 foot
    (C) 1.05 feet
    (D) 1.40 feet
    (E) 2.10 feet

    A B C D E
    ○ ○ ○ ○ ○

16. If a rectangle with a perimeter of 48 inches is equal in area to a right triangle with legs of 12 inches and 24 inches, what is the rectangle's diagonal?

    (A) 12 inches
    (B) $12\sqrt{2}$ inches
    (C) $12\sqrt{3}$ inches
    (D) 24 inches
    (E) The answer cannot be determined from the given information.

    A B C D E
    ○ ○ ○ ○ ○

17. What is the approximate area that remains after a circle $3\frac{1}{2}''$ in diameter is cut from a square piece of cloth with a side of 8″? (Use $\pi = \frac{22}{7}$.)

    (A) 25.5 square inches
    (B) 54.4 square inches
    (C) 56.8 square inches
    (D) 142.1 square inches
    (E) 284.2 square inches

    A B C D E
    ○ ○ ○ ○ ○

18. A container is shaped like a rectangular solid with sides of 3 inches, 3 inches, and 11 inches. What is its approximate capacity, if 1 gallon equals 231 cubic inches? (1 gallon = 128 fluid ounces.)

    (A) 14 ounces
    (B) 27 ounces
    (C) 55 ounces
    (D) 110 ounces
    (E) 219 ounces

    A B C D E
    ○ ○ ○ ○ ○

19. The 20-inch-diameter wheels of one car travel at a rate of 24 revolutions per minute, while the 30-inch-diameter wheels of a second car travel at a rate of 18 revolutions per minute. What is the ratio of the speed of the second car to that of the first?

    (A) 1 : 1
    (B) 3 : 2
    (C) 4 : 3
    (D) 6 : 5
    (E) 9 : 8

    A B C D E
    ○ ○ ○ ○ ○

20. A circular garden 20 feet in diameter is surrounded by a path 3 feet wide. What is the area of the path?

    (A) 9π square feet
    (B) 51π square feet
    (C) 60π square feet
    (D) 69π square feet
    (E) 90π square feet

    A B C D E
    ○ ○ ○ ○ ○

21. What is the area of a semicircle with a diameter of 16 inches?

(A) 32π square inches
(B) 64π square inches
(C) 128π square inches
(D) 256π square inches
(E) 512π square inches

A B C D E
○ ○ ○ ○ ○

22. If the edges of a cube add up to 4 feet in length, what is the volume of the cube?

(A) 64 cubic inches
(B) 125 cubic inches
(C) 216 cubic inches
(D) 512 cubic inches
(E) none of these

A B C D E
○ ○ ○ ○ ○

23. The inside of a trough is shaped like a rectangular solid, 25 feet long, 6 inches wide, and filled with water to a depth of 35 inches. If we wish to raise the depth of the water to 38 inches, how much water must be let into the tank?

(A) $\dfrac{25}{96}$ cubic foot

(B) $\dfrac{25}{8}$ cubic feet

(C) $\dfrac{75}{2}$ cubic feet

(D) 225 cubic feet
(E) 450 cubic feet

A B C D E
○ ○ ○ ○ ○

24. If 1 gallon of water equals 231 cubic inches, approximately how much water will fill a cylindrical vase 7 inches in diameter and 10 inches high? (Assume $\pi = \dfrac{22}{7}$.)

(A) 1.7 gallons
(B) 2.1 gallons
(C) 3.3 gallons
(D) 5.3 gallons
(E) 6.7 gallons

A B C D E
○ ○ ○ ○ ○

25. Tiles of linoleum, measuring 8 inches × 8 inches, cost 9¢ apiece. At this rate, what will it cost a man to cover a floor with these tiles, if his floor measures 10 feet by 16 feet?

(A) $22.50
(B) $25.00
(C) $28.00
(D) $32.40
(E) $36.00

A B C D E
○ ○ ○ ○ ○

26. Which of the following figures has the largest area?

(A) a 3–4–5 triangle with a hypotenuse of 25 inches
(B) a circle with a diameter of 20 inches
(C) a square with a 20-inch diagonal
(D) a regular hexagon with a side equal to 10 inches
(E) a rectangle with sides of 10 inches and 30 inches

A B C D E
○ ○ ○ ○ ○

27. If the radius of the base of a cylinder is tripled and its height is divided by three, what is the ratio of the volume of the new cylinder to the volume of the original cylinder?

(A) 1 : 9
(B) 1 : 3
(C) 1 : 1
(D) 3 : 1
(E) 9 : 1

A B C D E
○ ○ ○ ○ ○

28. If 1 cubic foot of water equals 7.5 gallons, how long will it take for a faucet that flows at a rate of 10 gal/min to fill a cube 2 feet on each side (to the nearest minute)?

(A) 4 minutes
(B) 5 minutes
(C) 6 minutes
(D) 7 minutes
(E) 8 minutes

A B C D E
○ ○ ○ ○ ○

29. The ratio of the area of a square to the square of its diagonal is which of the following?

   (A) 2 : 1
   (B) √2 : 1
   (C) 1 : 1
   (D) 1 : √2
   (E) 1 : 2

   A B C D E
   ○ ○ ○ ○ ○

30. If *ABCD* is a square, with side *AB* = 4 inches, and *AEB* and *CED* are semicircles, what is the area of the shaded portion of the diagram below?

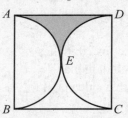

   (A) 8 − π square inches
   (B) 8 − 2π square inches
   (C) 16 − 2π square inches
   (D) 16 − 4π square inches
   (E) 16 − 8π square inches

   A B C D E
   ○ ○ ○ ○ ○

31. If the area of a circle is equal to the area of a rectangle, one of whose sides is equal to π, express the other side of the rectangle, *x*, in terms of the radius of the circle, *r*.

   (A) $x = r$
   (B) $x = \pi r$
   (C) $x = r^2$
   (D) $x = \sqrt{r}$
   (E) $x = \dfrac{1}{r}$

   A B C D E
   ○ ○ ○ ○ ○

32. If the volume of a cube is 27 cubic meters, find the surface area of the cube.

   (A) 9 square meters
   (B) 18 square meters
   (C) 54 square meters
   (D) 3 square meters
   (E) 1 square meter

   A B C D E
   ○ ○ ○ ○ ○

33. What is the area of a regular hexagon one of whose sides is 1 inch?

   (A) $\dfrac{3\sqrt{3}}{4}$
   (B) √3
   (C) $\dfrac{3\sqrt{3}}{2}$
   (D) 3
   (E) 6

   A B C D E
   ○ ○ ○ ○ ○

34. What is the area of the triangle pictured below?

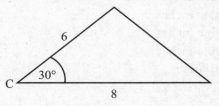

   (A) 18 square units
   (B) 32 square units
   (C) 24 square units
   (D) 12 square units
   (E) 124 square units

   A B C D E
   ○ ○ ○ ○ ○

35. If a wheel travels 1 mile in 1 minute, at a rate of 600 revolutions per minute, what is the diameter of the wheel, in feet? (Use $\pi = \dfrac{22}{7}$.)

   (A) 2.2 feet
   (B) 2.4 feet
   (C) 2.6 feet
   (D) 2.8 feet
   (E) 3.0 feet

   A B C D E
   ○ ○ ○ ○ ○

36. Which of the following figures has the largest perimeter?

   (A) a square with a diagonal of 5 feet
   (B) a rectangle with sides of 3 feet and 4 feet
   (C) an equilateral triangle with a side of 48 inches
   (D) a regular hexagon whose longest diagonal is 6 feet
   (E) a parallelogram with sides of 6 inches and 7 feet

   A B C D E
   ○ ○ ○ ○ ○

37. A man has two containers: The first is a rectangular solid, measuring 3 inches × 4 inches × 10 inches; the second is a cylinder having a base with a radius of 2 inches and a height of 10 inches. If the first container is filled with water, and then this water is poured into the second container, which of the following occurs?

   (A) There is room for more water in the second container.
   (B) The second container is completely filled, without overflowing.
   (C) The second container overflows by less than 1 cubic inch.
   (D) The second container overflows by less than 2 (but not less than 1) cubic inches.
   (E) The second container overflows by 2 or more cubic inches.

   A B C D E
   ○ ○ ○ ○ ○

38. If, in this diagram, A represents a square with a side of 4 inches and B, C, D, and E are semicircles, what is the area of the entire figure?

   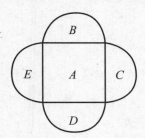

   (A) $16 + 4\pi$ square inches
   (B) $16 + 8\pi$ square inches
   (C) $16 + 16\pi$ square inches
   (D) $16 + 32\pi$ square inches
   (E) $16 + 64\pi$ square inches

   A B C D E
   ○ ○ ○ ○ ○

39. The area of a square is $81p^2$. What is the length of the square's diagonal?

   (A) $9p$
   (B) $9p\sqrt{2}$
   (C) $18p$
   (D) $9p^2$
   (E) $18p^2$

   A B C D E
   ○ ○ ○ ○ ○

40. The following diagram represents the floor of a room that is to be covered with carpeting at a price of $2.50 per square yard. What will be the cost of the carpeting?

   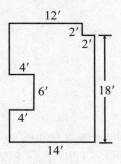

   (A) $70
   (B) $125
   (C) $480
   (D) $630
   (E) none of these

   A B C D E
   ○ ○ ○ ○ ○

41. Which of the following has the largest perimeter?

   (A) a square with a diagonal of 10 inches
   (B) a 3–4–5 right triangle with a hypotenuse of 15 inches
   (C) a pentagon, each of whose sides is 5 inches
   (D) a right isosceles triangle with an area of 72 square inches
   (E) a regular hexagon with a radius of 5 inches

   A B C D E
   ○ ○ ○ ○ ○

42. If you double the area of the base of a rectangular solid and also triple the solid's height, what is the ratio of the new volume to the old volume?

   (A) $2:3$
   (B) $3:2$
   (C) $1:6$
   (D) $6:1$
   (E) none of these

   A B C D E
   ○ ○ ○ ○ ○

43. A certain type of linoleum costs $1.50 per square yard. If a room measures 27 feet by 14 feet, what will be the cost of covering it with linoleum?

    (A) $44.10
    (B) $51.60
    (C) $63.00
    (D) $132.30
    (E) $189.00

    A B C D E
    ○ ○ ○ ○ ○

44. How many circles, each with a 4-inch radius, can be cut from a rectangular sheet of paper measuring 16 inches × 24 inches?

    (A) 6
    (B) 7
    (C) 8
    (D) 12
    (E) 24

    A B C D E
    ○ ○ ○ ○ ○

45. The ratio of the area of an equilateral triangle, in square inches, to its perimeter, in inches, is

    (A) 3 : 4
    (B) 4 : 3
    (C) $\sqrt{3}$: 4
    (D) 4 : $\sqrt{3}$
    (E) The answer cannot be determined from the given information.

    A B C D E
    ○ ○ ○ ○ ○

46. What is the volume of a cylinder whose radius is 4 inches and whose height is 10 inches? (Assume that $\pi = 3.14$.)

    (A) 125.6 cubic inches
    (B) 134.4 cubic inches
    (C) 144.0 cubic inches
    (D) 201.2 cubic inches
    (E) 502.4 cubic inches

    A B C D E
    ○ ○ ○ ○ ○

47. The area of a square is $144s^2$. What is the square's diagonal?

    (A) $12s$
    (B) $12s\sqrt{2}$
    (C) $24s$
    (D) $144s$
    (E) $144s^2$

    A B C D E
    ○ ○ ○ ○ ○

48. A circular pool is 10 feet in diameter and 5 feet deep. What is its volume, in cubic feet?

    (A) 50 cubic feet
    (B) 50π cubic feet
    (C) 125π cubic feet
    (D) 250π cubic feet
    (E) 500π cubic feet

    A B C D E
    ○ ○ ○ ○ ○

49. A certain type of carpeting is 30 inches wide. How many yards of this carpet will be needed to cover a floor that measures 20 feet by 24 feet?

    (A) 48
    (B) 64
    (C) 144
    (D) 192
    (E) none of these

    A B C D E
    ○ ○ ○ ○ ○

50. Two wheels have diameters of 12 inches and 18 inches, respectively. Both wheels roll along parallel straight lines at the same linear speed until the large wheel has revolved 72 times. At this point, how many times has the small wheel revolved?

    (A) 32
    (B) 48
    (C) 72
    (D) 108
    (E) 162

    A B C D E
    ○ ○ ○ ○ ○

Answer Key for Session 3 Practice Test

1. B	14. B	27. D	39. B
2. A	15. E	28. C	40. A
3. B	16. B	29. E	41. D
4. B	17. B	30. B	42. D
5. E	18. C	31. C	43. C
6. B	19. E	32. C	44. A
7. D	20. D	33. C	45. E
8. C	21. A	34. D	46. E
9. C	22. A	35. D	47. B
10. B	23. B	36. D	48. C
11. D	24. A	37. A	49. B
12. C	25. D	38. B	50. D
13. E	26. B		

Answers and Solutions for Session 3 Practice Test

1. Choice B is correct. This is a fairly difficult comparison problem, but the use of diagrams simplifies it considerably.

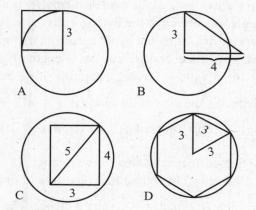

From diagram A it is apparent that the circle is larger than the square. Diagram B shows that the circle is larger than the right triangle. And, since a rectangle with a diagonal of 5 inches is made up of two right triangles, as shown in diagram C, the circle is larger than the rectangle. Finally, as shown in diagram D, the circle is larger than the hexagon. Thus, the circle is the largest of the five figures described. (Refresher 302)

2. Choice A is correct. This is a formula problem: Letting V_o represent the original volume, B_o represent the original area of the base, and h_o represent the original height of the figure, we have the formula $V_o = h_o B_o$. The new volume, V, is equal to $3h_o B_o$. Thus, the new volume is three times the original volume—an *increase* of 200%. (Refresher 301)

3. Choice B is correct. Here, we must find the length of carpeting needed to cover an area of 12 feet × 13 feet, or 156 square feet. The formula needed is: $A = lw$, where l = length and w = width, both expressed in *feet*. Now, since we know that $A =$ 156 square feet, and $w = 26$ inches, or $\frac{26}{12}$ feet, we can calculate l as $156 \div \left(\frac{26}{12}\right)$, or 72 feet. But since the answer must be expressed in yards, we express 72 feet as 24 yards. (Refresher 304)

4. Choice B is correct. First we must calculate the volume of the tank in cubic feet. Converting the dimensions of the box to feet, we get $1\frac{1}{2}$ feet × $2\frac{2}{3}$ feet × $2\frac{1}{4}$ feet, so the total volume is $\frac{3}{2} \times \frac{8}{3} \times \frac{9}{4}$, or 9, cubic feet. Thus, at a rate of 6 cubic feet per minute, it would take $\frac{9}{6}$, or $1\frac{1}{2}$, minutes to fill the tank. (Refreshers 312, 201)

5. Choice E is correct. Here, we use the formula $A = \pi r^2$, where A = area, and r = radius. Thus, the ratio of A to r is just $\frac{A}{r} = \pi r$. Since r is not a constant, the ratio cannot be determined. (Refresher 310)

6. Choice B is correct.

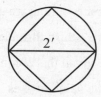

First, we diagram the circle and the square and see that the square has a smaller perimeter. Next, we notice that the circle, which has a larger circumference than the square, has circumference 2π, or about 6.3 feet. But the perimeters of the rectangle (9 feet), of the pentagon (5 × 16 inches = 80 inches = 6 feet, 8 inches), and of the hexagon (6 × 14 inches = 84 inches = 7 feet) are all greater than the circumference of the circle, and therefore also greater than the perimeter of the square. Thus, the square has the smallest perimeter. (Refresher 302)

7. Choice D is correct. The formula involved here is $A_1 : A_2 = s_1{}^2 : s_2{}^2$, where A_1 represents the area of the triangle with one side of length s_1 and A_2 represents the area of the triangle corresponding to s_2. If we let s_1 represent AE and s_2 represent AC, so that A_1 is the area of ADE and A_2 is the area of ABC, then we have the resulting formula $\dfrac{AE}{AC} = \dfrac{s_1}{s_2} = \sqrt{\dfrac{A_1}{A_2}}$. The area of the trapezoid $DECB$ is twice the area of ADE, or $2A_1$, so the area of ABC is equal to the sum of the area of ADE and $DECB$, which equal A_1 and $2A_1$, respectively; thus, the area of ABC is $3A_1$. So, $A_1 : A_2 = 1 : 3$. Thus, $s_1 : s_2 = \sqrt{\dfrac{1}{3}} = 1 : \sqrt{3}$.

(Refresher 318)

8. Choice C is correct. Since the radius of the circle is 10 inches, its circumference is $2\pi(10 \text{ inches})$, or $2\left(\dfrac{22}{7}\right)(10 \text{ inches})$, which equals $\dfrac{440}{7}$ inches. This is the distance the wheel will travel in one revolution. To travel 10 feet, or 120 inches, it must travel $120 \div \dfrac{440}{7}$, or $\dfrac{21}{11}$ revolutions. At a speed of 22 revolutions per minute, or $\dfrac{11}{30}$ revolutions per second, it will take $\dfrac{21}{11} \div \dfrac{11}{30}$, or $\dfrac{630}{121}$ seconds. Carrying the division to the nearest tenth of a second, we get 5.2 seconds. (Refresher 310)

9. Choice C is correct. If we let d represent the diagonal of a square, s represent the length of one side, and A represent the area, then we have two formulas: $d = s\sqrt{2}$ and $A = s^2$, relating the three quantities. However, from the first equation, we can see that $s^2 = \dfrac{d^2}{2}$, so we can derive a third formula, $A = \dfrac{d^2}{2}$, relating A and d. We are given that d equals 16 inches, so we can calculate the value of A as $\dfrac{(16 \text{ inches})^2}{2}$, or 128 square inches.

(Refresher 303)

10. Choice B is correct. The area of the shaded figure is equal to the difference between the areas of the rectangle and the circle. The area of the rectangle is defined by the formula $A = bh$, where b and h are the two adjacent sides of the rectangle. In this case, A is equal to 4 inches $\times$ 6 inches, or 24 square inches. The area of the circle is defined by

the formula $A = \pi r^2$, where r is the radius. Since BE equals the diameter of the circle and is equal to 4 inches, then the radius must be 2 inches. Thus, the area of the circle is $\pi(2 \text{ inches})^2$, or 4π square inches. Subtracting, we obtain the area of the shaded portion: $24 - 4\pi$ square inches.

(Refreshers 304, 310)

11. Choice D is correct. We use the formula for the area of an equilateral triangle, $\dfrac{\sqrt{3}s^2}{4}$, where s is a side. If $s = 1$, then the area of the triangle is $\dfrac{\sqrt{3}}{4}$.

(Refresher 308)

12. Choice C is correct.

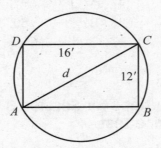

An angle, inscribed in a circle, whose sides cut off an arc of 180° (that is, whose sides intersect the circle at the two ends of the circle's diameter) is a right angle. According to the Pythagorean theorem, the diameter AC, being the hypotenuse of a triangle with sides of 12 feet and 16 feet, has a length of $\sqrt{12^2 + 16^2} = \sqrt{400} = 20$ feet. Therefore, if we call d the diameter, the area of the circle is $A = \pi\left(\dfrac{d}{2}\right)^2 = \pi\left(\dfrac{20}{2}\right)^2 = 100\pi$ square feet. (Refresher 310)

13. Choice E is correct. The area of the room $= 12$ feet $\times 18$ feet $= 216$ square feet. The area of one tile $= \dfrac{3}{4}$ inch $\times 2$ inches $= \dfrac{3}{2}$ square inches. The number of tiles

$=$ area of the room $\div$ area of one tile

$= \dfrac{216 \text{ square feet}}{\frac{3}{2} \text{ square inches}} = \dfrac{216 \times 144 \text{ square inches}}{\frac{3}{2} \text{ square inches}}$

$= 216 \times \overset{48}{\cancel{144}} \times \dfrac{2}{\cancel{3}} = 20{,}736$ tiles. (Refresher 304)

14. Choice B is correct. The volume of a sphere is found by using the formula $\frac{4}{3}\pi r^3$, where r is the radius. In this case, the radius is 4 meters, so the volume is $\frac{256}{3}\pi$ cubic meters. This is equal to the volume of a cylinder of radius 8 meters, so $\frac{256}{3}\pi$ $= \pi 8^2 h$, since the volume of a cylinder is $\pi r^2 h$, where h is the height and r is the radius of the base. Solving $\frac{256\pi}{3} = \pi 8^2 h$:

$$h = \frac{\frac{256\pi}{3}}{\pi 64} = \frac{256}{3} \times \frac{1}{64} = \frac{4}{3} \text{ meters}$$

(Refreshers 314, 315)

15. Choice E is correct. 33 yards = 99 feet = 15 revolutions. Thus, 1 revolution = $\frac{99}{15}$ feet = $\frac{33}{5}$ feet = 6.6 feet. Since 1 revolution = the circumference of the wheel, the wheel's diameter = circumference ÷ π. 6.6 feet ÷ $\frac{22}{7}$ = 2.10 feet.   (Refresher 310)

16. Choice B is correct. The area of the right triangle is equal to $\frac{1}{2}ab$, where a and b are the legs of the triangle. In this case, the area is $\frac{1}{2} \times 12 \times 24$, or 144 square inches. If we call the sides of the rectangle x and y we get $2x + 2y = 48$, or $y = 24 - x$. The area of the rectangle is xy, or $x(24 - x)$. This must be equal to 144, so we get the equation $24x - x^2 = 144$. Adding $x^2 - 24x$ to both sides of this last equation gives us $x^2 - 24x + 144 = 0$, or $(x - 12)^2 = 0$. Thus, $x = 12$. Since $y = 24 - x$, $y = 24 - 12$, or $y = 12$. By the Pythagorean theorem, the diagonal of the rectangle = $\sqrt{12^2 + 12^2}$ = $\sqrt{144 + 144}$ = $\sqrt{2(144)}$ = $(\sqrt{2})(\sqrt{144})$ = $12\sqrt{2}$.

(Refreshers 304, 306, 317)

17. Choice B is correct. The area of the square is 64 square inches, since $A = s^2$ where s is the length of a side and A is the area. The area of the circle is $\pi\left(\frac{7}{4}\right)^2 = \frac{22}{7} \times \frac{49}{16} = \frac{77}{8} = 9.625$. Subtracting, $64 - 9.625 = 54.375 = 54.4$ (approximately).

(Refreshers 304, 310)

18. Choice C is correct. The volume of the container ($V = lwh$, where l, w, h are the adjacent sides of the solid) = (3 inches)(3 inches)(11 inches) = 99 cubic inches. Since 1 gallon equals 231 cubic inches, 99 cubic inches equal $\frac{99}{231}$ gallon (the fraction reduces to $\frac{3}{7}$). One gallon equals 128 ounces (1 gallon = 4 quarts; 1 quart = 2 pints; 1 pint = 16 ounces), so the container holds $\frac{384}{7}$ ounces = 55 ounces (approximately).   (Refresher 312)

19. Choice E is correct. The speed of the first wheel is equal to its rate of revolution multiplied by its circumference, which equals 24 × 20 inches × π = 480π inches per minute. The speed of the second is 18 × 30 inches × π = 540π inches per minute. Thus, their ratio is $540\pi : 480\pi = 9 : 8$.

(Refresher 310)

20. Choice D is correct.

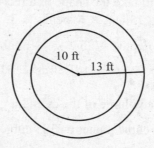

The area of the path is equal to the area of the ring between two concentric circles of radii 10 feet and 13 feet. This area is obtained by subtracting the area of the smaller circle from the area of the larger circle. The area of the larger circle is equal to π × its radius squared = $\pi(13)^2$ square feet = 169π square feet. By the same process, the area of the smaller circle = 100π square feet. The area of the path = $169\pi - 100\pi = 69\pi$ square feet.   (Refresher 310)

21. Choice A is correct. The diameter = 16 inches, so the radius = 8 inches. Thus, the area of the whole circle = $\pi(8 \text{ inches})^2 = 64\pi$ square inches. The area of the semicircle is one-half of the area of the whole circle, or 32π square inches.

(Refresher 311)

22. Choice A is correct.

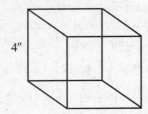

A cube has 12 equal edges, so the length of one side of the cube is $\frac{1}{12}$ of 4 feet, or 4 inches. Thus, its volume is 4 inches $\times$ 4 inches $\times$ 4 inches = 64 cubic inches. (Refresher 313)

23. Choice B is correct.

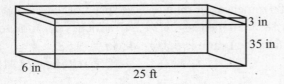

The additional water will take the shape of a rectangular solid measuring 25 feet $\times$ 6 inches $\times$ 3 inches (3″ = the added depth) = $25 \times \frac{1}{2} \times \frac{1}{4}$ cubic feet = $\frac{25}{8}$ cubic feet. (Refresher 312)

24. Choice A is correct. The volume of the cylinder = $\pi r^2 h = \left(\frac{22}{7}\right)\left(\frac{7}{2}\right)^2 (10)$ cubic inches = 385 cubic inches. 231 cubic inches = 1 gallon, so 385 cubic inches = $\frac{385}{231}$ gallons = $\frac{5}{3}$ gallons = 1.7 gallons (approximately). (Refresher 314)

25. Choice D is correct. The area of floor = 10 feet $\times$ 16 feet = 160 square feet. Area of one tile = 8 inches $\times$ 8 inches = 64 square inches = $\frac{64}{144}$ square feet = $\frac{4}{9}$ square foot. Thus, the number of tiles = area of floor $\div$ area of tile = $160 \div \frac{4}{9}$ = 360. At 9¢ apiece, the tiles will cost $32.40. (Refresher 304)

26. Choice B is correct. Looking at the following three diagrams, we can observe that the triangle, square, and hexagon are all smaller than the circle.

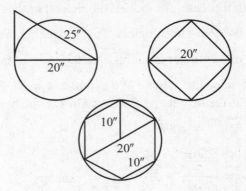

Comparing the areas of the circle and the rectangle, we notice that the area of the circle is $\pi(10 \text{ inches})^2 = 100\pi$ square inches, which is greater than (10 inches) (30 inches) = 300 square inches, the area of the rectangle. (π is approximately 3.14.) (Refresher 302)

27. Choice D is correct. In a cylinder, $V = \pi r^2 h$, where r is the radius of the base and h is the height. The new volume $V' = \pi(3r)^2 \left(\frac{h}{3}\right) = 3\pi r^2 h = 3V$. Thus, the ratio of the new volume to the old volume is $3:1$. (Refresher 314)

28. Choice C is correct. A cube 2 feet on each side has a volume of $2 \times 2 \times 2 = 8$ cubic feet. Since 1 cubic foot equals 7.5 gallons, 8 cubic feet equals 60 gallons. If the faucet flows at the rate of 10 gallons/minute, it will take 6 minutes to fill the cube. (Refresher 313)

29. Choice E is correct. Let s = the side of the square. Then, the area of the square is equal to s^2. The diagonal of the square is $s\sqrt{2}$, so the square of the diagonal is $2s^2$. Thus, the ratio of the area of the square to the square of the diagonal is $s^2 : 2s^2$, or $1:2$. (Refresher 303)

30. Choice B is correct. The area of the square $ABCD$ is equal to 4 inches $\times$ 4 inches = 16 square inches. The two semicircles can be placed together diameter-to-diameter to form a circle with a radius of 2 inches,

and thus, an area of 4π. Subtracting the area of the circle from the area of the square, we obtain the combined areas of *AED* and *BEC*. But, since the figure is symmetrical, *AED* and *BEC* must be equal. The area of the remainder is $16 - 4\pi$; *AED* is one-half of this remainder, or $8 - 2\pi$ square inches.

(Refreshers 303, 310)

31. Choice C is correct. The area of the circle is equal to πr^2, and the area of the rectangle is equal to πx. Since these areas are equal, $\pi r^2 = \pi x$, and $x = r^2$.

(Refreshers 304, 310)

32. Choice C is correct. The volume of a cube is e^3, where e is the length of an edge. If the volume is 27 cubic meters, then $e^3 = 27$ and $e = 3$ meters. The surface area of a cube is $6e^2$, and if $e = 3$ meters, then the surface area is 54 square meters.

(Refresher 313)

33. Choice C is correct.

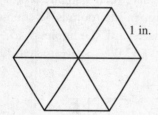

The area of a regular hexagon, one of whose sides is 1 inch, is equal to the sum of the areas of 6 equilateral triangles, each with a side of 1 inch. The area of an equilateral triangle with a side of 1 inch is equal to $\frac{\sqrt{3}}{4}$ square inch. (The formula for the area of an equilateral triangle with a side of s is $A = \frac{1}{4}s^2\sqrt{3}$.) The sum of 6 such triangles is $\frac{6\sqrt{3}}{4}$, or $\frac{3\sqrt{3}}{2}$.

(Refresher 308)

34. Choice D is correct. Draw a perpendicular line from the top of the triangle to the side, which is 8. You have created a 30–60–90 right triangle. The line drawn is $\frac{1}{2}$ of $6 = 3$. The area of the whole triangle is the altitude multiplied by the base divided by 2. The altitude is 3 and the base is 8, so the area is $3 \times \frac{8}{2} = 12$.

(Refresher 307)

35. Choice D is correct. Since the wheel takes 1 minute to make 600 revolutions and travels 1 mile in that time, we have the relation 1 mile = 5,280 feet = 600 revolutions. Thus 1 revolution = $\frac{5,280}{600}$ feet = 8.8 feet = circumference = π(diameter) = $\left(\frac{22}{7}\right)$ (diameter). Therefore, the diameter = 8.8 feet ÷ $\left(\frac{22}{7}\right)$ = 2.8 feet.

(Refresher 310)

36. Choice D is correct. In this case, it is easiest to calculate the perimeters of the 5 figures. According to the Pythagorean theorem, a square with a diagonal of 5 feet has a side of $\frac{5}{\sqrt{2}}$, which is equal to $\frac{5\sqrt{2}}{2}$. (This is found by multiplying the numerator and denominator of $\frac{5}{\sqrt{2}}$ by $\sqrt{2}$.) If each side of the square is $\frac{5\sqrt{2}}{2}$, then the perimeter is $4 \times \frac{5\sqrt{2}}{2} = 10\sqrt{2}$ feet. A rectangle with sides of 3 feet and 4 feet has a perimeter of $2(3) + 2(4)$, or 14 feet. An equilateral triangle with a side of 48 inches, or 4 feet, has a perimeter of 12 feet. A regular hexagon whose longest diagonal is 6 feet has a side of 3 feet and, therefore, a perimeter of 18 feet. (See the diagram for Solution 41.) Finally, a parallelogram with sides of 6 inches, or $\frac{1}{2}$ foot, and 7 feet has a perimeter of 15 feet. Therefore, the hexagon has the largest perimeter.

(Refreshers 302, 317)

37. Choice A is correct. The volume of the first container is equal to 3 inches $\times$ 4 inches $\times$ 10 inches, or 120 cubic inches. The volume of the second container, the cylinder, is equal to $\pi r^2 h$ = $\pi(2 \text{ inches})^2(10 \text{ inches})$, or 40π cubic inches, which is greater than 120 cubic inches (π is greater than 3). So the second container can hold more than the first. If the first container is filled and the contents poured into the second, there will be room for more water in the second.

(Refreshers 312, 314)

38. Choice B is correct. The area of the square is 16 square inches. The four semicircles can be added to form two circles, each of radius 2 inches, so the area of each circle is 4π square inches, and the two circles add up to 8π square inches. Thus, the total area is $16 + 8\pi$ square inches.

(Refreshers 303, 311)

39. Choice B is correct. Since the area of the square is $81p^2$, one side of the square will equal $9p$. According to the Pythagorean theorem, the diagonal will equal $\sqrt{81p^2 + 81p^2} = 9p\sqrt{2}$.

(Refreshers 303, 317)

40. Choice A is correct. We can regard the area as a rectangle, 20 ft × 14 ft, with two rectangles, measuring 4 ft × 6 ft and 2 ft × 2 ft, cut out. Thus, the area is equal to 280 sq ft − 24 sq ft − 4 sq ft = 252 sq ft = $\frac{252}{9}$ sq yd = 28 sq yds. (Remember, 1 square yard equals 9 square feet.) At $2.50 per square yard, 28 square yards will cost $70.

(Refresher 304)

41. Choice D is correct.

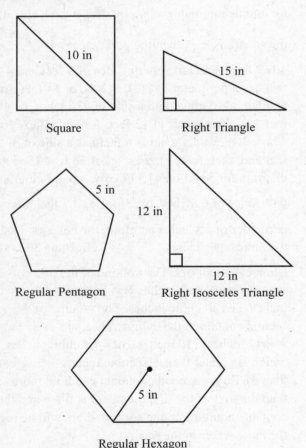

Square

Right Triangle

Regular Pentagon

Right Isosceles Triangle

Regular Hexagon

The perimeter of the square is equal to four times its side; since a side is $\frac{1}{\sqrt{2}}$, or $\frac{\sqrt{2}}{2}$ times the diagonal, the perimeter of the square in question is $4 \times 5\sqrt{2} = 20\sqrt{2}$, which is approximately equal to 28.28 inches. The perimeter of a right triangle with sides that are in a 3–4–5 ratio, i.e., 9 inches, 12 inches, and 15 inches, is $9 + 12 + 15 = 36$ inches. The

perimeter of the pentagon is 5 × 5 inches, or 25 inches. The perimeter of the right isosceles triangle (with sides of 12 inches, 12 inches, and $12\sqrt{2}$ inches) is $24 + 12\sqrt{2}$ inches, which is approximately equal to 40.968 inches. The perimeter of the hexagon is 6 × 5 inches, or 30 inches. Thus, the isosceles right triangle has the largest perimeter of those figures mentioned. You should become familiar with the approximate value of $\sqrt{2}$, which is 1.414.

(Refresher 302)

42. Choice D is correct. For rectangular solids, the following formula holds:

$V = Ah$, where A is the area of the base, and h is the height.

If we replace A with $2A$, and h with $3h$, we get $V' = (2A)(3h) = 6V$. Thus, $V' : V = 6 : 1$.

(Refresher 312)

43. Choice C is correct. The area of the room is 27 feet × 14 feet = 378 square feet. 9 square feet = 1 square yard, so the area of the room is 42 square yards. At $1.50 per square yard, the linoleum to cover the floor will cost $63.00.

(Refresher 304)

44. Choice A is correct.

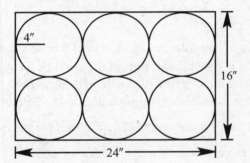

A circle with a 4-inch radius has an 8-inch diameter, so there can be only 2 rows of 3 circles each, or 6 circles.

(Refresher 310)

45. Choice E is correct. Let one side of the triangle be s. Then the area of the triangle is $\frac{s^2\sqrt{3}}{4}$. (Either memorize this formula or remember that it is derived by drawing an altitude to divide the triangle into two congruent 30–60–90 right triangles.) The perimeter of the equilateral triangle is $3s$, so the ratio of the area to the perimeter is $\frac{s^2\sqrt{3}}{4} : 3s$, or $s : 4\sqrt{3}$, which cannot be determined unless we know the value of s.

(Refresher 308)

46. Choice E is correct. The formula for volume of a cylinder is $V = \pi r^2 h$, where r is the radius of the base and h is the height. Here, $r = 4$ inches and $h = 10$ inches, while $\pi \approx 3.14$. (The symbol $\approx$ means "approximately equal to.") Thus $V \approx (4)^2(10)(3.14) = 160(3.14) = 502.4$ cubic inches.

(Refresher 314)

47. Choice B is correct. If the area of a square is $144s^2$, then one side will equal $12s$, so the diagonal will equal $12s\sqrt{2}$. (The Pythagorean theorem may be used here to get $d = \sqrt{144s^2 + 144s^2}$, where d is the diagonal.) (Refreshers 303, 317)

48. Choice C is correct. The inside of the pool forms a cylinder of radius 5 feet and height 5 feet. The volume is $\pi r^2 h$, or $\pi \times 5 \times 5 \times 5 = 125\pi$ cubic feet. (Refresher 314)

49. Choice B is correct. The area of the floor is 20 feet $\times$ 24 feet = 480 square feet. 30 inches is equal to $2\frac{1}{2}$ feet, and we must find the length that, when multiplied by $2\frac{1}{2}$ feet, will yield 480 square feet. This length is 192 feet, which equals 64 yards (3 feet = 1 yard). (Refresher 304)

50. Choice D is correct. The circumference of the larger wheel is 18π inches ($C = \pi d$). After 72 revolutions, the larger wheel will have gone a distance of $72(18\pi)$ inches. Since the smaller wheel moves at the same linear speed, it will also have gone $72(18\pi)$ inches. The circumference of the smaller wheel is 12π inches, and if we call the number of revolutions that the smaller wheel makes r, then we know that $12\pi r = 72(18\pi)$. Dividing both sides by 12π gives us $r = 6(18)$ or 108 revolutions. Note that in this problem we have used the relation *distance = rate $\times$ time*, where the time for both wheels is a fixed quantity.

(Refresher 310)

MATH REFRESHER SESSION 4

Algebra Problems

Algebraic Properties

Algebra is the branch of mathematics that applies the laws of arithmetic to symbols that represent unknown quantities. The most commonly used symbols are the letters of the alphabet, such as A, B, C, x, y, z, etc. These symbols can be added, subtracted, multiplied, and divided like numbers. For example, $3a + 2a = 5a$, $2x - x = x$, $3(5b) = 15b$, $\frac{6x}{3x} = 2$. These symbols can be raised to powers like a^3 or y^2. Remember that raising a number to a power means multiplying the number by itself a number of times. For example, $a^3 = a \cdot a \cdot a$. The power is 3, and a is multiplied by itself 3 times.

Generally, in algebra, a *variable* (an unknown represented by a symbol) appears in an expression that defines the relationship (whether an equation or an inequality) between certain quantities. The numerical value of a variable that satisfies this relationship can usually be found if the expressions contain numerical values (e.g., $26, -5, \frac{1}{2}$). For example, the equation $6a = 12$ is satisfied when the variable a is equal to 2. This section is a discussion on how to solve complicated algebraic equations and other related topics.

Fundamental Laws of Our Number System

The following list of laws applies to all numbers, and it is necessary to adhere to these laws when doing arithmetic and algebra problems. Remember these laws and use them in solving problems.

401. If $x = y$ and $y = z$, then $x = z$. This is called *transitivity*. For example, if $a = 3$ and $b = 3$, then $a = b$.

402. If $x = y$, then $x + z = y + z$, and $x - z = y - z$. This means that the same quantity can be added to or subtracted from both sides of an equation. For example, if $a = b$, then add any number to both sides, say 3, and $a + 3 = b + 3$. Or if $a = b$, then $a - 3 = b - 3$.

403. If $x = y$, then $x \cdot z = y \cdot z$ and $x \div z = y \div z$, unless $z = 0$ (see Section 404). This means that both sides of an equation can be multiplied by the same number. For example, if $a = n$, then $5a = 5n$. It also means that both sides of an equation can be divided by the same nonzero number. If $a = b$, then $\frac{a}{3} = \frac{b}{3}$.

404. *Never divide by zero.* This is a very important rule that must be remembered. The quotient of *any* quantity (except zero) divided by zero is infinity.

405. $x + y = y + x$, and $x \cdot y = y \cdot x$. Therefore, $2 + 3 = 3 + 2$, and $2 \cdot 3 = 3 \cdot 2$. Remember that this does not work for division and subtraction. $3 \div 2$ does not equal $2 \div 3$, and $3 - 2$ does not equal $2 - 3$. The property described above is called *commutativity*.

Algebraic Expressions

405a. Since the letters in an algebraic expression stand for numbers, and since we add, subtract, multiply, or divide them to get the algebraic expression, the algebraic expression itself stands for a number. When we are told what value each of the letters in the expression has, we can evaluate the expression. Note that $(+a) \times (+b) = +ab$; $(+a) \times (-b) = -ab$; $(-a) \times (+b) = -ab$; and $-a \times -b = +ab$.

In evaluating algebraic expressions, place the value you are substituting for a letter in parentheses. (This is important when a letter has a negative value.)

Example: What is the value of the expression $a^2 - b^3$ when $a = -2$, and $b = -1$?

$a^2 - b^3 = (-2)^2 - (-1)^3 = 4 - (-1) = 4 + 1 = 5$.

If you can, simplify the algebraic expression before you evaluate it.

Example: Evaluate $\frac{32a^6b^2}{8a^4b^3}$ if $a = 4$, and $b = -2$.

First we divide:

$\frac{32a^6b^2}{8a^4b^3} = \frac{4a^2}{b}$. Then $\frac{4a^2}{b} = \frac{4(+4)^2}{-2} = -32$.

Note: $\frac{a^6}{a^4} = a^2$ and $\frac{b^2}{b^3} = \frac{1}{b}$. Remember, in division, you subtract the exponents if they belong to the same variable.

Equations

406. *Linear equations in one unknown.* An equation of this type has only one variable, and that variable is always in the first power, i.e., x or y or a, but never a higher or fractional power, i.e., x^2, y^3, or $a^{\frac{1}{2}}$. Examples of linear equations in one unknown are $x + 5 = 7$, $3a - 2 = 7a + 1$, $2x - 7x = 8 + x$, $8 = -4y$, etc. To solve these equations, follow these steps:

Step 1. Combine the terms on the left and right sides of the equality. That is, (1) add all of the numerical terms on each side, and (2) add all of the terms with variables on each side. For example, if you have $7 + 2x + 9 = 4x - 3 - 2x + 7 + 6x$, combining terms on the left gives you $16 + 2x$, because $7 + 9 = 16$, and $2x$ is the only variable term on that side. On the right we get $8x + 4$, since $4x - 2x + 6x = 8x$ and $-3 + 7 = 4$. Therefore the new equation is $16 + 2x = 8x + 4$.

Step 2. Put all of the numerical terms on the right side of the equation and all of the variable terms on the left side. This is done by subtracting the numerical term on the left from both sides of the equation and by subtracting the variable term on the right side from both sides of the equation. In the example $16 + 2x = 8x + 4$, subtract 16 from both sides and obtain $2x = 8x - 12$; then subtracting $8x$ from both sides gives $-6x = -12$.

Step 3. Divide both sides by the coefficient of the variable. In this case, where $-6x = -12$, dividing by -6 gives $x = 2$. This is the final solution to the problem.

Example: Solve for a in the equation $7a + 4 - 2a = 18 + 17a + 10$.

Solution: From Step 1, we combine terms on both sides to get $5a + 4 = 28 + 17a$. As in Step 2, we then subtract 4 and $17a$ from both sides to give $-12a = 24$. In Step 3, we then divide both sides of the equation by the coefficient of a, which is -12, to get $a = -2$.

Example: Solve for x in $2x + 6 = 0$.

Solution: Here Step 1 is eliminated because there are no terms to combine on either side. Step 2 requires that 6 be subtracted from both sides to get $2x = -6$. Then Step 3, dividing by 2, gives $x = -3$.

407. *Simultaneous equations in two unknowns.* These are problems in which two equations, each with two unknowns, are given. These equations must be solved together (simultaneously) in order to arrive at the solution.

Step 1. Rearrange each equation so that both have the x term on the left side and the y term and the constant on the right side. In other words, put the equations in the form $Ax = By + C$, where A, B, and C are numerical constants. For example, if one of the equations is $9x - 10y + 30 = 11y + 3x - 6$, then subtract $-10y$ and 30 from both sides to get $9x = 21y + 3x - 36$. Subtracting $3x$ from both sides gives $6x = 21y - 36$, which is in the form of $Ax = By + C$.

The first equation should be in the form $Ax = By + C$, and the second equation should be in the form $Dx = Ey + F$, where A, B, C, D, E, and F are numerical constants.

Step 2. Multiply the first equation by the coefficient of x in the second equation (D). Multiply the second equation by the coefficient of x in the first equation (A). Now the equations are in the form $ADx = BDy + CD$ and $ADx = AEy + AF$. For example, in the two equations $2x = 7y - 12$ and $3x = y + 1$, multiply the first by 3 and the second by 2 to get $6x = 21y - 36$ and $6x = 2y + 2$.

Step 3. Equate the right sides of both equations. This can be done because both sides are equal to ADx. (See Section 401 on transitivity.) Thus, $BDy + CD = AEy + AF$. So $21y - 36$ and $2y + 2$ are both equal to $6x$ and are equal to each other: $21y - 36 = 2y + 2$.

Step 4. Solve for y. This is done in the manner outlined in Section 406. In the equation $21y - 36 = 2y + 2$, $y = 2$. By this method

$$y = \frac{AF - CD}{BD - AE}.$$

Step 5. Substitute the value of y into either of the original equations and solve for x. In the general equations we would then have either

$$x = \frac{B}{A}\left[\frac{AF - CD}{BD - AE}\right] + \frac{C}{A} \text{ or } x = \frac{E}{D}\left[\frac{AF - CD}{BD - AE}\right] + \frac{F}{D}.$$

In the example, if $y = 2$ is substituted into either $2x = 7y - 12$ or $3x = y + 1$, then $2x = 14 - 12$ or $3x = 3$ can be solved to get $x = 1$.

Example: Solve for a and b in the equations $3a + 4b = 24$ and $2a + b = 11$.

Solution: First note that it makes no difference in these two equations whether the variables are a and b instead of x and y. Subtract $4b$ from the first equation and b from the second equation to get the equations $3a = 24 - 4b$ and $2a = 11 - b$. Multiply the first by 2 and the second by 3. Thus, $6a = 48 - 8b$ and $6a = 33 - 3b$. Equate $48 - 8b$ and $33 - 3b$ to get $48 - 8b = 33 - 3b$. Solving for b in the usual manner gives us $b = 3$. Substituting the value of $b = 3$ into the equation $3a + 4b = 24$ obtains $3a + 12 = 24$. Solving for a gives $a = 4$. Thus the complete solution is $a = 4$ and $b = 3$.

408. *Quadratic equations.** Quadratic equations are expressed in the form $ax^2 + bx + c = 0$, where a, b, and c are constant numbers (for example, $\frac{1}{2}$, 4, -2, etc.) and x is a variable. An equation of this form may be satisfied by two values of x, one value of x, or no values of x. Actually, when there are no values of x that satisfy the equation, there are only *imaginary* solutions. On the SAT, you will not have questions where you will have to use these formulas. To determine the number of solutions, find the value of the expression $b^2 - 4ac$, where a, b, and c are the constant coefficients of the equation $ax^2 + bx + c = 0$.

> If $b^2 - 4ac$ is *greater* than 0, there are two solutions.
>
> If $b^2 - 4ac$ is *less* than 0, there are no solutions.
>
> If $b^2 - 4ac$ is *equal* to 0, there is one solution.

*On the SAT, you will not need to know the quadratic equations formula.

If solutions exist, they can be found by using the formulas:

$$x = \frac{-b + \sqrt{b^2 - 4ac}}{2a} \text{ and } x = \frac{-b - \sqrt{b^2 - 4ac}}{2a}$$

Note that if $b^2 - 4ac = 0$, the two solutions above will be the same and there will be one solution.

Example: Determine the solutions, if they exist, to the equation $x^2 + 6x + 5 = 0$.

Solution: First, noting $a = 1$, $b = 6$, and $c = 5$, calculate $b^2 - 4ac$, or $6^2 - 4(1)(5)$. Thus, $b^2 - 4ac = 16$. Since this is greater than 0, there are two solutions. They are, from the formulas:

$$x = \frac{-6 + \sqrt{6^2 - 4 \cdot 1 \cdot 5}}{2 \cdot 1}$$

$$\text{and } x = \frac{-6 - \sqrt{6^2 - 4 \cdot 1 \cdot 5}}{2 \cdot 1}$$

Simplify these to:

$$x = \frac{-6 + \sqrt{16}}{2} \text{ and } x = \frac{-6 - \sqrt{16}}{2}$$

As $\sqrt{16} = 4$, $x = \frac{-6 + 4}{2} = \frac{-2}{2}$ and $x = \frac{-6 - 4}{2} = \frac{-10}{2}$. Thus, the two solutions are $x = -1$ and $x = -5$.

Another method of solving quadratic equations is to *factor* the $ax^2 + bx + c$ into two expressions. This will be explained in the next section.

409. *Factoring.* Factoring is breaking down an expression into two or more expressions, the product of which is the original expression. For example, 6 can be factored into 2 and 3 because $2 \cdot 3 = 6$. $x^2 - x$ can be factored into x and $(x - 1)$ because $x^2 - x = x(x - 1)$. Then, if $x^2 + bx + c$ is factorable, it will be factored into two expressions in the form $(x + d)$ and $(x + e)$. If the expression $(x + d)$ is multiplied by the expression $(x + e)$, their product is $x^2 + (d + e)x + de$. For example, $(x + 3) \cdot (x + 2)$ equals $x^2 + 5x + 6$. To factor an expression such as $x^2 + 6x + 8$, find d and e such that $d + e = 6$ and $de = 8$. Of the various factors of 8, we find that $d = 4$ and $e = 2$. Thus $x^2 + 6x + 8$ can be factored into the expressions $(x + 4)$ and $(x + 2)$. Below are factored expressions.

$$x^2 + 2x + 1 = (x + 1)(x + 1)$$
$$x^2 + 4x + 4 = (x + 2)(x + 2)$$
$$x^2 - 4x + 3 = (x - 3)(x - 1)$$
$$x^2 + 10x + 16 = (x + 8)(x + 2)$$
$$x^2 - 5x + 6 = (x - 2)(x - 3)$$

$$x^2 + 3x + 2 = (x + 2)(x + 1)$$
$$x^2 + 5x + 6 = (x + 3)(x + 2)$$
$$x^2 - 4x - 5 = (x - 5)(x + 1)$$
$$x^2 + 4x - 5 = (x + 5)(x - 1)$$
$$x^2 - \;\; x - 6 = (x - 3)(x + 2)$$

An important rule to remember in factoring is that $a^2 - b^2 = (a + b)(a - b)$. For example, $x^2 - 9 = (x + 3)(x - 3)$. You don't get a middle term in x because the $3x$ cancels with the $-3x$ in the product $(x + 3)(x - 3)$. To apply factoring in solving quadratic equations, factor the quadratic expression into two terms and set each term equal to zero. Then, solve the two resulting equations.

Example: Solve $x^2 - x - 6 = 0$.

Solution: First factor the expression $x^2 - x - 6$ into $x - 3$ and $x + 2$. Setting each of these equal to 0 gives $x - 3 = 0$ and $x + 2 = 0$. Solving these equations gives us $x = 3$ and $x = -2$.

Algebra of Graphs

410a. *Number lines*. Numbers, positive and negative, can be represented as points on a straight line. Conversely, points on a line can also be represented by numbers. This is done by use of the number line.

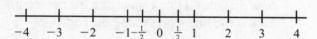

The diagram above is an example of a number line. On a number line, a point is chosen to represent the number zero. Then a point that is 1 unit to the right of 0 represents $+1$; a point that is $\frac{1}{2}$ unit to the right of 0 is $+\frac{1}{2}$; a point that is 2 units to the right of 0 is $+2$; and so on. A point that is 1 unit to the left of 0 is -1; a point that is $\frac{1}{2}$ unit to the left of 0 is $-\frac{1}{2}$; a point that is 2 units to the left of 0 is -2; and so on. As you can see, all points to the right of the 0 point represent positive numbers, and all those to the left of the 0 point represent negative numbers.

To find the distance between two points on the line:
1. Find the numbers that represent the points.
2. The distance is the smaller number subtracted from the larger.

Example: Find the distance between point A and point B on the number line.

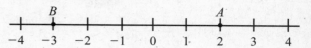

Solution: Point A is $+2$ on the number line and point B is -3. $+2$ is larger than -3, so the distance is $+2 - (-3)$ or $+2 + 3 = 5$. By counting the number of units between A and B, we can also find the distance to be 5.

410b. *Coordinate geometry*. These problems deal with the algebra of graphs. A graph consists of a set of points whose position is determined with respect to a set of axes, usually labeled the x-axis and the y-axis and divided into appropriate units. Locate a point on the graph with an "x-coordinate" of a units and a "y-coordinate" of b units. First move a units along the x-axis (either to the left or the right depending on whether a is negative or positive). Then move b units along the y-axis (either up or down depending on the sign of b). A point with an x-coordinate of a and a y-coordinate of b is represented by (a,b). The points $(2,3)$, $(-1,4)$, $(-2,-3)$, and $(4,-2)$ are shown on the following graph.

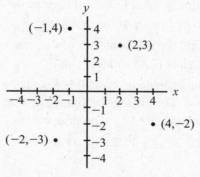

411. *Distance between two points*. If the coordinates of point A are (x_1, y_1) and the coordinates of point B are (x_2, y_2), then the distance on the graph between the two points is $d = \sqrt{(x_2 - x_1)^2 + (y_2 - y_1)^2}$.

Example: Find the distance between the point $(2, -3)$ and the point $(5, 1)$.

Solution: In this case $x_1 = 2$, $x_2 = 5$, $y_1 = -3$, and $y_2 = 1$. Substituting into the above formula gives us

$$d = \sqrt{(5 - 2)^2 + [1 - (-3)]^2} = \sqrt{3^2 + 4^2} = \sqrt{25} = 5$$

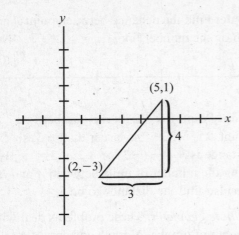

Note: This formula is a consequence of the Pythagorean theorem. Pythagoras, an ancient Greek mathematician, discovered that the square of the length of the hypotenuse (longest side) of a right triangle is equal to the sum of the squares of the lengths of the other two sides. See Sections 317 and 509.

412. *Midpoint of the line segment joining two points.* If the coordinates of the first point are (x_1, y_1) and the coordinates of the second point are (x_2, y_2), then the coordinates of the midpoint will be $\left(\dfrac{x_1 + x_2}{2}, \dfrac{y_1 + y_2}{2}\right)$. In other words, each coordinate of the midpoint is equal to the *average* of the corresponding coordinates of the endpoints.

Example: Find the midpoint of the segment connecting the points (2,4) and (6,2).

Solution: The average of 2 and 6 is 4, so the first coordinate is 4. The average of 4 and 2 is 3; thus the second coordinate is 3. The midpoint is (4,3).

$$\left[\frac{2 + 6}{2} = 4, \frac{4 + 2}{2} = 3\right]$$

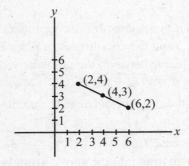

413. *Plotting the graph of a line.* An equation that can be put in the form of $y = mx + b$, where m and b are numerical constants, can be represented as a line on a graph. This means that all of the points on the graph that the line passes through will satisfy the equation. Remember that each point has an x and a y value that can be substituted into the equation. To plot a line, follow the steps below:

Step 1. Select two values of x and two values of y that will satisfy the equation. For example, in the equation $y = 2x + 4$, the point $(x = 1, y = 6)$ will satisfy the equation, as will the point $(x = -2, y = 0)$. There is an infinite number of such points on a line.

Step 2. Plot these two points on the graph. In this case, the two points are (1,6) and (−2,0). These points are represented below.

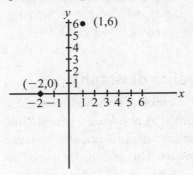

Step 3. Draw a line connecting the two points. This is the line representing the equation.

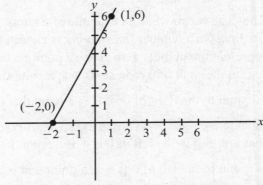

(*Note:* A straight line is completely specified by two points.)

Example: Graph the equation $2y + 3x = 12$.

Solution: Two points that satisfy this equation are (2,3) and (0,6). Plotting these points and drawing a line between them gives:

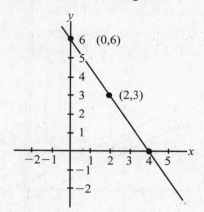

414. *y-intercept.* The *y*-intercept of a line is the point where the line crosses the *y*-axis. At any point where a line crosses the *y*-axis, $x = 0$. To find the *y*-intercept of a line, simply substitute $x = 0$ into the equation of the line, and solve for *y*.

Example: Find the *y*-intercept of the equation $2x + 3y = 6$.

Solution: If $x = 0$ is substituted into the equation, it simplifies to $3y = 6$. Solving for *y* gives $y = 2$. Thus, 2 is the *y*-intercept.

> **If an equation can be put into the form of $y = mx + b$, then b is the *y*-intercept.**

415. *x-intercept.* The point where a line intersects the *x*-axis is called the *x*-intercept. At this point $y = 0$. To find the *x*-intercept of a line, substitute $y = 0$ into the equation and solve for *x*.

Example: Given the equation $2x + 3y = 6$, find the *x*-intercept.

Solution: Substitute $y = 0$ into the equation, getting $2x = 6$. Solving for *x*, find $x = 3$. Thus the *x*-intercept is 3.

In the diagram below, the *y*- and *x*-intercepts of the equation $2x + 3y = 6$ are illustrated.

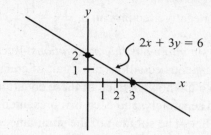

416. *Slope.* The slope of a line is the change in *y* caused by a 1-unit increase in *x*. If an equation is in the form of $y = mx + b$, then as *x* increases 1 unit, *y* will increase *m* units. Therefore the slope is *m*.

Example: Find the slope of the line $2x + 3y = 6$.

Solution: First put the equation into the form of $y = mx + b$. Subtract $2x$ from both sides and divide by 3. The equation becomes $y = -\frac{2}{3}x + 2$. Therefore the slope is $-\frac{2}{3}$.

The slope of the line joining two points, (x_1, y_1) and (x_2, y_2), is given by the expression $m = \frac{y_2 - y_1}{x_2 - x_1}$.

Example: Find the slope of the line joining the points (3,2) and (4,−1).

Solution: Substituting into the formula above gives us $m = \frac{-3}{1} = -3$, where $x_1 = 3$, $x_2 = 4$, $y_1 = 2$, $y_2 = -1$.

If two lines are perpendicular, the slope of one is the negative reciprocal of the other.

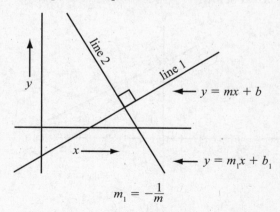

Example: What is the slope of a line perpendicular to the line $y = -3x + 4$?

Solution: Since the slope of the line $y = -3x + 4$ is -3, the slope of the line perpendicular to that line is the negative reciprocal, or $\frac{-1}{-3} = \frac{+1}{+3}$.

417. *Graphing simultaneous linear equations.* Recall that simultaneous equations are a pair of equations in two unknowns. Each of these equations is graphed separately, and each is represented by a straight line. The solution of the simultaneous equations (i.e., the pair of values that satisfies *both* at the same time) is represented by the intersection of two lines. Now, for any pair of lines, there are three possible relationships:

1. The lines intersect at one and only one point; in this case, this point represents the unique solution to the pair of equations. This is most often the case. Such lines are called *consistent*.

2. The lines coincide exactly; this represents the case where the two equations are equivalent (just different forms of the same mathematical relation). Any point that satisfies *either* of the two equations automatically satisfies *both*.

3. The lines are parallel and never intersect. In this case the equations are called *inconsistent*, and they have *no* solution at all. Two lines that are parallel will have the same slope.

Example: Solve graphically the equations $4x - y = 5$ and $2x + 4y = 16$.

Solution: Plot the two lines represented by the two equations. (See Section 413.) The graph is shown below.

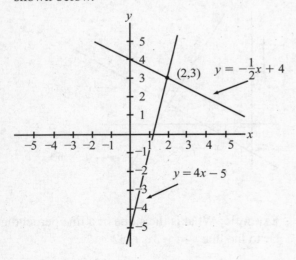

The two lines intersect in the point (2,3), which represents the solution $x = 2$ and $y = 3$. This can be checked by solving the equations as is done in Section 407.

Example: Solve $x + 2y = 6$ and $2x + 4y = 8$.

Solution: Find a point that satisfies each equation. You cannot. The two graphs will look like this:

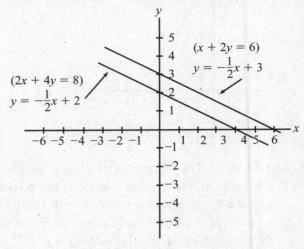

These lines will never intersect, and these equations are termed inconsistent. There is no solution.

> **Remember that two parallel lines have the same slope. This is an easy way to see whether two lines are consistent or inconsistent.**

Example: Find the solution to $2x - 3y = 8$ and $4x = 6y + 16$.

Solution: On the graph these two lines are identical. This means that there is an infinite set of points that satisfy both equations.

Equations of identical lines are multiples of each other and can be reduced to a single equation.

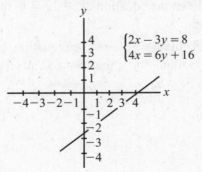

418. *Areas of polygons.* Often, an elementary geometric figure is placed on a graph to calculate its area. This is usually simple for figures such as triangles, rectangles, squares, parallelograms, etc.

Example: Calculate the area of the triangle in the figure below.

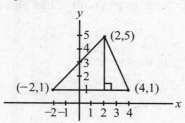

Solution: The area of a triangle is $\frac{1}{2}$(base)(height).

On the graph the length of the line joining $(-2,1)$ and $(4,1)$ is 6 units. The height, which goes from point $(2,5)$ to the base, has a length of 4 units.

Therefore the area is $\frac{1}{2}(6)(4) = 12$.

Example: Calculate the area of the square pictured below.

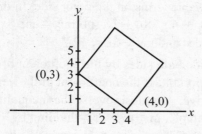

Solution: The area of a square is given by the square of the side. To find this area, first find the length of one side. The length of a segment whose endpoints are (x_1,y_1) and (x_2,y_2) is given by the formula $\sqrt{(x_2 - x_1)^2 + (y_2 - y_1)^2}$. Substituting in $(0,3)$ and $(4,0)$ gives a length of 5 units. Thus the length of one side of the square is 5. Using the formula area $=$ (side)^2 gives an area of 5^2, or 25 square units.

To find the area of more complicated polygons, divide the polygon into simple figures whose areas can be calculated. Add these areas to find the total area.

Example: Find the area of the figure below:

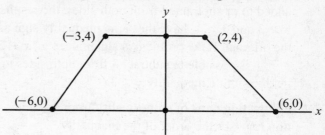

Solution: Divide the figure into two triangles and a rectangle by drawing vertical lines at $(-3,4)$ and $(2,4)$. Thus the polygon is now two triangles and a rectangle.

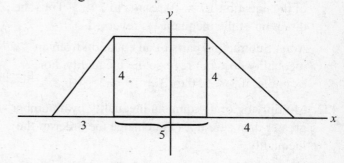

The height of the left triangle is 4 units, and the base is 3. Using $A = \frac{1}{2}bh$ gives the area as 6. The height of the right triangle is 4, and the base is 4. The area is 8. The length of one side of the rectangle is 4, and the other side is 5. Using the formula area $=$ base $\cdot$ height gives the area as 20. Thus the total area is $6 + 8 + 20 = 34$.

Inequalities

419. *Inequalities.* These problems deal with numbers that are less than, greater than, or equal to other numbers. The following laws apply to all inequalities:

$<$ means "less than," thus $3 < 4$
$>$ means "greater than," thus $5 > 2$
$\leq$ means "less than or equal to," thus $x \leq y$
    means $x < y$ or $x = y$
$\geq$ means "greater than or equal to," thus $x \geq y$
    means $x > y$ or $x = y$

420. If equal quantities are added to or subtracted from both sides of an inequality, the direction of the inequality does *not* change.

If $x < y$, then $x + z < y + z$ and $x - z < y - z$.
If $x > y$, then $x + z > y + z$ and $x - z > y - z$.

For example, given the inequality $4 > 2$, with 1 added to or subtracted from both sides, the results, $5 > 3$ and $3 > 1$, have the same inequality sign as the original. If the problem is algebraic, e.g., $x + 3 < 6$, it is possible to subtract 3 from both sides to get the simple inequality $x < 3$.

421. Subtracting parts of an inequality from an equation *reverses* the order of the inequality.

Given $z = z$ and $x < y$, then $z - x > z - y$.
Given $z = z$ and $x > y$, then $z - x < z - y$.

For example, given that $3 < 5$, subtracting 3 from the left-hand side and 5 from the right-hand side of the equation $10 = 10$ results in $7 > 5$. Thus the direction of the inequality is reversed.

Note: Subtracting parts of an equation from an inequality does not reverse the inequality. For example, if $3 < 5$, then $3 - 10 < 5 - 10$.

422. Multiplying or dividing an inequality by a number greater than zero does not change the order of the inequality.

If $x > y$ and $a > 0$, then $xa > ya$ and $\dfrac{x}{a} > \dfrac{y}{a}$.

If $x < y$ and $a > 0$, then $xa < ya$ and $\dfrac{x}{a} < \dfrac{y}{a}$.

For example, if $4 > 2$, multiplying both sides by any arbitrary number (for instance, 5) gives $20 > 10$, which is still true. Or, if algebraically $6h < 3$, dividing both sides by 6 gives $h < \dfrac{1}{2}$, which is true.

423. Multiplying or dividing an inequality by a number less than 0 reverses the order of the inequality.

If $x > y$ and $a < 0$, then $xa < ya$ and $\dfrac{x}{a} < \dfrac{y}{a}$.

If $x < y$ and $a < 0$, then $xa > ya$ and $\dfrac{x}{a} > \dfrac{y}{a}$.

If $-3 < 2$ is multiplied through by -2 it becomes $6 > -4$, and the order of the inequality is reversed.

Note that negative numbers are always less than positive numbers. Note also that the greater the absolute value of a negative number, the smaller it actually is. Thus, $-10 < -9$, $-8 < -7$, etc.

424. The product of two numbers with like signs is positive.

If $x > 0$ and $y > 0$, then $xy > 0$.
If $x < 0$ and $y < 0$, then $xy > 0$.

For example, -3 times -2 is 6.

425. The product of two numbers with unlike signs is negative.

If $x < 0$ and $y > 0$, then $xy < 0$.
If $x > 0$ and $y < 0$, then $xy < 0$.

For example, -2 times 3 is -6; 8 times -1 is -8; etc.

426. *Linear inequalities in one unknown*. In these problems a first-power variable is given in an inequality, and this variable must be solved for in terms of the inequality. Examples of linear inequalities in one unknown are $2x + 7 > 4 + x$, $8y - 3 \le 2y$, etc.

Step 1. By ordinary algebraic addition and subtraction (as if it were an equality), get all of the constant terms on one side of the inequality and all of the variable terms on the other side. In the inequality $2x + 4 < 8x + 16$ subtract 4 and $8x$ from both sides and get $-6x < 12$.

Step 2. Divide both sides by the coefficient of the variable. Important: If the coefficient of the variable is negative, you must reverse the inequality sign. For example, in $-6x < 12$, dividing by -6 gives $x > -2$. (The inequality is reversed.) In $3x < 12$, dividing by 3 gives $x < 4$.

Example: Solve for y in the inequality $4y + 7 \ge 9 - 2y$.

Solution: Subtracting $-2y$ and 7 from both sides gives $6y \ge 2$. Dividing both sides by 6 gives $y \ge \dfrac{1}{3}$.

Example: Solve for a in the inequality $10 - 2a < 0$.

Solution: Subtracting 10 from both sides gives $-2a < -10$. Dividing both sides by -2 gives $a > \dfrac{-10}{-2}$ or $a > 5$. Note that the inequality sign has been reversed because of the division by a negative number.

427. *Simultaneous linear inequalities in two unknowns.* These are two inequalities, each one in two unknowns. The same two unknowns are to be solved for in each equation. This means the equations must be solved simultaneously.

Step 1. Plot both inequalities on the same graph. Replace the inequality sign with an equals sign and plot the resulting line. The side of the line that makes the inequality true is then shaded in. For example, graph the inequality $2x - y > 4$. First replace the inequality sign, getting $2x - y = 4$; then, plot the line. The x-intercept is where $y = 0$. The y-intercept is where $x = 0$. So in the equation $2x - y = 4$, the x-intercept is where $2x = 4$, or where $x = 2$. Similarly, in the equation $2x - y = 4$, the y-intercept is where $-y = 4$, or where $y = -4$. (See Sections 414 and 415 for determining x- and y-intercepts.)

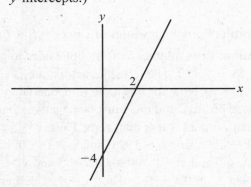

To decide which side of the line satisfies the inequality, choose a convenient point on each side and determine which point satisfies the inequality. Shade in that side of the line. In this case, choose the point (0,0). With this point the equation becomes $2(0) - 0 > 4$, or $0 > 4$. This is not true. Therefore, shade in the other side of the line.

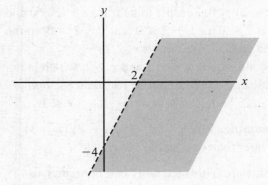

Step 2. After both inequalities have been solved, the area that is common to both shaded portions is the solution to the problem.

Example: Solve $x + y > 2$ and $3x < 6$.

Solution: First graph $x + y > 2$ by plotting $x + y = 2$ and using the point (4,0) to determine the region where the inequality is satisfied:

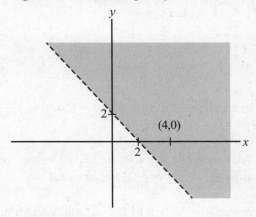

Graph the inequality $3x < 6$ on the same axes and get:

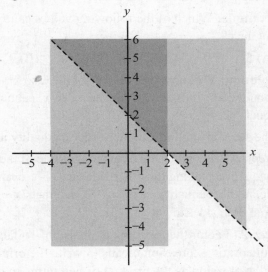

The solution is the double-shaded area.

428. *Higher-order inequalities in one unknown.* These are inequalities that deal with variables multiplied by themselves. For example, $x^2 + 3 \geq 0$, $(x - 1)(x + 2) < 4$, and $x^3 - 7x > 0$ are such inequalities. The basic rules to remember in doing such problems are:

1. The product of any number of positive numbers is positive.

For example, $2 \times 3 \times 4 \times 5 = 120$, which is positive, or $\frac{1}{2} \times \frac{1}{2} = \frac{1}{4}$, which is positive.

2. The product of an even number of negative numbers is positive.

For example, $(-3)(-2) = 6$ or $(-3)(-1)(-9)(-2) = 54$, which is positive.

3. The product of an odd number of negative numbers is negative.

For example, $(-1)(-2)(-3) = -6$ or $(-\frac{1}{2})(-2)(-3)(-6)(-1) = -18$.

4. Any number squared or raised to an even power is always positive or zero.

For example, $x^2 \geq 0$ or $a^4 \geq 0$ for all x and for all a. Often these basic rules will make the solution to an inequality problem obvious.

Example: Which of the following values can x^2 not have?

(A) 5   (B) −2   (C) 0   (D) 144   (E) 9

Solution: We know that $x^2 \geq 0$ for all x, so x^2 cannot be negative. −2 is negative, so x^2 cannot equal −2.

The steps in solving a higher-order inequality are:

Step 1. Bring all of the terms to one side of the inequality, making the other side zero. For example, in the inequality $x^2 > 3x - 2$, subtract $3x - 2$ from both sides to get $x^2 - 3x + 2 > 0$.

Step 2. Factor the resulting expression. To factor a quadratic expression means to write the original expression as the product of two terms in the first power, i.e., $x^2 = x \cdot x$. x is a factor of x^2. (See Section 409 for a detailed explanation of factoring.) The quadratic expression $x^2 - 3x + 2$ when factored is $(x - 2)(x - 1)$. Note that $x \cdot x = x^2$, $-2x - x = -3x$, and $(-1)(-2) = 2$. Most quadratic expressions can easily be factored by taking factors of the last term (in this case 2 and 1) and adding or subtracting them to or from x. Through trial and error, the right combination is found. An important fact to remember when factoring is: $(a + b)(c + d) = ac + ad + bc + bd$. Example: $(x + 4)(x + 2) = x^2 + 4x + 2x + 8 = x^2 + 6x + 8$. Another is that $a^2 - b^2 = (a + b)(a - b)$. Example: $x^2 - 16 = (x + 4)(x - 4)$.

Step 3. Investigate which terms are positive and which terms are negative. For example, in $(x - 3)(x + 2) > 0$, either $(x - 3)$ and $(x + 2)$ are both positive or $(x - 3)$ and $(x + 2)$ are both negative. If one were positive and the other were negative, the product would be negative and would not satisfy the inequality. If the factors are positive, then $x - 3 > 0$ and $x + 2 > 0$, which yields $x > 3$ and $x > -2$. For x to be greater than 3 and to be greater than −2, it must be greater than 3. If it is greater than 3, it is automatically greater than −2. Thus, with positive factors $x > 3$ is the answer. If the factors are negative, $x - 3 < 0$ and $x + 2 < 0$, or $x < -2$. For x to be less than 3 and less than −2, it must be less than −2. Thus, with negative factors $x < -2$ is the answer. As both answers are possible from the original equation, the solution to the original problem is $x > 3$ or $x < -2$.

Example: For which values of x is $x^2 + 5 < 6x$?

Solution: First subtract $6x$ from both sides to get $x^2 - 6x + 5 < 0$. The left side factors into $(x - 5)(x - 1) < 0$. Now for this to be true, one factor must be positive and one must be negative, that is, their product is less than zero. Thus, $x - 5 > 0$ and $x - 1 < 0$, or $x - 5 < 0$ and $x - 1 > 0$. If $x - 5 < 0$ and $x - 1 > 0$, then $x < 5$ and $x > 1$, or $1 < x < 5$. If $x - 5 > 0$ and $x - 1 < 0$, then $x > 5$ and $x < 1$, which is impossible because x cannot be less than 1 *and* greater than 5. Therefore, the solution is $1 < x < 5$.

Example: For what values of x is $x^2 < 4$?

Solution: Subtract 4 from both sides to get $x^2 - 4 < 0$. Remember that $a^2 - b^2 = (a + b)(a - b)$; thus $x^2 - 4 = (x + 2)(x - 2)$. Hence, $(x + 2)(x - 2) < 0$. For this to be true, $x + 2 > 0$ and $x - 2 < 0$, or $x + 2 < 0$ and $x - 2 > 0$. In the first case $x > -2$ and $x < 2$, or $-2 < x < 2$. The second case is $x < -2$ and $x > 2$, which is impossible because x cannot be less than −2 *and* greater than 2. Thus, the solution is $-2 < x < 2$.

Example: When is $(x^2 + 1)(x - 2)^2(x - 3)$ greater than or equal to zero?

Solution: This inequality can be written as $(x^2 + 1)(x - 2)^2(x - 3) \geq 0$. This is already in factors. The individual terms must be investigated.

$x^2 + 1$ is always positive because $x^2 \geq 0$, so $x^2 + 1$ must be greater than 0. $(x - 2)^2$ is a number squared, so this is always greater than or equal to zero. Therefore, the product of the first two terms is positive or equal to zero for all values of x. The third term, $x - 3$, is positive when $x > 3$ and negative when $x < 3$. For the entire expression to be positive, $x - 3$ must be positive, that is, $x > 3$. For the expression to be equal to zero, $x - 3 = 0$, that is, $x = 3$, or $(x - 2)^2 = 0$, that is, $x = 2$. Thus, the entire expression is positive when $x > 3$ and zero when $x = 2$ or $x = 3$.

Exponents and Roots

429. *Exponents.* An exponent is an easy way to express repeated multiplication. For example, $5 \times 5 \times 5 \times 5 = 5^4$. The 4 is the exponent. In the expression $7^3 = 7 \times 7 \times 7$, 3 is the exponent. 7^3 means 7 is multiplied by itself three times. If the exponent is 0, the expression always has a value of 1. Thus, $6^0 = 15^0 = 1$, etc. If the exponent is 1, the value of the expression is the number base. Thus, $4^1 = 4$ and $9^1 = 9$.

In the problem $5^3 \times 5^4$, we can simplify by counting the factors of 5. Thus, $5^3 \times 5^4 = 5^{3+4} = 5^7$. When we multiply and the base number is the same, we keep the base number and add the exponents. For example, $7^4 \times 7^8 = 7^{12}$.

For division, we keep the same base number and subtract exponents. Thus, $8^8 \div 8^2 = 8^{8-2} = 8^6$.

A negative exponent indicates the reciprocal of the expression with a positive exponent, thus $3^{-2} = \dfrac{1}{3^2}$.

430. *Roots.* The square root of a number is a number whose square is the original number. For example, $\sqrt{16} = 4$, since $4 \times 4 = 16$. (The $\sqrt{}$ symbol always means a positive number.) Note that $(-4)(-4) = 16$, so if we have an equation such as $x^2 = 16$, then $x = \pm\sqrt{16} = \pm 4$.

To simplify a square root, we factor the number.
$$\sqrt{32} = \sqrt{16 \cdot 2} = \sqrt{16} \cdot \sqrt{2} = 4\sqrt{2}$$
$$\sqrt{72} = \sqrt{36 \cdot 2} = \sqrt{36} \cdot \sqrt{2} = 6\sqrt{2}$$
$$\begin{aligned}
\sqrt{300} &= \sqrt{25 \cdot 12} = \sqrt{25} \cdot \sqrt{12} \\
&= 5 \cdot \sqrt{12} \\
&= 5 \cdot \sqrt{4 \cdot 3} \\
&= 5 \cdot \sqrt{4} \cdot \sqrt{3} \\
&= 5 \cdot 2\sqrt{3} \\
&= 10\sqrt{3}
\end{aligned}$$

We can add expressions with the square roots only if the numbers inside the square root sign are the same. For example,
$$3\sqrt{7} + 2\sqrt{7} = 5\sqrt{7}$$
$$\begin{aligned}
\sqrt{18} + \sqrt{2} &= \sqrt{9 \cdot 2} + \sqrt{2} \\
&= \sqrt{9} \cdot \sqrt{2} + \sqrt{2} \\
&= 3\sqrt{2} + \sqrt{2} \\
&= 4\sqrt{2}
\end{aligned}$$

431. *Evaluation of expressions.* To evaluate an expression means to substitute a value in place of a letter. For example: Evaluate $3a^2 - c^3$ if $a = -2$, $c = -3$.
$$\begin{aligned}
3a^2 - c^3 &= 3(-2)^2 - (-3)^3 \\
&= 3(4) - (-27) \\
&= 12 + 27 \\
&= 39
\end{aligned}$$

Given: $a \triangledown b = ab + b^2$. Find: $-2\triangledown 3$.

Using the definition, we get
$$\begin{aligned}
-2\triangledown 3 &= (-2)(3) + (3)^2 \\
&= -6 + 9 \\
-2\triangledown 3 &= 3
\end{aligned}$$

SESSION 4 PRACTICE TEST

Algebra Problems

Correct answers and solutions follow this test.

1. For what values of x is the following equation satisfied: $3x + 9 = 21 + 7x$?

   (A) -3 only
   (B) 3 only
   (C) 3 or -3 only
   (D) no values
   (E) an infinite number of values

   A B C D E
   ○ ○ ○ ○ ○

2. What values may z have if $2z + 4$ is greater than $z - 6$?

   (A) any values greater than -10
   (B) any values greater than -2
   (C) any values less than 2
   (D) any values less than 10
   (E) none of these

   A B C D E
   ○ ○ ○ ○ ○

3. If $ax^2 + 2x - 3 = 0$ when $x = -3$, what value(s) can a have?

   (A) -3 only
   (B) -1 only
   (C) 1 only
   (D) -1 and 1 only
   (E) -3, -1, and 1 only

   A B C D E
   ○ ○ ○ ○ ○

4. If the coordinates of point P are $(0,8)$, and the coordinates of point Q are $(4,2)$, which of the following points represents the midpoint of PQ?

   (A) $(0,2)$
   (B) $(2,4)$
   (C) $(2,5)$
   (D) $(4,8)$
   (E) $(4,10)$

   A B C D E
   ○ ○ ○ ○ ○

5. In the formula $V = \pi r^2 h$, what is the value of r, in terms of V and h?

   (A) $\dfrac{\sqrt{V}}{\pi h}$
   (B) $\pi\sqrt{\dfrac{V}{h}}$
   (C) $\sqrt{\pi V h}$
   (D) $\dfrac{\pi h}{\sqrt{V}}$
   (E) $\sqrt{\dfrac{V}{\pi h}}$

   A B C D E
   ○ ○ ○ ○ ○

6. Solve the inequality $x^2 - 3x < 0$.

   (A) $x < -3$
   (B) $-3 < x < 0$
   (C) $x < 3$
   (D) $0 < x < 3$
   (E) $3 < x$

   A B C D E
   ○ ○ ○ ○ ○

7. Which of the following lines is parallel to the line represented by $2y = 8x + 32$?

   (A) $y = 8x + 32$
   (B) $y = 8x + 16$
   (C) $y = 16x + 32$
   (D) $y = 4x + 32$
   (E) $y = 2x + 16$

   A B C D E
   ○ ○ ○ ○ ○

8. In the equation $4.04x + 1.01 = 9.09$, what value of x is necessary to make the equation true?

(A) -1.5

(B) 0

(C) 1

(D) 2

(E) 2.5

A B C D E
○ ○ ○ ○ ○

9. What values of x satisfy the equation $(x + 1)(x - 2) = 0$?

(A) 1 only

(B) -2 only

(C) 1 and -2 only

(D) -1 and 2 only

(E) any values between -1 and 2

A B C D E
○ ○ ○ ○ ○

10. What is the largest possible value of the following expression:

$$(x + 2)(3 - x)(2 + x)^2(2x - 6)(2x + 4)?$$

(A) -576

(B) -24

(C) 0

(D) 12

(E) cannot be determined

A B C D E
○ ○ ○ ○ ○

11. For what value(s) of k is the following equation satisfied:

$$2k - 9 - k = 4k + 6 - 3k?$$

(A) -5 only

(B) 0

(C) $\frac{5}{2}$ only

(D) no values

(E) more than one value

A B C D E
○ ○ ○ ○ ○

12. In the equation $p = aq^2 + bq + c$, if $a = 1$, $b = -2$, and $c = 1$, which of the following expresses p in terms of q?

(A) $p = (q - 2)^2$

(B) $p = (q - 1)^2$

(C) $p = q^2$

(D) $p = (q + 1)^2$

(E) $p = (q + 2)^2$

A B C D E
○ ○ ○ ○ ○

13. If $A + B + C = 10$, $A + B = 7$, and $A - B = 5$, what is the value of C?

(A) 1

(B) 3

(C) 6

(D) 7

(E) The answer cannot be determined from the given information.

A B C D E
○ ○ ○ ○ ○

14. If $5x + 15$ is greater than 20, which of the following best describes the possible values of x?

(A) x must be greater than 5.

(B) x must be greater than 3.

(C) x must be greater than 1.

(D) x must be less than 5.

(E) x must be less than 1.

A B C D E
○ ○ ○ ○ ○

15. If $\frac{t^2 - 1}{t - 1} = 2$, then what value(s) may t have?

(A) 1 only

(B) -1 only

(C) 1 or -1

(D) no values

(E) an infinite number of values

A B C D E
○ ○ ○ ○ ○

16. If $4m = 9n$, what is the value of $7m$, in terms of n?

(A) $\frac{63n}{4}$

(B) $\frac{9n}{28}$

(C) $\frac{7n}{9}$

(D) $\frac{28n}{9}$

(E) $\frac{7n}{4}$

A B C D E
○ ○ ○ ○ ○

17. The coordinates of a triangle are (0,2), (2,4), and (1,6). What is the area of the triangle in square units (to the nearest unit)?

    (A) 2 square units
    (B) 3 square units
    (C) 4 square units
    (D) 5 square units
    (E) 6 square units

    A B C D E
    ○ ○ ○ ○ ○

18. In the formula $s = \frac{1}{2}gt^2$, what is the value of t, in terms of s and g?

    (A) $\frac{2s}{g}$

    (B) $2\sqrt{\frac{s}{g}}$

    (C) $\frac{s}{2g}$

    (D) $\sqrt{\frac{s}{2g}}$

    (E) $\sqrt{\frac{2s}{g}}$

    A B C D E
    ○ ○ ○ ○ ○

19. In the triangle ABC, angle A is a 30° angle, and angle B is obtuse. If x represents the number of degrees in angle C, which of the following best represents the possible values of x?

    (A) $0 < x < 60$
    (B) $0 < x < 150$
    (C) $60 < x < 180$
    (D) $120 < x < 180$
    (E) $120 < x < 150$

    A B C D E
    ○ ○ ○ ○ ○

20. Which of the following sets of coordinates does *not* represent the vertices of an isosceles triangle?

    (A) (0,2), (0,−2), (2,0)
    (B) (1,3), (1,5), (3,4)
    (C) (1,3), (1,7), (4,5)
    (D) (2,2), (2,0), (1,1)
    (E) (2,3), (2,5), (3,3)

    A B C D E
    ○ ○ ○ ○ ○

21. If $2 < a < 5$, and $6 > b > 3$, what are the possible values of $a + b$?

    (A) $a + b$ must equal 8.
    (B) $a + b$ must be between 2 and 6.
    (C) $a + b$ must be between 3 and 5.
    (D) $a + b$ must be between 5 and 8.
    (E) $a + b$ must be between 5 and 11.

    A B C D E
    ○ ○ ○ ○ ○

22. The area of a square will be doubled if:

    (A) the length of the diagonal is divided by 2
    (B) the length of the diagonal is divided by $\sqrt{2}$
    (C) the length of the diagonal is multiplied by 2
    (D) the length of the diagonal is multiplied by $\sqrt{2}$
    (E) none of the above

    A B C D E
    ○ ○ ○ ○ ○

23. Find the value of y that satisfies the equation $8.8y - 4 = 7.7y + 7$.

    (A) 1.1
    (B) 7.7
    (C) 8.0
    (D) 10.0
    (E) 11.0

    A B C D E
    ○ ○ ○ ○ ○

24. Which of the following is a factor of the expression $2x^2 + 1$?

    (A) $x + 2$
    (B) $x - 2$
    (C) $x + \sqrt{2}$
    (D) $x - \sqrt{2}$
    (E) none of these

    A B C D E
    ○ ○ ○ ○ ○

25. A manager has ten employees. The manager's salary is equal to six times the *average* of the employees' salaries. If the eleven of them received a total of $640,000 in one year, what was the manager's salary that year?

    (A) $40,000
    (B) $60,000
    (C) $240,000

(D) $400,000
(E) $440,000

A B C D E
○ ○ ○ ○ ○

26. If $6x + 3 = 15$, what is the value of $12x - 3$?

(A) 21
(B) 24
(C) 28
(D) 33
(E) 36

A B C D E
○ ○ ○ ○ ○

27. If $2p + 7$ is greater than $3p - 5$, which of the following best describes the possible values of p?

(A) p must be greater than 2.
(B) p must be greater than 12.
(C) p must be less than 2.
(D) p must be less than 12.
(E) p must be greater than 2 but less than 12.

A B C D E
○ ○ ○ ○ ○

28. What is the value of q if $x^2 + qx + 1 = 0$, if $x = 1$?

(A) -2
(B) -1
(C) 0
(D) 1
(E) 2

A B C D E
○ ○ ○ ○ ○

29. What is the area (to the nearest unit) of the shaded figure in the diagram below, assuming that each of the squares has an area of 1?

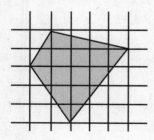

(A) 12
(B) 13
(C) 14

(D) 15
(E) 16

A B C D E
○ ○ ○ ○ ○

30. Which of the following statements is *false*?

(A) Any two numbers, a and b, have a sum equal to $a + b$.
(B) Any two numbers, a and b, have a product equal to $a \cdot b$.
(C) Any two numbers, a and b, have a difference equal to $a - b$.
(D) Any two numbers, a and b, have a quotient equal to $\dfrac{a}{b}$.
(E) Any two numbers, a and b, have an average equal to $\dfrac{(a + b)}{2}$.

A B C D E
○ ○ ○ ○ ○

31. If $(x - 1)(x - 2)(x^2 - 4) = 0$, what are the possible values of x?

(A) -2 only
(B) $+2$ only
(C) $-1, -2$, or -4 only
(D) $+1, +2$, or $+4$ only
(E) $+1, -2$, or $+2$ only

A B C D E
○ ○ ○ ○ ○

32. If $P + Q = R$ and $P + R = 2Q$, what is the ratio of P to R?

(A) $1 : 1$
(B) $1 : 2$
(C) $2 : 1$
(D) $1 : 3$
(E) $3 : 1$

A B C D E
○ ○ ○ ○ ○

33. For what value(s) of r is $\dfrac{r^2 + 5r + 6}{r + 2}$ equal to 0?

(A) -2 only
(B) -3 only
(C) $+3$ only
(D) -2 or -3
(E) $+2$ or $+3$

A B C D E
○ ○ ○ ○ ○

34. What is the value of $a^2b + 4ab^2 + 4b^3$, if $a = 15$ and $b = 5$?

    (A) 1,625
    (B) 2,125
    (C) 2,425
    (D) 2,725
    (E) 3,125

    A B C D E
    ○ ○ ○ ○ ○

35. If $m + 4n = 2n + 8m$, what is the ratio of n to m?

    (A) 1 : 4
    (B) 1 : −4
    (C) −4 : 1
    (D) 2 : 7
    (E) 7 : 2

    A B C D E
    ○ ○ ○ ○ ○

36. If the value of a lies between −5 and +2, and the value of b lies between −7 and +1, what are the possible values for the product $a \cdot b$?

    (A) between −14 and +2
    (B) between −35 and +2
    (C) between +2 and +35
    (D) between −12 and +3
    (E) between −14 and +35

    A B C D E
    ○ ○ ○ ○ ○

37. What is the area, in square units, of a triangle whose vertices lie on points $(−5,1)$, $(−5,4)$, and $(2,4)$?

    (A) 10.5 square units
    (B) 12.5 square units
    (C) 15.0 square units
    (D) 20.0 square units
    (E) 21.0 square units

    A B C D E
    ○ ○ ○ ○ ○

38. If $A + B = 12$ and $B + C = 16$, what is the value of $A + C$?

    (A) −4
    (B) −28
    (C) +4

    (D) +28
    (E) The answer cannot be determined from the given information.

    A B C D E
    ○ ○ ○ ○ ○

39. What is the solution to the equation $x^2 + 2x + 1 = 0$?

    (A) $x = 1$
    (B) $x = 0$
    (C) $x = 1$ and $x = −1$
    (D) $x = −1$
    (E) no real solutions

    A B C D E
    ○ ○ ○ ○ ○

40. Which of the following equations will have a vertical line as its graph?

    (A) $x + y = 1$
    (B) $x − y = 1$
    (C) $x = 1$
    (D) $y = 1$
    (E) $xy = 1$

    A B C D E
    ○ ○ ○ ○ ○

41. For what value(s) of x does $x^2 + 3x + 2$ equal zero?

    (A) −1 only
    (B) +2 only
    (C) −1 or −2 only
    (D) 1 or 2 only
    (E) none of these

    A B C D E
    ○ ○ ○ ○ ○

42. If $a + b$ equals 12, and $a − b$ equals 6, what is the value of b?

    (A) 0
    (B) 3
    (C) 6
    (D) 9
    (E) The answer cannot be determined from the given information.

    A B C D E
    ○ ○ ○ ○ ○

43. For what value(s) of m is $m^2 + 4$ equal to $4m$?

    (A) -2 only
    (B) 0 only
    (C) $+2$ only
    (D) $+4$ only
    (E) more than one value

    A B C D E
    ○ ○ ○ ○ ○

44. If $x = 0$, $y = 2$, and $x^2yz + 3xz^2 + y^2z + 3y + 4x = 0$, what is the value of z?

    (A) $-\dfrac{4}{3}$

    (B) $-\dfrac{3}{2}$

    (C) $+\dfrac{3}{4}$

    (D) $+\dfrac{4}{3}$

    (E) The answer cannot be determined from the given information.

    A B C D E
    ○ ○ ○ ○ ○

45. If $c + 4d = 3c - 2d$, what is the ratio of c to d?

    (A) $1 : 3$
    (B) $1 : -3$
    (C) $3 : 1$
    (D) $2 : 3$
    (E) $2 : -3$

    A B C D E
    ○ ○ ○ ○ ○

46. If $3 < x < 7$ and $6 > x > 2$, which of the following best describes x?

    (A) $2 < x < 6$
    (B) $2 < x < 7$
    (C) $3 < x < 6$
    (D) $3 < x < 7$
    (E) No value of x can satisfy both of these conditions.

    A B C D E
    ○ ○ ○ ○ ○

47. What are the coordinates of the midpoint of the line segment whose endpoints are $(4,9)$ and $(5,15)$?

    (A) $(4,5)$
    (B) $(5,9)$
    (C) $(4,15)$
    (D) $(4.5,12)$
    (E) $(9,24)$

    A B C D E
    ○ ○ ○ ○ ○

48. If $\dfrac{t^2 + 2t}{2t + 4} = \dfrac{t}{2}$, what does t equal?

    (A) -2 only
    (B) $+2$ only
    (C) any value except $+2$
    (D) any value except -2
    (E) any value

    A B C D E
    ○ ○ ○ ○ ○

49. If $x + y = 4$, and $x + z = 9$, what is the value of $(y - z)$?

    (A) -5
    (B) $+5$
    (C) -13
    (D) $+13$
    (E) The answer cannot be determined from the given information.

    A B C D E
    ○ ○ ○ ○ ○

50. Of the following statements, which are equivalent?

    I. $-3 < x < 3$

    II. $x^2 < 9$

    III. $\dfrac{1}{x} < \dfrac{1}{3}$

    (A) I and II only
    (B) I and III only
    (C) II and III only
    (D) I, II, and III
    (E) none of the above

    A B C D E
    ○ ○ ○ ○ ○

Answer Key for Session 4 Practice Test

1. A	14. C	27. D	39. D
2. A	15. D	28. A	40. C
3. C	16. A	29. B	41. C
4. C	17. B	30. D	42. B
5. E	18. E	31. E	43. C
6. D	19. A	32. D	44. B
7. D	20. E	33. B	45. C
8. D	21. E	34. E	46. C
9. D	22. D	35. E	47. D
10. C	23. D	36. E	48. D
11. D	24. E	37. A	49. A
12. B	25. C	38. E	50. A
13. B	26. A		

Answers and Solutions for Session 4 Practice Test

1. Choice A is correct. The original equation is $3x + 9 = 21 + 7x$. First subtract 9 and $7x$ from both sides to get $-4x = 12$. Now divide both sides by the coefficient of x, -4, obtaining the solution, $x = -3$.
(Refresher 406)

2. Choice A is correct. Given $2z + 4 > z - 6$. Subtracting equal quantities from both sides of an inequality does not change the order of the inequality. Therefore, subtracting z and 4 from both sides gives a solution of $z > -10$.
(Refreshers 419, 420)

3. Choice C is correct. Substitute -3 for x in the original equation to get the following:
$$a(-3)^2 + 2(-3) - 3 = 0$$
$$9a - 6 - 3 = 0$$
$$9a - 9 = 0$$
$$a = 1$$
(Refresher 406)

4. Choice C is correct. To find the midpoint of the line segment connecting two points, find the point whose x-coordinate is the average of the two given x-coordinates, and whose y-coordinate is the average of the two given y-coordinates. The midpoint here will be $\left(\frac{0+4}{2}, \frac{8+2}{2}\right)$, or (2,5).
(Refresher 412)

5. Choice E is correct. Divide both sides of the equation by πh:
$$\frac{V}{\pi h} = r^2$$
Take the square root of both sides:
$$r = \sqrt{\frac{V}{\pi h}}$$
(Refresher 403)

6. Choice D is correct. Factor the original expression into $x(x - 3) < 0$. In order for the product of two expressions to be less than 0 (negative), one must be positive and the other must be negative. Thus, $x < 0$ and $x - 3 > 0$; or $x > 0$ and $x - 3 < 0$. In the first case, $x < 0$ and $x > 3$. This is impossible because x cannot be less than 0 *and* greater than 3 at the same time. In the second case $x > 0$ and $x < 3$, which can be rewritten as $0 < x < 3$.
(Refresher 428)

7. Choice D is correct. Divide both sides of the equation $2y = 8x + 32$ by 2 to get $y = 4x + 16$. Now it is in the form of $y = mx + b$, where m is the slope of the line and b is the y-intercept. Thus the slope of the line is 4. Any line parallel to this line must have the same slope. The answer must have a slope of 4. This is the line $y = 4x + 32$. Note that all of the choices are already in the form of $y = mx + b$.
(Refresher 416)

8. Choice D is correct. Subtract 1.01 from both sides to give: $4.04x = 8.08$. Dividing both sides by 4.04 gives a solution of $x = 2$.
(Refresher 406)

9. Choice D is correct. If a product is equal to zero, then one of the factors must equal zero. If $(x + 1)(x - 2) = 0$, either $x + 1 = 0$, or $x - 2 = 0$. Solving these two equations, we see that either $x = -1$ or $x = 2$.
(Refreshers 408, 409)

10. Choice C is correct. It is possible, but time-consuming, to examine the various ranges of x, but it will be quicker if you realize that the same factors appear, with numerical multiples, more than once in the expression. Properly factored, the expression becomes:
$$(x + 2)(2 + x)^2(2)(x + 2)(3 - x)(-2)(3 - x)$$
$$= -4(x + 2)^4(3 - x)^2$$
Since squares of real numbers can never be negative, the whole product has only one negative term and is therefore negative, except when one of the terms is zero, in which case the product is also zero. Thus, the product cannot be larger than zero for any x.
(Refresher 428)

11. Choice D is correct. Combine like terms on both sides of the given equations and obtain the equivalent form: $k - 9 = k + 6$. This is true for no values of k. If k is subtracted from both sides, -9 will equal 6, which is impossible. (Refresher 406)

12. Choice B is correct. Substitute for the given values of a, b, and c, and obtain $p = q^2 - 2q + 1$; or, rearranging terms, $p = (q - 1)^2$. (Refresher 409)

13. Choice B is correct. $A + B + C = 10$. Also, $A + B = 7$. Substitute the value 7 for the quantity $(A + B)$ in the first equation and obtain the new equation: $7 + C = 10$ or $C = 3$. $A - B = 5$ could be used with the other two equations to find the values of A and B. (Refresher 406)

14. Choice C is correct. If $5x + 15 > 20$, then subtract 15 from both sides to get $5x > 5$. Now divide both sides by 5. This does not change the order of the inequality because 5 is a positive number. The solution is $x > 1$. (Refreshers 419, 426)

15. Choice D is correct. Factor $(t^2 - 1)$ to obtain the product $(t + 1)(t - 1)$. For any value of t, except 1, the equation is equivalent to $(t + 1) = 2$, or $t = 1$. One is the only possible value of t. However, this value is not possible as $t - 1$ would equal 0, and the quotient $\dfrac{t^2 - 1}{t - 1}$ would not be defined. (Refreshers 404, 409)

16. Choice A is correct. If $4m = 9n$, then $m = \dfrac{9n}{4}$. Multiplying both sides of the equation by 7, we obtain: $7m = \dfrac{63n}{4}$. (Refresher 403)

17. Choice B is correct. As the diagram shows, the easiest way to calculate the area of this triangle is to start with the area of the enclosing rectangle and subtract the three shaded triangles.

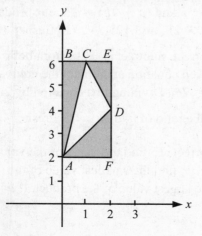

The area of the rectangle $ABEF = (2)(4) = 8$ square units.

The area of the triangle $ABC = \dfrac{1}{2}(1)(4) = 2$ square units.

The area of the triangle $CDE = \dfrac{1}{2}(1)(2) = 1$ square unit.

The area of the triangle $ADF = \dfrac{1}{2}(2)(2) = 2$ square units.

Thus the area of the triangle $ACD = 8 - 5 = 3$ square units. (Refresher 418)

18. Choice E is correct. Since $s = \dfrac{1}{2}gt^2$, divide both sides of the equation by $\dfrac{1}{2}g$ to obtain the form, $\dfrac{2s}{g} = t^2$. Then, after taking the square roots, $t = \sqrt{\dfrac{2s}{g}}$. (Refresher 403)

19. Choice A is correct. The sum of the three angles of a triangle must be 180°. Since angle A is 30°, and angle B is between 90° and 180° (it is obtuse), their sum is greater than 120° and less than 180° (the sum of all three angles is 180°). Their sum subtracted from the total of 180° gives a third angle greater than zero but less than 60°. (Refresher 419)

20. Choice E is correct. An isosceles triangle has two equal sides. To find the length of the sides, we use the distance formula, $\sqrt{(x_2 - x_1)^2 + (y_2 - y_1)^2}$. In the first case the lengths of the sides are 4, $2\sqrt{2}$, and $2\sqrt{2}$. Thus two sides have the same length, and it is an isosceles triangle. The only set of points that is not an isosceles triangle is the last one. (Refresher 411)

21. Choice E is correct. The smallest possible value of a is greater than 2, and the smallest possible value of b is greater than 3, so the smallest possible value of $a + b$ must be greater than $2 + 3 = 5$. Similarly, the largest values of a and b are less than 5 and 6, respectively, so the largest possible value of $a + b$ is less than 11. Therefore, the sum must be between 5 and 11. (Refresher 419)

22. Choice D is correct. If the sides of the original square are each equal to s, then the area of the square is s^2, and the diagonal is $s\sqrt{2}$. Now, a new square, with an area of $2s^2$, must have a side of $s\sqrt{2}$. Thus, the diagonal is $2s$, which is $\sqrt{2}$ times the original length of the diagonal. (Refreshers 303, 406)

23. Choice D is correct. First place all of the variable terms on one side and all of the numerical terms on the other side. Subtracting 7.7y and adding 4 to both sides of the equation gives $1.1y = 11$. Now divide both sides by 1.1 to solve for $y = 10$.

(Refresher 406)

24. Choice E is correct. To determine whether an expression is a factor of another expression, give the variable a specific value in both expressions. An expression divided by its factor will be a whole number. If we give x the value 0, then the expression $2x^2 + 1$ has the value of 1 and $x + 2$ has the value of 2. 1 is not divisible by 2, so the first choice is not a factor. The next choice has the value of -2, also not a factor of 1. Similarly $x + \sqrt{2}$ and $x - \sqrt{2}$ take on the values of $\sqrt{2}$ and $-\sqrt{2}$, respectively, when $x = 0$, and are not factors of $2x^2 + 1$. Therefore, the correct choice is (E).

(Refresher 409)

25. Choice C is correct. Let x equal the average salary of the employees. Then the employees receive a total of $10x$ dollars, and the manager receives six times the average, or $6x$. Together, the eleven of them receive a total of $10x + 6x = 16x$, which equals $640,000. Thus, x equals $40,000, and the manager's salary is $6x$, or $240,000.

(Refresher 406)

26. Choice A is correct. We are given $6x + 3 = 15$. Subtract 3 from both sides of the equation. We get $6x = 12$. Now divide this equation by 6. We get $x = 2$. Substituting $x = 2$ into the expression $12x - 3$ gives $24 - 3$, which equals 21.

(Refresher 406)

27. Choice D is correct. $2p + 7 > 3p - 5$. To both sides of the inequality add 5. We get $2p + 12 > 3p$. Now subtract $2p$. We get $12 > p$. Thus, p is less than 12.

(Refreshers 419, 426)

28. Choice A is correct. Substituting 1 for x in the given equation obtains $1 + q + 1 = 0$, or $q + 2 = 0$. This is solved only for $q = -2$.

(Refresher 406)

29. Choice B is correct.

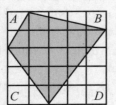

The area of the shaded figure can most easily be found by taking the area of the square surrounding it (25) and subtracting the areas of the four triangles marked A (1), B (2), C (3), and D (6), leaving an area of $25 - (1 + 2 + 3 + 6) = 13$ square units.

(Refresher 418)

30. Choice D is correct. If the number b is equal to zero, the quotient $\frac{a}{b}$ is not defined. For all other pairs, all five statements are true.

(Refreshers 401–405)

31. Choice E is correct. If a product equals zero, one of the factors must be equal to zero also. Thus, either $x - 1 = 0$, or $x - 2 = 0$, or $x^2 - 4 = 0$. The possible solutions, therefore, are $x = 1$, $x = 2$, and $x = -2$.

(Refresher 408)

32. Choice D is correct. Solve the equation $P + Q = R$, for Q (the variable we wish to eliminate), to get $Q = R - P$. Substituting this for Q in the second equation yields $P + R = 2(R - P) = 2R - 2P$, or $3P = R$. Therefore, the ratio of P to R is $\frac{P}{R}$, or $\frac{1}{3}$.

(Refresher 406)

33. Choice B is correct. The fraction in question will equal zero if the numerator equals zero and the denominator is nonzero. The expression $r^2 + 5r + 6$ can be factored into $(r + 2)(r + 3)$. As long as r is not equal to -2, the equation is defined, and $r + 2$ can be canceled in the original equation to yield $r + 3 = 0$, or $r = -3$. For r equals -2, the denominator is equal to zero, and the fraction in the original equation is not defined.

(Refreshers 404, 409)

34. Choice E is correct. This problem can be shortened considerably by factoring the expression $a^2b + 4ab^2 + 4b^3$ into the product $(b)(a + 2b)^2$. Now, since $b = 5$ and $(a + 2b) = 25$, our product equals $5 \times 25 \times 25$, or 3,125. (Refresher 409)

35. Choice E is correct. Subtract $m + 2n$ from both sides of the given equation and obtain the equivalent form, $2n = 7m$. Dividing this equation by $2m$ gives $\frac{n}{m} = \frac{7}{2}$, the ratio of n to m. (Refresher 406)

36. Choice E is correct. To find the range of the values of the product ab, find the smallest value of the product and the largest value of the product. If a lies

between -5 and $+2$ and b lies between -7 and $+1$, then the largest value of ab is $-5 \times -7 = +35$. The smallest value of ab is $+2 \times -7 = -14$. So the possible values of ab are between -14 and 35.

(Refresher 419)

37. Choice A is correct.

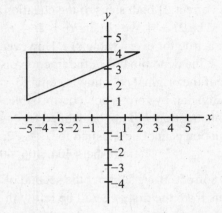

As can be seen from a diagram, this triangle must be a right triangle, since the line from $(-5,1)$ to $(-5,4)$ is vertical, and the line from $(-5,4)$ to $(2,4)$ is horizontal. The lengths of these two perpendicular sides are 3 and 7, respectively. Since the area of a right triangle is half the product of the perpendicular sides, the area is equal to $\frac{1}{2} \times 3 \times 7$, or 10.5.

(Refreshers 410, 418)

38. Choice E is correct. Solving the first equation for A gives $A = 12 - B$. Solving the second equation for C gives $C = 16 - B$. Thus, the sum $A + C$ is equal to $28 - 2B$. There is nothing to determine the value of B, so the sum of A and C is not determined from the information given.

(Refresher 406)

39. Choice D is correct. Factor $x^2 + 2x + 1$ to get $(x + 1)(x + 1) = 0$. Thus $x + 1 = 0$, so $x = -1$.

(Refresher 409)

40. Choice C is correct. If we graph the five choices we will get:

A

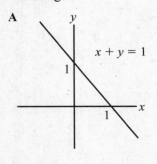

$x + y = 1$

B

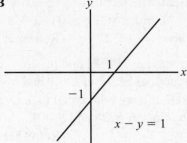

$x - y = 1$

C

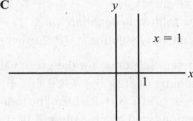

$x = 1$

D

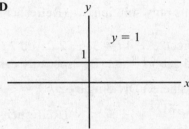

$y = 1$

E

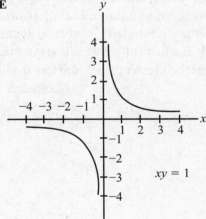

$xy = 1$

The only choice that is a vertical line is Choice C, $x = 1$.

(Refresher 413)

41. Choice C is correct. The factors of $x^2 + 3x + 2$ are $(x + 1)$ and $(x + 2)$. Either $x + 1 = 0$ or $x + 2 = 0$. x may equal either -1 or -2. (Refresher 408)

42. Choice B is correct. $a + b = 12$ and $a - b = 6$. Rewrite these equations as $a = 12 - b$ and $a = 6 + b$. $12 - b$ and $6 + b$ are both equal to a. Or, $12 - b = 6 + b$. Thus, $6 = 2b$ and $b = 3$. (Refresher 407)

43. Choice C is correct. Let $m^2 + 4 = 4m$. Subtracting $4m$ from both sides yields $m^2 - 4m + 4 = 0$. Factor to get the following equation: $(m - 2)^2 = 0$. Thus, $m = 2$ is the only solution. (Refresher 408)

44. Choice B is correct. Substitute for the given values of x and y, obtaining: $(0)^2(2)(z) + (3)(0)(z)^2 + (2)^2(z) + (3)(2) + (4)(0) = 0$. Perform the indicated multiplications, and combine terms. $0(z) + 0(z^2) + 4z + 6 + 0 = 4z + 6 = 0$. This equation has $z = -\dfrac{3}{2}$ as its only solution. (Refresher 406)

45. Choice C is correct. $c + 4d = 3c - 2d$. Add $2d - c$ to each side and get $6d = 2c$. (Be especially careful about your signs here.) Dividing by $2d$; $\dfrac{c}{d} = \dfrac{6}{2} = \dfrac{3}{1}$. Thus, $c : d = 3 : 1$. (Refresher 406)

46. Choice C is correct. x must be greater than 3, less than 7, greater than 2, and less than 6. These conditions can be reduced as follows: If x is less than 6, it is also less than 7. Similarly, x must be greater than 3, which automatically makes it greater than 2. Thus, x must be greater than 3 *and* less than 6. (Refresher 419)

47. Choice D is correct. To obtain the coordinates of the midpoint of a line segment, average the corresponding coordinates of the endpoints. Thus, the midpoint will be $\left(\dfrac{4 + 5}{2}, \dfrac{9 + 15}{2}\right)$, or (4.5,12). (Refresher 412)

48. Choice D is correct. If both sides of the equation are multiplied by $2t + 4$, we obtain: $t^2 + 2t = t^2 + 2t$, which is true for every value of t. However, when $t = -2$, the denominator of the fraction on the left side of the original equation is equal to zero. Since division by zero is not a permissible operation, this fraction will not be defined for $t = -2$. The equation cannot be satisfied for $t = -2$. (Refreshers 404, 406, 409)

49. Choice A is correct. If we subtract the second of our equations from the first, we will be left with the following: $(x + y) - (x + z) = 4 - 9$, or $y - z = -5$. (Refresher 402)

50. Choice A is correct. If x^2 is less than 9, then x may take on any value greater than -3 and less than $+3$; other values will produce squares greater than or equal to 9. If $\dfrac{1}{x}$ is less than $\dfrac{1}{3}$, x is restricted to positive values greater than 3 and all negative values. For example, if $x = 1$, then conditions I and II are satisfied, but $\dfrac{1}{x}$ equals 1, which is greater than $\dfrac{1}{3}$. (Refresher 419)

MATH REFRESHER SESSION 5

Geometry Problems

Basic Definitions

500. *Plane geometry* deals with points and lines. A point has no dimensions and is generally represented by a dot (·). A line has no thickness, but it does have length. Lines can be straight or curved, but here it will be assumed that a line is straight unless otherwise indicated. All lines have infinite length. A part of a line that has a finite length is called a line segment.

> Remember that the *distance* between two lines or from a point to a line always means the perpendicular distance. Thus, the distance between the two parallel lines pictured below (top diagram) is the length of line segment *A*, as this is the only perpendicular line segment. Also, as shown in bottom diagram, the distance from a line to a point is the length of perpendicular line segment *AB* from the point to the line. Thus, *AB* is the distance from point *A* to the line segment *CBD*.

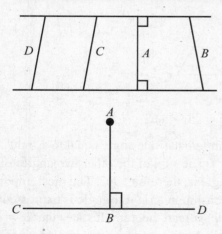

501. *Angles.* An angle is formed when two lines intersect at a point. Angle *B*, angle *ABC*, ∠*B*, and ∠*ABC* are all possible names for the angle shown.

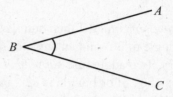

The measure of the angle is given in degrees. If the sides of the angle form a straight line, then the angle is said to be a straight angle and has 180°. A circle has 360°, and a straight angle is a turning through a half circle. All other angles are either greater or less than 180°.

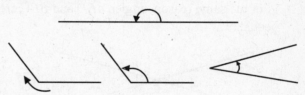

Angles are classified in different ways:

An *acute* angle has less than 90°.

A *right* angle has exactly 90°. In the diagram, the small square in the corner of the angle indicates a right angle (90°).

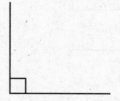

An *obtuse* angle has between 90° and 180°.

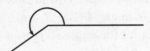

A *straight* angle has exactly 180°.

A *reflex* angle has between 180° and 360°.

502. Two angles are *complementary* if their sum is 90°. For example, an angle of 30° and an angle of 60° are complementary. Two angles are *supplementary* if their sum is 180°. If one angle is 82°, then its supplement is 98°.

503. *Vertical angles.* These are pairs of opposite angles formed by the intersection of two straight lines. Vertical angles are always equal to each other.

Example: In the diagram shown, angles *AEC* and *BED* are equal because they are vertical angles. For the same reason, angles *AED* and *BEC* are equal.

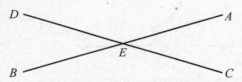

504. When two parallel lines are crossed by a third straight line (called a *transversal*), then all the acute angles formed are equal, and all of the obtuse angles are equal.

Example: In the diagram below, angles 1, 4, 5, and 8 are all equal. Angles 2, 3, 6, and 7 are also equal.

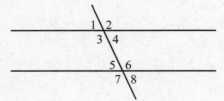

Triangles

505. *Triangles.* A triangle is a closed figure with three sides, each side being a line segment. The sum of the angles of a triangle is *always* 180°.

506. *Scalene triangles* are triangles with no two sides equal. Scalene triangles also have no two angles equal.

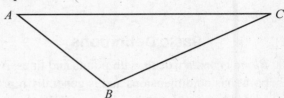

507. *Isosceles triangles* have two equal sides and two equal angles formed by the equal sides and the unequal side. See the figure below.

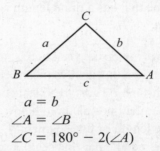

$$a = b$$
$$\angle A = \angle B$$
$$\angle C = 180° - 2(\angle A)$$

508. *Equilateral triangles* have all three sides and all three angles equal. Since the sum of the three angles of a triangle is 180°, each angle of an equilateral triangle is 60°.

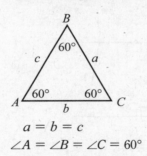

$$a = b = c$$
$$\angle A = \angle B = \angle C = 60°$$

509. A *right triangle* has one angle equal to a right angle (90°). The sum of the other two angles of a right triangle is, therefore, 90°. The most important relationship in a right triangle is expressed by the Pythagorean theorem. It states that $c^2 = a^2 + b^2$, where c, the hypotenuse, is the length of the

side opposite the right angle, and a and b are the lengths of the other two sides. Recall that this was discussed in Section 317.

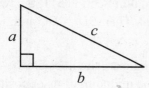

Example: If the two sides of a right triangle adjacent to the right angle are 3 inches and 4 inches respectively, find the length of the side opposite the right angle.

Solution:

Use the Pythagorean theorem, $c^2 = a^2 + b^2$, where $a = 3$ and $b = 4$. Then, $c = 3^2 + 4^2$ or $c^2 = 9 + 16 = 25$. Thus $c = 5$.

> Certain sets of integers will always fit the formula $c^2 = a^2 + b^2$. These integers can always represent the lengths of the sides of a right triangle. For example, a triangle whose sides are 3, 4, and 5 will always be a right triangle. Further examples are 5, 12, and 13, and 8, 15, and 17. Any multiples of these numbers also satisfy this formula. For example, 6, 8, and 10; 9, 12, and 15; 10, 24, and 26; 24, 45, and 51; etc.

509a. In a triangle, the greater angle lies opposite the greater side.

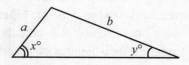

If $a < b$, then $y < x$
If $y < x$, then $a < b$

Properties of Triangles

510. Two triangles are said to be *similar* (having the same shape) if their corresponding angles are equal. The sides of similar triangles are in the same proportion. The two triangles below are similar because they have the same corresponding angles.

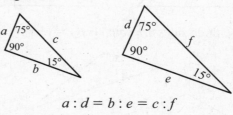

$$a : d = b : e = c : f$$

Example: Two triangles both have angles of 30°, 70°, and 80°. If the sides of the triangles are as indicated below, find the length of side x.

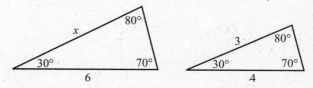

Solution: The two triangles are similar because they have the same corresponding angles. The corresponding sides of similar triangles are in proportion, so $x : 3 = 6 : 4$. This can be rewritten as $\frac{x}{3} = \frac{6}{4}$. Multiplying both sides by 3 gives $x = \frac{18}{4}$, or $x = 4\frac{1}{2}$.

511. Two triangles are *congruent* (*identical* in shape and size) if any one of the following conditions is met:

1. Each side of the first triangle equals the corresponding side of the second triangle.

2. Two sides of the first triangle equal the corresponding sides of the second triangle, and their included angles are equal. The included angle is formed by the two sides of the triangle.

3. Two angles of the first triangle equal the corresponding angles of the second triangle, and any pair of corresponding sides are equal.

Example: Triangles *ABC* and *DEF* in the diagrams below are congruent if any one of the following conditions can be met:

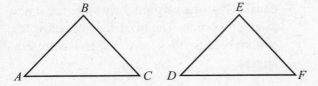

1. The three sides are equal (*sss*) = (*sss*).

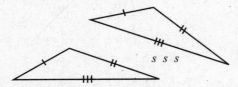

2. Two sides and the included angle are equal (*sas*) = (*sas*).

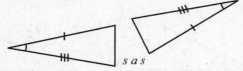

3. Two angles and any one side are equal (*aas*) = (*aas*) or (*asa*) = (*asa*).

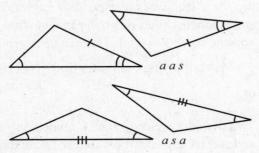

Example: In the equilateral triangle below, line *AD* is perpendicular (forms a right angle) to side *BC*. If the length of *BD* is 5 feet, what is the length of *DC*?

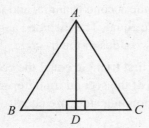

Solution: Since the large triangle is an equilateral triangle, each angle is 60°. Therefore ∠*B* is 60° and ∠*C* is 60°. Thus, ∠*B* = ∠*C*. *ADB* and *ADC* are both right angles and are equal. Two angles of

each triangle are equal to the corresponding two angles of the other triangle. Side *AD* is shared by both triangles and side *AB* = side *AC*. Thus, according to condition 3 in Section 511, the two triangles are congruent. Then *BD* = *DC* and, since *BD* is 5 feet, *DC* is 5 feet.

512. The *medians* of a triangle are the lines drawn from each vertex to the midpoint of its opposite side. The medians of a triangle cross at a point that divides each median into two parts: one part is one-third the length of the median and the other part is two-thirds the length.

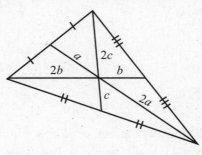

513. The *angle bisectors* of a triangle are the lines that divide each angle of the triangle into two equal parts. These lines meet in a point that is the center of a circle inscribed in the triangle.

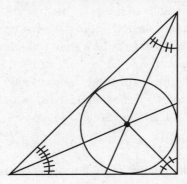

514. The *altitudes* of the triangle are lines drawn from the vertices perpendicular to the opposite sides. The lengths of these lines are useful in calculating the area of the triangle, since the area of the triangle is $\frac{1}{2}$(base)(height), and the height is identical to the altitude.

 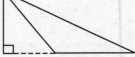

515. The *perpendicular bisectors* of the triangle are the lines that bisect and are perpendicular to each of the three sides. The point where these lines meet is the center of the circumscribed circle.

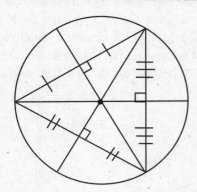

516. The sum of any two sides of a triangle is greater than the third side.

Example: If the three sides of a triangle are 4, 2, and x, then what is known about the value of x?

Solution: Since the sum of two sides of a triangle is always greater than the third side, then $4 + 2 > x$, $4 + x > 2$, and $2 + x > 4$. These three inequalities can be rewritten as $6 > x$, $x > -2$, and $x > 2$. For x to be greater than -2 and 2, it must be greater than 2. Thus, the values of x are $2 < x < 6$.

Four-Sided Figures

517. A *parallelogram* is a four-sided figure with each pair of opposite sides parallel.

A parallelogram has the following properties:

1. Each pair of opposite sides is equal. ($AD = BC$, $AB = DC$)

2. The diagonals bisect each other. ($AE = EC$, $DE = EB$)

3. The opposite angles are equal. ($\angle A = \angle C$, $\angle D = \angle B$)

4. One diagonal divides the parallelogram into two congruent triangles. Two diagonals divide the parallelogram into two pairs of congruent triangles.

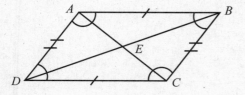

518. A *rectangle* is a parallelogram in which all the angles are right angles. Since a rectangle is a parallelogram, all of the laws that apply to a parallelogram apply to a rectangle. In addition, the diagonals of a rectangle are equal.

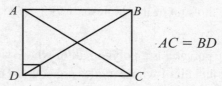

$AC = BD$

519. A *rhombus* is a parallelogram with four equal sides. Since a rhombus is a parallelogram, all of the laws that apply to a parallelogram apply to a rhombus. In addition, the diagonals of a rhombus are perpendicular to each other and bisect the vertex angles.

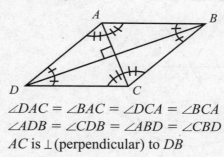

$\angle DAC = \angle BAC = \angle DCA = \angle BCA$
$\angle ADB = \angle CDB = \angle ABD = \angle CBD$
AC is $\perp$ (perpendicular) to DB

520. A *square* is a rectangular rhombus. Thus a square has the following properties:

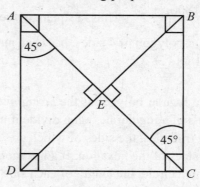

1. All four sides are equal. ($AB = BC = CD = DA$)

2. Opposite pairs of sides are parallel. ($AD \| BC$, $AB \| DC$)

3. Diagonals are equal, are perpendicular to each other, and bisect each other. ($AC = BD$, $AC \perp BD$, $AE = EC = DE = EB$)

4. All the angles are right angles (90°). ($\angle A = \angle B = \angle C = \angle D = 90°$)

5. Diagonals intersect the vertices at 45°. ($\angle DAC = \angle BCA = 45°$, and similarly for the other 3 vertices.)

Many-Sided Figures

521. A *polygon* is a closed plane figure whose sides are straight lines. The sum of the angles in any polygon is equal to $180(n - 2)°$, where n is the number of sides. Thus, in a polygon of 3 sides (a triangle), the sum of the angles is $180(3 - 2)°$, or $180°$.

522. A *regular polygon* is a polygon all of whose sides are equal and all of whose angles are equal. These polygons have special properties:

1. A regular polygon can be inscribed in a circle and can be circumscribed about another circle. For example, a hexagon is inscribed in a circle in the diagram below.

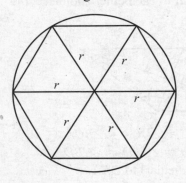

2. Each angle of a regular polygon is equal to the sum of the angles divided by the number (n) of sides, $\dfrac{180(n - 2)°}{n}$. Thus, a square, which is a regular polygon of 4 sides, has each angle equal to $\dfrac{180(4 - 2)°}{4}$ or $90°$.

523. An important regular polygon is the *hexagon*. The diagonals of a regular hexagon divide it into 6 equilateral triangles, the sides of which are equal to the sides of the hexagon. If a hexagon is inscribed in a circle, the length of each side is equal to the length of the radius of the circle. (See diagram of hexagon above.)

Circles

524. A *circle* (also see Section 310) is a set of points equidistant from a given point, the *center*. The distance from the center to the circle is the *radius*. Any line that connects two points on the circle is a *chord*. A chord through the center of the circle is a *diameter*. On the circle below, O is the center, line segment OF is a radius, DE is a diameter, and AC is a chord.

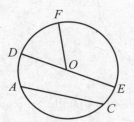

The length of the diameter of a circle is twice the length of the radius. The circumference (distance around the circle) is 2π times the length of the radius. π is a constant approximately equal to $\dfrac{22}{7}$ or 3.14. The formula for the circumference of a circle is $C = 2\pi r$, where C = circumference and r = radius.

525. A *tangent* to a circle is a line that is perpendicular to a radius and that passes through only one point of the circle. In the diagram below, AB is a tangent.

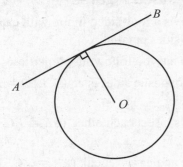

526. A *central angle* is an angle whose sides are two radii of the circle. The vertex of this angle is the center of the circle. The number of degrees in a central angle is equal to the amount of arc length that the radii intercept. As the complete circumference has 360°, any other arc lengths are less than 360°.

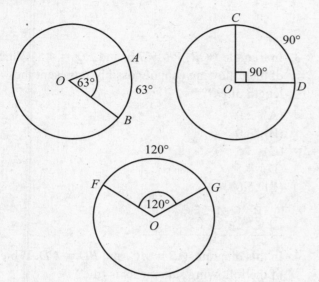

Angles *AOB*, *COD*, and *FOG* are all central angles.

527. An *inscribed angle* of a circle is an angle whose sides are two chords. The vertex of the angle lies on the circumference of the circle. The number of degrees in the inscribed angle is equal to one-half the intercepted arc.

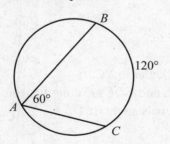

∠*BAC* is an inscribed angle.

528. An angle inscribed in a semicircle is always a right angle. ∠*ABC* and ∠*ADC* are inscribed in semicircles *AOCB* and *AOCD*, respectively, and are thus right angles.

Note: A semicircle is one-half of a circle.

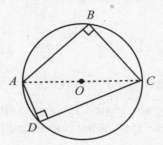

529. Two tangents to a circle from the same point outside of the circle are always equal.

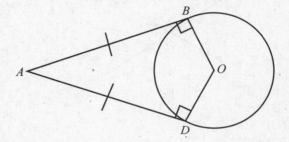

Tangents *AB* and *AD* are equal.

SESSION 5 PRACTICE TEST

Geometry Problems

Correct answers and solutions follow this test.

1. In the following diagram, angle 1 is equal to 40°, and angle 2 is equal to 150°. What is the number of degrees in angle 3?

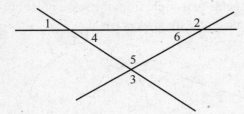

(A) 70°
(B) 90°
(C) 110°
(D) 190°
(E) The answer cannot be determined from the given information.

A B C D E
○ ○ ○ ○ ○

2. In this diagram, *AB* and *CD* are both perpendicular to *BE*. If *EC* = 5 and *CD* = 4, what is the ratio of *AB* to *BE*?

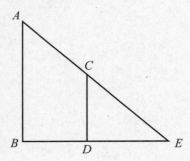

(A) 1 : 1
(B) 4 : 3
(C) 5 : 4
(D) 5 : 3
(E) none of these

A B C D E
○ ○ ○ ○ ○

3. In triangle *PQR*, *PR* = 7.0, and *PQ* = 4.5. Which of the following cannot possibly represent the length of *QR*?

(A) 2.0
(B) 3.0
(C) 3.5
(D) 4.5
(E) 5.0

A B C D E
○ ○ ○ ○ ○

4. In this diagram, *AB* = *AC*, and *BD* = *CD*. Which of the following statements is true?

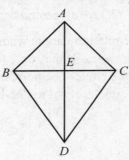

(A) *BE* = *EC*.
(B) *AD* is perpendicular to *BC*.
(C) Triangles *BDE* and *CDE* are congruent.
(D) Angle *ABD* equals angle *ACD*.
(E) All of these.

A B C D E
○ ○ ○ ○ ○

5. In the following diagram, if $BC = CD = BD = 1$, and angle ADC is a right angle, what is the perimeter of triangle ABD?

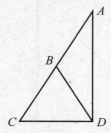

(A) 3
(B) $2 + \sqrt{2}$
(C) $2 + \sqrt{3}$
(D) $3 + \sqrt{3}$
(E) 4

A B C D E
○ ○ ○ ○ ○

6. In this diagram, if $PQRS$ is a parallelogram, which of the following can be deduced?

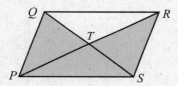

I. $QT + PT = RT + ST$.
II. QS is perpendicular to PR.
III. The area of the shaded portion is exactly three times the area of triangle QRT.

(A) I only
(B) I and II only
(C) II only
(D) I and III only
(E) I, II, and III

A B C D E
○ ○ ○ ○ ○

7. James lives on the corner of a rectangular field that measures 120 yards by 160 yards. If he wants to walk to the opposite corner, he can either travel along the perimeter of the field or cut directly across in a straight line. How many yards does he save by taking the direct route? (Express to the nearest 10 yards.)

(A) 40 yards
(B) 60 yards

(C) 80 yards
(D) 100 yards
(E) 110 yards

A B C D E
○ ○ ○ ○ ○

8. In a square, the perimeter is how many times the length of the diagonal?

(A) $\dfrac{\sqrt{2}}{2}$
(B) $\sqrt{2}$
(C) 2
(D) $2\sqrt{2}$
(E) 4

A B C D E
○ ○ ○ ○ ○

9. How many degrees are there in the angle formed by two adjacent sides of a regular nonagon (nine-sided polygon)?

(A) 40°
(B) 70°
(C) 105°
(D) 120°
(E) 140°

A B C D E
○ ○ ○ ○ ○

10. In the diagram below, $AB = CD$. From this we can deduce that:

(*Note*: Figure is not drawn to scale.)

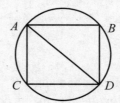

(A) AB is parallel to CD.
(B) AB is perpendicular to BD.
(C) $AC = BD$.
(D) Angle ABD equals angle BDC.
(E) Triangle ABD is congruent to triangle ACD.

A B C D E
○ ○ ○ ○ ○

11. If two lines, *AB* and *CD*, intersect at a point *E*, which of the following statements is *not* true?

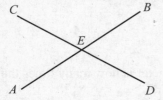

(A) Angle *AEB* equals angle *CED*.
(B) Angles *AEC* and *BEC* are complementary.
(C) Angle *CED* is a straight angle.
(D) Angle *AEC* equals angle *BED*.
(E) Angle *BED* plus angle *AED* equals 180°.

A B C D E
○ ○ ○ ○ ○

12. In the following diagram, *AC* = *CE* and *BD* = *DE*. Which of these statements is (are) true?

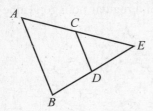

I. *AB* is twice as long as *CD*.
II. *AB* is parallel to *CD*.
III. Triangle *AEB* is similar to triangle *CED*.

(A) I only
(B) II and III only
(C) I and III only
(D) I, II, and III
(E) none of these

A B C D E
○ ○ ○ ○ ○

13. In triangle *ABC,* angle *A* is obtuse, and angle *B* equals 30°. Which of the following statements *best* describes angle *C*?

(A) Angle *C* must be less than 60°.
(B) Angle *C* must be less than or equal to 60°.
(C) Angle *C* must be equal to 60°.
(D) Angle *C* must be greater than or equal to 60°.
(E) Angle *C* must be greater than 60°.

A B C D E
○ ○ ○ ○ ○

14. In this diagram, *ABCD* is a parallelogram, and *BFDE* is a square. If *AB* = 20 and *CF* = 16, what is the perimeter of the parallelogram *ABCD*?

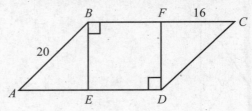

(A) 72
(B) 78
(C) 86
(D) 92
(E) 96

A B C D E
○ ○ ○ ○ ○

15. The hypotenuse of a right triangle is exactly twice as long as the shorter leg. What is the number of degrees in the smallest angle of the triangle?

(A) 30°
(B) 45°
(C) 60°
(D) 90°
(E) The answer cannot be determined from the given information.

A B C D E
○ ○ ○ ○ ○

16. The legs of an isosceles triangle are equal to 17 inches each. If the altitude to the base is 8 inches long, how long is the base of the triangle?

(A) 15 inches
(B) 20 inches
(C) 24 inches
(D) 25 inches
(E) 30 inches

A B C D E
○ ○ ○ ○ ○

17. The perimeter of a right triangle is 18 inches. If the midpoints of the three sides are joined by line segments, they form another triangle. What is the perimeter of this new triangle?

(A) 3 inches
(B) 6 inches
(C) 9 inches

(D) 12 inches

(E) The answer cannot be determined from the given information.

A B C D E
○ ○ ○ ○ ○

18. If the diagonals of a square divide it into four triangles, the triangles *cannot* be

(A) right triangles
(B) isosceles triangles
(C) similar triangles
(D) equilateral triangles
(E) equal in area

A B C D E
○ ○ ○ ○ ○

19. In the diagram below, *ABCDEF* is a regular hexagon. How many degrees are there in angle *ADC*?

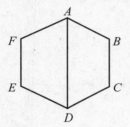

(A) 45°
(B) 60°
(C) 75°
(D) 90°
(E) none of these

A B C D E
○ ○ ○ ○ ○

20. This diagram depicts a rectangle inscribed in a circle. If the measurements of the rectangle are 10″ × 14″, what is the area of the circle in inches?

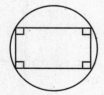

(A) 74π
(B) 92π
(C) 144π
(D) 196π
(E) 296π

A B C D E
○ ○ ○ ○ ○

21. How many degrees are included between the hands of a clock at 5:00?

(A) 50°
(B) 60°
(C) 75°
(D) 120°
(E) 150°

A B C D E
○ ○ ○ ○ ○

22. *ABCD* is a square. If the midpoints of the four sides are joined to form a new square, the perimeter of the old square is how many times the perimeter of the new square?

(A) 1
(B) $\sqrt{2}$
(C) 2
(D) $2\sqrt{2}$
(E) 4

A B C D E
○ ○ ○ ○ ○

23. Angles *A* and *B* of triangle *ABC* are both acute angles. Which of the following *best* describes angle *C*?

(A) Angle *C* is between 0° and 180°.
(B) Angle *C* is between 0° and 90°.
(C) Angle *C* is between 60° and 180°.
(D) Angle *C* is between 60° and 120°.
(E) Angle *C* is between 60° and 90°.

A B C D E
○ ○ ○ ○ ○

24. The angles of a quadrilateral are in the ratio 1 : 2 : 3 : 4. What is the number of degrees in the largest angle?

(A) 72
(B) 96
(C) 120
(D) 144
(E) 150

A B C D E
○ ○ ○ ○ ○

25. *ABCD* is a rectangle; the diagonals *AC* and *BD* intersect at *E*. Which of the following statements is *not necessarily true*?

(A) *AE = BE*.
(B) Angle *AEB* equals angle *CED*.
(C) *AE* is perpendicular to *BD*.
(D) Triangles *AED* and *AEB* are equal in area.
(E) Angle *BAC* equals angle *BDC*.

A B C D E
○ ○ ○ ○ ○

26. City A is 200 miles from City B, and City B is 400 miles from City C. Which of the following best describes the distance between City A and City C? (*Note*: The cities A, B, and C do *not* all lie on a straight line.)

(A) It must be greater than zero.
(B) It must be greater than 200 miles.
(C) It must be less than 600 miles and greater than zero.
(D) It must be less than 600 miles and greater than 200 miles.
(E) It must be exactly 400 miles.

A B C D E
○ ○ ○ ○ ○

27. At 7:30, how many degrees are included between the hands of a clock?

(A) 15°
(B) 30°
(C) 45°
(D) 60°
(E) 75°

A B C D E
○ ○ ○ ○ ○

28. If a ship is sailing in a northerly direction and then turns to the right until it is sailing in a southwesterly direction, it has gone through a rotation of:

(A) 45°
(B) 90°
(C) 135°
(D) 180°
(E) 225°

A B C D E
○ ○ ○ ○ ○

29. *x, y,* and *z* are the angles of a triangle. If $x = 2y$ and $y = z + 30°$, how many degrees are there in angle *x*?

(A) 22.5°
(B) 37.5°
(C) 52.5°
(D) 90.0°
(E) 105.0°

A B C D E
○ ○ ○ ○ ○

30. In the diagram below, *AB* is parallel to *CD*. Which of the following statements is *not necessarily true*?

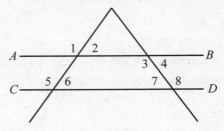

(A) $\angle 1 + \angle 2 = 180°$
(B) $\angle 4 = \angle 7$
(C) $\angle 5 + \angle 8 + \angle 2 + \angle 4 = 360°$
(D) $\angle 2 + \angle 3 = 180°$
(E) $\angle 2 = \angle 6$

A B C D E
○ ○ ○ ○ ○

31. What is the ratio of the diagonal of a square to the hypotenuse of the isosceles right triangle having the same area?

(A) 1 : 2
(B) 1 : $\sqrt{2}$
(C) 1 : 1
(D) $\sqrt{2}$: 1
(E) 2 : 1

A B C D E
○ ○ ○ ○ ○

32. How many degrees are there between two adjacent sides of a regular ten-sided figure?

(A) 36°
(B) 72°
(C) 120°
(D) 144°
(E) 154°

A B C D E
○ ○ ○ ○ ○

33. Which of the following sets of numbers *cannot* represent the lengths of the sides of a right triangle?

    (A) 5, 12, 13
    (B) 4.2, 5.6, 7
    (C) 9, 28, 35
    (D) 16, 30, 34
    (E) 7.5, 18, 19.5

    A B C D E
    ○ ○ ○ ○ ○

34. How many degrees are there in the angle that is its own supplement?

    (A) 30°
    (B) 45°
    (C) 60°
    (D) 90°
    (E) 180°

    A B C D E
    ○ ○ ○ ○ ○

35. If a central angle of 45° intersects an arc 6 inches long on the circumference of a circle, what is the radius of the circle?

    (A) $\dfrac{24}{\pi}$ inches

    (B) $\dfrac{48}{\pi}$ inches

    (C) 6π inches
    (D) 24 inches
    (E) 48 inches

    A B C D E
    ○ ○ ○ ○ ○

36. What is the length of the line segment connecting the two most distant vertices of a 1-inch cube?

    (A) 1 inch
    (B) $\sqrt{2}$ inches
    (C) $\sqrt{3}$ inches
    (D) $\sqrt{5}$ inches
    (E) $\sqrt{6}$ inches

    A B C D E
    ○ ○ ○ ○ ○

37. Through how many degrees does the hour hand of a clock move in 70 minutes?

    (A) 35°
    (B) 60°
    (C) 80°
    (D) 90°
    (E) 120°

    A B C D E
    ○ ○ ○ ○ ○

38. In the diagram pictured below, AB is tangent to circle O at point A. CD is perpendicular to OA at C. Which of the following statements is (are) true?

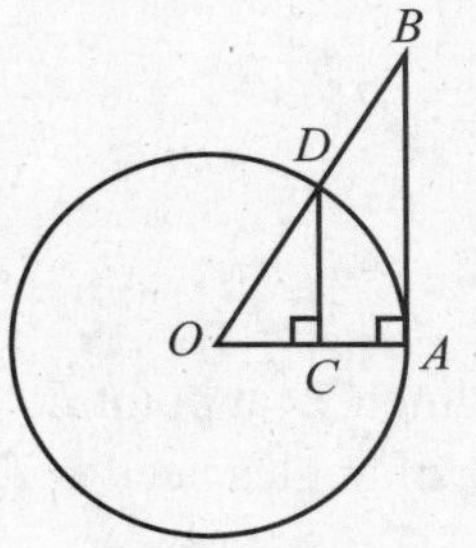

    I.   Triangles ODC and OBA are similar.
    II. $OA : CD = OB : AB$.
    III. AB is twice as long as CD.

    (A) I only
    (B) III only
    (C) I and II only
    (D) II and III only
    (E) none of the above combinations

    A B C D E
    ○ ○ ○ ○ ○

39. The three angles of triangle ABC are in the ratio 1 : 2 : 6. How many degrees are in the largest angle?

    (A) 45°
    (B) 90°
    (C) 120°
    (D) 135°
    (E) 160°

    A B C D E
    ○ ○ ○ ○ ○

40. In this diagram, $AB = AC$; angle $A = 40°$, and BD is perpendicular to AC at D. How many degrees are there in angle DBC ?

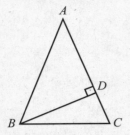

   (A) 20°
   (B) 40°
   (C) 50°
   (D) 70°
   (E) none of these

   A B C D E
   ○ ○ ○ ○ ○

41. If the line AB intersects the line CD at point E, which of the following pairs of angles need *not* be equal?

   (A) $\angle AEB$ and $\angle CED$
   (B) $\angle AEC$ and $\angle BED$
   (C) $\angle AED$ and $\angle CEA$
   (D) $\angle BEC$ and $\angle DEA$
   (E) $\angle DEC$ and $\angle BEA$

   A B C D E
   ○ ○ ○ ○ ○

42. All right isosceles triangles must be

   (A) similar
   (B) congruent
   (C) equilateral
   (D) equal in area
   (E) none of these

   A B C D E
   ○ ○ ○ ○ ○

43. What is the area of a triangle whose sides are 10 inches, 13 inches, and 13 inches?

   (A) 39 square inches
   (B) 52 square inches
   (C) 60 square inches
   (D) 65 square inches
   (E) The answer cannot be determined from the given information.

   A B C D E
   ○ ○ ○ ○ ○

44. If each side of an equilateral triangle is 2 inches long, what is the triangle's altitude?

   (A) 1 inch
   (B) $\sqrt{2}$ inches
   (C) $\sqrt{3}$ inches
   (D) 2 inches
   (E) $\sqrt{5}$ inches

   A B C D E
   ○ ○ ○ ○ ○

45. In the parallelogram $ABCD$, diagonals AC and BD intersect at E. Which of the following must be true?

   (A) $\angle AED = \angle BEC$
   (B) $AE = EC$
   (C) $\angle BDC = \angle DBA$
   (D) Two of the above must be true.
   (E) All three of the statements must be true.

   A B C D E
   ○ ○ ○ ○ ○

46. If $ABCD$ is a square and diagonals AC and BD intersect at point E, how many isosceles right triangles are there in the figure?

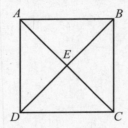

   (A) 4
   (B) 5
   (C) 6
   (D) 7
   (E) 8

   A B C D E
   ○ ○ ○ ○ ○

47. How many degrees are there in each angle of a regular hexagon?

   (A) 60°
   (B) 90°
   (C) 108°
   (D) 120°
   (E) 144°

   A B C D E
   ○ ○ ○ ○ ○

48. The radius of a circle is 1 inch. If an equilateral triangle is inscribed in the circle, what will be the length of one of the triangle's sides?

   (A) 1 inch

   (B) $\frac{\sqrt{2}}{2}$ inches

   (C) $\sqrt{2}$ inches

   (D) $\frac{\sqrt{3}}{2}$ inches

   (E) $\sqrt{3}$ inches

   A B C D E
   ○ ○ ○ ○ ○

49. If the angles of a triangle are in the ratio 2 : 3 : 4, how many degrees are there in the largest angle?

   (A) 20°

   (B) 40°

   (C) 60°

   (D) 80°

   (E) 120°

   A B C D E
   ○ ○ ○ ○ ○

50. Which of the following combinations may represent the lengths of the sides of a right triangle?

   (A) 4, 6, 8

   (B) 12, 16, 20

   (C) 7, 17, 23

   (D) 9, 20, 27

   (E) none of these

   A B C D E
   ○ ○ ○ ○ ○

Answer Key for Session 5 Practice Test

1. C	14. E	27. C	39. C
2. B	15. A	28. E	40. A
3. A	16. E	29. E	41. C
4. E	17. C	30. D	42. A
5. C	18. D	31. B	43. C
6. D	19. B	32. D	44. C
7. C	20. A	33. C	45. E
8. D	21. E	34. D	46. E
9. E	22. B	35. A	47. D
10. D	23. A	36. C	48. E
11. B	24. D	37. A	49. D
12. D	25. C and D	38. C	50. B
13. A	26. D		

Answers and Solutions for Session 5 Practice Test

1. Choice C is correct.

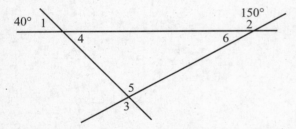

In the problem it is given that ∠1 = 40° and ∠2 = 150°. The diagram makes it apparent that: (1) ∠1 = ∠4 and ∠3 = ∠5 (vertical angles); (2) ∠6 + ∠2 = 180° (straight angle); (3) ∠4 + ∠5 + ∠6 = 180° (sum of angles in a triangle). To solve the problem, ∠3 must be related through the above information to the known quantities in ∠1 and ∠2. Proceed as follows: ∠3 = ∠5, but ∠5 = 180° − ∠4 − ∠6. ∠4 = ∠1 = 40° and ∠6 = 180° − ∠2 = 180° − 150° = 30°. Therefore, ∠3 = 180° − 40° − 30° = 110°.
(Refreshers 501, 503, 505)

2. Choice B is correct. Since CD is perpendicular to DE, CDE is a right triangle, and using the Pythagorean theorem yields $DE = 3$. Thus, the ratio of CD to DE is 4 : 3. But triangle ABE is similar to triangle CDE. Therefore, $AB : BE = CD : DE = 4 : 3$.
(Refreshers 509, 510)

3. Choice A is correct. In a triangle, it is impossible for one side to be longer than the sum of the other two (a straight line is the shortest distance between two points). Thus 2.0, 4.5, and 7.0 cannot be three sides of a triangle.
(Refresher 516)

4. Choice E is correct. $AB = AC$, $BD = CD$, and AD equal to itself is sufficient information (three sides) to prove triangles ABD and ACD congruent. Also, since $AB = AC$, $AE = AE$, and $∠BAE = ∠CAE$ (by the previous congruence), triangles ABE and ACE are congruent. Since $BD = CD$, $ED = ED$, and angle BDE equals angle CDE (by initial congruence), triangles BDE and CDE are congruent. Through congruence of triangle ABE and triangle ACE, angles BEA and CEA are equal, and their sum is a straight angle (180°). They must both be right angles. Thus, from the given information, we can deduce all the properties given as choices.
(Refresher 511)

5. Choice C is correct. The perimeter of triangle ABD is $AB + BD + AD$. The length of BD is 1. Since $BC = CD = BD$, triangle BCD is an equilateral triangle. Therefore, angle $C = 60°$ and angle $BDC = 60°$. Angle A + angle $C = 90°$ (the sum of two acute angles in a right triangle is 90°), and angle BDC + angle $BDA = 90°$ (these two angles form a right angle). Since angle C and angle BDC both equal 60°, angle A = angle $BDA = 30°$. Now two angles of triangle ADB are equal. Therefore, triangle ADB is an isosceles triangle with side BD = side AB. Since $BD = 1$, then $AB = 1$. AD is a leg of the right triangle, with side $CD = 1$ and hypotenuse $AC = 2$. ($AC = AB + BC = 1 + 1$.) Using the relationship $c^2 = a^2 + b^2$ gives us the length of AD as $\sqrt{3}$. Thus the perimeter is $1 + 1 + \sqrt{3}$, or $2 + \sqrt{3}$.
(Refreshers 505, 507, 509)

6. Choice D is correct. Statement I must be true, since the diagonals of a parallelogram bisect each other, so $QT = ST$, and $PT = RT$. Thus, since the sums of equals are equal, $QT + PT = RT + ST$. II is not necessarily true and, in fact, can be true only if the parallelogram is also a rhombus (all four sides equal). III is true, since the four small triangles each have the same area. The shaded portion

contains three such triangles. This can be seen by noting that the altitudes from point P to the bases of triangles PQT and PTS are identical. We have already seen from part (I) that these bases (QT and TS) are also equal. Therefore, only I and III can be deduced from the given information.

(Refreshers 514, 517)

7. Choice C is correct.

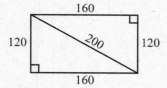

The diagonal path divides the rectangular field into two right triangles. The Pythagorean theorem gives the length of the diagonal as 200 yards. If James takes the route around the perimeter, he will travel 120 + 160, or 280 yards. Thus, the shorter route saves him 80 yards.

(Refreshers 509, 518)

8. Choice D is correct. Let one side of a square be s. Then the perimeter must be $4s$. The diagonal of a square with side s is equal to $s\sqrt{2}$. Dividing the perimeter by the diagonal produces $2\sqrt{2}$. The perimeter is $2\sqrt{2}$ times the diagonal.

(Refreshers 509, 520)

9. Choice E is correct. The sum of the angles of any polygon is equal to $180°(n - 2)$, where n is the number of sides. Thus the total number of degrees in a nonagon = $180°(9 - 2) = 180° \times 7 = 1{,}260°$. The number of degrees in each angle is $\frac{1{,}260°}{n} = \frac{1{,}260°}{9} = 140°$. (Refreshers 521, 522)

10. Choice D is correct.

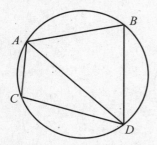

Since chord AB equals chord CD, it must be true that arc AB equals arc CD. By adding arc AC to arc CD and to arc AB, it is apparent that arc ACD

is equal to arc CAB. These arcs are intersected by inscribed angles ABD and BDC. Therefore, the two inscribed angles must be equal. If we redraw the figure as shown above, the falseness of Choices A, B, C, and E becomes readily apparent.

(Refresher 527)

11. Choice B is correct. $\angle AEC + \angle BEC = \angle AEB$, a straight angle (180°). Thus, angles AEC and BEC are *supplementary*. (*Complementary* means that the two angles add up to a *right* angle, or 90°.)

(Refreshers 501, 502)

12. Choice D is correct. Since $AC = CE$ and $BD = DE$, triangles AEB and CED are similar, and AB is twice as long as CD, since by proportionality, $AB : CD = AE : CE = 2 : 1$. From the similarity it is found that angle ABE equals angle CDE, and, therefore, that AB is parallel to CD. Thus, all three statements are true. (Refreshers 504, 510)

13. Choice A is correct. Angle A must be greater than 90°; angle B equals 30°. Thus, the sum of angles A and B must be greater than 120°. Since the sum of the three angles A, B, and C must be 180°, angle C must be *less than* 60°. (It cannot equal 60°, because then angle A would be a right angle instead of an obtuse angle.) (Refreshers 501, 505)

14. Choice E is correct. CDF is a right triangle with one side of 16 and a hypotenuse of 20. Thus, the third side, DF, equals 12. Since $BFDE$ is a square, BF and ED are also equal to 12. Thus, $BC = 12 + 16 = 28$, and $CD = 20$. $ABCD$ is a parallelogram, so $AB = CD$, $AD = BC$. The perimeter is $28 + 20 + 28 + 20 = 96$. (Refreshers 509, 517, 520)

15. Choice A is correct.

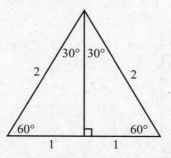

Recognize that the sides of a 30°-60°-90° triangle are in the proportion $1 : \sqrt{3} : 2$, and the problem is solved. 30° is the smallest angle. (Refresher 509)

16. Choice E is correct.

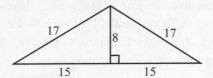

The altitude to the base of an isosceles triangle divides it into two congruent right triangles, each with one leg of 8 inches, and a hypotenuse of 17 inches. By the Pythagorean theorem, the third side of each right triangle must be 15 inches long. The base of the isosceles triangle is the sum of two such sides, totaling 30 inches.

(Refreshers 507, 509, 514)

17. Choice C is correct.

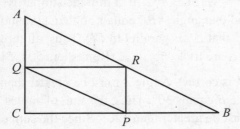

Call the triangle ABC, and the triangle of midpoints PQR, where P is the midpoint of BC, Q is the midpoint of AC, and R is the midpoint of AB. Then, PQ is equal to half the length of AB, $QR = \frac{1}{2}BC$, and $PR = \frac{1}{2}AC$. This has nothing to do with the fact that ABC is a right triangle. Thus, the perimeter of the small triangle is equal to $PQ + QR + PR = \frac{1}{2}(AB + BC + AC)$. The new perimeter is half the old perimeter, or 9 inches.

(Refreshers 509, 510, 512)

18. Choice D is correct.

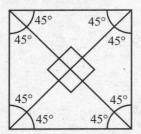

The diagonals of the square form four right triangles, each of which is isosceles because each has two 45° angles. The triangles are all identical in shape and size, so they all are similar and have

the same area. The only choice left is equilateral, which cannot be true, since the sum of the angles at the intersection of the diagonals must be 360°. The sum of four 60° angles would be only 240°.

(Refresher 520)

19. Choice B is correct.

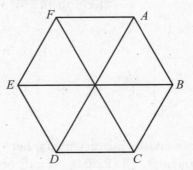

First, draw in the lines CF and BE. These intersect AD at its midpoint (also the midpoint of CF and BE) and divide the hexagon into six equilateral triangles. Since ADC is an angle of one of these equilateral triangles, it must be equal to 60°. (Another way to do this problem is to calculate the number of degrees in one angle of a regular hexagon and divide this by 2.)   (Refreshers 508, 523)

20. Choice A is correct. The diagonal of an inscribed rectangle is equal to the diameter of the circle. To find this length, use the Pythagorean theorem on one of the two triangles formed by two of the sides of the rectangle and the diagonal. Thus, the square of the diagonal is equal to $10^2 + 14^2 = 100 + 196 = 296$. The area of the circle is equal to π times the square of the radius. The square of the radius of the circle is one-fourth of the diameter squared (since $d = 2r$, $d^2 = 4r^2$), or 74. Thus, the area is 74π.   (Refreshers 509, 518, 524)

21. Choice E is correct.

Each number (or hour marking) on a clock represents an angle of 30°, as 360° divided by 12 is 30° (a convenient fact to remember for other clock problems). Since the hands of the clock are on the 12 and the 5, there are five hour units between the hands; $5 \times 30° = 150°$. (Refreshers 501, 526)

22. Choice B is correct.

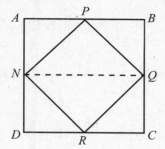

Let S represent the side of the large square. Then the perimeter is $4S$. Let s represent the side of the smaller square. Then the smaller square's perimeter is $4s$. Line NQ is the diagonal of the smaller square, so the length of NQ is $\sqrt{2}s$. (The diagonal of a square is $\sqrt{2}$ times the side.) Now, NQ is equal to DC, or S, which is the side of the larger square. So now $S = \sqrt{2}s$. The perimeter of the large square equals $4S = 4\sqrt{2}s = \sqrt{2}(4s) = \sqrt{2} \times$ perimeter of the small square. (Refresher 520)

23. Choice A is correct. Angles A and B are both greater than 0° and less than 90°, so their sum is between 0° and 180°. Then angle C must be between 0° and 180°. (Refreshers 501, 505)

24. Choice D is correct. Let the four angles be x, $2x$, $3x$, and $4x$. The sum of the angles in a quadrilateral is 360°. Thus, the sum, $10x$, must equal 360° and therefore $x = 36°$. The largest angle is then $4x$, which is equal to 144°. (Refresher 505)

25. Choices C and D are correct.

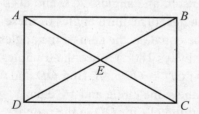

For Choice C, the diagonals of a rectangle are perpendicular only when the rectangle is a square. AE is part of the diagonal AC, so AE will not necessarily be perpendicular to BD. For Choice D, triangles AED and AEB are equal in area when the rectangle is a square. Triangles AED and AEB are also equal in area, in general, when $h_2 \times AD = h_1 \times AB$, where h_2 and h_1 are, respectively, the

altitudes to side AD and side AB. When $h_2 \times AD \neq h_1 \times AB$, triangles AED and AEB are not equal in area. (Refresher 518)

26. Choice D is correct.

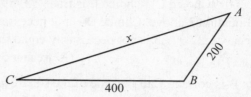

Draw the three cities as the vertices of a triangle. The length of side CB is 400 miles, the length of side AB is 200 miles, and x, the length of side AC, is unknown. The sum of any two sides of a triangle is greater than the third side, or in algebraic terms: $400 + 200 > x$, $400 + x > 200$, and $200 + x > 400$. These simplify to $600 > x$, $x > -200$, and $x > 200$. For x to be greater than 200 and -200, it must be greater than 200. Thus, the values of x are $200 < x < 600$. (Refreshers 506, 516)

27. Choice C is correct. At 7:30, the hour hand is *halfway between the 7 and the 8*, and the minute hand is on the 6. Thus, there are one and one-half "hour units," each equal to 30°, so the whole angle is 45°. (Refreshers 501, 526)

28. Choice E is correct. If a ship is facing north, a right turn of 90° will face it eastward. Another 90° turn will face it south, and an additional 45° turn will bring it to southwest. Thus, the total rotation is $90° + 90° + 45° = 225°$. (Refresher 501)

29. Choice E is correct. Since $y = z + 30°$ and $x = 2y$, then $x = 2(z + 30°) = 2z + 60°$. Thus, $x + y + z$ equals $(2z + 60°) + (z + 30°) + z = 4z + 90°$. This must equal 180° (the sum of the angles of a triangle). So $4z + 90° = 180°$, and the solution is $z = 22\frac{1}{2}°$; $x = 2z + 60° = 45° + 60° = 105°$. (Refresher 505)

30. Choice D is correct. Choice A is true: $\angle 1 + \angle 2 = 180°$ because they are supplementary angles (since AB is a straight line). Choice B is true: $\angle 4 = \angle 7$ because AB is parallel to CD making the alternate interior angles $\angle 4$ and $\angle 7$ equal. Choice C is true: $\angle 5 + \angle 6 = 180°$ (Equation 1) (supplementary angles). But $\angle 2 = \angle 6$ (Equation 2) (because AB is parallel to CD). Thus adding Equation 1 and Equation 2, we get $\angle 5 + \angle 2 = 180°$ (Equation 3). Now

$\angle 8 + \angle 7 = 180°$ (supplementary angles). But $\angle 4 = \angle 7$ (alternate interior angles from parallel lines). Thus $\angle 8 + \angle 4 = 180°$ (Equation 4). Adding Equation 3 and Equation 4, we get $\angle 5 + \angle 2 + \angle 8 + \angle 4 = 360°$ (Choice C). Choice E is true: $\angle 2 = \angle 6$ from Equation 2 above. Choice D is not necessarily true because $\angle 2 + \angle 3$ is not necessarily equal to 180°. (Refresher 504)

31. Choice B is correct. Call the side of the square s. Then, the diagonal of the square is $s\sqrt{2}$ and the area is s^2. The area of an isosceles right triangle with leg r is $\frac{1}{2}r^2$. Now, the area of the triangle is equal to the area of the square, so $s^2 = \frac{1}{2}r^2$. Solving for r gives $r = s\sqrt{2}$. The hypotenuse of the triangle is $\sqrt{r^2 + r^2}$. Substituting $r = s\sqrt{2}$, the hypotenuse is $\sqrt{2s^2 + 2s^2} = \sqrt{4s^2} = 2s$. Therefore, the ratio of the diagonal to the hypotenuse is $s\sqrt{2} : 2s$. Since $s\sqrt{2} : 2s$ is $\frac{s\sqrt{2}}{2s}$ or $\frac{\sqrt{2}}{2}$, multiply by $\frac{\sqrt{2}}{\sqrt{2}}$, which has a value of 1. $\frac{\sqrt{2}}{2} \cdot \frac{\sqrt{2}}{\sqrt{2}} = \frac{2}{2\sqrt{2}} = \frac{1}{\sqrt{2}}$ or $1 : \sqrt{2}$, which is the final result. (Refreshers 507, 509, 520)

32. Choice D is correct. The formula for the number of degrees in the angles of a polygon is $180(n - 2)$, where n is the number of sides. For a ten-sided figure this is $180°(10 - 2) = 180°(8) = 1,440°$. Since the ten angles are equal, they must each equal 144°. (Refreshers 521, 522)

33. Choice C is correct. If three numbers represent the lengths of the sides of a right triangle, they must satisfy the Pythagorean theorem: The squares of the smaller two combined must equal the square of the largest one. This condition is met in all the sets given except the set 9, 28, 35. There, $9^2 + 28^2 = 81 + 784 = 865$, but $35^2 = 1,225$. (Refresher 509)

34. Choice D is correct. Let the angle be x. Since x is its own supplement, then $x + x = 180°$, or, since $2x = 180°$, $x = 90°$. (Refresher 502)

35. Choice A is correct. The length of the arc intersected by a central angle of a circle is proportional to the number of degrees in the angle. Thus, if a 45° angle cuts off a 6-inch arc, a 360° angle intersects an arc eight times as long, or 48 inches. The length of the arc of a 360° angle is equal to the circle's circumference, or 2π times the radius. Thus, to obtain the radius, divide 48 inches by 2π.

48 inches $\div 2\pi = \frac{24}{\pi}$ inches. (Refreshers 524, 526)

36. Choice C is correct.

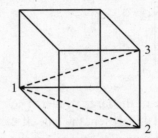

Refer to the diagram above. Calculate the distance from vertex 1 to vertex 2. This is simply the diagonal of a 1-inch square and equal to $\sqrt{2}$ inches. Now, vertices 1, 2, and 3 form a right triangle, with legs of 1 and $\sqrt{2}$. By the Pythagorean theorem, the hypotenuse is $\sqrt{3}$. This is the distance from vertex 1 to vertex 3, the two most distant vertices. (Refreshers 509, 520)

37. Choice A is correct. In one hour, the hour hand of a clock moves through an angle of 30° (one "hour unit"). 70 minutes equals $\frac{7}{6}$ hours, so during that time the hour hand will move through $\frac{7}{6} \times 30°$, or 35°. (Refreshers 501, 526)

38. Choice C is correct. In order to be similar, two triangles must have equal corresponding angles. This is true of triangles ODC and OBA, since angle O equals itself, and angles OCD and OAB are both right angles. (The third angles of these triangles must be equal, as the sum of the angles of a triangle is always 180°.) Since the triangles are similar, $OD : CD = OB : AB$. But, OD and OA are radii of the same circle and are equal. Therefore, substitute OA for OD in the proportion above. Hence, $OA : CD = OB : AB$. There is, however, no information given on the relative sizes of any of the line segments, so statement III may or may not be true. (Refreshers 509, 510, 524)

39. Choice C is correct. Let the three angles equal x, $2x$, and $6x$. The sum of the angles in a triangle is 180°. Thus, $x + 2x + 6x = 180°$, or $9x = 180°$. Therefore, $x = 20°$ and the largest angle is $6x = 120°$.

(Refresher 505)

40. Choice A is correct. Since $AB = AC$, angle ABC must equal angle ACB. (Base angles of an isosceles triangle are equal.) As the sum of angles BAC, ABC, and ACB is 180°, and angle BAC equals 40°, angle ABC and angle ACB must each equal 70°. Now, DBC is a right triangle, with angle $BDC = 90°$ and angle $DCB = 70°$. (The three angles must add up to 180°.) Angle DBC must equal 20°.

(Refreshers 507, 514)

41. Choice C is correct.

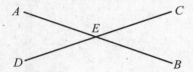

$\angle AEB$ and $\angle CED$ are both straight angles, and are equal; similarly, $\angle DEC$ and $\angle BEA$ are both straight angles. $\angle AEC$ and $\angle BED$ are vertical angles, as are $\angle BEC$ and $\angle DEA$, and are equal. $\angle AED$ and $\angle CEA$ are supplementary and need not be equal.

(Refreshers 501, 502, 503)

42. Choice A is correct. All right isosceles triangles have angles of 45°, 45°, and 90°. Since all triangles with the same angles are similar, all right isosceles triangles are similar. (Refreshers 507, 509, 510)

43. Choice C is correct.

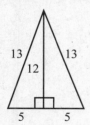

As the diagram shows, the altitude to the base of the isosceles triangle divides it into two congruent right triangles, each with 5–12–13 sides. Thus, the base is 10, the height is 12, and the area is $\frac{1}{2}(10)(12) = 60$.

(Refreshers 505, 507, 509)

44. Choice C is correct.

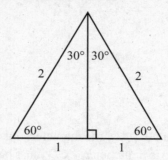

The altitude to any side divides the triangle into two congruent 30°-60°-90° right triangles, each with a hypotenuse of 2 inches and a leg of 1 inch. The other leg equals the altitude. By the Pythagorean theorem, the altitude is equal to $\sqrt{3}$ inches. (The sides of a 30°-60°-90° right triangle are always in the proportion $1 : \sqrt{3} : 2$.)

(Refreshers 509, 514)

45. Choice E is correct.

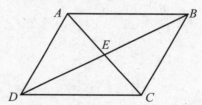

As the diagram illustrates, angles AED and BEC are vertical and, therefore, equal. $AE = EC$, because the diagonals of a parallelogram bisect each other. Angles BDC and DBA are equal because they are alternate interior angles of parallel lines ($AB \| CD$).

(Refreshers 503, 517)

46. Choice E is correct. There are eight isosceles right triangles: ABE, BCE, CDE, ADE, ABC, BCD, CDA, and ABD. (Refresher 520)

47. Choice D is correct.

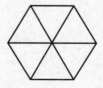

Recall that a regular hexagon may be broken up into six equilateral triangles. Since the angles of each triangle are 60°, and two of these angles make up each angle of the hexagon, an angle of the hexagon must be 120°. (Refresher 523)

48. Choice E is correct.

Since the radius equals 1″, *AD*, the diameter, must be 2″. Now, since *AD* is a diameter, *ACD* must be a right triangle, because an angle inscribed in a semi-circle is a right angle. Thus, because ∠*DAC* = 30°, it must be a 30°-60°-90° right triangle. The sides will be in the proportion 1 : √3 : 2. As *AD* : *AC* = 2 : √3, so *AC*, one of the sides of the equilateral triangle, must be √3 inches long.

(Refreshers 508, 524)

49. Choice D is correct. Let the angles be $2x$, $3x$, $4x$. Their sums are equal to $9x = 180°$ and $x = 20°$. Thus, the largest angle, $4x$, is 80°.

(Refresher 505)

50. Choice B is correct. The sides of a right triangle must obey the Pythagorean theorem. The only group of choices that does so is the second: 12, 16, and 20 are in the 3 : 4 : 5 ratio, and the relationship $12^2 + 16^2 = 20^2$ is satisfied. (Refresher 509)

MATH REFRESHER SESSION 6

Miscellaneous Problems: Averages, Standard Deviation, Properties of Integers, Approximations, Combinations, Permutations, Probability, the Absolute Value Sign, and Functions

Averages, Medians, and Modes

601. *Averages*. The average of *n* numbers is merely their sum, divided by *n*.

Example: Find the average of 20, 0, 80, and 12.

Solution: The average is the sum divided by the number of entries, or:

$$\frac{20 + 0 + 80 + 12}{4} = \frac{112}{4} = 28$$

Another way of obtaining an average of a set of numbers that are close together is the following:

Step 1. Choose any number that will approximately equal the average.

Step 2. Subtract this approximate average from each of the numbers (this sum will give some positive and negative results). Add the results.

Step 3. Divide this sum by the number of entries.

Step 4. Add the result of Step 3 to the approximate average chosen in Step 1. This will be the true average.

Example: Find the average of 92, 93, 93, 96, and 97.

Solution: Choose 95 as an approximate average. Subtracting 95 from 92, 93, 93, 96, and 97 gives −3, −2, −2, 1, and 2. The sum is −4. Divide −4 by 5 (the number of entries) to obtain −0.8. Add −0.8 to the original approximation of 95 to get the true average, 95 − 0.8, or 94.2.

601a. *Medians*. The median of a set of numbers is that number which is in the *middle* of all the numbers.

Example: Find the median of 20, 0, 80, 12, and 30.

Solution: Arrange the numbers in increasing order:

0
12
20
30
80

The *middle* number is 20, so 20 is the *median*.

Note: If there is an *even* number of items, such as 0, 12, 20, 24, 30, and 80, there is no *middle* number.

So in this case we take the average of the two middle numbers, 20 and 24, to get 22, which is the *median*.

In the above set of 6 numbers, if 24 was replaced by 22, the median would be 21 (just the average of 20 and 22).

601b. *Modes*. The mode of a set of numbers is the number that occurs most frequently.

If we have numbers 0, 12, 20, 30, and 80, there is *no* mode, since no one number appears with the greatest frequency. But consider this:

Example: Find the mode of 0, 12, 12, 20, 30, and 80.

Solution: 12 appears most frequently, so it is the mode.

Example: Find the mode of 0, 12, 12, 20, 30, 30, and 80.

Solution: Here *both* 12 and 30 are modes.

Standard Deviation

602. Let's consider what a standard deviation is with an example:

Consider a population consisting of the following eight values:

$$2, 4, 4, 4, 5, 5, 7, 9$$

The eight data points have a *mean* (or average) value of 5:

$$\frac{2 + 4 + 4 + 4 + 5 + 5 + 7 + 9}{8} = 5$$

To calculate the population standard deviation, first compute the difference of each data point from the mean, and *square* the result of each:

$$(2 - 5)^2 = (-3)^2 = 9 \qquad (5 - 5)^2 = 0^2 = 0$$
$$(4 - 5)^2 = (-1)^2 = 1 \qquad (5 - 5)^2 = 0^2 = 0$$
$$(4 - 5)^2 = (-1)^2 = 1 \qquad (7 - 5)^2 = 2^2 = 4$$
$$(4 - 5)^2 = (-1)^2 = 1 \qquad (9 - 5)^2 = 4^2 = 16$$

Next divide the sum of these values by the number of values and take the *square root* to give the standard deviation:

$$\sqrt{\frac{9 + 1 + 1 + 1 + 0 + 0 + 4 + 16}{8}} = 2$$

Therefore, the above has a population standard deviation of 2.

So to calculate the standard deviation of a set of numbers, subtract each number from the average of the numbers, then square what you get for each of the numbers. Add all those results, and then divide by how many numbers you originally had. Take the square root of the result. That is your standard deviation.

Properties of Integers

An integer is a whole number; for example, –5, –2, 0, 1, 3, etc.

603. *Even–Odd.* These are problems that deal with even and odd numbers. An even number is divisible by 2, and an odd number is not divisible by 2. All even numbers end in the digits 0, 2, 4, 6, or 8; odd numbers end in the digits 1, 3, 5, 7, or 9. For example, the numbers 358, 90, 18, 9,874, and 46 are even numbers. The numbers 67, 871, 475, and 89 are odd numbers. It is important to remember the following facts:

604. The sum of *two even* numbers is *even*, and the sum of *two odd* numbers is *even*, but the sum of an *odd* number *and* an *even* number is *odd*. For example, $4 + 8 = 12$, $5 + 3 = 8$, and $7 + 2 = 9$.

Example: If m is any integer, is the number $6m + 3$ an even or odd number?

Solution: $6m$ is even, since 6 is a multiple of 2. 3 is odd. Therefore $6m + 3$ is odd, since even + odd = odd.

605. The product of *two odd* numbers is *odd*, but the product of an *even* number and *any other* number is an *even* number. For example, $3 \times 5 = 15$ (odd); $4 \times 5 = 20$ (even); $4 \times 6 = 24$ (even).

Example: If m is any integer, is the product $(2m + 3)(4m + 1)$ even or odd?

Solution: Since $2m$ is even and 3 is odd, $2m + 3$ is odd. Likewise, since $4m$ is even and 1 is odd, $4m + 1$ is odd. Thus $(2m + 3)(4m + 1)$ is (odd $\times$ odd), which is odd.

606. Even numbers are expressed in the form $2k$, where k may be any integer. Odd numbers are expressed in the form of $2k + 1$ or $2k - 1$, where k may be any integer. For example, if $k = 17$, then $2k = 34$ and $2k + 1 = 35$. If $k = 6$, then we have $2k = 12$ and $2k + 1 = 13$.

Example: Prove that the product of two odd numbers is odd.

Solution: Let one of the odd numbers be represented as $2x + 1$. Let the other number be represented as $2y + 1$. Now multiply $(2x + 1)(2y + 1)$. We get $4xy + 2x + 2y + 1$. Since $4xy + 2x + 2y$ is even because it is a multiple of 2, that quantity is even. Since 1 is odd, we have $4xy + 2x + 2y + 1$ is odd, since even + odd = odd.

607. *Divisibility.* If an integer P is divided by an integer Q, and an integer is obtained as the quotient, then P is said to be divisible by Q. In other words, if P can be expressed as an integral multiple of Q, then P is said to be divisible by Q. For example, dividing 51 by 17 gives 3, an integer. 51 is divisible by 17, or 51 equals 17 times 3. On the other hand, dividing 8 by 3 gives $2\frac{2}{3}$, which is not an integer. 8 is not divisible by 3, and there is no way to express 8 as an integral multiple of 3. There are various tests to see whether an integer is divisible by certain numbers. These tests are listed below:

1. Any integer is divisible *by 2* if the last digit of the number is a 0, 2, 4, 6, or 8.

   Example: The numbers 98, 6,534, 70, and 32 are divisible by 2 because they end in 8, 4, 0, and 2, respectively.

2. Any integer is divisible *by 3* if the sum of its digits is divisible by 3.

   Example: Is the number 34,237,023 divisible by 3?

   Solution: Add the digits of the number. 3 + 4 + 2 + 3 + 7 + 0 + 2 + 3 = 24. Now, 24 is divisible by 3 (24 ÷ 3 = 8), so the number 34,237,023 is also divisible by 3.

3. Any integer is divisible *by 4* if the last two digits of the number make a number that is divisible by 4.

   Example: Which of the following numbers is divisible by 4?

   3,456; 6,787,612; 67,408; 7,877; 345; 98.

   Solution: Look at the last two digits of the numbers: 56, 12, 08, 77, 45, 98. Only 56, 12, and 08 are divisible by 4, so only the numbers 3,456; 6,787,612; and 67,408 are divisible by 4.

4. An integer is divisible *by 5* if the last digit is either a 0 or a 5.

   Example: The numbers 780, 675, 9,000, and 15 are divisible by 5, while the numbers 786, 5,509, and 87 are not divisible by 5.

5. Any integer is divisible *by 6* if it is divisible by both 2 and 3.

   Example: Is the number 12,414 divisible by 6?

   Solution: Test whether 12,414 is divisible by 2 and 3. The last digit is a 4, so it is divisible by 2. Adding the digits yields 1 + 2 + 4 + 1 + 4 = 12. 12 is divisible by 3, so the number 12,414 is divisible by 3. Since it is divisible by both 2 and 3, it is divisible by 6.

6. Any integer is divisible *by 8* if the last three digits are divisible by 8. (Since 1,000 is divisible by 8, you can ignore all multiples of 1,000 in applying this rule.)

   Example: Is the number 342,169,424 divisible by 8?

   Solution: 424 ÷ 8 = 53, so 342,169,424 is divisible by 8.

7. Any integer is divisible *by 9* if the sum of its digits is divisible by 9.

   Example: Is the number 243,091,863 divisible by 9?

   Solution: Adding the digits yields 2 + 4 + 3 + 0 + 9 + 1 + 8 + 6 + 3 = 36. 36 is divisible by 9, so the number 243,091,863 is divisible by 9.

8. Any integer is divisible *by 10* if the last digit is a 0.

   Example: The numbers 60, 8,900, 5,640, and 34,000 are all divisible by 10 because the last digit in each is a 0.

Note that if a number P is divisible by a number Q, then P is also divisible by all the factors of Q. For example, 60 is divisible by 12, so 60 is also divisible by 2, 3, 4, and 6, which are all factors of 12.

608. *Prime numbers.* A prime number is one that is divisible only by 1 and itself. The first few prime numbers are 2, 3, 5, 7, 11, 13, 17, 19, 23, 29, 31, 37. . . . Note that the number 1 is not considered a prime number. To determine if a number is prime, follow these steps:

Step 1. Determine a very rough approximate square root of the number. Remember that the square root of a number is that number which, when multiplied by itself, gives the original number. For example, the square root of 25 is 5 because 5 × 5 = 25.

Step 2. Divide the number by all of the primes that are less than the approximate square root. If the number is not divisible by any of these primes, then it is prime. If it is divisible by one of the primes, then it is not prime.

Example: Is the number 97 prime?

Solution: An approximate square root of 97 is 10. All of the primes less than 10 are 2, 3, 5, and 7. Divide 97 by 2, 3, 5, and 7. No integer results, so 97 is prime.

Example: Is the number 161 prime?

Solution: An approximate square root of 161 is 13. The primes less than 13 are 2, 3, 5, 7, and 11. Divide 161 by 2, 3, 5, 7, and 11. 161 is divisible by 7 (161 ÷ 7 = 23), so 161 is not prime.

Approximations

609. *Rounding off numbers with decimal points.* A number expressed to a certain number of places is rounded off when it is approximated as a number with fewer places of accuracy. For example, the number 8.987 is expressed more accurately than the number rounded off to 8.99. To round off to *n* places, look at the digit that is to the right of the *n*th digit. (The *n*th digit is found by counting *n* places to the right of the decimal point.) If this digit is less than 5, eliminate all of the digits to the right of the *n*th digit. If the digit to the right of the *n*th digit is 5 or more, then add 1 to the *n*th digit and eliminate all of the digits to the right of the *n*th digit.

Example: Round off 8.73 to the nearest tenth.

Solution: The digit to the right of the 7 (.7 is seven-tenths) is 3. Since this is less than 5, eliminate it, and the rounded-off answer is 8.7.

Example: Round off 986 to the nearest tens place.

Solution: The number to the right of the tens place is 6. Since this is 5 or more, add 1 to the 8 and replace the 6 with a 0 to get 990.

610. *Approximating sums with decimal points.* When adding a small set of numbers (10 or fewer) and the answer must have a given number of places of accuracy, follow the steps below.

Step 1. Round off each addend (number being added) to one less place than the number of places the answer is to have.

Step 2. Add the rounded addends.

Step 3. Round off the sum to the desired number of places of accuracy.

Example: What is the sum of 12.0775, 1.20163, and 121.303, correct to the nearest hundredth?

Solution: Round off the three numbers to the nearest thousandth (one less place than the

accuracy of the sum): 12.078, 1.202, and 121.303. The sum of these is 134.583. Rounded off to the nearest hundredth, this is 134.58.

611. *Approximating products.* To multiply certain numbers and have an answer to the desired number of places of accuracy (significant digits), follow the steps below.

Step 1. Round off the numbers being multiplied to the number of places of accuracy (significant digits) desired in the answer.

Step 2. Multiply the rounded-off factors (numbers being multiplied).

Step 3. Round off the product to the desired number of places (significant digits).

Example: Find the product of 3,316 and 1,432 to the nearest thousand.

Solution: First, round off 3,316 to 3 places, to obtain 3,320. Round off 1,432 to 3 places to give 1,430. The product of these two numbers is 4,747,600. Rounded off to 3 places, this is 4,748,000.

612. *Approximating square roots.* The square root of a number is that number which, when multiplied by itself, gives the original number. For example, 6 is the square root of 36. Often on tests, a number with different choices for the square root is given. Follow this procedure to determine which is the best choice.

Step 1. Square all of the choices given.

Step 2. Select the closest choice that is too large and the closest choice that is too small (assuming that no choice is the exact square root). Find the average of these two *choices* (not of their squares).

Step 3. Square this average; if the square is greater than the original number, choose the lower of the two choices; if its square is lower than the original number, choose the higher.

Example: Which of the following is closest to the square root of 86: 9.0, 9.2, 9.4, 9.6, or 9.8?

Solution: The squares of the five numbers are 81, 84.64, 88.36, 92.16, and 96.04, respectively. (Actually, it is not necessary to calculate the last two, since they are greater than the third square, which is already greater than 86.) The two closest choices are 9.2 and 9.4; their average is 9.3. The square of 9.3 is 86.49. Therefore, 9.3 is greater than the square root of 86. So, the square root must be closer to 9.2 than to 9.4.

Combinations

613. Suppose that a job has 2 different parts. There are m different ways of doing the first part, and there are n different ways of doing the second part. The problem is to find the number of ways of doing the entire job. For each way of doing the first part of the job, there are n ways of doing the second part. Since there are m ways of doing the first part, the total number of ways of doing the entire job is $m \times n$. The formula that can be used is

$$\text{Number of ways} = m \times n$$

For any problem that involves 2 actions or 2 objects, each with a number of choices, and asks for the number of combinations, this formula can be used. For example: A man wants a sandwich and a drink for lunch. If a restaurant has 4 choices of sandwich and 3 choices of drink, how many different ways can he order his lunch?

Since there are 4 choices of sandwich and 3 choices of drink, use the formula

$$\text{Number of ways} = 4(3)$$
$$= 12$$

Therefore, the man can order his lunch 12 different ways.

If we have objects a, b, c, and d and want to arrange them two at a time—that is, like ab, bc, cd, etc.—we have four combinations taken two at a time. This is denoted as $_4C_2$. The rule is that $_4C_2 = \dfrac{(4)(3)}{(2)(1)}$. In general, n combinations taken r at a time is represented by the formula:

$$_nC_r = \frac{(n)(n-1)(n-2)\ldots(n-r+1)}{(r)(r-1)(r-2)\ldots(1)}$$

Examples: $_3C_2 = \dfrac{3 \times 2}{2 \times 1}$; $_8C_3 = \dfrac{8 \times 7 \times 6}{3 \times 2 \times 1}$

Suppose there are 24 people at a party and each person shakes another person's hand (only once). How many handshakes are there?

Solution: Represent the people at the party as a, b, c, d, etc.

The combinations of handshakes would be ab, ac, bc, bd, etc., or 24 combinations taken 2 at a time: $_{24}C_2$. This is $\dfrac{24 \times 23}{2 \times 1} = 276$.

Permutations

613a. *Permutations* are like combinations, except in permutations the order is important. As an example, if we want to find how many permutations there are of 3 objects taken 2 at a time, we would have for a, b, c, ab, ba, ac, ca, bc, cb. Thus, as an example, ba would be one permutation and ab would be another. The permutations of 3 objects taken 2 at a time would be $_3P_2 = 3 \times 2$ and not $\dfrac{(3 \times 3)}{(2 \times 1)}$ as in combinations. The number of permutations of n objects taken r at a time would be

$$_nP_r = (n)(n-1)\ldots(n-r+1).$$

Example: How many permutations of the digits 142 are there, where the digits are taken two at a time?

Solution: You have 14, 41, 12, 21, 42, 24. That is, $_3P_2 = 3 \times 2 = 6$.

Probability

614. The *probability* that an event will occur equals the number of favorable ways divided by the total number of ways. If P is the probability, m is the number of favorable ways, and n is the total number of ways, then

$$P = \frac{m}{n}$$

Example: What is the probability that a head will turn up on a single throw of a penny?

The favorable number of ways is 1 (a head).

The total number of ways is 2 (a head and a tail).

Thus, the probability is $\dfrac{1}{2}$.

If a and b are two mutually exclusive events, then the probability that a or b will occur is the sum of the individual probabilities.

Suppose P_a is the probability that an event a occurs. Suppose that P_b is the probability that a second independent event b occurs. Then the probability that the first event a occurs *and* the second event b occurs subsequently is $P_a \times P_b$.

The Absolute Value Sign

615. The symbol $|\ |$ denotes *absolute value*. The absolute value of a number is the numerical value of the number without the plus or minus sign in front of it. Thus all absolute values are positive. For example, $|+3|$ is 3, and $|-2|$ is 2. Here's another example:

   If x is positive and y is negative $|x| + |y| = x - y$. Because y is negative, we must have $x - y$ to make the term positive.

Functions

616. Suppose we have a *function* of x. This is denoted as $f(x)$ or $g(y)$ or $h(z)$, etc. As an example, if $f(x) = x$, then $f(3) = 3$.

   In this example we substitute the value 3 wherever x appears in the function. Similarly, $f(-2) = -2$.

   Consider another example: If $f(y) = y^2 - y$, then $f(2) = 2^2 - 2 = 2$. $f(-2) = (-2)^2 - (-2) = 6$. $f(z) = z^2 - z$. $f(2z) = (2z)^2 - (2z) = 4z^2 - 2z$.

Let us consider still another example: Let $f(x) = x + 2$ and $g(y) = 2^y$. What is $f[g(-2)]$? Now $g(-2) = 2^{-2} = \frac{1}{4}$. Thus $f[g(-2)] = f\left(\frac{1}{4}\right)$. Since $f(x) = x + 2$, $f\left(\frac{1}{4}\right) = \frac{1}{4} + 2 = 2\frac{1}{4}$.

Imaginary Numbers

617. An imaginary number, $i = \sqrt{-1}$, is a number that when multiplied by itself will give you the value -1. Obviously there is no number in the real world that can be multiplied by itself to give a negative number: If the number is positive, positive $\times$ positive $=$ positive, and if the number is negative, negative $\times$ negative $=$ positive, and if it is 0, $0 \times 0 = 0$. Thus the number is called "imaginary." So if $i = \sqrt{-1}$, $i^2 = -1$.

Example: Find another expression for $(2 + 3i)$ $(3 + 5i)$.

Solution: Multiply the factors: We get $2 \times 3 + 3i \times 3 + 2 \times 5i + 3i \times 5i$. This becomes $6 + 9i + 10i + 15i^2 = 6 + 19i + 15(-1) = 6 + 19i - 15 = 19i - 9$.

SESSION 6 PRACTICE TEST

Miscellaneous Problems: Averages, Standard Deviation, Properties of Integers, Approximations, Combinations, Permutations, Probability, the Absolute Value Sign, and Functions

Correct answers and solutions follow this test.

1. If *n* is the first of five consecutive odd numbers, what is their average?

   (A) *n*
   (B) *n* + 1
   (C) *n* + 2
   (D) *n* + 3
   (E) *n* + 4

   A B C D E
   ○ ○ ○ ○ ○

2. What is the average of the following numbers: 35.5, 32.5, 34.0, 35.0, 34.5?

   (A) 33.0
   (B) 33.8
   (C) 34.0
   (D) 34.3
   (E) 34.5

   A B C D E
   ○ ○ ○ ○ ○

3. If *P* is an even number and *Q* and *R* are both odd, which of the following *must* be true?

   (A) *P* · *Q* is an odd number.
   (B) *Q* − *R* is an even number.
   (C) *PQ* − *PR* is an odd number.
   (D) *Q* + *R* cannot equal *P*.
   (E) *P* + *Q* cannot equal *R*.

   A B C D E
   ○ ○ ○ ○ ○

4. If a number is divisible by 102, then it is also divisible by:

   (A) 23
   (B) 11
   (C) 103
   (D) 5
   (E) 2

   A B C D E
   ○ ○ ○ ○ ○

5. Which of the following numbers is divisible by 36?

   (A) 35,924
   (B) 64,530
   (C) 74,098
   (D) 152,640
   (E) 192,042

   A B C D E
   ○ ○ ○ ○ ○

6. How many prime numbers are there between 45 and 72?

   (A) 4
   (B) 5
   (C) 6
   (D) 7
   (E) 8

   A B C D E
   ○ ○ ○ ○ ○

7. Which of the following represents the smallest possible value of $\left(M - \frac{1}{2}\right)^2$, if *M* is an integer?

   (A) 0.00
   (B) 0.25
   (C) 0.50
   (D) 0.75
   (E) 1.00

   A B C D E
   ○ ○ ○ ○ ○

8. Which of the following best approximates $\dfrac{7.40096 \times 10.0342}{0.2001355}$?

   (A) 0.3700
   (B) 3.700
   (C) 37.00
   (D) 370.0
   (E) 3,700

   A B C D E
   ○ ○ ○ ○ ○

9. In a class with 6 boys and 4 girls, the students all took the same test. The boys' scores were 74, 82, 84, 84, 88, and 95, while the girls' scores were 80, 82, 86, and 86. Which of the following statements is true?

   (A) The boys' average was 0.1 higher than the average for the whole class.
   (B) The girls' average was 0.1 lower than the boys' average.
   (C) The class average was 1.0 higher than the boys' average.
   (D) The boys' average was 1.0 higher than the class average.
   (E) The girls' average was 1.0 lower than the boys' average.

   A B C D E
   ○ ○ ○ ○ ○

10. Which of the following numbers *must* be odd?

    (A) The sum of an odd number and an odd number.
    (B) The product of an odd number and an even number.
    (C) The sum of an odd number and an even number.
    (D) The product of two even numbers.
    (E) The sum of two even numbers.

    A B C D E
    ○ ○ ○ ○ ○

11. Which of the following numbers is the best approximation of the length of one side of a square with an area of 12 square inches?

    (A) 3.2 inches
    (B) 3.3 inches
    (C) 3.4 inches
    (D) 3.5 inches
    (E) 3.6 inches

    A B C D E
    ○ ○ ○ ○ ○

12. If n is an odd number, then which of the following *best* describes the number represented by $n^2 + 2n + 1$?

    (A) It can be odd or even.
    (B) It must be odd.
    (C) It must be divisible by four.

   (D) It must be divisible by six.
   (E) The answer cannot be determined from the given information.

   A B C D E
   ○ ○ ○ ○ ○

13. What is the average of the following numbers: $3\frac{1}{2}$, $4\frac{1}{4}$, $2\frac{1}{4}$, $3\frac{1}{4}$, 4?

    (A) 3.25
    (B) 3.35
    (C) 3.45
    (D) 3.50
    (E) 3.60

    A B C D E
    ○ ○ ○ ○ ○

14. Which of the following numbers is divisible by 24?

    (A) 76,300
    (B) 78,132
    (C) 80,424
    (D) 81,234
    (E) 83,636

    A B C D E
    ○ ○ ○ ○ ○

15. In order to graduate, a boy needs an average of 65 percent for his five major subjects. His first four grades were 55, 60, 65, and 65. What grade does he need in the fifth subject in order to graduate?

    (A) 65
    (B) 70
    (C) 75
    (D) 80
    (E) 85

    A B C D E
    ○ ○ ○ ○ ○

16. If t is any integer, which of the following represents an odd number?

    (A) $2t$
    (B) $2t + 3$
    (C) $3t$
    (D) $2t + 2$
    (E) $t + 1$

    A B C D E
    ○ ○ ○ ○ ○

17. If the average of five whole numbers is an even number, which of the following statements is *not* *true*?

(A) The sum of the five numbers must be divisible by 2.
(B) The sum of the five numbers must be divisible by 5.
(C) The sum of the five numbers must be divisible by 10.
(D) At least one of the five numbers must be even.
(E) All of the five numbers must be odd.

A B C D E
○ ○ ○ ○ ○

18. What is the product of 23 and 79 to one significant digit?

(A) 1,600
(B) 1,817
(C) 1,000
(D) 1,800
(E) 2,000

A B C D E
○ ○ ○ ○ ○

19. Which of the following is closest to the square root of $\frac{1}{2}$?

(A) 0.25
(B) 0.5
(C) 0.6
(D) 0.7
(E) 0.8

A B C D E
○ ○ ○ ○ ○

20. How many prime numbers are there between 56 and 100?

(A) 8
(B) 9
(C) 10
(D) 11
(E) none of the above

A B C D E
○ ○ ○ ○ ○

21. If you multiply 1,200,176 by 520,204, and then divide the product by 1,000,000,000, your result will be closest to:

(A) 0.6
(B) 6
(C) 600
(D) 6,000
(E) 6,000,000

A B C D E
○ ○ ○ ○ ○

22. The number 89.999 rounded off to the nearest tenth is equal to which of the following?

(A) 90.0
(B) 89.0
(C) 89.9
(D) 89.99
(E) 89.90

A B C D E
○ ○ ○ ○ ○

23. a, b, c, d, and e are integers; M is their average and S is their sum. What is the ratio of S to M?

(A) 1 : 5
(B) 5 : 1
(C) 1 : 1
(D) 2 : 1
(E) It depends on the values of a, b, c, d, and e.

A B C D E
○ ○ ○ ○ ○

24. The sum of five odd numbers is always:

(A) even
(B) divisible by 3
(C) divisible by 5
(D) a prime number
(E) none of the above

A B C D E
○ ○ ○ ○ ○

25. If E is an even number and F is divisible by 3, then what is the *largest* number by which E^2F^3 *must* be divisible?

    (A) 6
    (B) 12
    (C) 54
    (D) 108
    (E) 144

    A B C D E
    ○ ○ ○ ○ ○

26. If the average of five consecutive even numbers is 8, which of the following is the smallest of the five numbers?

    (A) 4
    (B) 5
    (C) 6
    (D) 8
    (E) none of the above

    A B C D E
    ○ ○ ○ ○ ○

27. If a number is divisible by 23, then it is also divisible by which of the following?

    (A) 7
    (B) 24
    (C) 9
    (D) 3
    (E) none of the above

    A B C D E
    ○ ○ ○ ○ ○

28. What is the average (to the nearest tenth) of the following numbers: 91.4, 91.5, 91.6, 91.7, 91.7, 92.0, 92.1, 92.3, 92.3, 92.4?

    (A) 91.9
    (B) 92.0
    (C) 92.1
    (D) 92.2
    (E) 92.3

    A B C D E
    ○ ○ ○ ○ ○

29. Which of the following numbers is divisible by 11?

    (A) 30,217
    (B) 44,221
    (C) 59,403
    (D) 60,411
    (E) none of the above

    A B C D E
    ○ ○ ○ ○ ○

30. Which of the following is the best approximation of the product (1.005)(20.0025)(0.0102)?

    (A) 0.02
    (B) 0.2
    (C) 2.0
    (D) 20
    (E) 200

    A B C D E
    ○ ○ ○ ○ ○

31. If a, b, and c are all divisible by 8, then their average must be

    (A) divisible by 8
    (B) divisible by 4
    (C) divisible by 2
    (D) an integer
    (E) none of the above

    A B C D E
    ○ ○ ○ ○ ○

32. Which of the following numbers is divisible by 24?

    (A) 13,944
    (B) 15,746
    (C) 15,966
    (D) 16,012
    (E) none of the above

    A B C D E
    ○ ○ ○ ○ ○

33. Which of the following numbers is a prime?

    (A) 147
    (B) 149
    (C) 153
    (D) 155
    (E) 161

    A B C D E
    ○ ○ ○ ○ ○

34. The sum of four consecutive odd integers must be:
    (A) even, but not necessarily divisible by 4
    (B) divisible by 4, but not necessarily by 8
    (C) divisible by 8, but not necessarily by 16
    (D) divisible by 16
    (E) none of the above

    A B C D E
    ○ ○ ○ ○ ○

35. Which of the following is closest to the square root of $\frac{3}{5}$?

    (A) $\frac{1}{2}$

    (B) $\frac{2}{3}$

    (C) $\frac{3}{4}$

    (D) $\frac{4}{5}$

    (E) 1

    A B C D E
    ○ ○ ○ ○ ○

36. The sum of an odd and an even number is
    (A) a perfect square
    (B) negative
    (C) even
    (D) odd
    (E) none of the above

    A B C D E
    ○ ○ ○ ○ ○

Answer Key for Session 6 Practice Test

1. E	10. C	19. D	28. A
2. D	11. D	20. B	29. A
3. B	12. C	21. C	30. B
4. E	13. C	22. A	31. E
5. D	14. C	23. B	32. A
6. C	15. D	24. E	33. B
7. B	16. B	25. D	34. C
8. D	17. E	26. A	35. C
9. E	18. E	27. E	36. D

Answers and Solutions for Session 6 Practice Test

1. Choice E is correct. The five consecutive odd numbers must be $n, n + 2, n + 4, n + 6$, and $n + 8$. Their average is equal to their sum, $5n + 20$, divided by the number of addends, 5, which yields $n + 4$ as the average. (Refresher 601)

2. Choice D is correct. Choosing 34 as an approximate average results in the following addends: $+1.5, -1.5, 0, +1.0$, and $+0.5$. Their sum is $+1.5$. Now, divide by 5 to get $+0.3$ and add this to 34 to get 34.3. (To check this, add the five original numbers and divide by 5.) (Refresher 601)

3. Choice B is correct. Since Q is an odd number, it may be represented by $2m + 1$, where m is an integer. Similarly, call R $2n + 1$, where n is an integer. Thus, $Q - R$ is equal to $(2m + 1) - (2n + 1)$, $2m - 2n$, or $2(m - n)$. Now, since m and n are integers, $m - n$ will be some integer p. Thus, $Q - R = 2p$. Any number in the form of $2p$, where p is any integer, is an even number. Therefore, $Q - R$ *must* be even. (A) and (C) are wrong, because an even number multiplied by an odd is always even. (D) and (E) are only true for specific values of P, Q, and R. (Refresher 604)

4. Choice E is correct. If a number is divisible by 102, then it must be divisible by all of the factors of 102. The only choice that is a factor of 102 is 2. (Refresher 607)

5. Choice D is correct. To be divisible by 36, a number must be divisible by both 4 and 9. Only (A)

and (D) are divisible by 4. (Recall that only the last two digits must be examined.) Of these, only (D) is divisible by 9. The sum of the digits of (A) is 23, which is not divisible by 9; the sum of the digits of (D) is 18. (Refresher 607)

6. Choice C is correct. The prime numbers between 45 and 72 are 47, 53, 59, 61, 67, and 71. All of the others have factors other than 1 and themselves. (Refresher 608)

7. Choice B is correct. Since M must be an *integer*, the closest value it can have to $\frac{1}{2}$ is either 1 or 0. In either case, $\left(M - \frac{1}{2}\right)^2$ is equal to $\frac{1}{4}$, or 0.25. (Refresher 603)

8. Choice D is correct. Approximate each of the numbers to only one significant digit (this is permissible because the choices are so far apart; if they had been closer together, two or three significant digits should be used). After this approximation, the expression is: $\frac{7 \times 10}{0.2}$, which is equal to 350. This is closest to 370. (Refresher 609)

9. Choice E is correct. The average for the boys alone was $\frac{74 + 82 + 84 + 84 + 88 + 95}{6}$, or $507 \div 6$ = 84.5. The girls' average was $\frac{80 + 82 + 86 + 86}{4}$, or $334 \div 4 = 83.5$, which is 1.0 below the boys' average. (Refresher 601)

10. Choice C is correct. The sum of an odd number and an even number can be expressed as $(2n + 1) + (2m)$, where n and m are integers. ($2n + 1$ must be odd, and $2m$ must be even.) Their sum is equal to $2n + 2m + 1$, or $2(m + n) + 1$. Since $(m + n)$ is an integer, the quantity $2(m + n) + 1$ *must* represent an odd integer. (Refreshers 604, 605)

11. Choice D is correct. The actual length of one of the sides would be the square root of 12. Square each of the five choices to find the square of 3.4 is 11.56, and the square of 3.5 is 12.25. The square root of 12 must lie between 3.4 and 3.5. Squaring 3.45 (halfway between the two choices) yields 11.9025, which is less than 12. Thus the square root of 12 must be greater than 3.45 and therefore closer to 3.5 than to 3.4. (Refresher 612)

12. Choice C is correct. Factor $n^2 + 2n + 1$ to $(n + 1)$ $(n + 1)$ or $(n + 1)^2$. Now, since n is an odd number, $n + 1$ must be even (the number after every odd number is even). Thus, representing $n + 1$ as $2k$ where k is an integer ($2k$ is the standard representation for an even number), yields the expression: $(n + 1)^2 = (2k)^2$ or $4k^2$. Thus, $(n + 1)^2$ is a multiple of 4, and it must be divisible by 4. A number divisible by 4 must also be even, so (C) is the best choice. (Refreshers 604–607)

13. Choice C is correct. Convert to decimals. Then calculate the value of $\frac{3.50 + 4.25 + 2.25 + 3.25 + 4.00}{5}$. This equals $17.25 \div 5$, or 3.45. (Refresher 601)

14. Choice C is correct. If a number is divisible by 24, it must be divisible by 3 and 8. Of the five choices given, only Choice C is divisible by 8. Add the digits in 80,424 to get 18. As this is divisible by 3, the number is divisible by 3. The number, therefore, is divisible by 24. (Refresher 607)

15. Choice D is correct. If the boy is to average 65 for five subjects, the total of his five grades must be five times 65, or 325. The sum of the first four grades is $55 + 60 + 65 + 65$, or 245. Therefore, the fifth mark must be $325 - 245$, or 80. (Refresher 601)

16. Choice B is correct. If t is any integer, then $2t$ is an even number. Adding 3 to an even number always produces an odd number. Thus, $2t + 3$ is always odd. (Refresher 606)

17. Choice E is correct. Call the five numbers a, b, c, d, and e. Then the average is $\frac{(a + b + c + d + e)}{5}$. Since this must be even, $\frac{(a + b + c + d + e)}{5}$ $= 2k$, where k is an integer. Thus $a + b + c + d + e = 10k$. Therefore, the sum of the 5 numbers is divisible by 10, 2, and 5. Thus the first three choices are eliminated. If the five numbers were 1, 1, 1, 1, and 6, then the average would be 2. Thus, the average is even, but not all of the numbers are even. Thus, Choice D can be true. If all the numbers were odd, the sum would have to be odd. This contradicts the statement that the average is even. Thus, Choice E is the answer. (Refreshers 601, 607)

18. Choice E is correct. First, round off 23 and 79 to one significant digit. The numbers become 20 and 80. The product of these two numbers is 1,600, which rounded off to one significant digit is 2,000. (Refresher 611)

19. Choice D is correct. 0.7 squared is 0.49. Squaring 0.8 yields 0.64. Thus, the square root of $\frac{1}{2}$ must lie between 0.7 and 0.8. Take the number halfway between these two, 0.75, and square it. This number, 0.5625, is more than $\frac{1}{2}$, so the square root must be closer to 0.7 than to 0.8. An easier way to do problems concerning the square roots of 2 and 3 and their multiples is to memorize the values of these two square roots. The square root of 2 is about 1.414 (remember fourteen-fourteen), and the square root of three is about 1.732 (remember that 1732 was the year of George Washington's birth). Apply these as follows: $\frac{1}{2} = \frac{1}{4} \times 2$. Thus, $\sqrt{\frac{1}{2}} = \sqrt{\frac{1}{4}} \times \sqrt{2} = \frac{1}{2} \times 1.414 = 0.707$, which is very close to 0.7. (Refresher 612)

20. Choice B is correct. The prime numbers can be found by taking all the odd numbers between 56 and 100 (the even ones cannot be primes) and eliminating all the ones divisible by 3, by 5, or by 7. If a number under 100 is divisible by none of these, it must be prime. Thus, the only primes between 56 and 100 are 59, 61, 67, 71, 73, 79, 83, 89, and 97. (Refresher 608)

21. Choice C is correct. Since all the answer requires is an order-of-ten approximation, do not calculate the exact answer. Approximate the answer in the following manner: $\frac{1,000,000 \times 500,000}{1,000,000,000} = 500$. The only choice on the same order of magnitude is 600. (Refresher 609)

22. Choice A is correct. To round off 89.999, look at the number in the hundredths place. 9 is more than 5, so add 1 to the number in the tenths place and eliminate all of the digits to the right. Thus, we get 90.0. (Refresher 609)

23. Choice B is correct. The average of five numbers is found by dividing their sum by five. Thus, the sum is five times the average, so $S : M = 5 : 1$ (Refresher 601)

24. Choice E is correct. None of the first four choices is necessarily true. The sum, $5 + 7 + 9 + 13 + 15 = 49$, is not even, not divisible by 3, not divisible by 5, and not prime. (Refreshers 604, 607, 608)

25. Choice D is correct. Any even number can be written as $2m$, and any number divisible by 3 can be written as $3n$, where m and n are integers. Thus, E^2F^3 equals $(2m)^2(3n)^3 = (4m^2)(27n^3) = 108(m^2n^3)$, and 108 is the largest number by which E^2F^3 must be divisible. (Refresher 607)

26. Choice A is correct. The five consecutive even numbers can be represented as $n, n + 2, n + 4, n + 6,$ and $n + 8$. Taking the sum and dividing by five yields an average of $n + 4$. Thus, $n + 4 = 8$, the given average, and $n = 4$, the smallest number. (Refresher 601)

27. Choice E is correct. If a number is divisible by 23, then it is divisible by all of the factors of 23. But 23 is a prime with no factors except 1 and itself. Therefore, the correct choice is E. (Refresher 607)

28. Choice A is correct. To find the average, it is convenient to choose 92.0 as an approximate average and then find the average of the differences between the actual numbers and 92.0. Thus, add up: $(-0.6) + (-0.5) + (-0.4) + (-0.3) + (-0.3) + (0.0) + 0.1 + 0.3 + 0.3 + 0.4 = -1.0$; divide this by 10 (the number of quantities to be averaged) to obtain -0.1. Finally, add this to the approximate average, 92.0, to obtain a final average of 91.9. (Refresher 601)

29. Choice A is correct. To determine if a number is divisible by 11, take each of the digits separately and, beginning with either end, subtract the second from the first, add the following digit, subtract the next one, add the one after that, etc. If this result is divisible by 11, the entire number is. Thus, because $3 - 0 + 2 - 1 + 7 = 11$, we know that 30,217 is divisible by 11. Using the same method, we find that the other four choices are not divisible by 11. (Refresher 607)

30. Choice B is correct. This is simply an order-of-ten approximation, so round off the numbers and work the following problem. $(1.0)(20.0)(0.01) = 0.20$. The actual answer is closest to 0.2. (Refresher 611)

31. Choice E is correct. Represent the three numbers as $8p$, $8q$, and $8r$, respectively. Thus, their sum is $8p + 8q + 8r$, and their average is $\frac{(8p + 8q + 8r)}{3}$. This need not even be a whole number. For example, the average of 8, 16, and 32 is $\frac{56}{3}$, or $18\frac{2}{3}$. (Refreshers 601, 607)

32. Choice A is correct. To be divisible by 24, a number must be divisible by both 3 and 8. Only 13,944 and 15,966 are divisible by 3; of these, only 13,944 is divisible by 8 ($13,944 = 24 \times 581$). (Refresher 607)

33. Choice B is correct. The approximate square root of each of these numbers is 13. Merely divide each of these numbers by the primes up to 13, which are 2, 3, 5, 7, and 11. The only number not divisible by any of these primes is 149. (Refreshers 608, 612)

34. Choice C is correct. Call the first odd integer $2k + 1$. (This is the standard algebraic expression for an odd integer.) Thus, the next 3 odd integers are $2k + 3, 2k + 5,$ and $2k + 7$. (Each one is 2 more than the previous one.) The sum of these integers is $(2k + 1) + (2k + 3) + (2k + 5) + (2k + 7) = 8k + 16$. This can be written as $8(k + 2)$, which is divisible by 8, but not necessarily by 16. (Refreshers 606, 607)

35. Choice C is correct. By squaring the five choices, it is evident that the two closest choices are $\left(\frac{3}{4}\right)^2 = 0.5625$ and $\left(\frac{4}{5}\right)^2 = 0.64$. Squaring the number halfway between $\frac{3}{4}$ and $\frac{4}{5}$ gives $(0.775)^2 = 0.600625$. This is greater than $\frac{3}{5}$, so the square root of $\frac{3}{5}$ must be closer to $\frac{3}{4}$ than to $\frac{4}{5}$. (Refresher 612)

36. Choice D is correct. Let the even number be $2k$, where k is an integer, and let the odd number be $2m + 1$, where m is an integer. Thus, the sum is $2k + (2m + 1)$, $2k + 2m + 1$, or $2(k + m) + 1$. Now $k + m$ is an integer since k and m are integers. Call $k + m$ by another name, p. Thus, $2(k + m) + 1$ is $2p + 1$, which is the representation of an odd number. (Refreshers 604, 606)

MATH REFRESHER SESSION 7

Tables, Charts, and Graphs

Introduction

701. *Graphs* and *charts* show the relationship of numbers and quantities in visual form. By looking at a graph, you can see at a glance the relationship between two or more sets of information. If such information were presented in written form, it would be hard to read and understand.

Here are some things to remember when doing problems based on graphs or charts:

1. Understand what you are being asked to do before you begin figuring.

2. Check the dates and types of information required. Be sure that you are looking in the proper columns, and on the proper lines, for the information you need.

3. Check the units required. Be sure that your answer is in thousands, millions, or whatever the question calls for.

4. In computing averages, be sure that you add the figures you need and no others, and that you divide by the correct number of years or other units.

5. Be careful in computing problems asking for percentages.

    (a) Remember that to convert a decimal into a percent you must multiply it by 100. For example, 0.04 is 4%.

    (b) Be sure that you can distinguish between such quantities as 1% (1 percent) and .01% (one one-hundredth of 1 percent), whether in numerals or in words.

    (c) Remember that if quantity X is greater than quantity Y, and the question asks what percent quantity X is of quantity Y, the answer must be greater than 100 percent.

Tables and Charts

702. A table or chart shows data arranged in rows and columns. Each column usually is headed by a brief description of the type of data in the column, and the far-left column lists items for which these different data points are displayed in the rows.

Example:

Test Score	Number of Students
90	2
85	1
80	1
60	3

Example: How many students took the test?

Solution: To find out the number of students who took the test, just add up the numbers in the column marked "Number of Students." That is, add $2 + 1 + 1 + 3 = 7$.

Example: What was the difference in scores between the highest and the lowest score?

Solution: First look at the highest score: 90. Then look at the lowest score: 60. Now calculate the difference: $90 - 60 = 30$.

Example: What was the *median* score?

Solution: The median score means the score that is in the *middle* of all the scores. That is, there are just as many scores above the median as below it.

So in this example, the scores are 90, 90 (there are two 90s), 85, 80, and 60, 60, 60 (there are three 60s). So we have:

$$90$$
$$90$$
$$85$$
$$80$$
$$60$$
$$60$$
$$60$$

80 is right in the middle. That is, there are three scores above it and three scores below it. So 80 is the median.

Example: What was the *mean* score?

Solution: The mean score is defined as the *average* score. That is, it is the

$$\frac{\text{sum of the scores}}{\text{total number of scores}}$$

The sum of the scores is 90 + 90 + 85 + 80 + 60 + 60 + 60 = 525. The total number of scores is 2 + 1 + 1 + 3 = 7, so divide 7 into 525 to get the average: 75.

Graphs

703. To read a graph, you must know what *scale* the graph has been drawn to. Somewhere on the face of the graph will be an explanation of what each division of the graph means. Sometimes the divisions will be labeled. At other times, this information will be given in a small box called a *scale* or *legend*. For instance, a map, which is a specialized kind of graph, will always carry a scale or legend on its face telling you such information as $1'' = 100$ miles or $\frac{1''}{4} = 2$ miles.

Bar Graphs

704. A *bar graph* shows how information is compared by using broad lines, called *bars*, of varying lengths. Sometimes single lines are used as well. Bar graphs are good for showing a quick comparison of the information involved; however, the bars are difficult to read accurately unless the end of the bar falls exactly on one of the divisions of the scale. If the end of the bar falls between divisions of the scale, it is not easy to arrive at the precise figure represented by the bar. In bar graphs, the bars can run either vertically or horizontally. The sample bar graph following is a horizontal graph.

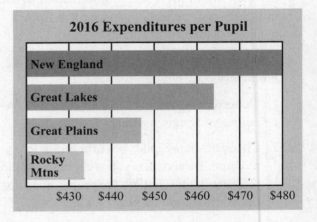

The individual bars in this kind of graph may carry a label within the bar, as in this example. The label may also appear alongside each bar. The scale used on the bars may appear along one axis, as in the example, or it may be noted somewhere on the face of the graph. Each numbered space on the *x*-axis, or horizontal axis, represents an expenditure of $10 per pupil. A wide variety of questions may be answered by a bar graph, such as:

1. Which area of the country spends least per pupil? Rocky Mountains.

2. How much does the New England area spend per pupil? $480.

3. How much less does the Great Plains spend per pupil than the Great Lakes?

$$\$464 - 447 = \frac{\$17}{\text{pupil}}.$$

4. How much more does New England spend on a pupil than the Rocky Mountains area?

$$\$480 - 433 = \frac{\$47}{\text{pupil}}$$

Circle Graphs

705. A *circle graph* or *pie chart* shows how an entire quantity has been divided or apportioned. The circle represents 100 percent of the quantity; the different parts into which the whole has been divided are shown by sections, or wedges, of the circle. Circle graphs are good for showing how money is distributed or collected, and for this reason they are widely used in financial graphing. The information is usually presented on the face of each section, telling you exactly what the section stands for and the value of that section in comparison to the other parts of the graph.

Sources of Income—Public Colleges of the U.S.*

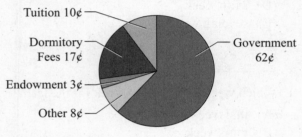

*Amounts represent cents per dollar of income.

The circle graph above indicates where the money originates that is used to maintain public colleges in the United States. The sizes of the sections tell you at a glance which source is most important (government) and which is least important (endowments). The sections total 100¢, or $1.00. This graph may be used to answer the following questions:

1. What is the most important source of income to the public colleges? Government.

2. What part of the revenue dollar comes from tuition? 10¢.

3. Dormitory fees bring in how many times the money that endowments bring in? $5\frac{2}{3}$ times $\left(\frac{17}{3} = 5\frac{2}{3}\right)$.

4. What is the least important source of revenue to public colleges? Endowments.

Line Graphs

706. *Line graphs* display the relationship of two types of information, one arranged vertically on a *y*-axis and the other horizontally on an *x*-axis. When we are asked to compare two values, we subtract the smaller from the larger.

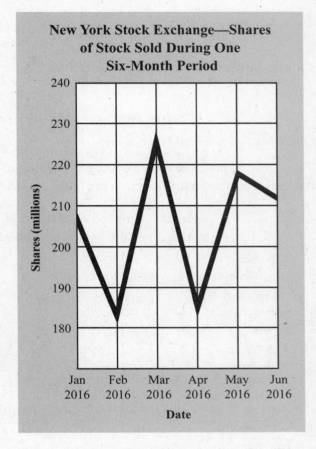

Our sample line graph represents the total shares of stock sold on the New York Stock Exchange between January and June of 2016. The months are placed along the *x*-axis, while the sales, in units of 1,000,000 shares, are placed along the *y*-axis.

1. How many shares were sold in March? 225,000,000.

2. What is the trend of stock sales between April and May? The volume of sales rose.

3. Compare the share sales in January and February. 25,000,000 fewer shares were sold in February.

4. During which months of the period was the increase in sales largest? February to March.

SESSION 7 PRACTICE TEST

Tables, Charts, and Graphs

Correct answers and solutions follow this test.

Table Test

Questions 1–5 are based on this table.

The following table is a record of the performance of a baseball team for the first seven weeks of the season.

	Games Won	Games Lost	Total No. of Games Played
First week	5	3	8
Second week	4	4	16
Third week	5	2	23
Fourth week	6	3	32
Fifth week	4	2	38
Sixth week	3	3	44
Seventh week	2	4	50

1. How many games did the team win during the first seven weeks?

   (A) 32
   (B) 29
   (C) 25
   (D) 21
   (E) 50

   A B C D E
   ○ ○ ○ ○ ○

2. What percent of the games did the team win?

   (A) 75%
   (B) 60%
   (C) 58%
   (D) 29%
   (E) 80%

   A B C D E
   ○ ○ ○ ○ ○

3. According to the table, which week was the worst for the team?

   (A) second week
   (B) fourth week
   (C) fifth week
   (D) sixth week
   (E) seventh week

   A B C D E
   ○ ○ ○ ○ ○

4. Which week was the best week for the team?

   (A) first week
   (B) third week
   (C) fourth week
   (D) fifth week
   (E) sixth week

   A B C D E
   ○ ○ ○ ○ ○

5. If there are fifty more games to play in the season, how many more games must the team win to end up winning 70% of the games?

   (A) 39
   (B) 35
   (C) 41
   (D) 34
   (E) 32

   A B C D E
   ○ ○ ○ ○ ○

Pie Chart Test

Questions 6–10 are based on this pie chart.

Population by Region

Total = 191.3 million = 100%

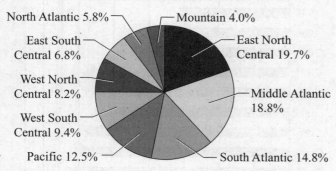

North Atlantic 5.8% — Mountain 4.0%

East South Central 6.8% — East North Central 19.7%

West North Central 8.2%

Middle Atlantic 18.8%

West South Central 9.4%

Pacific 12.5% — South Atlantic 14.8%

6. Which region is the most populated region?

(A) East North Central
(B) Middle Atlantic
(C) South Atlantic
(D) Pacific
(E) North Atlantic

A B C D E
○ ○ ○ ○ ○

7. What part of the entire population lives in the Mountain region?

(A) $\frac{1}{10}$

(B) $\frac{1}{30}$

(C) $\frac{1}{50}$

(D) $\frac{1}{25}$

(E) $\frac{1}{8}$

A B C D E
○ ○ ○ ○ ○

8. What is the approximate population in the Pacific region?

(A) 20 million
(B) 24 million
(C) 30 million
(D) 28 million
(E) 15 million

A B C D E
○ ○ ○ ○ ○

9. Approximately how many more people live in the Middle Atlantic region than in the South Atlantic?

(A) 4.0 million
(B) 7.7 million
(C) 5.2 million
(D) 9.3 million
(E) 8.5 million

A B C D E
○ ○ ○ ○ ○

10. What is the total population in all the regions combined?

(A) 73.3 million
(B) 100.0 million
(C) 191.3 million
(D) 126.8 million
(E) 98.5 million

A B C D E
○ ○ ○ ○ ○

Line Graph Test

Questions 11–15 are based on this line graph.

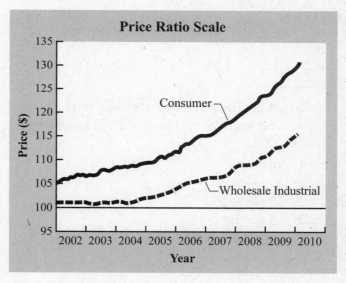

Price Ratio Scale

Consumer

Wholesale Industrial

11. On the ratio scale, what was the consumer price at the end of 2005?

(A) 95
(B) 100
(C) 105
(D) 110
(E) 115

A B C D E
○ ○ ○ ○ ○

12. During what year did consumer prices rise fastest?

(A) 2003
(B) 2005
(C) 2007
(D) 2008
(E) 2009

A B C D E
○ ○ ○ ○ ○

13. When wholesale and industrial prices were recorded as 110, consumer prices were recorded as

(A) between 125 and 120
(B) between 120 and 115
(C) between 115 and 110
(D) between 110 and 105
(E) between 105 and 100

A B C D E
○ ○ ○ ○ ○

14. For the 8 years from 2002 to 2009 inclusive, the average increase in consumer prices was

(A) 1 point
(B) 2 points
(C) 3 points
(D) 4 points
(E) 5 points

A B C D E
○ ○ ○ ○ ○

15. The percentage increase in wholesale and industrial prices between the beginning of 2002 and the end of 2009 was

(A) 1 percent
(B) 5 percent
(C) 10 percent
(D) 15 percent
(E) less than 1 percent

A B C D E
○ ○ ○ ○ ○

Bar Graph Test

Questions 16–18 are based on this bar graph.

Soft Plywood Shows Growth

Billion Square Feet

16. What was the approximate ratio of soft plywood produced in 1998 as compared with that produced in 2007?

(A) 1 : 1
(B) 2 : 3
(C) 4 : 7
(D) 3 : 4
(E) 1 : 3

A B C D E
○ ○ ○ ○ ○

17. For the years 1998 through 2003, excluding 2002, how many billion square feet of plywood were produced altogether?

(A) 23.2
(B) 29.7
(C) 34.1
(D) 49.8
(E) 52.6

A B C D E
○ ○ ○ ○ ○

18. Between which consecutive odd years and between which consecutive even years did plywood production have the greatest increase?

(A) 2005 and 2007; 1998 and 2000
(B) 2003 and 2005; 2004 and 2006
(C) 1999 and 2001; 2000 and 2002
(D) 2001 and 2003; 2000 and 2002
(E) 2003 and 2005; 2002 and 2004

A B C D E
○ ○ ○ ○ ○

Cumulative Graph Test

Questions 19–23 are based on this cumulative graph.

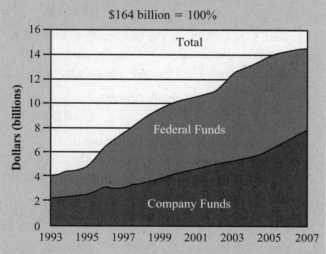

Spending for Research & Development (R&D) by Type of Research, 2007

$164 billion = 100%

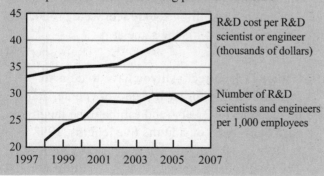

Scientists and engineers engaged full time in R&D and full-time equivalent of those working part time in R&D.

R&D cost per R&D scientist or engineer (thousands of dollars)

Number of R&D scientists and engineers per 1,000 employees

19. About how much in government funds was spent for research and development in 2007?

(A) $4 billion
(B) $6 billion

(C) $12 billion
(D) $16 billion
(E) $24 billion

A B C D E
○ ○ ○ ○ ○

20. In 2007, about what percent of the total spending in research and development was company funds?

(A) 27%
(B) 37%
(C) 47%
(D) 57%
(E) 67%

A B C D E
○ ○ ○ ○ ○

21. What was the change in the relative number of research and development scientists and engineers with respect to all employees from 2004 to 2005?

(A) 10%
(B) 5%
(C) 2%
(D) 3%
(E) 0%

A B C D E
○ ○ ○ ○ ○

22. What was the increase in company funds in research and development from 1993 to 2007?

(A) $12 billion
(B) $6 billion
(C) $8 billion
(D) $4 billion
(E) $14 billion

A B C D E
○ ○ ○ ○ ○

23. What was the percent of increase in the company funds spent on research and development from 1993 to 2007?

(A) 100%
(B) 50%
(C) 300%
(D) 400%
(E) 1,000%

A B C D E
○ ○ ○ ○ ○

Answer Key for Session 7 Practice Test

1. B	7. D	13. A	19. B
2. C	8. B	14. C	20. D
3. E	9. B	15. D	21. E
4. B	10. C	16. C	22. B
5. C	11. D	17. D	23. C
6. A	12. E	18. E	

Answers and Solutions for Session 7 Practice Test

1. Choice B is correct. To find the total number of games won, add the number of games won for all the weeks, $5 + 4 + 5 + 6 + 4 + 3 + 2 = 29$. (Refresher 702)

2. Choice C is correct. The team won 29 out of 50 games, or 58%. (Refresher 702)

3. Choice E is correct. The seventh week was the only week in which the team lost more games than it won. (Refresher 702)

4. Choice B is correct. During the third week the team won 5 games and lost 2, or it won about 70% of the games that week. Compared with the winning percentages for other weeks, the third week's was the highest. (Refresher 702)

5. Choice C is correct. To win 70% of all the games, the team must win 70 out of 100. Since it won 29 games out of the first 50 games, it must win $70 - 29$, or 41 games out of the next 50 games. (Refresher 702)

6. Choice A is correct. East North Central, with 19.7% of the total population, has the largest population. (Refresher 705)

7. Choice D is correct. The Mountain region has 4.0% of the population. 4.0% is $\frac{1}{25}$. (Refresher 705)

8. Choice B is correct. Pacific has 12.5% of the population. 12.5% of 191.3 million is $.125 \times 191.3$, or about 24 million. (Refresher 705)

9. Choice B is correct. Middle Atlantic has 18.8% and South Atlantic has 14.8% of the population. So, Middle Atlantic has 4.0% more. 4.0% of 191.3 million is $.04 \times 191.3$, or about 7.7 million. (Refresher 705)

10. Choice C is correct. All the regions combined have 100% of the population, or 191.3 million. (Refresher 705)

11. Choice D is correct. Drawing a vertical line at the end of 2005, we reach the consumer price graph at about the 110 level. (Refresher 706)

12. Choice E is correct. The slope of the consumer graph is clearly steepest in 2009. (Refresher 706)

13. Choice A is correct. Wholesale and industrial prices were about 110 at the beginning of 2009, when consumer prices were between 120 and 125. (Refresher 706)

14. Choice C is correct. At the beginning of 2002 consumer prices were about 105; at the end of 2009 they were about 130. The average increase is $\frac{130 - 105}{8} = \frac{25}{8}$, or about 3 points. (Refresher 706)

15. Choice D is correct. At the beginning of 2002 wholesale prices were about 100; at the end of 2009 they were about 115. The percent increase is about $\frac{115 - 100}{100} \times 100\%$, or 15%. (Refresher 706)

16. Choice C is correct. To answer this question, you will have to measure the bars. In 1998, about 8 billion square feet of plywood were produced. In 2007, about 14 billion square feet were produced. The ratio of $8 : 14$ is the same as $4 : 7$. (Refresher 704)

17. Choice D is correct. All you have to do is to measure the bar for each year—of course, don't include the 2002 bar—and estimate the length of each bar. Then you add the five lengths. $1998 = 8$; $1999 = 10$; $2000 = 10$; $2001 = 10$; $2003 = 12$. The total is close to 50. (Refresher 704)

18. Choice E is correct. The jumps from 2001 to 2003, from 2003 to 2005, and from 2007 to 2009 were all about 2 billion square feet, so you can eliminate answers A and C. The jump from 2002 to 2004 was from 11 to 13.5 = 2.5 billion square feet. None of the other choices shows such broad jumps.

(Refresher 704)

19. Choice B is correct. Total spending was about $14 billion, and company spending was about $8 billion. So, government spending was about $6 billion.

(Refresher 706)

20. Choice D is correct. Company funds totaled about $8 billion, and the total funds were about $14 billion. So, company funds were $\frac{4}{7}$ of total funds, or 57%.

(Refresher 706)

21. Choice E is correct. The graph showing the relative employment of research and development scientists and engineers was horizontal between 2004 and 2005. This means no change, or 0%.

(Refresher 706)

22. Choice B is correct. Company funds totaled $8 billion in 2007 and $2 billion in 1993. The increase was $6 billion.

(Refresher 706)

23. Choice C is correct. Company funds totaled $2 billion in 1993, and the increase from 1993 to 2007 was $6 billion, or 300% of $2 billion.

(Refresher 706)

MATH REFRESHER SESSION 8

Modern Math: Sets, Relations, Solution Sets, Axioms, Closed Sets, and Mathematical Symbols

Sets

801. A *set* is a collection of anything: numbers, letters, objects, etc. The members, or elements, of the set are written between braces like this: {1, 2, 3, 4, 5}. The elements of this set are simply the numbers 1, 2, 3, 4, and 5. Another example of a set is {apples, peaches, pears}. Two sets are equal if they have the same elements. The order in which the elements of the set are listed does not matter. Thus {1, 2, 3, 4, 5} = {5, 4, 3, 2, 1}. We can use one letter to stand for a whole set; for example, $A = \{1, 2, 3, 4, 5\}$.

802. To find the *union* of two sets:

Write down every member in both of the two sets. The union of two sets is a new set. The union of sets A and B is written $A \cup B$.

For example: If $A = \{1, 2, 3, 4\}$ and $B = \{2, 4, 6\}$, find $A \cup B$. All the elements in both A and B are 1, 2, 3, 4, and 6. Therefore $A \cup B = \{1, 2, 3, 4, 6\}$.

803. To find the *intersection* of two sets:

Write down every member that the two sets have in common. The intersection of the sets A and B is a set written $A \cap B$.

Example: If $A = \{1, 2, 3, 4\}$ and $B = \{2, 4, 6\}$, find $A \cap B$. The elements in both A and B are 2 and 4. Therefore $A \cap B = \{2, 4\}$.

If two sets have no elements in common, then their intersection is the null or empty set, written as $\varnothing$ or { }.

Example: The intersection of {1, 3, 5, 7} with {2, 4, 6, 8} is $\varnothing$ since they have no members in common.

804. To perform several union and intersection operations, first operate on sets within parentheses.

Example: If $A = \{1, 2, 3\}$ and $B = \{2, 3, 4, 5, 6\}$ and $C = \{1, 4, 6\}$ find $A \cup (B \cap C)$.

First we find $B \cap C$ by listing all the elements in both B and C. $B \cap C = \{4, 6\}$.

Then $A \cup (B \cap C)$ is just the set of all members in at least one of the sets A and {4, 6}.

Therefore, $A \cup (B \cap C) = \{1, 2, 3, 4, 6\}$.

805. A *subset* of a set is a set, all of whose members are in the original set. Thus, {1, 2, 3} is a subset of the set {1, 2, 3, 4, 5}. Note that the null set (a set with no members) is a subset of every set, and also that every set is a subset of itself. In general, a set with n elements has 2^n subsets. For example: How many subsets does $\{x, y, z\}$ have? This set has 3 elements and therefore 2^3, or 8 subsets.

Relations

806. When the elements of a set are ordered pairs, then the set is called a *relation*. An ordered pair is written (x, y). The order of the two components of the ordered pair matters. Therefore the ordered pairs (x, y) and (y, x) are not equal.

The *domain* of a relation is the set of the first components of the ordered pairs. The *range* of a relation is the set of the second components of the ordered pairs. A relation is a *function* if each element of the domain occurs only once as a first component.

Example: $R = \{(a, b), (a, c), (b, c), (c, d)\}$. Find the domain and range of R. Is the relation R a function?

The domain is the set of first components. These are a, a, b, and c, so that the domain is $\{a, b, c\}$. The range is the set of second components. These are b, c, c, and d. Thus the range is $\{b, c, d\}$. R is not a function since the letter a occurred twice as a first component.

807. The *inverse* of a relation is the relation with all the ordered pairs reversed. Thus, the inverse of $R = \{(1, 2), (3, 4), (5, 6)\}$ is $\{(2, 1), (4, 3), (6, 5)\}$.

Example: Find the domain of the inverse of $\{(m, n), (p, q), (r, s)\}$.

The domain of the inverse is simply the range of the original relation. So, the domain of the inverse is $\{n, q, s\}$. Similarly, the range of the inverse is the domain of the original relation.

Solution Sets

808. Sets can be used to indicate solutions to equations or inequalities. These sets are called *solution sets*. A solution set is just the set of the solutions to an equation. We may also demand that the elements of the solution set meet another condition. Thus, the solution set for the equation $10x - 5 = 0$ is simply $\left\{\frac{1}{2}\right\}$, since only $x = \frac{1}{2}$ solves the equation.

If we demanded that the solution set consist only of whole numbers, then the solution set would be $\varnothing$ since no whole number solves this equation.

The solution set in the positive integers (whole numbers) for the inequality $x < 4$ is $\{1, 2, 3\}$ since these are the only positive integers less than 4.

> When finding a solution set, first solve the equation or inequality and then use only the solutions that satisfy the condition required.

Example: Find the solution set in the positive integers for the inequality $4x < x + 13$.

First, $4x < x + 13$ means $3x < 13$, or $x < 4\frac{1}{3}$. Since x must be a positive integer, the solution set is the set of positive integers less than $4\frac{1}{3}$, or $\{1, 2, 3, 4\}$. Sometimes we use the following notation:

$$R = \{x : x \geq 10\}$$

This would be read as "the set of all x such that x is greater than or equal to 10."

Axioms

809. On your test, there may be a list of *axioms*, or rules, about arithmetical operations with numbers. The list will contain examples of the use of the axioms. Problems will then ask you to identify which axiom is used to make a specific statement. An example of these axioms is the distributive law. A problem may ask you: Which axiom is used to justify $3(4 + 1) = 3 \cdot 4 + 3 \cdot 1$? The *distributive* axiom is used to justify this statement.

Another axiom is the *commutative* axiom of addition and multiplication. The equations $5 + 3 = 3 + 5$ and $5 \cdot 3 = 3 \cdot 5$ illustrate these rules.

The last two rules are the *associative* axioms of addition and multiplication. Examples of these operations are the equations $(3 + 5) + 6 = 3 + (5 + 6)$ and $(3 \cdot 5)6 = 3(5 \cdot 6)$.

Closed Sets

810. A set is called *closed* under an operation if any two members of the set constitute an element of the set. Consider, for example, the set $\{0, 1\}$. This set is closed under the operation of multiplication because $0 \times 0 = 0$, $1 \times 1 = 1$, and $0 \times 1 = 0$. Note that in order for the set to be closed, the elements multiplied by themselves must also be elements of the set $\{0 \times 0 = 0$ and $1 \times 1 = 1\}$.

SESSION 8 PRACTICE TEST

Modern Math: Sets, Relations, Solution Sets, Axioms, Closed Sets, and Mathematical Symbols

Correct answers and solutions follow this test.

Sets Test

1. Which set equals {1, 2, 3, 4}?

   (A) {a, b, c, d}
   (B) {4, 5, 6, 7}
   (C) {1, 3, 5, 7, 9}
   (D) {4, 3, 2, 1}
   (E) none of the above

   A B C D E
   ○ ○ ○ ○ ○

2. $A = \{1, 2, 3, 4, 5\}$. $B = \{2, 4, 6, 8\}$. $A \cap B$ equals

   (A) {1, 2, 3, 4, 5, 6, 7, 8}
   (B) {2, 4}
   (C) {1, 2, 3, 4, 5, 6, 8, 10}
   (D) {9}
   (E) {1, 2, 6, 8}

   A B C D E
   ○ ○ ○ ○ ○

3. $C = \{a, b, c, d\}$. $D = \{3, 4, b\}$. $C \cup D$ equals

   (A) {a, b, c, d, 3, 4}
   (B) {b}
   (C) {3, 4}
   (D) {b, d, 4}
   (E) {a, c, 3, 4}

   A B C D E
   ○ ○ ○ ○ ○

4. $A = \{1, 2, 3\}$. $B = \{2, 3, 4\}$. $C = \{3, 4, 5\}$. $(A \cap B) \cap C$ equals

   (A) {1, 2, 3, 4, 5}
   (B) {1, 3, 5}
   (C) {2, 3, 4}
   (D) {1}
   (E) {3}

   A B C D E
   ○ ○ ○ ○ ○

5. How many elements are there in the set of even integers from 2 through 10 inclusive?

   (A) 3
   (B) 5
   (C) 7
   (D) 9
   (E) 10

   A B C D E
   ○ ○ ○ ○ ○

6. How many subsets does {a, b, c} have?

   (A) 6
   (B) 7
   (C) 8
   (D) 9
   (E) 10

   A B C D E
   ○ ○ ○ ○ ○

Use the following information to answer Questions 7–10.

$A = \{1, 3, 2, 5\}$. $B = \{2, 4, 6\}$. $C = \{1, 3, 5\}$.

7. $(A \cup B) \cap C$ equals

   (A) {1, 2, 3}
   (B) {2, 4, 5}
   (C) {1, 2, 5}
   (D) {1, 3, 5}
   (E) {3, 4, 5}

   A B C D E
   ○ ○ ○ ○ ○

8. $(A \cap B) \cup C$ equals

   (A) {1, 2, 3, 5}
   (B) {4}
   (C) {2, 4}
   (D) {1, 3, 5}
   (E) {1, 2, 3, 4, 5}

   A B C D E
   ○ ○ ○ ○ ○

9. How many subsets does $A \cup (B \cup C)$ have?

   (A) 2
   (B) 4
   (C) 16
   (D) 32
   (E) 64

   A B C D E
   ○ ○ ○ ○ ○

10. Which set is not a subset of $A \cup C$?

    (A) ∅
    (B) A
    (C) C
    (D) {4}
    (E) {1, 2, 5}

    A B C D E
    ○ ○ ○ ○ ○

Relations Test

11. Which of the following sets are relations?

    I.   {(1, 2), (a, c)}
    II. {(3, 8), (8, 3)}
    III. {(1, a), (2, c)}

    (A) I only
    (B) II only
    (C) III only
    (D) I and III only
    (E) I, II, and III

    A B C D E
    ○ ○ ○ ○ ○

12. Which of the following relations equals the relation {(a, b), (1, 2), (x, y)}?

    (A) {(a, b), (1, x), (2, y)}
    (B) {(x, y), (a, b), (1, 2)}
    (C) {(12, xy), (a, b)}
    (D) {(b, a), (2, 1), (x, y)}
    (E) none of the above

    A B C D E
    ○ ○ ○ ○ ○

13. What is the range of {(1, 2), (3, 4), (5, 6)}?

    (A) {1, 2, 3, 4, 5, 6}
    (B) {(1, 2)}
    (C) {(1, 2), (3, 4), (5, 6)}

    (D) {1, 3, 5}
    (E) none of the above

    A B C D E
    ○ ○ ○ ○ ○

14. What is the domain of {(1, 2), (2, 1), (1, 5)}?

    (A) {1, 2}
    (B) {(1, 2)}
    (C) {1, 2, 5}
    (D) {8}
    (E) {3}

    A B C D E
    ○ ○ ○ ○ ○

15. Which relation is a function?

    (A) {(1, 1), (2, 2), (3, 3)}
    (B) {(1, 1), (1, 2), (1, 3)}
    (C) {(a, b), (b, a), (b, b)}
    (D) {(1, 3), (1, 5), (1, 7)}
    (E) {(1, a), (2, b), (2, 1)}

    A B C D E
    ○ ○ ○ ○ ○

16. What is the inverse of {(1, 2), (3, 6), (4, 2)}?

    (A) {1, 2, 3, 4, 5, 6}
    (B) {(1, 3), (1, 4), (1, 6)}
    (C) {(2, 1), (6, 3), (2, 4)}
    (D) {(3, 2), (6, 4), (4, 1)}
    (E) none of the above

    A B C D E
    ○ ○ ○ ○ ○

17. Which relation equals its inverse?

    (A) {(1, 2)}
    (B) {(1, 2), (3, 3)}
    (C) {(1, 2), (3, 3), (2, 1)}
    (D) {(4, 4), (2, 3), (3, 4)}
    (E) {(1, 2), (2, 3), (3, 1)}

    A B C D E
    ○ ○ ○ ○ ○

18. What is the domain of the inverse of {(a, 1), (b, 3), (c, 5)}?

    (A) {a, b, c}
    (B) {1, 3, 5}
    (C) {1, a, 2, b, 3, c}

(D) {a, 5}
(E) {(a, 5)}

A B C D E
○ ○ ○ ○ ○

19. The inverse of which of the following is a function?

(A) {(1, 1), (1, 2), (1, 3)}
(B) {(a, 0), (b, 0), (c, 0)}
(C) {(a, j), (r, j), (a, r)}
(D) {(1, 2), (2, 3), (3, 2)}
(E) {(u, v), (w, v), (y, x)}

A B C D E
○ ○ ○ ○ ○

20. What is the range of the inverse of {(P, Q), (R, S), (T, V)}?

(A) {1, 2, 3}
(B) {P, Q, R}
(C) {Q, S, V}
(D) {P, R, T}
(E) {P, Q, R, S, T, V}

A B C D E
○ ○ ○ ○ ○

Solution Sets Test

Find the solution sets in Questions 21–23.

21. $2x - 4 = 0$

(A) {2}
(B) {4}
(C) {−4}
(D) {0}
(E) {2, −4}

A B C D E
○ ○ ○ ○ ○

22. $x + 9 = 3 - x$

(A) {−3}
(B) {9}
(C) {3}
(D) {−3, 9}
(E) ∅

A B C D E
○ ○ ○ ○ ○

23. $(x + 2)(x - 1) = 0$

(A) {−1}
(B) {−2, −1}
(C) {1}
(D) {−2, 1}
(E) {2, 1}

A B C D E
○ ○ ○ ○ ○

Find the solution sets in the positive integers for Questions 24–27.

24. $x + 7 = 9$

(A) {7}
(B) {9}
(C) {16}
(D) {2}
(E) {9, 7}

A B C D E
○ ○ ○ ○ ○

25. $x - 3 = -4$

(A) {−3}
(B) {−4}
(C) {1}
(D) {−1}
(E) ∅

A B C D E
○ ○ ○ ○ ○

26. $x > 2x - 4$

(A) {1}
(B) {2, 3}
(C) {1, 2, 3}
(D) {1, 2, 3, 4}
(E) ∅

A B C D E
○ ○ ○ ○ ○

27. $(x + 1)(x - 4) = 0$

(A) {4}
(B) {1, 4}
(C) {−1, 1, 4}
(D) {0}
(E) {−4}

A B C D E
○ ○ ○ ○ ○

Find the solution set in the negative integers for Questions 28–30.

28. $(x + 3)(x + 6) = 0$

    (A) {3, 6}
    (B) {−3, −6}
    (C) {−3}
    (D) {−6}
    (E) ∅

    A B C D E
    ○ ○ ○ ○ ○

29. $(2x + 7)(x − 3) = 0$

    (A) {2, 7, −3}
    (B) {−3}
    (C) $\left\{-3\frac{1}{2}\right\}$
    (D) {2}
    (E) ∅

    A B C D E
    ○ ○ ○ ○ ○

30. $10 + 2x > 0$

    (A) {−1, −2}
    (B) {−10, −8, −6}
    (C) {−1, −2, −3, −4, −5}
    (D) {−1, −2, −3, −4}
    (E) {1, 2, 3, 4}

    A B C D E
    ○ ○ ○ ○ ○

Axioms Test

Use the following axioms to answer Questions 31–35.

I. Commutative axiom for addition:
    $a + b = b + a$

II. Associative axiom for addition:
    $a + (b + c) = (a + b) + c$

III. Commutative axiom for multiplication:
    $ab = ba$

IV. Associative axiom for multiplication:
    $(ab)c = a(bc)$

V. Distributive axiom:
    $a(b + c) = ab + ac$

In Questions 31–34, which axiom can be used to justify the given statements?

31. $3 \cdot 5 = 5 \cdot 3$

    (A) I
    (B) II
    (C) III
    (D) IV
    (E) V

    A B C D E
    ○ ○ ○ ○ ○

32. $(3 + 7) + 4 = 3 + (7 + 4)$

    (A) I
    (B) II
    (C) III
    (D) IV
    (E) V

    A B C D E
    ○ ○ ○ ○ ○

33. $(2 \cdot 5) \cdot 3 = (5 \cdot 2) \cdot 3$

    (A) I
    (B) II
    (C) III
    (D) IV
    (E) V

    A B C D E
    ○ ○ ○ ○ ○

34. $3(6 + 2) = 18 + 6$

    (A) I
    (B) II
    (C) III
    (D) IV
    (E) V

    A B C D E
    ○ ○ ○ ○ ○

35. Which two axioms can be used to justify the following:

    $5(3 + 4) = 20 + 15?$

    (A) I and II
    (B) I and III
    (C) III and V
    (D) IV and V
    (E) V and I

    A B C D E
    ○ ○ ○ ○ ○

Answer Key for Session 8 Practice Test

1. D	10. D	19. A	28. B
2. B	11. E	20. D	29. E
3. A	12. B	21. A	30. D
4. E	13. E	22. A	31. C
5. B	14. A	23. D	32. B
6. C	15. A	24. D	33. C
7. D	16. C	25. E	34. E
8. A	17. C	26. C	35. E
9. E	18. B	27. A	

Answers and Solutions for Session 8 Practice Test

1. Choice D is correct. $\{4, 3, 2, 1\}$ contains the same elements as $\{1, 2, 3, 4\}$. Since the order does not matter, the sets are equal. (Refresher 801)

2. Choice B is correct. $A \cap B$ means the set of elements in both A and B, or $\{2, 4\}$. (Refresher 803)

3. Choice A is correct. $C \cup D$ means the set of elements in at least one of C and D, or $\{a, b, c, d, 3, 4\}$. (Refresher 802)

4. Choice E is correct. $(A \cap B) \cap C$ is the set of elements in all three sets. Only 3 is a member of all three sets, so $(A \cap B) \cap C = \{3\}$. (Refresher 803)

5. Choice B is correct. The set of even integers from 2 through 10 inclusive is $\{2, 4, 6, 8, 10\}$, which has 5 elements. (Refresher 801)

6. Choice C is correct. $\{a, b, c\}$ has 3 elements and therefore 2^3, or 8 subsets. (Refresher 805)

7. Choice D is correct. First $(A \cup B) = \{1, 2, 3, 4, 5, 6\}$.
Then $\{1, 2, 3, 4, 5, 6\} \cap \{1, 3, 5\} = \{1, 3, 5\}$. (Refresher 804)

8. Choice A is correct. First $(A \cap B) = \{2\}$.
Then $\{2\} \cup \{1, 3, 5\} = \{1, 2, 3, 5\}$. (Refresher 804)

9. Choice E is correct. $A \cup (B \cup C)$ is the set of elements in at least one of the three sets, or $\{1, 2, 3, 4, 5, 6\}$, which has 2^6, or 64 subsets. (Refresher 805)

10. Choice D is correct. $A \cup C = \{1, 2, 3, 5\}$. Since 4 is not an element of this set, $\{4\}$ is not a subset of $A \cup C$. (Refreshers 802, 805)

11. Choice E is correct. A set is a relation if all its elements are ordered pairs; I, II, and III meet this condition. (Refresher 806)

12. Choice B is correct. Two relations are equal if their elements are equal. Though it doesn't matter in what order the ordered pairs are listed, if the elements of the ordered pairs are switched, the relation is changed. (Refresher 806)

13. Choice E is correct. The range of a relation is the set of second elements of the ordered pairs. The range of $\{(1, 2), (3, 4), (5, 6)\}$ is $\{2, 4, 6\}$. (Refresher 806)

14. Choice A is correct. The domain is the set of first elements of the ordered pairs. The domain of $\{(1, 2), (2, 1), (1, 5)\}$ is $\{1, 2\}$. (Refresher 806)

15. Choice A is correct. To be a function, a relation must not repeat any of the first elements of its ordered pairs. The first elements of $\{(1, 1), (2, 2), (3, 3)\}$ are all distinct. (Refresher 806)

16. Choice C is correct. To find the inverse, simply reverse all the ordered pairs. (Refresher 807)

17. Choice C is correct. Reversing $(1, 2)$ we get $(2, 1)$; reversing $(3, 3)$ we get $(3, 3)$; reversing $(2, 1)$ we get $(1, 2)$. Though they are in a different order, the ordered pairs of the inverse of (C) are the same as the ordered pairs of (C). (Refresher 807)

18. Choice B is correct. The domain of the inverse is the range of the relation, or $\{1, 3, 5\}$. (Refreshers 806, 807)

19. Choice A is correct. If the inverse of the relation is to be a function, the second elements must all be distinct. The second elements of the ordered pairs of (A) are 1, 2, and 3, all distinct. (Refreshers 806, 807)

20. Choice D is correct. The range of the inverse is the domain of the function, or $\{P, R, T\}$. (Refreshers 806, 807)

21. Choice A is correct. $2x - 4 = 0$. $x = 2$, so the solution set is $\{2\}$. (Refresher 808)

22. Choice A is correct. $x + 9 = 3 - x$. $2x = -6$, or $x = -3$. The solution set is $\{-3\}$.

(Refresher 808)

23. Choice D is correct. $(x + 2)(x - 1) = 0$, so $x = -2$ or 1. The solution set is $\{-2, 1\}$.

(Refresher 808)

24. Choice D is correct. $x + 7 = 9$, or $x = 2$, which is a positive integer. The solution set is $\{2\}$.

(Refresher 808)

25. Choice E is correct. $x - 3 = -4$, or $x = -1$, which is not a positive integer. The solution set is $\varnothing$.

(Refresher 808)

26. Choice C is correct. $x > 2x - 4$, or $x < 4$. The positive integers less than 4 are 1, 2, and 3. The solution set is $\{1, 2, 3\}$.

(Refresher 808)

27. Choice A is correct. $(x + 1)(x - 4) = 0$. $x = -1$, or 4. 4 is a positive integer, but -1 is not, so the solution set is $\{4\}$.

(Refresher 808)

28. Choice B is correct. $(x + 3)(x + 6) = 0$. $x = -3$, or -6, both of which are negative integers, so the solution set is $\{-3, -6\}$.

(Refresher 808)

29. Choice E is correct. $(2x + 7)(x - 3) = 0$. $x = -3\frac{1}{2}$, or 3, neither of which is a negative integer. The solution set is $\varnothing$.

(Refresher 808)

30. Choice D is correct. $10 + 2x > 0$. $2x > -10$ or $x > -5$. The negative integers greater than -5 are $-1, -2, -3$, and -4. The solution set is $\{-1, -2, -3, -4\}$.

(Refresher 808)

31. Choice C is correct. To go from $3 \cdot 5$ to $5 \cdot 3$, we switch the order of multiplication. The axiom that deals with order of multiplication is the commutative axiom for multiplication, III.

(Refresher 809)

32. Choice B is correct. Switching parentheses in addition involves the associative axiom for addition, II.

(Refresher 809)

33. Choice C is correct. To go from $(2 \cdot 5) \cdot 3$ to $(5 \cdot 2) \cdot 3$, we switch the order of multiplying inside the parentheses. This is justified by the commutative axiom for multiplication, III.

(Refresher 809)

34. Choice E is correct. To go from $3(6 + 2)$ to $3 \cdot 6 + 3 \cdot 2$, or $18 + 6$, we use the distributive axiom, V.

(Refresher 809)

35. Choice E is correct. To go from $5(3 + 4)$ to $5 \cdot 3 + 5 \cdot 4$, or $15 + 20$, we use the distributive axiom, V. To go from $15 + 20$ to $20 + 15$, we use the commutative axiom of addition, I.

(Refresher 809)

MATH REFRESHER SESSION 9

Trigonometry

Diagnostic Test on Trigonometry

Questions 1–5 refer to the following diagram:

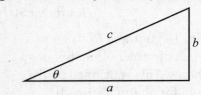

1. $\sin \theta =$

   (A) $\dfrac{a}{b}$

   (B) $\dfrac{b}{c}$

   (C) $\dfrac{a}{c}$

   (D) $\dfrac{c}{b}$

   (E) $\dfrac{b}{a}$

   A B C D E
   ○ ○ ○ ○ ○

2. $\cos \theta =$

   (A) $\dfrac{a}{b}$

   (B) $\dfrac{b}{c}$

   (C) $\dfrac{a}{c}$

   (D) $\dfrac{c}{b}$

   (E) $\dfrac{b}{a}$

   A B C D E
   ○ ○ ○ ○ ○

3. $\tan \theta =$

   (A) $\dfrac{a}{b}$

   (B) $\dfrac{b}{c}$

   (C) $\dfrac{a}{c}$

   (D) $\dfrac{c}{b}$

   (E) $\dfrac{b}{a}$

   A B C D E
   ○ ○ ○ ○ ○

4. $\sin^2 \theta + \cos^2 \theta =$

   (A) 1
   (B) 2
   (C) $\tan \theta$
   (D) $\tan^2 \theta$
   (E) $\dfrac{1}{\tan^2 \theta}$

   A B C D E
   ○ ○ ○ ○ ○

5. $1 + \tan^2 \theta =$

   (A) $\dfrac{1}{\cos^2 \theta}$

   (B) $\cos^2 \theta$

   (C) $\dfrac{1}{\sin^2 \theta}$

   (D) $\sin^2 \theta$

   (E) $\cos^2 \theta$

   A B C D E
   ○ ○ ○ ○ ○

Answers for Diagnostic Test

Refer to the 19 Trig Identities to Know below.

1. Choice B is correct.
   See 19 Trig Identities to Know #1.

2. Choice C is correct.
   See 19 Trig Identities to Know #2.

3. Choice E is correct.
   See 19 Trig Identities to Know #3.

4. Choice A is correct.
   See 19 Trig Identities to Know #7.

5. Choice A is correct.
   See 19 Trig Identities to Know #8.

---

19 Trig Identities to Know

901.

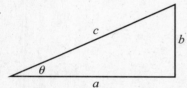

Remember the letter sequence:

$\underline{S} \ \underline{O} \ \underline{H} \ \underline{C} \ \underline{A} \ \underline{H} \ \underline{T} \ \underline{O} \ \underline{A}$

1. $\underline{S}$in $\theta = \underline{O}$pposite side (from angle θ) divided by $\underline{H}$ypotenuse (longest side c)

   So we get $\sin \theta = \dfrac{b}{c}$

2. $\underline{C}$os $\theta = \underline{A}$djacent side (to angle θ) divided by $\underline{H}$ypotenuse

   So we get $\cos \theta = \dfrac{a}{c}$

3. $\underline{T}$an $\theta = \underline{O}$pposite side (from angle θ) divided by $\underline{A}$djacent side

   So we get $\tan \theta = \dfrac{b}{a}$

Other definitions for cotangent θ, secant θ, and cosecant θ are:

4. $\cot \theta = \dfrac{a}{b}$

5. $\sec \theta = \dfrac{c}{a}$

6. $\csc \theta = \dfrac{c}{b}$

$\sin^2 \theta + \cos^2 \theta = \dfrac{b^2}{c^2} + \dfrac{a^2}{c^2} + \dfrac{(a^2 + b^2)}{c^2} = \dfrac{c^2}{c^2}$
$= 1$

So

7. $\sin^2 \theta + \cos^2 \theta = 1$

   $1 + \tan^2 \theta = 1 + \dfrac{b^2}{a^2} = \dfrac{(a^2 + b^2)}{a^2} = \dfrac{c^2}{a^2} = \dfrac{1}{\cos^2\theta}$
   $= \sec^2 \theta$

So

8. $1 + \tan^2 \theta = \dfrac{1}{\cos^2\theta} = \sec^2 \theta$

   $\dfrac{\sin\theta}{\cos\theta} = \dfrac{\frac{b}{c}}{\frac{a}{c}} = \dfrac{b}{a} = \tan \theta$

So

9. $\dfrac{\sin\theta}{\cos\theta} = \tan \theta$

Other things to know:

10. $\sin(x + y) = \sin(x)\cos(y) + \cos(x)\sin(y)$

11. $\sin(x - y) = \sin(x)\cos(y) - \cos(x)\sin(y)$

12. $\cos(x + y) = \cos(x)\cos(y) - \sin(x)\sin(y)$

13. $\cos(x - y) = \cos(x)\cos(y) + \sin(x)\sin(y)$

You can prove using (10), where $y = x$, and using (12), where $y = x$, that

14. $\sin 2x = 2\sin x \cos x$

15. $\cos 2x = \cos^2 x - \sin^2 x = 1 - 2\sin^2 x$

Also note:

16. $\cos \dfrac{x}{2} = \pm\sqrt{\dfrac{1 + \cos x}{2}}$

and

17. $\sin \dfrac{x}{2} = \pm\sqrt{\dfrac{1 - \cos x}{2}}$

18. $\cos(-x) = +\cos x$

19. $\sin(-x) = -\sin x$

SESSION 9 PRACTICE TEST

Trigonometry

Refer to the following diagrams for questions 1–5:

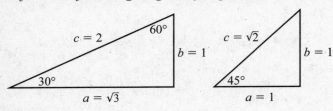

1. sin 30° =

   (A) $\dfrac{1}{2}$

   (B) $\dfrac{1}{\sqrt{3}}$

   (C) $\dfrac{\sqrt{3}}{2}$

   (D) $\sqrt{3}$

   (E) 2

   A B C D E
   ○ ○ ○ ○ ○

2. sin 60° =

   (A) $\dfrac{1}{2}$

   (B) $\dfrac{1}{\sqrt{3}}$

   (C) $\dfrac{\sqrt{3}}{2}$

   (D) $\sqrt{3}$

   (E) 2

   A B C D E
   ○ ○ ○ ○ ○

3. tan 30° =

   (A) $\dfrac{1}{2}$

   (B) $\dfrac{1}{\sqrt{3}}$

   (C) $\dfrac{\sqrt{3}}{2}$

   (D) $\sqrt{3}$

   (E) 2

   A B C D E
   ○ ○ ○ ○ ○

4. tan 45° =

   (A) 1

   (B) $\sqrt{2}$

   (C) 2

   (D) $\dfrac{1}{2}$

   (E) $\dfrac{1}{4}$

   A B C D E
   ○ ○ ○ ○ ○

5. sin 45° =

   (A) 1

   (B) $\dfrac{1}{\sqrt{2}}$

   (C) 2

   (D) $\dfrac{1}{2}$

   (E) $\dfrac{1}{4}$

   A B C D E
   ○ ○ ○ ○ ○

Answers for Session 9 Practice Test

1. Choice A is correct.

2. Choice C is correct.

3. Choice B is correct.

4. Choice A is correct.

5. Choice B is correct.

PART 7

Vocabulary Building That Is Guaranteed to Raise Your SAT Score

KNOWING WORD MEANINGS IS ESSENTIAL FOR A HIGHER SAT SCORE

Improving your vocabulary is essential if you want to get a high score on the Reading Section of the SAT.

Almost all SAT exam takers come across many "tough" words in this part, whose meanings they do not know. These students thereby lose many points because if they do not know the meanings of the words in the questions, they aren't able to answer the questions confidently—and so, they are likely to answer incorrectly.

Every correct answer on the SAT gives you approximately 10 points.

Several "tough" words show up in the Reading Comprehension passages of every SAT exam. Knowing the meanings of these difficult words will, of course, help you to understand the passages better. It follows that knowing what the passages are all about will help you correctly answer the Reading Comprehension questions that appear in the SAT—*and each correct answer nets you approximately 10 points.*

5 STEPS TO WORD POWER

1. Learn those Latin and Greek roots, prefixes, and suffixes that make up many English words. It has been estimated that more than half of all English words come from Latin and Greek. "The Gruber Prefix-Root-Suffix List" begins on page 309. Also learn the "Hot Prefixes and Roots" in Appendix A beginning on page 627.

2. Read—read—read. By reading a great deal, you will encounter new and valuable words. You will learn the meanings of many of these words by context—that is, you will perceive a clear connection between a new word and the words that surround that word. In this way, you will learn the meaning of that new word.

3. Listen to what is worth listening to. Listen to good radio and TV programs. Listen to people who speak well. Go to selected movies and plays. Just as you will increase your vocabulary by reading widely, you will increase your vocabulary by listening to English that is spoken well.

4. Play word games like crossword puzzles, anagrams, and Scrabble. Take advantage of online word games and word game apps.

5. Make sure you learn the 3 Vocabulary Strategies beginning on page 148.

NO ONE CAN DISPUTE THIS FACT!

You will pile up SAT points by taking advantage of
the valuable Vocabulary Building study and practice
materials that are offered to you in the following pages
of this chapter.

THE GRUBER PREFIX-ROOT-SUFFIX LIST

That Gives You the Meanings of More than 150,000 Words

Word Building with Roots, Prefixes, and Suffixes

According to some linguistic studies, approximately 60 percent of our English words are derived from Latin and Greek. One reliable study has shown that a selected list of 20 prefixes and 14 root elements pertain to more than 100,000 words in an unabridged dictionary. Here we have done even better—we've given you a list of prefixes and roots that will give you meanings of more than 150,000 words! The following entries of Latin and Greek roots, prefixes, and suffixes frequently show up in some of the words in the SAT Verbal areas, such as Reading Comprehension. Learn these Latin and Greek word parts to increase your vocabulary immensely— and thus score well in the Verbal part of your SAT.

The shortest and best way of learning a language is to know the roots of it; that is, those original primitive words from which other words are formed.

—Lord Chesterfield, British statesman (1694–1773)

Lord Chesterfield is, in effect, saying that roots are used as important "building blocks" of many of our English words. As you study the following list of Latin and Greek roots, prefixes, and suffixes, have a dictionary by your side. Look up the meanings of the word examples that are given if you do not know their meanings.

ROOTS

A Root Is the Basic Element—Fundamental or Essential Part—of a Word

The roots marked with a bullet (♦) are especially important.
Refer to a dictionary for word meanings you don't know.

Root	Meaning and Example
♦ ag, act	do, act; *agent, counteract*
agr, agora	field; *agriculture, agoraphobia*
alt	high; *altitude, altar*
alter	other; *altercation, alternative*
♦ am	friend, love; *amity, amorous*
anim	mind, life, spirit; *animate, animal, animosity*
ann, annu, enni	year; *annuity, annual, anniversary, perennial*
anthrop	man; *philanthropy, anthropoid*
aper	open; *aperture, aperient*
apt	fit; *adapt, aptitude*
aqu	water; *aqueous, aquacade*
arch	rule, govern; *anarchy, matriarch*
aster, astr	star; *asteroid, disaster, astronomy*
aud	hear; *audible, audition*
aur	gold; *auriferous*
♦ bas	low; *debase, basement*
bell	war; *bellicose, antebellum*
ben	good, well; *benevolent, benefactor*
bibl	book; *biblical, bibliography*
bio	life; *biology, biopsy*
brev	short; *brevity, abbreviation*
cad, cas, cid	fall; *cascade, casualty, incident*
cand	white, shining; *candid, candidate*
♦ cap, capt, cept	take, hold; *capable, captive, intercept*

Root	Meaning and Example
capit	head; *capital, decapitate, captain*
carn	flesh; *carnal, carnivorous*
♦ ced, cess	yield, go; *cede, procession*
celer	swift; *celerity, accelerate*
cent	hundred; *century, centipede*
chrom	color; *chromium, chromatic*
chron	time; *chronology, chronic*
cid, cis	cut, kill; *suicide, precision*
clin	lean, bend; *inclination, recline*
clud, clus	close, shut; *conclude, recluse*
cogn	know; *incognito, cognizant*
cord	heart; *cordial, accord*
corp	body; *corpulent, corpse*
cosm	world; *cosmic, cosmopolitan*
♦ cred	believe; *incredible, credentials*
♦ curr, curs	run; *current, cursory*
dec	ten; *decimal, decade*
dem	people; *democracy, demographic*
derm	skin; *epidermis, dermatologist*
di	day; *diary, sundial*
♦ dic, dict	speak, say; *indicate, contradict*
dign	worthy; *dignity, indignant*
domin	lord, master; *dominate, indomitable*
dorm	sleep; *dormant, dormitory*
♦ duc, duct	lead; *induce, ductile*
ego	I; *egotism, egomaniac*
equ	equal; *equity, equanimity*

Root	Meaning and Example
◆ **fac, fact, fect, fic**	make, do; *facile, factory, infection, fiction*
◆ **fer**	bear, carry; *fertile, confer*
fid	faith, trust; *confide, infidelity*
fin	end; *infinite, final*
flect, flex	bend; *reflect, flexible*
form	shape; *conform, reformation*
◆ **fort**	strong; *fortitude, fortify*
frag, fract	break; *fragile, fracture*
fug	flee; *fugitive, refugee*
fus	pour; *confuse, fusion*
◆ **gen**	kind, race, birth; *generate, generic, generation*
gest	carry, bring; *congestion, gestation*
grad, gress	step, go; *graduate, digress*
graph	write; *autograph, graphic*
grat	pleasing; *gratitude, congratulate*
hydr	water; *dehydrated, hydrant*
integr	entire, whole; *integrate, integral*
◆ **ject**	throw; *inject, projection*
junct	join; *conjunction, juncture*
lat	carry; *translation, dilate*
leg, lig, lect	choose, gather; *legible, eligible, collect*
liber	free; *liberate, libertine*
◆ **loc**	place; *dislocate, local*
log	word, study; *catalog, psychology*
loqu, locut	speak, talk; *loquacious, circumlocution*
luc, lum	light; *translucent, illuminate*
magn	great; *magnitude, magnificent*
◆ **man**	hand; *manufacture, manual*
mar	sea; *marine, maritime*
mater, matri	mother; *maternal, matrimony*
mega	large; *megaton, megaphone*

Root	Meaning and Example
ment	mind; *mentality, mentally*
merg	plunge, sink; *submerge, merger*
meter	measure; *chronometer, symmetry*
micro	small; *microscope, microfilm*
migr	wander; *migrate, immigration*
mir	look; *admire, mirror*
◆ **mit, miss**	send; *admit, submission*
mon	advise, remind; *admonish, monument*
◆ **mort**	death; *immortality, mortal*
mot, mov	move; *motor, motility, movable*
◆ **mult**	many; *multitude, multifarious*
◆ **mut**	change; *mutation, transmute, immutable*
◆ **nat**	born; *natal, innate*
nav	ship; *naval, navigate*
neg	deny; *negate, renege*
nomen	name; *nominee, nomenclature, cognomen*
nov	new; *novelty, novice, innovation*
ocul	eye; *oculist, binocular*
oper	work; *cooperation, operate*
pater, patri	father; *paternal, patriot*
ped	child; *pediatrics, pedagogue*
ped, pod	foot; *impede, biped, tripod*
pel, puls	drive; *compel, expulsion*
pend, pens	hang; *pendant, pension*
pet	seek; *impetus, petition*
petr, petri, petro	stone, rock; *petrify, petroglyph*
phil	loving; *philosophy*
phob	fear; *claustrophobia*
phon	sound; *phonic, phonetics*
◆ **plic**	fold, bend; *complicate, implicate*
◆ **pon, pos**	place, put; *component, compose*

Root	Meaning and Example
◆ port	carry, bring; *porter, import*
pot	drink; *potion, potable*
poten	powerful; *potentate, impotent*
prehend, prehens	take, grasp; *apprehend, comprehension*
prot	first; *protagonist, prototype*
psych	mind; *psychological, psychic*
quer, quir, quis, ques	ask, seek; *query, inquiry, inquisition, quest*
reg, rig, rect	rule, govern; *regent, rigid, corrective*
rid, ris	laugh; *ridiculous, risible*
rupt	break; *rupture, erupt, interruption*
sacr	holy; *sacred, sacrificial*
sanct	holy; *sanction, sanctify*
sci, scio	know; *science, conscious, omniscient*
scop	watch; *periscope, horoscope*
◆ scrib, script	write; *describe, prescription*
sec, sect	cut; *secant, bisect*
sed, sid, sess	sit, seat; *sedate, reside, session*
sent, sens	feel, think; *sentiment, sensible*
◆ sequ, secut	follow; *sequel, consecutive*
serv	keep; *reserve, conservation*
sist	place, stand; *assist, resistance*
solv, solu	loosen; *dissolve, absolution*
somn	sleep; *somnambulist, insomnia*
soph	wisdom; *sophisticated, philosophy*
◆ spec, spect, spic	look, appear; *specimen, prospect, conspicuous*
spir	breathe; *conspire, respiration*
◆ stat, stab	stand; *status, stability*

Root	Meaning and Example
string, strict	bind; *stringent, stricture*
stru, struct	build; *construe, destructive*
sum, sumpt	take; *assume, presumption*
tang, ting, tact, tig	touch; *tangent, contingency, contact, contiguous*
teg, tect	cover; *tegument, detect*
tele	distance; *telescope, teletype*
tempor	time; *temporary, extemporaneous*
◆ ten, tain	hold, reach; *tenant, tension, retain*
term	end; *terminal, terminate*
ter, terr	land, earth; *inter, terrace*
therm	heat; *thermometer, thermos*
tort, tors	twist; *contort, torsion*
◆ tract	draw; *attract, extract*
trit	rub; *trite, attrition*
trud, trus	thrust; *intrude, abstruse*
umbra	shade; *umbrella, umbrage*
urb	city; *suburb, urban*
vac	empty; *vacate, evacuation*
vad, vas	go; *evade, evasive*
val, vail	be strong; *valid, prevail*
◆ ven, vent	come; *convene, prevention*
◆ ver	true; *veracity, aver*
verb	word; *verbose, verbatim*
◆ vert, vers	turn; *convert, reverse*
vid, vis	see; *evident, visible*
vinc, vict	conquer; *invincible, evict*
viv, vit	live; *vivacity, vital*
voc, vok	call; *vocation, revoke*
volv, volut	roll, turn; *involve, revolution*

PREFIXES

A Prefix Is Part of a Word That May Be Placed before the Basic Element (Root) of a Word

The prefixes marked with a bullet (♦) are especially important.

Prefix	Meaning and Example
♦ a, ab, abs	from, away; *avert, abjure, absent*
♦ ad	to; *adhere.* By assimilation, *ad* takes the forms of **a, ac, af, al, an, ap, as, at;** *aspire, accord, affect, allude, annex, appeal, assume, attract*
ambi, amphi	around, both; *ambidextrous, amphibious*
♦ ante, anti	before; *antedate, anticipate*
♦ anti	against; *antidote, antislavery*
arch	first, chief; *archangel, archenemy*
auto	self; *autobiography, automatic*
ben	good, well; *benediction, benefactor*
♦ bi	two; *bilateral, bisect*
♦ circum	around; *circumnavigate, circumvent*
♦ com, con, col, cor, co	together; *commit, concord, collect, correct, coworker*
♦ contra, contro, counter	against; *contradict, controvert, counteract*
♦ de	down, away from, about; *descend, depart, describe*
demi	half; *demigod, demitasse*
dia	across, through; *diameter, diastole*
♦ dis, di, dif	apart, not; *dissension, division, diffident*
♦ equi	equal; *equinox, equivalent*
♦ ex, e, ef	out of, from; *extract, eject, efface*

Prefix	Meaning and Example
extra	out of, beyond; *extraordinary, extraterrestrial*
♦ hyper	too much; *hypercritical, hypersensitive*
hypo	too little, under; *hypochondriac, hypodermic*
♦ in, il, im, ir	into, in, on; *invade, illustrate, immerse, irritate*
♦ in, il, im, ir	not; *indistinct, illegal, impossible, irresponsible*
inter, intro	between, among; *interpose, introduce*
♦ mal, mis	bad; *malevolent, mistreat*
mono	one, single; *monotone, monorail*
neo	new; *neoplasm, neophyte*
♦ non	not; *nonentity, nonconformist*
♦ ob, of, op	against; *obviate, offend, oppose*
♦ omni	all; *omniscient, omnipresent*
ortho	straight; *orthodox, orthopedic*
pan	all; *pantheism, Pan-American*
♦ peri	around; *perimeter, periscope*
♦ poly	many; *polygon, polygamy*
♦ post	after; *postpone, postmortem*
♦ pre	before; *predict, precursory*
♦ pro	forward, before; *proceed, provide*
♦ re	back, again; *recur, recede*
retro	backward; *retrogress, retrospect*

Prefix	Meaning and Example	Prefix	Meaning and Example
se	apart, away; *seduce, sedition*	◆ trans	across; *transcontinental, transmit*
semi	half; *semicircle, semiconscious*	ultra	beyond; *ultraliberal, ultramodern*
◆ sub	under; *submarine, subversive*	◆ un	not; *unaware, uninformed*
◆ super	above, beyond; *superpose, superimpose, supernatural*	◆ uni	one; *unanimous, uniform*
syn, sym	with, at the same time; *synonymous, sympathetic*	vice	instead of; *vice-chancellor, viceroy*

SUFFIXES

A Suffix Is Part of a Word That May Follow the Basic Element (Root) of a Word

The suffixes marked with a bullet (◆) are especially important.

Suffix	Meaning and Example	Suffix	Meaning and Example
◆ able, ible	able; *pliable, returnable, comestible*	◆ ion	act of; *desperation, perspiration*
acious, cious	having the quality of; *capacious, meretricious*	◆ ious	characterized by; *spacious, illustrious*
age	act, condition; *courage, foliage*	◆ ish	like; *boyish, foolish*
al	belonging or related to; *legal, regal*	ism	belief in or practice of; *idealism, capitalism*
◆ ance, ence	state of; *abundance, indulgence*	ist	one who practices or is devoted to; *anarchist, harpist*
ary, eer, er	one who, concerning; *visionary, engineer, mariner*	◆ ive	relating to; *abusive, plaintive*
◆ ate, ent, ant, ante	one who; *candidate, advocate, resident, tenant, debutante*	mony	state of; *harmony, matrimony*
◆ cy	state, position of; *adequacy, presidency*	◆ ness	quality of; *willingness, shrewdness*
dom	state of; *freedom, serfdom*	ory	a place for; *factory, depository*
◆ ence	state of; *presence, credence*	◆ ous, ose	full of; *ponderous, verbose*
er, or	one who; *player, actor, monitor, employer*	ship	state of, skill; *friendship, gamesmanship*
◆ escent	becoming; *adolescent, putrescent*	◆ some	characteristic of; *loathsome, fearsome*
◆ fy	make; *beautify, sanctify*	tude	state of; *lassitude, rectitude*
hood	state of; *knighthood, childhood*	ward	in the direction of; *windward, backward*
ic, id	of, like; *bucolic, acrid*	◆ y	full of; *unruly, showy*
◆ il, ile	capable of being; *evil, servile*		

250 MOST COMMON SAT VOCABULARY WORDS

Based on Analysis of 50 Recent SAT Tests

abdicate   to yield, to give up

aberration   abnormality, deviation

abstruse   hard to understand

adage   a familiar saying

adamant   stubborn, unyielding

aesthetic   pertaining to beauty

affable   friendly, agreeable

alleviate   to lessen, to relieve

ambiguous   unclear, open to one or more
interpretations

ambivalent   having conflicting feelings toward
something or someone

amenable   agreeable

amiable   friendly, pleasant

ample   roomy, abundant

annihilate   totally destroy

apt   inclined, suitable, able

arbiter   a judge, an umpire

archaic   outdated, old-fashioned

arduous   difficult, strenuous

arid   dry

assiduous   diligent, careful

asylum   a safe place, a refuge

auspicious   favorable

austere   severe, stern, self-disciplined

benevolent   generous, kindly

benign   harmless, gentle

biased   preferential, prejudicial

brittle   fragile, likely to crack or break

brusque   abrupt in manner, blunt, rough

burgeoning   to flourish, to grow rapidly

camaraderie   loyalty, friendliness

candor   honesty, openness, frankness

cantankerous   bad-tempered, quarrelsome

capacious   spacious, roomy

capricious   erratic, impulsive

catalog   a list systematically displayed

caustic   corrosive, sarcastic

charlatan   a fake, a quack

clandestine   secretive and private

clarity   clearness or lucidity

cogent   convincing

cohesive   tending to stick together

compelling   forceful

conflagration   a large and destructive fire

conscientious   attentive, dedicated

contemptuous   scornful

convoluted   twisted, coiled

copious   plentiful, abundant

cordial   friendly, courteous

coup   a brilliant move, a successful and sudden attack

curtailed   cut short

debunk   quash, disprove

decorous   tasteful, respectable

deleterious   harmful

despotic   tyrannical

dictatorial   undemocratic

didactic   instructive, inclined to lecture others too much

dilatory   slow, late in doing things

dilettante   a dabbler in the fine arts, one who is not an expert

diligent   hard-working, industrious

disdain   to scorn

disingenuous   untruthful, insincere

disparage   to belittle, to put down

disparate   different, dissimilar, distinct

dogged   single-minded, persistent

dogmatic   expressing or adhering to doctrines as if they are correct and cannot be doubted

dubious   doubtful, questionable

ebullience   enthusiasm

eclectic   selecting, choosing from various sources

effusive   unrestrained, enthusiastic

egregious   remarkably bad, outrageous

embellish   to decorate

emollient   something that soothes or softens

emphatic   vehement, forceful

emulate   to imitate

enervate   to weaken

enmity   hostility, hatred

ephemeral   temporary, short-lived

epiphany   revelation, appearance of a deity (God)

equanimity   calmness, evenness of temperament

exculpate   to free from blame, to vindicate

exemplary   worthy of imitation

fabricate   to construct, to lie

facetious   joking, sarcastic

facile   easy, effortless

farce   foolish show, mockery, a ridiculous sham

fastidious   meticulous, exacting

feasible   capable of being accomplished, likely, logical

feral   untamed, wild

florid   flowery, ornate

fractious   irritable, quarrelsome, stubborn

frank   forthright

frenetic   frantic, wild

furtive   stealthy, secretive

futile   useless

garrulous   talkative

genre   an art form or class

glower   to frown, to stare angrily at

gratuitous   free of cost, unnecessary

gregarious   sociable, friendly

hackneyed   trite, commonplace, overused

harbinger   an omen or a sign

haughty   snobbish or arrogant

heinous   hateful or abominable

heresy   sacrilege, dissent from accepted orthodoxy

idyllic   tranquil, carefree, scenic, picturesque

immutable   unchangeable

impede   to hinder or obstruct

impenetrable   incapable of being passed through or into

imperious   domineering, haughty

impetuous   acting without thought, impulsive

impinge   to strike, to collide, to encroach

implacable   unbending, inflexible, merciless

impromptu   without preparation, offhand

inconsequential   unimportant

incontrovertible   certain, undeniable

incorrigible   bad beyond correction or reform

incumbent   resting in or lying upon; one who holds a political office

indigenous   native to a particular area, inborn

indolent   lazy

ingrate   ungrateful person

innate   inborn, existing from birth

innocuous   harmless, insipid

insightful   having a penetrating understanding of things, mentally alert and sharp

insolvent   bankrupt, unable to pay creditors

insipid   tasteless, dull

intrepid   fearless, courageous

intuitive   insightful, knowing by a hidden sense

inveterate   firmly established, deep-rooted

itinerant   traveling from place to place

jurisprudence   science of law

laconic   using few words, concise

lament   to mourn

lampoon   a sharp, often harmful satire

laudatory   complementary, flattering

liquid   fluid, free running

listless   feeling no interest in anything, indifferent

lucid   clear, easy to understand, rational or sane

malevolent   showing ill will or hatred, very dangerous, harmful

malfeasance   wrongdoing

malice   spite, intent to act with ill will

maverick   a rebel, a nonconformist

medley   a mixture, a musical selection combining parts from various sources

mercurial   changeable, fickle, erratic

meticulous   excessively careful, finicky

milk   to draw something from, to take advantage of

mitigate   to make less severe, to become milder

mollify   to calm, to pacify, to appease

morose   gloomy, ill-humored

mundane   worldly, ordinary

mural   a painting depicted directly on a wall

naïve   simple, unsophisticated

nascent   coming into being, being born

nocturnal   pertaining to the night

notorious   having a bad reputation, infamous

novel   new, original

novice   a beginner

obdurate   stubborn, hard-headed

obscure   dim, not clear, not easily understood

obsolete   outdated

obstinate   stubborn

ominous   threatening, indicating evil or harm

omnipotent   all-powerful

opulent   rich, luxurious

ornate   showy, highly decorative

ostentatious   showing off and boastful

pander   to indulge others' wants and weaknesses

paramount   chief, supreme

parochial   local, narrow, limited

parody   a work that imitates another in a ridiculous manner

parsimonious   stingy, miserly

patronizing   talking down to someone

paucity   scarcity, lack

penitent   expressing sorrow for sin or wrongdoing

pejorative   having a negative effect, insulting

permeate   to spread throughout

pervasive   widespread, extensive

plagiarism   the claiming of another's work as one's own

plausible   apparently true, fair, or reasonable

poignant   keenly distressing, affecting the emotions

ponderous   heavy, burdensome

portend   foretell, foreshadow

pragmatic   practical

pristine   uncorrupted, in its original state

prodigious   enormous, vast

prophetic   predictive

propriety   conformity, appropriateness

prosaic dull, commonplace, unimaginative

prudent cautious

pugnacious eager to fight, quarrelsome

punctilious very exact, precise

purist perfectionist

quandary a puzzling situation, a dilemma

rancorous bitter, resentful

rapport friendly or close friendship, harmony

recalcitrant disobedient, hard to manage

reclamation the act of restoring or rehabilitating

remote far-off, distant

replete filled

repugnant distasteful, disgusting

reticent silent or reserved in manner

ruse a skillful trick or deception

salutary healthful, wholesome

sanction to authorize, to give permission

sanguine cheerful, optimistic

sedentary sitting most of the time

serene calm, peaceful

slander to make a false statement against someone

solvent having the ability to pay a debt, a substance that dissolves another

sonorous producing a deep, rich sound

soporific causing sleep

specious not genuine, pleasing to the eye but deceptive

spurious deceitful, counterfeit

squalor filth, dirt

staid sedate, settled

stoic showing no emotion, indifferent to pleasure or pain

stratagem a plan, a scheme or trick

stupor daze

stymied hindered, blocked

substantiate to prove, to confirm, to support

superfluous excessive, unnecessary

suppress to keep from public knowledge, to put down by authority

surreptitious acting in a sneaky way

tacit silent, conveyed or indicated without words

temperate not extreme, moderate

tenacity holding on, persistent, stubborn

tenet a doctrine, a belief

tenuous slender, flimsy, without substance

terse brief, to the point

thwart to prevent or hinder

timorous fearful, cowardly

torpor laziness, lethargy

toxic poisonous or harmful

transitory brief, passing, lasting a short time

trenchant keen or incisive, vigorous, effective

trepidation fear, alarm

trite worn out, stale, commonplace

truncate to shorten, to cut off

unfettered unconstrained, unrestricted

unpalatable unappetizing, not desirable

urbane refined, suave, citified

usurp to supplant or to seize illegally

vacuous empty-headed, unintelligent, vacant

vilify to speak evil of, to defame

vindicate to clear of guilt or blame

wane to gradually decrease in size or intensity

wary cautious, watchful

whimsical unpredictable, changeable

wily tricky or sly

wry produced by distorting the face (a wry grin), ironic

zealous ardently active, devoted, diligent

THE MOST IMPORTANT/FREQUENTLY USED SAT WORDS AND THEIR OPPOSITES

A List of Popular SAT Words and Their Opposites

Note: These words fit into specific categories, and it may be a little easier memorizing the meanings of these important words knowing what category they fit into.

Positive	Negative	Positive	Negative
To Praise	*To Belittle*	*To Calm or Make Better*	*To Agitate or Make Worse*
acclaim	admonish	abate	alienate
applaud	assail	accede	antagonize
commend	berate	accommodate	contradict
eulogize	calumniate	allay	dispute
exalt	castigate	ameliorate	embitter
extol	censure	appease	estrange
flatter	chastise	assuage	incense
hail	chide	comply	infuriate
laud	decry	concede	nettle
panegyrize	denigrate	conciliate	oppose
resound	denounce	gratify	oppugn
tout	disparage	mitigate	repulse
	excoriate	mollify	snub
	execrate	pacify	
	flay	palliate	
	lambaste	placate	
	malign	propitiate	
	reprimand	quell	
	reproach	satiate	
	scold		
	upbraid		
	vilify		

Positive	Negative	Positive	Negative
Pleasant	*Unpleasant*	*Abundant or Rich*	*Scarce or Poor*
affable	callous	affluent	dearth
agreeable	cantankerous	bounteous	deficit
amiable	captious	copious	destitute
captivating	churlish	luxuriant	exiguous
congenial	contentious	multifarious	impecunious
cordial	gruff	multitudinous	impoverished
courteous	improper	myriad	indigent
decorous	ireful	opulent	insolvent
engaging	obstinate	plenteous	meager
gracious	ornery	plentiful	paltry
obliging	peevish	plethoric	paucity
sportive	perverse	profuse	penurious
unblemished	petulant	prosperous	scanty
undefiled	querulous	superabundant	scarce
	testy	teeming	sparse
	vexing	wealthy	
	wayward		
		Yielding	*Not Yielding*
Generous	*Cheap*	accommodating	adamant
altruistic	frugal	amenable	determinate
beneficent	miserly	compliant	immutable
benevolent	niggardly	deferential	indomitable
charitable	parsimonious	docile	inflexible
effusive	penurious	flexible	intractable
hospitable	provident	hospitable	intransigent
humanitarian	skinflinty	inclined	recalcitrant
magnanimous	spartan	malleable	relentless
munificent	tight-fisted	obliging	resolute
philanthropic	thrifty	pliant	steadfast
		submissive	tenacious
		subservient	
		tractable	

Positive	Negative	Positive	Negative
Courageous	**Timid**	**Humble**	**Haughty**
audacious	diffident	demure	affected
dauntless	indisposed	diffident	aristocratic
gallant	reserved	indisposed	arrogant
intrepid	reticent	introverted	audacious
stalwart	retiring	plebeian	authoritarian
undaunted	subdued	restrained	autocratic
valiant	timorous	reticent	condescending
valorous		subdued	disdainful
		subservient	egotistical
Lively	**Bleak**	unassuming	flagrant
brisk	dejected	unostentatious	flippant
dynamic	dismal	unpretentious	imperious
ebullient	forlorn		impertinent
exhilarating	lackluster		impudent
exuberant	lugubrious		insolent
inspiring	melancholy		ostentatious
provocative	muted		pompous
scintillating	prostrate		proud
stimulating	somber		supercilious
titillating	tenebrous		vainglorious

Note: In many cases you can put the prefix *im-* or *un-* in front of the word to change its meaning to its opposite.

Examples: Balance. *Opposite*: Imbalance

Ostentatious. *Opposite*: Unostentatious

Positive	Negative
Careful	**Careless**
chary	culpable
circumspect	felonious
conscientious	indifferent
discreet	insouciant
exacting	lackadaisical
fastidious	lax
gingerly	negligent
heedful	perfunctory
judicious	rash
meticulous	remiss
provident	reprehensible
prudent	temerarious
punctilious	
scrupulous	
scrutinous	
wary	

PRACTICE QUESTIONS

Find the OPPOSITES of the following words.

1. EXTOL:

   (A) oppose
   (B) restrain
   (C) enter
   (D) deviate
   (E) denigrate

2. ALLAY:

   (A) incense
   (B) drive
   (C) berate
   (D) signify
   (E) determine

3. DECOROUS:

   (A) scanty
   (B) improper
   (C) musty
   (D) pliant
   (E) rigid

4. AMENABLE:

   (A) tiresome
   (B) uncultured
   (C) intransigent
   (D) soothing
   (E) careless

5. MUNIFICENT:

   (A) simple
   (B) pallid
   (C) crafty
   (D) penurious
   (E) stable

6. PLETHORIC:

   (A) impecunious
   (B) slothful
   (C) indifferent
   (D) reticent
   (E) sly

7. METICULOUS:

   (A) timid
   (B) plenteous
   (C) peevish
   (D) intractable
   (E) perfunctory

8. IMPERIOUS:

   (A) restrained
   (B) lackadaisical
   (C) insolvent
   (D) churlish
   (E) immutable

9. TIMOROUS:

   (A) judicious
   (B) intrepid
   (C) multifarious
   (D) benevolent
   (E) tenebrous

10. LUGUBRIOUS:

   (A) flexible
   (B) unblemished
   (C) ebullient
   (D) conciliatory
   (E) impertinent

ANSWERS TO PRACTICE QUESTIONS

1. Choice E is correct. EXTOL fits into the category of TO PRAISE. *Denigrate* fits into the category TO BELITTLE—the opposite category.

2. Choice A is correct. ALLAY fits into the category of TO CALM. *Incense* fits into the opposite category—TO AGITATE or MAKE WORSE.

3. Choice B is correct. DECOROUS fits into the category of PLEASANT. The opposite category is UNPLEASANT. *Improper* fits into this category.

4. Choice C is correct. AMENABLE fits into the category of YIELDING. *Intransigent* fits into the opposite category—NOT YIELDING.

5. Choice D is correct. MUNIFICENT fits into the category of GENEROUS. *Penurious* fits into the category of CHEAP, the opposite category.

6. Choice A is correct. PLETHORIC fits into the category of ABUNDANT or RICH. *Impecunious* fits into the opposite category of SCARCE or POOR.

7. Choice E is correct. METICULOUS fits into the category of CAREFUL. *Perfunctory* fits into the category of CARELESS (or mechanical).

8. Choice A is correct. IMPERIOUS fits into the category of HAUGHTY (highbrow). *Restrained* fits into the category of HUMBLE, the opposite category.

9. Choice B is correct. TIMOROUS fits into the category of TIMID. *Intrepid* fits into the opposite category of COURAGEOUS.

10. Choice C is correct. LUGUBRIOUS fits into the category of BLEAK or dismal. *Ebullient* fits into the opposite category of LIVELY.

PART 8

Grammar and Usage Refresher

The following pages will be very helpful in your preparation for the writing ability parts of the SAT. You will find in these pages a brief but to-the-point review for just about every type of writing ability question that appears on the actual SAT.

These are the areas covered in this study section:

- The Parts of Speech
- Clauses and Phrases
- The Sentence and Its Parts
- Verbs

- Nouns and Pronouns
- Subject-Verb Relationship
- Tense
- Verbals
- Mood and Voice
- Adjective Modifiers
- Adverbial Modifiers
- Connectives
- Correct Usage—Choosing the Right Word

THE PARTS OF SPEECH*

1a. Noun

A **noun** is a word that names a **person**, **place**, **thing**, or **idea**.

Persons	Places
nurse	forest
Henry	Miami
uncle	house
Chicano	airport

Things	Ideas
banana	love
shoe	democracy
television	hunger
notebook	cooperation

A noun that is made up of more than one word is called a **compound noun**.

Persons	Places
Martin Luther King	high school
cab driver	Puerto Rico
movie star	dining room
federal judge	Middle East

Things	Ideas
cell phone	foresight
car key	inflation
post office	light year
ice cream	market value

1b. Pronoun

A **pronoun** is a word used **in place of a noun**.

Buy a newspaper and bring **it** home. (The pronoun "it" stands for the noun "newspaper.")

Marlene went to the party, but **she** didn't stay long. (The pronoun "she" stands for the noun "Marlene.")

A **pronoun** may be used **in place of a noun or a group of nouns**.

Pedro wanted to see the polar bears, camels, and tropical birds, **which** were at the zoo. (The pronoun "which" stands for the nouns "polar bears, camels, and tropical birds.")

When Mark, Steven, Teresa, and Barbara turned eighteen, **they** registered to vote. (The pronoun "they" stands for the nouns "Mark, Steven, Teresa, and Barbara.")

The **noun that the pronoun replaces** is called the **antecedent** of the pronoun.

The **plates** broke when **they** fell. (The noun "plates" is the antecedent of the pronoun "they.")

Avoid confusion by repeating the noun instead of using a pronoun if more than one noun might be considered to be the antecedent.

The lamp hit the table when **the lamp** was knocked over. (**Not:** The lamp hit the table when **it** was knocked over.)

1c. Verb

A **verb** is a word or group of words that **expresses action or being**.

The plane **crashed** in Chicago. (action)

Soccer **is** a popular sport. (being)

1d. Adjective

An **adjective** is a word that **modifies a noun or pronoun**.

Note: In grammar, to modify a noun means to describe, talk about, explain, limit, specify, or change the character of a noun.

Susan brought us **red** flowers. (The adjective "red" describes the noun "flowers.")

---

* An index to this entire Grammar Refresher section begins on page 370.

Everyone at the party looked **beautiful**. (The adjective "beautiful" describes the pronoun "everyone.")

Several people watched the parade. (The adjective "several" does not actually describe the noun "people"; it limits or talks about how many "people" watched the parade.)

Those shoes are her **favorite** ones. (The adjective "favorite" defines or specifies which "ones.")

They have **two** children. (The adjective "two" limits or specifies how many "children.")

1e. Adverb

An **adverb** is a word that **modifies** the meaning of **a verb, an adjective, or another adverb**.

The librarian spoke **softly**. (The adverb "softly" describes or explains how the librarian "spoke.")

Bill Gates is **extremely** rich. (The adverb "extremely" talks about or specifies how "rich" Bill Gates is.)

The job is **very** nearly completed. (The adverb "very" limits or specifies how "nearly" the job is completed.)

1f. Preposition

A **preposition** is a word that **connects a noun or pronoun to another word** in the sentence.

The mayor campaigned **throughout** the city. (The preposition "throughout" connects the noun "city" to the verb "campaigned.")

A **preposition connects** a noun or pronoun to another word in the sentence **to show a relationship**.

The wife **of** the oil executive was kidnapped.

A friend **of** mine is a good lawyer.

The strainer **for** the sink is broken.

The floor **under** the sink is wet.

David wants to work **in** the city.

The accident occurred **about** eight o'clock.

1g. Conjunction

A **conjunction** is a word that **joins words, phrases, or clauses**.

Alan's father **and** mother are divorced. (two words joined)

      phrase   phrase

Is your favorite song at the end **or** at the beginning of the movie? (two phrases joined)

You may swim in the pool, **but** don't stay long. (two clauses joined)

(See "Connectives" for a discussion of how prepositions and conjunctions act as connectives.)

1h. Interjection

An **interjection** is a word (or group of words) that **expresses surprise, anger, pleasure, or some other emotion**.

Aha! I've caught you.

Oh no! What have you done now?

An **interjection** has **no grammatical relation** to another word.

Ouch! I've hurt myself.

1i. A word may belong to more than one part of speech, depending on its meaning.

Example 1:

Everyone **but** Kara was invited to the wedding. (preposition)

Phil Mickelson won the British Open, **but** Tiger Woods came close to winning. (conjunction)

Harry has **but** ten dollars left in his bank account. (adverb)

Example 2:

He lives **up** the street. (preposition)

It's time to get **up**. (adverb)

The sun is **up**. (adjective)

Every life has its **ups** and downs. (noun)

I'll **up** you five dollars. (verb)

Note: Just for fun—what is the part of speech of the word *behind* in this sentence?

Attempting to save Annie, the fireman ran for the door, dragging her **behind**.

Our answer is an adverb, meaning "at the rear." If your answer was a noun—oh my! The noun means a certain part of the human body. We won't tell you which part.

CLAUSES AND PHRASES

2a. Clauses

A **clause** is a **group of words** within a sentence.

From his room, **he could see the park**. (one clause)

The children loved the man who sold ice cream. (two clauses)

A clause contains a subject and a verb.

subject   verb
↓   ↓
Before the race, **the jockeys inspected their horses**. (one clause)

subject verb   subject verb
↓   ↓   ↓   ↓
When the rain stopped, the air was cooler. (two clauses)

2b. There are two types of clauses: **main** and **subordinate**.*

subordinate clause | main clause
During the riot, several people got hurt.

subordinate clause
When she won the lottery,

main clause
Mrs. Ya-ching shouted with joy.

A **main clause** makes sense by itself.

We got the day off.

A **main clause** expresses a complete thought.

The fire was put out.
(**Not:** When the fire was put out.)

It rained this morning.
(**Not:** Because it rained this morning.)

A **subordinate clause** does not make sense by itself.

While the washing machine was broken, we couldn't wash anything.
(The subordinate clause does not make sense without the rest of the sentence.)

Because a subordinate clause does not make sense by itself, a subordinate clause cannot stand as a complete sentence.

While the washing machine was broken . . .

A subordinate clause depends on a particular word in a main clause to make the subordinate clause mean something.

main clause | subordinate clause
Jayden abandoned the car **that had two flat tires**.
(The subordinate clause depends on the noun "car" in the main clause to describe the car.)

main clause
The job was offered to Ava

subordinate clause
because she was best qualified.
(The subordinate clause depends on the verb "**was** offered" in the main clause to explain **why** the job was offered.)

main clause | subordinate clause
My new neighbor is the one **who is waving**.
(The subordinate clause depends on the pronoun "one" in the main clause to tell who is waving.)

*A main clause may be called an independent clause. A subordinate clause may be called a dependent clause.

A **subordinate clause** may be used in a sentence as an **adjective**, an **adverb**, or a **noun**.

> Pixar's *Toy Story 3* is the most successful movie **that the company has made yet**.
> (The subordinate clause acts like an adjective because it modifies—talks about—the noun "movie.")

> The child giggled **while he was asleep**.
> (The subordinate clause functions like an adverb because it modifies the verb "giggled.")

> Please tell me **what this is all about**.
> (The subordinate clause acts like a noun because it is the object of the action verb "tell.")

2c. **Phrases**

A phrase is a group of words within a sentence that forms a grammatical unit.

> Jenny Rivera died **in a plane crash**. (one phrase)

> Let's sit **under that apple tree**. (one phrase)

> **At the top of the hill** there were some cows grazing. (two phrases)

The phrase itself does not contain a subject or a verb.

> subject   verb
> ↓   ↓
> Many streets **in the city** need repairs.

A phrase does not make sense by itself.

> Ellen has a collection **of beautiful earrings**.
> (The phrase "of beautiful earrings" does not make sense by itself; therefore, the phrase cannot stand alone as a complete sentence.)

A phrase may begin with a preposition, a participle, a gerund, or an infinitive.

> preposition
> ↓
> Put the milk **into the refrigerator**. (prepositional phrase)

> participle
> ↓
> There are several people **waiting in line**. (participial phrase)

> gerund
> ↓
> **Running ten miles a day** is hard work. (gerund phrase)

> infinitive
> ↓
> **To sing well** takes a lot of practice. (infinitive phrase)

A **phrase** may be used as a **noun**, an **adjective**, or an **adverb**.

> A doctor's job is **to heal people**.
> (The infinitive phrase acts like a noun because it names the doctor's job.)

> **Raising his hands,** the Pope blessed the crowd.
> (The participial phrase acts like an adjective because it describes the Pope.)

> Most stores close **at five o'clock**.
> (The prepositional phrase acts like an adverb because it tells when most stores close.)

THE SENTENCE AND ITS PARTS

3a. A **sentence** is a **group of words** that has a **subject** and a **verb**.

        subject verb
         ↓   ↓

The **concert began** at midnight.

                subject verb
                 ↓   ↓

During the storm, the **electricity was knocked out**.

3b. A sentence may be **declarative, interrogative**, or **exclamatory**.

A **declarative** sentence **states or asserts**.

    Inflation is a serious problem.

An **interrogative** sentence **asks a question**.

    How long must we suffer?

An **exclamatory** sentence **expresses emotion.** The sentence ends with an exclamation point (!).

    What a fool he is!

An **imperative** sentence **makes a request** or **gives a command**. (The subject, "You," is present but hiding—it is always built into the verb that commands or requests.)

    Don't be afraid to try something new.

A **sentence** expresses a **complete thought**.

    The price of gold has gone up.

    Bus service will resume on Friday morning.

Note: Because a sentence expresses a complete thought, a sentence makes sense by itself.

    Owen likes to play his electric guitar. (complete thought)

    Owen likes. (incomplete thought—not a sentence)

    The tornado caused much damage. (complete thought)

    The tornado. (incomplete thought—not a sentence)

3c. **The four types of sentences according to structure are the following:**

(1) **Simple**
Everyone likes music.

(2) **Compound**
The Simons put their house up for sale on Friday, and it was sold by Monday.

(3) **Complex**
If you want good Szechuan cooking, you should go to the Hot Wok Restaurant.

(4) **Compound-Complex**
Bob met Sally, who was in town for a few days, and they went to a museum.

3d. **Simple sentence**

A **simple sentence** is made up of only **one main (independent) clause**.

    I love you.

A simple sentence may be of any length.

    The elderly couple sitting on the park bench are parents of a dozen children besides being the grandparents of nearly forty children.

Note: A simple sentence **does not have a subordinate clause** in it.

3e. **Compound sentence**

A **compound sentence** has **two or more main clauses**.

        main clause   conjunction
                               ↓
    William and Kate got married, and
                main clause
    they invited several friends to a party.

      main clause   conjunction

Sebastian attended college, but

    main clause

he left after a year.

Each main clause in a compound sentence may stand by itself as a simple sentence—as long as the conjunction is left out.

             conjunction

Carlos will arrive by plane tonight, and Maria will go to the airport to meet him. (compound sentence)

Carlos will arrive by plane tonight. (simple sentence)

Maria will go to the airport to meet him. (simple sentence)

Note: A compound sentence does not have any subordinate clauses.

3f. Complex sentence

A complex sentence contains only one main clause and one or more subordinate clauses.

     subordinate clause

After he signed the treaty,

        main clause

President Obama asked the Senate to ratify it. (one main clause and one subordinate clause)

      subordinate clause

Although they are expensive to install,

       main clause

solar heating systems save money and energy,

     subordinate clause

which are hard to get these days. (one main clause and two subordinate clauses)

      subordinate clause

Because he came from the planet Krypton,

       main clause

Superman had special powers

     subordinate clause

that no one on Earth could equal,

      subordinate clause

though many people have tried. (one main clause and three subordinate clauses)

3g. Compound-complex sentence

A compound-complex sentence is made up of **two or more main clauses and one or more subordinate clauses**.

      subordinate clause

After his store burned down,

       main clause

Mr. Garcia rented the store across the street,

       main clause

and his business continued to do well. (two main clauses and one subordinate clause)

      main clause

Zachary wanted to go to the new club,

      subordinate clause

which he had heard was a great place,

      main clause

but he did not want to see his ex-girlfriend,

     subordinate clause

who worked there. (two main clauses and two subordinate clauses)

3h. The parts of a sentence

The basic parts of a sentence are a **subject**, a **verb**, and a **complement**.*

    subject   verb   complement

The waiter brought the soup.

compound subject verb   complement

Mason and Lily sold me their computer.

*The complement is discussed on page 336.

3i. **Subject**

The **subject** of the sentence is the noun (or word that functions as a noun, such as a gerund) that performs the action indicated by the verb—including the verb "to be."

> **Dr. Phil** gives advice to millions of Americans.
>
> **Dr. Phil** (subject) *gives* (verb) or performs the action of the sentence.
>
> High **taxes** caused many businesses to close.
>
> **Taxes** (noun/subject) *caused* (verb). . . .
>
> **Whoever** goes to bed last should shut off the lights.
>
> **Whoever** (pronoun) *goes* (verb). . . .
>
> **Brushing one's teeth and getting checkups regularly** are two important parts of good dental care.
>
> *Brushing* one's teeth and *getting* checkups (compound subject formed by two connected gerunds) *are* (verb "to be"). . . .

3j. A **subject** may be a **noun, pronoun, verbal, phrase,** or **clause** that functions as a noun.

(1) A subject is usually a **noun**.

> Our **wedding** will be held outdoors.
>
> The **White House** is the home of the president.
>
> The **police** arrested the burglars.

(2) A subject may be a **pronoun**.

> **He** always gets his way. (personal pronoun used as the subject)
>
> **Hers** is the tan raincoat. (possessive pronoun used as the subject)
>
> **What** did you do? (interrogative pronoun used as the subject)
>
> **That** is my car. (demonstrative pronoun used as the subject)
>
> **Everyone** was happy. (indefinite pronoun used as the subject)

(3) A subject may be a **verbal**.*

> **To begin** is the hardest part of the job. (infinitive used as the subject)

> **Swimming** is good exercise. (gerund used as a subject)
>
> *Note*: A participle may not be used as a subject because it is a verb form that only does the work of an adjective.

(4) A subject may be a **phrase**.

> **Consuming sugary drinks** is unhealthy. (gerund phrase used as a subject)
>
> **To obey the law** is everyone's duty. (infinitive phrase used as a subject)

(5) A subject may be a **clause**.

> **Whatever you decide** is all right.
>
> **That Danny had cancer** saddened his friends.
>
> **What will happen** is going to surprise you.
>
> **Whoever is on your team** will help you win.

3k. **Verb**

A verb is a word or group of words that **usually tells what the subject does**.

> Avery **skated** down the street.
>
> Your baby **has dropped** his toy.
>
> President Nixon **resigned**.
>
> The cell phone **is ringing**.

Two or more verbs may have one subject.

> They **defeated** the Cubs but **lost** to the Pirates.
>
> Brayden **works** during the day and **goes** to school at night.

A verb may express a state or condition.

> Taylor **appears** puzzled. (Or: Taylor **appears to be** puzzled.)
>
> The stew **tastes** delicious.
>
> Jason and Madison **are** good friends.

3l. The three kinds of verbs are **transitive, intransitive, and linking**.

3m. A transitive verb tells what its subject does to someone or to something (the direct object).

> The cat **caught** the mouse.
>
> Zach **washed** the dishes.
>
> Chloe's mother **slapped** the boy.

---

*See "Verbals" on page 348.

3n. **An intransitive verb tells what its subject does. The action of the intransitive verb does not affect someone or something else.**

> The old man **slept** in his chair.
>
> The audience **applauded**.
>
> All of the job applicants **waited** patiently.

Note: **Many verbs may be transitive or intransitive.**

> He **will return** the book tomorrow. (transitive)
>
> The manager **will return** in an hour. (intransitive)

Whether a verb is transitive or intransitive depends on how it is used in the sentence.

> Colton **opened** the package.
> (The verb is transitive because the action was carried out on something.)
>
> The door **opened** slowly.
> (The verb is intransitive because the action by the subject "door" did not affect anything else.)

3o. **A linking verb links the subject with a noun or a pronoun or an adjective.**

> *The Grey* was a terrifying **film**. (noun)
>
> It's **I**.* (pronoun)
>
> The child in this old photograph is **I**. (pronoun)
>
> The girl who loves Peter is **she**. (pronoun)
>
> The Beatles were **popular** in the 1960s. (adjective)

A linking verb may link the subject with an infinitive, a gerund, or a noun clause.

> Stephanie's greatest pleasure is **to sing**. (infinitive)
>
> The senator's mistake was **lying**. (gerund)
>
> David's new job seemed **what he had hoped for**. (noun clause)

Linking verbs are **to be, to appear, to grow, to seem, to remain, to become,** and verbs that involve the senses, such as **to look, to smell, to feel, to sound,** and **to taste**.

> Kaylee and Ashley **are** sisters.
>
> Ben **is** strong.

*In spoken English, it is acceptable to say, "It's me" or "It's us." It is not acceptable, however, to say, "It's him," "It's her," or "It's them." For formal tests such as the SAT, follow the rules for case.

> Caleb **appears** healthy.
>
> The situation at the prison **remains** tense.
>
> Mia **feels** better.
>
> Josh **sounds** angry.

A verb that appears to be a sense-linking verb may not actually be a sense-linking verb.

> The milk **smells** sour. (linking verb)
>
> The dog **smells** the fire hydrant. (transitive verb)
>
> Troy **looked** sad. (linking verb)
>
> Layla **looked** through the window. (intransitive verb)

Note: The use of a particular verb determines whether that verb is sense-linking **or** transitive **or** intransitive.

3p.

Transitive Verb

1. Expresses action.
2. Is followed by a direct object that receives the action.

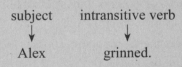

Intransitive Verb

1. Expresses action.
2. Is not followed by a direct object.

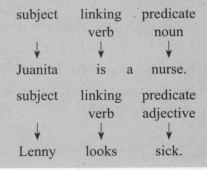

VERBS

4a. Five characteristics of every verb are number, person, tense, mood, and voice.

4b. Number shows whether the subject of the verb is singular or plural. A good rule to keep in mind is that nouns ending in *s* are plural, while verbs ending in *s* are singular.

> Melissa **drives** well. (singular)
>
> Arthur's parents **are** from Texas. (plural)
>
> Julia's grandmother **is** in Atlanta. (singular)
>
> Anthony and Peter **drive** dangerously. (plural)

A verb must always agree in number with its subject.

> subject verb
> ↓ ↓
> Emily **lives** alone. (subject and verb both singular)
>
> subject subject verb
> ↓ ↓ ↓
> Dennis and Michael **live** together. (subject and verb both plural)

4c. Person tells whether the subject of the verb is speaking, being spoken to, or being spoken about.

> I **am** the person in charge. (first person)
>
> You **are** my best friend. (second person)
>
> Bill **is** not here. (third person)
>
> I **swim** at the YMCA. (first person)
>
> You **come** with me. (second person)
>
> Rosa **speaks** Spanish and French. (third person)

All three persons may be singular or plural in number.

	Singular	Plural
First person	I run	we run
Second person	you run	you run
Third person	he runs	
	she runs	they run
	it runs	

Note: The same verb form frequently is used for different persons and different numbers.

> I **love** ice cream. (first person singular)
>
> We **love** ice cream. (first person plural)
>
> They **love** ice cream. (third person plural)

4d. Tense shows when the action of the verb takes place—whether in the present, the past, or the future.

> A plane **is passing** over our house right now. (present)
>
> Our guests **are** here. (present)
>
> Two U.S. astronauts **walked** on the moon in 1969. (past)
>
> The workers **were** here yesterday. (past)
>
> We'll **pay** you tomorrow. (future)
>
> Many people **will be** at the party tomorrow. (future)

4e. Mood indicates how a sentence is used—whether it is a statement or a question, a command or a request, a wish or a condition.

> Dinner **is** ready. (statement)
>
> Does Lillian **work** in New Jersey? (question)
>
> **Go** away! (command)
>
> Please **pass** me the bread. (request)
>
> If it **doesn't** rain, we can go. (condition)

The three kinds of mood are indicative, imperative, and subjunctive.

The indicative mood is used to express a statement or a question.

> Two firemen were injured in the blaze. (statement)

> Are you going out tonight? (question)

The imperative mood expresses a command or a request.

> Turn off your cell phones! (command)

> May I have a menu? (request—not question)

Note: The imperative mood is frequently indicated by leaving out the pronoun "you."

> (You) Stop that!

The subjunctive mood may be used to show that a wish rather than a fact is being expressed.

> I wish I **were** ten years younger.

4f. **Voice indicates whether the subject acts or is acted upon.**

> The dog **barked** at the stranger. (acts)

> The baby **was kissed** several times. (is acted upon)

A verb in the active voice shows that the subject is doing something.

> The thieves **wounded** the bank teller. (active voice)

> The curtains **blocked** our view. (active voice)

A verb in the passive voice shows that something is being done to the subject.

> The garbage **was picked up** this morning. (passive voice)

> Tyrone's car **is being washed**. (passive voice)

4g. **Complement**

> A complement may be one or more words that come after either a transitive or a linking verb.

> complement
> ↓
> Fire destroyed the **building**. (transitive verb)

> complement
> ↓
> The cat seemed **startled**. (linking verb)

complement   complement
↓   ↓
Tony bought his **wife** a silver **necklace**. (transitive verb)

complement
↓
Adam will be **president** someday. (linking verb)

A complement completes the meaning of the verb.

> The junta took **control of the government**.

> A baseball broke the **window**.

4h. **The four ways that a complement may be used in a sentence are (1) as a direct object of the verb, (2) as an indirect object of the verb, (3) as a predicate noun,* and (4) as a predicate adjective.**

> Samantha waters her **garden** every day. (direct object, receiving the action of the verb)

> Vincent gave his **brother** a basketball. (indirect object, telling to whom the action of the verb was directed)

Note: The noun "basketball" is the direct object of the transitive verb "gave"; therefore, "basketball" is also a complement.

> Arthur Fiedler was the **conductor** of the Boston Pops. (predicate noun, renaming the subject after the linking verb)

> Alaska is **huge**. (predicate adjective, describing the subject after the linking verb)

4i. **A complement used as a direct object of the verb may be a noun, a pronoun, or a subordinate clause.**

> Uncle Nate plants **vegetables** each spring. (noun used as direct object)

> You should see **her** now. (pronoun used as direct object)

> Tell me **what you know about life insurance**. (subordinate clause used as direct object)

---

*A predicate noun is also called a predicate nominative.

4j. **A complement used as an indirect object of the verb may also be a noun, a pronoun, or a subordinate clause.**

> The nurse sent the **patient** a bill. (noun used as indirect object)
>
> Will you do **me** a favor? (pronoun used as indirect object)
>
> Give **whoever calls today** this information. (subordinate clause used as indirect object)

Note: This applies only to sentences that contain both direct and indirect objects.

The three previous sentences—which have indirect objects—may be expressed in a different way.

> The nurse sent a bill **to the patient**.
>
> Will you do a favor **for me**?
>
> Give this information **to whoever calls today**.

In these three sentences, the prepositional phrases serve the purpose of indirect objects.

4k. **A complement that acts as a predicate noun may be a noun, a pronoun, a verbal, a phrase, or a clause.**

> Juan's uncle is **a bus driver**. (noun)
>
> It is **she**. (pronoun)
>
> Isaac's favorite sport is **sailing**. (gerund)
>
> President Sadat's desire was **to make peace**. (infinitive phrase)
>
> Fixing cars is **what Tom does best**. (noun clause)

4l. **A complement that acts like a predicate adjective may be an adjective or an adjective phrase.**

> Leonard and Sheldon **are funny**. (adjective)
>
> The lecture was **about athletics**. (adjective phrase)

Note: Both predicate nouns and predicate adjectives may be called predicate complements.

NOUNS AND PRONOUNS

5a. **Nouns**

The five types of nouns are **(1) proper, (2) common, (3) collective, (4) concrete,** and **(5) abstract**.*

5b. **A proper noun names a particular person, place, or thing**.

> Nelson Mandela, San Clemente, Statue of Liberty
> (Proper nouns always begin with a capital letter.)

5c. **A common noun names a general sort of person, place, or thing**.

> waitress, store, table

5d. **A collective noun names a group of individuals**.

> congregation, class, political party
> (A collective noun is singular in form, but it refers to many people.)

5e. **A concrete noun names any material object that is inanimate**.

> apple, hat, ball, box, desk, book, shirt

5f. **An abstract noun names a quality, state, or idea**.

> truth, motion, beauty

5g. **Pronouns**

The six kinds of pronouns are **(1) personal, (2) relative, (3) interrogative, (4) indefinite, (5) demonstrative,** and **(6) reflexive**.

5h. **A personal pronoun stands for the speaker, the person spoken to, or the person or thing spoken about.**

> **I** am going out.
> (The first person "I" is speaking.)

You should see the traffic jam downtown.
(The second person "you" is being spoken to.)

She wants to become a lawyer.
(The third person "she" is being spoken about.)

The **personal pronouns** are the following:

> I, you, he, she, it, we, they, me, us, him, her, them

The **possessive** forms of the personal pronouns are the following:

> my, mine, yours, his, hers, its, our, ours, their, theirs

A pronoun should be in the same person as the noun or pronoun it refers to.

> The tree was damaged when lightning struck **it**. (noun and pronoun in third person)
> **Everyone** knows that **he** [or **she** if a group of women is referenced] should dress well to make a good impression. (both pronouns in third person)
> (Not: **Everyone** knows that "you" or "they" should . . .)

5i. The **relative pronouns** are the following:

> who (whom), which, what, that

A relative pronoun may begin a subordinate clause.

> The child, **who** was alone, looked unhappy.

A relative pronoun connects the main clause to the subordinate clause.

> The problem was in the gas line, **which** was rusty.
> (The relative pronoun "which" joins the main clause to the subordinate clause it begins.)

A relative pronoun stands for a noun in the main clause.

> Savannah gave me the money **that** I needed.
> (The relative pronoun "that" stands for the noun "money" in the main clause.)

---

*A noun may be of more than one type. For example, "table" is both a common noun and a concrete noun.

When to use the relative pronoun "whom"
"Whom" is the objective case form of "who." We use "whom" as a **direct object,** an **indirect object,** or an **object of the preposition.**

> The men **whom** you see are waiting for work.
> (The relative pronoun "whom" is the direct object of the verb "see.")
>
> Hansen is the person to **whom** Wilmot gave the bribe money.
> (The relative pronoun "whom" is the indirect object of the verb "gave." It's also the object of the preposition "to.")
>
> The tablet was stolen by the messenger about **whom** the office manager had been suspicious.
> (The relative pronoun "whom" is the object of the preposition "about.")

5j. **An interrogative pronoun asks a question.**

> **Who** wants to start first?
>
> **What** did Richard do then?
>
> **Which** should I take?
>
> **Whose** is this jacket?
>
> **Whom** do you want to speak to?

5k. **An indefinite pronoun refers to a number of persons, places, or things in a general way.**

> **None** of the dishes was broken.
>
> Mark finds **everything** about boats interesting.
>
> I'll bring you **another.**
>
> **Some** of my friends buy lottery tickets.

Other commonly used indefinite pronouns are the following:

> **any, both, few, many, most, one, other, several, such**

5l. **A demonstrative pronoun points out a specific person or thing.**

> **This** is not my handwriting.
>
> May I have two of **those?**
>
> **That** is my brother.
>
> **These** are my best friends.

Note: **Interrogative, indefinite, and demonstrative pronouns may be used as adjectives.**

> **Which** dessert do you want? (interrogative adjective)
>
> **Every** time I try to skate I fall down. (indefinite adjective)

> **That** dress costs too much. (demonstrative adjective)

5m. **A reflexive pronoun refers back to the noun it stands for.**

> I hurt **myself** while jogging.
>
> Amy considers **herself** an adult.

A reflexive pronoun may be the **direct object of a verb,** the **indirect object of a verb,** the **object of a preposition,** or a **predicate noun.**

> Kim pushed **himself** and finished the race. (direct object)
>
> Ray bought **himself** a new watch. (indirect object)
>
> Amanda likes to be by **herself.** (object of a preposition)
>
> Mr. Thompson is just not **himself** lately. (predicate nominative)

Note: **Do not use "hisself" for "himself," or "theirselves" for "themselves." "Hisself" and "theirselves" are always incorrect.**

5n. **Three characteristics shared by all nouns and pronouns are gender, number, and case.**

5o. **Gender indicates the sex of the person or thing named—whether masculine, feminine, or neuter.**

> **Adam** wants some ice cream, but **he** is on a diet.
> ("Adam" and the pronoun "he" are both masculine in gender.)
>
> **Alice** said **she** was ready.
> ("Alice" and the pronoun "she" are both feminine in gender.)
>
> The **movie** was good, but **it** was too long.
> ("Movie" and the pronoun "it" are neither masculine nor feminine; therefore, they are both neuter in gender.)

A pronoun should be in the same gender as the noun it refers to.

5p. **Number indicates whether one or more than one person or thing is named.**

> Here is a **letter** for you.
> (The one "letter" is singular in number.)
>
> Many **cars** were involved in the accident.
> (Many "cars" are plural in number.)

Note: A collective noun is singular in form but usually plural in meaning.

> The audience was upset by the delay. ("Audience" is singular in number, although many people are in the audience.)

A pronoun should be in the same number as the noun it refers to.

> The **dishes** are not clean, so don't use **them**. ("Dishes" and the pronoun "them" are both plural in number.)

> **Hockey** is a lot of fun, but **it** is rough. ("Hockey" and the pronoun "it" are both singular in number.)

A pronoun that refers to a collective noun that is considered as a unit should be singular in number.

> The home team won **its** final game of the season.

A pronoun that refers to a collective noun that is considered as a group of individuals should be plural.

> The visiting team felt **they** deserved to win.

A pronoun that refers to an indefinite pronoun antecedent must be singular.

> Almost anyone can earn a good living if **he** or **she** works hard.

A pronoun must be singular if it refers to singular antecedents joined by "or" or "nor."

> Neither **Earle** nor **Jeff** could find **his** coat.

5q. **Case shows how a noun or pronoun is used in a sentence**.

> **They** stayed out all night. ("They" is the subject.)

> Natalie knew **him**. ("Him" is the object of the transitive verb.)

> Craig thinks this hat is **his**. ("His" is a pronoun that shows ownership.)

The three cases are nominative, objective, and possessive.

5r. **The nominative case names the subject of a verb or the predicate noun of a linking verb**.

> **Sophie** and **I** will call you tonight. (subjects)

> My best friends are **Katherine** and **you**. (predicate nouns)

A noun in the nominative case is usually placed before a verb.

> **Mr**. **Garcia** opened a dry-cleaning business.

> **Zoe** answered the telephone.

Personal pronouns in the nominative case have the following forms:

> I, you, he, she, it, we, they

The subject of a subordinate clause must be in the nominative case even if the clause itself acts as a direct object or an object of a preposition.

> Show me **who** is waiting to see me. (subordinate clause as direct object)

> Discuss this form with **whoever** applies for the job. (subordinate clause **as** object of a preposition)

5s. **The objective case indicates that nouns and pronouns act as direct objects, indirect objects, or objects of prepositions**.

> The storm forced **them** to stay home. (direct object)

> Michael enjoyed meeting **her**. (direct object)

> Samantha called **us, Mary** and **me,** into her office. (direct objects)

> The cab driver gave **me** good directions. (indirect object)

> Our supervisor showed **him** and **me** some contracts. (indirect objects)

> Christina had trouble teaching **them** how to type. (indirect object)

> Several of **us** want more food. (object of the preposition)

> Between **you** and **me,** I don't like our boss. (objects of the preposition)

Note: Each noun or pronoun in a compound object must be in the objective case.

A noun is in the objective case if it is placed after a transitive verb or after a preposition.

> He saw **Selena Gomez**.

> Ernie went into the **store**.

Personal pronouns in the objective case have the following forms:

> me, you, him, her, it, us, them

5t. Only three personal pronouns—**we**, **us**, and **you**—may also be used as **adjective pronouns**.

> **We** students have responded to the challenge of the 2000s.

> They are discriminating against **us** women.

> **You** boys should play more quietly.

Note: **The adjective pronoun "we" is in the nominative case when it modifies a subject. The adjective pronoun "us" is in the objective case when it modifies an object of a verb or an object of a preposition.**

> **We** Republicans support the President's bid for re-election. (nominative case when modifying subject)

> Mom sent **us** children to bed. (objective case when modifying direct object of verb)

> Won't you give **us** boys a chance to earn some money? (objective case when modifying indirect object of verb)

> Many children were on the plane with **us** adults. (objective case when modifying object of a preposition)

5u. **The objective case is used by nouns and pronouns that are the subject of an infinitive.**

> Paul's father wants **him** to help paint the house.

> Should Fred ask **her** to join the club?

A noun or pronoun following the infinitive **to be** must, like its subject, be in the objective case.

> Pat didn't expect my friend to be **him**.

Note: If the infinitive **to be** has no subject, the noun or pronoun that comes after the infinitive is in the nominative case.

> My twin brother is often thought to be **I**. (nominative case)

5v. **The possessive case indicates ownership.**

> **Melissa's** home is in Ohio.

> This book is **mine**.

Possession is generally shown by using an apostrophe and *s*:

> Bumbry's error

> men's room

> child's toy

> ship's crew

Ownership may be shown by an "of" phrase.

> The handle **of the door** is broken.

The "of" phrase is used in formal English to show possession by inanimate things or to avoid awkward constructions.

> The passage **of the bill** now in Congress will mean lower taxes.

> The sister **of my uncle's wife** is eighty years old.

Personal and relative pronouns have distinct forms to show the possessive case.

The following are personal pronouns (possessive form): my, mine, your, yours, his, her, hers, our, ours, their, theirs, its*

> That dress is **hers**.

> **Ours** is the house on the left.

"Whose" is a relative pronoun. (possessive form)†

> No one knows **whose** it is.

The possessive forms **my, your, his, our, their,**‡ and **whose** are called adjective pronouns because they modify nouns.

> **Your** shirt has a button missing.

> **My** family is very large.

> **Their** apartment costs a lot of money.

> The woman **whose** laptop I borrowed, gave it to me.

The possessive case is used by nouns and pronouns that come before a gerund.

> **Bubba's** shouting attracted a large crowd. (noun)

> **My** being sick caused me to miss an important lecture. (pronoun)

The possessive case of a compound noun is indicated by adding '*s* to the **last word of the compound noun**.

> A **movie star's** life is glamorous.

> The **Governor of California's** speech attacked the president.

---

*"Its" is the possessive form of the personal pronoun "it." "It's" is a contraction of "it is."

†"Whose" is the possessive form of the relative pronoun "who"; "who's" is a contraction of "who is."

‡"Their" is the possessive form of the relative pronoun "they"; "they're" is a contraction of "they are."

Pope John Paul II's visit to the United States pleased millions.

Note: **The plural of a compound noun** is formed by adding *s* to the principal noun.

chief of police (singular)

chief of police's (singular possessive)

chiefs of police (plural)

chiefs of police's (plural possessive)

5w. An **appositive** is a **noun or pronoun** usually placed next to another noun or pronoun to rename it.

Two guys, **Nestar and his cousin**, were already there. (identifies the subject)

Clarinda's dog **Sonya** eats only hamburgers. (renames the subject)

Note: An appositive must always be in the same case as the noun it renames.

We, **my brother and I,** are going skiing together. (both subject and appositive in nominative case)

Uncle Joe gave us, **Seb and me,** tickets to the World Series. (both object and appositive in case)

5x. **Direct address** and **nominative absolute** constructions are **always in the nominative case**.

Direct address consists of a noun (or pronoun) that names a particular person when someone else addresses that person.

Noah, please come here immediately.

A nominative absolute consists of a noun plus a participle.

The money having been spent, the children decided to go home.

SUBJECT-VERB RELATIONSHIP

6a. **A verb must agree with its subject in number and in person.**

> Dr. Shu has office hours from 8 until 4. (The third person singular form of "to have" agrees with the subject "Dr. Shu.")
>
> Robin and I **play** squash every Tuesday. (The first person plural form of "to play" agrees with the compound subject "Robin and I.")

6b. **Collective nouns are followed by singular or plural verbs according to the sense of the sentence.**

> The jury **has** asked for more time. (The third person singular is used because the jury is considered to be a unified body.)
>
> The jury **are** unable to agree. (The third person plural is used because the jury is considered to be a group of twelve persons.)

To summarize, a **collective noun** is **singular** when it refers to a group as a single unit.

> A minority in Congress **is** delaying passage of the bill.

A **collective noun** is **plural** when it refers to the individual members of the group.

> A minority of senators **want** to defeat the bill.

6c. **Some indefinite pronouns are always singular in meaning.**

> **Each** of the candidates **wants** an opportunity to discuss his beliefs.
>
> **Anyone is** allowed to use the public beach.
>
> **Any one** of us **is** willing to help.

Some indefinite pronouns are always plural in meaning.

> **Many** of the drawings **were** beautiful.
>
> A **few** of the windows **were** broken.
>
> **Several** of Joe's friends **are** sorry that he left.

6d. A verb should be **singular** if its subject has "every" or "many a" just before it.

> **Many a celebrity feels** entitled to more privacy than the paparazzi allow.
>
> **Every man, woman, and child wants** to be happy.

Some **indefinite pronouns** may be **singular or plural,** depending on the meaning of the sentence.

> **Some** of the books **have** been lost.
>
> **Some** of the work **was** completed.
>
> **All** of the ice cream **is** gone.
>
> **All** of the men **have** left.
>
> **Most** of the talk **was** about football.
>
> **Most** of the people **were** dissatisfied.

6e. **When singular subjects are joined by "or" or "nor," the subject is considered to be singular.**

> **Neither** the mother **nor** her daughter **was** ever seen again.
>
> **One** or the **other** of us **has** to buy the tickets.

6f. **When one singular and one plural subject are joined by "or" or "nor," the subject closer to the verb determines the number of the verb.**

> Neither the plumber nor the painters **have** finished.
>
> Either the branch offices or the main office **closes** at 4.

6g. **When the subjects joined by "or" or "nor" are of different persons, the subject nearer the verb determines the person.**

> She or you **are** responsible.
>
> You or she **is** responsible.

To avoid such awkward sentences, place a verb next to each subject.

> Either she **is** responsible or you **are.**
>
> Either you **are** responsible or she **is.**

6h. **Even if the verb comes before the subject, the verb agrees with the true subject in number and person**.

> **Are** the cat and the dog fighting? (The cat and the dog are . . .)
>
> Coming at us from the left **was** an ambulance. (An ambulance was . . .)
>
> There **are** two things you can do.* (Two things are . . .)
>
> There **is** only one bottle left.* (Only one bottle is . . .)

6i. **Interrogative pronouns and the adverbs "where," "here," and "there" do not affect the number or person of the verb when they introduce a sentence**.

> subject
> ↓
> What **is** the **name** of your friend?
>
> subject
> ↓
> What **are** the **addresses** of some good restaurants?
>
> subject
> ↓
> Who **is** the **man** standing over there?

> subject
> ↓
> Who **are** those **people?**
>
> subject
> ↓
> Here **comes** my **friend**.
>
> subject
> ↓
> Here **come** my **parents**.

6j. **When a predicate noun (following a linking verb) differs in number from the subject, the verb must agree with the subject**.

> Our biggest problem **is** angry customers.
>
> More gas guzzlers **aren't** what this country needs.

6k. **Parenthetical phrases** or other modifiers that come between the subject and verb **do not change the number or person of the true subject—** which the verb agrees with.

> The amount shown, plus interest, **is** due on Friday.
>
> The president, together with his advisers, **is** at Camp David.

---

*In these sentences, *there* is an expletive. An expletive is a word that gets a sentence started, but it is not a subject. Another expletive is *it*.

TENSE

7a. Tense specifies the moment of an action or condition.

> We **are walking** to the park. (present moment)
>
> We **will walk** to the park tomorrow. (future moment)
>
> We **walked** to the park yesterday. (past moment)
>
> I **have worked** here for three years. (action begun in the past and continued into the present)
>
> I **had worked** in Chicago for four years before I left. (past action completed **before** another past action)
>
> I **will have worked** here six months next Friday. (action to be completed sometime in the future)

7b. The six tenses are present, past, future, present perfect, past perfect, and future perfect.

7c. The present tense shows that an action is **happening in the present** or that a condition exists now.

> I **live** here. (action)
>
> He **is** busy now. (condition)

The **present-tense** forms of **to work, to have,** and **to be** follow:

to work	to have	to be
I work	I have	I am
you work	you have	you are
he ⎤	he ⎤	he ⎤
she ⊢ works	she ⊢ has	she ⊢ is
it ⎦	it ⎦	it ⎦
we work	we have	we are
you work	you have	you are
they work	they have	they are

The present tense may indicate **habitual action** or **habitual condition** or **a general truth**.

> Judy **leaves** her office every day at 5 o'clock. (habitual action)
>
> Dana **is** allergic to chocolate. (habitual condition)
>
> Two and two **are** four. (general truth)

The present tense may express **future time with the help of an adverb**.

> adverb
> ↓
> Gary flies to Washington **tomorrow**.
>
> adverb
> ↓
> We are going to see a movie **tonight**.

7d. The present perfect tense shows that an action that **began in the past** is **still going on in the present**.

> Betsy and I **have been** in New York for two years. (and are still in New York)
>
> The Johnson family **has owned** a plumbing supply company for sixty years. (and still owns it)

The **present perfect tense** may show that an action **begun in the past was just completed at the present time**.

> Our men **have worked** on your car until now.
>
> Charlayne **has** just **walked** in.

The **present perfect tense** is formed with **have or has and a past participle**.

> I **have eaten** too much.
>
> Nina **has** always **loved** music.

7e. The **past tense** shows that an action **occurred some time in the past** but has **not continued into the present**.

> Laura's doctor **advised** her to lose weight.
>
> The plane **landed** on time.
>
> Sarah **was living** in Philadelphia then. (progressive form)
>
> We **went** along for the ride.

If the verb in the main clause is in the past tense, the verb in the subordinate clause must also be in the past tense.

> The surgeon told his patient that an operation **was** necessary.
> (**Not:** The surgeon told his patient that an operation **is** necessary.)
>
> Lenny said that he **would meet** Frank at 7:30.
> (**Not:** Lenny said that he **will meet** Frank at 7:30.)

The past tense (first, second, and third person—singular and plural) is often formed by adding "ed" to the infinitive (without "to").

> James **helped** us many times.
>
> We **called** you last night.

7f. The **past perfect tense** indicates that an **action was completed before another action began**.

> I remembered the answer after **I had handed in** my exam.
>
> Kevin **had bought** the tickets before he met Angela.
>
> Madelyn **had worked** very hard, so she took a vacation.

Note: The **past tense** shows that an event happened at any time in the past, but the **past perfect tense** indicates that an event happened before another event in the past.

> Amelia **had finished** dressing before I woke up.
> (Not: Amelia **finished** dressing before I woke up.)
>
> Jake **had** already **left** by the time I arrived.
> (Not: Jake already **left** by the time I arrived.)

The past perfect tense is formed with "had" and a past participle.

> Cameron **had said** he would call before twelve.

7g. The **future tense** indicates that an **action is going to take place sometime in the future**.

> All of us **will pay** more for heat this winter.
>
> The weatherman says it **will rain** tomorrow.
>
> **Will** you **join** us for lunch, Eric?
>
> **I'll go** away this weekend.

The future tense is formed with "will" and the infinitive (without "to").

> Dylan **will take** you to the airport.

7h. The **future perfect tense** is used to express a **future action that will be completed before another future action**.

> By the time we get home,* my parents **will have gone** to bed.
>
> We'll start eating after you (**will**) **have washed** your hands.
>
> Helena **will have finished** her work when we meet her at the office.

The future perfect tense is formed with "will have" and a past participle.

> Alison **will have quit** her job by Christmas.

7i. **All six tenses may be expressed in a progressive form by adding the present participle of a verb to the appropriate form of "to be."**

> The Cosmos **are winning**. (present progressive)
>
> The Cosmos **were winning**. (past progressive)
>
> The Cosmos **have been winning**. (present perfect progressive)
>
> The Cosmos **had been winning**. (past perfect progressive)
>
> The Cosmos **will be winning**. (future progressive)
>
> The Cosmos **will have been winning**. (future perfect progressive)

7j. **Principal parts of irregular verbs**

We call a verb like "eat" an irregular verb. Any verb that changes internally to form the past participle is an irregular verb.

---

*See page 345, which discusses how a present tense may express future time.

Present Tense	Past Tense	Past Participle	Present Participle
begin	began	begun	beginning
blow	blew	blown	blowing
break	broke	broken	breaking
burst	burst	burst	bursting
catch	caught	caught	catching
choose	chose	chosen	choosing
come	came	come	coming
do	did	done	doing
drink	drank	drunk	drinking
drive	drove	driven	driving
eat	ate	eaten	eating
fall	fell	fallen	falling
find	found	found	finding
fly	flew	flown	flying
freeze	froze	frozen	freezing
give	gave	given	giving
go	went	gone	going
grow	grew	grown	growing
know	knew	known	knowing
lay (place)	laid	laid	laying
lie (rest)	lay	lain	lying
raise	raised	raised	raising
ring	rang	rung	ringing
rise	rose	risen	rising
run	ran	run	running
set	set	set	setting
sit	sat	sat	sitting
speak	spoke	spoken	speaking
steal	stole	stolen	stealing
swim	swam	swum	swimming
take	took	taken	taking
throw	threw	thrown	throwing
wear	wore	worn	wearing
write	wrote	written	writing

VERBALS

8a. **A verbal is a word formed from a verb.**

> **Skiing** can be dangerous.
>
> We could hear our neighbors **arguing**.
>
> Alexandra and Zachary worked hard **to succeed**.

8b. **The three kinds of verbals are gerunds, participles, and infinitives.**

8c. **A gerund acts like a noun.**

> **Texting** is not allowed while you drive.
>
> **Traveling** by train can be fun.
>
> Mark's favorite sport is **boating**.

A gerund ends in "-ing."

> Beyoncé's **singing** is beautiful.
>
> **Flying** is the fastest way to get there.

A phrase that begins with a gerund is called a gerund phrase.

> **Paying bills on time** is a good habit.
>
> **Leaving my friends** made me sad.

8d. **A participle acts like an adjective.**

> The police stopped the **speeding** car.
>
> The **tired** children were sent to bed.

A present participle ends in "-ing."

> A priest comforted the **dying** woman.
>
> **Running**, the girl caught up with her friends.

Note: **A present participle looks like a gerund because they both end in "-ing." A present participle, however, is used as an adjective, not as a noun.**

A past participle usually ends in "-d," "-ed," "-t," "-n," or "-en."

> **Used** clothing is cheaper than new clothes.
>
> Ella left **written** instructions for her assistant.

A phrase that begins with a participle is called a participial phrase.

> **Getting off the elevator**, I met a friend.
>
> **Questioned by the police**, several witnesses described the robbery.

8e. **An infinitive is used as a noun or an adjective or an adverb.**

> Hunter loves **to dance**. (noun)
>
> Our candidate has the ability **to win**. (adjective)
>
> Lily practices every day **to improve**. (adverb)

An infinitive usually begins with "to," but not always.

> Samantha wants **to know** if you need a ride.
>
> Help me wash my car. (Or: Help me **to wash** my car.)

A phrase introduced by an infinitive is called an infinitive phrase.

> His only desire **was to save money**. (infinitive phrase used as a noun)
>
> There must be **a way to solve this problem**. (infinitive phrase used as an adjective)
>
> The doctor is too busy **to see you now**. (infinitive phrase used as an adverb)

8f. **Gerunds may be present or perfect.**

> Good **cooking** is his specialty. (present)
>
> Your **having arrived** on time saved me. (perfect)

A gerund in the present form refers to an action happening at the same time as the action of the main verb.

> **Swimming** is fun.
>
> **Running** a mile tired him out.
>
> **Taking** driving lessons will help you drive better.

A **gerund in the perfect** form refers to an **action that was completed before the time of the main verb**.

> He believes his recovery is a result of his **having prayed**.

> Our **having read** the book made the movie boring.

8g. **Participles may be present, past, or perfect.**

> The woman **sitting** on the couch is my mother. (present)

> **Warned** by his doctor, Jack began to exercise. (past)

> **Having been recognized,** Jay-Z was mobbed by his fans. (perfect)

A **present participle** refers to **action happening at the same time as the action of the main verb**, whether that verb is in the present tense or the past tense.

present
↓

> **Smiling** broadly, the president **answers** questions from the audience.

past
↓

> **Smiling** broadly, the president **answered** questions from the audience.

present
↓

> **Holding up** his hands, the teacher **is asking** for silence.

past
↓

> **Holding up** his hands, the teacher **asked** for silence.

A **past participle sometimes refers to action happening at the same time as the action of the main verb.**

> **Irritated** by his sister, Raphael yelled at her.

> **Dressed up,** Tom looks like a new man.

A **past participle sometimes refers to action that happened before the action of the main verb.**

> **Burned** by the sun, Melissa is suffering.

> **Awakened** by the noise, we looked outside.

The **perfect participle always refers to action occurring before the action of the main verb.**

> **Having finished** work, we can leave.

> **Having seen** that movie, we went for ice cream.

> **Having left** home in a hurry, Michael forgot his umbrella.

8h. **Infinitives may be present or perfect.**

> Justin likes **to read** all day. (present)

> Taylor was supposed **to have brought** the money. (perfect)

The **present infinitive shows an action occurring at the same time as the action of the main verb.**

> I **am trying to finish** this puzzle. (both present)

> Henry **looked** around **to see** who was there. (both past)

> Dana **will call to ask** you for some advice. (both future)

The **present infinitive may indicate action or a state of being at some future time.**

> I hope **to see** you again.

> I expect **to be** there in an hour.

> He intended **to write** to us.

An **infinitive is never used in a subordinate clause that begins with "that."**

> I expect everyone to remain seated.

> I expect that everyone will remain seated. (**Not:** I expect that everyone to remain seated.)

The **perfect infinitive expresses action occurring before that of the main verb.**

> I am sorry not **to have met** you before.

> He claims **to have seen** a UFO.

Avoid using the perfect infinitive after main verbs in the past or past perfect tense.

> I had expected **to receive** my mail today. (**Not:** I had expected **to have received** . . .)

> They hoped **to join** us for dinner. (**Not:** They hoped **to have joined** us . . .)

> Mike would have liked to **ask** Alice for a date, but he **was** too shy. (**Not:** Mike would have liked **to have asked** Alice . . .)

MOOD AND VOICE

9a. **Mood**

The **three moods** that a verb may express are **indicative, imperative,** and **subjunctive**.

9b. **The indicative mood indicates that the action or state is something believed to be true**.

I **am** the greatest.

She **sings** beautifully.

The **indicative** mood is **used in asking a question**.

Are you Mr. Martin?

Does Austin **want** to watch *Saturday Night Live*?

9c. **The imperative mood expresses a command or a request or a suggestion**.

Answer the phone. (command)

Give me a chance, please. (request)

Try turning the handle the other way. (suggestion)

The imperative mood is not only more emphatic than the indicative mood—it is more quickly and easily understood.

Give me that letter. (imperative)

I **would appreciate** it if you would give me that letter. (indicative)

9d. **The subjunctive mood is often used to express a wish or a condition that is not real—that is, contrary to fact**.

I wish the weather **were** nicer.

If this paint **were** dry, we could sit on the bench.

Zoe suggested that Carol **stay** at her apartment.

Carl asked that Samuel **agree** to pay for the damage.

The subjunctive mood is also used to express purpose or intention.

Connie said that she **would visit** her mother at Easter.

(**Not:** Connie said that she **will visit** her mother at Easter.)

We bought coolers so that we **would have** fresh food for the trip.

(**Not:** We bought coolers so that we **had** fresh food for the trip.)

The subjunctive mood is mainly indicated by **two forms of the verb "to be."** The forms are **"be"** and **"were."**

Be good.

If I **were** president, I'd nationalize the oil industry.

The present subjunctive uses "be" for all three persons, both singular and plural.

I be, you be, he be, we be, they be

I have one wish—that I **be** president some day.

Mrs. Diggs insists that you **be** given a bonus.

I asked that the child not **be** punished.

The judge ordered that the tenants **be** allowed to stay.

The more common form of the subjunctive is the past subjunctive form "were" for all three persons, both singular and plural.

If $\begin{bmatrix} \text{I} \\ \text{you} \\ \text{he} \\ \text{we} \\ \text{they} \end{bmatrix}$ **were** here, everything would be all right.

The subjunctive mood for verbs other than "to be" is formed by using the present-tense first person singular form for all persons.

> Madison suggested that Robert **keep** an extra pair of eyeglasses.

> The umpire insisted that the manager **leave** the field.

9e. Choosing between the subjunctive and indicative mood.

People express how they see a situation—whether **contrary to fact** or **within the realm of possibility**—by choosing either the subjunctive mood or the indicative mood.

> If his statement **be** true, this is a case of fraud. (subjunctive)
> (The writer thinks it is highly improbable that the statement is true.)

> If his statement **is** true, this may be a case of fraud. (indicative)
> (The writer indicates that it is quite possible that the statement may be true.)

> If he **were** at the meeting, he would . . . (subjunctive)
> (The speaker tells the listener that the man is not at the meeting.)

> If he **was** at the meeting, he would have been able to speak to the point. (indicative)
> (Perhaps the man **was** at the meeting; one doesn't know.)

> **Had** the first payment been made in April, the second would be due in September. (subjunctive)
> (The speaker indicates that the payment was **not** made in April.)

> If the first payment **was** made in April, the second will be due in September. (indicative)
> (Perhaps it was made; perhaps not—the speaker doesn't know.)

Do not use "would have" instead of "had" in "if" clauses to express the past perfect tense of the subjunctive.

> If he **had worked** harder, he would have a better job.
> (**Not:** If he **would have worked** harder . . .)

9f. Voice

A verb is either in the **active voice** or in the **passive voice**.

9g. A verb in the active voice indicates that the subject performs an action.

> Arianna **reads** every night before going to sleep.

> The fire **burned** the entire house.

A verb in the active voice stresses the subject or actor rather than the action.

9h. A verb in the passive voice indicates that something is being done to the subject.

> The children **were given** lunches to take to school.

> The television **was turned off** by my dad.

A verb in the passive voice stresses the action rather than the actor.

9i. All transitive verbs—verbs whose action affects something or someone—**can be used in the passive voice**.

> Carlos Beltrán **caught** the ball. (active)

> The ball **was caught** by Carlos Beltrán. (passive)

9j. To form the passive, the object of the transitive verb in the active voice is moved ahead of the verb, thus becoming the subject. A form of "to be" is added to the main verb. The subject of the active sentence is either left out or expressed in a prepositional phrase.

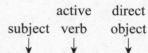

> The **tow truck pulled** the **car** out of the ditch. (active voice)

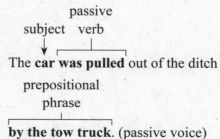

> The **car was pulled** out of the ditch

by the tow truck. (passive voice)

9k. **If the active sentence has an indirect object as well as a direct object, either the indirect object or the direct object may be the subject of the passive sentence.**

active   indirect direct
verb   object   object
↓   ↓   ↓

Tom **gave** his **sister a kitten**. (active)

passive
subject   verb
↓   ↓

A **kitten was given** by Tom to his sister. (passive)

passive
subject   verb
↓   ↓

Tom's **sister was given** a kitten by Tom. (passive)

9l. **The passive voice is appropriate** to express an action **when the actor is unknown**.

The door **had been locked** before we arrived.

Note: In general, avoid the passive voice for clearer, more forceful sentences.

MODIFIERS—ADJECTIVES, ADJECTIVE PHRASES, AND ADJECTIVE CLAUSES

10a. Modifiers

A modifier adds information to another word in the sentence.

> **Blue** flowers were growing in the field. (The adjective "blue" adds color to the noun "flowers.")
>
> Harper paints **beautifully**. (The adverb "beautifully" tells how Harper paints.)

Note: Adverbs and adverbial phrases are introduced in this section and covered in greater detail the next section starting on page 358.

10b. Modifiers may be a word, a phrase, or a clause.

> Ben put on a **clean** shirt. (word)
>
> The wristband **of her watch** was broken. (phrase)
>
> Landon liked the painting **that was done by his friend**. (clause)

There are **various types** of modifiers.

> Jill brought us **fresh** fruit. (adjective as modifier)
>
> Bob's friends greeted him **warmly**. (adverb as modifier)
>
> Rudy enjoyed the ride **from Birmingham to Atlanta**. (adjective phrase as modifier)
>
> The rent will increase **after this month**. (adverb phrase as modifier)
>
> Lillian holds two jobs **because she supports her sons in college**. (subordinate clause as adverbial modifier)
>
> The houses **where American presidents were born** are museums. (subordinate clause as adjectival modifier)

10c. Adjectives modify nouns.

The six kinds of adjectives are the following:

> **Limiting: Many** children are bused to school.
>
> **Numerical: Four** days have passed since I saw her.
>
> **Descriptive: Striped** wallpaper hung in the hall.
>
> **Proper: American** and **Russian** flags lined the parade route.
>
> **Pronoun: My** book has a torn cover.
>
> **Article: A** letter has arrived.

10d. Articles

The **article "a"** or **"an"** (indefinite article) indicates that the **noun it modifies is an example of a general type.**

> **A** dove symbolizes peace. (any dove)
>
> **A** doctor saves lives. (any doctor)
>
> **An** ambulance brings people to hospitals. (any ambulance)

Note: Do not use the articles "a" or "an" after "kind of," "type of," or "sort of."

> A mango is **a kind of fruit**. (Not: . . . **a kind of a fruit**.)
>
> The hybrid is **a new type of car**. (Not: . . . **a new type of a car**.)
>
> That sound gives me **a sort of weird feeling**. (Not: . . . **a sort of a weird feeling**.)

The **article "the"** (definite article) indicates that the **noun it modifies is a particular noun.**

> **The** winner received ten thousand dollars. (specific person)
>
> **The** lamp over there is sold. (specific thing)

10e. Single adjectives and compound adjectives

A single adjective usually comes immediately before the word it modifies.

> Help me carry this **heavy** package.

A compound adjective consists of **two or more words serving as a single adjective**.

> The drought made the earth **bone dry**.

> My dictionary is **up to date**.

When a **compound adjective** comes **before a noun,** the words are **joined by a hyphen**.

> Denzel Washington was my **next-door** neighbor.

> A **large-scale** map is hanging on the wall.

When the modifying words follow a noun, they are not hyphenated, unless they are normally hyphenated compounds.

> This book is **well written**.

> My new watch is **self-winding**. (normally hyphenated)

When two or more adjectives come before a noun but do not act jointly, they are not hyphenated.

> Jordan was wearing a **white silk** shirt.

> I've had a **long, hard** day.

Note: If the word *and* can be inserted between two adjectives that come before a noun without destroying the meaning of the sentence, put a comma in between the two adjectives; otherwise, do not.

> Ms. Davis is a **kind, generous** person. (kind **and** generous)

> Show us your **new suit**.
> (**Not:** . . . your and new suit, so **not** your, new suit.)

10f. Two or more adjectives may follow the word they modify to make the sentence read more smoothly.

> The children, **tired and hungry,** were difficult to control.

10g. Most adjectives may show greater or lesser degrees of their characteristic quality.

> Today was **cold**. (characteristic quality)
> Tomorrow will be **colder** than today. (greater)

The day after will be the **coldest**. (still greater)

Yesterday was **less cold** than today. (lesser)

The day before was the **least cold** this week. (lesser still)

Some adjectives do not show comparison.

> Jennifer is **pregnant**.
> (She cannot be **more** or **less** pregnant.)

> This salad dressing is **perfect**.
> (**Not:** . . . is **more** or **less** perfect.)

10h. The three degrees of comparison are positive, comparative, and superlative.

> Brianna is **happy**. (positive degree)

> Christopher is **happier** than Frank. (comparative degree)

> Brandon is the **happiest** of all. (superlative degree)

The positive degree simply names the quality expressed by an adjective.

> I like **spicy** food.

The **comparative degree** indicates that the quality described by an adjective exists in one person to a **greater or lesser degree** than in another person or thing.

> Valentina looks **older** than Liz. (greater)

> Amelia was **more excited** than her brother. (greater)

> This street is **less clean** than the one where I live. (lesser)

The greater form of the comparative degree is formed by adding "-er" to the positive degree or by inserting "more" before the positive form.

> **rich + er = richer**

> **rich + more = more rich**

The lesser form of the comparative degree is formed by inserting "less" before the positive form.

> **rich + less = less rich**

Note: **Use the comparative degree when comparing only two things.**

The **superlative degree** indicates that the quality described by an adjective exists in the **greatest or least degree** in one person or thing.

Toby is the **friendliest** dog I know. (greatest)

Charlotte seems the **least nervous** of us all. (least)

Note: **Use the superlative degree when comparing more than two things**.

10i. **Some adjectives do not follow the regular methods of forming their comparative and superlative degrees.**

Positive Degree	Comparative Degree	Superlative Degree
good	better	best
bad	worse	worst
little	less, lesser	least

(A dictionary will provide the irregular comparatives of such adjectives.)

Most adjectives of three syllables or more are compared by the use of "more" and "most," rather than by the endings "-er" and "-est."

Alejandro is **more capable** of managing a business than Jon.

Luciana is the **most wonderful** girl I know.

10j. **Avoid double comparisons, which are formed by adding both "more" or "most" and "-er" or "-est."**

Alan is the **brightest** little boy.
(**Not**: . . . the **most brightest** . . .)

Eric is a **better** eater than his brother.
(**Not**: . . . a **more better** eater . . .)

10k. **When two things are compared, both things should be clearly accounted for**.

These clothes look cleaner than **those (clothes)**.

George looks older than **he** used to.

An **ellipsis** is the leaving out of one or more words that are grammatically important but that are understood by the reader.

Audrey plays soccer better than I (do).

While (he was) waiting for the pitch, Alex clenched the bat tightly.

Incomplete subordinate clauses that cause confusion, similar to the confusion caused

by **dangling modifiers,** may be corrected by supplying the missing words.

Melissa's dress was torn while **she was** climbing over the fence.
(**Not**: Melissa's dress was torn while climbing over the fence.)

Use the word *other* or *else* to separate the thing being compared from the rest of the group of which the word is a part.

This car gets better mileage than all the **other** cars.

Marisol is more beautiful than anyone **else** around.

10l. **Infinitives, infinitive phrases, participles, and participial phrases may act as adjectives**.

Ms. Garcia is the person **to know** if you want a bank loan. (infinitive as adjective)

This is a day **to remember always**. (infinitive phrase as adjective)

Screaming, Nancy woke up from her nightmare. (present participle as adjective)

Covering his face, the defendant walked past the reporters. (participial phrase as adjective)

10m. **Infinitive and participial phrases that begin a sentence must be able to refer, both logically and grammatically, to the subject of the main clause**.

To qualify for the job, you need a high school diploma.
(**Not**: To qualify for the job, a high school diploma is needed. A "high school diploma" cannot apply for the job.)

Rushing to finish, Tanya made some errors.
(**Not**: Rushing to finish, some errors were made by Tanya. "Errors" cannot rush to finish.)

10n. **Infinitive and participial phrases are called dangling modifiers if they cannot logically and grammatically attach to the subject of the main clause**.

To apply for a credit card, an application form must be filled out. (infinitive phrase as dangling modifier)

Being an only child, my parents spoiled me. (participial phrase as dangling modifier)

Sentences with dangling modifiers may be corrected either by supplying the subject that the phrase can sensibly modify or by changing the phrase to an introductory adverbial clause.

To apply for a credit card, **one** (or **you** or **a person**) must fill out an application. (Or: **When one applies for a credit card,** an application form must be filled out.)

Being an only child, **I** was spoiled by my parents. (Or: **Because I am an only child,** I was spoiled by my parents.)

10o. **A prepositional phrase may act as an adjective.**

The violent storm damaged the roof **of our house.**

Her leaving **without saying a word** irritated me. (also considered a **gerund phrase**)

10p. **A subordinate clause may act as an adjective.**

Thanks for the present **that you gave me.**

The person **who can help you** is not at her desk.

This ring, **which belonged to my grandmother,** is valuable.

The building **where they used to live** is being torn down.

There is never a time **when Ed isn't busy.**

Subordinate clauses that act as adjectives may state essential information or nonessential information.

The train **that you need to take** is leaving from Track 12. (information essential to describe which train)

Robert loves his car, **which he hasn't finished paying for.** (information that is nonessential to describe which car)

10q. **Restrictive and nonrestrictive clauses**

Restrictive clauses, which contain essential information (that is, information that is necessary to identify the *specific* thing we are discussing), **are not set apart by commas.**

The secondhand TV **that I bought for twenty dollars** works beautifully. (restrictive clause)

Nonrestrictive clauses, which contain secondary information (information that is not essential to identify the specific thing being discussed), **are set off by commas.**

My friend Dina, **whom I've known for years,** wants me to visit her. (nonrestrictive clause)

10r. **"Whose" is the possessive form for the relative pronouns "who," "which," and "that."**

The boy **whose** father died had to get a job.

The dog **whose** leg was broken runs well now.

Mr. Temple, **whose** wife is a ballerina, teaches French.

The book **whose** cover is damaged is half price.

Note: "Whose" can be used with objects as well as people.

10s. **A word, phrase, or clause should be placed as close as possible to the word it modifies.**

Give me a glass of **cold** water.
(**Not:** Give me a cold glass . . .)

We need someone **with experience** to cook breakfast.
(**Not:** We need someone to cook breakfast with experience.)

On his head Grant wore a felt hat **that was obviously too small.**
(**Not:** Grant wore a felt hat on his head that was obviously too small.)

10t. **A misplaced modifier is a word, phrase, or clause that is misplaced in the sentence so that it modifies the wrong word.**

Wrong: Kara was injured while running on the treadmill **in a horrible manner.**

Right: Kara was injured **in a horrible manner** while running on the treadmill.

Wrong: The old farmer went to the barn to milk the cow **with a cane.**

Right: The old farmer **with a cane** went to the barn to milk the cow.

Wrong: The flames were extinguished before any damage was done **by the Fire Department**.

Right: The flames were extinguished **by the Fire Department** before any damage was done.

10u. **Squinting modifiers** are modifiers that are misplaced so that the reader cannot tell if the word, phrase, or clause modifies the words immediately before the modifier or immediately after.

Wrong: Henry said **today** he would wash his car.

Right: **Today** Henry said he would wash his car. (Or: Henry said he would wash his car **today**.)

Wrong: The dentist told him **frequently** to use dental floss.

Right: The dentist **frequently** told him to use dental floss. (**Or:** The dentist told him to use dental floss **frequently**.)

MODIFIERS—ADVERBS, ADVERBIAL PHRASES, AND ADVERBIAL CLAUSES

11a. **Adverbs modify verbs, adjectives, and adverbs.**

Dan runs **slowly**. (modifies verb)

Emily is an **extremely** gifted pianist. (modifies adjective)

Jimmie Johnson drives **incredibly** well. (modifies adverb)

11b. **The five kinds of adverbs are classified by the questions they answer.**

How? Adverbs of manner.

She sings **well**. He speaks **clearly**.

Where? Adverbs of place or direction.

Take me **home**. She was just **here**. He went **out**.

When? Adverbs of time.

Bring it **immediately**. I'll see you **tomorrow**.

How much? Adverbs of degree or measure.

That's **enough**. A little **more**, please.

Why? Adverbs of cause, reason, or purpose.

He left **because** he was afraid.

He bought a car **so** he could get to work.

11c. **The following words can be either adjectives or adverbs, depending on their use.**

above
better
cheap
deep
early
fast
first
hard
long
much
only
slow
well

The instructor warned her not to drive **fast**. (adverb)

Fast drivers can be dangerous. (adjective)

Michael Phelps can swim **better** than I can. (adverb)

Lily feels **better** now. (adjective)

11d. Distinguish carefully **when an adverb should follow a linking verb** and **when a predicate adjective should be used** to follow the linking verb.

Sarah looks **bad**. (predicate adjective meaning that Sarah doesn't look healthy)

Miguel looks **badly**. (adverb meaning that Miguel is doing a poor job looking for something)

Caramel smells **sweet**. (predicate adjective meaning that caramel has a sweet scent)

Roses smell **sweetly**. (adverb **incorrectly** meaning that roses sniff the air sweetly!)

11e. While speaking, one may incorrectly drop the "-ly" ending from common adverbs.

I'm **real** glad you called.
(**Correct:** I'm **really** glad you called.)

He **sure** is lucky.
(**Correct:** He **surely** is lucky.)

Do not drop the "-ly" ending unless a shorter form is correct.

I bought it **cheaply**. (Or: I bought it **cheap**.)

Come **quickly**! (Or: Come **quick**!)

The adverbs "hardly," "scarcely," "only," and "barely" should not be used with a negative verb construction.

Dale has **hardly** any free time.
(**Not:** Dale **hasn't** hardly any free time.)

Rose and I have **scarcely** worked this week. (**Not:** Rose and I **haven't** scarcely worked this week.)

11f. **An adverb may show greater or lesser degrees** of its characteristic quality.

> Peter arrived **early**.
>
> Anthony came **earlier** than Peter.
>
> Tiana came **earliest** of all.

The positive degree simply names the quality expressed by an adverb.

> Stephanie runs **quickly**.

The **comparative degree** indicates that the quality described by an adverb exists for one person or thing to **a greater or lesser degree** than for another person or thing.

> New air conditioners run **more efficiently** than old ones.
>
> Nat draws **less well** than Monica.

The **comparative degree** of adverbs is formed by inserting **"more" or "less" before the positive degree form,** unless there is an irregular form for the comparative degree.

> Sarita works **more diligently** than Mark.
>
> Victoria gets angry **less often** than Ethan.
>
> This amplifier sounds **better** than mine. (irregular form)

The **superlative degree** indicates the quality described by the adverb exists in the **greatest or least degree** for one person or thing.

> Ben works **most carefully** when someone is watching.
>
> Evelyn explained the problem the **most clearly**.
>
> His was the **least carefully** written report.

The **superlative degree** of adverbs is formed by inserting **"most" or "least" before the positive degree form**.

> Who was voted "**most likely** to succeed"?
>
> Maria Sharapova played **least skillfully** during the first set.

When two persons or things are being compared, the comparison should be clear.

> I love chocolate more than **Umberto** does. (**Not:** I love chocolate more than Umberto. Such an incomplete comparison might be interpreted to mean that I love chocolate more than I love Umberto.)

11g. An infinitive or an infinitive phrase may be used as an adverb.

> Robert was willing **to go**. (infinitive used as adverb)
>
> I am writing **to explain my behavior** last night. (infinitive phrase used as adverb)

11h. A prepositional phrase may be used as an adverb.

> We left **for the weekend**.
>
> The elderly couple sat **on the park bench**.
>
> The coach supported his team **in every way**.

11i. A subordinate clause may be used as an adverb.

> Mrs. Maurillo forgot her umbrella **when she left**.
>
> **Because they cooperated with him,** the president thanked several members of Congress.

11j. **An adverb or an adverbial phrase should be placed as close as possible to the word it modifies**.

> Joanne worked **without complaining** while her husband went to school.
> (**Not:** Joanne worked while her husband went to school **without complaining**.)

Note how an adverbial misplacement may change the meaning of a sentence.

> The room can be painted **only** by me. (not by anyone else)
>
> The room can **only** be painted by me. (not wallpapered)
>
> **Only** the room can be painted by me. (not the outside of the house)

11k. **An adverbial clause may be placed either at the beginning of a sentence or, in its natural order, after the main clause.**

> **After you have read this letter,** you will understand my reasons.

> You will understand my reasons **after you have read this letter**.

Note: An adverbial clause is followed by a comma when it is used to introduce a sentence.

11l. **Adverbial phrases and clauses should be placed so that only one meaning is possible.**

> **After the movie** we all agreed to go for some ice cream. (Or: We all agreed to go for some ice cream **after the movie**.)
> (**Not:** We all agreed **after the movie** to go for some ice cream.)

> Ask Kay to call me **when she gets in**. (Or: **When she gets in,** ask Kay to call me.)
> (**Not:** Ask Kay **when she gets in** to call me.)

CONNECTIVES

12a. A connective joins one part of a sentence to another part.

> Ryan **and** Lucas are giving a concert tonight.
> (The connective "and" joins the two parts of the compound subject.)

> Did you go out, **or** did you stay home last night?
> (The connective "or" joins the two independent clauses.)

> The banks are closed **because** today is a holiday.
> (The connective "because" joins the main clause to the subordinate clause.)

> The investigation **of** the robbery has been completed.
> (The connective "of" joins the noun "robbery" to the noun "investigation.")

12b. A connective may be a preposition, a conjunction, an adverb, or a pronoun.

> Josie left her scarf **on** the bus. (preposition)

> Mr. Colbert campaigned for the presidency, **but** he lost. (conjunction)

> Kevin looked back **because** someone was shouting. (conjunction)

> Ernie left his home an hour ago; **therefore,** he should be here any minute. (adverb)

> The letter **that** was mailed this morning should arrive tomorrow. (pronoun)

12c. Prepositions as connectives

A preposition may be **a word or a compound**. A compound consists of two or more words that function as one word.

> Come **over** here. (word)

> Women live longer than men, **according to** statistics. (compound)

12d. A preposition joins a noun or pronoun to the rest of the sentence.

> preposition
> ↓
> One of the **windows** is broken. (noun)

> preposition
> ↓
> Josh is worried about his **health**. (noun)

> preposition
> ↓
> These bags have nothing in **them**. (pronoun)

Choosing the correct preposition is often based on **idiomatic usage**—that is, the way English is used, whether or not it contradicts strict grammatical rules.

12e. Some commonly used prepositional idioms are the following:

Word	Preposition	Meaning
absolve	from	[blame]
abstain	from	[drinking]
accede	to	[a request]
accommodate	to	[a situation]
accompanied	by	[a lady (a person)]
accompanied	with	[applause (a thing)]
account	for	[one's actions]
account	to	[one's superior]
acquit	of	[a crime]
adapted	to	[his requirements]
adapted	from	[a novel]
adept	in	[selling a product]
adequate	to	[the demand]
adequate	for	[her needs]
agree	to	[a proposal (an idea)]
agree	with	[the teacher (a person)]
amenable	to	[an offer]
angry	with	[my cousin (a person)]
angry	at	[a remark (a thing)]
annoyed	by	[the noise (a thing)]
annoyed	with	[the child (a person)]
appreciative	of	[their efforts]
averse	to	[hard work (an idea)]
basis	for	[agreement]
capable	of	[getting high marks]
concur	with	[the mayor (a person)]
concur	in	[the decision (an idea)]
confer	with	[someone (a person)]
confer	about	[something (a thing)]
conform	to	[the rules]
correspond	to	[what I said (a thing)]
correspond	with	[his lawyer (a person)]
differs	from	[her sister (a person)]
differs	with	[what was done (a thing)]

Word	Preposition	Meaning
disappointed	in	[you (a person)]
disappointed	with	[the result (a thing)]
enter	into	[an agreement]
enter	upon	[a career]
excepted	from	[further responsibility]
exempt	from	[taxes]
expect	from	[your investment (a thing)]
expect	of	[his assistant (a person)]
familiar	to	[me (a person)]
familiar	with	[the proceedings (a thing)]
free	of	[his wife (a person)]
free	from	[her nagging (a thing)]
identical	with	[something else]
ignorant	of	[his rights]
incompatible	with	[fellow workers]
independent	of	[his relative]
infer	from	[a statement]
involved	in	[a project (a thing)]
involved	with	[a friend (a person)]
liable	to	[damages (a thing)]
necessity	for	[food (a thing)]
necessity	of	[avoiding trouble (doing something)]
proficient	in	[a skill]
profit	by	[knowledge]
responsible	to	[the owner (a person)]
responsible	for	[paying a debt (a thing)]
talk	to	[the group (one person talks)]
talk	with	[my friends (all talk)]
variance	with	[another]
wait	at	[the church (a place)]
wait	for	[your uncle (a person)]
worthy	of	[consideration]

12f. Prepositions should not be used needlessly.

Where is your brother?
(**Not:** Where is your brother **at?**)

Where are you going?
(**Not:** Where are you going **to?**)

Pete started on another project.
(**Not:** Pete started **in** on another project.)

We agreed to divide the housework.
(**Not:** We agreed to divide **up** the housework.)

Prepositions are sometimes left out by mistake.

Harley talked to me **about** her new job and **about** why she left her old one.
(**Not:** Harley talked to me about her new job and why . . .)

Dr. Rosen was puzzled **by** and concerned **about** Ellen's nightmares.
(**Not:** Dr. Rosen was puzzled and concerned about . . .)

Note: Two different prepositions are needed for this last sentence.

12g. Conjunctions as connectives

A conjunction is a word that joins words, phrases, clauses, or sentences.

Nixon **and** Agnew ended their political careers by resigning. (words joined)

The mouse ran out of the kitchen **and** into the living room. (phrases joined)

Casino gambling in Atlantic City has helped some, **but** it has hurt others. (clauses joined)

Sally has the ability to do the job; **however,** she has too many prior commitments. (clauses joined)

12h. Conjunctions are coordinate, correlative, or subordinate.

A **coordinate conjunction** and a **correlative conjunction** connect grammatical elements of equal rank. A **subordinate conjunction** connects grammatical elements of unequal rank.

12i. Coordinate conjunctions connect two equal elements. They include the following words:

and, but, or, nor, so, yet, for

On our vacation we will go to Boston **or** to Cape Cod. (two phrases)

My two favorite colors are blue **and** green. (two words)

I told Matías that I couldn't leave my house, **so** he should come over tonight. (two subordinate clauses)

Phil was eager to try the new restaurant, **but** he moved away before trying it. (two independent clauses)

12j. Correlative conjunctions include the following **word pairs** in order to connect two equal elements.

either . . . or, neither . . . nor, not only . . . but also, both . . . and, if . . . then

Take **either** the dark meat **or** the light meat. (two words)

Rick **not only** quit school **but also** left town. (two predicate clauses)

Both the Baltimore Orioles **and** the Pittsburgh Pirates won the pennant in 1979. (two words)

I have seen her **neither** in the movies **nor** on television. (two prepositional phrases)

Note: The correlative conjunctions "neither . . . nor" should never be written "neither . . . or."

Each member of the pair of correlative conjunctions must be followed by the same grammatical construction; this is known as *parallel construction.*

same construction

Ben Affleck is **not only** a good **actor but also**

same construction

a good film **director**.

different construction

(**Not:** Ben Affleck **not only** is a good actor

different construction

but **also** a good film director.)

same construction

Either we should spend the night here **or**

same construction

we should leave right now.

different construction

(**Not: Either** we should spend the night here

different construction

or leave right now.)

12k. Conjunctive adverbs

A **conjunctive adverb** may be considered a **type of coordinate conjunction**.

Conjunctive adverbs include the following words, which **serve to connect two equal elements**.

> therefore, however, consequently, accordingly, furthermore, besides, moreover, nevertheless, still

Although the clause introduced by a conjunctive adverb is *grammatically* independent, it is *logically* dependent on the preceding clause for complete meaning.

> A storm knocked down our electric wires; **therefore,** we had to eat by candlelight.

> A bad traffic accident ahead of us caused us to be delayed; **nevertheless,** we made the party on time.

> You have not paid your rent for six months; **accordingly,** I am going to see a lawyer.

Independent clauses joined by a conjunctive adverb should be separated by a semicolon (;) or a period.

> Frank and Marty delayed their vacation one week; **consequently,** I was able to join them.

> The judge awarded custody of the child to his mother. **Moreover,** the judge set strict guidelines for visiting privileges.

Certain phrases may act as conjunctive adverbs.

> Amelia wanted to buy a fur coat; **on the other hand,** she was trying to save money for a car.

> We saw many interesting towns and cities on our tour. **In addition,** we met several nice people.

12l. Join only the same parts of speech with coordinate conjunctions or with correlative conjunctions. Faulty parallelism will result if different parts of speech are combined.

> Correct: Jim's day consisted of waking up early, working all day, **and** going back to bed. (three gerund phrases)

> Faulty: Jim's day consisted of waking up early, working all day, **and** then to go back to bed. (two gerund phrases combined with an infinitive phrase)

> Correct: The president's plan was a disappointment **not only** to the leaders of big business **but also** to the leaders of organized labor. (two prepositional phrases)

> Faulty: The president's plan was a disappointment **not only** to the leaders of big business **but also** the leaders of organized labor. (one prepositional phrase and one noun phrase)

12m. Connecting elements of unequal rank

A less important idea should be put into a subordinate clause; the more important idea should be expressed in the main or independent clause.

main idea

Bill is going to work for his father,

subordinate idea

although he was offered other jobs.

12n. Subordination may be introduced by a subordinate conjunction, by a relative pronoun, or by a relative adverb.

> Eva will want to go straight to bed **after** she comes back from her exercise class. (subordinate conjunction)

> I bought the sneakers **that** you wanted. (relative pronoun)

We saw the house **where** they filmed the *Twilight Saga*. (relative adverb)

A subordinate conjunction introduces an adverbial clause.

My mother can knit a sweater **while** she watches television. (adverbial clause tells **when**)

Tell me what he looks like **so that** I'll recognize him. (adverbial clause tells **why**)

12o. **Some relative pronouns introduce adjective clauses.**

Everyone wants a job **that** he likes.

The woman **who** walked across the United States has written a book about her experience.

Bobby gave Connie a new tennis racket, **which** she needed.

Other relative pronouns introduce noun clauses.

Tell me **what** you did.

This book has **whatever** you want to know about scuba diving.

Invite **whomever** you like.

12p. **A relative adverb introduces an adjective clause.**

Do you remember the night **when** we locked ourselves out of the house?

Chris will be at the place **where** we met him last time.

CORRECT USAGE—CHOOSING THE RIGHT WORD

The difference between the almost right word and the right word is . . . the difference between the lightning bug (firefly) and the lightning.

—Mark Twain

A, an. The indefinite article *a* is used before a consonant sound; the indefinite article *an* is used before a vowel sound. Say *a plan, an idea.*

Accept, except. *Accept* means *to receive; except* when used as a verb means *to leave out.* (We *accepted* the gift. Pedro's name was *excepted* from the honor roll.) The word *except* is used most often as a preposition. *Everyone went except me.*

Affect, effect. *Affect* is a verb that means to *influence.* (Winning the sweepstakes will *affect* his attitude.) *Effect,* as a noun, means *an influence.* (Smoking has an *effect* on one's health.) *Effect,* as a verb, means to *bring about.* (The teacher's praise *effected* a change in the student.)

Affected, as an adjective, has the meaning of *false.* (She had an *affected* way of speaking.)

Aggravate, irritate. *Aggravate* means to make worse. (Drinking iced water will *aggravate* your cold.) *Irritate* means to *annoy* or *exasperate.* (Mary's continuous chattering *irritated* me.)

Ain't. Do not use this expression.

Already, all ready. *Already* means *before* or *by a certain time.* (Mike said that he had *already* done the job.) *All ready* means *completely ready.* (When the buzzer sounded, the horses were *all ready* to start running.)

All right, alright. The only correct spelling is *all right.*

Altogether, all together. *Altogether* means *entirely, wholly.* (Jane is *altogether* too conceited to get

along with people.) *All together* means *as a group.* (After the explosion, the boss was relieved to find his workers *all together* in front of the building.)

Among, between. *Among* is used with more than two persons or things. (The manager distributed the gifts *among* all of the employees.) *Between* is used only with two persons or things. (The steak was divided *between* the two children.)

Amount, number. *Amount* is used to refer to things in bulk. (The war costs a great *amount* of money.) *Number* is used to refer to things that can be counted. (A large *number* of pupils attend this school.)

And etc. This is incorrect. The abbreviation *etc.* stands for the Latin *et cetera.* The *et* means *and;* the *cetera* means *other things.* It is wrong to say *and etc.* because the idea of *and* is already included in *etc.*

Anyways, anywheres, everywheres, somewheres. These expressions are not correct. Omit the final *s* after each.

As, like. *As,* used as a conjunction, is followed by a clause. (Please do it *as* I told you to.) *Like* may not be used as a conjunction. If it is used as a preposition, it is not followed by a verb. (This ice cream looks *like* custard.)

Awful. See **Terrific, terrible**.

Being that. *Being that* is incorrect for *since* or *because.* (*Since* you are tired, you ought to rest.)

Beside, besides. *Beside* means *alongside of; besides* means *in addition to.* (Kevin sat *beside* Kyle at the baseball game.) (There is nobody *besides* her husband who understands Ann.)

Between. See **Among**.

Bring, take. Consider the speaker as a starting point. *Bring* is used for something carried in the direction of the speaker. (When you return from lunch, please *bring* me a ham sandwich.) *Take* is used for something carried away from the speaker. (If you are going downtown, please *take* this letter to the post office.)

Bunch. *Bunch* means cluster. Do not use *bunch* for group or crowd. (This is a large *bunch* of grapes.) (A *crowd* of people were at the scene of the accident.)

But that, but what. Do not use these expressions in place of *that* in constructions like the following: I do not question *that* (not *but that*) you are richer than I am.

Can't hardly. Don't use this double negative. Say *can hardly*.

Continual, continuous. *Continual* means happening at intervals. (Salespeople are *continually* walking into this office.) *Continuous* means going on without interruption. (Without a moment of dry weather, it rained *continuously* for forty days and forty nights.)

Could of. Do not use for *could have*.

Data. Although *data* is the plural of *datum,* idiom permits the use of this word as a singular. Some authorities still insist on *Data are gathered* rather than *Data is gathered* or *these data* rather than *this data.* Most persons in computer programming now say *Data is gathered* or *this data.*

Deal. Do not use this colloquial term for *arrangement* or *transaction* in formal expression. (He has an *excellent arrangement* [not *deal*] *with the manager.*)

Different from, different than. *Different from* is correct. *Different than* is incorrect. (His method of doing this is *different from* mine.)

Discover, invent. *Discover* means to see or learn something that has not been previously known. (They say the Vikings, not Columbus, *discovered* America.) *Invent* means to create for the first time. (Douglas Engelbart *invented* the computer mouse.)

Disinterested, uninterested. *Disinterested* means without bias. (An umpire must be *disinterested* to judge fairly in a baseball game.) *Uninterested* means not caring about a situation. (I am totally *uninterested* in your plan.)

Doesn't, don't. *Doesn't* means *does not; don't* means *do not.* Do not say *He don't* (*do not*) when you mean *He doesn't* (*does not*).

Due to. At the beginning of a sentence, *due to* is always incorrect. Use, instead, *on account of, because of,* or a similar expression. (*On account of* bad weather, the contest was postponed.) As a predicate adjective construction, *due to* is correct. His weakness was *due to* his hunger.

Each other, one another. *Each other* is used for two persons. (The executive and his assistant antagonize *each other.*) *One another* is used for more than two persons. (The members of the large family love *one another.*)

Effect. See **Affect**.

Enthuse. Do not use this word. Say *enthusiastic.* (The art critic was *enthusiastic* about the painting.)

Equally as. This expression is incorrect. Say, instead, *just as.* (This car is *just as good* as that.)

Farther, further. *Farther* is used for a distance that is measurable. (The farmer's house is about 100 yards *farther* down the road.) *Further* is used to express the extension of an idea. (A *further* explanation may be necessary.)

Fewer, less. *Fewer* applies to what may be counted. (Greenwich Village has *fewer* conservatives than liberals.) *Less* refers to degree or amount. (*Less* rain fell this month than the month before.)

Flout, flaunt. *Flout* means to mock, insult, or work against. (The king *flouted* the wise man when the latter offered advice. The rioters *flouted* the rules.) *Flaunt* means to make a pretentious display of. (The upstart *flaunted* his diamond ring.)

Further. See **Farther**.

Get. *Get* means *to obtain* or *receive. Get* should not be used in the sense of *to excite, to interest,* or *to* *understand.* Say: His guitar playing *fascinates* (not *gets*) me. Say: When you talk about lifestyles, I just don't *understand* (not *get*) *you.*

Good, well. Do not use the adjective *good* in place of the adverb *well* in structures like the following: John works *well* (not *good*) in the kitchen. Jim Palmer pitched *well* (not *good*) in last night's game.

Graduate. One *graduates from,* or *is graduated from,* a school. One does not *graduate a school.* (The student *graduated* [or *was graduated*] from high school.)

Had of. Avoid this for *had.* Say: My father always said that he wished he *had* (not *had of*) gone to college.

Had gone. Never use *had* to refer to the simple past. Say: Yesterday I went to the store. Not: Yesterday I *had gone* to the store.

Hanged, hung. When a person is *executed,* he is *hanged.* When anything is *suspended* in space, it is *hung.*

Hardly. See **Can't hardly**.

Healthful, healthy. *Healthful* applies to *conditions that promote health. Healthy* applies to *a state of health.* Say: Stevenson found the climate of Saranac Lake very *healthful.* Say: Mary is a very *healthy* girl.

If, whether. Use *whether*—not *if*—in structures that follow verbs like *ask, doubt, know, learn, say.* Say: Hank Aaron didn't know *whether* (not *if*) he was going to break Babe Ruth's home run record.

Imply, infer. The speaker *implies* when he suggests or hints at. (The owner of the store *implied* that the patron stole a box of toothpicks.) The listener *infers* when he draws a conclusion from facts or evidence. (From what you say, I *infer* that I am about to be discharged.)

In, into. *In* is used to express a location, without the involvement of motion. (The sugar is *in* the cupboard.) *Into* is used to express motion from one place to another. (The housekeeper put the sugar *into* the cupboard.)

In regards to. This is incorrect. Say *in regard to* or *with regard to.*

Invent. See **Discover**.

Irregardless. Do not use *irregardless.* It is incorrect for *regardless.* (You will not be able to go out tonight *regardless* of the fact that you have done all of your homework.)

Its, it's. *Its* is the possessive of *it; it's* is the contraction for *it is.*

Kind of, sort of. Do not use these expressions as adverbs. Say: Ali was *quite* (not *kind of* or *sort of*) witty in his postfight interview.

Kind of a, sort of a. Omit the *a.* Say: What *kind of* (not *kind of a* or *sort of a*) game is lacrosse?

Lay, lie. See "Principal Parts of Irregular Verbs"— pages 346–347.

Learn, teach. *Learn* means *to gain knowledge. Teach* means *to impart knowledge.* Say: He *taught* (not *learned*) his brother how to swim.

Leave, let. The word *leave* means *to depart.* (I *leave* today for San Francisco.) The word *let* means to allow. (*Let* me take your place.)

Less, fewer. See **Fewer, less**.

Liable, likely. *Liable* means subject to something unpleasant. (If you speed, you are *liable* to get a summons.) *Likely* means probable, with reference to either a pleasant or unpleasant happening. (It is *likely* to snow tomorrow.)

Locate. Do not use *locate* to mean *settle* or *move to.* Say: We will *move to* (not *locate in*) Florida next year.

Might of, must of. Omit the *of.*

Myself, himself, yourself. These pronouns are to be used as intensives. (The Chairman *himself* will open the meeting.) Do not use these pronouns when *me, him,* or *you* will serve. Say: We shall be happy if Joe and *you* (not *yourself*) join us for lunch at the Plaza.

Nice. See **Terrific, terrible**.

Number, amount. See **Amount, number**.

Of, have. Do not use *of* for *have* in structures like *could have*.

Off of. Omit the *of.* Say: The book fell *off* (not *off of*) the shelf.

Pour, spill. When one *pours,* he does it deliberately. (He carefully *poured* the water into her glass.) When one *spills,* he does it accidentally. (I carelessly *spilled* some water on her dress.)

Pour, pore. Beware of homonyms—words that sound the same but have different meanings. *Pour* means *to cause a liquid to flow,* as from a container into a different vessel. *Pore* means *to examine,* as when you *pore over* these SAT strategies.

Practical, practicable. *Practical* means *fitted for actual work. Practicable* means *feasible* or *possible.* Say: My business partner is a *practical man.* Say: The boss did not consider the plan *practicable* for this coming year.

Principal, principle. *Principal* applies to a *chief* or the *chief part* of something. *Principle* applies to a *basic law.* Say: Mr. Jones is the *principal* of the school. Professor White was the *principal* speaker. Honesty is a good *principle* to follow.

Raise, rise. See "Principal Parts of Irregular Verbs"— pages 346–347.

Reason is because. Do not use the expression *reason is because*—it is always incorrect. Say the *reason is that.* (The *reason* Jack failed the course *is that* he didn't study.)

Regardless. See **Irregardless**.

Respectfully, respectively. *Respectfully* means *with respect* as in the complimentary close of a letter, *respectfully yours. Respectively* means that each item will be considered *in the order given.* Say: This paper is *respectfully* submitted. Say: The hero, the heroine, and the villain will be played by Albert, Joan, and Harry, *respectively.*

Rise, raise. See "Principal Parts of Irregular Verbs"— pages 346–347.

Said. Avoid the legalistic use of *said,* like *said letter, said plan, said program,* except in legal writing.

Should of. Do not use for *should have.*

Sit, set. See "Principal Parts of Irregular Verbs"— pages 346–347.

Some. Do not use *some* when you mean *somewhat.* Say: I'm confused *somewhat* (not *some*).

Spill, pour. See **Pour, spill**.

Suspicion. Do not use *suspicion* as a verb when you mean *suspect.*

Take, bring. See **Bring, take**.

Teach, learn. See **Learn, teach**.

Terrific, terrible. Avoid "lazy words." Many people don't want to take the trouble to use the exact word. They will use words like *terrific, awesome, nice, great, beautiful,* etc., to describe anything and everything that is favorable. And they will use words like *terrible, awful, lousy, miserable,* etc., for whatever is unfavorable. Use the exact word. Say: We had a *delicious* (not terrific) meal. Say: We had a *boring* (not *terrible*) weekend.

This kind, these kind. *This kind* is correct—as is *that kind, these kinds,* and *those kinds.* (My little brother likes *this kind* of pears.) *These kind* and *those kind* are incorrect.

Try and. Do not say *try and.* Say *try to.* (*Try to* visit me while I am in Florida.)

Uninterested. See **Disinterested**.

Wait for, wait on. *Wait for* means *to await; wait on* means *to serve.* Say: I am waiting *for* (not *on*) Carter to call me on the telephone.

Way, ways. Do not use *ways* for *way.* Say: It is a long *way* (not *ways*) to Japan.

Where. Do not use *where* in place of *that* in expressions like the following: I see in the newspaper *that* (not *where*) a nuclear reactor may be built a mile away from our house.

Would of. Do not use for *would have.*

GRAMMAR AND USAGE INDEX*

---

*This index does not include items listed in "Correct Usage—Choosing the Right Word" (page 366). Since these correct-usage items are in alphabetical order, it will be easy for you to locate any correct-usage explanation whatsoever.

PART 9

Practice for the Reading, Writing and Language, and Optional Essay Sections

ANSWER SHEET

It is recommended that you use a No. 2 pencil. It is very important that you fill in the entire circle darkly and completely. If you change your response, erase as completely as possible. Incomplete marks or erasures may affect your score.

Complete Mark ● **Examples of Incomplete Marks** ◓ ⊗ ⊖ ◐ ◑ ◔ ◕ ●

SECTION 1: READING QUIZZES

	A B C D E		A B C D E		A B C D E		A B C D E		A B C D E
1	○ ○ ○ ○ ○	14	○ ○ ○ ○ ○	27	○ ○ ○ ○ ○	40	○ ○ ○ ○ ○	53	○ ○ ○ ○ ○
2	○ ○ ○ ○ ○	15	○ ○ ○ ○ ○	28	○ ○ ○ ○ ○	41	○ ○ ○ ○ ○	54	○ ○ ○ ○ ○
3	○ ○ ○ ○ ○	16	○ ○ ○ ○ ○	29	○ ○ ○ ○ ○	42	○ ○ ○ ○ ○	55	○ ○ ○ ○ ○
4	○ ○ ○ ○ ○	17	○ ○ ○ ○ ○	30	○ ○ ○ ○ ○	43	○ ○ ○ ○ ○	56	○ ○ ○ ○ ○
5	○ ○ ○ ○ ○	18	○ ○ ○ ○ ○	31	○ ○ ○ ○ ○	44	○ ○ ○ ○ ○	57	○ ○ ○ ○ ○
6	○ ○ ○ ○ ○	19	○ ○ ○ ○ ○	32	○ ○ ○ ○ ○	45	○ ○ ○ ○ ○	58	○ ○ ○ ○ ○
7	○ ○ ○ ○ ○	20	○ ○ ○ ○ ○	33	○ ○ ○ ○ ○	46	○ ○ ○ ○ ○	59	○ ○ ○ ○ ○
8	○ ○ ○ ○ ○	21	○ ○ ○ ○ ○	34	○ ○ ○ ○ ○	47	○ ○ ○ ○ ○	60	○ ○ ○ ○ ○
9	○ ○ ○ ○ ○	22	○ ○ ○ ○ ○	35	○ ○ ○ ○ ○	48	○ ○ ○ ○ ○	61	○ ○ ○ ○ ○
10	○ ○ ○ ○ ○	23	○ ○ ○ ○ ○	36	○ ○ ○ ○ ○	49	○ ○ ○ ○ ○	62	○ ○ ○ ○ ○
11	○ ○ ○ ○ ○	24	○ ○ ○ ○ ○	37	○ ○ ○ ○ ○	50	○ ○ ○ ○ ○	63	○ ○ ○ ○ ○
12	○ ○ ○ ○ ○	25	○ ○ ○ ○ ○	38	○ ○ ○ ○ ○	51	○ ○ ○ ○ ○	64	○ ○ ○ ○ ○
13	○ ○ ○ ○ ○	26	○ ○ ○ ○ ○	39	○ ○ ○ ○ ○	52	○ ○ ○ ○ ○		

SECTION 2: WRITING AND LANGUAGE QUIZ 1

	A B C D		A B C D		A B C D		A B C D		A B C D
1	○ ○ ○ ○	16	○ ○ ○ ○	31	○ ○ ○ ○	46	○ ○ ○ ○	61	○ ○ ○ ○
2	○ ○ ○ ○	17	○ ○ ○ ○	32	○ ○ ○ ○	47	○ ○ ○ ○	62	○ ○ ○ ○
3	○ ○ ○ ○	18	○ ○ ○ ○	33	○ ○ ○ ○	48	○ ○ ○ ○	63	○ ○ ○ ○
4	○ ○ ○ ○	19	○ ○ ○ ○	34	○ ○ ○ ○	49	○ ○ ○ ○	64	○ ○ ○ ○
5	○ ○ ○ ○	20	○ ○ ○ ○	35	○ ○ ○ ○	50	○ ○ ○ ○	65	○ ○ ○ ○
6	○ ○ ○ ○	21	○ ○ ○ ○	36	○ ○ ○ ○	51	○ ○ ○ ○	66	○ ○ ○ ○
7	○ ○ ○ ○	22	○ ○ ○ ○	37	○ ○ ○ ○	52	○ ○ ○ ○	67	○ ○ ○ ○
8	○ ○ ○ ○	23	○ ○ ○ ○	38	○ ○ ○ ○	53	○ ○ ○ ○	68	○ ○ ○ ○
9	○ ○ ○ ○	24	○ ○ ○ ○	39	○ ○ ○ ○	54	○ ○ ○ ○	69	○ ○ ○ ○
10	○ ○ ○ ○	25	○ ○ ○ ○	40	○ ○ ○ ○	55	○ ○ ○ ○	70	○ ○ ○ ○
11	○ ○ ○ ○	26	○ ○ ○ ○	41	○ ○ ○ ○	56	○ ○ ○ ○	71	○ ○ ○ ○
12	○ ○ ○ ○	27	○ ○ ○ ○	42	○ ○ ○ ○	57	○ ○ ○ ○	72	○ ○ ○ ○
13	○ ○ ○ ○	28	○ ○ ○ ○	43	○ ○ ○ ○	58	○ ○ ○ ○	73	○ ○ ○ ○
14	○ ○ ○ ○	29	○ ○ ○ ○	44	○ ○ ○ ○	59	○ ○ ○ ○	74	○ ○ ○ ○
15	○ ○ ○ ○	30	○ ○ ○ ○	45	○ ○ ○ ○	60	○ ○ ○ ○	75	○ ○ ○ ○

SECTION 3: WRITING AND LANGUAGE QUIZ 2

	A B C D		A B C D		A B C D		A B C D		A B C D
1	○ ○ ○ ○	16	○ ○ ○ ○	31	○ ○ ○ ○	46	○ ○ ○ ○	61	○ ○ ○ ○
2	○ ○ ○ ○	17	○ ○ ○ ○	32	○ ○ ○ ○	47	○ ○ ○ ○	62	○ ○ ○ ○
3	○ ○ ○ ○	18	○ ○ ○ ○	33	○ ○ ○ ○	48	○ ○ ○ ○	63	○ ○ ○ ○
4	○ ○ ○ ○	19	○ ○ ○ ○	34	○ ○ ○ ○	49	○ ○ ○ ○	64	○ ○ ○ ○
5	○ ○ ○ ○	20	○ ○ ○ ○	35	○ ○ ○ ○	50	○ ○ ○ ○	65	○ ○ ○ ○
6	○ ○ ○ ○	21	○ ○ ○ ○	36	○ ○ ○ ○	51	○ ○ ○ ○	66	○ ○ ○ ○
7	○ ○ ○ ○	22	○ ○ ○ ○	37	○ ○ ○ ○	52	○ ○ ○ ○	67	○ ○ ○ ○
8	○ ○ ○ ○	23	○ ○ ○ ○	38	○ ○ ○ ○	53	○ ○ ○ ○	68	○ ○ ○ ○
9	○ ○ ○ ○	24	○ ○ ○ ○	39	○ ○ ○ ○	54	○ ○ ○ ○	69	○ ○ ○ ○
10	○ ○ ○ ○	25	○ ○ ○ ○	40	○ ○ ○ ○	55	○ ○ ○ ○	70	○ ○ ○ ○
11	○ ○ ○ ○	26	○ ○ ○ ○	41	○ ○ ○ ○	56	○ ○ ○ ○	71	○ ○ ○ ○
12	○ ○ ○ ○	27	○ ○ ○ ○	42	○ ○ ○ ○	57	○ ○ ○ ○	72	○ ○ ○ ○
13	○ ○ ○ ○	28	○ ○ ○ ○	43	○ ○ ○ ○	58	○ ○ ○ ○	73	○ ○ ○ ○
14	○ ○ ○ ○	29	○ ○ ○ ○	44	○ ○ ○ ○	59	○ ○ ○ ○	74	○ ○ ○ ○
15	○ ○ ○ ○	30	○ ○ ○ ○	45	○ ○ ○ ○	60	○ ○ ○ ○	75	○ ○ ○ ○

15 READING QUIZZES

Here Are 15 Reading Quizzes.
See How You Do.

Turn to Section 1 of your answer sheet (page 374) to answer the questions in this section.

Note: For instructional purposes we have included 5 answer choices. On the actual test you will have only 4 choices.

Reading Quiz 1

Questions 1–4 are based on the following passage.

The following passage is from Henry David Thoreau's Walden; or, Life in the Woods, *1854.*

I went to the woods because I wished to live deliberately, to front only the essential facts of life, and see if I could not learn what it had to teach, and not, when I came to die, discover that I had not lived. I did not
5 wish to live what was not life, living is so dear; nor did I wish to practice resignation, unless it was quite necessary. I wanted to live deep and suck out all the marrow of life, to live so sturdily and Spartan-like as to put to rout all that was not life, to cut a broad swath
10 and shave close, to drive life into a corner, and reduce it to its lowest terms, and, if it proved to be mean, why then to get the whole and genuine meanness of it, and publish its meanness to the world; or if it were sublime, to know it by experience, and be able to give a
15 true account of it in my next excursion. For most men, it appears to me, are in a strange uncertainty about it, whether it is of the devil or of God, and have somewhat hastily concluded that it is the chief end of man here to "glorify God and enjoy him forever."
20   Still we live meanly, like ants; though the fable tells us that we were long ago changed into men; like pygmies we fight with cranes; it is error upon error, and clout upon clout, and our best virtue has for its occasion a superfluous and evitable wretchedness.

25 Our life is frittered away by detail. An honest man has hardly need to count more than his ten fingers, or in extreme cases he may add his ten toes, and lump the rest. Simplicity, simplicity, simplicity! I say, let your affairs be as two or three, and not a hundred or a thou-
30 sand; instead of a million count half a dozen, and keep your accounts on your thumb-nail. In the midst of this chopping sea of civilized life, such are the clouds and storms and quicksands and thousand-and-one items to be allowed for, that a man has to live, if he would not
35 founder and go to the bottom and not make his port at all, by dead reckoning, and he must be a great calculator indeed who succeeds. Simplify, simplify. . . . Why should we live with such hurry and waste of life? We are determined to be starved before we are hungry. Men
40 say that a stitch in time saves nine, and so they take a thousand stitches today to save nine tomorrow.

Quiz 1 Questions

1. The author decided to move to the woods in order to

   (A) engage with life's basic realities
   (B) escape the rat race of civilization
   (C) reject the evils of society
   (D) enjoy greater peace of mind
   (E) become more spiritual

2. What does the passage suggest about the author's attitude toward religion?

   (A) He denies the existence of God.
   (B) He believes man's first duty is to glorify God.
   (C) He thinks religion is the opiate of the people.
   (D) He thinks religion can distract us from a true experience of life.
   (E) He believes that the devil and God have equal power over life.

3. According to the author, too many people "live meanly" because they are

   (A) lazy
   (B) disorganized
   (C) simple-minded
   (D) prone to error
   (E) preoccupied with irrelevant details

4. Which of the following best summarizes the point made in the second paragraph?

   (A) We can waste our lives preparing for what may never happen.
   (B) Dishonest men live overly complicated lives.
   (C) People should work and save for hard times.
   (D) Most people live their lives in fear.
   (E) It is best to avoid too many activities.

Reading Quiz 2

Questions 5–8 are based on the following passage.

In New York, as much as in most communities in America, basketball is more religious rite than sport. Kids are at the playground as long as ten hours a day, actually playing as many as six. Seventeen- and
5 eighteen-year-olds already have rheumatoid knees from the constant pounding of their feet on the asphalt. They play in the heat of the afternoon with not much more to fuel them than a can of soda and a store-bought pastry, and they play at night in the dim illu-
10 mination of nearby street lights and flashing neon. In a single summer, typical city ballplayers will wear out four or five pairs of sneakers. They play even in the dead of winter, bundled in jackets and sweaters and belching up little puffs of steam as they bang away at
15 the netless rims.

Quiz 2 Questions

5. When the author states that basketball is a religious rite, he is referring to the players'

   (A) joy
   (B) pride
   (C) team spirit
   (D) dedication
   (E) skill

6. This passage as a whole tends to

   (A) create an image
   (B) defend religion
   (C) ridicule basketball players
   (D) uphold the American tradition of fair play
   (E) describe an exception to city life

7. In writing the passage, the author points out the

   (A) many advantages of playing basketball
   (B) values of basketball as an escape from reality
   (C) reasons basketball should be curtailed
   (D) possible dangers to health of playing basketball
   (E) cost of many items of basketball equipment

8. Which statement can best be defended on the basis of the passage?

   (A) The basketball court is open twenty-four hours.
   (B) The playground is not fenced off.
   (C) The playground has a hard surface.
   (D) Kids would rather play in the afternoon than at night.
   (E) The kids are easily fatigued.

Reading Quiz 3

Questions 9–12 are based on the following passage.

This passage is from Richard Katz, "A Solo-Survival Experience as Education for Personal Growth," in Educational Opportunity Forum *vol. 1, no. 4, pp. 38–53. Albany, University of the State of New York and State Education Department, Fall 1969.*

I was exploring the far side of the island on the third day. I was also observing myself, an animal covering his territory. It was very quiet, even still. Suddenly a thunderous sound in the leaves and there was a pheas-
5 ant, frozen in fear, three feet from my face. I wasn't sure whether I looked as scared; I certainly had been deeply frightened. The stillness had become noise, and since I was alone on the island, my fantasies at that instant were elaborate. But I unfroze and the pheasant
10 did not. The myth of man, the primitive hunter, began to unfold as I reached for a stick. But before any action, another myth took hold and there was no taking of life. The basic need of hunger; the basic force of life. I can't forget that encounter.

Quiz 3 Questions

9   As used in line 9, the word *elaborate* most nearly
means

   (A) quiet

   (B) great

   (C) groundless

   (D) expensive

   (E) unnecessary

10. In line 12, the phrase "another myth" refers to

   (A) a need for food

   (B) a respect for primitive customs

   (C) a need for action

   (D) a respect for living things

   (E) the powerlessness of animals

11. From the passage, we can most safely conclude
that the

   (A) pheasant was an easy prey

   (B) narrator disliked exploring

   (C) narrator was familiar with the island

   (D) pheasant flew away

   (E) island was a noisy place

12. By the end of this episode, the narrator feels that
he has

   (A) created a new myth

   (B) learned how to survive

   (C) grown in perception

   (D) become a creature of fantasy

   (E) exploded several myths

Reading Quiz 4

Questions 13–15 are based on the following passage.

The ancient Egyptians believed strongly in life after
death. They also believed that a person would need his
body to exist in this afterlife. Therefore, they carefully
preserved the body by treating it with spices and oils
5   and wrapping it in linen cloth. The wrapped body was
then placed in a tomb. A body that is treated in this way
is called a mummy.

Egyptian kings and nobles wanted to be certain
that their mummies would be kept in safe places for-
10 ever. They had great tombs built for themselves and
their families. Many kings were buried in secret tombs
carved out of solid rock in a place near Thebes called
the Valley of the Kings.

About eighty kings built towering pyramid-shaped
15 stone tombs. These pyramids have become famous as
one of the Seven Wonders of the Ancient World.

One of the most amazing things about these pyramids
is that they were constructed without using wheels or
heavy equipment to move or raise the rocks. Egypt did
20 not learn about the wheel until long after the pyramids
were built. Workmen used levers to get large blocks
of stone on and off sledges and hauled them into place
over long ramps built around the pyramids.

Quiz 4 Questions

13. The term *mummy* was used to describe

   (A) kings of ancient Egypt

   (B) ancient Egyptian nobles

   (C) the place where Egyptian kings were buried

   (D) the preserved body of a dead person

   (E) one of the Seven Wonders of the Ancient
World

14. The pyramids were built

   (A) before the Egyptians developed a sophisticated technology

   (B) after the Egyptians developed a sophisticated
technology

   (C) to house the tombs of all ancient Egyptian
kings and nobles

   (D) with the use of spices, oils, and linen cloth

   (E) to keep mummies safe forever

15. Which of the following practices is most closely
associated with ancient Egyptian belief in an afterlife?

   (A) placing the dead in tombs carved out of solid
rock

   (B) building pyramids to house the bodies of dead
kings

   (C) preserving dead bodies with oils and spices

   (D) creating the Valley of the Kings near Thebes

   (E) constructing tombs without the use of wheels
or heavy equipment

Reading Quiz 5

Questions 16–18 are based on the following passage.

This passage is Walt Whitman's poem "I Hear America Singing," 1860.

I hear America singing, the varied carols I hear,

Those of mechanics, each one singing his as it should
be blithe and strong,

The carpenter singing his as he measures his plank or
5   beam,

The mason singing his as he makes ready for work, or
leaves off work,

The boatman singing what belongs to him in his boat,
the deckhand singing on the steamboat deck,

10 The shoemaker singing as he sits on his bench, the
hatter singing as he stands.

The wood-cutter's song, the ploughboy's on his way
in the morning, or at noon intermission or at sun-
down,

15 The delicious singing of the mother, or of the young
wife at work, or of the girl sewing or washing,

Each singing what belongs to him or her and to none
else,

The day what belongs to the day—at night the party of
20   young fellows, robust, friendly,

Singing with open mouths their strong melodious
songs.

Quiz 5 Questions

16. Judging from this poem, it is most probable that
the poet favors

    (A) teachers

    (B) workingmen

    (C) executives

    (D) singers

    (E) athletes

17. The poet's main purpose in this poem is to

    (A) indicate that women belong in the house

    (B) criticize America's economy

    (C) celebrate the American worker

    (D) speak out in favor of socialism

    (E) show that all work is basically the same

18. The tone of this poem can best be described as

    (A) joyful

    (B) humorous

    (C) impatient

    (D) peaceful

    (E) careless

Reading Quiz 6

Questions 19–24 are based on the following passage.

This passage is adapted from Jacques Barzun's Teacher
in America, *1945.*

The whole aim of good teaching is to turn the young
learner, by nature a little copycat, into an independent,
self-propelling creature who can work as his own boss
to the limit of his powers. This is to turn pupils into
5 students, and it can be done on any rung of the ladder of learning. When I was a child, the multiplication
table was taught from a printed sheet which had to be
memorized one square at a time—the ones and the twos
and so on up to nine. It never occurred to the teacher
10 to show us how the answers could be arrived at also by
addition, which we already knew. No one said, "Look:
if four times four is sixteen, you ought to be able to figure out, without aid from memory, what five times four
is, because that amounts to four more ones added to the
15 sixteen." This would at first have been puzzling, *more*
complicated and difficult than memory work, but once
explained and grasped, it would have been an instru-
ment for learning and checking the whole business of
multiplication. We could temporarily have dispensed
20 with the teacher and cut loose from the printed table.

    This is another way of saying that the only thing
worth teaching anybody is a principle. Naturally, principles involve facts and some facts must be learned
"bare" because they do not rest on any principle. The
25 capital of Alaska is Juneau and, so far as I know, that
is all there is to it; but a European child ought not to
learn that Washington is the capital of the United States
without fixing firmly in his mind the relation between
the city and the man who led his countrymen to free-
30 dom. That would be missing an association, which is
the germ of a principle. And just as a complex athletic
feat is made possible by rapid and accurate coordination, so all valuable learning hangs together and *works*
by associations which make sense.

Quiz 6 Questions

19. The title that best expresses the ideas of this passage is:

(A) How to Teach Arithmetic
(B) A Good Memory Makes a Good Student
(C) Principles—the Basis of Learning
(D) Using Addition to Teach Multiplication
(E) How to Dispense with the Teacher

20. The author implies that the difference between a pupil and a student is the difference between

(A) youth and maturity
(B) learning and knowing
(C) beginning and ending
(D) memorizing and understanding
(E) learning and teaching

21. The author indicates that children are naturally

(A) deceitful
(B) perceptive
(C) independent
(D) logical
(E) imitative

22. The author would be most likely to agree that the most desirable way to teach is by

(A) relating facts to principles
(B) stressing the importance of learning
(C) insisting that pupils work independently
(D) recognizing that a knowledge of facts is useless
(E) developing pupils' ability to memorize

23. As it is used in the passage, the word *germ* (line 31) most nearly means

(A) result
(B) beginning
(C) polish
(D) image
(E) weakness

24. In this passage, the author develops his paragraphs primarily by the use of

(A) narration
(B) comparison
(C) definitions
(D) description
(E) examples

Reading Quiz 7

Questions 25–30 are based on the following passage.

This passage is from W. Douglas Burden, Look to the Wilderness, *1956.*

Next morning I saw for the first time an animal that is rarely encountered face to face. It was a wolverine. Though relatively small, rarely weighing more than 40 pounds, he is, above all animals, the one most hated by
5 the Indians and trappers. He is a fine tree climber and a relentless destroyer. Deer, reindeer, and even moose succumb to his attacks. We sat on a rock and watched him come, a bobbing rascal in blackish-brown. Since the male wolverine occupies a very large hunting area
10 and fights to the death any other male that intrudes on his domain, wolverines are always scarce, and in order to avoid extinction need all the protection that man can give. As a trapper, Henry wanted me to shoot him, but I refused, for this is the most fascinating and little known
15 of all our wonderful predators. His hunchback gait was awkward and ungainly, lopsided yet tireless. He advanced through all types of terrain without change of pace and with a sense of power that seemed indestructible. His course brought him directly to us, and he did
20 not notice our immobile figures until he was ten feet away. Obviously startled, he rose up on his hind legs with paws outstretched and swayed from side to side like a bear undecided whether to charge. Then he tried to make off at top speed and watch us over his shoulder
25 at the same time, running headlong into everything in his path.

Quiz 7 Questions

25. Wolverines are very scarce because

(A) their food supply is limited
(B) they are afraid of all humankind
(C) they are seldom protected by man
(D) trappers take their toll of them
(E) they suffer in the survival of the fittest

26. The reason the author did not kill the wolverine seems to be that

(A) the wolverine's ungainly gait made him miss the target
(B) conservation laws protected the animal

(C) the roughness of the terrain made tracking difficult

(D) he admired the skill of the animal

(E) he felt sorry for the animal

27. The wolverine ran headlong into everything in his path because of his

(A) anxiety and curiosity

(B) helplessness in the face of danger

(C) snow blindness

(D) ferocious courage

(E) pursuit by the trappers

28. The author of this selection is most probably

(A) an experienced hunter

(B) a conscientious naturalist

(C) an inexperienced trapper

(D) a young Indian

(E) a farmer

29. The author's chief purpose in writing this passage seems to be to

(A) defend the wolverine from further attacks by man

(B) point out the fatal weakness of the wolverine

(C) show why the wolverine is scarce

(D) characterize a rarely seen animal

(E) criticize Henry's action

30. As a whole, this passage suggests that the wolverine

(A) is every bit as awesome as his reputation

(B) will eventually destroy the deer herds

(C) will one day be able to outwit man

(D) does not really need the protection of man

(E) is too smart for other animals

Reading Quiz 8

Questions 31–33 are based on the following passage.

This passage is from John Burroughs, "The Still Small Voice," in The Atlantic Monthly: A Magazine of Litera- ture, Science, Art, and Politics, Volume CXVIII, *1916, p. 329.*

In the ordinary course of nature, the great beneficent changes come slowly and silently. The noisy changes, for the most part, mean violence and disruption. The roar of storms and tornadoes, the explosions of volcanoes,

5 the crash of thunder, are the result of a sudden break in the equipoise of the elements; from a condition of comparative repose and silence they become fearfully swift and audible. The still small voice is the voice of life and growth and perpetuity. . . . In the history of a

10 nation it is the same.

Quiz 8 Questions

31. The title below that best expresses the ideas of this passage is:

(A) Upsetting Nature's Balance

(B) Repose and Silence

(C) The Voice of Life and Growth

(D) Nature's Intelligence

(E) The Violent Elements

32. As used in the passage, the word *equipoise* (line 6) most nearly means

(A) stress

(B) balance

(C) course

(D) slowness

(E) condition

33. The author implies that growth and perpetuity in nature and in history are the result of

(A) quiet changes

(B) a period of silence

(C) undiscovered action

(D) storms and tornadoes

(E) violence and disruptions

Reading Quiz 9

Questions 34–37 are based on the following passage.

It is here, perhaps, that poetry may best act nowadays as corrective and complementary to science. When science tells us that the galaxy to which our solar system belongs is so enormous that light, traveling at

5 186,000 miles per second, takes between 60,000 and 100,000 years to cross from one rim to the other of the galaxy, we laymen accept the statement but find it meaningless—beyond the comprehension of heart or mind. When science tells us that the human eye has

10 about 137 million separate "seeing" elements, we are no less paralyzed, intellectually and emotionally. Man

is appalled by the immensities and the minuteness
which science has disclosed for him. They are indeed
unimaginable. But may not poetry be a possible way
15 of mediating them to our imagination? Of scaling them
down to imaginative comprehension? Let us remember
Perseus, who could not look directly at the nightmare
Gorgon without being turned to stone, but could look at
her image reflected in the shield the goddess of wisdom
20 lent him.

Quiz 9 Questions

34. The title below that best expresses the ideas of this
passage is:

   (A) Poetry and Imagination
   (B) A Modern Gorgon
   (C) Poetry as a Mediator
   (D) The Vastness of the Universe
   (E) Imaginative Man

35. According to the passage, the average man

   (A) should have a better memory
   (B) is impatient with science
   (C) cannot trust the scientists
   (D) is overwhelmed by the discoveries of
       science
   (E) does not understand either science or
       poetry

36. Perseus was most probably

   (A) a scientist
   (B) a legendary hero
   (C) an early poet
   (D) a horrible creature
   (E) a minor god

37. This passage is chiefly developed by means of

   (A) examples
   (B) cause and effect
   (C) narration
   (D) definition
   (E) anecdotes

Reading Quiz 10

Questions 38–40 are based on the following passage.

Hail is at once the cruelest weapon in Nature's armory,
and the most incalculable. It can destroy one farmer's
prospects of a harvest in a matter of seconds; it can
leave his neighbor's unimpaired. It can slay a flock
5 of sheep (it has killed children before now) in one
field, while the sun continues to shine in the next. To
the harassed meteorologist its behavior is even more
Machiavellian than that of an ice storm. Difficult as it
undoubtedly is for him to forecast the onset of an ice
10 storm, he knows pretty well what its course and dura-
tion will be once it has started; just about all he can do
with a hailstorm is to measure the size of the stones—
and they have a habit of melting as soon as he gets his
hands on them. He is not even too sure any more about
15 the way in which hail forms—and until he knows this,
of course, he isn't likely to stumble upon any very
satisfactory prognostic rules.

Quiz 10 Questions

38. The title below that best expresses the ideas of this
passage is:

   (A) Forecasting Ice Storms
   (B) The Way That Hail Forms
   (C) The Harassed Meteorologist
   (D) The Unpredictability of Hailstorms
   (E) Hail—the Killer

39. As used in the passage, the word *prognostic* (last
line) most nearly means

   (A) restraining
   (B) breakable
   (C) day-by-day
   (D) foretelling
   (E) regular

40. The author capitalized "Nature's" (line 1) most
probably because he wished to

   (A) talk with nature directly
   (B) contrast nature and science
   (C) emphasize the power of nature
   (D) show off his knowledge of figures of speech
   (E) call the reader's attention to the subject of the
       passage

Reading Quiz 11

Questions 41–43 are based on the following passage.

This passage is from the Janesville [Wisconsin] Daily Gazette, *October 19, 1954, p. 6.*

Windstorms have recently established a record which meteorologists hope will not be equaled for many years to come. Disastrous tornadoes along with devastating typhoons and hurricanes have cost thousands of lives
5 and left property damage totaling far into the millions. The prominence these storms have held in the news has led many people to ask about the difference between the three. Is a typhoon the same as a hurricane? Is a tornado the same as a typhoon? Basically, there is no
10 difference. All three consist of wind rotating counterclockwise (in the Northern Hemisphere) at a tremendous velocity around a low-pressure center. However, each type does have its own definite characteristics. Of the three the tornado is certainly the most treacherous.
15 The Weather Bureau can, with some degree of accuracy, forecast the typhoon and the hurricane; however, it is impossible to determine where or when the tornado will strike. And out of the three, if one had a choice, perhaps it would be safer to choose to withstand the
20 hurricane.

Quiz 11 Questions

41. The title below that best expresses the ideas of this passage is:

    (A) Recent Storms
    (B) Record-Breaking Storms
    (C) Predicting Windstorms
    (D) Treacherous Windstorms
    (E) Wind Velocity and Direction

42. Which is not common to all of the storms mentioned?

    (A) fairly accurate forecasting
    (B) violently rotating wind
    (C) high property damage
    (D) loss of human lives
    (E) public interest

43. The author indicates that

    (A) typhoons cannot be forecast
    (B) the Southern Hemisphere is free from hurricanes
    (C) typhoons are more destructive than hurricanes
    (D) hurricanes are not really dangerous
    (E) tornadoes occur around a low-pressure center

Reading Quiz 12

Questions 44–46 are based on the following passage.

The following is William Shakespeare's Sonnet 18.

Shall I compare thee to a summer's day?
Thou art more lovely and more temperate:
Rough winds do shake the darling buds of May,
And summer's lease hath all too short a date:
5 Sometime too hot the eye of heaven shines,
And often is his gold complexion dimm'd;
And every fair from fair sometime declines,
By chance or nature's changing course untrimm'd;
But thy eternal summer shall not fade
10 Nor lose possession of that fair thou owest;
Nor shall Death brag thou wander'st in his shade,
When in eternal lines to time thou growest:
So long as men can breathe or eyes can see,
So long lives this and this gives life to thee.

Quiz 12 Questions

44. The phrase "summer's lease hath all too short a date" (line 4) means that summer

    (A) ends in the first few days of September
    (B) cannot be dated because it lasts forever
    (C) rents time in our memories
    (D) is eternal
    (E) lasts for only a brief time

45. What does the poet mean by "eye of heaven" in line 5?

    (A) the moon
    (B) the sun
    (C) the rain
    (D) the stars
    (E) lightning

46. In the final line (line 14), what does Shakespeare mean by "this"?

    (A) eternal summer
    (B) his beloved
    (C) time
    (D) his sonnet
    (E) Death

Reading Quiz 13

Questions 47–50 are based on the following passage.

The man who reads well is the man who thinks well, who has a background for opinions and a touchstone for judgment. He may be a Lincoln who derives wisdom from a few books or a Roosevelt who ranges
5 from Icelandic sagas to *Penrod*. But reading makes him a full man, and out of his fullness he draws that example and precept which stand him in good stead when confronted with problems which beset a chaotic universe. Mere reading, of course, is nothing. It is but
10 the veneer of education. But wise reading is a help to action. American versatility is too frequently dilettantism, but reinforced by knowledge it becomes motive power. "Learning," as James L. Mursell says, "cashes the blank check of native versatility." And learning is a
15 process not to be concluded with the formal teaching of schooldays or to be enriched only by the active experience of later years, but to be broadened and deepened by persistent and judicious reading. "The true University of these days is a Collection of Books," said Car-
20 lyle. If that is not the whole of the truth it is enough of it for every young person to hug to this bosom.

Quiz 13 Questions

47. The title that best expresses the ideas of this passage is:

    (A) The Veneer of Education
    (B) The Wise Reader
    (C) The Reading Habits of Great Men
    (D) The Versatility of Americans
    (E) The Motivation of Readers

48. Which advice would the author of this passage most likely give to young people?

    (A) Develop a personal reading program.
    (B) Avoid reading too many books of the same type.
    (C) Spend more time in a library.
    (D) Read only serious books.
    (E) Learn to read more rapidly and accurately.

49. The quotation "Learning cashes the blank check of native versatility" (lines 13–14) means that

    (A) a good education is like money in the bank
    (B) to be versatile is to be learned
    (C) native intelligence has more value than acquired knowledge
    (D) education can make possible an effective use of natural capabilities
    (E) he who learns well will keep an open mind at all times

50. The author apparently believes that

    (A) the answer to the world's problems lies in a nation of learned men
    (B) America can overcome her dilettantism by broader reading programs for her citizens
    (C) people with wide reading backgrounds are likely to find right courses of action
    (D) active experience is the second-best teacher
    (E) the best book is one that is serious in tone

Reading Quiz 14

Questions 51–55 are based on the following passage.

This passage is from Aaron Copland, What to Listen for in Music, *1939.*

Most people want to know how things are made. They frankly admit, however, that they feel completely at sea when it comes to understanding how a piece of music is made. Where a composer begins, how he manages
5 to keep going—in fact, how and where he learns his trade—all are shrouded in impenetrable darkness. The composer, in short, is a man of mystery, and the composer's workshop an unapproachable ivory tower.

One of the first things the layman wants to hear
10 about is the part inspiration plays in composing. He finds it difficult to believe that composers are not much preoccupied with that question, that composing is as natural for the composer as eating or sleeping. Composing is something that the composer happens to have
15 been born to do, and because of that, it loses the character of a special virtue in the composer's eyes.

The composer, therefore, does not say to himself: "Do I feel inspired?" He says to himself: "Do I feel like composing today?" And if he feels like composing, he
20 does. It is more or less like saying to himself: "Do I feel sleepy?" If you feel sleepy, you go to sleep. If you don't feel sleepy, you stay up. If the composer doesn't feel like composing, he doesn't compose. It's as simple as that.

Quiz 14 Questions

51. The author of the passage indicates that creating music is an activity that is

    (A) difficult
    (B) rewarding
    (C) inspirational
    (D) fraught with anxiety
    (E) instinctive

52. When considering the work involved in composing music, the layman often

    (A) exaggerates the difficulties of the composer in commencing work
    (B) minimizes the mental turmoil that the composer undergoes
    (C) is unaware that a creative process is involved

    (D) loses the ability to enjoy the composition
    (E) loses his ability to judge the work apart from the composer

53. In this passage, composing music is compared with

    (A) having a feast
    (B) climbing an ivory tower
    (C) visualizing problems
    (D) going to sleep
    (E) going to sea

54. The author's approach toward his subject is

    (A) highly emotional
    (B) casually informative
    (C) negative
    (D) deeply philosophical
    (E) consciously prejudiced

55. We may most safely conclude that the author is

    (A) a layman
    (B) a violinist
    (C) a working composer
    (D) an amateur musician
    (E) a novelist

Reading Quiz 15

Questions 56–64 are based on the following double passage, *Social Science.*

Below are two excerpts from speeches that were made more than two thousand years apart and yet have much in common; both speeches address the issue of democracy and both concern those who had recently given their lives defending their government.

The first was reportedly made in 431 B.C. by the Greek general Pericles shortly after the outbreak of the Peloponnesian War; the second was delivered during the American Civil War at Gettysburg, Pennsylvania, on November 19, 1863, by President Abraham Lincoln.

Passage 1—Athens, Greece

Many of those who have spoken here in the past have praised the institution of this speech at the close of our ceremony. It seemed to them a mark of honor to our soldiers who have fallen in war that a speech should be
5 made over them. I do not agree. These men have shown themselves valiant in action, and it would be enough,

I think, for their glories to be proclaimed in action, as you have just seen it done at this funeral organized by the state. Our belief in the courage of so many should
10 not be hazarded on the goodness or badness of any single speech.

Let me say that our system of government does not copy the institutions of our neighbors. It is more the case of our being a model to others than of our imitat-
15 ing anyone else. Our constitution is called a democracy because power is in the hands not of a minority but of the whole people. When it is a question of settling private disputes, everyone is equal before the law; when it is a question of putting one person before another in
20 positions of public responsibility, what counts is not membership in a particular class, but the actual ability that the individual possesses. No one who could be of service to the state is kept in political obscurity because of poverty. And, just as our political life is free
25 and open, so is our day-to-day life in our relations with each other. We do not get into a state with our neighbors if they enjoy themselves in their own way, nor do we give anyone the kind of frowning looks that, though they do no real harm, still hurt people's feelings. We
30 are free and tolerant in our private lives; but in public affairs we keep to the law. This is because it commands our great respect. . . .

They gave Athens their lives, to her and to all of us, and for their own selves they won praises that never
35 grow old, the most splendid of sepulchers—not the sepulcher in which their bodies are laid, but where their glory remains eternal in others' minds, always there on the right occasion to stir them to speech or to action. For the famous have the whole earth for their tomb: it is not
40 only the inscriptions on their graves in their own country that marks them out; no, in foreign lands also, not in any visible form but in people's hearts, their memory abides and grows. It is for you to try to be like them. Make up your minds that happiness depends on being
45 free, and freedom depends on being courageous. Let there be no relaxation in the face of the perils of war. . . .

Passage 2—Gettysburg, Pennsylvania

But, in a larger sense, we cannot dedicate—we cannot consecrate—we cannot hallow—this ground. The brave men, living and dead, who struggled here, have con-
50 secrated it far above our poor power to add or detract. The world will little note nor long remember what we

say here, but it can never forget what they did here. It is for us, the living, rather, to be dedicated here to the unfinished work which they who fought here have
55 thus far so nobly advanced. It is rather for us to be here dedicated to the great task remaining before us—that from these honored dead we take increased devotion to the cause for which they gave their last full measure of devotion; that we here highly resolve that these dead
60 shall not have died in vain; that this nation under God, shall have a new birth of freedom; and that government of the people, by the people, for the people, shall not perish from the earth.

Quiz 15 Questions

56. Why does Pericles "not agree" (line 5) that a speech such as the one he is giving can further honor fallen soldiers?

    (A) Public officials give too many boring speeches.
    (B) Fallen soldiers are seldom the subject of speeches.
    (C) Past speakers concentrated too much on winning personal fame.
    (D) The potential inadequacies of the speech could detract from the glory of the fallen soldiers.
    (E) The glory achieved in battle is best remembered by loved ones, not by public officials.

57. The word *state* in line 26 means

    (A) stage of development
    (B) political unit
    (C) declaration
    (D) luxury
    (E) furor

58. In the second paragraph of Passage 1, Pericles primarily stresses that

    (A) a democratic spirit will help Athens win the war
    (B) Athens will always be remembered
    (C) people in neighboring countries envy Athenians
    (D) the customs of others seem strange to Athenians
    (E) the Athenian form of government is an admirable one

59. Which best summarizes the reason given in Passage 1 for the soldiers having earned "praises that never grow old" (lines 34–35)?

    (A) People in foreign lands will praise the Greeks for ages.
    (B) Memorials dedicated to heroic events will always be honored.
    (C) The Athenians will honor their military heroes annually.
    (D) The memory of great feats will repeatedly inspire others.
    (E) Relatives and friends of the heroes will never forget them.

60. It can be inferred from the content and tone of Passage 1 that Pericles' primary feeling was one of

    (A) sadness because Athens had lost so many courageous soldiers
    (B) dismay at his responsibility to guide the Athenians safely
    (C) annoyance because the Athenians might not appreciate the sacrifices that had been made for them
    (D) concern about whether the audience would agree with his views
    (E) pride in Athens and determination that it would continue into the future

61. In Passage 2, the word *consecrate* (line 48) means

    (A) absolve
    (B) adore
    (C) make sacred
    (D) begin praising
    (E) enjoy properly

62. The "unfinished work" referred to in line 54 is the

    (A) battle of Gettysburg
    (B) defense of freedom
    (C) establishment of a government
    (D) dedication of the battlefield
    (E) honoring of the fallen soldiers

63. Which statement from Passage 1 does NOT have a parallel idea conveyed in Passage 2?

    (A) "These men have shown themselves valiant in action" (lines 5–6)
    (B) "our system of government does not copy the institutions of our neighbors" (lines 12–13)
    (C) "They gave Athens their lives, to her and to all of us" (line 33)
    (D) "It is for you to try to be like them" (line 43)
    (E) "freedom depends on being courageous" (line 45)

64. Which statement is best supported by a comparison of the two excerpts?

    (A) Both excerpts urge an end to existing hostilities.
    (B) Both excerpts are appeals to the audience for personal political support.
    (C) Both excerpts emphasize the cruelty of the opponents of the state.
    (D) The intent and the development of ideas of both excerpts are similar.
    (E) The purpose of both excerpts is to prepare the audience for the eventual outbreak of war.

2 WRITING AND LANGUAGE QUIZZES

Writing and Language Quiz 1

Turn to Section 2 of your answer sheet (page 375) to answer the questions in this section.

Directions

Each passage below is accompanied by a number of questions. For some questions, you will consider how the passage might be revised to improve the expression of ideas. For other questions, you will consider how the passage might be edited to correct errors in sentence structure, usage, or punctuation.

Some questions will direct you to an underlined portion of a passage. Other questions will direct you to a location in a passage or ask you to think about the passage as a whole.

After reading each passage, choose the answer to each question that most effectively improves the quality of writing in the passage or that makes the passage conform to the conventions of standard written English. Many questions include a "NO CHANGE" option. Choose that option if you think the best choice is to leave the relevant portion of the passage as it is.

Questions 1–15 are based on the following passage, *Dolphin Ingenuity*.

Most of the intelligent land animals have (1) grasping organs for (2) an exploration of their environment—hands in man and his anthropoid relatives, the sensitive, inquiring trunk (3) in the elephant makeup.

One of the surprising things about the dolphin is (4) because his superior brain is unaccompanied by any type of manipulative organ. He has, however, a remarkable (5) ability for range finding involving some sort of echo sounding.

Perhaps this acute sense—(6) far more accurate (7) then any man has been able to devise (8) artificially brings him greater knowledge of his watery surroundings than might at first seem possible. Human beings think of intelligence as geared to things. The hand and the tool are (9) to us unconscious symbols of our intellectual attainment.

It is difficult for us to visualize another kind of lonely, almost disembodied intelligence floating in the wavering green fairyland of the sea—an intelligence (10) possible near or comparable to our own but without hands to build, (11) transmit knowledge (12) with writing, or to alter by one hair's breadth the planet's surface. Yet at the same time (13) they're indications that the dolphin's intelligence is a warm, friendly, and eager intelligence, quite capable of coming to the assistance of injured companions and striving to rescue them from drowning. (14)

Dolphin Ingenuity Questions

1. (A) NO CHANGE
   (B) organs to do grasping
   (C) grasp-organs
   (D) grasp-like organs

2. (A) NO CHANGE
   (B) to explore
   (C) exploration into
   (D) exploring

3. (A) NO CHANGE
   (B) that the elephant has
   (C) in the elephant
   (D) as in the elephant

4. (A) NO CHANGE
   (B) that
   (C) as
   (D) why

5. Which of the following alternatives to the underlined portion would NOT be acceptable?

   (A) range-finding ability involving

   (B) ability that lets him find his range and involves

   (C) range finding ability involving

   (D) ability to find his range involving

6. (A) NO CHANGE

   (B) far accurate

   (C) far accurater

   (D) more accurate by a long shot

7. (A) NO CHANGE

   (B) than any

   (C) any

   (D) as any

8. (A) NO CHANGE

   (B) artificially, brings

   (C) artificially—brings

   (D) artificially, bringing

9. All of the following would be acceptable placements for the underlined portion EXCEPT

   (A) where it is now

   (B) after the word *unconscious*

   (C) at the beginning of the sentence (revising capitalization accordingly)

   (D) after the word *tool*

10. (A) NO CHANGE

   (B) possibly near to that or comparable to

   (C) possibly near or comparable to

   (D) possible nearly or comparable to

11. (A) NO CHANGE

   (B) to transmit

   (C) transmitting

   (D) or to transmit

12. (A) NO CHANGE

   (B) to write

   (C) by the written word

   (D) of writing

13. (A) NO CHANGE

   (B) there is

   (C) their are

   (D) there are

14. The writer is considering adding the following true statement.

> In Monterey, California, dolphins encircled and saved a surfer being attacked by a great white shark after the shark had bitten the man three times.

Should the writer make this addition here?

   (A) Yes, because the sentence adds an interesting supporting example of dolphins' unique abilities.

   (B) Yes, because the sentence exemplifies dolphins' warm, friendly nature.

   (C) No, because the sentence strays from the paragraph's focus on the nature of dolphin intelligence.

   (D) No, because information about a dolphin confronting a shark contradicts the point that dolphins are friendly creatures.

Question 15 asks about the previous passage as a whole.

15. Upon reviewing the essay and finding that some information has been left out, the writer composes the following sentence:

> Although dolphins lack such an external symbol of intellect, researchers have discovered that they can use tools to solve problems and invent novel behaviors.

This sentence would most logically be placed after sentence

   (A) 1 in paragraph 1

   (B) 1 in paragraph 3

   (C) 3 in paragraph 3

   (D) 1 in paragraph 4

Questions 16–30 are based on the following passage, *Breeding Rumors*.

Repeating rumors is the (16) most crudest way of spreading stories—by passing them on from mouth to mouth. (17) But in civilized countries in normal times have better sources of news than rumor. (18) It has radio, television, and newspapers. In times of stress and (19) confusion; however, rumor emerges and becomes rife. At such times (20) these different kind of news media are in (21) competition; the press, television, and radio versus the grapevine.

Rumors are especially likely to spread when war requires censorship on many important matters. The customary news sources no longer give out enough information. (22) Although the people, cannot learn (23) all that they are anxious to know through legitimate channels, they pick up "news" wherever they (24) can, and rumor thrives.

Rumors are often repeated even (25) by people which do not (26) believe the stories. There is a fascination (27) about them. (28) The reason is that the cleverly designed rumor gives expression to something deep in the hearts of the tellers—the fears, suspicions, forbidden hopes, or daydreams that they hesitate to have voiced directly. (29) Pessimistic rumors about defeat and disasters show that the people who repeat these rumors are worried and anxious. Optimistic rumors about record production or peace to come soon point to complacency or confidence—(30) and often to overconfidence.

Breeding Rumors Questions

16. (A) NO CHANGE
    (B) way most crude
    (C) more crude way
    (D) crudest way

17. (A) NO CHANGE
    (B) But countries, that are civilized,
    (C) But civilized countries
    (D) But countries with civilization

18. (A) NO CHANGE
    (B) Countries have
    (C) They have
    (D) Such as

19. (A) NO CHANGE
    (B) confusion however,
    (C) confusion, however,
    (D) confusion, however

20. (A) NO CHANGE
    (B) this different kinds
    (C) these different kinds
    (D) all these different kind

21. (A) NO CHANGE
    (B) competition: the
    (C) competition. The
    (D) competition, the

22. (A) NO CHANGE
    (B) Since the people
    (C) Consequently, the people who
    (D) The people, if they

23. (A) NO CHANGE
    (B) through legitimate channels in all that they are anxious to know,
    (C) what they are anxious to know through legitimate channels,
    (D) through legitimate channels all that they are anxious to know,

24. (A) NO CHANGE
    (B) can, and rumor has thrived.
    (C) can, rumor thrives.
    (D) can, rumor thriving.

25. (A) NO CHANGE
    (B) by them as
    (C) by they who
    (D) by people who

26. (A) NO CHANGE
    (B) have belief of
    (C) dig
    (D) give credibility to

27. (A) NO CHANGE
    (B) with
    (C) over
    (D) because of

28. Upon reviewing the paragraph, the writer considers deleting this sentence. If the writer were to delete the sentence, the paragraph would lose primarily

    (A) an argument that spreading rumors is dangerous to national security
    (B) a defense of rumors as an inevitable part of human nature
    (C) an example of mass media's justification for repeating rumors
    (D) a generalization introducing examples of the root cause of people's participation in rumors

29. Which choice would best fit the paragraph's key point about why rumors spread?

    (A) NO CHANGE
    (B) Pessimistic rumors about defeat and disasters never fail to illustrate the gullibility of the public.

(C) Pessimistic rumors about defeat and disasters are evidence that mass media can play a major role in manipulating human behavior.

(D) Pessimistic rumors about defeat and disasters have often shaped the outcome of war and other crisis situations.

30. If the writer were to delete the underlined phrase, the sentence would lose primarily

(A) a sarcastic edge

(B) a tone of disdain for people who spread rumors

(C) the implication that people who spread false information are themselves misled

(D) a concrete example of a rumor that was eventually proved false

Questions 31–45 are based on the following passage, *There Is No Open-and-Shut Case.*

Average citizens today are knowledgeable about "land-mark" court decisions (31) as racial segregation, legislative apportionment, prayers in the public schools, or (32) that the defendant in a criminal prosecution has the right to have counsel. Too often, however, they think that (33) this settles matters once and for all. Actually, of course, these well-publicized court decisions are merely guideposts (34) that have the effect of pointing toward a virtually endless series of vexing legal questions (35). A person (36) whom the decisions (37) affects must often still endure lengthy court cases before his fate is decided. It is often more difficult to determine how far the courts should travel along a road (38) than deciding (39) whatever road should be taken.

(40) Illustrations of this difficulty exist in all areas of the law, especially in those with which the lay public is most familiar. For example, in the recent past, this nation could hardly have failed to agree that (41) state compelled racial segregation in the public schools (42) will be a denial of the equal protection of the laws guaranteed by the 14th Amendment. The real difficulty (43) lied in determining how desegregation (44) shall be accomplished and how to solve the problem of de facto school segregation, perpetuated by the practical if unfortunate realities of residential patterns.

There Is No Open-and-Shut Case **Questions**

31. (A) NO CHANGE
    (B) such as
    (C) like
    (D) concerning such questions as

32. (A) NO CHANGE
    (B) the right of the defendant to counsel in criminal prosecution.
    (C) the right in criminal prosecution to counsel of the defendant.
    (D) the defendant has a right to counsel in criminal prosecution.

33. (A) NO CHANGE
    (B) these decisions settle
    (C) these settle
    (D) those settle

34. (A) NO CHANGE
    (B) with the purpose of pointing
    (C) pointing
    (D) that are pointing

35. Which phrase when added to the end of the preceding sentence best clarifies the phrase "vexing legal questions"?

    (A) in the form of appeals and unanticipated social consequences.
    (B) that make agreement impossible.
    (C) that may never be answered.
    (D) that are argued in the media.

36. (A) NO CHANGE
    (B) who
    (C) which
    (D) as to whom

37. (A) NO CHANGE
    (B) effect
    (C) effects
    (D) affect

38. (A) NO CHANGE
    (B) than
    (C) than it is to decide
    (D) than to decide

39. (A) NO CHANGE
    (B) as to whose
    (C) what
    (D) whichever

40. Which choice would most effectively open this paragraph and introduce the supporting examples?

(A) NO CHANGE

(B) You are no doubt familiar with many highly publicized court cases.

(C) Several examples show how difficult it is for a high court to reach consensus.

(D) Many high-profile court decisions have caused unforeseen problems down the road.

41. (A) NO CHANGE

(B) state-compelled racial-segregation

(C) state compelled racial-segregation

(D) state-compelled racial segregation

42. (A) NO CHANGE

(B) will have been

(C) is

(D) had been

43. (A) NO CHANGE

(B) lay

(C) laid

(D) was lying

44. (A) NO CHANGE

(B) will be accomplished

(C) was to be accomplished

(D) were to be accomplished

Question 45 asks about the previous passage as a whole.

45. Suppose the writer had been asked to write a persuasive essay urging public support for laws with broad social significance once they are passed. Would this essay fulfill that assignment?

(A) Yes, because the essay describes how challenging it is for a judge to reach these decisions.

(B) Yes, because the essay clearly spells out the consequences of public polarization on legal issues of national significance.

(C) No, because the essay provides examples of decisions that turned out to have negative outcomes.

(D) No, because the essay's purpose is to describe a common public misperception about how historically significant court cases are resolved.

Questions 46–60 are based on the following passage, *The Highest Form of Education.*

The man who reads well is the man who thinks well, (46) he has a background for opinions and a touchstone for judgment. He may be a Lincoln (47) who derives wisdom from a few books or a Roosevelt who reads everything from Icelandic sagas to *Penrod*. But reading makes (48) his a full man, and out of his fullness (49) to draw that example and precept which (50) has stood him in good stead when confronted with problems (51) which beset a chaotic universe. Mere reading, of course, is nothing. (52) It is also the veneer of education. But wise reading is a help to action. (53) American versatility is too frequently dilettantism, but reinforced by knowledge, versatility becomes motive power. (54) "Learning" as James L. Mursell says, "cashes the (55) blank check of native versatility." (56) Ones learning is a process not to be concluded with the formal teaching of school days or (57) only to be enriched by the active experience of later years, but to be broadened and deepened by persistent and judicious reading. (58) "The true University of these days is a Collection of Books," said Carlyle. If that is not the whole of the truth, it is enough of the truth for every young person to hug to their breasts. Whoever follows this advice (59) will become a truly educated person.

The Highest Form of Education Questions

46. (A) NO CHANGE

(B) who

(C) and

(D) whom

47. (A) NO CHANGE

(B) , deriving wisdom

(C) , a deriver of wisdom

(D) , wisdom deriving

48. (A) NO CHANGE

(B) he

(C) him

(D) himself

49. (A) NO CHANGE

(B) draws

(C) drawing

(D) he draws

50. (A) NO CHANGE
    (B) stands
    (C) stood
    (D) stand

51. Which of the following alternatives to the under-lined portion would NOT be acceptable?

    (A) besetting
    (B) , that beset
    (C) that beset
    (D) that have always beset

52. (A) NO CHANGE
    (B) It is but the veneer
    (C) It is the veneer only
    (D) The veneer is

53. If the writer were to delete the sentence "American versatility . . .," the essay would lose primarily

    (A) an effective transitional statement between two different ideas
    (B) use of repetition to reinforce an argumentative point
    (C) an expansion and clarification of the distinction between reading and learning
    (D) a digression with no relationship to the essay's main point

54. (A) NO CHANGE
    (B) "Learning,"
    (C) "Learning,
    (D) "Learning"—

55. (A) NO CHANGE
    (B) blanked check
    (C) check that is blank
    (D) blanked out check

56. (A) NO CHANGE
    (B) One
    (C) One's
    (D) Ones'

57. (A) NO CHANGE
    (B) to be enriched only
    (C) to be only enriched
    (D) to only be enriched

58. If the writer were to delete the underlined quote, the paragraph would lose primarily

    (A) consideration of a viewpoint opposing the essay's central argument

    (B) a concrete example of the rich knowledge one can acquire from books
    (C) a comment by a well-known thinker that encapsulates the essay's point about reading and learning
    (D) an argument for pursuing a college education

59. (A) NO CHANGE
    (B) will be able to read even the most challenging material.
    (C) will love learning for the rest of his life.
    (D) will truly be ready to advance to university education.

Question 60 asks about the previous passage as a whole.

60. Suppose the writer had been asked to write an essay arguing the superiority of informal education to formal study. Would this essay fulfill that assignment?

    (A) Yes, because it argues that reading is the best substitute for an expensive education.
    (B) Yes, because the essay suggests that formal education is too restrictive and passive, while reading leads to activism.
    (C) No, because the essay points out that formal higher education is required in complex, chaotic times.
    (D) No, because the essay illustrates how formal education and informal learning complement and enrich each other.

Questions 61–75 are based on the following passage, *No Time to Lose*.

We streamlined our leisure hours for higher production, lived by the clock even when time did not matter, standardized and mechanized our homes, and (61) have sped the machinery of living so that we (62) can go to the most places and do the most things in the (63) shorter period of time possible. We tried to eat, sleep, and (64) loaf efficiently. (65) Even on holidays and Sundays, the efficient person relaxed on schedule with one eye on the clock and the other on an appointment sheet.

(66) To have squeezed the most out of each shining hour, we streamlined the opera, condensed the classics, (67) energize pellets, and culture into pocket-sized

packages. We made the busy bee look like an (68) <u>idler, the ant like a sluggard.</u> We lived sixty miles a minute and the great god (69) <u>efficiency</u> smiled. (70) <u>We wished we could have returned</u> to that pleasant day when we (71) <u>considered</u> time a friend instead of a competitor, when we had done things (72) <u>spontaneously</u> and because we had wanted to do them rather than (73) <u>on account of</u> our schedule had called for it. But (74) <u>that,</u> of course, had not been efficient; and every single one of us Americans (75) <u>are expected</u> to be efficient.

No Time to Lose Questions

61. (A) NO CHANGE
    (B) speed
    (C) speeding
    (D) sped

62. (A) NO CHANGE
    (B) could go
    (C) are able to go
    (D) go

63. (A) NO CHANGE
    (B) shortest
    (C) short
    (D) most short

64. (A) NO CHANGE
    (B) to loaf efficiently.
    (C) loaf efficient.
    (D) to loaf efficient.

65. Which sentence best emphasizes the paragraph's point about the American lifestyle?

    (A) NO CHANGE
    (B) Relaxation was so important to us, we scheduled it into our lives every day.
    (C) Being on time for scheduled appointments has been a hallmark of our efficiency.
    (D) Holidays and Sundays have traditionally been the days reserved for leisure.

66. (A) NO CHANGE
    (B) In order for squeezing
    (C) In order for having squeezed
    (D) To squeeze

67. (A) NO CHANGE
    (B) gave pellets energy,
    (C) energy into pellets,
    (D) and put energy into pellets

68. (A) NO CHANGE
    (B) idler, the ant as a sluggard.
    (C) idler. The ant like a sluggard.
    (D) idler; the ant as a sluggard.

69. (A) NO CHANGE
    (B) , efficiency,
    (C) Efficiency
    (D) , Efficiency,

70. (A) NO CHANGE
    (B) (DO NOT begin a new paragraph) We wished we could have returned,
    (C) (Begin a new paragraph) We wished we could have returned
    (D) (Begin a new paragraph) We wished, we could have returned

71. (A) NO CHANGE
    (B) had considered
    (C) consider
    (D) will consider

72. (A) NO CHANGE
    (B) with spontaneity
    (C) in a spontaneous manner
    (D) spontaneous

73. (A) NO CHANGE
    (B) because
    (C) when
    (D) OMIT

74. Given that all are true, which choice most clearly conveys the writer's message about American efficiency?

    (A) NO CHANGE
    (B) wasting time
    (C) wishing to live at a more relaxed pace
    (D) ignoring our responsibilities

75. (A) NO CHANGE
    (B) are to be expected
    (C) expect
    (D) is expected

Writing and Language
Quiz 2

Turn to Section 3 of your answer sheet (page 376) to answer the questions in this section.

Directions

Each passage below is accompanied by a number of questions. For some questions, you will consider how the passage might be revised to improve the expression of ideas. For other questions, you will consider how the passage might be edited to correct errors in sentence structure, usage, or punctuation.

Some questions will direct you to an underlined portion of a passage. Other questions will direct you to a location in a passage or ask you to think about the passage as a whole.

After reading each passage, choose the answer to each question that most effectively improves the quality of writing in the passage or that makes the passage conform to the conventions of standard written English. Many questions include a "NO CHANGE" option. Choose that option if you think the best choice is to leave the relevant portion of the passage as it is.

Questions 1–15 are based on the following passage, *The Money Behind Movie Musicals.*

Since (1) the origination of movies, (2) there had always been people interested (3) in being financially involved in films. Nowadays, these people are called backers. A backer is (4) someone who the director or the producer has chosen. But (5) between you and myself, when the money (6) he or she has paid mounts up to the staggering sums required to produce a movie musical, he or she becomes as important to the film (7) as any person involved. (8)

Why back a movie (9) which cost millions to shoot? How do backers recoup their investment in a project that looks and feels like a stage production people may have already seen? (10) Mostly to the point, why (11) except the arbitrary confines of the theater proscenium? Because the music and story are usually already well known and beloved by Broadway audiences, it pays to stay as faithful as possible to the original version. In doing so, however, producers can use the camera to

open up a world of fantasy and fun to larger audiences. Being faithful to the original story while *looking* original is only part of the (12) story, and not scarcely the most important part. To produce (13) any kind of stage presentation for film is purely handyman's work, a matter of picking the pieces and pasting them together. A truly successful adaptation from stage to screen, on the other hand, (14) will have called for imagination, finesse, and creativity. (15) Perhaps that is why it is so rare.

The Money Behind Movie Musicals Questions

1. Which of the following alternatives to the underlined portion would NOT be acceptable?

   (A) movies were invented,
   (B) the movies' invention,
   (C) the invention of movies,
   (D) having invented movies,

2. (A) NO CHANGE
   (B) there have always been
   (C) there were always
   (D) there will always be

3. (A) NO CHANGE
   (B) to finance
   (C) in financing
   (D) in finance

4. (A) NO CHANGE
   (B) someone who is the one
   (C) someone whom
   (D) someone, whomever

5. (A) NO CHANGE
   (B) you and me
   (C) you and I
   (D) you and also me

6. (A) NO CHANGE
   (B) they have paid
   (C) the backer has paid
   (D) the backer had paid

7. (A) NO CHANGE
   (B) as any other one
   (C) as anyone
   (D) as anyone else

8. The writer is considering adding the following true statement:

> Consider the fact that in 1978, the total budget for *Grease* was $6 million, whereas in 2007, *Hairspray* cost approximately $75 million, a relatively low budget by Hollywood standards.

Should the writer make this addition here?

(A) Yes, because the sentence supports the importance of the financial backer with a concrete example of increasing costs.

(B) Yes, because the example of successful movie musicals supports the writer's argument that movie financiers should see musicals as a good investment.

(C) No, because the sentence neglects to identify the backers of these films.

(D) No, because the sentence is irrelevant to the essay's focus on the producer's role.

9. (A) NO CHANGE
   (B) who costs
   (C) that costs
   (D) that costed

10. (A) NO CHANGE
    (B) Even better to the point,
    (C) Even more to the point,
    (D) More to the point is,

11. (A) NO CHANGE
    (B) accept
    (C) excepting
    (D) accepting

12. (A) NO CHANGE
    (B) story. And scarcely
    (C) story. Scarcely
    (D) story—and scarcely

13. (A) NO CHANGE
    (B) these kind of stage presentation
    (C) any of those kinds of stage presentation
    (D) some of these kinds of stage presentation

14. (A) NO CHANGE
    (B) called for
    (C) had called for
    (D) calls for

15. Given that all of the choices are true, which one is most relevant to the focus of this essay?

(A) NO CHANGE

(B) These qualities are rare among musical screenwriters.

(C) One of the finest examples of an artful adaptation is the movie version of *Chicago*.

(D) These qualities are rare, but they are often a hallmark of musical adaptations that do well at the box office and return their backers' investment.

Questions 16–30 are based on the following passage, *Diving Dangers*.

(16) Despite patience is the most important quality a treasure hunter can have, (17) the hunting about for treasure demands a certain amount of courage too. I have my share of guts but make no boast (18) in regards to ignoring the hazards of diving. (19) All good divers know, the business of plunging into an alien world with an artificial air supply as your only link to the world above (20) this occupation can be (21) more dangerous as stepping into a den of lions. Most of the danger rests within the diver himself. (22)

The (23) devil-may-care diver who shows great bravado underwater is the worst risk of all. He may lose his bearings in the glimmering dim light (24) that penetrates the sea and (25) become separate from his diving companions. He may dive too deep, too long, and suffer painful, sometimes fatal, bends.

Once, (26) when I was salvaging brass from the sunken hulk of an old steel ship, I brushed lightly against a huge engine cylinder that looked (27) like it was as solid as it was on the day the ship was launched. Although the pressure of my touch was hardly enough to topple a toy soldier, the heavy mass of cast iron collapsed, (28) having caused a chain reaction in which the rest of the old engine crumbled. Tons of iron dropped all around me. (29) Sheer luck saved me from being crushed. I (30) was wary of swimming around steel shipwrecks ever since.

Diving Dangers Questions

16. (A) NO CHANGE
    (B) Although
    (C) However
    (D) Because

17. (A) NO CHANGE
    (B) this
    (C) treasure hunting
    (D) it

18. (A) NO CHANGE
    (B) concerning ignorance of
    (C) to ignore
    (D) about ignoring

19. (A) NO CHANGE
    (B) As all good divers know,
    (C) Like all good divers know,
    (D) As all good divers are knowing,

20. (A) NO CHANGE
    (B) this can
    (C) can
    (D) doing this can

21. (A). NO CHANGE
    (B) as dangerous as
    (C) dangerous as
    (D) so dangerous as

22. Upon reviewing the essay's first paragraph, the writer considers deleting the preceding sentence. If the writer were to delete the sentence, the paragraph would lose primarily

    (A) an emotional appeal designed to inspire sympathy for divers
    (B) the element of suspense
    (C) a focusing statement suggesting a cause/effect relationship
    (D) a first-person perspective on treasure hunting

23. If the writer were to delete the underlined phrase, the paragraph would lose primarily

    (A) the connection the writer wants to make between the fate of the diver and spiritual questions

    (B) an essential part of the writer's classification of different types of divers
    (C) a visual image that helps the reader picture the diver
    (D) a vivid adjective reinforcing the writer's point about divers' responsibility for their own fate

24. (A) NO CHANGE
    (B). that is penetrating
    (C) that penetrated
    (D) that has penetrated

25. (A) NO CHANGE
    (B) became separated
    (C) become separated
    (D) became separate

26. (A) NO CHANGE
    (B) during salvaging
    (C) while salvaging
    (D) during the time that I was salvaging

27. (A) NO CHANGE
    (B) as if it was
    (C) as if it were
    (D) DELETE the underlined portion

28. (A) NO CHANGE
    (B) to cause
    (C) caused
    (D) causing

29. Which choice would most clearly communicate the precariousness of the diver's situation?

    (A) NO CHANGE
    (B) Good thing I didn't give the engine cylinder a stronger shove.
    (C) Another day, another near-death experience!
    (D) My experience saw me through yet again.

30. (A) NO CHANGE
    (B) am
    (C) had been
    (D) have been

Questions 31–45 are based on the following passage, *Who Makes the Music?*

Most people want to know (31) how are things made? They frankly (32) admit; however, that they feel completely at sea when it comes to understanding (33) how the making of a piece of music is done. Where the composer begins, how he or she manages to (34) keep going, how and where the composer learns the trade—(35) all is shrouded in impenetrable darkness. The composer, (36) fortunately, is a person of mystery and (37) the composers workshop an unapproachable ivory tower.

(38) One of the first things the layperson wants to hear the story of is the part inspiration plays in composing. He or she finds it difficult to believe that composers (39) are not much preoccupied with that question, that composing is as natural for the composer (40) as him or her eating or sleeping. Composing is something that the composer happens (41) to be born to do, and because of that, (42) lost the character of a special virtue in the composer's eyes.

The composer, therefore, does not say: "Do I feel inspired?" He or she says: "Do I feel like composing today?" And if the composer feels like composing, he or she composes. It is more or less (43) like saying to himself or to herself: "Do I feel sleepy?" If you feel sleepy, you go to sleep. If you don't feel sleepy, you stay up. If the composer doesn't feel like composing, (44) he or she doesn't. It's as simple as that.

Who Makes the Music? Questions

31. (A) NO CHANGE
    (B) how are things made.
    (C) how things are made.
    (D) how things are made?

32. (A) NO CHANGE
    (B) admit however
    (C) admit, however,
    (D) admit; however

33. (A) NO CHANGE
    (B) how to make a piece of music.
    (C) how making a piece of music is done.
    (D) how a piece of music is made.

34. Which choice would best clarify the underlined phrase as it is used in this sentence?
    (A) NO CHANGE
    (B) get through the day
    (C) stay in this competitive business
    (D) withstand the pressure

35. (A) NO CHANGE
    (B) all are
    (C) all this is
    (D) all them are

36. (A) NO CHANGE
    (B) nevertheless,
    (C) thereby,
    (D) in short,

37. (A) NO CHANGE
    (B) the composers' workshop
    (C) the composer's workshop
    (D) the workshop of the composer

38. Which choice would most effectively introduce the main idea of this paragraph?
    (A) NO CHANGE
    (B) The layperson doesn't understand the composer's methods.
    (C) Many would-be composers find it frustrating that the process seems to require inborn talent rather than skill that can be taught.
    (D) Laypeople and composers often disagree about the best approach to musical composition.

39. (A) NO CHANGE
    (B) are preoccupied not too much with
    (C) are not preoccupied very with
    (D) are not too very preoccupied with

40. (A) NO CHANGE
    (B) as eating or sleeping.
    (C) as that he or she eats or sleeps.
    (D) as that he or she is eating or sleeping.

41. (A) NO CHANGE
    (B) to have been born
    (C) to having been born
    (D) to be being born

42. (A) NO CHANGE
    (B) it lost
    (C) loses
    (D) it loses

43. (A) NO CHANGE
    (B) as if he or she says to him or to her:
    (C) like saying to his or to her own self:
    (D) like saying to he himself or to she herself:

44. (A) NO CHANGE
    (B) he or she doesn't do it.
    (C) he or she doesn't compose.
    (D) he or she doesn't do any composing.

Question 45 asks about the previous passage as a whole.

45. Suppose the writer had been asked to write a personal narrative describing his insights into the composer's creative process. Would this essay fulfill that goal?

    (A) Yes, because the writer shares his frustrations that the composer's talent is misunderstood.
    (B) Yes, because the writer includes first-person questions he asks himself in order to begin the creative process.
    (C) No, because the essay is a third-person, objective definition of "composer."
    (D) No, because the essay is a third-person exploration of what the writer knows about composers and what is unknown.

Questions 46–60 are based on the following passage, *A New View of Man*.

(46) The American museum of natural history (47) had long portrayed various aspects of man. Primitive cultures have been shown (48) kind of through habitat groups and displays of man's tools, utensils, and art. In more recent years, (49) there has been a tendency to delineate man's place in nature, displaying his destructive and constructive activities on the earth he inhabits. (50) For the first time, now, the museum has taken man apart, enlarged the delicate mechanisms that make him run, and examined him as a biological phenomenon. (51) In the new Hall of the Biology of Man, museum technicians have created a series of (52) displays that is instructive to a degree (53) never achieved in an exhibit hall. Using new techniques and new materials, (54) movement has been produced as well

as form and color. It is a human belief (55) that beauty is skin deep only. (56) But nature has proved to be a master designer, not only in the matter of man's bilateral symmetry (57) as well as in the marvelous packaging job that has arranged all man's organs and systems (58) inside his skin covered-case. When these are taken out of the case, greatly enlarged, and given color, they reveal form and design that give the lie to that old saying. (59) Visitors will surprise to discover that man's insides, too, are beautiful.

A New View of Man Questions

46. (A) NO CHANGE
    (B) The American Museum of Natural History
    (C) The American Museum of natural history
    (D) The American museum of Natural History

47. (A) NO CHANGE
    (B) portrayed for a long time
    (C) has long portrayed
    (D) portrays for a long time

48. (A) NO CHANGE
    (B) not only through
    (C) through
    (D) throughout

49. (A) NO CHANGE
    (B) it has been a tendency
    (C) a tendency being
    (D) a tendency is

50. (A) NO CHANGE
    (B) Now for the first time
    (C) Now, for the first time
    (D) Now, for the first time,

51. If the writer were to delete the opening sentence of this paragraph (so the paragraph would begin "In the new Hall of the Biology of Man"), the paragraph would lose primarily

    (A) a process analysis of the technology that makes the exhibit run
    (B) a transition introducing the theme and significance of the new exhibit
    (C) an argument for the museum's importance and relevance
    (D) a contrast between the American Museum of Natural History and other museums of its kind

52. (A) NO CHANGE
    (B) displays, which are instructive,
    (C) displays that are instructive
    (D) displays as are instructive

53. (A) NO CHANGE
    (B) never before achieved
    (C) never to be achieved
    (D) not never before achieved

54. (A) NO CHANGE
    (B) these technicians have been able to produce movement
    (C) it has been possible to produce movement
    (D) the possibility of producing movement has been realized

55. (A) NO CHANGE
    (B) that only beauty is skin deep.
    (C) only that beauty is skin deep.
    (D) that beauty is only skin deep.

56. If the writer were to delete the preceding sentence, the paragraph would lose primarily
    (A) a concrete example of a theme brought to life in the museum exhibit
    (B) a sentence setting up the writer's interpretation of the exhibit's meaning
    (C) a comment on the human condition
    (D) part of the writer's critique of the exhibit

57. (A) NO CHANGE
    (B) but also the marvelous
    (C) and in the marvelous
    (D) but also in the marvelous

58. (A) NO CHANGE
    (B) in his skin-covered case.
    (C) within his skin-covered case.
    (D) with his skin covered case.

59. Which choice would best tie the conclusion of the essay to its opening sentence?
    (A) NO CHANGE
    (B) Visitors may be upset by the unusually graphic nature of the display.
    (C) Thanks to the American Museum of Natural History, visitors will be surprised to discover that man's insides, too, are beautiful.
    (D) More visitors than ever will flock to American museums to see groundbreaking exhibits.

Question 60 asks about the previous passage as a whole.

60. Suppose the writer had been asked to write an essay that compares and contrasts representations of man in art and natural history museums. Would this essay fulfill that assignment?
    (A) Yes, because the essay describes use of form and color as well as other artistic choices in the exhibit.
    (B) Yes, because the essay implies that visiting the Museum of Natural History is a more instructive experience than visiting an art museum.
    (C) No, because the essay focuses on the purpose of all museums, to show the beauty of its subjects.
    (D) No, because the writer's analysis of the natural history exhibit as art is only implied.

Questions 61–75 are based on the following passage, *Modigliani's Art.*

The futurists (61) had broken passionately with Renaissance art. (62) Gone was its single center of interest, its naturalistic color, and its emphasis on humanism. (63) A year only or two later, however, Modigliani (64) is to turn back to (65) one of his ancestors, Botticelli, and, in a most daring union, attempt to join (66) this artists sinuous elegance to the primitive power of (67) newly discovering African American art. (68) Himself limited almost solely to the portraits, (69) to juxtapose Botticelli's fluent line and urbane individualism with tribal memories of Africa, miraculously inventing a language of his own as authentic as those he combined. Wistful, lost in reverie and loneliness, (70) he transcends the stylized conventions that produced his figures. (71) In other hands, these elongated necks, ovoid heads, and flattened noses might seem contrived, even "modernistic." With Modigliani they are not clever technical (72) exercises, they are engrossing human documents touched by humor, pathos, sensuality, and compassion. (73) Because his methods were easily imitated but his content unexpectedly evasive, he established no school. His was a brush as personal as those of the Renaissance masters he admired. A symbol of (74) our 20th century, Modigliani was in love with primitive art while remaining faithful to his own heritage. The transformation (75) he must of affected was not due to a gentle refurbishing of the past but to a new image forged from two alien cultures.

Modigliani's Art Questions

61. (A) NO CHANGE
    (B) were broke
    (C) broke
    (D) did break

62. (A) NO CHANGE
    (B) Far gone was
    (C) Gone were
    (D) Gone away were

63. (A) NO CHANGE
    (B) Only a year or two later,
    (C) A year or only two later,
    (D) A year or two later only,

64. (A) NO CHANGE
    (B) is to have turned
    (C) was to have turned
    (D) was to turn

65. (A) NO CHANGE
    (B) his ancestor, Botticelli,
    (C) Botticelli, his ancestor,
    (D) Botticelli his ancestor,

66. (A) NO CHANGE
    (B) this artist's
    (C) this artists'
    (D) this artist

67. (A) NO CHANGE
    (B) new discovered
    (C) new discovering
    (D) newly discovered

68. (A) NO CHANGE
    (B) Limiting he
    (C) Limiting him
    (D) Limiting himself

69. (A) NO CHANGE
    (B) juxtaposing
    (C) he juxtaposed
    (D) to have juxtaposed

70. (A) NO CHANGE
    (B) the stylized conventions that produced his figures are transcended.
    (C) transcending the stylized conventions that produced his figures.
    (D) his figures transcend the stylized conventions that produced them.

71. (A) NO CHANGE
    (B) (DO NOT begin a new paragraph) In other hands these elongated necks,
    (C) (Begin new paragraph) In other hands these elongated necks,
    (D) (Begin new paragraph) In other hands, these elongated necks,

72. (A) NO CHANGE
    (B) exercises; they
    (C) exercises and they
    (D) exercises: they

73. Which sentence would best express the writer's assessment of Modigliani's legacy in the art world?

    (A) NO CHANGE
    (B) Modigliani's works were often copied, but Modigliani himself has largely been forgotten.
    (C) Few artists study Modigliani's techniques because they are so difficult to understand.
    (D) Modigliani resisted teaching art because he did not want his techniques to be copied.

74. Which choice would most logically specify the writer's interpretation of Modigliani as a symbol in the essay's closing lines?

    (A) NO CHANGE
    (B) the art-obsessed 20th century
    (C) the abstract 20th-century style
    (D) both 20th-century innovation and embrace of folk traditions,

75. (A) NO CHANGE
    (B) he affected
    (C) he must of effected
    (D) he effected

ANSWERS

To Reading Quizzes

Quiz 1
1. A
2. D
3. E
4. A

Quiz 2
5. D
6. A
7. D
8. C

Quiz 3
9. B
10. D
11. A
12. C

Quiz 4
13. D
14. E
15. C

Quiz 5
16. B
17. C
18. A

Quiz 6
19. C
20. D
21. E

22. A
23. B
24. E

Quiz 7
25. E
26. D
27. A
28. B
29. D
30. A

Quiz 8
31. C
32. B
33. A

Quiz 9
34. C
35. D
36. B
37. A

Quiz 10
38. D
39. D
40. C

Quiz 11
41. D
42. A
43. E

Quiz 12
44. E
45. B
46. D

Quiz 13
47. B
48. A
49. D
50. C

Quiz 14
51. E
52. A
53. D
54. B
55. C

Quiz 15
56. D
57. E
58. E
59. D
60. E
61. C
62. B
63. B
64. D

EXPLANATORY ANSWERS

To Writing and Language Quizzes

Writing and Language
Quiz 1

1. Choice A is correct. Choice B is incorrect because it is wordy. Choice C ("grasp-organs") does not sound as effective as Choice A ("grasping organs"). Choice D does not convey the meaning intended.

2. Choice D is correct. Choice A is incorrect because it is wordy. Choice B is incorrect because, in modern idiomatic English, an infinitive is not used to complete a prepositional phrase. Choice C is incorrect because "exploration into" is unidiomatic.

3. Choice C is correct. The two phrases after the dash must be parallel in construction. Therefore, Choices A and B are incorrect. Choice D includes an unneeded "as."

4. Choice B is correct. You don't use the word *because* here; you are already stating a reason so *because* would be redundant. Use the subordinating conjunction *that* instead.

5. Choice C is correct. Choice A is acceptable because it correctly hyphenates the compound adjective "range-finding ability." Choice B is acceptable because it uses correct parallel structure. Choice C is the unacceptable choice because it omits the hyphen in the compound adjective "range finding." The hyphen is necessary when the compound adjective precedes the noun it describes, "ability" in this case. Choice D is also an acceptable/grammatical rewording.

6. Choice A is correct. Choice B is incorrect because it omits the comparative "more." Choice C is incorrect because it gives a nonexistent form. Choice D is incorrect because it is unnecessarily lengthy.

7. Choice B is correct. The comparative "more" is completed with "than." "Then" (Choice A) means "at that time." Choice C is incorrect because it omits "than." Choice D is incorrect because it substitutes "as" for "than."

8. Choice C is correct. The clause that begins after the dash ends with the word *artificially*, so the word should be followed by a dash. Dashes can be used to set off long parenthetical remarks, but they are used in pairs.

9. Choice B is correct. Choices A, C, and D are all acceptable placements of the phrase. Choice B is the unacceptable placement because it creates a misplaced modifier ("to us symbols") and an ambiguous meaning.

10. Choice C is correct. Choice A is incorrect because "possible" should be the adverb form, "possibly," to modify the adjectives "near" and "comparable." Choice B is incorrect because "that" is not needed. Choice D is incorrect because of "nearly."

11. Choice B is correct. Choice A is incorrect because, although "to" as the infinitive sign is often omitted in series, the third member of the series includes "to": "to alter." Therefore, "to" is needed with "transmit" for parallelism. Choices C and D are also incorrect because they destroy the parallel construction needed.

12. Choice A is correct. Choice B is unidiomatic. Choice C is wordy. Choice D distorts the meaning.

13. Choice D is correct. Choice A is incorrect because "they're" is a contraction for "they are," which does not fit here. Choice B is incorrect because the subject of the verb is "indications," which is plural. Choice C is incorrect because "their" is a possessive pronoun, which is out of place here.

14. Choice C is correct. Choices A and B are not appropriate reasons to add the sentence in the given location because they do not accurately reflect the essay's focus. Choice C correctly identifies the essay's focus and rejects the addition of the new sentence. Choice D is correct in rejecting the new sentence but misidentifies the essay's focus.

15. Choice C is correct. Choice A is incorrect because the essay has not yet introduced the subject of dolphins, the essay's focus. Choice B is incorrect because "such an external symbol of intellect" refers indirectly to a phrase ("symbols of our intellectual attainment") not used until a later sentence. Choice C is correct because the new sentence contains transitional phrases linking it directly back to sentence 3 in paragraph 3. Choice D is incorrect because the essay has transitioned to a new phase of discussion, away from the idea of intellectual "tools."

16. Choice D is correct. Choice A is incorrect because it has a double superlative. Either "the most crude way" or "the crudest way" would be correct. Choice B is awkward. Choice C is the comparative degree, whereas the superlative degree is called for.

17. Choice C is correct. "Civilized countries" is the subject of the sentence. Choice A is incorrect because it makes "civilized countries" the object of the preposition "in," thus depriving the sentence of a subject. Choice B makes "that are civilized" nonrestrictive, but the phrase should be restrictive. Choice D is indirect.

18. Choice C is correct. Choice A is incorrect because a plural subject is required, since the antecedent is plural ("countries"). Choice B is too general. Not all countries have radio, television, and newspapers. Choice C is correct. Choice D creates a sentence fragment.

19. Choice C is correct. Used parenthetically, "however" should be set off by commas. Only Choice C sets "however" off in this way.

20. Choice C is correct. The demonstrative adjectives "this" and "these" must agree in number with the word being modified. Only Choice C contains the required agreement.

21. Choice B is correct. "The press, television, and radio . . . the grapevine" are examples of news media; therefore, a colon is the correct punctuation after "competition."

22. Choice B is correct. Choice A is incorrect because the complete dependent clause ends with "channels." Choice A separates a subject ("people") from its verb ("cannot") with a comma. Choice C is incorrect because "who" makes "cannot . . . channels" a subordinate clause and at the same time makes "the people . . . they" redundant. The same is true of Choice D; in this case "if they . . . channels" is the subordinate clause that makes "the people . . . they" redundant.

23. Choice D is correct. "Through legitimate channels" modifies "learn," not "know," so the phrase should be placed close to "learn." Therefore, Choices A and C are incorrect. Choice B is incorrect because the preposition "in" is not to be used here.

24. Choice A is correct. Choice B is incorrect because the present ("thrives")—not the present perfect ("has thrived")—is the right tense here. Choice C is incorrect because it presents a run-on sentence. Choice D is incorrect because "rumor thriving" does not modify anything.

25. Choice D is correct. Choice A is incorrect because "which" cannot be used as a relative pronoun to refer to people. Choice B is bad usage. Choice C is incorrect—"by those who" would be correct.

26. Choice A is correct. Choices B and D are unnecessarily formal. Choice C is slang.

27. Choice B is correct. Choice A is incorrect because "fascination about" is not correct wording of the common idiom "fascination *with*." In addition, *about* used in this way is ambiguous, meaning either *regarding* or *near*. Choice B uses the correct preposition to create the two-word idiom. Choices C and D are nonstandard variations.

28. Choice D is correct. Choice A is incorrect because the essay refers to national crises, such as war, as a cause of rumors but makes no claims about the effect of rumors on national events. Choice B is incorrect because, while the essay does connect

rumors with universal human conditions such as fear, it is not primarily a defensive argument. Choice C is incorrect because, while the essay mentions media's role, it does not provide any examples of media perspective on the issue. Choice D best summarizes the essay's explanatory purpose.

29. Choice A is correct. Choice A is correct because the existing sentence is most consistent with the essay's tone and central point. Choice B is incorrect because the essay explains the public's participation in believing and spreading rumors but avoids explicitly judging those behaviors. Choice C is incorrect because, while media is mentioned, focus remains on the general public's role. Choice D is incorrect because the essay makes no claims about the effect of rumors.

30. Choice C is correct. Choices A and B are incorrect because they inaccurately represent the essay's tone and attitude toward its subject. Choice C is correct because the sentence implies that some types of rumors spring from people's false sense of confidence and thus that the people are misled. Choice D is incorrect because the essay includes no specific examples of popular rumors that were demonstrated to be false information.

31. Choice D is correct. Choices A, B, and C are incorrect because the decisions were not "segregation," etc., but were "about" or "concerning" these topics.

32. Choice B is correct. Choices A and D are not in parallel construction with the other elements of the series. Choice C is awkward because the prepositional phrase "of the defendant" is too far away from "the right," which the prepositional phrase modifies.

33. Choice B is correct. Choices A, C, and D are all incorrect because there is no definite antecedent for the pronouns "this," "these," and "those."

34. Choice C is correct. Although all the choices are grammatically correct, Choice C is best because it is most economical in the use of words.

35. Choice A is correct. Choice A is correct because it accurately summarizes and introduces the upcoming examples of situations that prevent full resolution of legal issues even after court cases are

closed. Choice B is incorrect because the essay never claims that agreement is impossible, only that decisions can be complex and lengthy. Choice C overstates the essay's point. Choice D is incorrect because the idea is never stated or implied in the essay.

36. Choice A is correct. Choice B is incorrect because the relative pronoun is the object of the verb "affect" (see question 37), so the objective case must be used (Choice A). Choice C is incorrect because "which" is not used with people. Choice D is incorrect because it is awkward.

37. Choice D is correct. *To affect* means "to influence" or "to produce a change in." *To effect* means "to bring about." Here, "affect" is appropriate, so choices B and C are incorrect. Choice A is incorrect because the subject of the verb is "decisions," a plural that demands a plural verb.

38. Choice D is correct. The words that follow a comparative adjective and "than" must be in parallel construction. Here the comparative adjective is "more difficult." An infinitive follows "more difficult," so an infinitive must follow "than." Therefore, Choice D is correct and the other choices are incorrect.

39. Choice C is correct. Here "what" is a relative adjective modifying "road." Choices A and D are incorrect because "whatever" and "whichever" indicate that any of a number of choices is acceptable. That meaning is not appropriate here. Choice B is incorrect because it is vague in meaning.

40. Choice A is correct. Choice B is incorrect because it uses second-person perspective inappropriately in a topic-focused essay. Choice C is incorrect because the essay does not specifically focus on high court decisions requiring consensus. Choice D is incorrect because the upcoming example does not illustrate problems *caused* by a legal decision but instead describes a decision that did not resolve a problem that already existed.

41. Choice D is correct. When two words jointly modify another, the two are often hyphenated for clarity. Here "state" and "compelled" jointly modify "segregation," so "state" and "compelled" should

be hyphenated. There is no reason to hyphenate "racial" and "segregation." "Racial" is an adjective modifying "segregation"; the two words do not jointly modify any other.

42. Choice C is correct. The present tense is used to state a lasting or universal truth. That "segregation . . . is a denial" is such a truth, so the present tense is needed.

43. Choice B is correct. We are dealing here with the verb "to lie," meaning "to rest." The past tense of *to lie* is "lay."

44. Choice C is correct. Since we have a past tense ("lay") in the main clause, sequence of tenses requires that we have a past tense ("was") with a future implication in the form of the infinitive ("to be accomplished") in the subordinate clause.

45. Choice D is correct. Choice A is incorrect because the essay alludes to challenges surrounding legal decisions but does not deal not specifically with the judge's role. Choice B is incorrect because public polarization is not discussed directly or even alluded to in the essay. Choice C is incorrect because it focuses on the difficulties of reaching closure on a legal decision, not the consequences *resulting from* legal decisions. Choice D correctly summarizes the essay's purpose.

46. Choice B is correct. Choice A is incorrect because it forms a run-on sentence. Choice B is correct because it creates a parallel construction with the previous "who" clause. Choice C is incorrect because it starts a clause that is not a logical follow-up of what precedes. Choice D is incorrect because "whom" is an object pronoun. A subject pronoun ("who") is needed here.

47. Choice A is correct. Choice A is the only choice that provides the parallelism required in this sentence. Any of the other choices would throw the style of the sentence out of balance.

48. Choice C is correct. The pronoun is the object of "makes." The only object pronoun given is "him," Choice C. Choice A is the possessive adjective or pronoun, Choice B the subject pronoun, and Choice D the reflexive pronoun.

49. Choice D is correct. The comma and "and" after "man" together indicate a compound sentence. A subject and verb for the second independent clause is therefore needed. Choice A is an infinitive. Choice B is a verb without the subject "he." The specific subject is necessary because the understood subject of "draws" would be "reading." Choice C is a participle, so it is incorrect. Choice D has a subject and a verb and is correct.

50. Choice D is correct. Choice A is incorrect because the antecedent of "which" is "example and precept," making "which" plural. Therefore, the verb "has stood" should be plural. Choice B is incorrect for the same reason: "stands" is singular. Choice C is incorrect because the past tense is not logical, since the rest of the sentence is in the present tense.

51. Choice B is correct. Choice A is incorrect because it is an acceptable use of a present participle to modify a noun (*problems*). Choice B is correct because it is unacceptable to place a comma before the restrictive relative pronoun *that*. Choice C is incorrect because it is an acceptable use of the restrictive relative pronoun *that*. Choice D is incorrect because it is an acceptable use of the restrictive relative pronoun and present perfect verb tense.

52. Choice B is correct. The meaning intended is best expressed by Choice B.

53. Choice C is correct. Choice A is incorrect because the writer is elaborating on an idea, not transitioning to a new one. Choice B is incorrect because the sentence adds a new dimension to the distinctions the writer is trying to make between reading and learning (a substantive and meaningful outcome of reading) by comparing dilettantism (superficial interest in art, culture, and so on) and versatility that is substantive and motivates people to act on their interests. Choice C is correct in identifying the sentence as an expansion and clarification of a point. Choice D is incorrect because, while the point may not be obvious, it is relevant as explained in Choice C.

54. Choice B is correct. The correct way to punctuate the first part of a broken quotation is quotation marks—comma—quotation marks.

55. Choice A is correct. The accepted term for a bank check bearing a signature but no stated amount is "blank check." The idea here is that "Learning" is the signature required so that "native versatility" will be of worth.

56. Choice C is correct. "Learning" is a gerund here, so it takes a possessive pronoun. Therefore, Choices A and B are incorrect. Choice D is incorrect because it gives the plural possessive, but the singular "one" is used as an impersonal pronoun, not the plural.

57. Choice B is correct. "Only" modifies "by the active experience . . ." so "only" should be placed before that phrase. Choices A, C, and D are therefore incorrect.

58. Choice C is correct. Choice A is incorrect because the quote supports rather than contradicts the essay's argument about the value of reading widely. Choice B is incorrect because the essay focuses on the general value of reading with no limiting specifics. Choice C correctly identifies the function of the quotation of Thomas Carlyle, an influential Victorian-era essayist and historian. Choice D is incorrect because the essay's main focus is on reading to learn, a process that complements a formal education. According to the essay, formal schooling alone is not sufficient to make someone a truly educated person.

59. Choice A is correct. Choice A is correct because it provides closure for the essay while reinforcing the essay's definition of an educated person. Choice B is incorrect because the essay's focus is not on how to read but on how reading becomes learning. Choice C is incorrect because it digresses somewhat from the essay's focus on the *nature* of learning and education. Choice D is incorrect because the sentence would contradict the essay's advice that formal education alone is insufficient to create well-rounded, educated individuals.

60. Choice D is correct. Choice A is incorrect because while the essay argues the importance of learning through books, it does not argue against formal schooling in general or criticize formal schooling on any specific basis such as cost. Choice B is incorrect because the essay does suggest that what one learns through reading can support action, but it does not state or imply that formal education restricts or discourages action. Choice C is incorrect because the essay emphasizes reading as the most important factor in shaping people's ability to exercise critical thinking and sound judgment when the times most demand them. Choice D is correct because it best summarizes the essay's stance on the relationship between the two forms of education.

61. Choice D is correct. Choice A is incorrect because it is not parallel to the other verbs in the series: e.g., "streamlined," "mechanized." Choice B is incorrect because it is the present tense and a past tense is needed. Choice C is incorrect because it is a participle, but a verb is needed.

62. Choice B is correct. The past tense ("could go") is required in the subordinate clause since the verb of the main clause is in the past tense.

63. Choice B is correct. The superlative form of the adjective is needed here, as indicated by the word *possible*. Choice A is the comparative, Choice C the positive degree. Choice D is incorrect because it is an awkward form of the superlative.

64. Choice A is correct. In a series, the infinitive sign "to" is often omitted in all but the first infinitive. That is the case here, so Choices B and D are incorrect. Choices C and D are incorrect because they contain the adjective form "efficient" instead of the adverb form "efficiently."

65. Choice A is correct. Choice A is correct because it best fits the theme that Americans do not relax even in their leisure time. Choice B is incorrect because it misrepresents the situation and loses the irony of the idea that we "relax on schedule." Choice C is incorrect because it changes the tone of the writer's remarks about American scheduling and time-consciousness. Choice D is incorrect for the same reason.

66. Choice D is correct. The present tense is required in this verbal construction to indicate a time that is the same as that of "streamlined." Therefore, Choices A and C are incorrect. The gerund construction of Choice B is awkward. The present infinitive construction of Choice D is correct.

67. Choice D is correct. Choice A is incorrect because "energize" is in the present tense, but a past tense is needed. Choice B does not sound right because it personalizes "pellets" unnecessarily. Choice C is incorrect because it does not supply a verb for either "energy into pellets" or "culture . . . packages." Choice D is correct.

68. Choice A is correct. "The ant like a sluggard" is elliptical—that is, some of its parts seem to be missing. Without ellipsis, this sentence would read: "We made the ant look like a sluggard." Since this form is the same as that of the first clause, ellipsis is acceptable; the parts left out are exactly the same and are used in exactly the same way as they are in the first clause. The correct punctuation in a case like this is a comma, so Choices C and D are incorrect. Choice B is incorrect because "as" is substituted for "like."

69. Choice C is correct. Choice C is correct because the concept of efficiency has here been personified. When a common noun is personified, the practice is to make it a proper noun by capitalizing it. Therefore, Choices A and B are incorrect. The noun here is not to be set off by commas since it has a restrictive function in this sentence. Therefore, Choices B (again) and D are incorrect.

70. Choice C is correct. Choice A is incorrect because the tone and topic shift, and therefore a new paragraph is called for. Choice B is incorrect because it fails to begin a new paragraph and adds an unnecessary comma. Choice C is correct because it begins a new paragraph and leaves punctuation as is. Choice D is incorrect because it adds an unnecessary comma between the subject and predicate.

71. Choice B is correct. Since "considering time a friend" preceded the "wishing," "had considered," the past perfect, is the correct answer. Another reason the past perfect tense is correct is that "had done," which is in parallel construction with "had considered," is in the past perfect.

72. Choice A is correct. There is no reason to use two words (Choice B) or four words (Choice C) when one word (Choice A) expresses the thought clearly. The adjective (Choice D) is incorrect. The adverb ("spontaneously") is required to modify the verb ("had done").

73. Choice B is correct. The prepositional phrase ("on account of") is incorrect. The conjunction "because" should be used to introduce the subordinate clause. Therefore, Choice A is wrong and Choice B is right. The conjunction "when" (Choice C) does not give the thought intended. The conjunction "because" (Choice B) is necessary. Therefore, Choice D is incorrect.

74. Choice C is correct. Choice A is incorrect because the antecedent of *that* in the long preceding sentence is unclear. Choice B is incorrect as a replacement for *that* because the preceding sentence is not intended to be interpreted literally as wasting time. The writer is using sarcasm to point out that this wishful, nostalgic thinking would be taken as inefficient in our time-conscious culture. Choice C correctly restates the specific antecedent of *that*. Choice D is incorrect because, similar to Choice B, it is not consistent with the writer's point.

75. Choice D is correct. Since the subject of the clause is "one," we must have a singular verb ("is expected"). Therefore, Choice D is correct and all the other choices are incorrect.

Writing and Language
Quiz 2

1. Choice D is correct. Choice A is incorrect because it is an acceptable use of past tense. Choice B is incorrect because it is an acceptable use of a possessive. Choice C is incorrect because it is an acceptable use of a prepositional phrase. Choice D is the correct answer because it is an unacceptable use of a passive adverb clause and is a dangling modifier (there is no subject for "having invented").

2. Choice B is correct. Choice A is incorrect because it uses the past perfect tense, whereas the present perfect tense is required (Choice B). Choices C and D also give the wrong tenses: Choice C, simple past; Choice D, simple future.

3. Choice C is correct. Choice A is wordy. Choice B is incorrect because the gerund "financing," not the infinitive, should be used in this construction. Choice D says that people have always been interested in films about finance; this statement does not make sense here.

4. Choice C is correct. Choice A is incorrect because "who" should be "whom" (Choice C), as the object of "has chosen." Choice B is wordy. Choice D makes "whomever . . . has chosen" a nonrestrictive clause, but it is actually restrictive.

5. Choice B is correct. The object pronoun is used after prepositions, so Choices A and C are incorrect. Choice D is incorrect because "also" is unnecessary and awkward.

6. Choice C is correct. Choice A is incorrect because there are three possible antecedents for "he or she": "backer," "director," and "producer." Choice B is incorrect because the antecedent of "they" is unclear and because the singular, referring to "backer," is needed logically. Choice D is incorrect because the present perfect tense is needed; the action of paying began in the past and continues in the present ("mounts up").

7. Choice D is correct. Choices A and C are incorrect because they omit "else" or "other," needed because the backer is himself involved in the film. Choice B is awkward.

8. Choice A is correct. Choice A is correct because by providing an example of the increasing cost of movie musicals, the sentence supports the essay's thesis that the financial backer is an important part of the films' production. Choice B is incorrect because the essay's purpose is primarily explanatory for a general audience, not argumentative or directed at an audience of financial backers. Choice C is incorrect because it suggests that the sentence should not be added unless irrelevant information (names of backers) is included. Choice D is incorrect because it misidentifies the essay's focus and rejects the new sentence.

9. Choice C is correct. Choice A is incorrect because the present tense "costs" is needed. Choice B is incorrect because "who" refers to people, not things. Choice D is incorrect for two reasons: (1) "costed" is not a word; (2) the past tense would be wrong.

10. Choice C is correct. Choices A and B are unidiomatic. Choice C is the idiomatic phrase. Choice D is incorrect because of the lack of subordination of the phrase "more to the point." Also, "More to the point is, why accept" is awkward.

11. Choice B is correct. Choices A and C wrongly substitute "except" for "accept." *To accept* means "to receive" or "to accommodate oneself to"; *to except* means "to exclude." Choice D is incorrect because a verb, not a verbal, is needed as the main verb of the sentence.

12. Choice D is correct. Choice A has a double negative: "not scarcely." Choices B and C produce sentence fragments: "And . . . way" and "Scarcely . . . way." Choice D gives an acceptable use of the dash— that is, to set up a parenthetical comment. (*Note*: Dashes are used in pairs; only one dash appears here because the sentence ends at the end of the comment.)

13. Choice A is correct. Choice B is ungrammatical because *this/these* and *kind/kinds* must both be either singular or plural. Choices C and D are awkward.

14. Choice D is correct. Choice A contains the future perfect tense. Choice B contains the simple past tense. Choice C contains the past perfect tense.

These are incorrect because the simple present tense (Choice D) is used to state a universal or lasting truth.

15. Choice D is correct. Choice A is incorrect because the sentence focuses on one of the essay's subtopics, adaptation, not the main topic of financial backers. Choice B is incorrect because it focuses on the screenwriter's, not the backer's, role. Choice C is incorrect because it causes the essay to digress toward the subject of successful/unsuccessful adaptation and away from the backer's role. Choice D is correct because it returns the essay's final sentence to the essay's primary focus, the backer, and how the backer makes money on the investment.

16. Choice B is correct. Choice A is incorrect because "despite" is a preposition and cannot introduce an independent clause. Choice C is incorrect because "however" (an adverb) does not make sense here. Choice D is incorrect since "because" gives the opposite meaning of that intended.

17. Choice C is correct. Choice A is too wordy. Choices B and D are incorrect because there is no logical antecedent for "this" or "it." The preceding noun is "hunter," which does not make sense as the antecedent. Choice C is clear and correct.

18. Choice D is correct. Choice A is incorrect because "in regards to" is unidiomatic ("in regard to" and "as regards" are acceptable). Choice B is incorrect because it is wordy and because "ignorance" does not have the desired meaning of "not paying attention to." Choice C is incorrect because it clouds the meaning intended.

19. Choice B is correct. Choice A is incorrect. It would be correct without the comma after "know" or without the comma and with *that* after "know." Choice C is incorrect because "like" cannot be used with clauses. Choice D is incorrect because the progressive present ("are knowing") is incorrect here.

20. Choice C is correct. The subject of this sentence is "the business," so any other noun or pronoun with a similar or the same meaning before the verb is redundant. Therefore, Choices A ("this occupation"), B ("this"), and D ("doing this") are incorrect.

21. Choice B is correct. The construction for comparison is "as . . . as." The construction *so . . . as* is used for negatives, "it is not so dangerous as. . . ." Choice A is unidiomatic. Choice C is incorrect because it omits the first "as." Choice D is incorrect because it uses "so . . . as" in a positive construction.

22. Choice C is correct. Choice A is incorrect because it is a declarative sentence placing responsibility on divers, not eliciting emotional reaction in divers' favor. Choice B is incorrect because it states a point explicitly and uses no suspense-building devices. Choice C is correct because it implies that the *cause* of a particular effect, diving hazards, is most often the actions of the diver. Choice D is incorrect because the sentence is not written from a first-person perspective.

23. Choice D is correct. Choice A is incorrect because "devil-may-care" has nothing to do with the Devil, and there is no pattern of spiritual references in the essay. Choice B is incorrect because the essay's focus is on the hazards of diving, not on classifying types of divers. Choice C is incorrect because the sentence is a third-person reference to divers of a particular type. Choice D is correct because "devil-may-care" is a way of restating the writer's point that divers themselves are responsible for the risks they take.

24. Choice A is correct. The penetration of the sea by the light is a constant truth, so the simple present is correct. Choice B is the present progressive. Choice C is the simple past. Choice D is the present perfect.

25. Choice C is correct. Parallel structure is required here. "He may lose . . ." balances with ". . . may become." Therefore Choices A and D are incorrect because "separate" does not make sense. The diver is always separate—that is, a separate person from his group. The danger is that he will become "separated" from his group. Choice B is incorrect. You wouldn't say, "became separated" because you are talking about a future situation.

26. Choice C is correct. Choices A and D are incorrect because they are too wordy. Choice B is incorrect because "during salvaging" is awkward.

27. Choice C is correct. Choice A is incorrect because "like" cannot be used with clauses. Choice B is incorrect because the "contrary to fact" subjunctive *were* is needed. (Choice A has this error also.) Choice D is incorrect because, if this clause were omitted, the construction would be incomplete.

28. Choice D is correct. Choice A is incorrect because the "causing" cannot logically precede in time the collapse of the heavy mass, so the past participle is incorrect. Choice B is incorrect because the infinitive is not idiomatic here. Choice C is incorrect because there is no coordinating conjunction to join "collapsed" and "caused." Choice D is correct because the present participle indicates an action that occurs at the same time as the action of the main verb.

29. Choice A is correct. Choice A is correct because this sentence emphasizes both the diver's lack of control after he touches the cylinder and the potential danger of being crushed. Choice B is incorrect because in its tone and in the information left out, the sentence doesn't communicate the possible consequences of touching the cylinder. Choice C is incorrect because it is too flippant to match the writer's serious point. Choice D is incorrect because the self-congratulatory content and first-person wording do not fit the writer's thesis.

30. Choice D is correct. The present perfect tense ("I have been") indicates action that began in the past but still continues in the present. This is the tense required in this sentence, so Choice D is correct and the other choices are incorrect. Choice A is the simple past. Choice B is the simple present. Choice C is the past perfect.

31. Choice C is correct. Choice A is incorrect because for a direct question, the clause should be preceded by a comma and the first word should be capitalized. Choice B is incorrect for the same reason. (The direct question is indicated in these two choices by the inverted word order: "are things.") Choice C is correct; it is an indirect question. Choice D is incorrect because indirect questions do not take question marks.

32. Choice C is correct. In this sentence, "however" is a parenthetical word—not a conjunctive adverb.

Therefore, it should be preceded and followed by a comma only, not preceded by a semicolon. Therefore, Choices A and D are incorrect, and Choice C is correct. Choice B is incorrect because it lacks commas.

33. Choice D is correct. Choices A and C are too wordy. Choice B implies that "people," not the composer, are going "to make" the piece of music. The passive voice, as in Choice D, is preferable.

34. Choice A is correct. Choice A is correct in the context of the sentence, and "keeps going" is a logical progression from "where the composer begins." Choice B is incorrect because it is inappropriately general. Choice C is incorrect because it refers to the business aspect of composing in a sentence focusing on the artistic process. Choice D is incorrect because it implies something about the process (that it is a high-pressure endeavor) not supported within the sentence or the essay.

35. Choice B is correct. Choice A is incorrect because "all" refers to those things described in the preceding three adverbial clauses, so "all" is plural, as in Choice B. Choice C is incorrect for the same reason; adding "this" does not help. Choice D is incorrect because "them" is an object pronoun, whereas a subject pronoun is needed (e.g., "all *these*," "*they* all").

36. Choice D is correct. Nothing in the passage suggests that it is good that composers and composing are difficult to understand, so Choice A does not make sense. The sentence referred to in question 36 says the same thing that the preceding sentences say, so "nevertheless," Choice B, does not make sense. The sentences preceding the one in question do not prove what is said in this sentence, so "thereby," Choice C, does not make sense. This sentence does, however, sum up what came before, so "in short," Choice D, does make sense and is correct.

37. Choice C is correct. What is needed here is the singular possessive. Choice A has no possessive. Choice B is the plural possessive. Choice D is a roundabout way to give the singular possessive; here, this method is not needed.

38. Choice A is correct. Choice A is correct and is the best topic sentence because the paragraph focuses on the role of inspiration in composing. Choice B is incorrect because although it reflects one implication in the paragraph, it is not specific enough to serve as the topic sentence. Choice C is incorrect because the idea of frustrated composers is never mentioned in the paragraph. Choice D is incorrect because the paragraph does address a misunderstanding about the process of composition, but it does not describe a disagreement about technique.

39. Choice A is correct. Choice B is incorrect because "not too much" should precede "preoccupied." Choice C is incorrect because "very" should precede "preoccupied." Choice D is incorrect because "too" and "very" are both intensifiers and have similar meanings, so including them both is redundant.

40. Choice B is correct. Choice A is incorrect because "eating" and "sleeping" are either participles or gerunds and in neither case would they be preceded by the objective pronouns "him" and "her." If "eating" and "sleeping" were functioning as gerunds (nouns), they would require the possessive "his or her"—an awkward construction here. Choices C and D are incorrect because they introduce unnecessary clauses. Choice B is the answer because it correctly compares one participle ("composing") with two others: ". . . *composing* is as natural for the composer as *eating* or *sleeping*."

41. Choice B is correct. Choice A is incorrect because the past infinitive (Choice B) is needed; being born preceded in time the composing. Choice C is incorrect because it is not an infinitive form. Choice D is incorrect because the progressive sense of "being" is inappropriate; the composer is completely born before he becomes a composer.

42. Choice D is correct. Choices A and C are incorrect because they omit the pronoun "it." This pronoun is needed as the subject of the second independent clause (if no coordinating conjunction is present, a semicolon joins two independent clauses). Choices A and B are incorrect because the present tense is needed, since the passage is in the present tense.

43. Choice A is correct. Choice B is incorrect because the reflexive "himself or herself" is needed. Choice C is incorrect because "his or her own self" is not acceptable English. Choice D is incorrect because "he or she" is not needed; moreover, the objective pronoun, not the subjective, must be used after a preposition ("to").

44. Choice C is correct. Choice A is incorrect because it is vague: the composer doesn't "feel like composing" or doesn't "compose"? Choice B is awkward. Choice D is too wordy.

45. Choice D is correct. Choice A is incorrect because the essay's purpose is expository; it is not a personal essay or argumentative piece. Choice B is incorrect because the writer uses a third-person, not a first-person, perspective. Choice C is incorrect because while the essay's perspective is third-person, defining "composer" is not its primary purpose. Choice D is correct because it accurately summarizes the essay's content and point of view.

46. Choice B is correct. The full name of the museum is the American Museum of Natural History. Each important word must be capitalized. ("The" is capitalized only because it is the first word in the sentence.) Therefore, Choices A, C, and D are incorrect.

47. Choice C is correct. The act of portraying began in the past and continues in the present. The present perfect tense is used to indicate this type of action. Choice A is the past perfect (used to show action that began in the past and ended before some other action in the past). Choice B uses the simple past tense (which indicates an action that began and ended in the past). Choice D uses the simple present tense.

48. Choice C is correct. Choice A is incorrect because "kind of through" is not an acceptable expression. Choice B is incorrect because "not only" works as a partner of "but also," and there is no "but also" in this sentence. Choice D is incorrect because "throughout" means "everywhere in," which does not make sense here.

49. Choice A is correct. Choice B is incorrect because the antecedent of "it" is unclear. Choice C is incorrect because the lack of a verb ("being" is a verbal) creates a fragmentary sentence. Choice D is incorrect because the tendency is not confined to the present—it has been going on for some years. Choice A is correct.

50. Choice D is correct. The complete clause is "Now the museum has taken man apart." "For the first time" is parenthetical. Therefore, "for the first time" must be set off by commas and Choices B and C are incorrect. Choice A is incorrect because it is awkward.

51. Choice B is correct. Choice A is incorrect because the sentence does not describe the workings of any mechanism or process in step-by-step order. Choice B is correct because the sentence transitions into the specific aspect of the museum that will be discussed and begins describing its uniqueness. Choice C is incorrect because the sentence is primarily descriptive, not argumentative. Choice D is incorrect because the sentence makes no direct comparison with any other museums.

52. Choice C is correct. It is the displays that are instructive, not the series, so the singular verb is incorrect (Choice A). The clause "which are instructive" is restrictive, so it should not be set off by commas and "which" is misused for "that" (Choice B). Choice D is incorrect because "as" should not be used to mean "that."

53. Choice B is correct. Choice A is illogical; the degree of instructiveness has been achieved in this museum, so it has not "never" been achieved. Choice B is correct because it says that this feat has never been achieved "before." Choice C is incorrect because it omits "before" and because the infinitive indicates that this feat will not be achieved in the present or in the future. This statement does not make sense since the feat has already been achieved. Choice D contains a double negative.

54. Choice B is correct. It is "they" (the technicians) who are "using," so "they" must be the subject of the sentence. Choices A, C, and D make "using new techniques and new materials" a dangling participial phrase. Choice D is also wordy.

55. Choice D is correct. In speech the placement of "only" is very loose, but in writing "only" should be placed as close as possible to the words it modifies. In this sentence "only" modifies "skin deep," so Choices B and C are incorrect. Choice A is incorrect because it is awkward.

56. Choice B is correct. Choice A is incorrect because the sentence cites a common belief without reference to any specific museum example. Choice B is correct because the common belief is referenced in order to contrast it with the idea the writer takes from the exhibit. Choice C is incorrect because the writer expresses no opinion about the human condition. Choice D is incorrect because the writer does not offer any criticism of the exhibit in the essay.

57. Choice D is correct. "Not only" works with "but also," so Choices A and C are incorrect. Choice B is incorrect because it is not in parallel construction with the "not only" phrase. The preposition "in" is needed: "not only in . . . but also in . . . ."

58. Choice C is correct. When two words work together to modify another word, they are often hyphenated for the sake of clarity. In this sentence "skin" and "covered" work together to modify "case," so "skin-covered" should be hyphenated. Choices A and D are therefore incorrect. Choice D is further incorrect, and Choice B is incorrect because a preposition that indicates "in the interior part" is needed. Neither "with" nor "in" so indicates.

59. Choice C is correct. Choice A is incorrect because the sentence as it is written does relate to the idea of beauty explored in the final paragraph, but it does not connect back to the first paragraph's focus on the museum. Choice B is incorrect because the writer describes the graphic display as beautiful, not shocking. Choice C is correct because it adds a reference to the museum, better reflecting the whole essay as opposed to the beauty of man's insides alone. Choice D is incorrect because neither the opening line nor the essay as a whole draws any conclusions about visitor reaction or how museums in general may benefit.

60. Choice D is correct. Choice A is incorrect because the essay does describe the exhibit from an artistic perspective, but it does not make any direct comparisons or contrasts with art museums. Choice B is incorrect because the essay does not compare the experiences of spectators at different types of museums. Choice C is incorrect because the essay does not state an opinion about what the purpose of this or any museum should be. Choice D is correct because it accurately summarizes how the writer handles the topic of art (only indirectly).

61. Choice C is correct. Choice C (the simple past tense) is correct here. Choice A is the past perfect tense. Choice B is incorrect because "were broke" means "had no money" and makes no sense here. Choice D is incorrect because the emphatic "did break" is not necessary; nothing is being emphasized.

62. Choice C is correct. Choice A is incorrect because the verb should be plural ("were"): the subject is "center, . . . color, and . . . emphasis." Choice B is incorrect because "far gone" (meaning "nearly exhausted") is not what is meant here. Moreover, the verb should be plural. Choice C is correct because the verb is plural. Choice D is incorrect because the adverb "away" is unnecessary.

63. Choice B is correct. "Only" modifies the whole phrase, so the word should not be in such a position that it modifies "a year" (Choice A) or "two" (Choice C). Choice D is awkward.

64. Choice D is correct. Choice A is incorrect because the main verb should be in the past tense, as is the rest of the passage. Choice B is incorrect for the same reason. Choice C is incorrect because the past infinitive ("to have turned") indicates that the turning occurred at some prior time, whereas "only a year or two later" indicates that the turning occurred at a later time. This is indicated by the present infinitive, as in Choice D.

65. Choice A is correct. Choice A is correct because "Botticelli" is in apposition to "one of his ancestors" and is therefore set off by commas. Choice B is incorrect because the apposition implies that Botticelli was Modigliani's only ancestor; this

implication does not make sense. Choice C is incorrect because "his ancestor" is not set off by commas; moreover, "his" has an indefinite antecedent: both "Botticelli" and "Modigliani" precede the singular third-person masculine pronoun "his." Choice D is incorrect because "his" has an indefinite antecedent and because "his ancestor" is not set off by commas.

66. Choice B is correct. The singular possessive is needed. Choice A contains no possessive. Choice C contains the plural possessive. Choice D contains no possessive.

67. Choice D is correct. The past participle ("discovered") acts as an adjective, so an adverb is needed as modifier. Therefore, Choices B and C are incorrect. Choice A is incorrect because the past participle is needed since African art was already discovered before Modigliani drew from it.

68. Choice D is correct. Choice A is incorrect because "himself limited" means that Modigliani was limited by nature, not that he consciously limited himself, as the passage indicates. Choice B and C are incorrect because the reflexive "himself" (Choice D) is needed. The person doing the limiting and the person limited are the same; this relationship is indicated by the reflexive pronoun.

69. Choice C is correct. A main verb is needed for the sentence. Only Choice C supplies a main verb. Choice A gives the infinitive. Choice B gives the present participle. Choice D gives the past infinitive.

70. Choice D is correct. Choices A and B make the introductory phrase a dangling construction. "His figures" are what are "wistful," etc., so "his figures" must be the subject of the sentence. Choice C creates a sentence fragment; there is no main verb given.

71. Choice D is correct. Choice A is incorrect because this sentence should begin a new paragraph. Choice B is incorrect because the sentence should begin a new paragraph and because the comma after the introductory phrase "In other hands" is incorrectly omitted. Choice C is incorrect because, although the sentence correctly begins a new

paragraph, the comma after the introductory phrase "In other hands" is incorrectly omitted. Choice D is correct because the sentence correctly begins a new paragraph and commas are correctly placed after the introductory phrase and the first item in a series ("elongated necks").

72. Choice B is correct. Choice A presents a run-on sentence. Choice B is correct; a semicolon joins independent clauses. Choice C is incorrect because, if we do use a conjunction here, it should be "but"—not "and." Choice D is incorrect because the second clause does not exemplify the first, as is indicated by the use of a colon.

73. Choice A is correct. Choice A is correct because the sentence offers two examples to explain a specific result, "he established no school." Choice B is incorrect because establishing no "school" of artistic style is not equivalent to being forgotten. The essay implies that Modigliani has not been forgotten. Choice C is incorrect because it makes

two points not supported anywhere else in the essay (that few artists study Modigliani and that his techniques are impossible to understand). Choice D is incorrect because it makes assertions not supported elsewhere in the essay.

74. Choice D is correct. Choice A is incorrect because it is too vague to be meaningful. Choice B is incorrect because it does not connect to or receive support from any other part of the essay. Choice C is incorrect because it only partially reflects the upcoming examples. Choice D is correct because it is the best synthesis of the upcoming examples and is therefore the best phrasing.

75. Choice D is correct. *To affect* means "to influence." *To effect* means "to bring about." In this case "to effect" has the logical meaning, so Choices A and B are incorrect. "Must of" is an illiteracy for "must have," so Choices A and C are incorrect. Choice D contains neither error and is correct.

THE SAT ESSAY

What the SAT Essay Measures

The SAT Essay is designed to measure your understanding of a passage and your ability to use it to build a well-written, well-thought-out discussion. Two people will score your essay, and each will award 1, 2, 3, or 4 points for each of these categories:

Reading

How well did you understand the passage? Did you comprehend the interplay of central ideas and important details? How effectively does your essay make use of textual evidence?

Analysis

How well does your essay show your understanding of the way the author builds an argument? How well did you:

- examine the author's use of reasoning, evidence, and stylistic and persuasive techniques?

- support and develop your claims with well-chosen evidence from the passage?

Writing

To achieve a high score on the SAT Essay, your essay will need to be organized, focused, and precise. Its tone and style will need to be appropriate to the topic. It will demonstrate a varied sentence structure and observe the rules and conventions of standard written English.

Who Should Take the SAT with Essay

The SAT Essay test is optional. If you choose to take it, however, you will be able to use your SAT results to apply to colleges that require a score for the SAT Essay. So you should be sure to find out those schools on your list that require the SAT with Essay exam. Even if your school just *recommends* the SAT Essay, it's a good idea to take it. You can add it later if didn't register for the SAT with Essay at first—SAT fee waivers cover the cost of the SAT with Essay.

Sending Scores

When you take the SAT with Essay, your essay scores are always reported along with your other scores from that test day. Remember that you can never send only *some* scores from a certain test day, even though the College Board's Score Choice™ service allows you to choose which day's scores you send to colleges. (For example, you can't choose to send Math scores but not SAT Essay scores.)

Note: Remember to check the Score Choice policies of every college you're applying to. Some schools require the scores from *every* time you took the SAT. The good news is that many colleges consider your best scores.

The Essay Prompt and Topic

There are two parts of the Essay: the prompt (a question) and the topic. The prompt will be very similar if not identical in every SAT with Essay, as follows:

As you read the passage below, consider how the author uses the following writing strategies:

- evidence, such as facts or examples, to support claims

- reasoning to develop ideas and to connect claims and evidence

- stylistic or persuasive elements, such as word choice or appeals to emotion, to add power to the ideas expressed

Write an essay in which you explain how [the author] builds an argument to persuade [his/her] audience that [author's claim]. In your essay, analyze how [the author] uses one or more of the features listed above (or features of your own choice) to strengthen the logic and persuasiveness of [his/her] argument. Be sure that your analysis focuses on the most relevant features of the passage. Your essay should not explain whether you agree with [the author's] claims, but rather explain how the author builds an argument to persuade [his/her] audience.

The Topic

Unlike the essay prompt, which will remain the same or nearly so across SAT exams, the essay topic will be different every time. However, all the passages on which your essay is based will:

- be written for a broad audience
- argue a point
- express subtle views on complex subjects
- use logical reasoning and evidence to support claims
- examine ideas, debates, or trends in the arts and sciences, or civic, cultural, or political life
- always be taken from published works

In your test, the passage, or the notes about the passage, will contain all the information you need to compose your essay.

Essay Prompt Example

As you read the passage below, consider how Paul Bogard uses

- evidence, such as facts or examples, to support claims
- reasoning to develop ideas and to connect claims and evidence
- stylistic or persuasive elements, such as word choice or appeals to emotion, to add power to the ideas expressed

This passage is adapted from Paul Bogard, "Let There Be Dark." ©2012 by Los Angeles Times. Originally published December 21, 2012.

At my family's cabin on a Minnesota lake, I knew woods so dark that my hands disappeared before my eyes. I knew night skies in which meteors left smoky trails across sugary spreads of stars. But now, when 8 of 10 children born in the United States will never know a sky dark enough for the Milky Way, I worry we are rapidly losing night's natural darkness before realizing its worth. This winter solstice, as we cheer the days' gradual movement back toward light, let us also remember the irreplaceable value of darkness.

All life evolved to the steady rhythm of bright days and dark nights. Today, though, when we feel the closeness of nightfall, we reach quickly for a light switch. And too little darkness, meaning too much artificial light at night, spells trouble for all.

Already the World Health Organization classifies working the night shift as a probable human carcinogen, and the American Medical Association has voiced its unanimous support for "light pollution reduction efforts and glare reduction efforts at both the national and state levels." Our bodies need darkness to produce the hormone melatonin, which keeps certain cancers from developing, and our bodies need darkness for sleep. Sleep disorders have been linked to diabetes, obesity, cardiovascular disease and depression, and recent research suggests one main cause of "short sleep" is "long light." Whether we work at night or simply take our tablets, notebooks and smartphones to bed, there isn't a place for this much artificial light in our lives.

The rest of the world depends on darkness as well, including nocturnal and crepuscular species of birds, insects, mammals, fish and reptiles. Some examples are well known—the 400 species of birds that migrate at night in North America, the sea turtles that come ashore to lay their eggs—and some are not, such as the bats that save American farmers billions in pest control and the moths that pollinate 80% of the world's flora. Ecological light pollution is like the bulldozer of the night, wrecking habitat and disrupting ecosystems several billion years in the making. Simply put, without darkness, Earth's ecology would collapse. . . .

In today's crowded, louder, more fast-paced world, night's darkness can provide solitude, quiet and stillness, qualities increasingly in short supply. Every religious tradition has considered darkness invaluable for a soulful life, and the chance to witness the universe has inspired artists, philosophers and everyday stargazers since time began. In a world awash with electric light . . . how would Van Gogh have given the world his "Starry Night"? Who knows what this vision of the night sky might inspire in each of us, in our children or grandchildren?

Yet all over the world, our nights are growing brighter. In the United States and Western Europe, the amount of light in the sky increases an average of about 6% every year. Computer images of the United States at night, based on NASA photographs, show that what was a very dark country as recently as the 1950s is now nearly covered with a blanket of light. Much of this light is wasted energy, which means wasted dollars. Those of us over 35 are perhaps among the last generation to have known truly dark nights. Even the northern lake where I was lucky to spend my summers has seen its darkness diminish.

It doesn't have to be this way. Light pollution is readily within our ability to solve, using new lighting technologies and shielding existing lights. Already, many cities and towns across North America and Europe are changing to LED streetlights, which offer dramatic possibilities for controlling wasted light. Other communities are finding success with simply turning off portions of their public lighting after midnight. Even Paris, the famed "city of light," which already turns off its monument lighting after 1 a.m., will this summer start to require its shops, offices and public buildings to turn off lights after 2 a.m. Though primarily designed to save energy, such reductions in light will also go far in addressing light pollution. But we will never truly address the problem of light pollution until we become aware of the irreplaceable value and beauty of the darkness we are losing.

Directions

Write an essay in which you explain how Paul Bogard builds an argument to persuade his audience that natural darkness should be preserved. In your essay, analyze how Bogard uses one or more of the features in the directions that precede the passage (or features of your own choice) to strengthen the logic and persuasiveness of his argument. Be sure that your analysis focuses on the most relevant features of the passage.

Your essay should not explain whether you agree with Bogard's claims, but rather explain how Bogard builds an argument to persuade his audience.

Essay Scoring Guide

The optional SAT Essay is scored by two different people after reading the essay carefully. Each scorer will give your essay a score of 1 to 4 points for each of three dimensions: *reading*, *analysis*, and *writing*. Therefore you will get *two* scores for each of those three dimensions. These are added together to give three scores: 2–8 points for *each* dimension. (There are no percentiles or composite scores for the SAT Essay.)

The College Board lists the criteria for each of the three dimensions as follows below.

Reading

Score of 4

- Demonstrates thorough comprehension of the source text.

- Shows an understanding of the text's central idea(s) and of most important details and how they interrelate, demonstrating a comprehensive understanding of the text.

- Is free of errors of fact or interpretation with regard to the text.

- Makes skillful use of textual evidence (quotations, paraphrases, or both), demonstrating a complete understanding of the source text.

Score of 3

- Demonstrates effective comprehension of the source text.
- Shows an understanding of the text's central idea(s) and important details.
- Is free of substantive errors of fact and interpretation with regard to the text.
- Makes appropriate use of textual evidence (quotations, paraphrases, or both), demonstrating an understanding of the source text.

Score of 2

- Demonstrates some comprehension of the source text.
- Shows an understanding of the text's central idea(s) but not of important details.
- May contain errors of fact and/or interpretation with regard to the text.
- Makes limited and/or haphazard use of textual evidence (quotations, paraphrases, or both), demonstrating some understanding of the source text.

Score of 1

- Demonstrates little or no comprehension of the source text.
- Fails to show an understanding of the text's central idea(s), and may include only details without reference to central idea(s).
- May contain numerous errors of fact and/or interpretation with regard to the text.
- Makes little or no use of textual evidence (quotations, paraphrases, or both), demonstrating little or no understanding of the source text.

Analysis

Score of 4

- Offers an insightful analysis of the source text and demonstrates a sophisticated understanding of the analytical task.
- Offers a thorough, well-considered evaluation of the author's use of evidence, reasoning, and/or stylistic and persuasive elements, and/or feature(s) of the student's own choosing.

- Contains relevant, sufficient, and strategically chosen support for claim(s) or point(s) made.
- Focuses consistently on those features of the text that are most relevant to addressing the task.

Score of 3

- Offers an effective analysis of the source text and demonstrates an understanding of the analytical task.
- Competently evaluates the author's use of evidence, reasoning, and/or stylistic and persuasive elements, and/or feature(s) of the student's own choosing.
- Contains relevant and sufficient support for claim(s) or point(s) made.
- Focuses primarily on those features of the text that are most relevant to addressing the task.

Score of 2

- Offers limited analysis of the source text and demonstrates only partial understanding of the analytical task.
- Identifies and attempts to describe the author's use of evidence, reasoning, and/or stylistic and persuasive elements, and/or feature(s) of the student's own choosing, but merely asserts rather than explains their importance, or one or more aspects of the response's analysis are unwarranted based on the text.
- Contains little or no support for claim(s) or point(s) made.
- May lack a clear focus on those features of the text that are most relevant to addressing the task.

Score of 1

- Offers little or no analysis or ineffective analysis of the source text and demonstrates little or no understanding of the analytic task.
- Identifies without explanation some aspects of the author's use of evidence, reasoning, and/or stylistic and persuasive elements, and/or feature(s) of the student's choosing.
- Or numerous aspects of the response's analysis are unwarranted based on the text.

- Contains little or no support for claim(s) or point(s) made, or support is largely irrelevant.
- May not focus on features of the text that are relevant to addressing the task.
- Or the response offers no discernible analysis (e.g., is largely or exclusively summary).

Writing

Score of 4

- Is cohesive and demonstrates a highly effective use and command of language.
- Includes a precise central claim.
- Includes a skillful introduction and conclusion. The response demonstrates a deliberate and highly effective progression of ideas both within paragraphs and throughout the essay.
- Has a wide variety in sentence structures. The response demonstrates a consistent use of precise word choice. The response maintains a formal style and objective tone.
- Shows a strong command of the conventions of standard written English and is free or virtually free of errors.

Score of 3

- Is mostly cohesive and demonstrates effective use and control of language.
- Includes a central claim or implicit controlling idea.
- Includes an effective introduction and conclusion. The response demonstrates a clear progression of ideas both within paragraphs and throughout the essay.
- Has variety in sentence structures. The response demonstrates some precise word choice. The response maintains a formal style and objective tone.
- Shows a good control of the conventions of standard written English and is free of significant errors that detract from the quality of writing.

Score of 2

- Demonstrates little or no cohesion and limited skill in the use and control of language.
- May lack a clear central claim or controlling idea or may deviate from the claim or idea over the course of the response.
- May include an ineffective introduction and/or conclusion. The response may demonstrate some progression of ideas within paragraphs but not throughout the response.
- Has limited variety in sentence structures; sentence structures may be repetitive.
- Demonstrates general or vague word choice; word choice may be repetitive. The response may deviate noticeably from a formal style and objective tone.
- Shows a limited control of the conventions of standard written English and contains errors that detract from the quality of writing and may impede understanding.

Score of 1

- Demonstrates little or no cohesion and inadequate skill in the use and control of language.
- May lack a clear central claim or controlling idea.
- Lacks a recognizable introduction and conclusion. The response does not have a discernible progression of ideas.
- Lacks variety in sentence structures; sentence structures may be repetitive. The response demonstrates general and vague word choice; word choice may be poor or inaccurate. The response may lack a formal style and objective tone.
- Shows a weak control of the conventions of standard written English and may contain numerous errors that undermine the quality of writing.

IMPORTANT TIPS ON
HOW TO WRITE THE BEST ESSAY

Making Your Sentences Effective

What Is Style?

Many good ideas are lost because they are expressed in a dull, wordy, involved way. We often have difficulty following—we may even ignore—instructions that are hard to read. Yet we find other instructions written in such a clear and simple way that a child could easily follow them. This way of writing—the words we choose and the way we use them—is called *style*.

No two people write exactly alike. Even when writing about the same thing, they probably will express ideas differently. Some will say what they think more effectively than others; what they say will be more easily read and understood. But there is seldom any one best way to say something. Rather, there are usually several equally good ways. This flexibility is what makes English such a rich language.

Style can't be taught; each person's style is like personality—it is unique to him or her. But we can each improve our styles. Let us consider how we can improve our writing styles by improving our sentences.

How to Write Effective Sentences

We speak in sentences; we write in sentences. A single word or phrase sometimes carries a complete thought, but sentences are more often the real units of thought communication.

Writing good sentences takes concentration, patience, and practice. It involves much more than just stringing words together, one after another, as they tumble from our minds. If writers aren't careful, their sentences may not mean to the reader what they want them to mean; they may mean what they *didn't* want to convey—or they may mean nothing at all.

This section discusses five things writers can do to write better sentences—or improve sentences already written:

1. Create interest.
2. Make your meaning clear.
3. Keep your sentences brief.
4. Make every word count.
5. Vary your sentence patterns.

Let's consider interest first.

1. Create Interest

We can make our writing more interesting by writing in an informal, conversational style. This style also makes our writing easier to understand and our readers more receptive to our thoughts.

Listen to two men meeting in the coffee shop. One tells the other, "Let me know when you need more paper clips." But how would he have written it? Probably as follows:

> Request this office be notified when your activity's supply of paper clips, wire, steel gem pattern, large type 1, stock No. 7510-634-6516, falls below 30-day level prescribed in AFR 67-1, Vol. II, Section IV, subject: Office Supplies. Requisition will be submitted as expeditiously as possible to preclude noncompliance with appropriate directives.

Judging from the formal, academic style of much of our writing, we want to *impress* rather than *express*. There seems to be something about writing that brings out our biggest words, our most complex sentences, and our most formal style. Obviously this is not effective writing. We wouldn't dare say it aloud this formally for fear someone would laugh at us, but we will write it.

Write to Express

One of the best ways to make our writing more interesting to the reader and, hence, more effective is to write as we talk. Of course we can't write *exactly* as we talk, and we shouldn't want to. We usually straighten out the sentence structure, make our sentences complete rather than fragmentary or run-on, substitute for obvious slang words, and so on. But we can come close to our conversational style without being folksy, ungrammatical, or wordy. This informal style is far more appropriate for the kind of writing we do and for the kind of readers we have than the old formal style. And it certainly makes better reading.

Be Definite, Specific, and Concrete

Another way—and one of the surest—to arouse and hold the interest and attention of readers is to be definite, specific, and concrete.

2. Make Your Meaning Clear

You do not need to be a grammarian to recognize a good sentence. After all, the first requirement of grammar is that you focus your reader's attention on the meaning you wish to convey. If you take care to make your meaning clear, your grammar will usually take care of itself. You can, however, do three things to make your meaning clearer to your reader: (1) emphasize your main ideas, (2) avoid wandering sentences, and (3) avoid ambiguity.

Emphasize the Main Ideas

When we talk, we use gestures, voice changes, pauses, smiles, frowns, and so on to emphasize our main ideas. In writing, we have to use different methods for emphasis. Some are purely mechanical; others are structural.

Mechanical devices include capital letters, underlining or italics, punctuation, and headings. Printers used to capitalize the first letter of a word they wanted to emphasize. We still occasionally capitalize or use a heavier type to emphasize words, phrases, or whole sentences. Sometimes we underline or italicize words that we want to stand out. Often we label or head main sections or subdivisions, as we have done in this book. This effectively separates main ideas and makes them stand out so that the reader doesn't have to search for them.

But mechanical devices for emphasizing an idea—capitalization, particularly—are often overused. The best way to emphasize an idea is to place it effectively in the sentence. The most emphatic position is at the end of the sentence. The next most emphatic position is at the beginning of the sentence. The place of least importance is anywhere in the middle. Remember, therefore, to put the important clause, phrase, name, or idea at the beginning or at the end of a sentence, and never hide the main idea in a subordinate clause or have it so buried in the middle of the sentence that the reader has to dig it out or miss it altogether.

Unemphatic: People drive on the left side of the road instead of the right side in England.

Better: Instead of driving on the right side of the road, people in England drive on the left.

Avoid Wandering Sentences

All parts of a sentence should contribute to one clear idea or impression. Long, straggling sentences usually contain a hodgepodge of unrelated ideas. You should either break long sentences up into shorter sentences or put the subordinate thoughts into subordinate form. Look at this sentence:

The sergeant, an irritable fellow who had been a truck driver, born and brought up in the corn belt of Iowa, strong as an ox and six feet tall, fixed an angry eye on the recruit.

You can see that the main idea is "The sergeant fixed an angry eye on the recruit." That he was an irritable fellow, strong as an ox and six feet tall, adds to the main idea. But the facts that he had been a truck driver and had been born in Iowa add nothing to the main thought, and the sentence is better without them.

The sergeant, an irritable fellow who was strong as an ox and six feet tall, fixed an angry eye on the recruit.

Avoid Ambiguity

If a sentence can be misunderstood, it will be misunderstood. A sentence that says, "The truck followed the Jeep until its tire blew out," may be perfectly clear to the writer, but the reader will not know which vehicle's tire blew out until the pronoun *its* is identified.

Make Sure That Your Modifiers Say What You Mean

"While eating oats, the farmer took the horse out of the stable." This sentence suggests that the farmer is simultaneously eating his breakfast until you add to the first part of the sentence a logical subject ("the horse"): "While the horse was eating oats, the farmer took him out of the stable." Sometimes simple misplacement of modifiers in sentences leads to misunderstanding: "The young lady went to the dance with her boyfriend wearing a low-cut gown." You can clarify this sentence by simply rearranging it: "Wearing a low-cut gown, the young lady went to the dance with her boyfriend."

3. Keep Your Sentences Brief

Sentences written like ten-word advertisements are hard to read. You cannot get the kind of brevity you want by leaving out the articles (*a*, *an*, and *the*). You can get brevity by dividing complex ideas into bite-sized sentences and by avoiding unnecessary words and phrases and needless repetition and elaboration. Here are some suggestions that will help you to write short, straightforward sentences.

Use Verbs That Work

The verb—the action word—is the most important word in a sentence. It is the power plant that supplies the energy, vitality, and motion in the sentence. So use strong verbs, verbs that really *work* in your sentences.

Use the Active Voice

Sentences written in the basic subject-verb-object pattern are said to be written in the *active voice*. In such sentences, someone or something *does* something to the object—there is a forward movement of the idea. In sentences written in the *passive voice,* the subject merely receives the action—it has something done to it by an unnamed someone or something, and there is no feeling of forward movement of the idea.

The active voice, in general, is preferable to the passive voice because it helps to give writing a sense of energy, vitality, and motion. When we use the passive voice predominantly, our writing doesn't seem to have much life, the actor in the sentences is not identified, and verbs become weak. So don't rob your writing of its power by using the passive voice when you can use the active voice. Nine out of ten sentences will be both shorter (up to 25 percent shorter) and stronger in the active voice.

Let's compare the two voices:

Active: The pilot flew the aircraft.
(*Actor*) (*action*) (*acted upon*)

Passive: The aircraft was flown by the pilot.
(*Acted upon*) (*action*) (*actor*)

Now let's see some typical passive examples:

The committee will be appointed by the principal.

Reports have been received . . .

Provisions will be made by the manager in case of a subway strike.

Aren't these familiar? In most of these, we should be emphasizing the actor rather than leaving out or subordinating him or her.

See how much more effective those sentences are when they are written in the active voice:

The principal will appoint the committee.

We have received reports . . .

The manager will make provisions in case of a subway strike.

Avoid Using the Passive Voice

The passive voice always takes more words to say what could be said just as well (and probably better) in the active voice. In the passive voice, the subject also becomes less personal and may seem less important, and the motion of the sentence grinds to a halt.

There are times, of course, when the passive voice is useful and justified—as when the person or thing doing the action is unknown or unimportant.

When we use the lifeless passive voice indiscriminately, we make our writing weak, ineffective, and dull. Remember that the normal English word order is subject-verb-object. There may be occasions in your writing when you feel that the passive voice is preferable. But should such an occasion arise, think twice before you write; the passive voice rarely improves your style. Before using a passive construction, make certain that you have a specific reason. After using it, check to see that your sentence is not misleading.

Take a Direct Approach

Closely related to passive voice construction is indirect phrasing.

It is requested . . .

It is recommended . . .

It has been brought to the attention of . . .

It is the opinion of . . .

Again this is so familiar to us that we don't even question it. But *who* requested? *Who* recommended? *Who* knows? *Who* believes? No one knows from reading such sentences!

This indirect way of writing, this use of the passive voice and the indirect phrase, is perhaps the most characteristic feature of the formal style of the past. There are many explanations for it. A psychiatrist might say the writer was afraid to take the responsibility for what he or she is writing or merely passing the buck. The writer may unjustifiably believe this style makes him or her anonymous or makes him or her sound less dogmatic and authoritarian.

Express your ideas immediately and directly. Unnecessary expressions like *it is, there is,* and *there are* weaken sentences and delay comprehension. They also tend to place part of the sentence in the passive voice.

It is the recommendation of the sales manager that the report be forwarded immediately.

is more directly expressed as

The sales manager recommends that we send the report immediately.

Change Long Modifiers . . .

Dr. Barnes, who is president of the board, will preside.

Vehicles that are defective are . . .

They gave us a month for accomplishment of the task.

. . . to Shorter Ones

Dr. Barnes, the board president, will preside.

Defective vehicles are . . .

They gave us a month to do the job.

Break Long Sentences . . .

There is not enough time available for the average executive to do everything that might be done and so it is necessary for him to determine wisely the essentials and do them first, then spend the remaining time on things that are "nice to do."

. . . into Shorter Ones

The average executive lacks time to do everything that might be done. Consequently, he must decide what is essential and do it first. Then he can spend the remaining time on things that are "nice to do."

4. Make Every Word Count

Don't cheat your readers. They are looking for ideas—for meaning—when they read your letter, report, or directive. If they have to read several words that have little to do with the real meaning of a sentence or if they have to read a number of sentences to get just a little meaning, you are cheating them. Much of their time and effort is wasted because they aren't getting full benefit. They expected something that you didn't deliver.

Make Each Word Advance Your Thought

Each word in a sentence should advance the thought of that sentence. To leave a word out would destroy the meaning you are trying to convey.

"Naturally," you might say. "Of course!" But reread the last school essay you wrote. Are some of your sentences rather wordy? Could you have said the same thing in fewer words? And finally, how many times did you use a whole phrase to say what could have been said in one word, or a whole clause for what could have been expressed in a brief phrase? In short, try tightening up a sentence like this:

The reason that prices rose was that the demand was increasing at the same time that the production was decreasing.

Rewritten:

Prices rose because the demand increased while production decreased.

Doesn't our rewrite say the same thing as the original? Yet we have saved the reader some effort by squeezing the unnecessary words out of a wordy sentence.

Now try this one:

Wordy: The following statistics serve to give a good idea of the cost of production.

Improved: The following statistics give a good idea of the production costs.

or

These statistics show production costs.

And this one:

Wordy: I have a production supervisor who likes to talk a great deal.

Improved: I have a talkative production supervisor.

In all of those rewritten sentences we have saved our reader some time. The same thing has been said in fewer words.

Of course you can be *too* concise. If your writing is too brief or terse, it may "sound" rude and abrupt, and you may lose more than you gain. You need, then, to be politely concise. What you are writing, what you are writing about, and whom you are writing for will help you decide just where to draw the line. However, the general rule, make every word count, still stands. Say what you have to say in as few words as clarity *and tact* will allow.

Consolidate Ideas

A second way to save the reader's effort is to consolidate ideas whenever possible. Pack as much meaning as possible into each sentence *without making the sentence structure too complicated.*

Each sentence is by definition an idea, a unit of thought. Each time the readers read one of these units, they should get as much meaning as possible. It takes just about as much effort to read a sentence with a simple thought as it does to read one with a strong idea or with two or three strong ideas.

There are several things we can do to pack meaning into a sentence. In general, they all have to do with summarizing, combining, and consolidating ideas.

Some people write sentences that are weak and insignificant, in both structure and thought. Ordinarily several such sentences can be summarized and the thought put into one good, mature sentence. For example:

We left Wisconsin the next morning. I remember watching three aircraft. They were F-4s. They were flying very low. I felt sure they were going to crash over a half a dozen times. The F-4 is new to me. I hadn't seen one before.

Rewritten:

When we left Wisconsin the next morning, I remember watching three F-4s, a type of aircraft I had never seen before. They were flying so low that over a half-dozen times I felt sure they were going to crash.

When summarizing like this, be sure to emphasize the main action. Notice in the next example how we have kept the main action as our verb and made the other actions subordinate by changing them to verbals.

Poor: It was in 2010 that he *retired* from teaching and he *devoted* his time to *writing* his autobiography. (three verbs, one verbal)

Improved: In 2010 he *retired* from teaching to *devote* his time to *writing* his autobiography. (one verb, two verbals)

Here is an example similar to ones we might find in a directive:

Poor: The evaluation forms will be picked up from your respective personnel offices. You should have these completed by 1700 hours, 18 May. They will be delivered immediately to the security section.

Notice that in the instructions above all of the actions are to be performed by the reader or "you." Now let's put these into one sentence, placing the things to be done in a series and using a single subject.

Improved: Pick up the evaluation forms from your personnel office; complete and deliver them to the security section by 1700 hours, 18 May. (The subject [you] is understood.)

The same thing can be done with subjects or predicates:

Poor: Horror stories shown on television appear to contribute to juvenile delinquency. Comic books with their horror stories seem to have the same effect. Even the reports of criminal activities which appear in our newspapers seem to contribute to juvenile delinquency.

Improved: Television, comic books, and newspapers seem to contribute to juvenile delinquency by emphasizing stories of horror and crime.

There is one more thing we can do to make our sentences better. We can vary their length and complexity. The following paragraphs suggest ways to do this.

5. Vary Your Sentence Patterns

We should, as a general rule, write predominantly short sentences. Similarly, we should keep our sentences simple enough for our readers to understand them easily and quickly.

But most people soon get tired of reading nothing but simple, straightforward sentences. So, give your reader an occasional change of pace. Vary both the length and the construction of your sentences.

Vary Sentence Length

Some writers use nothing but short, choppy sentences ("The road ended in a wrecked village. The lines were up beyond. There was much artillery around."). In the hands of Hemingway, from whom this example is taken, short sentences can give an effect of purity and simplicity; in the hands of a less skillful writer, choppy sentences are usually only monotonous.

The other extreme, of course, is just as bad. The writer who always writes heavy sentences of 20 to 30 words soon loses the reader. Some great writers use long sentences effectively, but most writers do not.

The readability experts suggest that, for the most effective *communication*, a sentence should rarely exceed 20 words. Their suggestion is a good rule of thumb, but sentence length should vary. And an occasional long sentence is not hard to read if it is followed by shorter ones. A fair goal for most letter writers is an average of 21 words per sentence. For longer types of writing, such as regulations and manuals, sentences should average 15 words or fewer. The sentences in opening paragraphs and in short letters may run a little longer than the average.

Vary Sentence Construction

Just as important as varied sentence length is variety of construction. Four common sentence categories are simple, compound, complex, and compound-complex.

A *simple sentence* consists of only one main (independent) clause:

Rain came down in torrents.

Rain and hail started falling. (Simple sentence with compound subject)

The storm began and soon grew in intensity. (Simple sentence with compound predicate)

A *compound sentence* has two or more main clauses:

Rain started falling, and all work stopped.

The storm began; all work stopped.

The storm began, the workers found shelter, and all work stopped.

A *complex sentence* has one main clause and at least one subordinate (dependent) clause. (Subordinate clauses are underlined in the following sentences.)

They were just starting their work <u>when the rain started.</u>

<u>Before they had made any progress,</u> the rain started falling.

The storm, <u>which grew rapidly in intensity,</u> stopped all work.

A *compound-complex sentence* has two or more main clauses and at least one subordinate clause. (Subordinate clauses are underlined in the following sentences.)

Rain started falling, and all work stopped <u>before they had made any progress.</u>

<u>Although the workers were eager to finish the job,</u> the storm forced them to stop, and they quickly found shelter.

They had made some progress <u>before the storm began,</u> but <u>when it started,</u> all work stopped.

The names of the categories are really not important except to remind you to vary your sentence structure when you write. But remember that sentence variety is not just a mechanical chore to perform after your draft is complete. Good sentence variety comes naturally as the result of proper coordination and subordination when you write.

For example, if two or more short sentences have the same subject, combine them into one simple sentence with a compound verb:

The NASCAR drivers were hot. They were tired, too. They were also angry.

The NASCAR drivers were hot and tired and angry.

If you have two ideas of equal weight or parallel thought, write them as two clauses in a compound sentence:

The day was hot and humid. The NASCAR drivers had worked hard.

The NASCAR drivers had worked hard, and the day was hot and humid.

The day was hot and humid, but the NASCAR drivers had worked hard.

If one idea is more important than others, put it in the main clause of a complex sentence:

Poor: The NASCAR drivers were tired, and they had worked hard, and the day was hot.

Better: The NASCAR drivers were tired because they had worked hard on a hot day.

    or

    Although the day was hot and the NASCAR drivers were tired, they worked hard.

If the adverbial modifier is the least important part of a complex sentence, put it first and keep the end position for the more important main clause:

Instead of: The painters finished the job in record time, even though the day was hot and humid and they were tired.

Better: Even though the day was hot and humid and the painters were tired, they finished the job in record time.

But be careful about having long, involved subordinate clauses come before the main clause. The reader may get lost or confused before getting to your main point or give up before getting to it. Also beware of letting too many modifying words, phrases, or clauses come between the subject and the verb. This is torture for the reader. The subject and the verb are usually the most important elements of a sentence; keep them close together whenever possible.

PART 10

Two
SAT Practice Tests

5 IMPORTANT REASONS

FOR TAKING THESE PRACTICE TESTS

Each of the two Practice SAT tests in the final part of this book is modeled very closely after the actual SAT. You will find that each of these Practice Tests has

(a) the same level of difficulty as the actual SAT

and

(b) the same question formats as the actual SAT questions.

Accordingly, *taking each of the following tests is like taking the actual SAT*. There are five important reasons for taking each of these Practice SAT tests:

1. To find out which areas of the SAT you still need to work on.

2. To know just where to concentrate your efforts to eliminate weaknesses.

3. To reinforce the Critical-Thinking Skills—19 Math Strategies and 13 Verbal Strategies—that you learned in Part 4 of this book, the Strategy Section.

As we advised you at the beginning of Part 4, diligent study of these strategies will result in a sharp rise in your SAT Math and Verbal scores.

4. To strengthen your basic Math skills that might still be a bit rusty. We hope that Part 6, the Complete SAT Math Refresher, helped you to polish your skills.

5. To strengthen your grammar and writing skills. Look at Part 8, the Grammar and Usage Refresher, and Part 9, Practice for the Reading, Writing and Language Sections; Essay Tips.

These five reasons for taking the two Practice Tests in this section of the book tie in closely with a very important educational principle:

WE LEARN BY DOING!

10 TIPS

FOR TAKING THESE PRACTICE TESTS

1. Observe the time limits exactly as given.

2. Allow no interruptions.

3. Permit no talking by anyone in the "test area."

4. Use the answer sheets provided at the beginning of each Practice Test. Don't make extra marks. Two answers for one question constitute an omitted question.

5. Use scratch paper to figure things out. (On your actual SAT, you are permitted to use the test book for scratchwork.)

6. Omit a question when you start "struggling" with it. Go back to that question later if you have time to do so.

7. Don't get upset if you can't answer several of the questions. You can still get a high score on the test. Even if only 40 to 60 percent of the questions you answer are correct, you will get an average or above-average score.

8. You get the same credit for answering an easy question correctly as you do for answering a tough question correctly.

9. It is advisable to guess if you are not sure of the answer since there is no penalty for a wrong answer.

10. *Your SAT score increases by approximately 10 points for every answer you get correct.*

SAT PRACTICE TEST 1

TO SEE HOW YOU WOULD DO ON AN SAT AND WHAT YOU SHOULD DO TO IMPROVE

Introduction

This SAT test is very much like the actual SAT. It follows the genuine SAT very closely. Taking this test is like taking the actual SAT. The following is the purpose of taking this test:

1. To find out what you are *weak* in and what you are *strong* in.

2. To know where to concentrate your efforts in order to be fully prepared for the actual test.

Taking this test will prove to be a very valuable TIMESAVER for you. Why waste time studying what you already know? Spend your time profitably by studying what you *don't* know. That is what this test will tell you.

In this book, we do not waste precious pages. We get right down to the business of helping you to increase your SAT scores.

Other SAT preparation books place their emphasis on drill, drill, drill. We do not believe that drill work is of primary importance in preparing for the SAT exam. Drill work has its place. In fact, this book contains a great variety of drill material featuring SAT-type questions (Reading and Math and Writing), practically all of which have explanatory answers also keyed to basic skills and strategies. Our drill work is coordinated with learning Critical-Thinking Skills. These skills will help you to think clearly and critically so that you will be able to answer many more SAT questions correctly.

Ready? Start taking the test. It's just like the real thing.

ANSWER SHEET

It is recommended that you use a No. 2 pencil. It is very important that you fill in the entire circle darkly and completely. If you change your response, erase as completely as possible. Incomplete marks or erasures may affect your score.

Complete Mark ●   **Examples of Incomplete Marks** ◉ ⊗ ⊖ ◐ ⊘ ◖ ◓ ◕ ●

SECTION 1: READING

	A B C D		A B C D		A B C D		A B C D		A B C D
1	○ ○ ○ ○	12	○ ○ ○ ○	23	○ ○ ○ ○	34	○ ○ ○ ○	45	○ ○ ○ ○
2	○ ○ ○ ○	13	○ ○ ○ ○	24	○ ○ ○ ○	35	○ ○ ○ ○	46	○ ○ ○ ○
3	○ ○ ○ ○	14	○ ○ ○ ○	25	○ ○ ○ ○	36	○ ○ ○ ○	47	○ ○ ○ ○
4	○ ○ ○ ○	15	○ ○ ○ ○	26	○ ○ ○ ○	37	○ ○ ○ ○	48	○ ○ ○ ○
5	○ ○ ○ ○	16	○ ○ ○ ○	27	○ ○ ○ ○	38	○ ○ ○ ○	49	○ ○ ○ ○
6	○ ○ ○ ○	17	○ ○ ○ ○	28	○ ○ ○ ○	39	○ ○ ○ ○	50	○ ○ ○ ○
7	○ ○ ○ ○	19	○ ○ ○ ○	29	○ ○ ○ ○	40	○ ○ ○ ○	51	○ ○ ○ ○
8	○ ○ ○ ○	19	○ ○ ○ ○	30	○ ○ ○ ○	41	○ ○ ○ ○	52	○ ○ ○ ○
9	○ ○ ○ ○	20	○ ○ ○ ○	31	○ ○ ○ ○	42	○ ○ ○ ○		
10	○ ○ ○ ○	21	○ ○ ○ ○	32	○ ○ ○ ○	43	○ ○ ○ ○		
11	○ ○ ○ ○	22	○ ○ ○ ○	33	○ ○ ○ ○	44	○ ○ ○ ○		

SECTION 2: WRITING AND LANGUAGE

	A B C D		A B C D		A B C D		A B C D		A B C D
1	○ ○ ○ ○	10	○ ○ ○ ○	19	○ ○ ○ ○	28	○ ○ ○ ○	37	○ ○ ○ ○
2	○ ○ ○ ○	11	○ ○ ○ ○	20	○ ○ ○ ○	29	○ ○ ○ ○	38	○ ○ ○ ○
3	○ ○ ○ ○	12	○ ○ ○ ○	21	○ ○ ○ ○	30	○ ○ ○ ○	39	○ ○ ○ ○
4	○ ○ ○ ○	13	○ ○ ○ ○	22	○ ○ ○ ○	31	○ ○ ○ ○	40	○ ○ ○ ○
5	○ ○ ○ ○	14	○ ○ ○ ○	23	○ ○ ○ ○	32	○ ○ ○ ○	41	○ ○ ○ ○
6	○ ○ ○ ○	15	○ ○ ○ ○	24	○ ○ ○ ○	33	○ ○ ○ ○	42	○ ○ ○ ○
7	○ ○ ○ ○	16	○ ○ ○ ○	25	○ ○ ○ ○	34	○ ○ ○ ○	43	○ ○ ○ ○
8	○ ○ ○ ○	17	○ ○ ○ ○	26	○ ○ ○ ○	35	○ ○ ○ ○	44	○ ○ ○ ○
9	○ ○ ○ ○	18	○ ○ ○ ○	27	○ ○ ○ ○	36	○ ○ ○ ○		

SECTION 3: MATHEMATICS *(NO CALCULATOR ALLOWED)*

	A B C D		A B C D		A B C D		A B C D		A B C D
1	○ ○ ○ ○	4	○ ○ ○ ○	7	○ ○ ○ ○	10	○ ○ ○ ○	13	○ ○ ○ ○
2	○ ○ ○ ○	5	○ ○ ○ ○	8	○ ○ ○ ○	11	○ ○ ○ ○	14	○ ○ ○ ○
3	○ ○ ○ ○	6	○ ○ ○ ○	9	○ ○ ○ ○	12	○ ○ ○ ○	15	○ ○ ○ ○

Only answers that are gridded will be scored. You will not receive credit for anything written in the boxes.

16   17   18   19   20

(grid-in answer bubbles for questions 16–20, digits 0–9 with fraction slash and decimal point)

SECTION 4: MATHEMATICS *(CALCULATOR ALLOWED)*

	A B C D		A B C D		A B C D		A B C D		A B C D
1	○ ○ ○ ○	7	○ ○ ○ ○	13	○ ○ ○ ○	19	○ ○ ○ ○	25	○ ○ ○ ○
2	○ ○ ○ ○	8	○ ○ ○ ○	14	○ ○ ○ ○	20	○ ○ ○ ○	26	○ ○ ○ ○
3	○ ○ ○ ○	9	○ ○ ○ ○	15	○ ○ ○ ○	21	○ ○ ○ ○	27	○ ○ ○ ○
4	○ ○ ○ ○	10	○ ○ ○ ○	16	○ ○ ○ ○	22	○ ○ ○ ○	28	○ ○ ○ ○
5	○ ○ ○ ○	11	○ ○ ○ ○	17	○ ○ ○ ○	23	○ ○ ○ ○	29	○ ○ ○ ○
6	○ ○ ○ ○	12	○ ○ ○ ○	18	○ ○ ○ ○	24	○ ○ ○ ○	30	○ ○ ○ ○

SECTION 4: MATHEMATICS *(CALCULATOR ALLOWED)* (CONTINUED)

Only answers that are gridded will be scored. You will not receive credit for anything written in the boxes.

31

32

33

34

35

36

37

38

SECTION 5: TEST 1 ESSAY *(OPTIONAL)*

Begin your essay on this page. If you need more space, continue on the next page. Do not write outside of the essay box.

Continue on the next page if necessary.

Continuation of Section 5: Test 1 Essay from previous page. Write below only if you need more space.

SECTION 1: READING TEST

65 Minutes, 52 Questions

Turn to Section 1 of your answer sheet (page 433) to answer the questions in this section.

Directions

Each passage or pair of passages below is followed by a number of questions. After reading each passage or pair, choose the best answer to each question based on what is stated or implied in the passage or passages and in any accompanying graphics (such as a table or graph).

Questions 1–11 are based on the following passage.

This passage is from Rajiv Nehru, "The Flight Home," 1999, by Rajiv Nehru. The setting is Chicago in 1947. Achal, who is in his late twenties, moved six months ago to the United States from his native India.

Again Achal looked at the address he had penciled on the back of an envelope and then up at the imposing building. Nowhere did he see a sign for The Superior Driving School. He entered the revolving doors and
5 found himself forced to move with swift little steps to match the pace of a young man hurrying out the building. He was deposited into a wide lobby that extended upwards the full six floors of the building's height. Several dozen people rushed around him, and he was
10 lightly brushed by a man twice his age hustling to catch a set of closing elevator doors. "Scuse," said the man, only half-turning around as he passed.

As Achal approached a large directory of businesses hung on the wall, the names of the businesses
15 embossed in gold on heavy slate, he sensed a uniformed man approaching from one side. He did not want this encounter, whatever it entailed, but the man called out,

"Hey Mac. Help you with something?" The lobby
20 guard smiled. Achal was reminded of something Punit had told him:

"Americans love to help. They long to show you that they have figured out everything that anyone should ever need to know."

25 Achal smiled back. "I think I can find here the Superior Driving School."

"Sure, they're here, up on 3. They take you out to a lot on Grand for your lesson. Let's see . . . here . . . 322. There's the elevators. You'll see signs when you get
30 out."

"Yes I see, thanks,"—Achal gave a little bow as he crossed to the elevators.

The guard called after him, "322—just look for the signs."

35 "Yes, yes," Achal muttered with embarrassed annoyance. He entered the elevator without looking at those around him, a fixed tight smile on his face.

In the driving school office, Achal was told by the man behind the counter to take a seat and wait for the
40 instructor. As he was flipping through the leaflet "Rules of the Road," a short young woman, a few years older than Achal, came into the waiting area, thrust out her hand, and announced:

"Hi. I'm Shirl. You . . . Atchel?"
45 "Yes, A-*chal*." He shook her hand and turned to the man at the counter, who grinned as he looked back down at his work.

"Well, Achal, I'm your instructor. Ready to go?"

"Yes. Umm . . ." He again looked at the other man.
50 "Well, let's go then!" she said, with sing-song trace irritation in her voice, and briskly led them out of the office and down the hall. A few others were in the elevator, and they said little on the way down. Achal knew his discomfort at having this woman as his instructor
55 was obvious. He was, once again, in a state of doubled annoyance—at this place, at America and its rush to

Go on to the next page. ⇨

upend tradition, and at himself for not wholeheartedly joining in. Wasn't he, after all, just as eager to break with tradition back home? He thought again of Punit,
60 and of his brother's widow, Lakshmi, and how they had lost so much defying their own families—good people helplessly mired in the past—and the British authorities who controlled India.

As they crossed the street, Shirley asked whether he
65 had any driving experience.

"Not in a car. But I have driven a tank."

She took a closer look at Achal as they made their way into the parking lot.

"Where?"

70 He did not wish to speak much about his experiences in the war. He had come to realize that doing so would be a sure road to a form of acceptance in the eyes of Americans who were slow to treat him with the casual intimacy that they used with each other, but
75 he did want to "earn" acceptance this way. Talk of his military service seemed to him a sort of short-cut to a respect that left him half-way to his destination.

"In Burma. Do you know it?"

"Sure." She pointed to a car they then entered, he on
80 the driver's side. "My brother was in the Flying Tigers. He trained in Burma."

Her side of the car, the passenger side, had a duplicate steering wheel, and she now gripped it tightly. "He didn't make it back."

85 Achal allowed himself to look at the woman sitting next to him. She stared ahead, and he saw that through her grim expression she was struggling to keep her emotions in check. He clasped his own wheel. Without knowing why, he spoke of Punit.

90 "My brother lost his life at a protest. He left behind a wife and young child."

"He was fighting for independence?"

"Yes."

"That's a good thing to fight for," said Shirley, and
95 as she sat there, staring straight ahead, she silently let tears fall, and Achal, without confusion or shame, did the same.

The Driving Lesson **Questions**

1. Which choice best describes the developmental pattern of the passage?

   (A) a summary of background information about a character who then relates key parts of his history to another character

   (B) a description of key elements of a place and time and the exploration of how one character fits into this setting

   (C) a comparison between two people who have more in common than they at first realize, but whose differences gradually become more significant

   (D) some introductory material describing a setting and a main character followed by an emotional exchange

2. The passage indicates that Achal does not like to say much about his military service because he

   (A) wants Americans to accept him for other reasons

   (B) is embarrassed about the nature of his service during the war

   (C) believes that Americans, with their casual manner of speech, will not want to discuss such matters

   (D) thinks that Americans will consider this an overly simplistic approach to impressing them

3. As used in line 62, "mired in" most nearly means

   (A) buried in

   (B) running from

   (C) stalled in

   (D) found in

4. The main purpose of the first paragraph is to

   (A) show that Achal is nervous about having to take driving lessons

   (B) demonstrate that Achal has just arrived in the United States

   (C) present Achal as someone who is not entirely at home in his surroundings

   (D) introduce the dramatic elements that will become the main focus of the passage

5. How does Achal regard his feelings about having Shirley as his instructor?

   (A) He is ashamed.
   (B) He is conflicted.
   (C) He is bitter.
   (D) He is secretly pleased.

6. Which choice provides the best evidence for the answer to the previous question?

   (A) Lines 53–55 ("Achal . . . obvious.")
   (B) Lines 55–58 ("He was . . . in.")
   (C) Lines 58–59 ("Wasn't he . . . home?")
   (D) Lines 75–77 ("Talk . . . destination.")

7. The tone of Punit's comments regarding Americans is

   (A) self-serving
   (B) mocking
   (C) horrified
   (D) admiring

8. The author emphasizes the change in the way that Achal and Shirley relate to each other by

   (A) putting them in similar physical poses
   (B) having Shirley lead Achal out of the office
   (C) having Shirley mispronounce Achal's name
   (D) placing Achal in the driver's seat

9. The passage indicates that the "independence" that Punit fought for refers to

   (A) personal freedom
   (B) physical well-being for his family
   (C) victory in a military struggle
   (D) political liberation

10. Which choice provides the best evidence for the answer to the previous question?

   (A) Lines 22–24 ("*They long . . . know.*")
   (B) Lines 58–59 ("Wasn't he . . . home?")
   (C) Lines 59–63 ("He thought . . . India.")
   (D) Lines 94–97 ("That's a good . . . same.")

11. Why does Achal look several times at the man behind the counter at the driving school?

   (A) He wishes that he had more time to prepare for the lesson.
   (B) He wants to share his amusement at the situation with someone.
   (C) He is not comfortable with having Shirley as his instructor.
   (D) He is waiting to see if the man has anything else to say before the lesson begins.

Go on to the next page. ⇨

Directions

The two passages below are followed by questions based on their content and on the relationship between the two passages. Answer the questions on the basis of what is *stated* or *implied* in the passages and in any introductory material that may be provided.

Questions 12–23 are based on the following passages.

The following two passages describe different time periods. Passage 1 is adapted from Johan Huizinga's The Waning of the Middle Ages, *1919, and discusses life during the medieval time period. Passage 2 is adapted from P.V.N. Meyers,* A General History for Colleges and High Schools, *1902, and describes the rise of the Industrial Age in the nineteenth century.*

Passage 1

To the world when it was half a thousand years younger, the outlines of all things seemed more clearly marked than to us. The contrast between suffering and joy, between adversity and happiness, appeared more strik-
5 ing. All experience had yet to the minds of men the directness and absoluteness of the pleasure and pain of child life. Every event, every action, was still embodied in expressive and solemn forms, which raised them to the dignity of a ritual.
10 Misfortunes and poverty were more afflicting than at present; it was more difficult to guard against them, and to find solace. Illness and health presented a more striking contrast; the cold and darkness of winter were more real evils. Honors and riches were relished with
15 greater avidity and contrasted more vividly with surrounding misery. We, at the present day, can hardly understand the keenness with which a fur coat, a good fire on the hearth, a soft bed, a glass of wine, were formerly enjoyed.
20 Then, again, all things in life were of a proud or cruel publicity. Lepers sounded their rattles and went about in processions, beggars exhibited their deformity and their misery in churches. Every order and estate, every rank and profession, was distinguished by its
25 costume. The great lords never moved about without a glorious display of arms and liveries, exciting fear and envy. Executions and other public acts of justice, hawking, marriages and funerals, were all announced by cries and processions, songs and music. The lover
30 wore the colors of his lady; companions the emblem of their brotherhood; parties and servants the badges of their lords. Between town and country, too, the contrast was very marked. A medieval town did not lose itself in extensive suburbs of factories and villas; girded by
35 its walls, it stood forth as a compact whole, bristling with innumerable turrets. However tall and threatening the houses of noblemen or merchants might be, in the aspect of the town, the lofty mass of the churches always remained dominant.
40 The contrast between silence and sound, darkness and light, like that between summer and winter, was more strongly marked than it is in our lives. The modern town hardly knows silence or darkness in their purity, nor the effect of a solitary light or a single
45 distant cry.
All things presenting themselves to the mind in violent contrasts and impressive forms lent a tone of excitement and passion to everyday life and tended to produce that perpetual oscillation between despair and
50 distracted joy, between cruelty and pious tenderness which characterize life in the Middle Ages.

Passage 2

During the last fifty years the distinctive features of society have wholly changed. The battles now being waged in the religious and the political world are only
55 faint echoes of the great battles of the sixteenth, seventeenth, and eighteenth centuries. A new movement of human society has begun. Civilization has entered upon what may be called the Industrial Age, or the Age of Material Progress.
60 The decade between 1830 and 1840 was, in the phrase of Herzog, "the cradle of the new epoch." In that decade several of the greatest inventions that have marked human progress were first brought to practical perfection. Prominent among these were ocean steam
65 navigation, railroads, and telegraphs. In the year 1830 Stephenson exhibited the first really successful locomotive. In 1836 Morse perfected the telegraph. In 1838 ocean steamship navigation was first practically solved. . . . Within the last fifty years the continents
70 have been covered with a perfect network of railroads, constructed at an enormous cost of labor and capital. . . .
By these inventions the most remote parts of the earth have been brought near together. A solidarity of commercial interests has been created. Thought has
75 been made virtually cosmopolitan: a new and helpful

Go on to the next page. ⇒

idea or discovery becomes immediately the common
possession of the world. Facilities for travel, by bringing men together, and familiarizing them with new
scenes and different forms of society and belief, have
80 made them more liberal and tolerant. Mind has been
broadened and quickened. And by the virtual annihila-
tion of time and space, governmental problems have
been solved. . . . Furthermore, the steps of human
progress have been accelerated a hundred-fold. The
85 work of years, and of centuries even, is crowded into a
day. Thus Japan, on the outskirts of the world, has been
modified more by our civilization within the last decade
or two, than Britain was modified by the civilization of
Rome during the four hundred years that the island was
90 connected with the empire. . . .

The history of this wonderful age, so different from
any preceding age, cannot yet be written, for no one
can tell whether the epoch is just opening or is already
well advanced. It may well be that we have already
95 seen the greatest surprises of the age, and that the
epoch is nearing its culmination, and that other than
material development—let us hope intellectual and
moral development—will characterize future epochs.

Questions for Passages 1 and 2

12. Conditions like those described in Passage 1 would
most likely have occurred about

   (A) the year 55
   (B) the year 755
   (C) the year 1055
   (D) the year 1455

13. The phrase "with greater avidity" in lines 14–15 is
best interpreted to mean with greater

   (A) desire
   (B) sadness
   (C) terror
   (D) silence

14. In Passage 1, all of the following are stated or
implied about towns in the Middle Ages *except*

   (A) Towns had no suburbs.
   (B) Towns were always quite noisy.
   (C) Towns served as places of defense.
   (D) Towns always had large churches.

15. The author's main purpose in Passage 1 is to

   (A) describe the miseries of the period
   (B) show how life was centered on the town
   (C) emphasize the uncontrolled and violent course
       of life at the time
   (D) point out how the upper classes mistreated the
       lower classes

16. According to Passage 1, people at that time, as
compared with people today, were

   (A) better off
   (B) less intelligent
   (C) more subdued
   (D) more sensitive to certain events

17. Passage 2 expresses an overall mood of

   (A) blatant despair
   (B) poignant nostalgia
   (C) muted pessimism
   (D) qualified optimism

18. Which of the following best explains the author's
meaning when he says "Thought has become virtually cosmopolitan" (lines 74–75)?

   (A) New technologies have accelerated the ability
       to share new ideas.
   (B) Human beings are blessed with a new free-
       dom to practice their beliefs.
   (C) People's beliefs are becoming increasingly
       similar across the globe.
   (D) It has become easier to steal other people's
       ideas and inventions.

19. Most of the specific advancements mentioned in
Passage 2 are related to

   (A) manufacturing and engineering
   (B) transportation and communication
   (C) labor and finance
   (D) moral and intellectual development

20. The groups involved in forming a "solidarity of
commercial interests" (lines 73–74) consist mainly
of

   (A) American cities and states
   (B) nations and societies across the globe
   (C) rural areas and urban centers
   (D) past and present societies

Go on to the next page. ⇨

21. If you were living in the world of Passage 1, which of the following characteristics of Passage 2's world would you see as the most different from the medieval world?

    (A) More ritual among the people of Passage 2.
    (B) A greater fear of the future in the world of Passage 2.
    (C) Less poverty among the people of Passage 2.
    (D) An overpopulated earth in the world of Passage 2.

22. Based on the information in each passage, what is the main difference between the worlds presented in Passage 1 and Passage 2?

    (A) The life of the people in Passage 1 is marked by greater experiential contrasts.
    (B) The people in Passage 2 are morally superior to the people in Passage 1.

    (C) The world of Passage 1 is more violent than the world of Passage 2.
    (D) The people in Passage 1 are more religious than the people of Passage 2.

23. From a reading of both passages, one may conclude that

    (A) the technology of transportation is of great importance to the people of both periods
    (B) the evolution of science has created great differences in the social classes
    (C) the future mirrors the past
    (D) the people in Passage 1 are more preoccupied with everyday living, whereas the people in Passage 2 are more inclined to look toward the future

Go on to the next page. ⟹

Questions 24–32 are based on the following passage.

The following passage is from Christopher Lehmann-Haupt, "Books of the Times," The New York Times, May 29, 1974. In it he discusses the pros and cons of B. F. Skinner's work on behaviorism.

In his compact and modestly titled book *About Behaviorism*, Dr. B. F. Skinner, the noted behavioral psychologist, lists the 20 most salient objections to "behaviorism or the science of behavior," and he has
5 gone on to answer them both implicitly and explicitly. He has answers and explanations for everyone.

For instance, to those who object that behaviorists "deny the existence of feelings, sensations, ideas, and other features of mental life," Dr. Skinner concedes that
10 "a good deal of clarification" is in order. What such people are really decrying is "methodological behaviorism," an earlier stage of the science whose goal was precisely to close off mentalistic explanations of behavior, if only to counteract the 2,500-year-old influence of mental-
15 ism. But Dr. Skinner is a "radical behaviorist." "Radical behaviorism . . . takes a different line. It does not deny the possibility of self-observation or self-knowledge or its possible usefulness. . . . It restores introspection. . . ."

For instance, to those who object that behaviorism
20 "neglects innate endowment and argues that all behavior is acquired during the lifetime of the individual," Dr. Skinner expresses puzzlement. Granted, "A few behaviorists . . . have minimized if not denied a genetic contribution, and in their enthusiasm for what may be done
25 through the environment, others have no doubt acted as if a genetic endowment were unimportant, but few would contend that behavior is 'endlessly malleable.'" And Dr. Skinner himself, sounding as often as not like some latter-day Social Darwinist, gives as much weight
30 to the "contingencies of survival" in the evolution of the human species as to the "contingencies of reinforcement" in the lifetime of the individual.

For instance, to those who claim that behaviorism "cannot explain creative achievements—in art, for
35 example, or in music, literature, science, or mathematics"—Dr. Skinner provides an intriguing ellipsis. "Contingencies of reinforcement also resemble contingencies of survival in the production of novelty. . . . In both natural selection and operant conditioning the appearance
40 of 'mutations' is crucial. Until recently, species evolved because of random changes in genes or chromosomes, but the geneticist may arrange conditions under which mutations are particularly likely to occur. We can also discover some of the sources of new forms of behavior
45 which undergo selection by prevailing contingencies or reinforcement, and fortunately the creative artist or thinker has other ways of introducing novelties."

And so go Dr. Skinner's answers to the 20 questions he poses—questions that range all the way from
50 asking if behaviorism fails "to account for cognitive processes" to wondering if behaviorism "is indifferent to the warmth and richness of human life, and . . . is incompatible with the . . . enjoyment of art, music, and literature and with love for one's fellow men."
55 But will it wash? Will it serve to silence those critics who have characterized B. F. Skinner variously as a mad, manipulative doctor, as a naïve 19th-century positivist, as an unscientific technician, and as an arrogant social engineer? There is no gainsaying that *About Behavior-*
60 *ism* is an unusually compact summary of both the history and "the philosophy of the science of human behavior" (as Dr. Skinner insists on defining behaviorism). It is a veritable artwork of organization. And anyone who reads it will never again be able to think of behaviorism as a
65 simplistic philosophy that reduces human beings to black boxes responding robotlike to external stimuli.

Still, there are certain quandaries that *About Behaviorism* does not quite dispel. For one thing, though Dr. Skinner makes countless references to the advances in
70 experiments with human beings that behaviorism has made since it first began running rats through mazes many decades ago, he fails to provide a single illustration of these advances. And though it may be true, as Dr. Skinner argues, that one can extrapolate from
75 pigeons to people, it would be reassuring to be shown precisely how.

More importantly, he has not satisfactorily rebutted the basic criticism that behaviorism "is scientistic rather than scientific. It merely emulates the sciences." A true
80 science doesn't predict what it will accomplish when it is firmly established as a science, not even when it is posing as "the philosophy of that science." A true science simply advances rules for testing hypotheses.

But Dr. Skinner predicts that behaviorism will pro-
85 duce the means to save human society from impending disaster. Two key concepts that keep accreting to that prediction are "manipulation" and "control." And so, while he reassures us quite persuasively that his science

would practice those concepts benignly, one can't
90 shake off the suspicion that he was advancing a science
just in order to save society by means of "manipulation" and "control." And that is not so reassuring.

About Behaviorism Questions

24. According to the passage, Skinner would be most
likely to agree that

   (A) studies of animal behavior are applicable to
   human behavior
   (B) introspection should be used widely to analyze conscious experience
   (C) behaviorism is basically scientific
   (D) behavioristic principles and techniques will be
   of no use in preventing widespread disaster

25. The reader may infer that

   (A) behaviorism, in its early form, and mentalism
   were essentially the same
   (B) the book *About Behaviorism* is difficult to
   understand because it is not well structured
   (C) methodological behaviorism preceded both
   mentalism and radical behaviorism
   (D) the author of the article has found glaring weaknesses in Skinner's defense of behaviorism

26. When Skinner speaks of "contingencies of survival"
(line 30) and "contingencies of reinforcement"
(lines 31–32), the word *contingency* most accurately means

   (A) frequency of occurrence
   (B) something incidental
   (C) a quota
   (D) dependence on chance

27. The author of the article says that Skinner sounds
"like some latter-day Social Darwinist" (line 29)
most probably because Skinner

   (A) is a radical behaviorist who has differed from
   methodological behaviorists
   (B) has predicted that human society faces disaster
   (C) has been characterized as a 19th-century
   positivist
   (D) has studied animal behavior as applicable to
   human behavior

28. It can be inferred from the passage that "extrapolate" (line 74) means

   (A) to gather unknown information by extending
   known information

(B) to determine how one organism may be used
to advantage by another organism
(C) to insert or introduce between other things or
parts
(D) to change the form or the behavior of one
thing to match the form or behavior of another
thing

29. One *cannot* conclude from the passage that

   (A) Skinner is a radical behaviorist but not a
   methodological behaviorist
   (B) *About Behavior* does not show how behaviorists have improved in experimentation with
   human beings
   (C) only human beings are used in experiments
   conducted by behaviorists
   (D) methodological behaviorism rejects the introspective approach

30. In Skinner's statement that "few would contend
that behavior is 'endlessly malleable'" (line 27), he
means that

   (A) genetic influences are of primary importance
   in shaping human behavior
   (B) environmental influences may be frequently
   supplemented by genetic influences
   (C) self-examination is the most effective way of
   improving a behavior pattern
   (D) the learning process continues throughout life

31. According to the author, which of the following are
true concerning *scientistic* and *scientific* disciplines?

   I. The scientific one develops the rules for testing the theory; the scientistic one does not.
   II. There is no element of prediction in scientistic
   disciplines.
   III. Science never assumes a philosophical nature.

   (A) I only
   (B) I and III only
   (C) I and II only
   (D) II and III only

32. The word *veritable* (line 63) means

   (A) abundant
   (B) careful
   (C) political
   (D) true

Go on to the next page. ⇨

Questions 33–41 are based on the following passage.

The following passage is excerpted from the essay "Self-Reliance" by the American writer Ralph Waldo Emerson.

Infancy conforms to nobody: all conform to it, so that one babe commonly makes four or five out of the adults who prattle and play to it. So God has armed youth and puberty and manhood no less with its own piquancy
5 and charm, and made it enviable and gracious and its claims not to be put by, if it will stand by itself. Do not think the youth has no force, because he cannot speak to you and me. Hark! in the next room his voice is sufficiently clear and emphatic. It seems he knows how to
10 speak to his contemporaries. Bashful or bold, then, he will know how to make us seniors very unnecessary.

The nonchalance of boys who are sure of a dinner, and would disdain as much as a lord to do or say aught to conciliate one, is the healthy attitude of
15 human nature. A boy is in the parlor what the pit is in the playhouse; independent, irresponsible, looking out from his corner on such people and facts as pass by, he tries and sentences them on their merits, in the swift, summary way of boys, as good, bad, interesting, silly,
20 eloquent, troublesome. He lumbers himself never about consequences, about interests; he gives an independent, genuine verdict. You must court him: he does not court you. But the man is, as it were, clapped into jail by his consciousness. As soon as he has once acted or spoken
25 with eclat, he is a committed person, watched by the sympathy or the hatred of hundreds, whose affections must now enter into his account. There is no Lethe for this. Ah, that he could pass again into his neutrality.

These are the voices which we hear in solitude, but
30 they grow faint and inaudible as we enter into the world. Society everywhere is in conspiracy against the manhood of every one of its members. Society is a joint-stock company, in which the members agree, for the better securing of his bread to each shareholder, to surrender the liberty
35 and culture of the eater. The virtue in most request is conformity. Self-reliance is its aversion. It loves not realities and creators, but names and customs.

Whoso would be a man must be a nonconformist. He who would gather immortal palms must not be hin-
40 dered by the name of goodness, but must explore if it be goodness. Nothing is at last sacred but the integrity of your own mind.

No law can be sacred to me but that of my nature. Good and bad are but names very readily transfer-
45 able to that or this; the only right is what is after my constitution, the only wrong what is against it. A man is to carry himself in the presence of all opposition as if every thing were titular and ephemeral but he. I am ashamed to think how easily we capitulate to badges
50 and names, to large societies and dead institutions. Every decent and well-spoken individual affects and sways me more than is right. I ought to go upright and vital, and speak the rude truth in all ways.

I shun father and mother and wife and brother, when
55 my genius calls me. I would write on the lintels of the doorpost, *Whim.* I hope it is somewhat better than whim at last, but we cannot spend the day in explanation. Expect me not to show cause why I seek or why I exclude company. Then, again, do not tell me, as a
60 good man did to-day, of my obligation to put all poor men in good situations. Are they *my* poor? I tell thee, thou foolish philanthropist, that I grudge the dollar, the dime, the cent, I give to such men as do not belong to me and to whom I do not belong. There is a class of
65 persons to whom by all spiritual affinity I am bought and sold; for them I will go to prison, if need be; but your miscellaneous popular charities; the education at college of fools; the building of meeting-houses to the vain end to which many now stand; alms to sots; and
70 the thousandfold Relief Societies;—though I confess with shame I sometimes succumb and give the dollar, it is a wicked dollar which by and by I shall have the manhood to withhold.

For nonconformity the world whips you with its
75 displeasure. And therefore a man must know how to estimate a sour face. The by-standers look askance on him in the public street or in the friend's parlor. If this aversion had its origin in contempt and resistance like his own, he might well go home with a sad coun-
80 tenance; but the sour faces of the multitude, like their sweet faces, have no deep cause, but are put on and off as the wind blows and a newspaper directs. Yet is the discontent of the multitude more formidable than that of the senate and the college.

85 The other terror that scares us from self-trust is our consistency; a reverence for our past act or word, because the eyes of others have no other data for computing our orbit than our past acts, and we are loath to disappoint them.

90 But why should you keep your head over your shoulder? Why drag about this corpse of your memory,

Go on to the next page. ⇨

lest you contradict somewhat you have stated in this or that public place? Suppose you should contradict yourself; what then?

95   A foolish consistency is the hobgoblin of little minds, adored by little statesmen and philosophers and divines. With consistency a great soul has simply nothing to do. He may as well concern himself with his shadow on the wall. Speak what you think now in hard
100 words, and to-morrow speak what to-morrow thinks in hard words again, though it contradict everything you said to-day.—"Ah, so you shall be sure to be misunderstood."—Is it so bad, then, to be misunderstood? Pythagoras was misunderstood, and Socrates, and
105 Jesus, and Luther, and Copernicus, and Galileo, and Newton, and every pure and wise spirit that ever took flesh. To be great is to be misunderstood.

Self Reliance Questions

33. The main theme of the selection is best expressed as follows:

    (A) "A foolish consistency is the hobgoblin of little minds."

    (B) "Eternal youth means eternal independence."

    (C) "Whoso would be a man must be a nonconformist."

    (D) "Colleges are designed to educate fools."

34. We are most nonconformist during our period of

    (A) infancy

    (B) puberty

    (C) youth

    (D) manhood

35. According to the author, "To be great is to be misunderstood" means that

    (A) one should never say exactly what one means

    (B) to be misunderstood is to be great

    (C) all great men have always been misunderstood

    (D) a man should not hesitate to change his mind if he sees the need to, even at the risk of being considered inconsistent

36. The refusal of young people to cater to accepted public opinion is, according to the author,

    (A) characteristic of the rebelliousness of youth

    (B) a healthy attitude of human nature

    (C) a manifestation of deep-seated immaturity

    (D) simply bad manners

37. From the selection, one may infer that the "pit in the playhouse" was

    (A) a section containing the best seats in the theater

    (B) favored by independent, outspoken, unselfconscious playgoers

    (C) an underground theater

    (D) a generally staid, quiet section of the theater, favored by young people only

38. "Society is a joint-stock company," etc., is one way in which the author shows

    (A) that the public is anticulture

    (B) society is highly organized and structured

    (C) how society rejects self-reliance

    (D) that there is no room for solitude in our world

39. The word *eclat* (line 25), as used in this selection, means

    (A) violence and force

    (B) disrespect and resistance

    (C) reason and logic

    (D) spirit and enthusiasm

40. "I would write on the lintels of the doorpost, *Whim*." By this, the author means

    (A) that one should renounce his immediate family

    (B) that signposts have an important educational function in our society

    (C) that an impulsive action may have a subsequent rational explanation

    (D) that one must never be held responsible for what one says and does

41. The statement that best sums up the spirit and sense of this selection is

    (A) "Nothing is at last sacred but the integrity of your own mind."

    (B) "With consistency a great soul has simply nothing to do."

    (C) "Do not think the youth has no force, because he cannot speak to you and me."

    (D) "The virtue in most request is conformity."

Go on to the next page. ⇨

Questions 42–52 are based on the following passage and supplementary material.

This passage is adapted from D. Weddle, "The Neuro-anatomy of Birdsong," SciPress Ltd., 2014.

Like humans and other mammals, birds that vocalize (not all birds do) use the controlled flow of air to resonate a finely-tuned organ in their throats. The avian organ is the *syrinx*, a bony structure that is placed at
5 the bottom of the throat, unlike the mammalian *larynx*, which is found at the top of the trachea. In both cases, air is pushed past membranes that can be adjusted to raise and lower pitch, while the force of the breath changes the sound's volume. Songbirds have split
10 syrinxes, giving some of the birds the ability to create two pitches simultaneously—the Wood Thrush is even capable of singing rising and falling notes at the same time. Another particularly adept singer is the Northern Cardinal, which can produce a lengthy burst of pitches
15 far faster than any human singer or other musician, and which takes advantage of its two-sided syrinx by switching its song from one side to the other without a break, eliminating any need to stop to take a breath. (The showiness of these performances is intentional, as
20 intricate singing sends a message of vitality and health to potential mates in the listening "audience.")

Though born with the basic mechanism for vocalization, a young bird must still learn to sing specific songs from a "tutor" bird of its own species, most
25 often its father. (In much of the Americas and Eurasia, males birds are generally the singers, while in the desert regions of Australia and Africa, females are just as likely to sing.) This stage of the learning process is known as *sensory* learning. The juvenile listens and
30 memorizes the pitch, timing, and timbre of the tutor's song. After learning this song "template," the juvenile attempts to mirror what it has heard through *sensorimotor* learning, a process that can be likened to the way that infants learn to talk. Indeed, the "sub-song" pro-
35 duced by the young bird during the beginning of this process may make as much sense as the vocalizations of a 6-month old child. Eventually, certain species-specific sounds will become recognizable in what is

termed the young bird's "plastic song," and ultimately
40 this song will *crystallize* as the bird becomes capable of emitting a consistent order of sounds that match that of the songs it has been absorbing from its family and others of its species.

Experiments have shown that a bird raised apart
45 from tutor birds will still sing, though its song will lack the more intricate elements of the standard song. Furthermore, a bird that loses its hearing during the sensorimotor stage will create vocalizations that are distinct from both the standard song and the song cre-
50 ated by birds isolated from tutors. These findings have led investigators to look for the neural pathways that allow a juvenile bird to learn from others and from its own vocalizations.

It seems clear that the two areas of the bird's brain
55 directly involved in learning and producing songs are the anterior forebrain pathway (AFP) and the posterior descending pathway (PDP). The AFP contains a region that is comparable to the human basal ganglia, an area associated with—among other functions—procedural
60 learning and certain routine behaviors. The PDP, which literally descends into the trachea, makes it physically possible for a bird to sing throughout its life. Messages travel from a level of the PDP called the HVC (high vocal area) and eventually to the other parts of the brain
65 involved in the song system, including the nerve that controls the contractions of the syrinx.

A number of similarities exist between the mechanisms and practices by which birds learn song and humans learn language. For example, just as humans
70 have regional dialects, birds often exhibit distinct varieties of song, especially when the birds are geographically isolated from other populations of their own species. And just as people differ in the manner and speed at which they acquire language, birds exhibit dif-
75 ferent learning modes. Some species are "close-ended learners," unable to learn new songs after the first year or so of their lives, while other birds—"open-ended" learners—develop new songs well into their maturity. Understanding this difference might help us understand
80 the relative ability of individuals to learn, process, and create human speech.

Go on to the next page. ⇨

The Neuroanatomy of Birdsong Questions

42. The main purpose of the third paragraph is to

    (A) explain the manner in which birds that are not raised in the wild under typical conditions are able to create their own songs

    (B) summarize findings that have led to areas of study described in the following paragraph

    (C) compare the three major styles by which birds learn to sing

    (D) show that juvenile birds that are isolated from tutor birds will create songs that are essentially unrelated to the typical song of their species

43. The phrase "plastic song" is used to emphasize

    (A) the ability of the juvenile bird to match the pitch, timing, and timbre of the adult bird

    (B) the nonsensical quality of the juvenile bird's song as it tries to imitate its tutor

    (C) the lack of consistency in the song of the juvenile bird during this stage

    (D) the simplicity of the juvenile bird's song relative to that of the adult bird

44. Regarding the neural pathways involved in song production in birds, the author of the passage indicates that

    (A) the ability of birds to engage in the learning of routine procedures is controlled by the animal's basal ganglia

    (B) the PDP gives birds the ability to learn new songs throughout its life

    (C) the mechanisms by which both pathways operate are essentially the same as those found in the neural pathways of mammals

    (D) relative to the function of the AFP, the PDP is more directly associated with the origin of the signals involved in the physical production of sound

45. What choice provides the best evidence for the answer to the previous question?

    (A) Lines 62–66 ("Messages . . . syrinx.")

    (B) Lines 60–62 ("The PDP . . . life.")

    (C) Lines 67–69 ("A number . . . language.")

    (D) Lines 75–78 ("Some species . . . maturity.")

46. As used in line 75, "modes" most nearly means

    (A) levels

    (B) skills

    (C) methods

    (D) dialects

47. The information in the passage most strongly supports which of the following statements?

    (A) In areas where there is little rain, food supplies can be so low that both sexes need to be actively involved in finding mates.

    (B) Birds raised in Africa are more likely to learn their songs from their mothers.

    (C) During the sensorimotor stage of learning, a bird switches from having one main tutor bird to learning its song from others in its family.

    (D) Female juveniles birds learning to sing will more quickly arrive at the crystallization stage than will males of the same age.

48. According to the passage, both mammals and birds

    (A) go through a stage during which they learn a "template" of sounds from a parent or other older member of its species

    (B) need to be geographically distant from other members of their own species in order to develop a dialect

    (C) have tracheas involved in the production of sound

    (D) have membranes that they use to control the relative loudness of their sounds

49. It can be inferred from the passage that a stork, a bird that does not sing,

    (A) does not have a fully developed syrinx

    (B) has a syrinx that is placed at the top of its trachea

    (C) is a close-ended learner

    (D) would be unlikely to share the same habitat as a Northern Cardinal

50. What choice provides the best evidence for the answer to the previous question?

    (A) Lines 1–3 ("Like humans . . . throats.")

    (B) Lines 3–6 ("The avian . . . trachea.")

    (C) Lines 13–18 ("Another . . . breath.")

    (D) Lines 73–75 ("And just . . . modes.")

Go on to the next page. ⇨

Bird Species	Natural Habitat	Learning Type	Sensory Period	Sensorimotor Period	Crystallization
Zebra finch	Central Australia	Limited	30–65 days after hatching	35–90 days after hatching	120 days after hatching
Canary	Micronesia	Open-ended	Early spring (shortly after hatching) through mid-autumn of that year	Late spring of the same year through late winter	The following spring during which the process may repeat

51. According to the table and the passage, 85 days after hatching, juvenile zebra finches will most likely be

   (A) creating sounds that resemble, though incompletely, the songs of their tutor birds
   (B) able to accurately reproduce the song of their tutor birds
   (C) listening to and trying to memorize the song of their tutor birds
   (D) producing sub-songs

52. According to the table and the passage, canaries

   (A) learn fewer songs during their lifetimes than do zebra finches
   (B) are the only birds native to Micronesia that are classified as "open-ended" learners
   (C) may achieve mastery of one song during the same season that they are beginning to learn another
   (D) reach maturity at about the same time that they learn the regional dialect of the local canary population

STOP!

If you finish before time is called, you may check your work on this section only.
Do not turn to any other section in the test.

SECTION 2: WRITING AND LANGUAGE TEST

35 Minutes, 44 Questions

Turn to Section 2 of your answer sheet (page 433) to answer the questions in this section.

Directions

Each passage below is accompanied by a number of questions. For some questions, you will consider how the passage might be revised to improve the expression of ideas. For other questions, you will consider how the passage might be edited to correct errors in sentence structure, usage, or punctuation. A passage or a question may be accompanied by one or more graphics (such as a table or graph) that you will consider as you make revising and editing decisions.

Some questions will direct you to an underlined portion of a passage. Other questions will direct you to a location in a passage or ask you to think about the passage as a whole.

After reading each passage, choose the answer to each question that most effectively improves the quality of writing in the passage or that makes the passage conform to the conventions of standard written English. Many questions include a "NO CHANGE" option. Choose that option if you think the best choice is to leave the relevant portion of the passage as it is.

Questions 1–11 are based on the following *Role of Celebrities* passage.

The role that celebrities play within (1) their cultures is a curious one. The very existence of these renowned people affects how we structure our lives, how we view ourselves, and how we relate to one another. Their impact, furthermore, has grown in both reach and breadth. Today's superstars are simply *more* famous than the idols of yesteryear, (2) however the raw number of public figures has multiplied to include an ever-widening assortment of individuals whose fame stems from the rapidly proliferating media sources that we use to communicate with and observe each other.

(3) The most popular people are not necessarily the most ethical. Centuries ago, the names of monarchs, military leaders, and religious figures spread across continents with a remarkable speed given the limited means by which news traveled. People, it seems, have always *needed* to know that certain individuals among us have greater privilege, authority, (4) notoriety.

The reasons for this need are sometimes contradictory. (5) On the one hand, the "viewer" gets the sense that *I too can achieve success and renown.* This is a viewpoint especially prevalent today, when fame can be acquired without the difficulties involved in, let's say, conquering a nation or managing to be born to royalty. A convincing case can be made that this facet of celebrity-worship actually reflects the rise in importance of the individual brought on by enlightenment ideals and democratic principles. (6) These values are held in high esteem all over the world, especially in places where they are not enshrined in law.

On the other hand, the celebrated can function as authorities (7) who possess magical abilities to protect those destined to remain "beneath." Such a notion seems quaint today, but witness the cyclical appearance of political and religious figures who (8) appear to have the best interest of the general public in mind.

Even a fixation with people of dubious talent can reap positive results, *especially* in this age of confession. The tweets of a supermodel publicly coming to grips with her emotional unavailability can provide some solace to the individual who suspects (9) that: he or she might suffer from the same problem. Yes, some "haters" will respond with derision, but there is little harm done, and perhaps it's best that anger of any kind gets directed down such a benign path.

(10) [1] However, I would suggest that the role of the (non-dictatorial) celebrity is generally beneficial. [2] Certainly there are dangers associated with hero-worship of a certain kind, as the sad and bizarre state of affairs in North Korea makes clear. [3] Prominent

Go on to the next page. ⇨

figures unify our fragmented world. [4] A preoccupation with a singer might be shared by teenagers in Bangladesh and Detroit. [5] An accountant in Milwaukee might be spurred to do charitable work because of the actions of a political activist in Nairobi.

So three cheers for the celebrities among us. They're so unappreciated.

Role of Celebrities Questions

1. (A) NO CHANGE
   (B) its
   (C) the
   (D) one's

2. (A) NO CHANGE
   (B) since
   (C) and
   (D) this is because

3. Which choice for replacing the underlined sentence is most relevant to the rest of this paragraph?

   (A) NO CHANGE
   (B) History is filled with example of people who took power by force.
   (C) In the past, people had limited means of expressing themselves.
   (D) Fame is, of course, nothing new.

4. (A) NO CHANGE
   (B) but even notoriety
   (C) but even of notoriety
   (D) or even notoriety

5. Which choice most effectively combines the underlined sentences?

   (A) On the one hand, the "viewer" gets the sense that *I too can achieve success and renown* a viewpoint especially prevalent today, when fame can be acquired without the difficulties involved in, let's say, conquering a nation or managing to be born to royalty.
   (B) On the one hand, the "viewer" gets the sense that *I too can achieve success and renown*, a viewpoint especially prevalent today, when fame can be acquired without the difficulties involved in, let's say, conquering a nation or managing to be born to royalty.

   (C) On the one hand, the "viewer" gets the sense that *I too can achieve success and renown*, viewpoints especially prevalent today, when fame can be acquired without the difficulties involved in, let's say, conquering a nation or managing to be born to royalty.
   (D) When fame can be acquired without the difficulties involved in, let's say, conquering a nation or managing to be born to royalty, the "viewer," on the one hand, gets the sense that *I too can achieve success and renown*, a viewpoint especially prevalent today.

6. The writer is considering deleting the underlined sentence. Should the sentence be kept or deleted?

   (A) Kept, because it provides a specific example of a general point made in the previous sentence.
   (B) Kept, because it summarizes the main idea of the paragraph.
   (C) Deleted, because it contradicts one of the main themes of the passage.
   (D) Deleted, because it makes a point that relates to the previous sentence but not the focus of the paragraph.

7. (A) NO CHANGE
   (B) of whom possess
   (C) who are in the possession with
   (D) possessed of

8. Which choice for replacing the underlined text best illustrates the type of celebrated people described in the previous sentence?

   (A) NO CHANGE
   (B) pretend to have been born with certain mystical powers.
   (C) exploit that craving for a man or woman with all the answers.
   (D) use their fame to increase their own wealth and power.

9. (A) NO CHANGE
   (B) that — he or she
   (C) that he or she
   (D) they

Go on to the next page. ⇨

10. To make this paragraph most logical, sentence 1
should be placed

(A) where it is now
(B) after sentence 2
(C) after sentence 3
(D) after sentence 4

*Think about the previous passage as a whole as you
answer question 11.*

11. To make the passage most logical, paragraph 6
should be placed

(A) where it is now
(B) after paragraph 2
(C) after paragraph 3
(D) after paragraph 4

Go on to the next page. ⇨

Questions 12–22 are based on the following passage, *Forcing Mechanisms*.

Factors that affect changes in the climate are known as forcing mechanisms. While the role that humans play in altering the climate gets the most attention, and (12) <u>understandably so,</u> it is worth reviewing some of the other important forcing mechanisms, including ocean circulation, life, solar output, and changes in the Earth's orbit.

Ocean circulation helps distribute the sun's heat across the globe by bringing warm waters from the equator to the poles, and cold waters back in the other direction. Any change in this process can significantly impact global temperatures and alter the amount of sea ice in the polar regions. Oceanic records show that rapid shifts in ocean currents and increased glacial melting (13) <u>has led</u> to major climate variations, including the Younger Dryas, a steep decline in temperatures throughout the northern hemisphere that occurred about 12,000 years ago.

The effect that living beings have had on the Earth's climate dates back at least as far as the Great Oxygenation Event (GOE) of about 2.3 billion years ago. (14) <u>At that time, bacteria used photosynthesis to produce so much oxygen that the gas accumulated in the atmosphere.</u> Oxygen is poisonous to anaerobic organisms, and so the GOE represents one of the largest extinction events in all of Earth's history. Once aerobic organisms began to evolve, they consumed enough oxygen to bring the presence of the gas down to levels (15) <u>comparable to</u> those that exist today.

Variations in the sun's output have had a profound effect on our atmosphere and therefore on our climate. (16) <u>Solar flares can occur several times a day or as infrequently as once a week, as is typical during an 11-year cycle.</u> The coolest period of the Little Ice Age (14th–19th centuries) and the warming in the early part of the 20th century were likely due to short-term solar cycling.

Changes in Earth's orbit can lead to changes in how the sun's energy is distributed across the globe. Because of these changes, the Earth's climate goes through what are known as Milankovitch cycles, named for (17) <u>Serbian geophysicist, Milutin</u> Milanković. These cycles last hundreds of thousands of years and are linked to the occurrence of ice ages.

And then there's us. It is well known that *greenhouse gases* in the atmosphere trap the sun's energy,

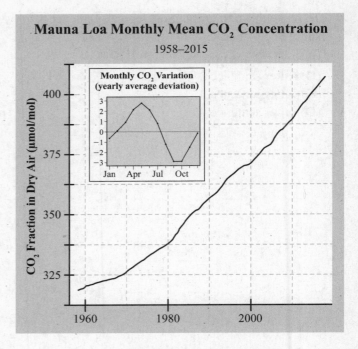

Mauna Loa Monthly Mean CO$_2$ Concentration
1958–2015

causing an increase in land and water temperatures and (18) <u>a host of</u> related issues. Because of our (19) <u>activities and especially with the burning of fossil fuels, more</u> of these gases, especially carbon dioxide, now exist in the atmosphere. The resulting change in the climate is such a pressing subject because of the dangerous rate at which this change is happening, the adverse affects of the change, and the opportunity we have to alter our behavior so as to minimize the negative consequences (20) <u>of this.</u>

Forcing Mechanisms Questions

12. (A) NO CHANGE
    (B) understandably, so
    (C) understandable, so
    (D) DELETE the underlined portion

13. (A) NO CHANGE
    (B) have led
    (C) leading
    (D) will lead

14. The writer is considering deleting the underlined sentence. Should the sentence be kept or deleted?

    (A) Kept, because it is a logical conclusion based on the previous sentence.
    (B) Kept, because it is important in connecting the sentence before this one to the sentence after this one.

(C) Deleted, because it states a detail that is essentially unimportant to this paragraph.

(D) Deleted, because it is simply a restatement of a fact found elsewhere in the passage.

15. (A) NO CHANGE
(B) compared to
(C) that are compared to
(D) comparing

16. Which choice most effectively sets up the information that follows?

(A) NO CHANGE
(B) The sun is the primary supplier of all our energy needs.
(C) Some of these variations take place over large expanses of time, but some are much shorter, as is the case with 11-year solar cycles.
(D) The sun has its own "lifespan," and will, billions of years from now, turn into a red giant and then a white dwarf.

17. (A) NO CHANGE
(B) Serbian geophysicist Milutin
(C) Serbian geophysicist: Milutin
(D) (Serbian) geophysicist Milutin

18. (A) NO CHANGE
(B) much
(C) numbers of
(D) a quantity of

19. (A) NO CHANGE
(B) activities—especially the burning of fossil fuels, more
(C) activities, like the burning especially of fossil fuels, more
(D) activities—especially the burning of fossil fuels—more

20. (A) NO CHANGE
(B) connected with them.
(C) of all those.
(D) of the change.

21. Based on the graph, the increase in CO_2 fraction in dry air from 1970 to 1980, measured in μmol/mol, is closest to which of the following?

(A) 10
(B) 12
(C) 15
(D) 25

22. For any given year, the CO_2 departure from the yearly average would be closest for which of the following pairs of months?

(A) January and February
(B) January and August
(C) March and July
(D) July and December

Go on to the next page. ⇨

Questions 23–33 are based on the following passage, *Music Appreciation*.

My habit for many years now (23) was to attend concerts with at least a passing familiarity with the works being performed. I am especially interested (24) with taking some prior knowledge of pieces that have the reputation of being "difficult," "thorny," or any of the other terms used for music that lacks the clear melody, harmony, and regular toe-tapping rhythm of most music written before the difficult and thorny 20th century.

Which brings me to a recent experience I had at a performance of Schoenberg's *Pierrot Lunaire*. (25) Arnold Schoenberg is, of course, the tremendously influential composer of the last century who jettisoned the rules of tonality, the rules that give us the sense that a piece is in the key of D, E minor, or whatever. If you've ever thought, "I can't stand modern music with its utter lack of tunefulness and its harsh dissonances," Schoenberg is the guy to blame.

Pierrot is scored for five instrumentalists, each playing a variety of (26) instruments and a female singer. The singer, however, does not actually sing in the traditional (27) sense; she uses a style that falls somewhere between speech and song, never landing on any one pitch for long. All this sliding around gives the piece a restless quality.

Restless is what much of the audience seemed during the performance of the piece. I sympathized with their impatience. *Pierrot* has no key, has little in the way of repeated melody, (28) and seldom has a regular pulse laying down for any length of time. It sabotages most attempts to follow it along its journey. (29) I found my mind wandering. I looked around at my surroundings and flipped through the program.

[1] By shutting down this most demanding of my senses, I can better absorb the sounds of the piece for *what they are* as opposed to *what they are not*. [2] My expectations and anticipations fade and I go along for the ride. [3] I often find that the best thing to do in this situation is to close my eyes. [4] I tried this and found that my appreciation of the piece immediately changed. [5] (30) Not only did I simply enjoy the sensual experience more, I understood the logic of the piece. [6] I noticed phrases. [7] (31) I felt the alternation of tension and release that is fundamental to all music everywhere. (32)

(33) As with any encounter with a great work of art, I doubt that I'll ever consider *Pierrot* among my favorite compositions, but I enjoyed the performance, which has enriched my life and broadened my tastes.

Music Appreciation Questions

23. (A) NO CHANGE
    (B) were
    (C) has been
    (D) have been

24. (A) NO CHANGE
    (B) by taking
    (C) with acquiring
    (D) in acquiring

25. (A) NO CHANGE
    (B) Arnold Schoenberg is, of course, the tremendously influential composer of the last century who jettisoned the rules of tonality; the rules that give us the sense that a piece is in the key of D, E minor, or whatever.
    (C) The rules that give us the sense that a piece is in the key of D, E minor, or whatever were jettisoned by Arnold Schoenberg, the tremendously influential composer, of course, of the last century.
    (D) The rules that give us the sense that a piece is in the key of D, E minor, or whatever were jettisoned by Arnold Schoenberg who is, of course, the tremendously influential composer of the last century.

26. (A) NO CHANGE
    (B) instruments as well as
    (C) instruments and also
    (D) instruments, and

27. (A) NO CHANGE
    (B) sense, however, she uses
    (C) sense that uses
    (D) sense, instead she

28. (A) NO CHANGE
    (B) and seldom lays down a regular pulse for any length of time.
    (C) or seldom lays down a regular pulse for any length of time.
    (D) seldom does it lay down a regular pulse for any length of time.

29. Which choice most effectively combines the under-lined sentences?

(A) I found my mind wandering as I looked around at my surroundings and flipped through the program.

(B) I found my mind wandering, I looked around at my surroundings and flipped through the program.

(C) I found my mind wandering, though I looked around at my surroundings and flipped through the program.

(D) I found my mind wandering, as I was look-ing around at my surroundings and flipped through the program.

30. If the word *better* is added to this sentence, which of the following would be the least effective place-ment of the word?

(A) between *I* and *understood*

(B) between *understood* and *the*

(C) between *the* and *logic*

(D) after *piece*, ending the sentence with a period after *better*

31. The writer is considering deleting the underlined sentence. Should the sentence be kept or deleted?

(A) Kept, because it shows that the author could appreciate the sensual quality of the music and then switch to appreciating its logic.

(B) Kept, because it gives another example of how the author's appreciation of the piece was heightened.

(C) Deleted, because it merely restates the fact that the author understood the piece differ-ently without providing new information.

(D) Deleted, because it makes an overgeneraliza-tion about music that would be out of charac-ter for the author.

32. To make this paragraph most logical, sentence 3 should be placed

(A) where it is now

(B) before sentence 1

(C) before sentence 2

(D) after sentence 7

33. (A) NO CHANGE

(B) As with any encounter with a great work of art, my life has been enriched and my tastes have been broadened, and I doubt, though I enjoyed the performance, that I'll ever con-sider *Pierrot* among my favorite composi-tions.

(C) My life has been enriched and my tastes have been broadened, as with any encounter with a great work of art, though I doubt that I'll ever consider that, even though I enjoyed the performance, *Pierrot* to be among my favorite compositions.

(D) I doubt that I'll ever consider *Pierrot* among my favorite compositions, but I enjoyed the performance and, as with any encounter with a great work of art, my life has been enriched and my tastes have been broadened.

Go on to the next page. ⇨

Questions 34–44 are based on the following passage, *Politics as a Career*.

The dwindling number of young people expressing an interest in political careers is a sad and telling state of affairs. Polls show that elected officials, especially those in Congress, are held in low esteem by a large majority of the (34) public; who would want to join the ranks of such an unloved and distrusted group of people?

(35) Therefore, the obstacles one must overcome in attaining political office seem daunting, even disreputable. The conventional wisdom is that if you're not privately wealthy, you have to constantly raise funds, begging and cajoling people for donations. If you do win an election, you immediately have to start thinking about repeating the whole process two, maybe four years down the road, or you're out of a job. (36) You have to again start talking to people about contributing to your campaign.

Even assuming that you (37) rise into office, your constituents love you, and no one seems eager to oust you from your position, what can you actually *get done*? American politics has developed a reputation for gridlock and partisan bickering that would put off the most dedicated would-be public servant.

(38) Career politicians, while there is some truth to all of the above, generally report high levels of satisfaction with their jobs. The negative perception that people have with politicians often falls away in one-on-one encounters. These men and women are, after all, people in positions of (39) power, admired and held in high regard by members of the public, even those who have radically different political philosophies.

Yes, incessant fund-raising and constant campaigning constitute the unpleasant reality of many a political career, but it's not all shaking hands, kissing babies, and meeting with potential donors looking for favors. (40) Using the Internet, large sums consisting of many small donations that are contributed without much involvement on the part of the candidate have been generated by campaign fund-raisers. As to always having to think about the next election, the truth is that, though (41) they complain about politicians in general, the typical voter does not have such a negative view of his or her own representatives, giving incumbents a large advantage that can last for decades.

It is also important to realize that some of the most important work gets done by locally elected officials. The pay for state legislators, city council members, and school board members is less than what members of the U.S. Congress receive, but (42) local politicians eventually become so entrenched in their communities that they know that they will always be able to find work in the area.

Yes, the political environment seems especially polarized these days, but that does not mean that progress (43) can't be done. Important laws get passed. Major policy initiatives are implemented. Relations between nations change, for the better or for the worse. The actions of elected officials affect us all.

Politics as a Career Questions

34. (A) NO CHANGE
    (B) public who
    (C) public, so: who
    (D) public; whom

35. (A) NO CHANGE
    (B) Nonetheless
    (C) Furthermore
    (D) Second,

36. The writer is considering deleting the underlined sentence. Should the sentence be kept or deleted?

    (A) Kept, because it strengthens an important point made in the paragraph.
    (B) Kept, because it functions as a transition into the following paragraph
    (C) Deleted, because it is not directly related to the main point of the paragraph.
    (D) Deleted, because it does not provide new information needed in the paragraph.

37. (A) NO CHANGE
    (B) sail
    (C) move
    (D) step

38. (A) NO CHANGE
    (B) Career politicians generally report high levels of satisfaction with their jobs, though there is some truth to all of the above things.

Go on to the next page. ⇨

(C) While there is some truth to all of the above, career politicians generally report high levels of satisfaction with their jobs.

(D) While there is some truth to all of the above, career politicians, who generally report high levels of satisfaction with their jobs.

39. (A) NO CHANGE
    (B) power, admiring and
    (C) power that is
    (D) power, which are admired and

40. (A) NO CHANGE
    (B) Using the Internet, campaign fund-raisers can generate large sums consisting of many small donations that are contributed without much involvement on the part of the candidate.
    (C) By using the Internet, large sums consisting of many small donations contributed without much involvement on the part of the candidate have been generated by campaign fund-raisers.
    (D) Using the Internet, the candidate has campaign fund-raisers that can generate large sums consisting of many small donations that are contributed without much involvement on the part of the candidate.

41. (A) NO CHANGE
    (B) they are complaining
    (C) it complains
    (D) citizens frequently complain

42. Paragraph 6 most logically leads to which of the following statements?
    (A) NO CHANGE
    (B) the expense of living in a small town or city is considerably less than the cost of living in the nation's capital.
    (C) the satisfaction of seeing firsthand the contributions you've made to the lives of the people you know best is powerful indeed.
    (D) locally elected officials have more to contribute to the workings of a democracy than do nationally elected politicians.

43. (A) NO CHANGE
    (B) is impossible.
    (C) is closed.
    (D) isn't anymore.

44. To make the passage most logical, paragraph 7 should be placed
    (A) where it is now
    (B) before paragraph 1
    (C) before paragraph 5
    (D) before paragraph 6

STOP!

If you finish before time is called, you may check your work on this section only.
Do not turn to any other section in the test.

SECTION 3: MATHEMATICS TEST, *NO CALCULATOR*

25 Minutes, 20 Questions

Turn to Section 3 of your answer sheet (page 434) to answer the questions in this section.

Directions

For questions 1–15, solve each problem, choose the best answer from the choices provided, and fill in the corresponding circle on your answer sheet. **For questions 16–20,** solve the problem and enter your answer in the grid on the answer sheet. Please refer to the directions before question 16 on how to enter your answers in the grid. You may use any available space in your test booklet for scratch work.

Notes

1. The use of a calculator **is not permitted**.
2. All variables and expressions used represent real numbers unless otherwise indicated.
3. Figures provided in this test are drawn to scale unless otherwise indicated.
4. All figures lie in a plane unless otherwise indicated.
5. Unless otherwise indicated, the domain of a given function f is the set of all real numbers x for which $f(x)$ is a real number.

Geometry Reference

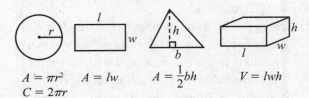

$A = \pi r^2$ $\quad A = lw$ $\quad A = \frac{1}{2}bh$ $\quad V = lwh$
$C = 2\pi r$

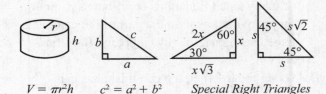

$V = \pi r^2 h$ $\quad c^2 = a^2 + b^2$ $\quad$ *Special Right Triangles*

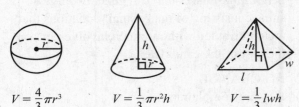

$V = \frac{4}{3}\pi r^3$ $\quad V = \frac{1}{3}\pi r^2 h$ $\quad V = \frac{1}{3}lwh$

The number of degrees of arc in a circle is 360.
The number of radians of arc in a circle is 2π.
The sum of the measures in degrees of the angles of a triangle is 180.

Go on to the next page. ⟹

1. If a and b are positive integers and $ab = 164$, what is the smallest possible value of $a + b$?

   (A) 34
   (B) 20
   (C) 16
   (D) 8

2. If a rectangle is drawn on the grid below with $\overline{MN}$ as one of its diagonals, which of the following could be the coordinates of another vertex of the rectangle?

   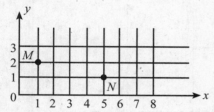

   (A) (1,0)
   (B) (2,0)
   (C) (3,3)
   (D) (5,2)

3. At 8:00 A.M. the outside temperature was $-15°$F. At 11:00 A.M. the temperature was $0°$F. If the temperature continues to rise at the same uniform rate, what will the temperature be at 5:00 P.M. on the same day?

   (A) $-5°$F
   (B) $0°$F
   (C) $15°$F
   (D) $30°$F

4. What is the slope of line l in the figure below?

   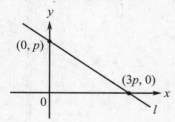

   (*Note*: Figure is not drawn to scale.)

   (A) -3
   (B) $-\dfrac{1}{3}$
   (C) $\dfrac{1}{3}$
   (D) 3

5. The average (arithmetic mean) of k scores is 20. The average of 10 of these scores is 15. Find the average of the remaining scores in terms of k.

   (A) $\dfrac{20k - 150}{10}$
   (B) $\dfrac{150 - 20k}{10}$
   (C) $\dfrac{150 - 20k}{k - 10}$
   (D) $\dfrac{20k - 150}{k - 10}$

6. At Jones College, there are a total of 100 students. If 30 of the students have cars on campus, and 50 have bicycles, and 20 have both cars and bicycles, then how many students have neither a car nor a bicycle on campus?

   (A) 80
   (B) 60
   (C) 40
   (D) 20

7. At a certain college, the number of freshmen is three times the number of seniors. If $\dfrac{1}{4}$ of the freshmen and $\dfrac{1}{3}$ of the seniors attend a football game, what fraction of the total number of freshmen and seniors attends the game?

   (A) $\dfrac{5}{24}$
   (B) $\dfrac{13}{48}$
   (C) $\dfrac{17}{48}$
   (D) $\dfrac{11}{24}$

8. In the figure below, each pair of intersecting segments is perpendicular with lengths as shown. Find the length of the dashed line segment.

   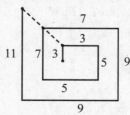

   (*Note*: Figure is not drawn to scale.)

   (A) 7
   (B) $4\sqrt{2}$
   (C) $\sqrt{46}$
   (D) $\sqrt{59}$

Go on to the next page. ⟹

9. A square has an area of R^2. An equilateral triangle has a perimeter of E. If r is the perimeter of the square and e is a side of the equilateral triangle, then, in terms of R and E, $e + r =$

   (A) $\dfrac{4R + 3E}{3}$

   (B) $\dfrac{3E + 4R}{12}$

   (C) $\dfrac{12E + R}{3}$

   (D) $\dfrac{E + 12R}{3}$

10. Given the volume of a cube is 8 cubic meters, find the distance from any vertex to the center point inside the cube.

    (A) $\sqrt{2}\ m$
    (B) $2\sqrt{2}\ m$
    (C) $2\sqrt{3}\ m$
    (D) $\sqrt{3}\ m$

11. The sum of a number of consecutive positive integers will always be divisible by 2 if the number of integers is a multiple of

    (A) 5
    (B) 4
    (C) 3
    (D) 2

12. A manufacturing plant has been hired for two projects. For one project, 12 identical electric components will be built. Afterward each of the components will be checked 3 times for defects. The entire process will take 61 hours. For the second project, 8 of these same components will be built, and each will be checked for defects 4 times. This will take 41 hours and 20 minutes. If the timing for creating one component is always the same, as is the time for checking it once for defects, what is the combined time required for creating one component and checking it once for defects?

    (A) 4 hours
    (B) 5 hours and 15 minutes
    (C) 5 hours and 20 minutes
    (D) 6 hours

13. The figure below shows two parabolas graphed on the xy-plane. If one of the parabolas can be described by the equation $y = -0.4(x - 3)^2 - 1$, which of the following could be the equation of the other parabola?

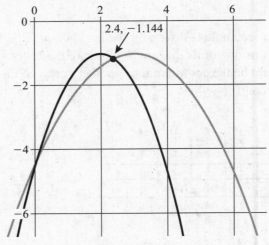

    (A) $y = -0.4(x + 3)^2 - 1$
    (B) $y = -0.4(x - 3)^2$
    (C) $y = -0.2(x - 3)^2 - 1$
    (D) $y = -0.9(x - 2)^2 - 1$

14. If the only solution for x in this equation is $9a$, what is the value of r?

    $$x^2 + rax + 81a^2 = 0$$

    (A) -81
    (B) -18
    (C) 18
    (D) 81

15. If $\sin \theta = \dfrac{a}{c}$, $c > 0$, and $\dfrac{5\pi}{4} < \theta < \dfrac{4\pi}{3}$, which of the following is $\tan \theta$?

    (A) $\dfrac{a}{-\sqrt{c^2 - a^2}}$

    (B) $\dfrac{a}{\sqrt{c^2 - a^2}}$

    (C) $\dfrac{\sqrt{c^2 - a^2}}{a}$

    (D) $\dfrac{c^2 - a^2}{a}$

Go on to the next page. ⇨

Directions

For questions 16–20, solve the problem and enter your answer in the grid, as described below, on the answer sheet.

1. Although not required, it is suggested that you write your answer in the boxes at the top of the columns to help you fill in the circles accurately. You will receive credit only if the circles are filled in correctly.

2. Mark no more than one circle in any column.

3. No question has a negative answer.

4. Some problems may have more than one correct answer. In such cases, grid only one answer.

5. **Mixed numbers** such as $3\frac{1}{2}$ must be gridded as 3.5 or 7/2. (If "31/2" is entered into the grid, it will be interpreted as $\frac{31}{2}$, not $3\frac{1}{2}$.)

6. **Decimal answers:** If you obtain a decimal answer with more digits than the grid can accommodate, it may be either rounded or truncated, but it must fill the entire grid.

Answer: $\frac{7}{12}$

Answer: 2.5

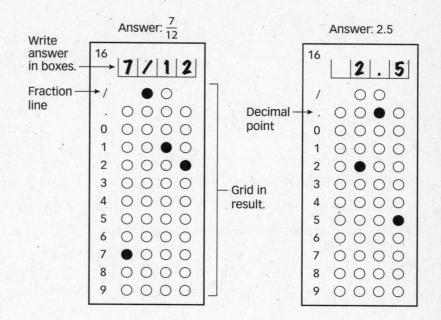

Write answer in boxes.

Fraction line

Decimal point

Grid in result.

Acceptable ways to grid $\frac{2}{3}$ are:

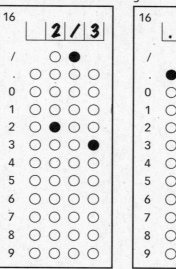

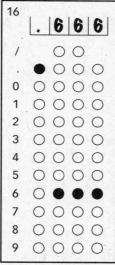

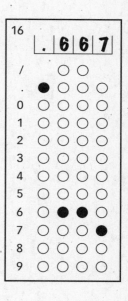

Answer: 201 – Either position is correct.

NOTE: You may start your answers in any column, space permitting. Columns you don't need to use should be left blank.

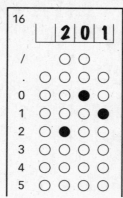

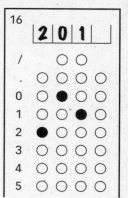

Go on to the next page. ⇨

16. If $\frac{1}{4} < x < \frac{1}{3}$ find one value of x.

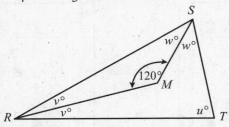

(*Note*: Figure is not drawn to scale.)

17. If $\angle RST = 80°$, find u.

18. How many ordered pairs of integers (x,y) satisfy $x^2 + y^2 < 9$?

19. The owners of a new store are determining how many hours the store should stay open on any given day. They use the equation $p = 35c - 1250$ to determine profit (p) given the number of customers to enter the store (c) that day if the store stays open 8 hours. If the store stays open 10 hours, the equation $p = 42c - 1700$ applies. What is the least number of customers the store would need to have in one day so that it would be more profitable staying open the extra 2 hours?

20. If $\left(2^{10}\right)^{y+1} = 8^{100}$, what is the value of y?

STOP!

If you finish before time is called, you may check your work on this section only.
Do not turn to any other section in the test.

SECTION 4: MATHEMATICS TEST, *WITH CALCULATOR*

55 Minutes, 38 Questions

Turn to Section 4 of your answer sheet (pages 434–435) to answer the questions in this section.

Directions

For questions 1–30, solve each problem, choose the best answer from the choices provided, and fill in the corresponding circle on your answer sheet. **For questions 31–37,** solve the problem and enter your answer in the grid on the answer sheet. Please refer to the directions before question 31 on how to enter your answers in the grid. You may use any available space in your test booklet for scratch work.

Notes

1. The use of a calculator **is permitted**.

2. All variables and expressions used represent real numbers unless otherwise indicated.

3. Figures provided in this test are drawn to scale unless otherwise indicated.

4. All figures lie in a plane unless otherwise indicated.

5. Unless otherwise indicated, the domain of a given function f is the set of all real numbers x for which $f(x)$ is a real number.

Geometry Reference

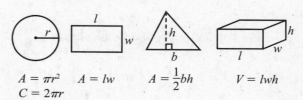

$A = \pi r^2$ $A = lw$ $A = \frac{1}{2}bh$ $V = lwh$
$C = 2\pi r$

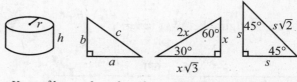

$V = \pi r^2 h$ $c^2 = a^2 + b^2$ *Special Right Triangles*

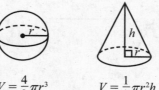

$V = \frac{4}{3}\pi r^3$ $V = \frac{1}{3}\pi r^2 h$ $V = \frac{1}{3}lwh$

The number of degrees of arc in a circle is 360.
The number of radians of arc in a circle is 2π.
The sum of the measures in degrees of the angles of a triangle is 180.

Go on to the next page. ⇨

1. If $a - 3 = 7$, then $2a - 14 =$
   (A) -4
   (B) 2
   (C) 4
   (D) 6

2. If $55,555 = y + 50,505$, find the value of $50,505 - 10y$.
   (A) -5.05
   (B) 0
   (C) 5
   (D) 5.05

3. If $5x^2 - 15x = 0$ and $x \neq 0$, find the value of x.
   (A) -3
   (B) 10
   (C) 5
   (D) 3

4. $m\|n$ in the figure below. Find y.

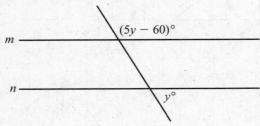

   (A) 10
   (B) 20
   (C) 40
   (D) 65

5. If an ant runs randomly through an enclosed circular field of radius 2 feet with an inner circle of radius 1 foot, what is the probability that the ant will be in the inner circle at any one time?
   (A) $\dfrac{1}{8}$
   (B) $\dfrac{1}{4}$
   (C) $\dfrac{1}{2}$
   (D) 1

6. According to the table below, which item has the greatest value when $P = 12$?

Item	Value
1	P
2	$P \times 3$
3	$(P \times 3) \div 2$
4	$[(P \times 3) \div 2] + 12$
5	$[(P \times 3) \div 2] + 12 - 1$

   (A) 2
   (B) 3
   (C) 4
   (D) 5

7. For how many two-digit positive numbers will tripling the tens digit give us a two-digit number that is triple the original number?
   (A) One
   (B) Two
   (C) Three
   (D) Four

8. At one instant, two meteors are 2,500 kilometers apart and traveling toward each other in straight paths along the imaginary line joining them. One meteor has a velocity of 300 meters per second while the other travels at 700 meters per second. Assuming that their velocities are constant and that they continue along the same paths, how many seconds elapse from the first instant to the time of their collision? (1 kilometer = 1,000 meters)
   (A) 250
   (B) 500
   (C) 1,250
   (D) 2,500

9. Given 4 percent of $(2a + b)$ is 18 and a is a positive integer, what is the *greatest* possible value of b?
   (A) 450
   (B) 449
   (C) 448
   (D) 43

Go on to the next page. ⇨

10. Find the circumference of a circle that has the same area as a square that has perimeter 2π.

    (A) $2\sqrt{2}$

    (B) $\pi\sqrt{\pi}$

    (C) $\dfrac{\pi}{2}$

    (D) $\dfrac{\sqrt{2}}{\pi}$

11. A plane left airport A and has traveled x kilometers per hour for y hours. In terms of x and y, how many kilometers from airport A had the plane traveled $\dfrac{2}{3}y$ hours ago?

    (A) $\dfrac{xy}{6}$

    (B) $\dfrac{xy}{3}$

    (C) xy

    (D) $\dfrac{3xy}{2}$

12. Using the formula $C = \dfrac{5}{9}(F - 32)$, if the Celsius (C) temperature increased 35°, by how many degrees would the Fahrenheit (F) temperature be increased?

    (A) $19\dfrac{4}{9}°$

    (B) $31°$

    (C) $51°$

    (D) $63°$

13. The length and width of a rectangle are $3w$ and w, respectively. The length of the hypotenuse of a right triangle, one of whose acute angles is 30°, is $2w$. What is the ratio of the area of the rectangle to that of the triangle?

    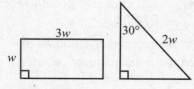

    (A) $2\sqrt{3} : 1$

    (B) $\sqrt{3} : 1$

    (C) $1 : \sqrt{3}$

    (D) $1 : 2\sqrt{3}$

14. In the figure below, two bicycles are being pedaled in opposite directions around a circular racetrack of circumference = 120 feet. Bicycle A is traveling at 5 feet/second in the counterclockwise direction, and Bicycle B is traveling at 8 feet/second in the clockwise direction. When Bicycle B has completed exactly 600 revolutions, how many complete revolutions will Bicycle A have made?

    (A) 180

    (B) 375

    (C) 475

    (D) 960

15. $[(3a^3b^2)^3]^2 =$

    (A) $27a^9b^6$

    (B) $54a^9b^6$

    (C) $729a^9b^6$

    (D) $729a^{18}b^{12}$

16. In the figure below, one side of a triangle has been extended. What is the value of $w + x + y$?

    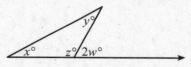

    (A) $3w$

    (B) $3z$

    (C) $2x + y$

    (D) $2x + 2y$

17. The ratio of Suri's age to Bob's age is 3 to 7. The ratio of Suri's age to Javier's age is 4 to 9. The ratio of Bob's age to Javier's age is

    (A) 28 to 27

    (B) 7 to 9

    (C) 27 to 28

    (D) 10 to 13

18. Find $(r - s)(t - s) + (s - r)(s - t)$ for all numbers r, s, and t.

    (A) 0

    (B) $2rt$

    (C) $2(s - r)(t - s)$

    (D) $2(r - s)(t - s)$

Go on to the next page. ⇨

19. In the figure below, squares I, II, and III are situated along the *x*-axis as shown. Find the area of square II

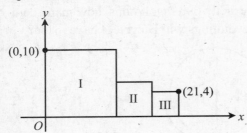

(*Note*: Figure is not drawn to scale.)

(A) 25
(B) 49
(C) 100
(D) 121

20. Which equation could represent the graph below?

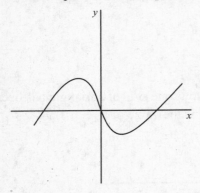

(A) $y = x^3 + 2$
(B) $y = x^3 + 2x + 4$
(C) $y = x^2$
(D) $y = x^3 - x$

21. A square of side *x* is inscribed inside an equilateral triangle of area $x^2\sqrt{3}$. If a rectangle with width *x* has the same area as the shaded region shown in the figure below, what is the length of the rectangle in terms of *x*?

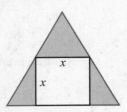

(A) $\sqrt{3}x - 1$
(B) $x\sqrt{3}$
(C) $\sqrt{3} - x$
(D) $x(\sqrt{3} - 1)$

22. For the complex number i, which of the following is equivalent to $\dfrac{3+i}{2-i}$?

(A) $1+i$
(B) $1-i$
(C) $1+5i$
(D) $5i$

Questions 23 and 24 refer to the following information.

Amount of money in $ provided to managers

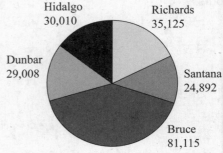

23. The owners of a business have decided to provide five of their regional managers with money that they can use as year-end bonuses for their employees. The circle graph (pie chart) shown above represents the amount of money in dollars the owners intend to provide to each of the managers for this purpose this year.

If a decision is made to take $20,000 of the money that had been intended for Bruce and instead give it to Dunbar, which of the following would be true?

I. The manager given the amount of money representing the median amount given to all five candidates would no longer be the same.

II. The average amount of money given to each of the managers would change.

III. The standard deviation of the amount of money given to all the managers would change.

IV. The range of the amount of money given to all the managers would change.

(A) I only
(B) I and II only
(C) II, III, and IV only
(D) I, III, and IV only

Go on to the next page. ⇨

24. The amount given to Santana represents a 10% increase from the amount he received a year ago, which was 5% more than the year before that. Which of the following represents the amount of money (in dollars) given to Santana two years ago?

(A) $0.85(24,892)$

(B) $\dfrac{24,892}{1.155}$

(C) $\dfrac{24,892}{1.15}$

(D) $1.15(24,892)$

25. A rectangular solid has dimensions of 2 feet × 2 feet × 1 foot. If it is sliced in small cubes, each of edge 0.1 foot, what is the maximum number of such cubes that can be formed?

(A) 40

(B) 1,000

(C) 2,000

(D) 4,000

26. The square in the figure below has two sides tangent to the circle. If the area of the circle is $9a^2\pi^2$, find the area of the square in terms of a and π.

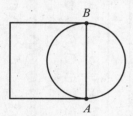

(A) $12a^2\pi^2$

(B) $36a^2\pi$

(C) $36a^2\pi^2$

(D) $18a^4\pi^2$

27. In $\triangle RST$ below, RS and ST have lengths equal to the same integer. All of the following could be the area of triangle RST *except*

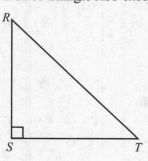

(A) 2

(B) $4\dfrac{1}{2}$

(C) $12\dfrac{1}{2}$

(D) 20

28. Equilateral polygon $ABCDEF$ is inscribed in the circle. If the length of arc BAF is 14π, find the length of the diameter of the circle.

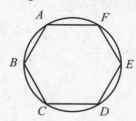

(A) 14

(B) 7π

(C) 21

(D) 42

29. The figure below shows part of the graph of a sine wave. Which of the following equations describes the sine wave?

(A) $y = \sin(x + 1)$

(B) $y = \sin x + 1$

(C) $y = 2\sin x + 1$

(D) $y = 2\left(\sin\dfrac{x}{2}\right) + 1$

30. If $f(x) = a^x$ then

(A) $f(x + y) = f(x) + f(y)$

(B) $f(x + y) = f(x)f(y)$

(C) $f(x - y) = f(x) - f(y)$

(D) $f(xy) = f(x)f(y)$

Go on to the next page. ⇨

Directions

For questions 31–38, solve the problem and enter your answer in the grid, as described below, on the answer sheet.

1. Although not required, it is suggested that you write your answer in the boxes at the top of the columns to help you fill in the circles accurately. You will receive credit only if the circles are filled in correctly.

2. Mark no more than one circle in any column.

3. No question has a negative answer.

4. Some problems may have more than one correct answer. In such cases, grid only one answer.

5. **Mixed numbers** such as $3\frac{1}{2}$ must be gridded as 3.5 or 7/2. (If "31/2" is entered into the grid, it will be interpreted as $\frac{31}{2}$, not $3\frac{1}{2}$.)

6. **Decimal answers:** If you obtain a decimal answer with more digits than the grid can accommodate, it may be either rounded or truncated, but it must fill the entire grid.

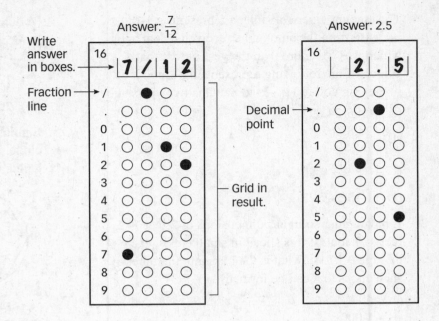

Answer: $\frac{7}{12}$ Answer: 2.5

Write answer in boxes.

Fraction line

Decimal point

Grid in result.

Acceptable ways to grid $\frac{2}{3}$ are:

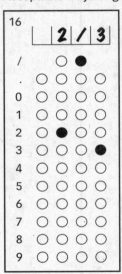
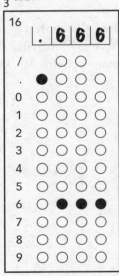
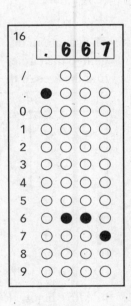

NOTE: You may start your answers in any column, space permitting. Columns you don't need to use should be left blank.

Answer: 201 – Either position is correct.

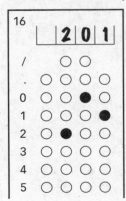
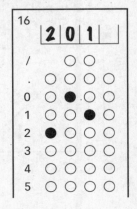

Go on to the next page. ⇨

31. There are 22 people on an island. A tram can carry at most 4 people at a time. What is the least number of trips that the tram must make to the mainland to get all the people to the mainland?

32. Given $3x + y = 17$ and $x + 3y = -1$, find the value of $3x + 3y$.

33. Natalie planned to buy some chocolate bars at 50 cents each but instead decided to purchase 30-cent chocolate bars. If she originally had enough money to buy 21 of the 50-cent bars, how many of the less expensive ones did she buy?

34. Let us define the operation $\odot$ as
$$a \odot b = (a + b)^2 - (a - b)^2$$
Find the value of $\sqrt{18} \odot \sqrt{2}$.

35. The figure below demonstrates that 5 straight lines can have 10 points of intersection. What is the maximum number of points of intersection of 4 straight lines?

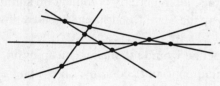

36. The number of degrees in one angle of a regular 8-sided polygon is how much more than the number of degrees in one angle of a regular 6-sided polygon?

37. If $\dfrac{3x - 1}{x - 1} = 3 + \dfrac{y}{x - 1}$, what is the value of y?

38. In the figure below, if sides LM and NM are cut apart from each other at point M, creating 2 free-swinging segments and each is folded down to LN in the directions shown by the arrows, what will be the length, in meters, of the overlap of the 2 segments? (Disregard the thickness of the segments.)

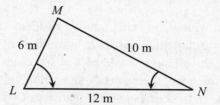

STOP!
If you finish before time is called, you may check your work on this section only.
Do not turn to any other section in the test.

SECTION 5: TEST 1 ESSAY *(OPTIONAL)*

50 Minutes

Turn to Section 5 of your answer sheet (pages 436–437) to write your essay.

Directions

Write an essay in which you explain how President Obama builds an argument to persuade his audience that constructing the pipeline would be a mistake. In your essay, analyze how Obama uses one or more of the features listed in the box below (or features of your own choice) to strengthen the logic and persuasiveness of his argument. Be sure that your analysis focuses on the most relevant features of the passage.

Your essay should not explain whether you agree with Obama's claims, but rather explain how Obama builds an argument to persuade his audience.

> As you read the passage below, consider how President Obama uses
> - evidence, such as facts or examples, to support claims.
> - reasoning to develop ideas and to connect claims and evidence.
> - stylistic or persuasive elements, such as word choice or appeals to emotion, to add power to the ideas expressed.

From President Barack Obama, "Statement by the President on the Keystone XL Pipeline." The speech was delivered at the White House on November 6, 2015.

Several years ago, the State Department began a review process for the proposed construction of a pipeline that would carry Canadian crude oil through our heartland to ports in the Gulf of Mexico and out into the world market.

This morning, Secretary Kerry informed me that, after extensive public outreach and consultation with other Cabinet agencies, the State Department has decided that the Keystone XL Pipeline would not serve the national interest of the United States. I agree with that decision.

Now, for years, the Keystone Pipeline has occupied what I, frankly, consider an overinflated role in our political discourse. It became a symbol too often used as a campaign cudgel by both parties rather than a serious policy matter. And all of this obscured the fact that this pipeline would neither be a silver bullet for the economy, as was promised by some, nor the express lane to climate disaster proclaimed by others.

To illustrate this, let me briefly comment on some of the reasons why the State Department rejected this pipeline.

First: The pipeline would not make a meaningful long-term contribution to our economy. So if Congress is serious about wanting to create jobs, this was not the way to do it. If they want to do it, what we should be doing is passing a bipartisan infrastructure plan that, in the short term, could create more than 30 times as many jobs per year as the pipeline would, and in the long run would benefit our economy and our workers for decades to come.

[Our businesses created 268,000 new jobs last month. They've created 13.5 million new jobs over the past 68 straight months—the longest streak on record. The pipeline would not have made a serious impact on those numbers and on the American people's prospects for the future.]

Second: The pipeline would not lower gas prices for American consumers. In fact, gas prices have already been falling—steadily. The national average gas price is down about 77 cents over a year ago. So while our politics have been consumed by a debate over whether or not this pipeline would create jobs and lower gas prices, we've gone ahead and created jobs and lowered gas prices.

Third: Shipping dirtier crude oil into our country would not increase America's energy security. What

Go on to the next page. ⇨

has increased America's energy security is our strategy over the past several years to reduce our reliance on dirty fossil fuels from unstable parts of the world. Three years ago, I set a goal to cut our oil imports in half by 2020. Between producing more oil here at home, and using less oil throughout our economy, we met that goal last year—five years early.

Now, the truth is, the United States will continue to rely on oil and gas as we transition—as we must transition—to a clean energy economy. That transition will take some time. But it's also going more quickly than many anticipated. Since I took office, we've doubled the distance our cars will go on a gallon of gas by 2025; tripled the power we generate from the wind; multiplied the power we generate from the sun 20 times over.

The old rules said we couldn't transition to clean energy without squeezing businesses and consumers. But this is America, and we have come up with new ways and new technologies to break down the old rules, so that today, homegrown American energy is booming, energy prices are falling, and over the past decade, even as our economy has continued to grow, America has cut our total carbon pollution more than any other country on Earth.

Today, the United States of America is leading on climate change with our investments in clean energy and energy efficiency. America is leading on climate change with new rules on power plants that will protect our air so that our kids can breathe. America is leading on climate change by working with other big emitters like China to encourage and announce new commitments to reduce harmful greenhouse gas emissions.

If we want to prevent the worst effects of climate change before it's too late, the time to act is now. Right here, right now. And I'm optimistic about what we can accomplish together. I'm optimistic because our own country proves, every day—one step at a time—that not only do we have the power to combat this threat, we can do it while creating new jobs, while growing our economy, while saving money, while helping consumers, and most of all, leaving our kids a cleaner, safer planet at the same time.

STOP!
If you finish before time is called, you may check your work on this section only.
Do not turn to any other section in the test.

HOW DID YOU DO ON THIS TEST?

Pages 476–477 will show you how to calculate your
scores on this test. Explanatory answers with strategies
and basic skills follow.

THERE'S ALWAYS ROOM
FOR IMPROVEMENT!

ANSWER KEY

Section 1: Reading Test Answers

1. D	14. B	27. D	40. C
2. A	15. C	28. A	41. A
3. C	16. D	29. C	42. B
4. C	17. D	30. B	43. C
5. B	18. A	31. A	44. D
6. B	19. B	32. D	45. A
7. B	20. B	33. C	46. C
8. A	21. C	34. A	47. A
9. D	22. A	35. D	48. C
10. C	23. D	36. B	49. A
11. C	24. A	37. B	50. A
12. D	25. D	38. C	51. A
13. A	26. D	39. D	52. C

Reading Test Raw Score
(number of correct answers) _____

Section 2: Writing and Language Test Answers

1. A	12. A	23. C	34. A
2. C	13. B	24. D	35. C
3. D	14. B	25. A	36. D
4. D	15. A	26. D	37. B
5. B	16. C	27. A	38. C
6. D	17. B	28. B	39. A
7. A	18. A	29. A	40. B
8. C	19. D	30. C	41. D
9. C	20. D	31. B	42. C
10. B	21. A	32. B	43. B
11. D	22. C	33. D	44. D

Writing and Language Test Raw Score *(number of correct answers)* _____

Section 3: Math Test Answers (No Calculator)

1. C	6. C	11. B	16. *
2. D	7. B	12. C	17. 60
3. D	8. B	13. D	18. 25
4. B	9. D	14. B	19. 65
5. D	10. D	15. A	20. 29

$* \frac{7}{24}, \frac{2}{7}, \frac{3}{10}, \frac{3}{11}$, or any number between .25 and .333

Math Test (No Calculator) Raw Score *(number of correct answers)* _____

Section 4: Math Test Answers (with Calculator)

1. D	11. B	21. D	31. 6
2. C	12. D	22. A	32. 12
3. D	13. A	23. D	33. 35
4. C	14. B	24. B	34. 24
5. B	15. D	25. D	35. 6
6. A	16. A	26. B	36. 15
7. C	17. A	27. D	37. 2
8. D	18. D	28. D	38. 4
9. C	19. B	29. D	
10. B	20. D	30. B	

Math Test (Calculator) Raw Score *(number of correct answers)* _____

RAW SCORE CONVERSION TABLE: SECTION AND TEST SCORES

Raw Score (# of correct answers)	Math Test Score	Reading Test Score	Writing and Language Test Score
0	200	10	10
1	200	10	10
2	210	10	10
3	230	11	10
4	240	12	11
5	260	13	12
6	280	14	13
7	290	15	13
8	310	15	14
9	320	16	15
10	330	17	16
11	340	17	16
12	360	18	17
13	370	19	18
14	380	19	19
15	390	20	19
16	410	20	20
17	420	21	21
18	430	21	21
19	440	22	22
20	450	22	23
21	460	23	23
22	470	23	24
23	480	24	25
24	480	24	25
25	490	25	26
26	500	25	26
27	510	26	27
28	520	26	28
29	520	27	28

Raw Score (# of correct answers)	Math Test Score	Reading Test Score	Writing and Language Test Score
30	530	28	29
31	540	28	30
32	550	29	30
33	560	29	31
34	560	30	32
35	570	30	32
36	580	31	33
37	590	31	34
38	600	32	34
39	600	32	35
40	610	33	36
41	620	33	37
42	630	34	38
43	640	35	39
44	650	35	40
45	660	36	
46	670	37	
47	670	37	
48	680	38	
49	690	38	
50	700	39	
51	710	40	
52	730	40	
53	740		
54	750		
55	760		
56	780		
57	790		
58	800		

CONVERSION EQUATION: SECTION AND TEST SCORES

Step 1. Using the table on the previous page, convert raw scores for Reading and for Writing and Language.

Reading Test Raw Score ⟶ Reading Test Score
(0–52)   (10–40)

_____ = _____

Writing and Language ⟶ Writing and Language
Test Raw Score   Test Score
(0–44)   (10–40)

_____ = _____

Step 2. Add Reading Test Score (10–40) and Writing and Language Test Score (10–40).

Reading Test Score _____

+ Writing and Language Test Score _____

= Reading and Writing Test Score _____

Step 3. Multiply combined Reading and Writing Test Score by 10 to get your Evidence-Based Reading and Writing Section Score (200–800).

Reading and Writing Test Score _____

× 10 _____

= Reading and Writing Section Score _____ *

Step 4. Add the two Math Scores.

Math Test Raw Score (No Calculator) (0–20) _____

+ Math Test Raw Score (Calculator) (0–38) _____

= Math Test Raw Score _____

Step 5. Using the table on the previous page, convert Math Test Raw Score to get your Math Section Score.

Math Test Raw Score ⟶ Math Section Score
(0–58)   (200–800)

_____ = _____ *

Step 6. Add the Evidence-Based Reading and Writing Section Score (200–800) and the Math Section Score (as marked by asterisks*) to get your Total SAT Score.

Reading and Writing Section Score _____

+ Math Section Score _____

= **TOTAL SAT SCORE** _____

EXPLANATORY ANSWERS

Section 1: Reading

As you read these Explanatory Answers, you are advised to refer to "13 Verbal Strategies" (beginning on page 123) whenever a specific strategy is referred to in the answer. Of particular importance is the Reading Comprehension Strategy 2 (page 135).

Note: All Reading questions use Reading Comprehension Strategies 1, 2, and 3 (pages 132–137) as well as other strategies indicated.

The Driving Lesson Answers

1. Choice D is correct. The passage begins by describing the office building, as well as Achal. This leads to an emotional exchange between Achal and Sylvia.

2. Choice A is correct. The author of the passage states that Achal "did want to 'earn' acceptance this way." He wanted to be accepted for reasons other than his military service.

3. Choice C is correct. Achal thinks of the parents of Punit and Lakshmi as "good people helplessly mired in the past" rather than people who can move forward and accept change that lies outside of the traditions they know. They were therefore "stalled" in the past.

4. Choice C is correct. The first paragraph shows that Achal is unsure of where he is. He also is forced to move quickly in the revolving door and is uncomfortable in the busy lobby. Furthermore, he wants to avoid the encounter with the guard in the lobby. He is clearly not at home (comfortable) in this situation.

5. Choice B is correct. The author states that Achal is in a state of "doubled annoyance." He is not comfortable with having Shirley as his instructor, but

he is also annoyed at himself for feeling this way. He is therefore conflicted.

6. Choice B is correct. The explanation to question 5 refers to this sentence.

7. Choice B is correct. Punit has said that "*Americans love to help. They long to show you that they have figured out everything that anyone should ever need to know.*" This implies that Americans have only "figured out" the kinds of things that *they* feel are important. Punit's tone is somewhat mocking; he clearly feels that Americans do not know many things, even if they don't think of these "other" things as being important.

8. Choice A is correct. There is tension between the two characters when they first meet. This clearly changes on the way to the car and then, most dramatically, in the car. They share their sadness about their lost brothers, and this sharing is emphasized by the fact that they're both sitting looking straight ahead with their hands on the steering wheels. Their physical positions are very similar.

9. Choice D is correct. The passage contains the line "He thought again of Punit, and of his brother's widow, Lakshmi, and how they had lost so much defying . . . the British authorities who controlled India." Punit was fighting so India could be liberated from (independent of) British rule.

10. Choice C is correct. The explanation to question 9 refers to this sentence.

11. Choice C is correct. The passage makes clear that Achal is uncomfortable with having a woman as his instructor. He does not quite know what to do and in his discomfort he looks at the man in the office as if he can help him out of the situation.

Answers for Passages 1 and 2

12. Choice D is correct. Line 1 ("To the world when it was half a thousand years younger . . .") indicates that the author is describing the world roughly five hundred years ago. Choice D—the year 1455—is therefore the closest date. Although Choice C is also in the Middle Ages, it is almost a thousand years ago. So it is an incorrect choice. Choices A and B are obviously incorrect choices.

13. Choice A is correct. We can see that "with greater avidity" is an adverbial phrase telling the reader how "honors and riches" were enjoyed and desired. See lines 16–19: "We, at the present day . . . formerly enjoyed." The reader thus learns that even simple pleasures such as a glass of wine were more keenly enjoyed then. Choices B, C, and D are incorrect because the passage does *not* state or imply that "with greater avidity" means "with greater sadness *or* terror *or* silence." See also **Reading Comprehension Strategy 5** (pages 139–140).

14. Choice B is not true—therefore it is the correct choice. See lines 40–42: "The contrast between silence and sound . . . than it is in our lives." The next sentence states that the modern town hardly knows silence. These two sentences together imply that the typical town of the Middle Ages did have periods of silence.

    Choice A is true—therefore an incorrect choice. See lines 33–34: "A medieval town . . . in extensive suburbs of factories and villas. . . ." Choice C is true—therefore an incorrect choice. See lines 35–36: ". . . it [a medieval town] stood forth . . . with innumerable turrets." Choice D is true—therefore an incorrect choice. See lines 38–39: ". . . the lofty mass of the churches always remained dominant."

15. Choice C is correct. Throughout Passage 1, the author is indicating the strong, rough, uncontrolled forces that pervaded the period. See, for example, the following references. Lines 10–11: "Misfortunes and poverty were more afflicting than at present. . . ." Lines 20–21: "Then, again, all things in life . . . cruel publicity." Lines 27–29: "Executions . . . songs and music." Therefore, Choice C is correct. Choice A is incorrect because the passage speaks of joys as well as miseries. See lines 16–19: "We, at the present day . . . formerly enjoyed." Choice

B is incorrect for this reason: Although the author contrasts town and country, he gives no indication as to which was dominant in that society. Therefore, Choice B is incorrect. Choice D is incorrect. The author contrasts how it felt to be rich or poor, but he does not indicate that the rich mistreated the poor.

16. Choice D is correct. See lines 5–7: "All experience . . . pain of child life." Throughout the passage, this theme is illustrated with specific examples. Choice A is incorrect because it is one-sided. In the passage, many conditions that may make the Middle Ages seem worse than today are matched with conditions that may make the Middle Ages seem better than today. Choice B is incorrect because nowhere in the passage is intelligence mentioned or implied. Choice C is incorrect because the third paragraph indicates that, far from being subdued, people went about their lives with a great deal of show and pageantry.

17. Choice D is correct. The overall mood of the passage is optimistic: "this wonderful age" (line 91). The author is hopeful for the future, although he qualifies his outlook by noting some uncertainty (lines 92–98).

18. Choice A is correct. The author immediately explains what he means by the assertion "Thought has become virtually cosmopolitan" when he states that new ideas and discoveries become "immediately the common possession of the world" (lines 76–77). Thus "ideas" is linked with technological progress and discovery, not personal, philosophical, or religious "beliefs" (Choices B and C). The new rapidity of communication may encourage others to "steal" these discoveries (Choice D), but nowhere does the passage refer to that possibility.

19. Choice B is correct. Most of the inventions and advancements listed in the passage, including the "prominent" ones—steam navigation, railroads, and telegraphs (lines 64–65)—have brought "the most remote parts of the earth together" (lines 72–73). Choices A and C are incorrect because these areas are not mentioned or are only indirectly alluded to. Choice D, "moral and intellectual development," is incorrect; the author refers to it as a possible future area of progress (lines 97–98), not a current one.

20. Choice B is correct. Choice B is the best choice because the groups benefiting from a new "solidarity of commercial interests" are found across the "world" (lines 73–74), implying other nations. The author also mentions Japan, Britain, and the earlier Roman civilization (lines 86–89). None of the other "groups" in Choices A, C, and D is either implied or specifically indicated.

21. Choice C is correct. The author specifically states at the beginning of Passage 1's second paragraph (lines 10–11) that "Misfortunes and poverty were more afflicting than at present." Since the modern world includes the late nineteenth century to the present day, this is the best answer. Choice A is incorrect; lines 7–9 suggest that "every event, every action, was still embodied in expressive and solemn forms, which raised them to the dignity of a ritual." Choice B is incorrect because the author of Passage 2 looks forward to the future with hope and enthusiasm (lines 97–98). Choice D is incorrect because there I no mention of the earth's being "overpopulated" in Passage 2.

22. Choice A is correct. The entire emphasis of Passage 1 is on the great contrasts that marked people's experience of everyday life during the Middle Ages, including those related to the tribalism of small communities and their loyalty to local lords (lines 23–32). Passage 2 highlights the advancements in communication and travel that, "by bringing men together, and familiarizing them with new scenes and different forms of society and belief, have made them more liberal and tolerant" (lines 77–80). Choice B is incorrect because the passages do not address the issue of moral superiority; don't fall into the trap of choosing the answer based on your opinion instead of the facts presented. While Choices C and D may be true, there is no information within Passage 2 that would allow one to conclude that the nineteenth-century world was any less violent or less religious than the world of the Middle Ages depicted in Passage 1.

23. Choice D is correct. Passage 1 emphasizes the contrasts in life during the Middle Ages; lines 10–19 particularly highlight the wide contrasts between, and vulnerability to, the personal experience of everyday life. Passage 2, by contrast, looks back a mere fifty years (to the mid to late nineteenth century) and marvels at the rapid progress in technology that has led to increased tolerance (line 80). Moreover, the author of Passage 2 expresses the hope that moral and intellectual progress may be expected in the future (lines 97–98). Choices A and B are incorrect because Passage 1 does not refer to transportation technology or to the effects of technological progress on social classes—only Passage 2 does that. Choice C is incorrect because neither passage indicates that the future mirrors the past, and in fact the author of Passage 2 asserts that "The battles now being waged in the religious and the political world are only faint echoes of the great battles of the sixteenth, seventeenth, and eighteenth centuries" (lines 53–56). In addition, a comparison of the two passages' depictions of their historical periods reveals stark contrasts between these two epochs.

About Behaviorism Answers

24. Choice A is correct. See lines 74–75: ". . . as Dr. Skinner argues, that one can extrapolate from pigeons to people. . . ." Choice B is incorrect because, though Skinner agrees that introspection may be of some use (lines 15–18), nowhere does the article indicate that he suggests wide use of the introspective method. Choice C is incorrect since Skinner, so the author says (lines 77–79), "has not satisfactorily rebutted the basic criticism that behaviorism 'is scientistic rather than scientific.'" Choice D is incorrect because lines 84–86 state that "Skinner predicts . . . impending disaster."

25. Choice D is correct. Choice A is incorrect. See lines 12–15: ". . . an earlier stage of . . . influence of mentalism." Choice B is incorrect. See lines 62–66: "It is a veritable . . . to external stimuli." Choice C is incorrect since mentalism evolved before methodological and radical behaviorism. See lines 10–18: "What such people . . . its possible usefulness." Choice D is correct. The passage, from line 67 to the end, brings out weaknesses in Skinner's presentation.

26. Choice D is correct. Skinner, in lines 26–27, says ". . . few would contend that behavior is 'endlessly malleable.'" Also, see lines 36–43: "Contingencies of reinforcement . . . likely to occur." Skinner is saying that behavior cannot always, by plan or design, be altered or influenced; behavior must depend, to some extent, on the element of chance.

27. Choice D is correct. Skinner is known for his experiments with pigeons. Also, rats have been used frequently by behaviorists in experimentation. See lines 67–76. In addition, see lines 38–40: "In both natural . . . is crucial." The other choices are not relevant to Darwin or his work.

28. Choice A is correct. From the context in the rest of the sentence where *extrapolate* appears, Choice A fits best. Note that the word *extrapolate* is derived from the Latin *extra* (outside) and *polire* (to polish). See also **Reading Comprehension Strategy 5** (pages 139–140).

29. Choice C is correct. Choice A is incorrect because Choice A is true according to line 15. Choice B is incorrect because Choice B is true according to lines 67–73. Choice C is correct because Choice C is *not* true according to lines 68–72. Choice D is incorrect because Choice D is true according to lines 9–18.

30. Choice B is correct. Choice A is incorrect; see lines 19–22: ". . . to those who object . . . Skinner expresses puzzlement." Choice B is correct because Skinner, a radical behaviorist, though believing that environmental influences are highly important in shaping human behavior, nevertheless states in lines 36–40: "Contingencies of reinforcement . . . [are] crucial." Operant conditioning is, according to behaviorists, a vital aspect of learning. Choice C is incorrect. Although Skinner accepts introspection (lines 16–18) as part of his system, nowhere does he place primary importance on introspection. Choice D is incorrect. Though Skinner may agree with this choice, nowhere in the passage does he state or imply this opinion. The word *malleable* means capable of being shaped or formed—from the Latin *malleare*, meaning "to hammer." The quote in the stem of the question says, in effect, that few people would say that behavior can always be shaped.

31. Choice A is correct. I is correct; see lines 83–84. II is incorrect; don't be fooled by what is in lines 79–82. It does not refer to *scientistic* areas. III is incorrect; see lines 79–82.

32. Choice D is correct. Given the context, *veritable* means "true." One may also note the "ver" in "veritable" and may associate that with the word *verify*, which means "to prove to be true." This is

the association strategy, which can be used to figure out clues to meanings of words. See also **Reading Comprehension Strategy 5** (pages 139–140).

Self-Reliance Answers

33. Choice C is correct. The theme of this essay, "Self-Reliance," by the American writer Ralph Waldo Emerson (1803–1882), is expressed in various other ways throughout the essay. For example: in referring to the independence of opinion that one loses with one's loss of early youth; in condemning our surrender of the freedom of solitude to the group actions of society at large; and in encouraging us not to fear the consequences of being inconsistent and misunderstood.

34. Choice A is correct. The infant can be, and is expected to be, completely irresponsible. "Infancy conforms to nobody: all conform to it, so that one babe commonly makes four or five out of the adults who prattle and play to it."

35. Choice D is correct. "Speak what you think now in hard words, and to-morrow speak what to-morrow thinks in hard words again, though it contradict everything you said to-day." The misunderstanding will occur because what you say may be the opposite of conventional opinion, or may be ahead of its time. But the risk is worth it.

36. Choice B is correct. It is a natural prerogative of youth to give "an independent, genuine verdict." He cares little about what older people may think because "It seems he knows how to speak to his contemporaries. Bashful or bold, then, he will know how to make us seniors very unnecessary."

37. Choice B is correct. The "pit" or gallery in a theater usually contains the least expensive seats. Consequently, it is favored by those less economically endowed, and, according to the author, less committed to conventional manners and highly dignified behavior. In effect, these are the people who go to the theater to see, rather than to be seen.

38. Choice C is correct. When people desert solitude (or individual action) to join society (group action), they surrender a large part of individual freedom in exchange for a livelihood. They thus become more reliant and dependent on others than on themselves.

The metaphor of the joint-stock company is a good one because such a company is faceless and without identity. No one member stands out above any other member.

39. Choice D is correct. "Spirit and enthusiasm" are something individualistic and definite. To be spirited and enthusiastic is to be spontaneous, natural, and uninhibited. One must (according to the author) be committed and courageous "As soon as he has once acted or spoken with eclat. . . ."

40. Choice C is correct. To act out of whim is to act impulsively and in an unpremeditated, spontaneous (and generally sincere) manner. The author, however, is not endorsing *whimsical* action simply because it is uninhibited ("I hope it is somewhat better than whim at last, but we cannot spend the day in explanation"), but because it is a way of speaking freely, and usually with complete honesty.

41. Choice A is correct. The essence of self-reliance and nonconformity is, as Shakespeare put it, "To thine own self be true." If one is dishonest with oneself, one will be dishonest with others; if one is honest with oneself, one will be honest with others.

Birdsong Answers

42. Choice B is correct. The paragraph refers to "experiments" and "findings," that have led to research regarding the "neural pathways that allow a juvenile bird to learn." These pathways (AFP and PDP) are then described in the following paragraph.

43. Choice C is correct. The word *plastic* is used here in the sense of *flexible* or *changeable*. The bird's song will "ultimately . . . *crystallize* as the bird becomes capable of emitting a consistent order of sounds." Therefore the song is not yet consistent.

44. Choice D is correct. According to the passage, "The PDP, which literally descends into the trachea, makes it *physically possible for a bird to sing* throughout its life. Messages travel from a level of the PDP called the HVC (high vocal area) and eventually to the other parts of the brain involved in the song system, **including the nerve that controls the contractions of the syrinx**." The author therefore connects the PDP (not the AFT, which is linked to "procedural learning") to messages that control the physical contractions of the bird's syrinx.

45. Choice A is correct. The sentences referred to in the explanation to question 44 include this line.

46. Choice C is correct. The passage makes a comparison between "the manner and speed at which [people] learn language" and the "learning modes" of birds. The word *mode* is used here as a parallel to "manner" or "method" of learning.

47. Choice A is correct. According to the passage, "in the desert regions of Australia and Africa, females are just as likely to sing." Earlier in the passage, the author makes it clear that singing is done, at least in part, to attract "potential mates." These statements lend strength to the idea that in regions without much rain—such as deserts—there's a reason why males *and* females sing—they both need to be actively looking for mates.

48. Choice C is correct. In the first paragraph, the author refers to the "mammalian larynx, which is found at the top of the trachea" and in the fourth paragraph to a bird's "PDP, which literally descends into the trachea."

49. Choice A is correct. The first paragraph clear that the reason a bird can sing at all is because of its syrinx. We are told that "birds that vocalize (not all birds do)" . . . use their "finely-tuned" syrinx. The author then discusses the advanced singing styles of birds that have a split syrinx. Clearly, a non-singing bird such as a stork would not have a finely-tuned, well-developed syrinx.

50. Choice A is correct. The sentences referred to in the explanation to question 49 include this line.

51. Choice A is correct. According to the table, by day 85, the zebra finch will be in the latter stages of its sensorimotor period. While the sub-song period comes at the beginning of this stage, the plastic song, in which "species-specific sounds . . . become recognizable" comes later, shortly before the sounds completely crystallize into the full, accurately reproduced song.

52. Choice C is correct. According to the table, the canary will achieve crystallization (mastery) of its song in the spring a year or so after it has hatched. This process may then repeat as a new song is learned that same spring.

EXPLANATORY ANSWERS

Section 2: Writing and Language

For further practice and information, please refer to Grammar and Usage Refresher starting on page 325.

The Role of Celebrities Answers

1. Choice A is correct. The pronoun "their" clearly refers back to the plural noun "celebrities." Choice B uses the singular (possessive) pronoun "its," but there is no singular noun for it to replace. Choice C refers to "*the* cultures" without making clear what those specific cultures might be. Choice D uses the possessive form of "one," but there is no noun that "one" is clearly replacing.

2. Choice C is correct. The conjunction "and" is all that is needed to connect the two parts of the sentence, each of which is an independent clause. The author states two things: Celebrities are more famous than those of the past *and* the number of celebrities has multiplied. Choices A and D create a comma splice—two independent clauses connected only by a comma. This is not allowed. In addition, "however" implies that there is some sort of contrast between the first and second clause, and this is not the case. Also, both "this is because" and "since" (choice B) imply that the second part of the sentence is the *cause* of the first part, and this too is not the case.

3. Choice D is correct. The correct sentence should lead the reader from the earlier paragraph, which discussed present-day celebrities, to this paragraph, which discusses celebrities from the past. This choice says that fame is not new, and then gives some general information relevant to that claim. Choice A makes an irrelevant comparison to popularity and ethics, something that is not discussed in the paragraph. Choice B incorrectly indicates that the paragraph will focus only on "people who took power by force." Choice C implies that the paragraph will focus on the manner in which people expressed themselves in the past; there is no mention of celebrities at all in this choice.

4. Choice D is correct. A conjunction is needed to join the final item in the list to the earlier two, and *or* does the job. The use of *even* emphasizes the surprising fact that notoriety (fame for bad behavior) would be on this list. Choice A does not use any kind of conjunction to connect the final item in the list to the earlier two. Choices B and C use the conjunction *but*, but this word serves no purpose in the list. In addition, *but* is typically used to connect only two parts of a sentence. Adding the word *of*, as in choice C, does nothing to improve the misuse of *but*.

5. Choice B is correct. "*I too can achieve success and renown*" is a viewpoint, so it is correct to separate it from the modifier (description) that follows—"a viewpoint especially prevalent today . . ."—with only a comma. Choice A incorrectly omits the comma needed to join "*I too can achieve success and renown*" to the modifying phrase that follows. Choice C uses the plural noun "viewpoints," but only one viewpoint is given. Choice D confuses the meaning by placing "on the one hand" in a location that doesn't clearly link it to a later point made "on the other hand."

6. Choice D is correct. The "values" mentioned in this sentence does refer to the "ideals" and "principles" mentioned in the previous sentence, but the fact that these values are not enshrined in law in some places is irrelevant to the paragraph (and the passage). Choices A, B, and C are incorrect because they inaccurately describe the sentence.

7. Choice A is correct. The word *who* clearly refers to "authorities" and the verb "possess" agrees with the plural subject of the verb—"authorities." Choice B incorrectly uses the prepositional phrase "of whom" without linking it to any other part of the sentence. Choice C incorrectly combines "possession" and "with." Choice D incorrectly forms the phrase "possessed of magical abilities to protect," which has no clear meaning.

8. Choice C is correct. The people described have magical abilities to "protect." Choice C implies that they might have "all" the answers to everyone's problems, a task that would be impossible for someone lacking magical powers. A political or religious figure in possession of all the answers would naturally be able to protect others. Choice A is too vague and mild to describe people of this sort. Choice B and D make no reference to "protection."

9. Choice C is correct. There is no need for any punctuation. "Suspects" is often followed by "that." In this example, "The individual suspects that he or she . . ." is clear. Choice A uses a colon, which typically is used following an independent clause in order to introduce a series of items or an explanation to demonstrate a preceding general statement. Choice B uses a dash when there is no need for this sort of "interrupting" punctuation. Choice D incorrectly uses the plural pronoun "they" to replace the singular "individual."

10. Choice B is correct. This sentence describes the beneficial role of celebrities, preceded by the word *However*. This implies that the statement preceding this one should indicate a non-beneficial (negative) aspect of celebrity. Sentence 2 provides this negative aspect. The remainder of the paragraph is all positive, so it makes sense to start with the negative sentence and then state "However" and continue with the benefits of celebrity. Choice A, C, and D are incorrect because each results in an illogical sentence progression. Sentence 1 *introduces* the beneficial aspects of celebrity by contrasting it with its "dangers" through the use of the word *However*. This sentence should therefore come before sentences 3, 4, and 5.

11. Choice D is correct. The focus of this paragraph is that, though celebrity can be a bad thing, it is "generally beneficial." Paragraph 5 also deals with beneficial aspects, and begins with "*Even* a fixation . . . can reap positive results." The word *even* implies that other positive features of celebrity have already been discussed. Without paragraph 6 placed between paragraphs 4 and 5, those two paragraphs have no logical connection. Choices A, B, and C are incorrect because each proposes a placement of paragraph 6 that prevents the entire passage from developing in a clear and logical order.

Forcing Mechanisms Answers

12. Choice A is correct. The meaning of the sentence is that the role humans play in altering the climate gets the most attention and *understandably* gets the most attention. The word *so* stands in for "gets the most attention." Choice B incorrectly places a comma between *understandably* and the word it is modifying—*so*. Choice C compounds this mistake by also changing the adverb *understandably* into the adjective *understandable*. Choice D results in the conjunction *and* connecting two parts of the sentence so that there is no longer a logical completion to the phrase that began with *while*.

13. Choice B is correct. The subject of this verb is both *rapid shifts in ocean currents and increased glacial melting* and so we need "have" to agree with this plural (compound) subject. Choice A incorrectly uses the singular "has." Choice C switches to the "ing" form (leading), thus depriving the subject of *any* verb. Choice D uses a future tense ("will lead") to refer to a past event.

14. Choice B is correct. The sentence before mentions the Great Oxygenation Event (GOE) without describing what that is. The sentence after states that the poisonous oxygen caused a large extinction. The underlined sentence explains how the bacteria-producing oxygen during the GOE would have led to that extinction. Choices A, C, and D are incorrect because they inaccurately describe the sentence in question.

15. Choice A is correct. This choice makes it clear that "past levels are comparable to (similar to) present levels." Choice B and C indicate only that the levels are just compared to each other, not that they are similar (comparable) to each other. Choice D makes it sound as though the levels are somehow themselves "comparing" something.

16. Choice C is correct. The information that follows refers to the results of short-term solar cycling, and this choice introduces short solar cycles. Choice A introduces solar flares, but the following sentence does not directly refer to them. Choice B provides broad background information that is not relevant at this point in the passage. Choice D in no way leads to the topic presented in the following sentence.

17. Choice B is correct. There is no reason for any punctuation separating "Serbian geophysicist" from his name. Choice A needlessly places a comma between the description of the man and his name, while choice C needlessly uses a colon. Choice D needlessly puts his nationality within parentheses.

18. Choice A is correct. The phrase "a host of" means "quite a few," which works perfectly in this context. Choice B would lead to "much issues" rather than "many issues," which would have been correct. Choice C leads to "numbers of issues" rather than "a number of issues," which would have been correct. Choice D leads to "a quantity of issues," a phrase that has no special meaning other than "some number of issues."

19. Choice D is correct. The phrase between dashes is an interruption; it can be taken out of the sentence without harming the sentence structure. Choice A incorrectly uses the phrase "especially *with* the burning of fossil fuels. The word *with* has no meaning in this context. Choice B incorrectly uses one dash and one comma to separate a phrase from the rest of the sentence. Choice C incorrectly places *especially* between *burning* and *of*.

20. Choice D is correct. By stating "of the change," the author makes clear that he or she is referring to the negative consequences of the change. Choices A,

B, and C use pronouns (*this*, *them*, and *those*) that do not clearly refer back to "change." Choice B and C are, in fact, plural, while "change" is singular.

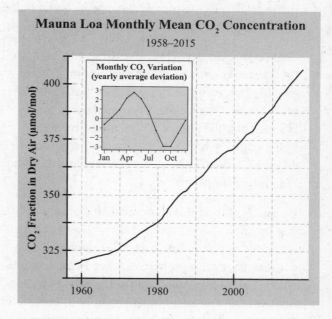

21. Choice B is correct. Looking at the larger graph, the CO_2 fraction in dry air value for 1970 appears to be very close to 325, and for 1980 appears to be very close to a point halfway between 325 and 350, which would be 337.5. This increase from 325 to 337.5 is 12.5, or about 12. The other choices are not as close to the actual increase as is Choice A.

22. Choice C is correct. Looking at the smaller graph (labeled Monthly CO_2 Variation), each point represents the "Departure from yearly average" value for a particular month. The point for March has a value of 1, and July's point is only slightly less than 1. The pairs of points in the other choices do not have values that are as close to each other as March's and July's values are.

Music Appreciation Answers

23. Choice C is correct. We need a verb tense that indicates that the author's habit existed in the past and still exists. Also, since "habit" is singular, it has to agree with the singular form of the verb. Therefore, the author's habit "has been" to attend concerts, with at least etc. Choice A puts the author's habit into the past, as if it's not ongoing, even though the author says "for many years *now*." Choice B also

puts the action into the past and also uses the plural form "were," though "habit" is singular. Choice D correctly indicates that the action is ongoing but incorrectly uses the plural "have been," which does not agree with "habit."

24. Choice D is correct. The author wants to "acquire" (get) knowledge, and the correct idiom is "interested in" acquiring. Choice A uses "interested with," which has no real meaning here. Choice B states that the author is "interested by taking knowledge," which also has no clear meaning. Choice C, like Choice A, incorrectly uses the idiom "interested with."

25. Choice A is correct. The dependent clause that begins after "the rules of tonality," should be separated from the first part of the sentence by a comma, as is the case here. Choice B uses a semicolon, but a semicolon joins independent clauses (clauses that can stand independently as complete sentences). Only the first part of this sentence is an independent clause, so the use of the semicolon is incorrect. Choice C places "of course" in an inappropriate place in the sentence, not clearly connecting this phrase to anything else. Choice D lacks a comma after "Arnold Schoenberg." A comma is generally needed after a person's name if it is then followed by a description of that person, as is the case here.

26. Choice D is correct. The phrase "each playing a variety of instruments" should be surrounded by a pair of commas, as is often the case when a phrase can be taken out of a sentence without disturbing its grammar. This choice provides the second comma. Choices A, B, and C lack the comma needed after "each playing a variety of instruments." This results in the absurd sense that the instrumentalists each played a female singer as well as several instruments.

27. Choice A is correct. Choice A uses a semicolon, and a semicolon joins independent clauses (clauses that can stand independently as complete sentences). Both parts of this sentence are independent clauses, so the semicolon use is correct. Choices B and D use a comma rather than a semicolon to connect two independent clauses. Choice C makes it

sound as though "the traditional sense uses a style that falls between speech and song . . .," which is clearly not what the author means.

28. Choice B is correct. The word *and* is all that is needed here to connect the final item in this list. Choice A uses the phrase " a regular pulse laying down," which has no definite meaning. Choice C uses *or*, though there is no choice between things (this *or* that) in the sentence. Choice D incorrectly states the final item in the list without a connecting conjunction such as *and*.

29. Choice A is correct. The use of *as*, makes it clear that the author's mind was wandering at the same time that the author looked around and flipped through the program. Choice B uses a comma to incorrectly connect two independent clauses. Choice C illogically uses *though* to connect the two parts. This sounds as though the author's mind was wandering *even though* the author looked around, etc. Choice D incorrectly uses a comma where none is needed.

30. Choice C is correct. The word *better* is used to show the that author's understanding of the logic of the piece was "better." This is not made clear in choice C, in which it sounds as though the "logic" was better, not the "understanding."

31. Choice B is correct. The author states that his or her appreciation of the piece changed. Then the author gives three examples of this. The underlined sentence is the third example of this. Choices A, C, and D are incorrect because they inaccurately describe the sentence.

32. Choice B is correct. Sentence 1 refers to "this most demanding of my senses." The meaning of this is not clear unless the sentence is preceded by sentence 3, which refers to the author's sight. Choice A, C, and D do not provide the information that is needed prior to sentence 1.

33. Choice D is correct. This choice makes clear that the author's meaning. The author doubts that *Pierrot* will be a favorite composition, *but* the author enjoyed the performance *and* as with any encounter with great art, the author's life has been

enriched and his or her tastes have broadened. Choice A begins with "As with any encounter with a great work of art, I doubt that I'll ever consider *Pierrot* among my favorite compositions," but there is no clear connection between these phrases. Choice B makes the meaning of the sentence unclear by leaving out "but," which shows that the author's life has been enriched *but* the piece will probably not be a favorite. In Choice C, the author "[doubts] that I'll ever consider that . . . *Pierrot* to be among my favorite composition." The two uses of "that" are incorrect.

Politics as a Career Questions

34. Choice A is correct. The semicolon correctly combines the two independent clauses. Choice B illogically suggests that it is the public that wants to join the ranks, etc. This is especially confusing given the question mark at the end of the sentence. Choice C incorrectly uses a colon after the conjunction *so*. Choice D incorrectly uses the objective "whom," when the subjective "who" is needed because it is followed by a verb ("would want").

35. Choice C is correct. After the first word of the sentence, negative consequences of running for political office are mentioned. This comes after the opening paragraph, which also mentions negative consequences (of holding political office). It therefore makes sense to join these two paragraphs with a "furthermore," indicating "here are more negatives." Choice A incorrectly implies that the following statement can be concluded *because* of the previous one. Choice B uses a word that means "despite this," which would be appropriate only if the following statement somehow were surprising or unusual given the previous statement. Choice D would be appropriate only if the author were clearly using a list. However there is no mention of a "first" or "third" item.

36. Choice D is correct. The author has already made it clear that the politician has to repeat "the whole process," which includes raising funds. Choices A, B, and C are incorrect because they inaccurately describe the sentence in question.

37. Choice B is correct. After first discussing the possible obstacles involved in getting elected, the author then poses possible problems even if one easily gets into office. The word *sails* in this context implies that getting elected was not a problem. Choices B and C use idioms that are not appropriate. One does not "rise into office" or "move into office." Choice D is somewhat more idiomatic but lacks the sense that one *easily* got elected.

38. Choice C is correct. The meaning of the sentence is clear. The first part of the sentence ("While x is true") leads logically from the previous paragraph into the second part of this sentence ("career politicians generally report . . ."). Choice A incorrectly places the phrase "while there is some truth to all of the above" in a location that needlessly separates the sentence's main subject and verb, thus confusing the sentence's meaning. Choice B places the phrase "though there is some truth to all of the above things" at the end of the sentence rather than immediately at the beginning, where it would more clearly refer to the previously described negative elements involved in running for and holding public office. Furthermore, the use of the word *things* is awkward. Choice D is not a complete sentence; there is no verb attached to "career politicians."

39. Choice A is correct. The phrase "admired and even held in awe by members of the public" clearly refers to "people in positions of power." Choice B does not make clear who is "admiring" whom. There is no clear subject of the verb "is" used in Choice C. The *people* are admired, not the "power." Choice D uses the pronoun *which*, but this word refers to the word immediately before it—power. This sounds as though "the power are admired," which makes no sense.

40. Choice B is correct. The sentence begins with the modifying phrase "Using the Internet," an action clearly performed by the subject (actor), which comes next—the campaign fund-raisers. In other words, the sentence could also read "Campaign fund-raisers, using the Internet. . . ." Choices A and C make it sound as though "large sums" are using the Internet. Choice D confusingly makes it sound

as though the candidate has, using the Internet, campaign fund-raisers that can generate. . . ." The candidate does not *have* these fund-raisers by using the Internet.

41. Choice D is correct. This avoids any of the pronoun problems found in the other choices. Choices A and B incorrectly use the plural "they" to refer to "the typical voter," which is singular. Choice C incorrectly uses "it" to refer to a person (the voter).

42. Choice C is correct. This paragraph begins by referring to the important work done by local officials. The author then admits that the pay isn't as high as it is for others but that these local positions do offer other meaningful rewards, such as "the satisfaction of seeing firsthand the contributions you've made to the lives of the people you know best." Choices A and B do not clearly follow from the first sentence, which refers to the importance of the work done by local officials. Choice D goes too far in saying that local officials are more important to democracy. This broad statement is nowhere supported in the passage.

43. Choice B is correct. The author states that the political environment seems polarized (sharply divided), but progress is still possible (not impossible). Choice A implies that progress can be "done," but there is no clear meaning to "doing progress." Similarly, progress cannot be "closed" as in Choice C, and progress cannot be "not anymore," as in Choice D.

44. Choice D is correct. This paragraph follows the pattern first established in paragraph 4, which starts to discuss the positive aspects of a career in politics by saying that there are problems *but*. . . ." Paragraph 5 continues this discussion, using the construction "Yes . . . but," after which it makes sense to place paragraph 7, which also uses this construction. The final paragraph will now be Paragraph 6, which no longer uses the "yes, but" pattern and instead brings up a new topic—locally elected officials. Choices A, B, and C are incorrect because each proposes a placement of paragraph 7 that prevents the entire passage from developing in a clear and logical order.

EXPLANATORY ANSWERS

Section 3: Mathematics, *No Calculator*

As you read these solutions, you are advised to do two things if you answered a math question incorrectly:

1. *When a specific Math Strategy is referred to in the solution, study that strategy, which you will find in "19 Math Strategies" (beginning on page 72).*

2. *When the solution directs you to the "Complete SAT Math Refresher" (beginning on page 163)—for example, Math Refresher #305—study the math principle to get a clear idea of the math operation that you needed to know in order to answer the question correctly.*

1. **Choice C is correct.**

   Given: ab = 64 and a and b are
       positive integers   ⬛1

   (Use Strategy 7: Use numerics to help find the answer.)

   If $a = 64$, $b = 1$, then ⬛1 is satisfied
      and $a + b = 65$ ⬛2
   If $a = 32$, $b = 2$, then ⬛1 is satisfied
      and $a + b = 34$ ⬛3
   If $a = 16$, $b = 4$, then ⬛1 is satisfied
      and $a + b = 20$ ⬛4
   If $a = 8$, $b = 8$, then ⬛1 is satisfied
      and $a + b = 16$ ⬛5

   The only other pairs of values that satisfy ⬛1 are each of the above pairs of values reversed for a and b. Thus ⬛5 , $a + b = 16$, is the smallest value of $a + b$.

   (Math Refresher #406)

2. **Choice D is correct.**

   (Use Strategy 8: When all choices must be tested, start with the last choice and work backward.)

   Since we must check all the choices, we should start with the last choice (here, Choice D). Clearly, if x is the point whose coordinates are (5,2), then $m\angle MXN = 90°$ and Choice D must be correct.

   (Math Refresher #410b)

3. **Choice D is correct.**

   Given: Temperature at 11:00 A.M. = 0°F   ⬛1
            Temperature at 8:00 A.M. = −15°F   ⬛2
   Let x = Temperature at 5:00 P.M.   ⬛3
      y = Temperature rise   ⬛4

   (Use Strategy 13: Find unknowns by subtracting.)

   Subtract ⬛2 from ⬛1 . We get
       Temperature rise in 3 hours = 15°F   ⬛5
   Subtract the times in ⬛1 and ⬛3 . We get
       Time change = 6 hours   ⬛6
   Use ⬛4 , ⬛5 , and ⬛6 to find temperature rise from 11:00 A.M. to 5:00 P.M. We get

   $$\frac{3 \text{ hours}}{6 \text{ hours}} = \frac{15°F}{y}$$
   $$3y = 6 \times 15°F$$
   $$y = 30°F \qquad ⬛7$$

   Use ⬛1 , ⬛3 , and ⬛7 to find the final temperature.
   $$x = 0°F + 30°F$$
   $$x = 30°F$$

   (Math Refresher #120)

4. Choice B is correct.

(Use Strategy 17: Use the given information effectively.)

Slope is defined as

$\dfrac{y_2 - y_1}{x_2 - x_1}$ where (x_1, y_1) is a point on the line and (x_2, y_2) is another point on the line. We are given that one point is $(0, p)$ and the other point is $(3p, 0)$ so,

$$\frac{y_2 - y_1}{x_2 - x_1} = \frac{p - 0}{0 - 3p} = \frac{p}{-3p} = -\frac{1}{3}$$

(Math Refresher #416)

5. Choice D is correct.

(Use Strategy 5: Know how to manipulate averages.)

We know that

$$\text{Average} = \frac{\text{sum of values}}{\text{total number of values}} \qquad \boxed{1}$$

Given: Average of k scores is 20 $\boxed{2}$

Substitute $\boxed{2}$ into $\boxed{1}$. We get

$$20 = \frac{\text{sum of } k \text{ scores}}{k}$$

$$20k = \text{sum of } k \text{ scores} \qquad \boxed{3}$$

Given: Average of 10 of these scores is 15. $\boxed{4}$

Substitute $\boxed{4}$ into $\boxed{1}$. We have

$$15 = \frac{\text{sum of 10 scores}}{10}$$

$$150 = \text{sum of 10 scores} \qquad \boxed{5}$$

There are $k - 10$ scores remaining. $\boxed{6}$

(Use Strategy 3: The whole equals the sum of its parts.)

We know: sum of 10 scores + sum of remaining scores = sum of k scores $\boxed{7}$

Substituting $\boxed{3}$ and $\boxed{5}$ into $\boxed{7}$, we get

150 + sum of remaining scores = $20k$

sum of remaining scores = $20k - 150$ $\boxed{8}$

Substituting $\boxed{6}$ and $\boxed{8}$ into $\boxed{1}$, we get

$$\text{Average of remaining scores} = \frac{20k - 150}{k - 10}$$

(Math Refresher #601)

6. Choice C is correct.

(Use Strategy 2: Translate from words into algebra.)

Set up a Venn diagram:

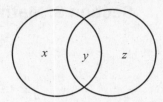

x = number of students with *only* a car

z = number of students with *only* a bicycle

y = number of students having a car and a bicycle

Total students = 100 $\boxed{1}$

We are given: $x + y = 30$ $\boxed{2}$

$z + y = 50$ $\boxed{3}$

$y = 20$ $\boxed{4}$

Substituting $\boxed{4}$ into $\boxed{2}$ and into $\boxed{3}$, we get

$$x = 10, z = 30 \qquad \boxed{5}$$

Using $\boxed{4}$ and $\boxed{5}$, we have:

The sum of $x + y + z$

$= 10 + 20 + 30$

$= 60$ $\boxed{6}$

This is the number of students who have either a car, a bicycle, or both.

Using $\boxed{1}$ and $\boxed{6}$, we get $100 - 60 = 40$ as the number who have neither a car nor a bicycle.

(Math Refreshers #200 and #406)

7. Choice B is correct.

(Use Strategy 2: Translate from words into algebra.)

Let f = number of freshmen

s = number of seniors

We are given $f = 3s$ $\boxed{1}$

$\dfrac{1}{4}$ of the freshmen = $\dfrac{1}{4} f$ $\boxed{2}$

$\dfrac{1}{3}$ of the seniors = $\dfrac{1}{4} s$ $\boxed{3}$

Total number of freshmen and seniors = $f + s$ $\boxed{4}$

(Use Strategy 17: Use the given information effectively.)

The desired fraction uses $\boxed{2}$, $\boxed{3}$, and $\boxed{4}$ as follows:

$$\frac{\frac{1}{4}f + \frac{1}{3}s}{f + s} \qquad \boxed{5}$$

Substituting 1 in 5, we get

$$\frac{\left(\frac{1}{4}(3s) + \frac{1}{3}s\right)}{3s + s} = \frac{\left(\frac{3}{4}s + \frac{1}{3}s\right)}{4s} \qquad 6$$

Multiplying 6, numerator and denominator, by 12, we get:

$$\left(\frac{12}{12}\right)\frac{\frac{3}{4}s + \frac{1}{3}s}{4s}$$

$$= \frac{9s + 4s}{48s}$$

$$= \frac{13s}{48s}$$

$$= \frac{13}{48}$$

(Math Refreshers #200 and #402)

8. Choice B is correct.

From the diagram we find that

$AB = 2$	1
$BC = 2$	2
$CD = 2$	3
$DE = 2$	4

(Use Strategy 3: The whole equals the sum of its parts.)

We know $AB + BC = AC$ 5

Substituting 1 and 2 into 5, we get

$$2 + 2 = AC$$
$$4 = AC \qquad 6$$

We know $CD + DE = CE$ 7

Substituting 3 and 4 into 7, we get

$$2 + 2 = CE$$
$$4 = CE \qquad 8$$

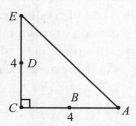

Filling 6 and 8 into the diagram and using the fact that all the segments drawn were perpendicular, we have ΔECA is an isosceles right triangle.

(Use Strategy 18: Know and use facts about triangles.)

In the isosceles right triangle, the

$$\text{hypotenuse} = \text{leg}(\sqrt{2}) \qquad 9$$

Substituting 6 or 8 into 9, we get

$$EA = 4\sqrt{2} \qquad 6$$

(Math Refreshers #507 and #509)

9. Choice D is correct.

Given:	
Area of square $= R^2$	1
Perimeter of equilateral triangle $= E$	2
Perimeter of square $= r$	3
Side of equilateral triangle $= e$	4

(Use Strategy 17: Use the given information effectively.)

We know perimeter of a square $= 4$ (side)   5
We know area of a square $=$ (side)^2 6

Substituting 1 into 6, we get

$$R^2 = (\text{side})^2$$
$$R = \text{side} \qquad 7$$

Substituting 7 and 3 into 5, we have

$$r = 4(R)$$
$$r = 4R \qquad 8$$

We know perimeter of an equilateral triangle $= 3$ (side)   9

Substituting 2 and 4 into 9, we get

$$E = 3(e)$$
$$E = 3e \qquad 10$$
$$\frac{E}{3} = e$$

We need $e + r$.   11

(Use Strategy 13: Know how to find unknown expressions by adding.)

Add 8 and 10 to get 11. We have

$$e + r = \frac{E}{3} + 4R$$

$$= \frac{E}{3} + 4R\left(\frac{3}{3}\right)$$

$$= \frac{E}{3} + \frac{12R}{3}$$

$$e + r = \frac{E + 12R}{3}$$

(Math Refreshers #303 and #308)

10. **Choice D is correct.**

    (Use Strategy 17: Use the given information effectively.)

    The center point inside a cube is the midpoint of an inner diagonal of the cube. Thus, the distance from any vertex to this center point is $\frac{1}{2}$ the length of the inner diagonal.

    We know length of inner diagonal of a cube

    $$= \sqrt{(edge)^2 + (edge)^2 + (edge)^2}$$
    $$= \sqrt{3(edge)^2} \qquad \boxed{1}$$
    $$= edge\sqrt{3} \qquad \boxed{2}$$

    Given: Volume = 8 cubic meters $\qquad \boxed{3}$

    We know volume of a cube = $(edge)^3 \qquad \boxed{4}$

    Substituting $\boxed{3}$ into $\boxed{4}$, we get

    $$8 \text{ cubic meters} = (edge)^3$$
    $$\sqrt[3]{8 \text{ cubic meters}} = \sqrt[3]{(edge)^3}$$
    $$2 \text{ meters} = edge \qquad \boxed{5}$$

    Substituting $\boxed{5}$ into $\boxed{2}$, we get

    $$\text{inner diagonal} = 2\sqrt{3} \text{ meters} \qquad \boxed{6}$$

    Using $\boxed{1}$ and $\boxed{6}$, we find

    $$\text{distance we need} = \frac{1}{2}(\text{inner diagonal})$$
    $$= \frac{1}{2}(2\sqrt{3} \text{ meters})$$
    $$= \sqrt{3} \text{ meters}$$
    $$\text{Distance we need} = \sqrt{3} \text{ m}$$

    (Math Refreshers #313, #429, #430, and #406

11. **Choice B is correct.**

    (Use Strategy 2: Translate from words into algebra.)

    Let a = a positive integer
    Then $a + 1, a + 2, a + 3, a + 4$, etc., are the next positive integers.

    (Use Strategy 13: Know how to find unknown expressions by adding.)

    Add the first 2 positive integers. We get
    Sum of first 2 positive integers
    $$= a + a + 1 = 2a + 1 \qquad \boxed{1}$$

    $\boxed{1}$ is not divisible by 2.

    Now add the third positive integer, $a + 2$, to $\boxed{1}$.
    We get
    Sum of first 3 positive integers
    $$= 2a + 1 + a + 2 = 3a + 3 \qquad \boxed{2}$$

    $\boxed{2}$ is not divisible by 2.

    Now add the fourth positive integer, $a + 3$, to $\boxed{2}$.
    We have

    Sum of first 4 positive integers
    $$= 3a + 3 + a + 3$$
    $$= 4a + 6 \qquad \boxed{3}$$

    Since $\boxed{3}$ can be written as $2(2a + 3)$, it is divisible by 2.

    Thus, if the number of integers is a multiple of 4, the sum of the consecutive positive integers will be divisible by 2.

    (Math Refreshers #200 and #607)

12. **Choice C is correct.**

    (Use Strategy 2: Translate English words into mathematical expressions.)

    Let b represent the number of hours it takes to build one component.
    Let c represent the number of hours it takes to check one component.

    For the first project we can translate the given information into

    $$12b + 3c = 61. \qquad \boxed{1}$$

    For the second project we can translate the given information into:

    $$8b + 4c = 41\frac{1}{3}. \qquad \boxed{2}$$

    (*Note*: 20 minutes is expressed as one-third of an hour.)

    One way to solve these equations is to use substitution. This involves using one equation to get one unknown in terms of the other, and then substituting this information into the other equation. You might, however, find it easier to use elimination, after first multiplying each term in the first equation by 4, and each term in the second equation by 3. This gives us:

    $$48b + 12c = 244 \qquad \boxed{3}$$
    $$24b + 12c = 124 \qquad \boxed{4}$$

    If we now subtract the second equation from the first, we'll get:

    $$48b + 12c = 244 \qquad \boxed{5}$$
    $$\underline{- \quad 24b + 12c = 124}$$
    $$24b = 120$$

This is what we wanted: One equation with only one unknown. This can now be easily solved by dividing each side by 24:

$$b = 5 \qquad \boxed{6}$$

This is the number of hours it takes to build one component. To find c, you can plug this information into either equation. Using 1, we get:

$$12(5) + 3c = 61 \qquad \boxed{7}$$
$$60 + 3c = 61$$
$$3c = 1$$
$$c = \frac{1}{3}$$

This means that the number of hours needed to check the component is one-third of an hour, or 20 minutes. If we add this to the 5 hours it takes to build the component, we get 5 hours and 20 minutes.

13. Choice D is correct.

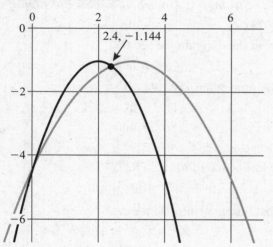

(Use Strategy 15: Know how to eliminate certain choices.)

The figure presents us with two parabolas. We don't know which is represented by the given equation, but it can be seen that these downward-facing parabolas have the same maximum value, whatever that is. In the equation that we are given, $y = -0.4(x - 3)^2 - 1$, the maximum value is the constant term at the end: -1. Therefore, the correct choice must have the same constant term at the end, and this information allows us to eliminate Choice B.

Furthermore, the two parabolas are at different places along the x-axis, so within the parentheses, they must have different values added to/subtracted from the x-value. The given equation shows $(x - 3)$

within the parentheses, so we can now eliminate Choice C, which (incorrectly) shows the same thing.

One parabola is wider than the other, so this means that the coefficient—the number *before* the x-value—must be different. The given equation has a coefficient of -0.4, so this eliminates Choice A, which has the same coefficient. This leaves us with Choice D, which represents the narrower parabola that is to the left.

14. Choice B is correct.

We are given

$$x^2 + rax + 81a^2 = 0 \qquad \boxed{1}$$

Since the *only* solution for x is $9a$, the equation can be written in factored form the following way:

$$(x - 9a)(x - 9a) = 0 \qquad \boxed{2}$$

As we see, the only solution to the equation above is $9a$. Now this equation can be expanded:

(Use Strategy 4: Remember classic expressions.)

$$x^2 - 18ax + 81a^2 = 0 \qquad \boxed{3}$$

Now the two forms of the equation—$\boxed{1}$ and $\boxed{3}$—can be set equal to each other. They are, remember, **both** equal to zero:

$$x^2 + rax + 81a^2 = x^2 - 18ax + 81a^2 \qquad \boxed{4}$$

If you subtract $x^2 + 81a^2$ from both sides you are left with

$$rax = -18ax \qquad \boxed{5}$$

Finally, dividing each side by ax gives you

$$r = -18.$$

15. Choice A is correct.

You are given the equation

$$\sin\theta = \frac{a}{c} \qquad \boxed{1}$$

Since the sine of an angle is equal to the side opposite the angle divided by the hypotenuse of the triangle, you know that

$$\frac{opposite}{hypotenuse} = \frac{a}{c} \qquad \boxed{2}$$

We need to find the tangent of the angle, which is equal to the opposite side divided by the adjacent side. If we call the adjacent side b, then

$$\tan\theta = \frac{opposite}{adjacent} = \frac{a}{b} \qquad \boxed{3}$$

We can use the Pythagorean theorem to express the adjacent side (b)—in terms of a and c.

(Use Strategy 18: Know and use facts about triangles.)

$$a^2 + b^2 = c^2, \text{ so } b^2 = c^2 - a^2 \qquad \boxed{4}$$

If we take the square root of each side we'll get

$$b = \pm\sqrt{c^2 - a^2} \qquad \boxed{5}$$

Using $\boxed{3}$ and $\boxed{5}$, we can now say that

$$\tan\theta = \frac{opposite}{adjacent} = \frac{a}{b} = \frac{a}{\sqrt{c^2 - a^2}}$$

$$\text{or} \quad \frac{a}{-\sqrt{c^2 - a^2}} \qquad \boxed{6}$$

To determine which of these two is the correct answer, you have to use more of the given information. You are told that

$$\frac{5\pi}{4} < \theta < \frac{4\pi}{3}$$

which puts the angle in Quadrant III. Only the tangent of an angle is positive in this quadrant. This means that the sine is negative. And since you are given 1 and $c > 0$, you know that a must be negative. $\qquad \boxed{6}$

That means that the answer must be

$$\frac{a}{-\sqrt{c^2 - a^2}}$$

since this gives us a negative divided by a negative, making the tangent positive, as it must be in Quadrant III.

16. $\dfrac{7}{24}, \dfrac{2}{7}, \dfrac{3}{10}, \dfrac{3}{11}$, or any number between 0.25 and 0.3333.

(Use Strategy 17: Use the given information effectively.)

Without a calculator:

Get a common denominator 12. Then write $\dfrac{1}{4} = \dfrac{3}{12}$

and $\dfrac{1}{3} = \dfrac{4}{12}$ to get a quantity *in between* $\dfrac{3}{12}$ and $\dfrac{4}{12}$.

Write $\dfrac{3}{12} = \dfrac{6}{24}$ and $\dfrac{4}{12} = \dfrac{8}{24}$

Thus $\dfrac{6}{24} < x < \dfrac{8}{24}$ and x can be $\dfrac{7}{24}$.

Or write $\dfrac{1}{4} = \dfrac{2}{8}$ and $\dfrac{1}{3} = \dfrac{2}{6}; \dfrac{2}{8} < \dfrac{2}{7} < \dfrac{2}{6}$, so $\dfrac{2}{7}$ is an

answer. $\dfrac{3}{10}$ and $\dfrac{3}{11}$ are also acceptable.

With a calculator:

Calculate $\dfrac{1}{4} = 0.25$; calculate $\dfrac{1}{3} = 0.3333\ldots$

"Grid" any number between 0.25 and 0.3333, like 0.26, 0.27, . . . , 0.332, 0.333.

(Math Refresher #419)

17. 60°

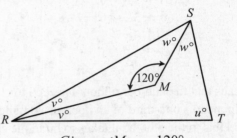

$$\text{Given: } \angle M = 120° \qquad \boxed{1}$$
$$\angle RST = 80° \qquad \boxed{2}$$

(Use Strategy 3: The whole equals the sum of its parts.)

From the diagram we see that

$$\angle RST = w + w \qquad \boxed{3}$$

Substitute $\boxed{2}$ into $\boxed{3}$. We get

$$80° = w + w$$
$$80° = 2w$$
$$40° = w \qquad \boxed{4}$$

We know that in triangle *RMS*

$$v + w + 120° = 180° \qquad \boxed{5}$$

Substituting $\boxed{4}$ into $\boxed{5}$, we get

$$v + 40° + 120° = 180°$$
$$v + 160° = 180°$$
$$v = 20° \qquad \boxed{6}$$

From the diagram we see that

$$\angle SRT = v + v \qquad \boxed{7}$$

Substitute $\boxed{6}$ into $\boxed{7}$. We get

$$\angle SRT = 20° + 20°$$
$$\angle SRT = 40° \qquad \boxed{8}$$

We know that in triangle *RST*

$$\angle RST + \angle SRT + u = 180° \qquad \boxed{9}$$

Substitute $\boxed{2}$ and $\boxed{8}$ into $\boxed{9}$. We get

$$80° + 40° + u = 180°$$
$$120° + u = 180°$$
$$u = 60°$$

(Math Refresher #505)

18. 25

If you have patience, it is not too hard to list all ordered pairs of integers (x, y) such that

$$x^2 + y^2 < 9$$

(Use Strategy 17: Use the given information effectively.)

However, to save time, try listing the possible values of each variable.

$$x = -2, -1, 0, 1, 2$$
$$y = -2, -1, 0, 1, 2$$

Since each variable has 5 possible values, the total number of ordered pairs for which $x^2 + y^2 < 9$ is:

(# of values for x)(# of values for y) = $5 \times 5 = 25$

Another way to do this problem is to note that $x^2 + y^2 = 9$ is the equation of a circle of radius 3 whose center is at (0, 0).

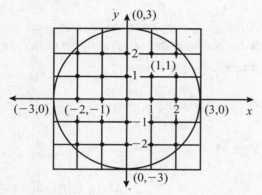

Thus, $x^2 + y^2 < 9$ is the region inside the circle. We want to find the number of ordered pairs of integers (x, y) inside the circle. As we can count from the picture above, there are 25 such ordered pairs.

(Math Refreshers #410 and #431)

19. 65

(Use Strategy 2: Translate English words into mathematical expressions.)

The question describes a situation in which it would be more profitable to stay open the extra 2 hours—that is, to stay open for 10 hours. The profit in this case is given as

$$42c - 1,700$$

Therefore, we can set up the inequality

$$42c - 1700 > 35c - 1,250 \qquad \boxed{1}$$

(Use Strategy 6: Know how to manipulate inequalities.)

To solve, you can first subtract $35c$ from each side:

$$7c - 1,700 > -1,250 \qquad \boxed{2}$$

Now you can add 1,700 to each side:

$$7c > 450 \qquad \boxed{3}$$

Finally, if you divide each side by 7, you get 64, with a remainder of 2, or

$$c > 64\frac{2}{7} \qquad \boxed{4}$$

Remember that c represents the number of customers. Since you can't have a fraction of a customer, there must be at least 65 customers for the profits on the longer day to be greater.

20. 29

(Use Strategy 12: Try not to make tedious calculations, since there is usually an easier way.)

This problem could not be solved with a standard calculator, even if you were allowed to use one on this section. In a situation like this, it helps to have the same base on both sides of the equation. Since 8 can be written as 2^3, you can rewrite the equation as

$$\left(2^{10}\right)^{y+1} = \left(2^3\right)^{100} \qquad \boxed{1}$$

You can now simplify each side by multiplying when a power is raised to another power.

$$2^{10y+10} = 2^{300} \qquad \boxed{2}$$

(Use Strategy 1: Cancel quantities to make the problem simpler.)

Since the bases are equal, the exponents must be equal as well. Therefore, you can set up this:

$$10y + 10 = 300 \qquad \boxed{3}$$

This can be easily solved by subtracting 10 from each side:

$$10y = 290$$

and then dividing each side by 10:

$$y = 29 \qquad \boxed{4}$$

EXPLANATORY ANSWERS

Section 4: Mathematics, *with Calculator*

As you read these solutions, you are advised to do two things if you answered a math question incorrectly:

1. *When a specific Math Strategy is referred to in the solution, study that strategy, which you will find in "19 Math Strategies" (beginning on page 72).*

2. *When the solution directs you to the "Complete SAT Math Refresher" (beginning on page 163)—for example, Math Refresher #305—study the math principle to get a clear idea of the math operation that you needed to know in order to answer the question correctly.*

1. Choice D is correct.

$$Given: a - 3 = 7 \qquad \boxed{1}$$

(Use Strategy 13: Know how to find unknown expressions by adding, subtracting, multiplying, or dividing equations or expressions.)

Fast Method: From $\boxed{1}$, we can subtract 7 from both sides, and then add 3 to both sides to get

$$a - 7 = 3 \qquad \boxed{2}$$

Multiplying $\boxed{2}$ by 2, we get

$$2a - 14 = 6$$

Slow Method: Solve $\boxed{1}$ to get

$$a = 10 \qquad \boxed{3}$$

Now substitute $\boxed{3}$:

$$2a - 14 = 2(10) - 14 = 6$$

(Math Refreshers #406 and #431)

2. Choice C is correct.

(Use Strategy 17: Use the given information effectively.)

$$Given: 55,555 = y + 50,505$$
$$5,050 = y \qquad \boxed{1}$$
$$We\ need: 50,505 - 10y \qquad \boxed{2}$$

Substitute $\boxed{1}$ into $\boxed{2}$. We get

$$50,505 - 10(5,050)$$
$$= 50,505 - 50,500$$
$$= 5$$

(Math Refresher #406)

3. Choice D is correct.

$$Given: 5x^2 - 15x = 0 \qquad \boxed{1}$$
$$x \neq 0 \qquad \boxed{2}$$

(Use Strategy 12: Try not to make tedious calculations, since there is usually an easier way.)

Factoring $\boxed{1}$, we get

$$5x(x - 3) = 0$$
$$5x = 0 \text{ or } x - 3 = 0$$
$$x = 0 \text{ or } x = 3 \qquad \boxed{3}$$

Applying $\boxed{2}$ to $\boxed{3}$, we get

$$x = 3$$

(Math Refresher #409)

4. Choice C is correct.

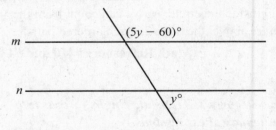

(Use Strategy 17: Use the given information effectively.)

$$Given: m \| n \qquad \boxed{1}$$

From $\boxed{1}$ we know that the two angles are supplementary. Thus,

$$(5y - 60)° + y° = 180°$$
$$6y - 60 = 180°$$
$$6y = 240°$$
$$y = 40°$$

(Math Refresher #504)

5. Choice B is correct.

(Use Strategy 17: Use the given information effectively.)

The probability is the number of favorable ways divided by the number of total ways. The total ways is the number of points in the large circle of radius 2 feet. We can look at that as the area of the large circle, which is $\pi r^2 = 2 \times 2\pi = 4\pi$. The favorable ways are the number of points in the inner circle, which we can look at as the area of that circle, which is $\pi r^2 = 1 \times 1\pi = 1\pi$. Thus the probability is

$$\frac{1\pi}{4\pi} = \frac{1}{4}$$

(Math Refresher #614)

6. Choice A is correct.

(Use Strategy 7: Use numerics to help find the answer.)

12 must be substituted for P in each of the five expressions and the results evaluated.

Item 1: $P = 12$ 12
Item 2: $P \times 3 = 12 \times 3 =$ 36
Item 3: $(P \times 3) \div 2 = (12 \times 3) \div 2 =$ 18
Item 4: $[(P \times 3) \div 2] + 12 =$
         $[(12 \times 3) \div 2] + 12 =$ 30
Item 5: $[(P \times 3) \div 2] + 12 - 1 =$
         $[(12 \times 3) \div 2] + 12 - 1 =$ 29

Item 2 has greatest in value.

(Math Refresher #431)

7. Choice C is correct.

(Use Strategy 11: Use new definitions and functions carefully.)

Two-digit numbers that have a units digit of zero and that can be tripled in value when the tens digit is tripled are the following:

Original *number*	*Tripled tens digit* *number*
10	30
20	60
30	90

The numbers above are the only numbers that result in a two-digit number as defined in the problem. Thus, 3 is the correct answer.

This problem can also be solved using a more sophisticated method.

Call the number $10t + u$ (where t is the tens digit and u is the units digit).

(Use Strategy 2: Translate English words into mathematical expressions.)

In the number $10t + u$, tripling the tens digit gives us the number $10(3t) + u$.

A two-digit number that is triple the original number translates to $3(10t + u)$.

Setting these quantities equal, we get:

$$10(3t) + u = 3(10t + u) \quad \boxed{1}$$
$$30t + u = 30t + 3u$$
$$u = 3u$$

Therefore $u = 0$.

So in the number $10t + u = 10t$, where $t = 1, 2,$ or 3 (three numbers), t can't be more than 3 because $\boxed{1}$ would not give us a two-digit number.

(Math Refresher #406)

8. Choice D is correct.

Given:

Meteor 1 travels at 300 meters/second $\boxed{1}$
Meteor 2 travels at 700 meters/second $\boxed{2}$

Draw a diagram:

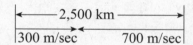

Let t be the time it takes the two meteors to meet. Call x the distance Meteor 1 travels. Then $2,500 - x$ is the distance Meteor 2 travels.

(Use Strategy 9: Know rate, time, and distance relationships.)

$$\text{Rate} \times \text{Time} = \text{Distance}$$
$$300 \text{ m/sec} \times t = x \quad \boxed{3}$$
$$700 \text{ m/sec} \times t = 2500 - x \quad \boxed{4}$$

(Use Strategy 13: Know how to find unknown expressions by adding.)

Add $\boxed{3}$ and $\boxed{4}$

$$(300 \text{ m/sec})t + (700 \text{ m/sec})t = 2,500 \text{ km}$$
$$(1,000 \text{ m/sec})t = 2,500 \text{ km} \quad \boxed{5}$$

(Use Strategy 10: Know how to use units.)

$$1 \text{ km} = 1,000 \text{ m} \quad \boxed{6}$$

Substitute 6 in 5:

$$(1{,}000 \text{ m/sec})t = 2{,}500(1{,}000) \text{ m} \qquad \boxed{7}$$

Divide 7 by 1,000 m:

$$t/\text{sec} = 2{,}500$$
$$t = 2{,}500 \text{ sec}$$

(Math Refreshers #121, #201, and #202)

9. Choice C is correct.

(Use Strategy 2: Translate from words into algebra.)

$$\textit{We have: } \frac{40}{100} \times (2a + b) = 18 \qquad \boxed{1}$$

(Use Strategy 13: Know how to find unknown expressions by multiplying.)

Multiply 1 by $\frac{100}{4}$. We get

$$\frac{100}{4}\left[\frac{4}{100} \times (2a + b)\right] = \frac{100}{4}(18)$$

(Use Strategy 19: Factor and reduce.)

$$2a + b = \frac{4 \times 25}{4}(18)$$
$$2a + b = 450$$
$$b = 450 - 2a \qquad \boxed{2}$$

(Use Strategy 17: Use the given information effectively.)

b will be greatest when a is smallest. $\qquad \boxed{3}$

Given: a is a positive integer $\qquad \boxed{4}$

Applying 4 to 3, we get

$$a = 1 \qquad \boxed{5}$$

Substituting 5 into 2, we have

$$b = 450 - 2(1)$$
$$= 450 - 2$$
$$b = 448$$

(Math Refresher #406)

10. Choice B is correct.

(Use Strategy 2: Translate from words into algebra.)

Given: Square has perimeter 2π $\qquad \boxed{1}$

Let $S =$ side of square.

We know perimeter of a square $= 4S$ $\qquad \boxed{2}$

Substitute 1 into 2. We get

$$\text{Perimeter of square} = 4S$$
$$2\pi = 4S$$
$$\frac{2\pi}{4} = S$$
$$\frac{\pi}{2} = S \qquad \boxed{3}$$

We are given that:

$$\text{area of circle} = \text{area of square} \qquad \boxed{4}$$

We know that:

area of circle $= \pi r^2$ $\qquad \boxed{5}$

area of square $= S^2$ $\qquad \boxed{6}$

Substituting 5 and 6 into 4, we get

$$\pi r^2 = S^2 \qquad \boxed{7}$$

Substitute 3 into 7. We get

$$\pi r^2 = \left(\frac{\pi}{2}\right)^2$$
$$\pi r^2 = \frac{\pi^2}{4}$$
$$r^2 = \frac{\pi^2}{4\pi}$$
$$r^2 = \frac{\pi}{4}$$
$$r = \sqrt{\frac{\pi}{4}} = \frac{\sqrt{\pi}}{2} \qquad \boxed{8}$$

We know the circumference of a circle $= 2\pi r$ $\qquad \boxed{9}$

Substitute 8 into 9. We have

$$\text{Circumference} = 2\pi\left(\frac{\sqrt{\pi}}{2}\right)$$
$$\text{Circumference} = \pi\sqrt{\pi}$$

(Math Refreshers #303 and #310)

11. Choice B is correct.

(Use Strategy 2: Translate from words into algebra.)

Given: Rate of plane $= x\dfrac{\text{km}}{\text{hour}}$ $\qquad \boxed{1}$

Time of flight $= y$ hours $\qquad \boxed{2}$

Need: Distance plane had flown $\frac{2}{3}y$ hours ago $\qquad \boxed{3}$

Subtracting 3 from 2, we get

Time plane had flown $\frac{2}{3}y$ hours ago $= y - \frac{2}{3}y$

Time plane had flown $\frac{2}{3}y$ hours ago $= \frac{1}{3}y$ hours $\qquad \boxed{4}$

(Use Strategy 9: Know rate, time, and distance relationships.)

We know: Rate $\times$ Time $=$ Distance $\qquad \boxed{5}$

Substitute 1 and 4 into 5. We get

$$x\frac{\text{km}}{\text{hour}} \times \frac{1}{3}y \text{ hours} = \text{distance}$$

$\frac{xy}{3} =$ distance plane had flown $\frac{2}{3}y$ hours ago.

(Math Refreshers #201 and #202)

12. Choice D is correct.

$$\textit{Given: } C = \frac{5}{9}(F - 32)$$

Call the number of degrees that the Fahrenheit temperature (F°) increases, x.

(Now use Strategy 17: Use the given information effectively.)

The Celsius temperature (C°) is given as

$$C = \frac{5}{9}(F - 32)$$

This can be rewritten as

$$C = \frac{5}{9}F - \frac{5}{9}(32) \qquad \boxed{1}$$

When the Celsius temperature increases by 35°, the Fahrenfeit temperature increases by $x°$, so we get:

$$C + 35 = \frac{5}{9}[(F + x) - 32]$$

$$C + 35 = \frac{5}{9}F + \frac{5}{9}x - \frac{5}{9}(32) \qquad \boxed{2}$$

(Now use Strategy 13: Find unknowns by subtraction.)

Subtract $\boxed{1}$ from $\boxed{2}$:

$$C + 35 = \frac{5}{9}F + \frac{5}{9}x - \frac{5}{9}(32) \qquad \boxed{2}$$

$$- \quad C = \frac{5}{9}F - \frac{5}{9}(32) \qquad \boxed{1}$$

$$\overline{\qquad \quad 35 = \frac{5}{9}x \qquad \boxed{3}}$$

Multiply $\boxed{3}$ by 9:

$$35 \times 9 = 5x \qquad \boxed{4}$$

(Use Strategy 19: Never multiply if you can reduce first.)

Divide $\boxed{4}$ by 5:

$$\frac{35 \times 9}{5} = x \qquad \boxed{5}$$

Now reduce $\frac{35}{5}$ to get 7 and we get for $\boxed{5}$

$$7 \times 9 = x$$

$$63 = x$$

(Math Refresher #406)

13. Choice A is correct.

(Use Strategy 18: Know and use facts about triangles.)

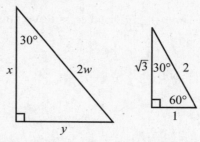

The triangle at left (given) is similar to the triangle at right, which is one of the standard triangles.

Corresponding sides of similar triangles are proportional. Thus,

$$\frac{2w}{2} = \frac{y}{1} \text{ and } \frac{2w}{2} = \frac{x}{\sqrt{3}}$$

or $y = w$ and $x = w\sqrt{3}$

$$\text{Area of triangle} = \frac{1}{2}(\text{base})(\text{height})$$

$$= \frac{1}{2}(y)(x)$$

$$= \frac{1}{2}(w)(w\sqrt{3})$$

$$\text{Area of triangle} = \frac{\sqrt{3}}{2} w^2 \qquad \boxed{1}$$

$$\text{Area of rectangle} = (3w)(w) = 3w^2 \qquad \boxed{2}$$

Using $\boxed{1}$ and $\boxed{2}$, we have

$$\frac{\text{area of rectangle}}{\text{area of triangle}} = \frac{3w^2}{\frac{\sqrt{3}}{2}w^2}$$

$$= \frac{3}{\frac{\sqrt{3}}{2}} = 3 \times \frac{2}{\sqrt{3}}$$

$$= \frac{6}{\sqrt{3}} = \frac{6\sqrt{3}}{3} = 2\sqrt{3}$$

or $2\sqrt{3} : 1$

(Math Refreshers #510, #509, #306, and #304)

14. Choice B is correct.

(Use Strategy 10: Use units of time, distance, etc.)

Since the track circumference is 120 feet:

$$\frac{\text{\# of feet}}{120} = \text{\# of revolutions}$$

(Use Strategy 9: Use the Rate × Time = Distance formula.)

Rate × Time = Distance

$$\frac{1}{120}\text{Rate} \times \text{Time} = \frac{1}{120}\text{Distance} = \text{Revolutions}$$

For Bicycle B:

$$\left(\frac{1}{120}\right)8 \times t = 600$$

For Bicycle A:

$$\left(\frac{1}{120}\right)5 \times t = a$$

The key is to realize that the time, t, is identical for both bicycles.

(Use Strategy 13: Know how to find unknown expressions by dividing equations.)

$$\frac{\left(\frac{1}{120}\right)8 \times t}{\left(\frac{1}{120}\right)5 \times t} = \frac{600}{a}$$

$$\frac{8}{5} = \frac{600}{a}$$

$$8a = 3,000$$

$$a = 375$$

(Math Refreshers #202, #403)

15. Choice D is correct.

(Use Strategy 17: Use the given information effectively.)

$$[(3a^3b^2)^3]^2 =$$
$$(3a^3b^2)^6 = 3^6a^{18}b^{12}$$

Checking the choices, we find only Choice D has $a^{18}b^{12}$ and must be correct.

Note: We did not have to calculate 3^6!

(Math Refresher #429)

16. Choice A is correct.

(Use Strategy 3: The whole equals the sum of its parts.)

From the given diagram, it is clear that

$$z + 2w = 180 \qquad \boxed{1}$$

Since the sum of the measures of the angles of a triangle is 180, then

$$x + y + z = 180 \qquad \boxed{2}$$

(Use Strategy 13: Find unknowns by subtracting equations.)

Subtracting $\boxed{2}$ from $\boxed{1}$,

$$2w - (x + y) = 0$$
$$\text{or} \quad 2w = x + y \qquad \boxed{3}$$

Using $\boxed{3}$, we calculate the unknown expression,

$$w + x + y = w + 2w$$
$$= 3w$$

(Math Refreshers #501, #505, and #406)

17. Choice A is correct.

(Use Strategy 2: Translate from words into algebra.)

"The ratio of Suri's age to Bob's age is 3 to 7" becomes

$$\frac{\text{Suri's age } (S)}{\text{Bob's age } (B)} = \frac{3}{7}$$

$$\text{or} \quad \frac{S}{B} = \frac{3}{7} \qquad \boxed{1}$$

"The ratio of Suri's age to Javier's age is 4 to 9" becomes

$$\frac{S}{J} = \frac{4}{9} \qquad \boxed{2}$$

Cross multiplying $\boxed{1}$, we have $7S = 3B$

$$\text{or} \quad \frac{7S}{3} = B$$

Cross multiplying $\boxed{2}$, we have $9S = 4J$

$$\text{or} \quad \frac{9S}{4} = J \qquad \boxed{4}$$

We need the ratio of Bob's age to Javier's age. $\boxed{5}$

Substituting $\boxed{3}$ and $\boxed{4}$ into $\boxed{5}$, we get

$$\frac{\text{Bob's age}}{\text{Javier's age}} = \frac{\frac{7S}{3}}{\frac{9S}{4}}$$

$$= \frac{7S}{3} \div \frac{9S}{4}$$

$$= \frac{7S}{3} \times \frac{4}{9S}$$

$$\frac{\text{Bob's age}}{\text{Javier's age}} = \frac{28}{27}$$

(Math Refreshers #200, #120, and #112)

18. Choice D is correct.

Method I:

Given:
$$(r - s)(t - s)$$
$$+ (s - r)(s - t) \qquad \boxed{1}$$

(Use Strategy 17: Use the given information effectively.)

Recognizing that $(s - r) = -1(r - s)$ $\qquad \boxed{2}$
$(s - t) = -1(t - s)$ $\qquad \boxed{3}$

Substituting $\boxed{2}$ and $\boxed{3}$ into $\boxed{1}$, we get
$$(r - s)(t - s) + [-1(r - s)][-1(t - s)]$$
$$= (r - s)(t - s) + (-1)(-1)(r - s)(t - s)$$
$$= 2(r - s)(t - s)$$

Method II:

Given: $(r - s)(t - s) + (s - r)(s - t)$ $\qquad \boxed{1}$

Multiply both pairs of quantities from $\boxed{1}$, giving
$$rt - rs - st + s^2 + s^2 - st - rs + rt$$
$$= 2rt - 2rs - 2st + 2s^2$$
$$= 2(rt - rs - st + s^2)$$
$$= 2[r(t - s) - s(t - s)]$$
$$= 2(r - s)(t - s)$$

(Math Refresher #409)

19. Choice B is correct.

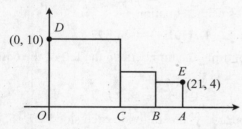

We want to find the area of the middle square, which is $(CB)^2$.

(Use Strategy 3: The whole equals the sum of its parts.)

$$OA = OC + CB + BA \qquad \boxed{1}$$

From the diagram, we get
$$OA = 21 \qquad \boxed{2}$$
$$AE = 4 \qquad \boxed{3}$$
$$OD = 10 \qquad \boxed{4}$$

Since each figure is a square, we get
$$BA = AE \qquad \boxed{5}$$
$$OC = OD \qquad \boxed{6}$$

Substituting $\boxed{5}$ into $\boxed{3}$, we get
$$AE = BA = 4 \qquad \boxed{7}$$

Substituting $\boxed{6}$ into $\boxed{4}$, we get
$$OD = OC = 10 \qquad \boxed{8}$$

Substituting $\boxed{2}$, $\boxed{7}$, and $\boxed{8}$ into $\boxed{1}$, we get
$$21 = 10 + CB + 4$$
$$21 = 14 + CB$$
$$7 = CB \qquad \boxed{9}$$

Area of square II $= (CB)^2$
Area of square II $= 7^2$ (from $\boxed{9}$)
Area of square II $= 49$

(Math Refreshers #410 and #303)

20. Choice D is correct.

(Use Strategy 15: Know how to eliminate certain choices.)

Since (according to the graph) $y = 0$ when $x = 0$, Choices A, B, and E are incorrect. Choice C is incorrect since the graph is not a parabola. The only feasible choice is Choice D.

(Math Refresher #410b)

21. Choice D is correct.

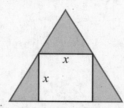

The key to this problem is to find the area of the shaded region in terms of known quantities.

(Use Strategy 3: The whole equals the sum of its parts.)

Area of shaded region and also the area of the rectangle
$$= \text{area of rectangle} - \text{area of square}$$
$$= x^2 \sqrt{3} - x^2$$
$$= x^2 (\sqrt{3} - 1)$$

We are given that an unknown rectangle has
width $= x$ $\qquad \boxed{1}$
and area $= x^2 (\sqrt{3} - 1)$ $\qquad \boxed{2}$

Since length = width = area,
length = area ÷ width $\qquad \boxed{3}$

Substituting $\boxed{1}$ and $\boxed{2}$ into $\boxed{3}$, we have
$$\text{length of rectangle} = \frac{x^2 (\sqrt{3} - 1)}{x}$$
$$\text{length of rectangle} = x (\sqrt{3} - 1)$$

(Math Refreshers #303, #304, and #306)

22. The correct answer is A.

(Use Strategy 17: Use the given information effectively.)

This expression has i, the imaginary number, in the denominator. This is not the preferred form for a fraction, so you'll need to express its value without the i in the bottom. To do so, you can multiply the top and bottom of the denominator by the *conjugate* of the denominator, which is $2 + i$. This gives us

$$\frac{3 + i}{2 - i} \times \frac{2 + i}{2 + i}$$

(The reason for doing this will become clear.)

If you multiply across the top and across the bottom, you'll get

$$\frac{3 + i}{2 - i} \times \frac{2 + i}{2 + i} = \frac{6 + 5i + i^2}{4 - i^2}$$

To simplify this, remember this key fact about imaginary numbers: $i^2 = -1$. This means that

$$\frac{6 + 5i + i^2}{4 - i^2}$$

$$= \frac{6 + 5i + (-1)}{4 - (-1)}$$

$$= \frac{6 + 5i - 1}{5}$$

$$= \frac{5 + 5i}{5}$$

$$= 1 + i$$

Notice that multiplying the denominator by its conjugate (by changing only the sign between the values), we eliminated the i in the bottom.

23. The correct answer is D.

(Use Strategy 12: Try not to make tedious calculations, since there is usually an easier way.)

I. Using the numbers in the graph, if each of the dollar amounts given to the managers were arranged from least to greatest, the amount given to **Hidalgo** would be in the middle. This represents the median value. If 20,000 is taken from Bruce and given to Dunbar, **Richards** would then be in the middle, changing the median.

(Use Strategy 5: Know how to manipulate averages.)

II. The average (arithmetic mean) is determined by dividing the sum of all the numbers by 5 (the number of managers). Since the sum and the number of managers would not change after the money was taken from Bruce and given to Dunbar, the average would *not* change.

III. The standard deviation represents how far the individual values differ from (deviate from) the average (arithmetic mean). By reducing the money given to Bruce (who currently gets substantially more than anyone else) and giving it to Dunbar (who would then be somewhere near the mean) the standard deviation *decreases*. Each manager would now be given an amount closer to the average. The transfer of dollars *flattens* the amount the managers get.

IV. The range is the difference between the least and greatest values. Clearly this would change after money is taken from Bruce (who currently gets substantially more than anyone else) and not changing the amount given to Santana, whose amount is the least.

24. The correct answer is B.

(Use Strategy 2: Translate English words into mathematical expressions.)

If we let x represent the amount Santana was given two years ago, then the following year, after he received 5% more than x, he got $1.05x$.

This year he received 10% more than *that*, so he got $1.1(1.05x)$, which we know to be equal to 24,892.

This gives us the equation

$$1.1(1.05x) = 24{,}892$$

If you multiply the numbers on the left of the equation, you'll get

$$1.155x = 24{,}892$$

To solve for x, you can divide each side by 1.155, giving you

$$\frac{24{,}892}{1.155}$$

25. Choice D is correct.

(Use Strategy 17: Use the given information effectively.)

Volume of rectangular solid $= l \times w \times h$ 1

Substituting the given dimensions into 1, we get

    Volume of solid $= 2$ feet $\times 2$ feet $\times 1$ foot

    Volume of solid $= 4$ cubic feet   2

    Volume of cube $= (\text{edge})^3$ 3

Substituting edge $= 0.1$ foot into 3, we get

    Volume of cube $= (0.1 \text{ foot})^3$

    Volume of cube $= 0.001$ cubic feet   4

(Use Strategy 3: The whole equals the sum of its parts.)

Since the volume of the rectangular solid must equal the sum of the small cubes, we need to know

$$\frac{\text{volume of rectangular solid}}{\text{volume of cube}} = \text{number of cubes} \quad \boxed{5}$$

Substituting $\boxed{2}$ and $\boxed{4}$ into $\boxed{5}$, we get

$$\frac{4 \text{ cubic feet}}{0.001 \text{ cubic feet}} = \text{number of cubes}$$

$$\frac{4}{0.001} = \text{number of cubes}$$

Multiply numerator and denominator by 1,000, we get

$$\frac{4}{0.001} \times \frac{1,000}{1,000} = \text{number of cubes}$$

$$\frac{4,000}{1} = \text{number of cubes}$$

$$4,000 = \text{number of cubes}$$

(Math Refreshers #312 and #313)

26. Choice B is correct.

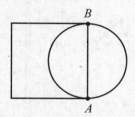

(Use Strategy 17: Use the given information effectively.)

Given: Area of circle $= 9a^2\pi^2$ $\boxed{1}$

Two sides of square are tangent to the circle $\boxed{2}$

We know that the area of a circle $= \pi r^2$ where r is the radius. $\boxed{3}$

Substituting $\boxed{1}$ into $\boxed{3}$, we have

$$9a^2\pi^2 = \pi r^2 \quad \boxed{4}$$

Dividing by π, we get

$$9a^2\pi = r^2 \quad \boxed{5}$$

Since $2r$ is the side of the square, the area of the square is

$$(2r)^2 = 4r^2$$

From $\boxed{5}$, multiplying both sides of the equation by 4, we get

$$4(9a^2\pi) = 4r^2$$

Thus $36a^2\pi = 4r^2 = $ area of square

(Math Refreshers #303, #310, and #406)

27. Choice D is correct.

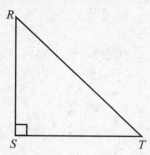

(Use Strategy 17: Use the given information effectively.)

We know that area of $\Delta = \frac{1}{2} \times$ base $\times$ height $\boxed{1}$

We are given that $RS = ST = $ an integer $\boxed{2}$

Substituting $\boxed{2}$ into $\boxed{1}$, we get

Area $\Delta RST = \frac{1}{2} \times$ (an integer) $=$ (same integer)

Area $\Delta RST = \frac{1}{2} \times$ (an integer)^2 $\boxed{3}$

Multiplying $\boxed{3}$ by 2, we have

2(area ΔRST) $=$ (an integer)^2 $\boxed{4}$

(Use Strategy 8: When each choice must be tested, start with the last choice and work backward.)

Substituting Choice D, 20, into $\boxed{4}$, we get

2(20) $=$ (an integer)^2

40 $=$ (an integer)^2 $\boxed{5}$

$\boxed{5}$ is *not* possible, since 40 isn't the square of an integer.

(Math Refreshers #307, #406, and #431)

28. Choice D is correct.

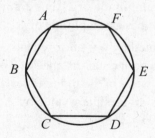

Given: $\overset{\frown}{BAF} = 14\pi$ $\boxed{1}$

$ABCDEF$ is equilateral $\boxed{2}$

From $\boxed{2}$ we know that all 6 sides are equal. $\boxed{3}$

From $\boxed{3}$ we know that all 6 arcs are equal. $\boxed{4}$

From $\boxed{1}$ and $\boxed{4}$ and noting that $\overset{\frown}{AB}$ equals $\frac{1}{2}\overset{\frown}{BAF}$, we find

$\overset{\frown}{AB} = \overset{\frown}{BC} = \overset{\frown}{CD} = \overset{\frown}{DE} = \overset{\frown}{EF} = \overset{\frown}{FA} = 7\pi$ $\boxed{5}$

(Use Strategy 3: The whole equals the sum of its parts.)

Circumference of circle

$$= 6 \times 7\pi \text{ (since there are 6 arcs)} \quad \boxed{6}$$

We know circumference $= 2\pi r$ $\quad \boxed{7}$

Using $\boxed{6}$ and $\boxed{7}$, we get

$$2\pi r = 6 \times 7\pi$$
$$2\pi r = 42\pi$$
$$2r = 42 \quad \boxed{8}$$

We know diameter $= 2 \times$ radius $\quad \boxed{9}$

So diameter $= 42$

(Math Refreshers #310 and #524)

29. The correct answer is D.

    (Use Strategy 15: Know how to eliminate certain choices.)

    A sine wave represented by $y = \sin x$ passes through the point $(0, 0)$. The sine wave in the figure has been shifted up 1, so that it passes through $(0, 1)$, meaning that a constant value of 1 should be found at the "end" of the equation, as we see in Choices B through D. This eliminates Choice A.

    The number found directly *before* sin x represents the amplitude of the wave, which refers to its vertical dimension (height). The sine wave represented by $y = \sin x$ has an amplitude of 1, though the number 1 does not need to be written; it's assumed. The sine wave in the figure goes up 2 to reach its maximum height of 3 (from its mid-level of 1) and down 2 to reach its minimum of -1 (from its mid-level). This gives it an amplitude of 2, thus eliminating Choice B, which has an amplitude of 1.

    The sine wave represented by $y = \sin x$ repeats after it has "traveled" a horizontal distance of 2π on the x-axis. The sine wave in the figure repeats (cycles) every 4π. This divides the x value by 2, as seen in correct Choice D.

30. Choice B is correct.

    (Use Strategy 13: Know how to find unknown expressions.)

    $f(x) = a^x$

    so $f(x + y) = a^{x+y}$

    $a^{x+y} = a^x a^y = f(x)f(y)$

    (Math Refreshers #616 and #429)

31. 6

    (Use Strategy 17: Use the given information effectively.)

    If the tram carries its maximum of 4 people then

    $$\dfrac{22 \; \text{people}}{\dfrac{4 \; \text{people}}{\text{trip}}} = 5\tfrac{1}{2} \; \text{trips}$$

    (Use Strategy 16: The obvious may be tricky!)

    There is no such thing as $\tfrac{1}{2}$ a trip. The $\tfrac{1}{2}$ arises because the last trip, the *6th* trip only, takes 2 people. So there are 6 trips.

    (Math Refresher #101)

32. 12

    $$\text{Given: } 3x + y = 17 \quad \boxed{1}$$
    $$x + 3y = -1 \quad \boxed{2}$$

    (Use Strategy 13: Know how to find unknowns by adding.)

    Adding $\boxed{1}$ and $\boxed{2}$, we get

    $$4x + 4y = 16 \quad \boxed{3}$$

    (Use Strategy 13: Know how to find unknowns by dividing.)

    Dividing $\boxed{3}$ by 4, we have

    $$x + y = 4 \quad \boxed{4}$$

    (Use Strategy 13: Know how to find unknowns by multiplying.)

    Multiply $\boxed{4}$ by 3. We get

    $$3x + 3y = 12$$

    (Math Refresher #407)

33. 35

    (Use Strategy 2: Translate from words into algebra.)

    Natalie originally had enough money to buy 21 bars at 50¢ per bar. Thus, she had $21 \times 50 = 1{,}050$ cents $= \$10.50$. Therefore,

    Number of 30¢ bars she bought

    $$= \frac{\text{total amount she had}}{\text{price of each bar}}$$
    $$= \frac{\$10.50}{\$.30}$$
    $$= 35 \text{ bars}$$

    (Math Refreshers #200 and #406)

34. 24

(Use Strategy 4: Remember classic expressions.)

Method I:

$$(a + b)^2 = a^2 + 2ab + b^2 \quad \boxed{1}$$
$$(a - b)^2 = a^2 - 2ab + b^2 \quad \boxed{2}$$

(Use Strategy 11: Use new definitions carefully. These problems are generally easy.)

Using $\boxed{1}$ and $\boxed{2}$, we have

$$a \odot b = (a + b)^2 - (a - b)^2$$
$$= a^2 + 2ab + b^2 - (a^2 - 2ab + b^2)$$
$$= 4ab \quad \boxed{3}$$

When we use $\boxed{3}$ with $a = \sqrt{18}$ and $b = \sqrt{2}$, we get

$$\sqrt{18} \odot \sqrt{2} = 4(\sqrt{18})(\sqrt{2})$$
$$= 4(\sqrt{36})$$
$$= 4(6)$$
$$= 24$$

Method II:

$$a \odot b = (a + b)^2 - (a - b)^2$$
$$2\sqrt{18} \odot \sqrt{2}$$
$$= (\sqrt{18} + \sqrt{2})^2 - (\sqrt{18} - \sqrt{2})^2$$
$$= 18 + 2\sqrt{36} + 2 - (18 - 2\sqrt{36} + 2)$$
$$= 18 + 12 + 2 - 18 + 12 - 2$$
$$= 24$$

The calculations in Method 2 are much more complex!

(Math Refreshers #409 and #431)

35. 6

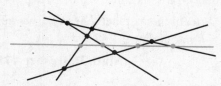

(Use Strategy 17: Use the given information effectively.)

Method I:

You can just take out one line (gray in the figure above) and you will have 6 points.

Method II:

There is a formula for finding the maximum number of points of intersection of n straight line segments.

It is $\dfrac{n(n - 1)}{2}$ \quad \boxed{1}

Substituting 4 into $\boxed{1}$, we get

$$\frac{4(4 - 1)}{2}$$
$$= \frac{4(3)}{2}$$
$$= \frac{12}{2}$$
$$= 6$$

(Math Refresher #405a)

36. 15

(Use Strategy 3: Know how to find unknown quantities.)

To determine the *total* number of degrees in all the angles of a polygon, you can use the following formula:

$$(n - 2)180$$

where n represents the number of sides.

For an 8-sided figure, we get

$$(8 - 2)180 = (6)(180)$$

For a 6-sided figure, we get

$$(6 - 2)180 = (4)(180)$$

A regular polygon has congruent angles, so you can determine the number of degrees by dividing the total found above by the number of angles.

For the 8-sided figure, we get

$$\frac{(6)(180)}{8} = 135$$

For the 6-sided figure, we get

$$\frac{(4)(180)}{6} = 120$$

The difference between these two values is

$$135 - 120 = 15$$

37. 2

(Use Strategy 13: Know how to find unknown expressions by adding, subtracting, multiplying, or dividing equations or expressions.)

You can divide $3x - 1$ by $x - 1$ the following way:

$$x - 1 \overline{)\begin{array}{l} 3 \\ 3x - 1 \end{array}}$$
$$\underline{3x - 3}$$
$$2$$

You now have a remainder of 2, and you can rewrite $\dfrac{3x - 1}{x - 1}$ as $3 + \dfrac{2}{x - 1}$. This makes y equal to 2.

If this is confusing, think of it this way: $\dfrac{5}{2}$ can be expressed as 2 with a remainder of 1 or as $2 + \dfrac{1}{2}$.

Alternate approach:

Given: $\dfrac{3x - 1}{x - 1} = 3 + \dfrac{y}{x - 1}$

we get common denominator $(x - 1)$.

$$\frac{3x - 1}{x - 1} = \frac{3(x - 1)}{x - 1} + \frac{y}{x - 1}$$
$$\frac{3x - 1}{x - 1} = \frac{3x - 3 + y}{x - 1}$$

Multiply by $x - 1$:

$$3x - 1 = 3x - 3 + y$$

Thus $2 = y$.

38. 4

(Use Strategy 17: Use the given information effectively.)

Method I:

Remembering that the sum of 2 sides of a triangle is greater than the third side, we know that

$$LM + MN > LN$$
$$6 + 10 > 12$$
$$16 > 12$$

The difference between 16 and 12, $16 - 12 = 4$, is the amount of overlap.

Method II:

(Use Strategy 14: Draw lines to make a problem easier.)

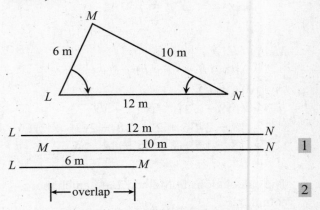

In the figure above, the segments have been redrawn so that the result can be easily discovered.

In 1 , the distance $LM = 12\text{ m} - 10\text{ m} = 2\text{ m}$ 3

Subtracting 3 from the distance LM in 2 , we get $6\text{ m} - 2\text{ m} = 4\text{ m}$ overlap.

(Math Refresher #419)

SECTION 5: TEST 1 ESSAY SCORING

SAT Essay responses are scored using a carefully designed process:

- Two different people will read and score your essay.
- Each scorer awards 1–4 points for each dimension: reading, analysis, and writing.
- The two scores for each dimension are added.
- You'll receive three scores for the SAT Essay—one for each dimension—ranging from 2 to 8 points.

Essay Scoring Rubric

Score Point 4: Advanced

Reading

- The response demonstrates thorough comprehension of the source text.
- The response shows an understanding of the text's central idea(s) and of most important details and how they interrelate, demonstrating a comprehensive understanding of the text.
- The response is free of errors of fact or interpretation with regard to the text.
- The response makes skillful use of textual evidence (quotations, paraphrases, or both), demonstrating a complete understanding of the source text.

Analysis

- The response offers an insightful analysis of the source text and demonstrates a sophisticated understanding of the analytical task.
- The response offers a thorough, well-considered evaluation of the author's use of evidence, reasoning, stylistic and persuasive elements, and/or feature(s) of the student's own choosing.

- The response contains relevant, sufficient, and strategically chosen support for claim(s) or point(s) made.
- The response focuses consistently on those features of the text that are most relevant to addressing the task.

Writing

- The response is cohesive and demonstrates a highly effective use and command of language.
- The response includes a precise central claim.
- The response includes a skillful introduction and conclusion. The response demonstrates a deliberate and highly effective progression of ideas both within paragraphs and throughout the esssay.
- The response has a wide variety in sentence structures. The response demonstrates a consistent use of precise woed choice. The response maintains a formal style and objective tone.
- The response shows a strong command of the conventions of standard written English and is free or virtually free of errors.

Score Point 3: Proficient

Reading

- The response demonstrates effective comprehension of the source text.
- The response shows an understanding of the text's central idea(s) and important details.
- The response is free of substantive errors of fact and interpretation with regard to the text.
- The response makes appropriate use of textual evidence (quotations, paraphrases, or both), demonstrating an understanding of the source text.

Analysis

- The response offers an effective analysis of the source text and demonstrates an understanding of the analytical task.

- The response competently evaluates the author's use of evidence, reasoning, stylistic and persuasive elements, and/or feature(s) of the student's own choosing.

- The response contains relevant and sufficient support for claim(s) or point(s) made.

- The response focuses primarily on those features of the text that are most relevant to addressing the task.

Writing

- The response is mostly cohesive and demonstrates effective use and control of language.

- The response includes a central claim or implicit controlling idea.

- The response includes an effective introduction and conclusion. The response demonstrates a clear progression of ideas both within paragraphs and throughout the essay.

- The response has variety in sentence structures. The response demonstrates some precise word choice. The response maintains a formal style and objective tone.

- The response shows a good control of the conventions of standard written English and is free of significant errors that detract from the quality of writing.

Score Point 2: Partial

Reading

- The response demonstrates some comprehension of the source text.

- The response shows an understanding of the text's central idea(s) but not of important details.

- The response may contain errors of fact and/or interpretation with regard to the text.

- The response makes limited and/or haphazard use of textual evidence (quotations, paraphrases, or both), demonstrating some understanding of the source text.

Analysis

- The response offers limited analysis of the source text and demonstrates only partial understanding of the analytical task.

- The response identifies and attempts to describe the author's use of evidence, reasoning, and/or stylistic and persuasive elements, and/or feature(s) of the student's own choosing, but merely asserts rather than explains their importance, or one or more aspects of the response's analysis are unwarranted based on the text.

- The response contains little or no support for claim(s) or point(s) made.

- The response may lack a clear focus on those features of the text that are most relevant to addressing the task.

Writing

- The response demonstrates little or no cohesion and limited skill in the use and control of language.

- The response may lack a clear central claim or controlling idea or may deviate from the claim or idea over the course of the response.

- The response may include an ineffective introduction and/or conclusion. The response may demonstrate some progression of ideas within paragraphs but not throughout the response.

- The response has limited variety in sentence structures; sentence structures may be repetitive.

- The response demonstrates general or vague word choice; word choice may be repetitive. The response may deviate noticeably from a formal style and objective tone.

- The response shows a limited control of the conventions of standard written English and contains errors that detract from the quality of writing and may impede understanding.

Score Point 1: Inadequate

Reading

- The response demonstrates little or no comprehension of the source text.

- The response fails to show an understanding of the text's central idea(s) and may include only details without reference to central idea(s).

- The response may contain numerous errors of fact and/or interpretation with regard to the text.

- The response makes little or no use of textual evidence (quotations, paraphrases, or both), demonstrating little or no understanding of the source text.

Analysis

- The response offers little or no analysis or ineffective analysis of the source text and demonstrates little or no understanding of the analytic task.

- The response identifies without explanation some aspects of the author's use of evidence, reasoning, and/or stylistic and persuasive elements, and/or feature(s) of the student's choosing, or numerous aspects of the response's analysis are unwarranted based on the text.

- The response contains little or no support for claim(s) or point(s) made, or support is largely irrelevant.

- The response may not focus on features of the text that are relevant to addressing the task, or the response offers no discernible analysis (e.g., is largely or exclusively summary).

Writing

- The response demonstrates little or no cohesion and inadequate skill in the use and control of language.

- The response may lack a clear central claim or controlling idea.

- The response lacks a recognizable introduction and conclusion. The response does not have a discernible progression of ideas.

- The response lacks variety in sentence structures; sentence structures may be repetitive. The response demonstrates general and vague word choice; word choice may be poor or inaccurate. Th response may lack a formal style and objective tone.

- The response shows a weak control of the conventions of standard written English and may contain numerous errors that undermine the quality of writing.

WHAT YOU MUST DO NOW TO RAISE YOUR SAT SCORE

1. Follow the directions on page 477 to determine your score for the SAT test you've just taken. These results will give you a good idea of how hard you'll need to study in order to achieve a certain score on the actual SAT.

2. Eliminate your weaknesses in each of the SAT test areas by taking the following Giant Steps toward SAT success:

Reading Part

Giant Step 1

Take advantage of the Verbal Strategies that begin on page 123. Read again the Explanatory Answer for each of the Reading questions that you got wrong. Refer to the reading comprehension strategy that applies to each of your incorrect answers. Learn each of these Reading Strategies thoroughly. These strategies are crucial if you want to raise your SAT Verbal score substantially.

Giant Step 2

You can improve your vocabulary by doing the following:

1. Study the Gruber Prefix-Root-Suffix List beginning on page 309.

2. Learn the Hot Prefixes and Roots beginning on page 627.

3. Read through 250 Most Common SAT Vocabulary Words on page 315.

4. Look through The Most Important/Frequently Used SAT Words and Their Opposites beginning on page 319.

5. Learn the 3 Vocabulary Strategies beginning on page 148.

6. Read as widely as possible—not only novels. Non-fiction is important too—and don't forget to read newspapers and magazines.

7. Listen to people who speak well. Tune in to worth-while TV programs.

8. Use the dictionary frequently and extensively—at home, on the bus, at work, etc.

9. Play word games—for example, crossword puzzles, anagrams, and Scrabble.

Math Part

Giant Step 3

Make good use of the 19 Math Strategies that begin on page 72. Read again the solutions for each Math question that you answered incorrectly. Refer to the Math Strategy that applies to each of your incorrect answers. Learn each of these Math Strategies thoroughly. I repeat that these strategies are crucial if you want to raise your SAT Math score substantially.

Giant Step 4

You may want to take the "101 Most Important Math Questions You Need to Know How to Solve" test beginning on page 35 and follow the directions after the test for a basic math skills diagnosis.

For each math question that you got wrong in the test, note the reference to the Complete SAT Math Refresher section beginning on page 163. This reference will explain clearly the mathematical principle involved in the solution of the question you answered incorrectly. Learn that particular mathematical principle thoroughly.

For Both the Math and Reading Parts

Giant Step 5

You may want to take the Strategy Diagnostic Test for the New SAT beginning on page 1 to assess whether you're using the best strategies for the questions.

Writing and Language Part

Giant Step 6

Make use of the Grammar and Usage Refresher—Part 8, page 325.

After you have done some of the tasks you have been advised to do in the suggestions, proceed to Practice Test 2, beginning on page 513.

After taking Practice Test 2, concentrate on the weaknesses that still remain.

Remember:

I am the master of my fate:
I am the captain of my soul.

—From the poem "Invictus"
by William Ernest Henley

SAT PRACTICE TEST 2

TO SEE HOW YOU WOULD DO ON AN SAT AND WHAT YOU SHOULD DO TO IMPROVE

Introduction

This SAT test is very much like the actual SAT. It follows the genuine SAT very closely. Taking this test is like taking the actual SAT. The following is the purpose of taking this test:

1. To find out what you are *weak* in and what you are *strong* in.

2. To know where to concentrate your efforts in order to be fully prepared for the actual test.

Taking this test will prove to be a very valuable TIMESAVER for you. Why waste time studying what you already know? Spend your time profitably by studying what you *don't* know. That is what this test will tell you.

In this book, we do not waste precious pages. We get right down to the business of helping you to increase your SAT scores.

Other SAT preparation books place their emphasis on drill, drill, drill. We do not believe that drill work is of primary importance in preparing for the SAT exam. Drill work has its place. In fact, this book contains a great variety of drill material featuring SAT-type questions (Reading and Math and Writing), practically all of which have explanatory answers also keyed to basic skills and strategies. Our drill work is coordinated with learning Critical-Thinking Skills. These skills will help you to think clearly and critically so that you will be able to answer many more SAT questions correctly.

Ready? Start taking the test. It's just like the real thing.

ANSWER SHEET

It is recommended that you use a No. 2 pencil. It is very important that you fill in the entire circle darkly and completely. If you change your response, erase as completely as possible. Incomplete marks or erasures may affect your score.

Complete Mark ●   **Examples of Incomplete Marks** ⊘ ⊗ ⊖ ◑ ◍ ◠ ◐ ◯

SECTION 1: READING

	A B C D		A B C D		A B C D		A B C D		A B C D
1	○ ○ ○ ○	12	○ ○ ○ ○	23	○ ○ ○ ○	34	○ ○ ○ ○	45	○ ○ ○ ○
2	○ ○ ○ ○	13	○ ○ ○ ○	24	○ ○ ○ ○	35	○ ○ ○ ○	46	○ ○ ○ ○
3	○ ○ ○ ○	14	○ ○ ○ ○	25	○ ○ ○ ○	36	○ ○ ○ ○	47	○ ○ ○ ○
4	○ ○ ○ ○	15	○ ○ ○ ○	26	○ ○ ○ ○	37	○ ○ ○ ○	48	○ ○ ○ ○
5	○ ○ ○ ○	16	○ ○ ○ ○	27	○ ○ ○ ○	38	○ ○ ○ ○	49	○ ○ ○ ○
6	○ ○ ○ ○	17	○ ○ ○ ○	28	○ ○ ○ ○	39	○ ○ ○ ○	50	○ ○ ○ ○
7	○ ○ ○ ○	19	○ ○ ○ ○	29	○ ○ ○ ○	40	○ ○ ○ ○	51	○ ○ ○ ○
8	○ ○ ○ ○	19	○ ○ ○ ○	30	○ ○ ○ ○	41	○ ○ ○ ○	52	○ ○ ○ ○
9	○ ○ ○ ○	20	○ ○ ○ ○	31	○ ○ ○ ○	42	○ ○ ○ ○		
10	○ ○ ○ ○	21	○ ○ ○ ○	32	○ ○ ○ ○	43	○ ○ ○ ○		
11	○ ○ ○ ○	22	○ ○ ○ ○	33	○ ○ ○ ○	44	○ ○ ○ ○		

SECTION 2: WRITING AND LANGUAGE

	A B C D		A B C D		A B C D		A B C D		A B C D
1	○ ○ ○ ○	10	○ ○ ○ ○	19	○ ○ ○ ○	28	○ ○ ○ ○	37	○ ○ ○ ○
2	○ ○ ○ ○	11	○ ○ ○ ○	20	○ ○ ○ ○	29	○ ○ ○ ○	38	○ ○ ○ ○
3	○ ○ ○ ○	12	○ ○ ○ ○	21	○ ○ ○ ○	30	○ ○ ○ ○	39	○ ○ ○ ○
4	○ ○ ○ ○	13	○ ○ ○ ○	22	○ ○ ○ ○	31	○ ○ ○ ○	40	○ ○ ○ ○
5	○ ○ ○ ○	14	○ ○ ○ ○	23	○ ○ ○ ○	32	○ ○ ○ ○	41	○ ○ ○ ○
6	○ ○ ○ ○	15	○ ○ ○ ○	24	○ ○ ○ ○	33	○ ○ ○ ○	42	○ ○ ○ ○
7	○ ○ ○ ○	16	○ ○ ○ ○	25	○ ○ ○ ○	34	○ ○ ○ ○	43	○ ○ ○ ○
8	○ ○ ○ ○	17	○ ○ ○ ○	26	○ ○ ○ ○	35	○ ○ ○ ○	44	○ ○ ○ ○
9	○ ○ ○ ○	18	○ ○ ○ ○	27	○ ○ ○ ○	36	○ ○ ○ ○		

SECTION 3: MATHEMATICS *(NO CALCULATOR ALLOWED)*

1 A B C D   4 A B C D   7 A B C D   10 A B C D   13 A B C D

2 A B C D   5 A B C D   8 A B C D   11 A B C D   14 A B C D

3 A B C D   6 A B C D   9 A B C D   12 A B C D   15 A B C D

Only answers that are gridded will be scored. You will not receive credit for anything written in the boxes.

16   17   18   19   20

SECTION 4: MATHEMATICS *(CALCULATOR ALLOWED)*

1 A B C D   7 A B C D   13 A B C D   19 A B C D   25 A B C D

2 A B C D   8 A B C D   14 A B C D   20 A B C D   26 A B C D

3 A B C D   9 A B C D   15 A B C D   21 A B C D   27 A B C D

4 A B C D   10 A B C D   16 A B C D   22 A B C D   28 A B C D

5 A B C D   11 A B C D   17 A B C D   23 A B C D   29 A B C D

6 A B C D   12 A B C D   18 A B C D   24 A B C D   30 A B C D

SECTION 4: MATHEMATICS *(CALCULATOR ALLOWED)* (CONTINUED)

Only answers that are gridded will be scored. You will not receive credit for anything written in the boxes.

31 32 33 34 35

36 37 38

SECTION 5: TEST 2 ESSAY *(OPTIONAL)*

Begin your essay on this page. If you need more space, continue on the next page. Do not write outside of the essay box.

Continue on the next page if necessary.

Continuation of Section 5: Test 2 Essay from previous page. Write below only if you need more space.

SECTION 1: READING TEST

65 Minutes, 52 Questions

Turn to Section 1 of your answer sheet (page 514) to answer the questions in this section.

Directions

Each passage or pair of passages below is followed by a number of questions. After reading each passage or pair, choose the best answer to each question based on what is stated or implied in the passage or passages and in any accompanying graphics (such as a table or graph).

Questions 1–11 are based on the following passage.

This passage is from Randolph Jones, "The Sussex Place," 1940. The setting is an elite private gentlemen's club in London in 1932. Lord Alton Sussex is a 25-year-old Englishman.

Lord Alton Sussex slouched in his heavily upholstered chair at the Brookshire club, stared deeply into his drink and raised the crystal glass up high, held it high up there for several moments, and exhaled rather noisily.
5　He relished the idea that he was attracting attention in the hushed room, was encouraging the viewpoint that he was insufficiently appreciative of his standing at the Brookshire. Playing on this, he made a series of fluttering noises with his lips and tongue—not loudly, just
10　carelessly. Finally, eyes closed, he brought the glass slowly down and polished off the golden brown liquid in one long gulp, eliciting another of his sighs.
　　Back to the matter at hand! He needed to hire a valet. He thought of Malcolm Dearing, his father's.
15　The gulf between Dearing and the family seemed, if not physically huge, uncrossable. The man had a wife and three children—four?—but never did the families gather in one place despite 16 years of the man's service. Alton hazily remembered visiting Dearing's son
20　when he was in hospital recovering from an injury. The visit, prompted by Alton's mother, was as awkward as he had feared. Dearing wasn't present—he was in fact accompanying Alton's father on a business trip—but the man's wife was there and she could do little to
25　alleviate the stuffy discomfort in the room. The two boys were both 14, they even looked alike, but Alton could think of nothing to say, and the other boy seemed too tired to talk, though perhaps there was resentment there as well. *Yes, there certainly was*, Alton thought
30　now, the scene coming more sharply into focus. *And dash it, I knew it at the time, though I pretended otherwise. He must have hated me. His father was my father's "man."*
　　Alton affected a shudder at the term. Nor did he care
35　much for the term his mother used: manservant. He did not want a house full of *servants*. No butler, just a cook and maid, a few gardeners and such, at least until he and Beatrice had children. He would drive his own car, even learn to fix the thing if it came to that. But he did
40　think a man in his position should have an assistant to help with travel plans, shopping errands, perhaps routine accounting.
　　"Another whisky, Lord Alton?"
　　It was Smetana, the lanky bald waiter, new at the
45　club, whose near-perfect English was at times made suddenly exotic by a thick Czech accent that appeared only on certain sounds.
　　"I don't know, old boy, what do you think?" And then, widening his eyes and lowering his voice con-
50　spiratorially, "Should I?"
　　Smetana picked up on the young man's playfulness and bent his tall frame down so that he could speak directly in Alton's ear. The seated man smiled, but withdrew a few inches. His eyes went to a table of
55　three men playing cribbage, who had turned to watch the scene.
　　"Sir," whispered Smetana, "I think you should have another one and then decide if you should have had it afterwards."

Go on to the next page. ⇨

60   Rather pleased at this remark, Alton relaxed a bit and laughed, using the opportunity to pull back a bit farther.

    "Sound advice my friend. I'll do just that and report afterwards."

65   The waiter now put his tray down on a side table and adopted a half-squatting posture next to Alton's chair. Alton saw that the cribbage players were eyeing him with amusement.

    "But before deciding the matter then, you must first
70 have another to . . ."

    "Yes, yes," said Alton in full voice as soon as the waiter took a breath. Smetana looked at him for a moment, nodded, stretched himself upwards, took the empty glass, and walked away. One of the cribbage
75 players, "Reg" Bowles, whom Alton knew from their time together at Eton, made his way over.

    "Hullo, Sussex. Still sneaking in past the man at the door, eh? Say, I heard you're marrying—bravo. Heard also that you're moving out of the old family manse.
80 Just a cozy cottage for two in the country?"

    "Something like that." Despite his distaste at Bowles' manner, he tried to be pleasant. "I'm in the market for a valet at the moment. Know of anyone?"

    "Pardon me, sir." It was Smetana, who had quickly
85 returned with the drink, though he did not set it down. "I was not trying to hear your conversation, but I believe you said you needed a valet. This is something that I have experience in."

    Bowles was clearly delighted. "Well then, problem
90 solved," he said, putting his arm around Smetana's shoulder. "He has experience in."

    Alton noticed that the headwaiter had entered the room and was standing by a wall, watching them closely.

95   "Well, that's interesting, but well, you're a waiter, yes?" Alton laughed awkwardly at the obviousness of his remark. "And, as a foreigner, that is, as someone not from England, well . . . I need someone who knows the lay of the land. Someone who knows the people I
100 know . . ."

    He stopped as the headwaiter now approached them.

    "Is everything all right, gentlemen? Did you need to discuss some matter with Smetana?"

    "Careful or Sussex here will steal your staff right
105 out from under you," said Bowles.

    "No, no, nothing of the sort," Alton quickly cut in. "No, were fine. We're done here. The drink, please," he said with some annoyance.

    Smetana put the drink down and exited the room
110 with the headwaiter close behind. Alton turned on Bowles.

    "You may have gotten that man sacked, you know."

    "You're a sensitive little thing, aren't you Sussex," Bowles replied, making his way back to the gaming
115 table.

    Lord Alton finished his drink as quickly as he could and left the club.

The Sussex Place Questions

1. What is the purpose of the description of Alton's memory of his visit to his father's valet's son?

  (A) to show that Alton was unable to show the proper level of sympathy for a boy that he hardly knew

  (B) to provide insight into how Alton viewed the consequences of the difference in status between his family and Dearing's

  (C) to give the reader a better indication of how Alton planned to resolve his problem regarding the hiring of a valet for himself

  (D) to indicate that Alton's memory of the event was inaccurate in a way that was typical of people in his position

2. It is clear from Alton's behavior that he

  (A) enjoys thinking of himself as someone who doesn't always conform to custom

  (B) is always aware of the effect that his actions have on others

  (C) would prefer not to concern himself with serious issues

  (D) is not concerned with what others in the club think of him

3. Which choice provides the best evidence for the answer to the previous question?

  (A) Lines 5–8 ("He relished . . . Brookshire.")

  (B) Line 13 ("*Back to the matter at hand!*")

  (C) Line 34 ("Alton affected a shudder at the term.")

  (D) Lines 60–62 ("Rather pleased . . . farther.")

Go on to the next page. ⟹

4. Which choice best describes how Alton interacts with Smetana?

   (A) He is disappointed that the waiter does not feel comfortable engaging in a conversation.
   (B) He interacts in a friendly manner with Smetana so as to show the waiter that he, Alton, does not care what the other men at the club think of him.
   (C) He at first enjoys conversing with Smetana, but then becomes more and more tense during the rest of their interactions throughout the passage.
   (D) He wishes to engage with him in a friendly manner, but he is somewhat uncomfortable with some of Smetana's actions.

5. As used in line 25, "alleviate" most nearly means

   (A) further
   (B) rearrange
   (C) reduce
   (D) repair

6. Bowles' attitude toward Smetana is best described in which of the following ways?

   (A) condescending
   (B) playful
   (C) instructive
   (D) harsh

7. The presence of the headwaiter serves mainly to

   (A) provide a comic element
   (B) increase the tension of the situation
   (C) introduce a character with a point of view similar to that of the narrator
   (D) help the reader picture the setting

8. In what way does Alton wish to have a home that differs from that of the one he knew as a boy?

   (A) He wants to consider the people who work for him as friends.
   (B) He would prefer to have a home far from any big city.
   (C) He wants to live in a less luxurious manner.
   (D) He prefers to have more assistance with certain daily matters than did his father.

9. Which choice provides the best evidence for the answer to the previous question?

   (A) Lines 15–16 ("The gulf . . . uncrossable.")
   (B) Lines 30–32 ("*And dash it . . . otherwise.*")
   (C) Lines 35–36 ("He did not . . . *servants.*")
   (D) Lines 39–42 ("But . . . accounting.")

10. One of the main ideas of the passage is that

    (A) Alton thinks of himself as less concerned with differences in social status than he actually is
    (B) the members of the club are actually rivals, regardless of how friendly they behave with each other
    (C) Alton has more in common with the people who work at the club than he does with the club's members
    (D) it is impossible for people who come from a privileged background to understand the concerns of people who have less wealth

11. As used in line 54, "withdrew" most nearly means

    (A) removed
    (B) lowered
    (C) leaned in
    (D) pulled back

Go on to the next page. ⇨

Questions 12–22 are based on the following passage.

The following passage is reprinted from John McDermott, "Technology: The Opiate of the Intellectuals," *which appeared originally in* The New York Review of Books, *July 31, 1969. The passage discusses advanced technological institutions and their relation to the workforce, with social implications.*

A second major hypothesis would argue that the most important dimension of advanced technological institutions is the social one; that is, the institutions are agencies of highly centralized and intensive social control.

5 Technology conquers nature, as the saying goes. But to do so it must first conquer man. More precisely, it demands a very high degree of control over the training, mobility, and skills of the workforce. The absence (or decline) of direct controls or of coercion should not

10 serve to obscure from our view the reality and intensity of the social controls which are employed (such as the internalized belief in inequality of opportunity, indebtedness through credit, advertising, selective service channeling, and so on).

15 Advanced technology has created a vast increase in occupational specialties, many of them requiring many, many years of highly specialized training. It must motivate this training. It has made ever more complex and "rational" the ways in which these occupational special-

20 ties are combined in our economic and social life. It must win passivity and obedience to this complex activity. Formerly, technical rationality had been employed only to organize the production of rather simple physical objects, for example, aerial bombs. Now technical rationality is

25 increasingly employed to organize all of the processes necessary to the utilization of physical objects, such as bombing systems, maintenance, intelligence and supply systems. For this reason it seems a mistake to argue that we are in a "post-industrial" age, a concept favored by the

30 *laissez innover* school. On the contrary, the rapid spread of technical rationality into organizational and economic life and, hence, into social life is more aptly described as a second and much more intensive phase of the industrial revolution. One might reasonably suspect that it will cre-

35 ate analogous social problems.

Accordingly, a third major hypothesis would argue that there are very profound social antagonisms or contradictions not less sharp or fundamental than

40 those ascribed by Marx to the development of nineteenth-century industrial society. The general form of the contradictions might be described as follows: a society characterized by the employment of advanced technology requires an ever more socially disciplined population, yet retains an ever declining capacity to

45 enforce the required discipline.

One may readily describe four specific forms of the same general contradiction. Occupationally, the workforce must be overtrained and underutilized. Here, again, an analogy to classical industrial practice serves

50 to shorten and simplify the explanation. I have in mind the assembly line. As a device in the organization of the work process, the assembly line is valuable mainly in that it gives management a high degree of control over the pace of the work and, more to the point in the

55 present case, it divides the work process into units so simple that the quality of the work performed is readily predictable. That is, since each operation uses only a small fraction of a worker's skill, there is a very great likelihood that the operation will be performed in a

60 minimally acceptable way. Alternately, if each operation taxed the worker's skill, there would be frequent errors in the operation, frequent disturbance of the work flow, and a thoroughly unpredictable quality to the end product. The assembly line also introduces

65 standardization in work skills and thus makes for a high degree of interchangeability among the workforce.

For analogous reasons the workforce in advanced technological systems must be relatively overtrained or, what is the same thing, its skills relatively underused.

70 My impression is that this is no less true now of sociologists than of welders, of engineers than of assemblers. The contradiction emerges when we recognize that technological progress requires a continuous increase in the skill levels of its workforce, skill levels which frequently

75 embody a fairly rich scientific and technical training, while at the same time the advance of technical rationality in work organization means that those skills will be less and less fully used.

Economically, there is a parallel process at work. It

80 is commonly observed that the workforce within technologically advanced organizations is asked to work not less hard but more so. This is particularly true for those with advanced training and skills. Brzezinski's conjecture that technical specialists undergo continuous

85 retraining is off the mark only in that it assumes such retraining only for a managing elite. To get people to

Go on to the next page. ⇨

work harder requires growing incentives. Yet the prosperity which is assumed in a technologically advanced
society erodes the value of economic incentives (while
90 of course, the values of craftsmanship are "irrational").
Salary and wage increases and the goods they purchase lose their overriding importance once necessities,
creature comforts, and an ample supply of luxuries are
assured. As if in confirmation of this point, it has been
95 pointed out that among young people, one can already
observe a radical weakening in the power of such incentives as money, status, and authority.

Questions

12. The term "technical rationality" in line 22 is used
    in conjunction with

    (A) a 20th-century euphemism for the industrial
        revolution
    (B) giving credibility to products of simple
        technology
    (C) the incorporation of unnecessary skills into
        economic social living
    (D) effective organization of production processes

13. The author states that advanced technological
    institutions exercise control by means of

    (A) the assembly-line work process
    (B) advertising, selective service channeling, etc.
    (C) direct and coercive pressures
    (D) salary incentives

14. The word "taxed" in line 61 means

    (A) a burdensome or excessive demand on the
        worker
    (B) a financial obstacle the worker must endure
    (C) the speed at which the worker must complete
        the job
    (D) the efficiency of the worker's performance on
        the job

15. The passage indicates that technologically advanced
    institutions

    (A) fully utilize worker skills
    (B) fare best under a democratic system
    (C) necessarily overtrain workers
    (D) find it unnecessary to enforce discipline

16. The value of the assembly line is that it
    I. minimizes the frequency of error
    II. allows for interchangeability among the work-
        force
    III. allows for full utilization of workers' skills

    (A) I and III only
    (B) I and II only
    (C) II and III only
    (D) I, II, and III

17. The article states that the workforce within the
    framework of a technologically advanced organiza-
    tion is

    (A) expected to work less hard
    (B) segregated into levels defined by the degree of
        technical training
    (C) familiarized with every process of production
    (D) expected to work harder

18. From the tone of the article, it can be inferred that
    the author is

    (A) in favor of increased employee control of
        industry
    (B) a social scientist objectively reviewing an
        industrial trend
    (C) vehemently opposed to the increase of
        technology
    (D) skeptical of the workings of advanced
        technological institutions

19. According to the author, economic incentives

    (A) are necessary for all but the managerial elite
    (B) are bigger and better in a society made pros-
        perous by technology
    (C) cease to have importance beyond a certain
        level of luxury
    (D) are impressive only to new members of the
        workforce

20. The "managing elite" in line 86 refers to

    (A) the assembly-line workers only
    (B) the craftsman only
    (C) the owners of the organizations
    (D) the top technical specialists

Go on to the next page. ⇨

21. According to the article, technological progress requires

    I.   increasing skill levels of workforce
    II. less utilization of work skills
    III. rich scientific and technical training

    (A) II and III only
    (B) I and III only
    (C) III only
    (D) I, II, and III

22. The article states that money, status, and authority

    (A) will always be powerful work incentives
    (B) are not powerful incentives for the young
    (C) are unacceptable to radical workers
    (D) are incentives that are a throwback to 19th-century industrial society

Go on to the next page. ⇨

Questions 23–33 are based on the following passage.

The following passage is based on the discovery of the Higgs boson particle.

Thanks to the startlingly successful discovery of the Higgs boson particle in 2012, much of the general public has at least heard of the Large Hadron Collider (LHC), the massive supercollider that sends particles
5 flying at near-light speeds around a 17-mile loop that lies beneath the France-Switzerland border. For perfectly understandable reasons, however, most people outside the scientific community (and a significant number within) who do know of the LHC are at best
10 unsure as to the reason for its existence. It therefore seems a good idea to outline some of the major purposes of the collider, the world's largest machine, one of the most expensive scientific devices ever created, and the product of the work of experts from over 100
15 countries. These purposes can seem quite specific, even trivial, but they are part of an effort to understand the deepest structure that lies behind space and time.

Physicists, naturally, are the most intellectually invested in the LHC, and those involved in the proj-
20 ect hope to shed light on one of the most problematic issues in contemporary physics: the nature of the relationship between quantum mechanics and general relativity, the two most important scientific theories to come out of the 20th century. Coming to a better under-
25 standing of this relationship should throw light on the basic laws behind the characteristics of elementary particles such as quarks, leptons, antiquarks, and bosons. (Atoms were once thought to be elementary particles, but it was discovered that they actually consisted of
30 other, *subatomic* particles.)

Of particular interest is whether the LHC experiments will corroborate what is known as the Standard Model or whether some alternative will prove more satisfactory. Briefly, the Standard Model, dating back
35 to the latter half of the 20th century, does a remarkable job in making unified sense of the electromagnetic force and the strong and weak nuclear forces. It also predicts that the decay width of the Higgs particle depends on the value of its mass. It does not, however,
40 resolve questions regarding gravity and general relativity. The collisions engendered by the LHC could very well lead to a new physics that incorporates all four of the forces, something that could even be called a Grand Unified Theory (GUT).

45 Speaking of GUTs, it is hoped that the LHC might help answer a related question that has bothered scientists for some time now. Of the four forces, gravity is by far the weakest. (By contrast the *weak nuclear force* is 10^{32} times stronger.) Why this should be is the major
50 *hierarchy problem* in particle physics. The existence of extra dimensions could help explain this discrepancy, as well as lead to an understanding of why the expansion of the universe is accelerating.

If the LHC can confirm or repudiate the existence of
55 extra dimensions, this would also have a great impact on *string theory*, in which the traditional idea of point-like particles is replaced by one-dimensional objects known a *strings*. This theory depends on the existence of more dimensions than the four we know of: length,
60 width, height, and time. While many physicists accept the existence of only these traditional four dimensions, others believe that certain mathematical calculations are better handled when one considers a different number of dimensions of spacetime. Superstring theory
65 proposes the existence of 10 dimensions, and bosonic string theory requires spacetime to have 26 dimensions. These extra dimensions are not graspable or observable by humans, but it is possible that the LHC, using its ATLAS detector—one of the two detectors responsible
70 for "sensing" the Higgs boson—could provide observational data confirming the validity of extra dimensions.

The LHC is also on the lookout for superpartner particles, sometimes called *sparticles*. These are elementary particles that are the *partners* of all the
75 particles that we now know of, as predicted by the supersymmetry theory. It may be that these sparticles share the exact same mass as their partners. However, if the symmetry is "broken," the sparticles may have masses thousands of times greater than their partners,
80 and producing them, even in an energy powerhouse like the LHC, will prove difficult. As of 2013, no evidence for sparticles had been found.

Another task of the LHC is to increase understanding of *dark matter*, the hypothetical stuff that accounts
85 for most of the universe's matter. It has been suggested that dark matter in the Milky Way Galaxy—our own—consists of WIMPs—that is, Weakly Interacting Massive Particles. If they do indeed exist, the collision of proton beams within the LHC may lead to their detec-
90 tion, though only indirectly. This is because a WIMP

Go on to the next page. ⇨

barely interacts with matter. If large amounts of energy go missing during collisions (and all the other collision products *are* detected), this would lend support to the existence of WIMPs. Direct detection would, however,
95 be needed to show that they actually account for dark matter.

ATLAS and the other three main detectors (there are seven in total) in the LHC have a range of other purposes, some of which directly deal with questions
100 regarding the time shortly after the Big Bang, the model for the universe's earliest periods and subsequent evolution. For example, the ALICE detector at the LHC investigates the nature of the "fluid" matter known as quark-gluon plasma, which is the densest
105 matter we know of outside of a black hole, and which is believed to have existed shortly after the Big Bang. The LHCb detector investigates what happened to the antimatter that went "missing" after the Big Bang.

So far, the LHC has produced nothing further to
110 rival the excitement surrounding the discovery of the Higgs boson, but of course there is a daunting amount of data to sort through: The collider creates 40 million collisions each second. It is a virtual certainty that from those events will come information that provides sur-
115 prising insights into the ultimate nature of reality.

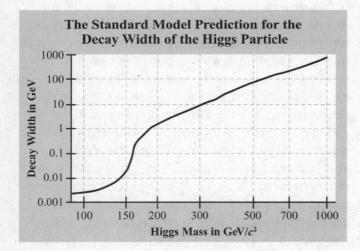

The Standard Model Prediction for the Decay Width of the Higgs Particle

Large Hadron Collider Questions

23. The author anticipates which of the following criticisms regarding the Large Hadron Collider (LHC)?

    (A) Not all the countries involved in constructing the LHC have benefited from the work being done with the collider.

    (B) Not enough scientists outside the field of physics are involved in the work being done with the LHC.

    (C) The reasons for the LHC are quite precise but not of great significance.

    (D) The physicists working with the LHC have a bias toward theories for which no good evidence exists.

24. According to the author, detections made by ATLAS could lead to

    (A) the confirmation that the Higgs boson exists only in "extra" dimensions that cannot be directly observed

    (B) better methods for calculating the number of dimensions in spacetime

    (C) the existence of sparticles

    (D) support for a theory that departs from the idea that all particles are point-like objects

25. Why does the author use the term "indirectly" when discussing the possibility that the LHC could add to our knowledge of dark matter?

    (A) The existence of WIMPs would not actually be detected.

    (B) There would still be many scientists who would insist that the existence of dark matter is purely hypothetical, regardless of the evidence.

    (C) There is little chance that all the collisions involved could be identified.

    (D) The LHC would not be able to detect every WIMP that would be produced by a collision.

Go on to the next page. ⇨

26. As used in line 111, "daunting" most nearly means
    (A) unlimited
    (B) intimidating
    (C) thrilling
    (D) incomprehensible

27. According to the passage, the Standard Model has not been able to answer certain key questions regarding
    (A) the relationship between general relativity and the weakest of the known forces
    (B) the underlying unity of the electromagnetic force and nuclear forces
    (C) why the strong nuclear force is so much stronger than the weak nuclear force
    (D) why bosons, but not atoms, are elementary particles

28. The ATLAS detector has the potential to provide confirming data regarding
    (A) "missing" antimatter
    (B) quark-gluon plasma
    (C) sparticles
    (D) string theory

29. The author suggests that, because of energy limitations, it may be very difficult for the LHC to
    (A) adequately analyze all the important data coming from the many collisions
    (B) address the most important elements of the hierarchy problem
    (C) create sparticles as predicted by broken symmetry
    (D) provide evidence leading to a Grand Unified Theory

30. What choice provides the best evidence for the answer to the previous question?
    (A) Lines 49–50 ("Why . . . physics.")
    (B) Lines 67–71 ("These . . . dimensions.")
    (C) Lines 77–81 ("However . . . difficult.")
    (D) Lines 109–113 ("So far . . . second.")

The information in the graph refers to Higgs particles that have masses up to 1,000 GeV/c^2 (GeV is the abbreviation for gigaelectron volts and c^2 is the speed of light squared.)

31. According to the passage, the information in the graph at the end of the passage lends support to
    (A) the Standard Model
    (B) the general theory of relativity
    (C) a Grand Unified theory
    (D) string theory

32. According to the graph, which of the following changes in the mass of a Higgs particle would result in the largest increase in its decay width? (All answers are given in GeV/c^2.)
    (A) from 100 to 130
    (B) from 140 to 180
    (C) from 200 to 350
    (D) from 900 to 1,000

33. Based on the information in the graph, a Higgs particle that had a mass of 1,500 GeV/c^2 would most likely have a decay width of
    (A) about 1,000 GeV
    (B) about 2,000 GeV
    (C) about 4,000 GeV
    (D) about 10,000 GeV

Go on to the next page. ⇨

Directions

The two passages below are followed by questions based on their content and on the relationship between the two passages. Answer the questions on the basis of what is *stated* or *implied* in the passages and in any introductory material that may be provided.

Questions 34–43 are based on the following passages.

The following two passages describe two views of the makeup and character of an artist. Passage 1 is from an essay by H. L. Mencken appearing in the Baltimore Evening Sun *on April 7, 1924, commonly known as "The Relation of Artists to Their Society." Passage 2 is from Ralph Waldo Emerson's famous speech delivered before the Phi Beta Kappa Society in Cambridge, Massachusetts, on August 31, 1837, known as "The American Scholar."*

Passage 1

The special quality which makes an artist of any worth might be defined, indeed, as an extraordinary capacity for irritation, a pathological sensitiveness to environmental pricks and stings. He differs from the rest of
5 us mainly because he reacts sharply and in an uncommon manner to phenomena which leave the rest of us unmoved, or, at most, merely vaguely annoyed. He is, in brief, a more delicate fellow than we are and hence less fitted to prosper and enjoy himself under the condi-
10 tions of life that he and we must face alike. Therefore, he takes to artistic endeavor, which is at once a criticism of life and an attempt to escape from life.

So much for the theory of it. The more the facts are studied, the more they bear it out. In those fields of art,
15 at all events, which concern themselves with ideas as well as with sensations, it is almost impossible to find any trace of an artist who was not actively hostile to his environment and thus an indifferent patriot. From Dante to Tolstoy and from Shakespeare to Mark Twain,
20 the story is ever the same. Names suggest themselves instantly: Goethe, Heine, Shelley, Byron, Thackeray, Balzac, Rabelais, Cervantes, Swift, Dostoevsky, Carlyle, Molière, Pope—all bitter critics of their time and nation, most of them piously hated by the contempo-
25 rary 100 percenters, some of them actually fugitives from rage and reprisal.

Dante put all of the patriotic Italians of his day into Hell and showed them boiling, roasting, and writhing on hooks. Cervantes drew such a devastating picture of
30 the Spain that he lived in that it ruined the Spaniards. Shakespeare made his heroes foreigners and his clowns Englishmen. Goethe was in favor of Napoleon. Rabelais, a citizen of Christendom rather than of France, raised a cackle against it that Christendom is still trying
35 in vain to suppress. Swift, having finished the Irish and then the English, proceeded to finish the whole human race. The exceptions are few and far between, and not many of them will bear examination. So far as I know, the only eminent writer in English history who was also
40 a 100 percent Englishman, absolutely beyond suspicion, was Samuel Johnson. But was Johnson actually an artist? If he was, then a kazoo player is a musician. He employed the materials of one of the arts, to wit, words, but his use of them was mechanical, not artis-
45 tic. If Johnson were alive today, he would be a United States senator, or a university president. He left such wounds upon English prose that it took a century to recover from them.

Passage 2

For the ease and pleasure of treading the old road,
50 accepting the fashions, the education, the religion of society, he takes the cross of making his own and, of course, the self-accusation, the faint heart, the frequent uncertainty and loss of time, which are the nettles and tangling vines in the way of the self-relying and self-
55 directed, and the state of virtual hostility in which he seems to stand to society, and especially to educated society. For all this loss and scorn, what offset? The artist is to find consolation in exercising the highest functions of human nature. The artist is one who raises
60 himself from private consideration and breathes and lives on public and illustrious thoughts. The artist is the world's eye. He is the world's heart. He is to resist the vulgar prosperity that retrogrades ever to barbarism, by preserving and communicating heroic sentiments,
65 noble biographies, melodious verse, and the conclusions of history. Whatsoever oracles the human heart, in all emergencies, in all solemn hours, has uttered as its commentary on the world of actions—these he shall receive and impart. And whatsoever new verdict Rea-
70 son from her inviolable seat pronounces on the passing men and women and events of today—this he shall hear and promulgate.

Go on to the next page. ⇨

These being his functions, it becomes the artist to
feel all confidence in himself and to defer never to
75 the popular cry. He and he alone knows the world.
The world of any moment is the merest appearance.
Some great decorum, some fetish of a government,
some ephemeral trade, or war, or man, is cried up by
half mankind and cried down by the other half, as if
80 all depended on this particular up or down. The odds
are that the whole question is not worth the poorest
thought which the scholar has lost in listening to the
controversy. Let him not quit his belief that a popgun
is a popgun, though the ancient and honorable of the
85 earth affirm it to be the crack of doom. In silence, in
steadiness, in severe abstraction, let him hold by himself; add observation to observation, patient of neglect,
patient of reproach, and bide his own time—happy
enough if he can satisfy himself alone that this day
90 he has seen something truly. Success treads on every
right step. For the instinct is sure that prompts him to
tell his brother what he thinks. The artist then learns
that in going down into the secrets of his own mind he
has descended into the secrets of all minds. He learns
95 that the artist who has mastered any law in his private
thoughts is master to that extent of all translated. The
poet, in utter solitude remembering his spontaneous
thoughts and recording them, is found to have recorded
that which men in crowded cities find true for them
100 also. The orator distrusts at first the fitness of his frank
confessions, his want of knowledge of the persons
he addresses, until he finds that he is the complement
of his hearers—that they drink his words because he
fulfills for them their own nature; the deeper he dives
105 into his most private, most secret presentiment, to his
wonder he finds this is the most acceptable, most public, and universally true. The people delight in it; the
better part of every man feels, This is my music; this is
myself.

Questions for Passages 1 and 2

34. Which of the following quotations is related most
closely to the principal idea of Passage 1?

(A) "When to her share some human errors fall,
Look on her face and you'll forget them all."

(B) "All human things are subject to decay, And,
when fate summons, monarchs must obey."

(C) "A little learning is a dangerous thing, Drink
deep or taste not the Pierian spring."

(D) "Great wits are sure to madness near allied,
And thin partitions do their bounds divide."

35. The author of Passage 1 seems to regard the artist as

(A) the best representative of his time
(B) an unnecessary threat to the social order
(C) one who creates out of discontent
(D) one who truly knows how to enjoy life

36. It can be inferred that the author of Passage 1
believes that United States senators and university
presidents

(A) must be treated with respect because of their
position
(B) are to be held in low esteem
(C) are generally appreciative of the great literary
classics
(D) have native writing ability

37. All of the following ideas about artists are mentioned in Passage 1 *except* that

(A) they are irritated by their surroundings
(B) they like to escape from reality
(C) they are lovers of beauty
(D) they are hated by their contemporaries

38. When the writer of Passage 2 speaks of the
"world's eye" and the "world's heart," he means

(A) the same thing
(B) culture and conscience
(C) culture and wisdom
(D) a scanning of all the world's geography and a
deep sympathy for every living thing

39. By the phrase "nettles and tangling vines" (lines
53–54), the author is probably referring to

(A) "faint heart" and "self-accusation"
(B) "the slings and arrows of outrageous fortune"
(C) a general term for the difficulties of a scholar's
life
(D) "self-accusation" and "uncertainty"

Go on to the next page. ⇨

40. The various ideas in Passage 2 are best summarized in which of these groups?

   I. truth versus society
      the artist and books
      the world and the artist

  II. the ease of living traditionally
      the glory of an artist's life
      true knowledge versus trivia

 III. the hardships of the scholar
      the artist's functions
      the artist's justifications for disregarding the world's business

(A) I and III only
(B) I only
(C) III only
(D) I, II, and III

41. In line 56, "seems to stand" means

(A) is
(B) ends probably in becoming
(C) gives the false impression of being
(D) is seen to be

42. The difference between the description of the artist in Passage 1 and the description of the artist in Passage 2 is that

(A) one is loyal to his fellow men and women, whereas the other is opposed to his or her environment
(B) one is sensitive to his or her environment, whereas the other is apathetic

(C) one has political aspirations; the other does not
(D) one has deep knowledge; the other has superficial knowledge

43. Which of the following describes statements that refer to the *same* one artist (either the one in Passage 1 *or* the one in Passage 2)?

   I. This artist's thoughts are also the spectator's thoughts.
      This artist lives modestly and not luxuriously.

  II. This artist admires foreigners over his own countrymen.
      This artist reacts to many things that most people would be neutral to.

 III. This artist is happy to be at his best.
      This artist accepts society.

(A) II only
(B) III only
(C) I and III only
(D) I, II, and III

Go on to the next page. ⇨

Questions 44–52 are based on the following passage.

The following passage explores how brilliant people think, how they may come up with their theories, and what motivates their thinking and creativity.

The discoveries made by scientific geniuses, from Archimedes through Einstein, have repeatedly revolutionized both our world and the way we see it. Yet no one really knows how the mind of a genius works.
5   Most people think that a very high IQ sets the great scientist apart. They assume that flashes of profound insight like Einstein's are the product of mental processes so arcane that they must be inaccessible to more ordinary minds.
10   But a growing number of researchers in psychology, psychiatry, and the history of science are investigating the way geniuses think. The researchers are beginning to give us tantalizing glimpses of the mental universe that can produce the discoveries of an Einstein, an
15   Edison, a Da Vinci—or any Nobel Prize winner.
Surprisingly, most researchers agree that the important variable in genius is not the IQ but creativity. Testers start with 135 as the beginning of the "genius" category, but the researchers seem to feel that, while an
20   IQ above a certain point—about 120—is very helpful for a scientist, having an IQ that goes much higher is not crucial for producing a work of genius. All human beings have at least four types of intelligence. The great scientist possesses the ability to move back and forth
25   among them—the logical-mathematical, the spatial, which includes visual perception, the linguistic, and the bodily kinesthetic.
Some corroboration of these categories comes from the reports of scientists who describe thought processes
30   centered on images, sensations, or words. Einstein reported a special "feeling at the tips of the fingers" that told him which path to take through a problem. The idea for a self-starting electric motor came to Nikola Tesla one evening as he was reciting a poem by Goethe and
35   watching a sunset. Suddenly he imagined a magnetic field rapidly rotating inside a circle of electromagnets.
Some IQ tests predict fairly accurately how well a person will do in school and how quickly he or she will master knowledge, but genius involves more than
40   knowledge. The genius has the capacity to leap significantly beyond his present knowledge and produce something new. To do this, he sees the relationship between facts or pieces of information in a new or unusual way.
45   The scientist solves a problem by shifting from one intelligence to another, although the logical-mathematical intelligence is dominant. Creative individuals seem to be marked by a special fluidity of mind. They may be able to think of a problem verbally, logically, and
50   also spatially.
Paradoxically, fluid thinking may be connected to another generally agreed-upon trait of the scientific genius—persistence, or unusually strong motivation to work on a problem. Persistence kept Einstein look-
55   ing for the solution to the question of the relationship between the law of gravity and his special theory of relativity. Yet surely creative fluidity enabled him to come up with a whole new field that included both special relativity and gravitation.
60   Many scientists have the ability to stick with a problem even when they appear not to be working on it. Werner Heisenberg discovered quantum mechanics one night during a vacation he had taken to recuperate from the mental jumble he had fallen into trying to solve the
65   atomic-spectra problem.

How Brilliant People Think Questions

44. Which statement is true, according to the passage?
    - (A) Nikola Tesla learned about magnets from his research on the works of Goethe.
    - (B) Archimedes and Einstein lived in the same century.
    - (C) Most scientists have IQ scores above 120.
    - (D) We ought to refer to intelligences rather than to intelligence.

45. The author believes that, among the four intelligences he cites, the most important one for the scientist is
    - (A) spatial
    - (B) bodily kinesthetic
    - (C) linguistic
    - (D) logical-mathematical

Go on to the next page. ⇨

46. The author focuses on the circumstances surrounding the work of great scientists in order to show that

    (A) scientific geniuses are usually eccentric in their behavior
    (B) the various types of intelligence have come into play during their work
    (C) scientists often give the impression that they are relaxing when they are really working on a problem
    (D) scientists must be happy to do their best work

47. The passage can best be described as

    (A) a comparison of how the average individual and the great scientist think
    (B) an account of the unexpected things that led to great discoveries by scientists
    (C) an explanation of the way scientific geniuses really think
    (D) a criticism of intelligence tests as they are given today

48. The passage suggests that a college football star who is majoring in literature is quite likely to have which intelligences to a high degree?

    I.   logical-mathematical
    II. spatial
    III. linguistic
    IV. bodily kinesthetic

    (A) II only
    (B) III only
    (C) I, II, and III only
    (D) II, III, and IV only

49. Which statement would the author most likely *not* agree with?

    (A) Some scientists may come up with a solution to a problem when they are working on something else.
    (B) Creativity is much more important than basic intelligence in scientific discovery.
    (C) Scientists and artists may think alike in their creative mode.
    (D) Scientists usually get the answer to a problem fairly quickly, and if they get stuck they usually go on to another problem.

50. "Fluidity" as described in lines 57–59 can best be defined as

    (A) persistence when faced with a problem
    (B) having a flighty attitude in dealing with scientific problems
    (C) being able to move from one scientific area to another
    (D) having an open mind in dealing with scientific phenomena

51. The word "paradoxically" in line 51 means

    (A) ironically
    (B) seemingly contradictorily
    (C) in a manner of speaking
    (D) experimentally

52. The author's attitude toward scientists in this passage can be seen as one of

    (A) objective intrigue
    (B) grudging admiration
    (C) subtle jealousy
    (D) growing impatience

STOP!

If you finish before time is called, you may check your work on this section only.
Do not turn to any other section in the test.

SECTION 2: WRITING AND LANGUAGE TEST

35 Minutes, 44 Questions

Turn to Section 2 of your answer sheet (page 514) to answer the questions in this section.

Directions

Each passage below is accompanied by a number of questions. For some questions, you will consider how the passage might be revised to improve the expression of ideas. For other questions, you will consider how the passage might be edited to correct errors in sentence structure, usage, or punctuation. A passage or a question may be accompanied by one or more graphics (such as a table or graph) that you will consider as you make revising and editing decisions.

Some questions will direct you to an underlined portion of a passage. Other questions will direct you to a location in a passage or ask you to think about the passage as a whole.

After reading each passage, choose the answer to each question that most effectively improves the quality of writing in the passage or that makes the passage conform to the conventions of standard written English. Many questions include a "NO CHANGE" option. Choose that option if you think the best choice is to leave the relevant portion of the passage as it is.

Questions 1–11 are based on the following passage, *Art as Destruction.*

One of the more curious of the many art movements of the 20th century, *Dadaism*—or simply *Dada*—was perhaps the ultimate example of modernist *avant-garde* thought. Even die-hard art enthusiasts of the time were confused by the goals of Dadaists, and the movement remains a puzzle to many today. (1)

Though Dada is associated with European (2) artists, especially those who first gathered at the Cabaret Voltaire in Switzerland in 1916, French artist Marcel Duchamp and others were engaged in something very similar a year or so earlier in New York. They did use the term *Dada*, but they also declared that they were fashioning *anti-art*, by which they meant that they were (3) opposed by the traditional process by which art was created and displayed in museums. Duchamp created what he called "readymades," pieces that were formed from existing objects. Most notoriously, he used a urinal to create a work titled *Fountain*, directly challenging the notion of art as a refined creation (4) thats consumed by elitists. Many angrily denounced the work, which has since become one of the most famous pieces of modern art.

[1] In Europe, which was then suffering from the horrors of the First World War, the Dadaists had a grimmer, more disillusioned approach to their work. (5) [2] The goal of Dada was therefore to be as *destructive* as previous art had been self-consciously *creative*. [3]They believed that the cultural conformity seen in the art world was the same dehumanized mindset that led to the war. [4] They also wrote papers and published manifestoes that (6) protested against what they saw as an oppressive middle-class logic that should be countered with chaos and illogic. [5] As Marcel Janco, an important Dadaist figure, said, "We had lost confidence in our culture. Everything had to be demolished."

Dada was an all-encompassing movement. Public protests, literary journals, and theater productions were all a part of a passionate attempt to overthrow accepted standards and traditions. (7) Theater-goers were scandalized by plays with absurd plots and shocking language. Poets created works that had no clear (8) meaning; some poets used seemingly random cut-and-paste processes to create poems. Concerts featured African music and jazz, music not considered "appropriate" for traditional concert halls.

After the war, Dadaism blurred into other art forms, (9) including notably surrealism and social realism. Some Dadaists emigrated to the United States. Others

Go on to the next page. ⇨

died at the hands of the Nazis, who considered their art degenerate and disgusting. The spirit of Dada lives on in the chaotic and anti-authoritarian tendencies found in various cultural practices. (10) Punk rock, for example, began as a rejection of the impulse to automatically question the traditions of the middle class. The belief that "everything has to be demolished" will no doubt find voice in our turbulent world (11) more and more times.

Art as Destruction Questions

1. At this point, the writer is considering adding the following sentence.

   The Dada movement is not unlike the post-modern movement that came at the end of the century.

   Should the writer make this addition here?

   (A) Yes, because it makes a relevant comparison that puts the Dada movement into perspective.
   (B) Yes, because it makes a point that is then expanded on in the following paragraph.
   (C) No, because the author provides no direct evidence for the claim made by the statement.
   (D) No, because it provides a comparison that has no direct relevance to the surrounding text.

2. (A) NO CHANGE
   (B) artists, especially those who were first gathered at the Cabaret Voltaire in Switzerland in 1916, French
   (C) artists—especially those who first gathered at the Cabaret Voltaire in Switzerland in 1916, French
   (D) artists, especially those who first gathered at the Cabaret Voltaire in Switzerland, in 1916 French

3. (A) NO CHANGE
   (B) opposed to
   (C) in opposition from
   (D) opposite from

4. (A) NO CHANGE
   (B) to be
   (C) which are
   (D) and that is

5. To make this paragraph most logical, sentence 2 should be placed

   (A) where it is now
   (B) before sentence 1
   (C) before sentence 4
   (D) before sentence 5

6. (A) NO CHANGE
   (B) dictated
   (C) railed
   (D) demonstrated

7. (A) NO CHANGE
   (B) People who went to the theater with plays that had absurd plots and shocking language were scandalized.
   (C) In the theater, plays with absurd plots and shocking language scandalized people who saw them.
   (D) Plays, with absurd plots and shocking language, made people who went to the theater scandalized.

8. (A) NO CHANGE
   (B) meaning, poets
   (C) meaning, for example: some
   (D) meaning while some

9. (A) NO CHANGE
   (B) forms, notably
   (C) forms, notably those of
   (D) forms, notably that of

10. Which of the following sentences most logically follows the sentence preceding it?

    (A) NO CHANGE
    (B) Early punk rockers, for example, began by rejecting the popular music of the day and went on to establish their own traditions.
    (C) Early punk rock was motivated in large part by a spirit not unlike the one that motivated the Dadaists.
    (D) Punk rock, like Dada, came about from a mix of American and European attitudes and influences.

11. (A) NO CHANGE
    (B) more times.
    (C) many times again.
    (D) many times more.

Go on to the next page. ⇨

Questions 12–22 are based on the following passage, *Racial Tension in New York*.

In July of 1863, with the American Civil War into its third bloody year, less than two weeks after the Battle of Gettysburg, officials in New York City, following the new draft laws passed by Congress, randomly drew numbers (12) to determine whom would be drafted into the Union Army. The drawing took place without a hitch. Two days later, however, a second drawing led to a terrible riot by men who did not support the Union cause, either for ideological reasons or because they feared that freed slaves would take their jobs. There was also (13) a great deal of resentment because wealthy citizens could pay a fee to avoid the draft.

At 10 in the morning, a mob of 500 or so attacked the provost marshal's office in Manhattan, (14) when the drafting took place there. The crowd, led by the volunteer firemen of Engine Company 33, hurled stones through windows, broke down doors, and set the building on fire. When the local fire department arrived on the scene, the firemen were prevented from doing their job. So as to keep other parts of the city from knowing what was going on and responding to the riot, the crowd cut telegraph lines. (15) This greatly hampered communication between different areas within New York.

(16) As usual, the state militia would have been called in to deal with the emergency, but the militia members had been sent to Pennsylvania to help the Union Army. The NYC Police Department eventually showed up and did what they could to contain the rioting, but they were outnumbered. The superintendent of police, John Alexander (17) Kennedy, though, not in uniform, was recognized by the mob, who then attacked him and left him barely conscious.

Throughout the day, the rioters destroyed buildings, including a bar that would not serve them alcohol and the Colored Orphan Asylum. African-Americans and people accused of sympathizing with them were attacked on the street, and at least 120 people were killed.

Fortunately, a heavy rain that night helped put out some of the fires. (18) Some of the rioters left for their homes. Many, however, returned the next day. In trying to restore calm, the (19) Governor of New York, Horatio Seymour, spoke from City Hall, claimed that the draft was unconstitutional. (20) Troops from surrounding areas brought in and militia forces were ordered back to the city.

On Wednesday, two days after the riots had started, a decision was made to delay the draft. News of this (21) alteration spread through the city and, after a final skirmish on Thursday in Gramercy Park, the riot came to an end. The draft was reinstated in August of that year, and eventually New York became one of the states most supportive of the Union cause as the war raged on. (22)

Racial Tension in New York Questions

Which answer choice represents the best substitute for the underlined word(s), if any?

12. (A) NO CHANGE
    (B) to determine who
    (C) for determining who
    (D) that determined which

13. (A) NO CHANGE
    (B) large amounts
    (C) much
    (D) a big deal

14. (A) NO CHANGE
    (B) in the place where the drafting occurred.
    (C) in the location where the drafting was taking place.
    (D) where the drafting took place.

15. The writer is considering deleting the underlined sentence. Should the sentence be kept or deleted?
    (A) Kept, because it helps convey the seriousness of the situation.
    (B) Kept, because it supports the main topic of the paragraph.
    (C) Deleted, because it is not relevant to the topic being discussed.
    (D) Deleted, because it needlessly repeats previously stated information.

16. (A) NO CHANGE
    (B) usually
    (C) more typically
    (D) frequently

17. (A) NO CHANGE
    (B) Kennedy, was, though not in uniform
    (C) Kennedy, despite not being in uniform, was
    (D) Kennedy was not in uniform, and was, however,

Go on to the next page. ⇨

18. (A) NO CHANGE
    (B) Some of the rioters left for their homes;
        though many returned the next day.
    (C) Some of the rioters left for their homes; but
        many returned the next day.
    (D) Some rioters left to go home, but also, many
        returned the next day.

19. (A) NO CHANGE
    (B) Governor Horatio Seymour, of New York,
        who spoke
    (C) New York governor Horatio Seymour,
        speaking
    (D) Governor of New York, Horatio Seymour,
        speaking

20. (A) NO CHANGE
    (B) Troops were brought in from surrounding
        areas and militia forces ordered
    (C) They brought in troops from surrounding
        areas, while militia forces were ordered
    (D) Troops, from surrounding areas, were brought
        in, and militia forces, ordered

21. (A) NO CHANGE
    (B) experience
    (C) turn of events
    (D) changed condition

22. At this point, the writer is considering adding the
    following sentence.

    The war finally ended in April of 1865, and
    we are still feeling the effects of that terrible
    conflict.

    Should the writer make this addition here?

    (A) Yes, because it summarizes the main events of
        the passage.
    (B) Yes, because it connects the end of the pas-
        sage to the beginning.
    (C) No, because it provides information that is too
        broad for the topic of this passage.
    (D) No, because its tone is too personal given the
        rest of the passage.

Go on to the next page. ⟹

Questions 23–33 are based on the following passage, *Modern Nursing*.

The practice of medicine has changed in many ways over the last 50 years. One important change is the increasingly important and diversified role that nurses play in patient care. (23) The patient receives more and more of their care directly from nurses, who work with a great deal of independence. Though the rules differ from state to state, advanced practice nurses in the United States can diagnose health problems, prescribe medicine, (24) and still perform many other important functions without the supervision of a physician.

Changes in the field of nursing are reflected in the educational process. Up until the mid-1990s, most nurses received their initial training at a school of nursing. Nowadays it is much more likely that an individual (25) going into nursing will first pursue an associate degree in nursing (ADN) in a 2-year undergraduate program given by a community college or 4-year college. (26) While pursuing an ADN, anatomy, physiology, chemistry, psychology, and other sciences are studied. Supervised clinical experience is also required.

(27) Some people opt for a bachelor of science in nursing (BSN) degree, which is awarded after a four-year program that places more emphasis on research and theory compared to taking the ADN program. Though having a BSN degree is not required for most nursing care, the degree does qualify a person for administrative and teaching positions that would not typically go to someone with an ADN.

After completing one of the programs outlined above (or an equivalent program), an individual can take an exam to become a registered nurse. (28) The shortage of registered nurses is expected to increase for years to come. He or she can also continue on to the graduate or post-graduate level. Some individuals become nurse practitioners or NPs.

NPs help patients who have acute and chronic medical conditions. An NP can diagnose, perform advanced (29) materials, and prescribe medicine. Some NPs work in clinics, private offices, or nursing homes, and some contract their services for private duty. Depending on the state in which they practice, NPs might not need to practice under the supervision of a (30) physician; in which case they might very well be a patient's primary health care provider. An NP can specialize in a range of areas, including cardiology, oncology, and women's health. They can also perform research, teach, and become involved in public policy issues.

Nurses can find work in many areas outside of a hospital setting. (31) Registered nurses can work for large companies or for themselves. Those who do work within a medical team collaborate closely with doctors and patients to treat serious illness and improve quality of life. (32) Also, nurses see up close the results of the effort and passion they bring to their work. (33) They have an enormous amount of responsibility and plenty of opportunities for personal growth.

Modern Nursing Questions

23. (A) NO CHANGE
    (B) A patient now receives
    (C) Patients now receive
    (D) The patients receive

24. (A) NO CHANGE
    (B) or even perform
    (C) performing
    (D) and perform

25. (A) NO CHANGE
    (B) whose going
    (C) goes
    (D) who will go

26. (A) NO CHANGE
    (B) While pursuing an ADN, students study anatomy, physiology, chemistry, psychology, and other sciences.
    (C) Students study anatomy, physiology, chemistry, psychology, and other sciences that are studied while pursuing an ADN.
    (D) One studies anatomy, physiology, chemistry, psychology, and other sciences when you pursue an ADN.

Go on to the next page. ⇨

27. Which of the following best combines the under-lined sentences?

    (A) Some people opt for a bachelor of science in nursing (BSN) degree, which is awarded after a four-year program that places more emphasis on research and theory compared to taking the ADN program.

    (B) Some people opt for a bachelor of science in nursing (BSN) degree, which is awarded after a four-year program that, in comparison to the ADN program, places more emphasis on research and theory.

    (C) In comparison to the ADN program, which places more emphasis on research and theory, some people opt for a bachelor of science in nursing (BSN) degree, which is awarded after a four-year program.

    (D) In comparison to the ADN program, which emphasizes more research and theory, a bachelor of science in nursing (BSN) degree, awarded after a four-year program, is opted by some people.

28. The writer is considering deleting the underlined sentence. Should the sentence be kept or deleted?

    (A) Kept, because it contains important information that is relevant to the topic of the paragraph.

    (B) Kept, because it provides a detail that leads directly into the following sentence.

    (C) Deleted, because it provides information that is not supported by the rest of the paragraph.

    (D) Deleted, because it provides information that is outside the specific focus of the paragraph.

29. (A) NO CHANGE
    (B) decisions
    (C) actions
    (D) procedures

30. (A) NO CHANGE
    (B) physician; they
    (C) physician, and yet they
    (D) physician, they therefore

31. At this point, the writer is considering adding the following sentence.

    > Some work for attorneys, schools, public health agencies, or insurance companies.

    Should the writer make this addition here?

    (A) Yes, because it provides examples relevant to the preceding sentence.

    (B) Yes, because it explains why some nurses prefer to work outside of a hospital setting.

    (C) No, because it interrupts the discussion with unnecessary details.

    (D) No, because the information it contains is too general given the topic of the paragraph.

32. (A) NO CHANGE
    (B) Finally, nurses
    (C) Nevertheless, nurses
    (D) Nurses

33. Which choice ends the passage with a statement that best summarizes the author's opinion on the main topic of the passage?

    (A) NO CHANGE

    (B) Few careers offer an individual a wider range of opportunities and a greater sense of purpose.

    (C) Over the course of a career, a nurse will have helped thousands of people go back to leading productive lives.

    (D) All nurses, whether they work in or out of a hospital setting, have opportunities every day to use the knowledge and skills they have received during their educational experience.

Go on to the next page. ⇨

Questions 34–44 are based on the following passage, *The Power of the Wind.*

Taking advantage of the power of the wind is nothing new. Travel, since before the days of the great explorers, would have been a much more limited (34) <u>investigation</u> without sailboats of course, but people have been harnessing wind power in inventive ways for thousands of years. Wind pumps brought water to livestock and carried water away from flooded (35) <u>areas, and yet</u> as early as 1887, windmills were used to generate electricity.

Today's wind farms can power millions of households. Many of these farms are located offshore so as to take advantage of the powerful winds that blow over large bodies of water and to minimize the aesthetic effects of placing hundreds or even thousands of turbines on land. (36) <u>It should be noted that</u> offshore wind farms do cost more to construct and maintain.

The advantages of using wind power rather than fossil fuels (37) <u>are obvious because wind</u> is easily available, renewable, clean, and far less destructive to the environment. (38) <u>The biggest obstacle to depending on wind power is that, though the strength and frequency of wind in any given area is quite consistent from year to year, there is a great deal of variation from day to day.</u> To compensate for a loss of power due to insufficient wind conditions, a power grid that heavily depends on wind must be able to replace this loss with power from another source.

Solar power is uniquely suited to compensate for losses of wind power since a day without strong winds (39) <u>is more likely than a sunny day.</u> Hydroelectricity (water power) also works well as a backup to wind power. Hydroelectric stations can hold back their water on windy days and speed up production on days when the wind drops. It is true that the amount of water needed might not be readily available, but *stored* hydroelectricity can be used in these situations.

The ability to forecast wind strength is helpful when designing and maintaining wind farms, (40) <u>but predictive success is low for any one wind farm or any given turbine.</u> Consequently, placing turbines over a greater area and linking farms can go a long way to smoothing over any unexpected loss of power at any one particular site. Another approach to making up for temporary losses of wind power is to equip wind turbines with their own backup batteries.

[1] Other challenges to the widespread use of wind power do exist. [2] However, this potential obstacle and others of its kind are being met and overcome with imagination and enterprise. [3] For example, the power generated at wind farms—typically located in thinly-populated areas—must be carried great distances to high population areas along the coasts. [4] The benefits of using an absolutely free energy source that has no environmentally degrading qualities (41) <u>are so exciting</u> that wind power will undoubtedly play an increasingly significant role in the high-tech energy grids of the future. (42)

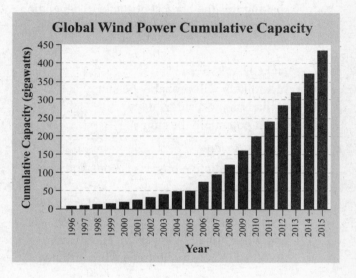

The Power of the Wind Questions

34. (A) NO CHANGE
    (B) venture
    (C) chance
    (D) plan

35. (A) NO CHANGE
    (B) areas. As early
    (C) areas and also
    (D) areas,

36. (A) NO CHANGE
    (B) Because of this
    (C) It should not come as a surprise, then, that
    (D) Additionally,

37. (A) NO CHANGE
    (B) are obvious; for wind
    (C) are: wind obviously
    (D) are obvious: wind

Go on to the next page. ⇨

38. (A) NO CHANGE
    (B) The biggest obstacle to depending on wind power is that, while the strength and frequency of wind in any given area is quite consistent from year to year, there is a great deal of variation from day to day.
    (C) Though wind strength and frequency varies a great deal from day to day—this is the biggest obstacle to depending on wind power—there is consistency from year to year.
    (D) Though from day to day there is a great deal of variety in wind strength and frequency, making this the biggest obstacle to depending on wind power, it is consistent from year to year.

39. (A) NO CHANGE
    (B) most likely will probably be sunny
    (C) is likely to be a sunny day
    (D) could potentially be sunny

40. (A) NO CHANGE
    (B) and the predictive process is constantly being refined.
    (C) though a certain avoidable unpredictability does exist.
    (D) and will ultimately lower the initial costs involved in constructing the wind turbines.

41. (A) NO CHANGE
    (B) are going to excite so much that
    (C) will be eventually exciting and
    (D) is so exciting that

42. To make this paragraph most logical, sentence 3 should be placed
    (A) where it is now
    (B) before sentence 1
    (C) before sentence 2
    (D) after sentence 4

43. According to the graph, the cumulative capacity of global wind power
    (A) increased at a steady rate between 1996 and 2014
    (B) rose more quickly between 2006 and 2010 than between 2000 and 2005
    (C) was most likely between 375 and 400 gigawatts in 2015
    (D) did not begin until 1996

44. From 2012 to 2013, the use of stored hydroelectricity as a backup to wind power increased globally. Based on this information, the passage, and the graph, which of the following conclusions (if any) can be made?
    (A) From 2013 to 2014, the global use of stored hydroelectricity as a backup to wind power increased more than it did from 2012 to 2013.
    (B) Between 2012 and 2013, the global use of stored hydroelectricity as a backup to wind power was greater than the global use of available (non-stored) hydroelectricity.
    (C) Globally, between 2012 and 2013, there were fewer windy days than there were days on which there was little or no wind.
    (D) None of the conclusions above can be made.

STOP!

If you finish before time is called, you may check your work on this section only.
Do not turn to any other section in the test.

SECTION 3: MATHEMATICS TEST, *NO CALCULATOR*

25 Minutes, 20 Questions

Turn to Section 3 of your answer sheet (page 515) to answer the questions in this section.

Directions

For questions 1–15, solve each problem, choose the best answer from the choices provided, and fill in the corresponding circle on your answer sheet. **For questions 16–20,** solve the problem and enter your answer in the grid on the answer sheet. Please refer to the directions before question 16 on how to enter your answers in the grid. You may use any available space in your test booklet for scratch work.

Notes

1. The use of a calculator **is not permitted**.

2. All variables and expressions used represent real numbers unless otherwise indicated.

3. Figures provided in this test are drawn to scale unless otherwise indicated.

4. All figures lie in a plane unless otherwise indicated.

5. Unless otherwise indicated, the domain of a given function f is the set of all real numbers x for which $f(x)$ is a real number.

Reference

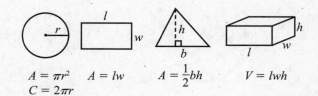

$A = \pi r^2$ $A = lw$ $A = \frac{1}{2}bh$ $V = lwh$
$C = 2\pi r$

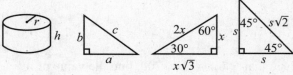

$V = \pi r^2 h$ $c^2 = a^2 + b^2$ *Special Right Triangles*

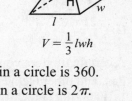

$V = \frac{4}{3}\pi r^3$ $V = \frac{1}{3}\pi r^2 h$ $V = \frac{1}{3}lwh$

The number of degrees of arc in a circle is 360.
The number of radians of arc in a circle is 2π.
The sum of the measures in degrees of the angles of a triangle is 180.

A = area, C = circumference, V = volume.

Go on to the next page. ⇨

1. If $\frac{3x}{4} = 9$, find $6x$.

   (A) 18
   (B) 27
   (C) 36
   (D) 72

2. If the sum of the four terms in each of the diagonal rows is the same, then $A =$

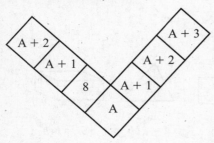

   (A) 4
   (B) 5
   (C) 6
   (D) 7

3. Given that $500w = 3 \times 700$, find the value of w.

   (A) $\frac{5}{21}$
   (B) 2
   (C) $\frac{11}{5}$
   (D) $\frac{21}{5}$

4. A certain mixture contains carbon, oxygen, hydrogen, and other elements in the percentages shown in the graph below. If the total mixture weighs 24 pounds, which number represents the closest number of pounds of carbon that is contained in the mixture?

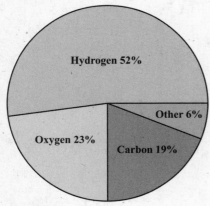

   (A) 5.2
   (B) 4.6
   (C) 2.1
   (D) 1.2

5. Parallel lines m and n are intersected by line l as shown. Find the value of $x + y$.

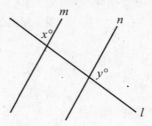

   (A) 180
   (B) 150
   (C) 120
   (D) 90

6. The two dials shown below operate simultaneously in the following manner. The hand in A turns *counterclockwise* while the hand in B turns *clockwise*. In the first move, the hand of A moves to 9 at exactly the same moment that the hand of B moves to 3. In the second move, the hand of A moves to 6 at exactly the same moment that the hand of B moves to 6, and so on. If each hand starts at 12, where will each hand be at the end of 17 moves?

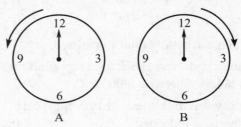

   (A) Both at 9
   (B) A at 3 and B at 12
   (C) A at 3 and B at 9
   (D) A at 9 and B at 3

7. The half-life of a certain radioactive substance is 6 hours. In other words, if you start with 8 grams of the substance, 6 hours later you will have 4 grams. If a sample of this substance contains x grams, how many grams remain after 24 hours?

   (A) $\frac{x}{32}$
   (B) $\frac{x}{16}$
   (C) $\frac{x}{8}$
   (D) $2x$

Go on to the next page. ⇨

8. In the rectangular coordinate system below, which of the following is true about line *l*?

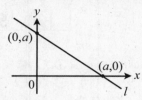

(*Note*: Figure is not drawn to scale.)

  I. The slope is −1.
  II. The distance of point $(0,a)$ to point $(a,0)$ is equal to $a\sqrt{2}$.
  III. The acute angle that line *l* makes with the *x*-axis is 45°.

(A) I only
(B) III only
(C) II and III only
(D) I, II, and III

9. In the *xy*-plane, the coordinates of point *A* are $(-1, -1)$ and the coordinates of point *B* are $(5, 1)$. What are the coordinates of the midpoint of line segment *AB*?

(A) $(0.5, 0.5)$
(B) $(2, 0)$
(C) $(2.0, 0.5)$
(D) $(3, 0)$

10. In the number line below, *a*, *b*, and *c* are real numbers. Which is true?

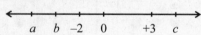

(A) $|b| < 2$
(B) $-|c| = c$
(C) $|b| > |a|$
(D) $|a| > |b|$

11. Given that $w = 7r + 6r + 5r + 4r + 3r$, which of the terms listed below may be added to *w* so that the resulting sum will be divisible by 7 for every positive integer *r*?

(A) $7r$
(B) $5r$
(C) $4r$
(D) $3r$

12. A ladder is set up against the wall as shown below. The bottom of the ladder is 5 feet from the wall. Which is true of the angle the ladder makes with the ground if the ladder is 8 feet in length?

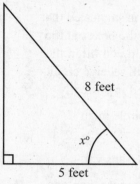

(A) $\cos x° = \dfrac{8}{5}$

(B) $\cot x° = \dfrac{5}{8}$

(C) $\tan x° = \dfrac{5}{8}$

(D) $\sec x° = \dfrac{8}{5}$

13. If $i^2 = -1$, what does $(3 + 4i)(6i - 1)$ equal?

(A) $14i - 27$
(B) $14i + 27$
(C) $42i - 3$
(D) $14i - 21$

14. If the graph of $y = (x - 3)^2 + 3$ is reflected over the line $y = 2$, what are the zeros of the reflected graph, if any?

(A) 3 only
(B) −3 and 3
(C) 2 and 4
(D) There are no zeros.

15. A circle in the xy plane is represented by the equation:

$$x^2 + y^2 - 8y + 4 = 0$$

What is the radius of the circle?

(A) $\sqrt{10}$
(B) $2\sqrt{3}$
(C) $\sqrt{14}$
(D) 4

Go on to the next page. ⇨

Directions

For questions 16–20, solve the problem and enter your answer in the grid, as described below, on the answer sheet.

1. Although not required, it is suggested that you write your answer in the boxes at the tops of the columns to help you fill in the circles accurately. You will receive credit only if the circles are filled in correctly.

2. Mark no more than one circle in any column.

3. No question has a negative answer.

4. Some problems may have more than one correct answer. In such cases, grid only one answer.

5. **Mixed numbers** such as $3\frac{1}{2}$ must be gridded as 3.5 or 7/2. (If "31/2" is entered into the grid, it will be interpreted as $\frac{31}{2}$, not $3\frac{1}{2}$.)

6. **Decimal answers:** If you obtain a decimal answer with more digits than the grid can accommodate, it may be either rounded or truncated, but it must fill the entire grid.

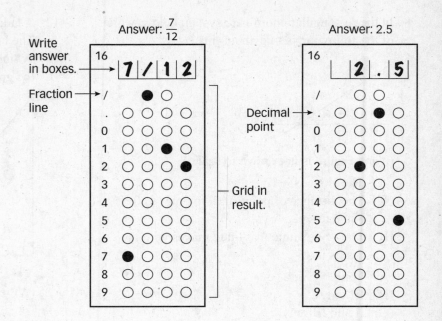

Answer: $\frac{7}{12}$ Answer: 2.5

Write answer in boxes.
Fraction line
Grid in result.
Decimal point

Acceptable ways to grid $\frac{2}{3}$ are:

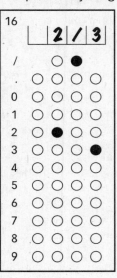 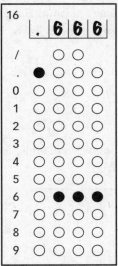 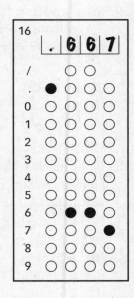

Answer: 201 – Either position is correct.

NOTE: You may start your answers in any column, space permitting. Columns you don't need to use should be left blank.

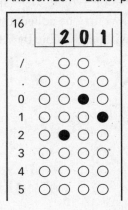 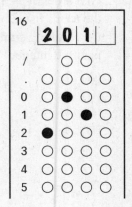

Go on to the next page. ➡

16. The managers of a new business estimate that for every p people who come into their offices, c of them will become clients. At the end of one year, 350 people had come into the offices, and 240 had become clients. If the original estimation had been accurate and the same number of people had come into the offices, 30 fewer people would have become clients. It can also be said that the original estimation would have been accurate if the same number of people had become clients, but x more people had come into the office. What is the value of x?

17. A construction company uses the following equations to determine how much to charge their clients as a function of the square footage (x) of the building involved.

$f(x) = 200x + 135{,}000$ for $5{,}000 \le x < 15{,}000$
$g(x) = 150x + 210{,}000$ for $5{,}000 \ge 15{,}000$

The company charges $\$2{,}535{,}000$ for work on a building of less than 15,000 square feet. If the square footage had been two times greater, the company would have charged $a \times 10^6$. What is the value of a?

18. In the addition problem shown below, if $\square$ is a constant, what must $\square$ equal in order for the answer to be correct?

$$\begin{array}{r} \square\,1 \\ 6\,\square \\ +\ \square\,9 \\ \hline 15\,\square \end{array}$$

19. If $\left(\dfrac{x}{y}\right)^{-10} = \sqrt{\left(\dfrac{w}{z}\right)^5}$ and $\left(\dfrac{y}{x}\right)^{p} = \left(\dfrac{w}{z}\right)^5$, what is the value of p?

20. Given the equation below, if $f(a) = a$ and $a \ne 0$, what is the value of $f(-2a)$?

$$f(x) = x^3 + x^2 + x$$

STOP!

If you finish before time is called, you may check your work on this section only.
Do not turn to any other section in the test.

SECTION 4: MATHEMATICS TEST, *WITH CALCULATOR*

55 Minutes, 38 Questions

Turn to Section 4 of your answer sheet (pages 515–516) to answer the questions in this section.

Directions

For questions 1–30, solve each problem, choose the best answer from the choices provided, and fill in the corresponding circle on your answer sheet. **For questions 31–38**, solve the problem and enter your answer in the grid on the answer sheet. Please refer to the directions before question 31 on how to enter your answers in the grid. You may use any available space in your test booklet for scratch work.

Notes

1. The use of a calculator **is permitted**.

2. All variables and expressions used represent real numbers unless otherwise indicated.

3. Figures provided in this test are drawn to scale unless otherwise indicated.

4. All figures lie in a plane unless otherwise indicated.

5. Unless otherwise indicated, the domain of a given function f is the set of all real numbers x for which $f(x)$ is a real number.

Reference

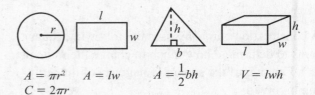

$A = \pi r^2$ $A = lw$ $A = \frac{1}{2}bh$ $V = lwh$
$C = 2\pi r$

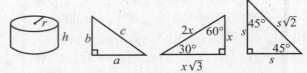

$V = \pi r^2 h$ $c^2 = a^2 + b^2$ *Special Right Triangles*

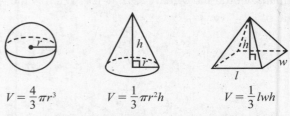

$V = \frac{4}{3}\pi r^3$ $V = \frac{1}{3}\pi r^2 h$ $V = \frac{1}{3}lwh$

The number of degrees of arc in a circle is 360.
The number of radians of arc in a circle is 2π.
The sum of the measures in degrees of the angles of a triangle is 180.

A = area, C = circumference, V = volume.

Go on to the next page. ⇨

1. If $\dfrac{3+y}{y} = 7$, then $y =$

   (A) 3
   (B) 2
   (C) 1
   (D) $\dfrac{1}{2}$

2. If 8 people share a winning lottery ticket and divide the cash prize equally, what percent of the prize do 2 of them together receive?

   (A) 8%
   (B) 10%
   (C) 20%
   (D) 25%
   (E) 40%

3. An athlete runs 90 laps in 6 hours. This is the same as how many laps per minute?

   (A) $\dfrac{1}{15}$
   (B) $\dfrac{1}{9}$
   (C) $\dfrac{1}{4}$
   (D) $\dfrac{1}{2}$

5. Which of the following is a graph of $y = 2x - 4$?

   (A)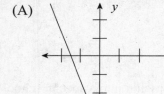

   (B)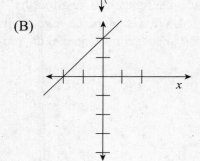

   (C)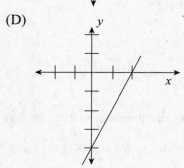

   (D)

5. The operation $\boxdot$ is defined for all numbers x and y by the following: $x \boxdot y = 3 + xy$. For example, $2 \boxdot 7 = 3 + 2(7) = 17$. If $y \neq 0$ and x is a number such that $x \boxdot y = 3$, then find x.

   (A) 0
   (B) $-\dfrac{3}{y}$
   (C) $-y + 3$
   (D) $\dfrac{3}{y}$

6. If $r - 3s = 9$ and $2r + 4s = -2$, what is the value of $3r + s$?

   (A) -11
   (B) 1
   (C) 7
   (D) 11

7. The chickens on a certain farm consumed 600 pounds of feed in half a year. During that time the total number of eggs laid was 5,000. If the feed cost $1.25 per pound, then the feed cost per egg was

   (A) $0.0750
   (B) $0.1250
   (C) $0.15
   (D) $0.25

Go on to the next page. ⇨

8. A circle is inscribed in a square. If the perimeter of the square is 40, what is the area of the circle?

   (A) 50π
   (B) 40π
   (C) 25π
   (D) 5π

9. If x is a positive integer, which of the following must be an even integer?

   (A) $x + 2$
   (B) $3x + 1$
   (C) $x^2 + x + 1$
   (D) $x^2 + x + 2$

10. Let represent the greatest even integer less than n that divides n, for any positive integer n. For example, ⊳24⊳ $= 12$. Find the value of ⊳20⊳.

    (A) 8
    (B) 10
    (C) 12
    (D) 14

11. In the figure below, the sides of rectangle $ABCD$ are parallel to the y-axis and x-axis as shown. If the rectangle is rotated clockwise about the origin through $90°$, what are the new coordinates of B?

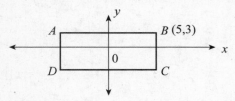

    (A) $(3,-5)$
    (B) $(-3,5)$
    (C) $(-3,-5)$
    (D) $(5,-3)$

12. The tables below show the number of uniforms ordered at two schools and the cost of the types of uniforms ordered in child and adult sizes. Find the total cost of all the uniforms in child sizes ordered at School B.

Number of Child Uniforms Ordered			
	Type A	Type B	Type C
School A	20	50	40
School B	30	60	50

Cost of Uniforms		
	Child	Adult
Type A	$9	$12
Type B	$10	$14
Type C	$11	$16

    (A) $30
    (B) $140
    (C) $1,420
    (D) $1,480

13. Diane's age is 8 less than five times Carlito's age. Belinda's age is 20 more than the combined age of Diane and Carlito. What is Belinda's age in terms of Carlito's age?

    (A) $12 + 4c$
    (B) $12 + 6c$
    (C) $28 - 4c$
    (D) $28 + 6c$

14. In order to obtain admission into a special school program, all applicants must take a special exam, which is passed by three out of every five applicants. Of those who pass the exam, one-fourth are finally accepted. What is the percentage of all applicants who *fail* to gain admission into the program?

    (A) 55
    (B) 60
    (C) 75
    (D) 85

Go on to the next page. ⇨

15. In the figure below, what is the sum of the degree measures of the marked angles?

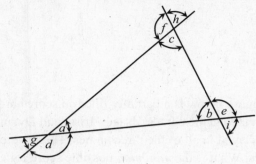

(A) 360°
(B) 720°
(C) 900°
(D) 1,080°

16. On a particular day, a restaurant has 8 waiters and 3 hosts on staff, and each table of customers at the restaurant is greeted by one of the hosts and served by one of the waiters. The number of possible combinations of one waiter and one host will increase by 16 if the restaurant adds which of the following to its staff that day?

(A) 2 waiters and 1 host
(B) 2 waiters and 2 hosts
(C) 2 waiters and 4 hosts
(D) 4 waiters and 4 hosts

17. If p is the average of x and y, and if q is the average of y and z, and if r is the average of x and z, then what is the average of x, y, and z?

(A) $\dfrac{p + q + r}{3}$

(B) $\dfrac{p + q + r}{2}$

(C) $\dfrac{2}{3}(p + q + r)$

(D) $p + q + r$

18. Given that $AC \perp BC$, $\angle DCB = 62°$, and $\angle ACE = 37°$, find $\angle DCE$ in degrees.

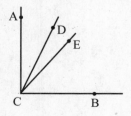

(A) 5°
(B) 9°
(C) 13°
(D) 25°

19. If K is the sum of three consecutive even integers and y is the sum of the greatest three consecutive *odd* integers that precede the least of the three even integers, express y in terms of K.

(A) $y = K - 5$
(B) $y = K - 10$
(C) $y = K - 15$
(D) $y = K - 20$

20. Container A holds twice as much as container B, and container C holds as much as A and B put together. If we start with A and B full, and C empty, and pour half the contents of A and a third of the contents of B into container C, what fraction of C's capacity will be filled?

(A) $\dfrac{5}{6}$

(B) $\dfrac{4}{9}$

(C) $\dfrac{5}{12}$

(D) $\dfrac{7}{12}$

21. For the five numbers marked by arrows, the best approximation to their product is

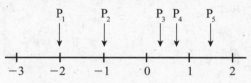

(A) $\dfrac{1}{3}$

(B) $\dfrac{2}{3}$

(C) $\dfrac{3}{2}$

(D) 3

Go on to the next page. ⇨

22. O is the center of a circle of diameter 20 and $\angle AOC$ = 108°. Find the sum of the lengths of minor arcs $\overset{\frown}{AC}$ and $\overset{\frown}{DB}$.

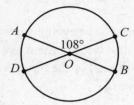

   (A) 5π
   (B) 8π
   (C) 10π
   (D) 12π

23. In a certain school, special programs in French and Spanish are available. If there are N students enrolled in the French program and M students enrolled in the Spanish program, including P students who enrolled in both programs, how many students are taking only one (but not both) of the language programs?

   (A) $N + M$
   (B) $N + M - P$
   (C) $N + M + P$
   (D) $N + M - 2P$

24. What is the diameter of a wheel which, when rotating at a speed of 10 revolutions per minute, takes 12 seconds to travel 16 feet?

   (A) $\dfrac{4}{\pi}$ feet
   (B) 8π feet
   (C) $\dfrac{8}{\pi}$ feet
   (D) $\dfrac{16}{\pi}$ feet

25. Lines l and n are parallel to each other, but line m is parallel to neither of the other two. Find $\dfrac{p}{q}$ if $p + q = 13$.

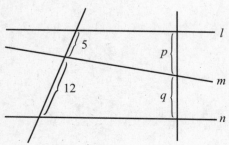

   (A) $\dfrac{13}{5}$
   (B) $\dfrac{12}{5}$
   (C) $\dfrac{7}{6}$
   (D) $\dfrac{1}{5}$

26. The figure below is a partially filled-in score card for a video game contest. Isaac, Arisa, and Dylan each played in all of the three games, There were no ties. What is the *minimum* possible score for Dylan in this tournament?

	First Place (6points)	Second Place (4 points)	Third Place (2 points)
Game 1			
Game 2		Arisa	
Game 3			Arisa

   (A) 2
   (B) 6
   (C) 8
   (D) 12

27. In the figure below, $ABCDEFGHIJKL$ is a regular dodecagon (a regular twelve-sided polygon). The curved path is made up of 12 semicircles, each of whose diameters is a side of the dodecagon. If the perimeter of the dodecagon is 24, find the area of the shaded region.

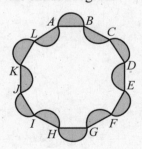

   (A) 6π
   (B) 12π
   (C) 24π
   (D) 36π

28. If $x > 0$ and $y > 0$ and $x^9 = 4$ and $x^7 = \dfrac{9}{y^2}$, which of the following is an expression for the value of x in terms of y?

(A) $\dfrac{4}{9}y$

(B) $\dfrac{2}{3}y$

(C) $\dfrac{3}{2}y^2$

(D) $6y$

29. 27 equal cubes, each with an edge of length r, are arranged so as to form a single larger cube with a volume of 81. If the larger cube has an edge of length s, then r divided by s equals

(A) $\dfrac{1}{3}$

(B) $\dfrac{1}{\sqrt{3}}$

(C) $\dfrac{1}{2}$

(D) $\dfrac{1}{8}$

30. $\overline{PM}$ and $\overline{PN}$ are tangent to circle O at M and N, respectively; $m \angle MON = 120°$ and $OM = ON = 5$. Find the perimeter of the shaded region.

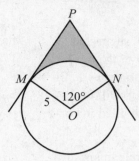

(A) $10 + 10\pi$

(B) $5\sqrt{3} + 10\pi$

(C) $5\sqrt{3} + \dfrac{10}{3}\pi$

(D) $10\sqrt{3} + \dfrac{10\pi}{3}$

Go on to the next page. ⇨

Directions

For questions 31–38, solve the problem and enter your answer in the grid, as described below, on the answer sheet.

1. Although not required, it is suggested that you write your answer in the boxes at the tops of the columns to help you fill in the circles accurately. You will receive credit only if the circles are filled in correctly.

2. Mark no more than one circle in any column.

3. No question has a negative answer.

4. Some problems may have more than one correct answer. In such cases, grid only one answer.

5. **Mixed numbers** such as $3\frac{1}{2}$ must be gridded as 3.5 or 7/2. (If "31/2" is entered into the grid, it will be interpreted as $\frac{31}{2}$, not $3\frac{1}{2}$.)

6. **Decimal answers:** If you obtain a decimal answer with more digits than the grid can accommodate, it may be either rounded or truncated, but it must fill the entire grid.

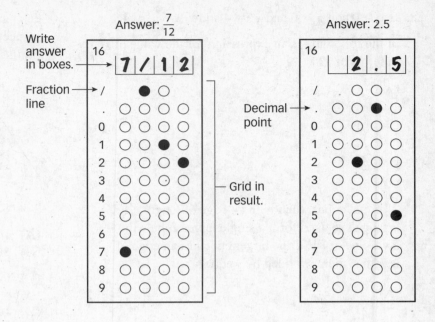

Answer: $\frac{7}{12}$ Answer: 2.5

Write answer in boxes.

Fraction line

Decimal point

Grid in result.

Acceptable ways to grid $\frac{2}{3}$ are:

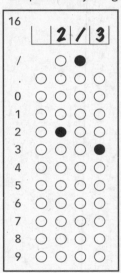

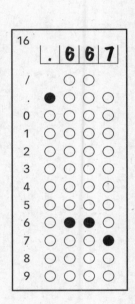

Answer: 201 – Either position is correct.

NOTE: You may start your answers in any column, space permitting. Columns you don't need to use should be left blank.

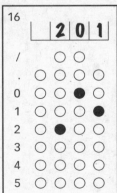

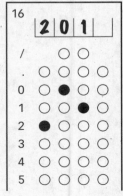

Go on to the next page. ⇨

31. If $\frac{5}{8}$ of a number is 3 less than $\frac{3}{4}$ of the number, what is the number?

32. A conference center has 9 rooms that have a maximum occupancy of 52 people and 10 rooms that have a maximum occupancy of 15 people. A group of 510 people are meeting at the conference center. If the maximum occupancy rules are followed, what is the least number of rooms needed so that everyone in the group is in one of these rooms?

33. A horizontal line has a length of 100 yards. A vertical line is drawn at one of its ends. If lines are drawn every ten yards thereafter, until the other end is reached, how many vertical lines are finally drawn?

34. The length of side AC in triangle ABC below is l. The length of side DE in triangle DBE is $0.9l$. The area of triangle DBE is what percentage of the area of triangle ABC? (Ignore the % sign when gridding your answer.)

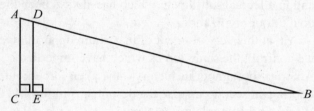

35. In a certain class containing 60 students, the average (arithmetic mean) age is 20. In another class containing 20 students, the average age is 40. Find the average age of all 80 students.

36. A lawn covers 108.6 square feet. Regan mowed all of the lawn in three evenings. She mowed $\frac{2}{9}$ of the lawn during the first evening. She mowed twice that amount on the second evening. On the third and final evening she mowed the remaining lawn. How many square feet were mowed on the third evening?

37. How many different *pairs* of parallel edges are there on a rectangular solid?

38. Triangle ABC is inscribed in the circle with center O, as shown below. If $\overline{BC}$ has a length of x, and $126\cos85° = x$, what is the length of minor arc BC rounded to the nearest tenth? Use 3.14 for the value of π.

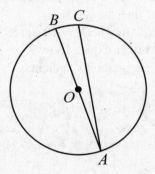

STOP!

If you finish before time is called, you may check your work on this section only.

Do not turn to any other section in the test.

SECTION 5: TEST 2 ESSAY (OPTIONAL)

50 Minutes

Turn to Section 5 of your answer sheet (pages 517–518) to write your essay.

Directions

Write an essay in which you explain how President Kennedy builds an argument to persuade his audience that they should join the Alliance for Progress. In your essay, analyze how Kennedy uses one or more of the features listed in the box below (or features of your own choice) to strengthen the logic and persuasiveness of his argument. Be sure that your analysis focuses on the most relevant features of the passage.

Your essay should not explain whether you agree with Kennedy's claims, but rather explain how Kennedy builds an argument to persuade his audience.

As you read the passage below, consider how President Kennedy uses

- evidence, such as facts or examples, to support claims.
- reasoning to develop ideas and to connect claims and evidence.
- stylistic or persuasive elements, such as word choice or appeals to emotion, to add power to the ideas expressed.

Adapted from President John F. Kennedy's address to a White House Reception for Members of Congress and the Diplomatic Corps of Latin America, March 13, 1961.

One hundred and thirty-nine years ago this week the United States, stirred by the heroic struggle of its fellow Americans, urged the independence and recognition of the new Latin American Republics. It was then, at the dawn of freedom throughout this hemisphere, that Bolivar spoke of his desire to see the Americas fashioned into the greatest region in the world, "greatest," he said, "not so much by virtue of her area and her wealth, as by her freedom and her glory."

Never in the long history of our hemisphere has this dream been nearer to fulfillment, and never has it been in greater danger.

The genius of our scientists has given us the tools to bring abundance to our land, strength to our industry, and knowledge to our people. For the first time we have the capacity to strike off the remaining bonds of poverty and ignorance—to free our people for the spiritual and intellectual fulfillment which has always been the goal of our civilization.

Yet at this very moment of maximum opportunity, we confront the same forces which have imperiled America throughout its history—the alien forces which once again seek to impose the despotisms of the Old World on the people of the New.

The revolutions which gave us birth ignited, in the words of Thomas Paine, "a spark never to be extinguished." And across vast, turbulent continents these American ideals still stir man's struggle for national independence and individual freedom. But as we welcome the spread of the American revolution to other lands, we must also remember that our own struggle—the revolution which began in Philadelphia in 1776, and in Caracas in 1811—is not yet finished. Our hemisphere's mission is not yet completed. For our unfulfilled task is to demonstrate to the entire world that man's unsatisfied aspiration for economic progress and social justice can best be achieved by free men working within a framework of democratic institutions.

Throughout Latin America, a continent rich in resources and in the spiritual and cultural achievements of its people, millions of men and women suffer the daily degradations of poverty and hunger. They lack decent shelter or protection from disease. Their children are deprived of the education or the jobs which are the gateway to a better life. And each day the problems

Go on to the next page. ⇨

grow more urgent. Population growth is outpacing economic growth—low living standards are further endangered and discontent—the discontent of a people who know that abundance and the tools of progress are at last within their reach—that discontent is growing. In the words of Jose Figueres, "once dormant peoples are struggling upward toward the sun, toward a better life."

Therefore I have called on all people of the hemisphere to join in a new Alliance for Progress—Alianza para Progreso—a vast cooperative effort, unparalleled in magnitude and nobility of purpose, to satisfy the basic needs of the American people for homes, work and land, health and schools—techo, trabajo y tierra, salud y escuela.

I propose that the American Republics begin on a vast new Ten Year Plan for the Americas, a plan to transform the 1960's into a historic decade of democratic progress.

And if we are successful, if our effort is bold enough and determined enough, then the close of this decade will mark the beginning of a new era in the American experience. The living standards of every American family will be on the rise, basic education will be available to all, hunger will be a forgotten experience, the need for massive outside help will have passed, most nations will have entered a period of self-sustaining growth, and though there will be still much to do, every American Republic will be the master of its own revolution and its own hope and progress.

And so I say to the men and women of the Americas—to the campesino in the fields, to the obrero in the cities, to the estudiante in the schools—prepare your mind and heart for the task ahead—call forth your strength and let each devote his energies to the betterment of all, so that your children and our children in this hemisphere can find an ever richer and a freer life.

STOP!
If you finish before time is called, you may check your work on this section only.
Do not turn to any other section in the test.

HOW DID YOU DO ON THIS TEST?

Pages 558–559 will show you how to calculate your
scores on this test. Explanatory answers with strategies
and basic skills follow.

THERE'S ALWAYS ROOM
FOR IMPROVEMENT!

ANSWER KEY

Section 1: Reading Test Answers

1. B	14. A	27. A	40. C
2. A	15. C	28. D	41. C
3. A	16. B	29. C	42. A
4. D	17. D	30. C	43. D
5. C	18. D	31. A	44. D
6. A	19. C	32. B	45. D
7. B	20. D	33. D	46. B
8. C	21. D	34. D	47. C
9. C	22. B	35. C	48. D
10. A	23. C	36. B	49. D
11. D	24. D	37. C	50. C
12. D	25. A	38. C	51. B
13. B	26. B	39. D	52. A

Reading Test Raw Score
(number of correct answers) _____

Section 2: Writing and Language Test Answers

1. D	12. B	23. C	34. B
2. A	13. A	24. D	35. B
3. B	14. D	25. A	36. A
4. B	15. D	26. B	37. D
5. D	16. B	27. B	38. B
6. C	17. C	28. D	39. C
7. A	18. A	29. D	40. A
8. A	19. D	30. B	41. A
9. B	20. B	31. A	42. C
10. C	21. C	32. D	43. B
11. D	22. C	33. B	44. D

Writing and Language Test Raw Score *(number of correct answers)* _____

Section 3: Math Test Answers (No Calculator)

1. D	6. D	11. D	16. 50
2. B	7. B	12. D	17. 3.81
3. D	8. D	13. A	18. 4
4. B	9. B	14. C	19. 20
5. A	10. D	15. B	20. 14

Math Test (No Calculator) Raw Score *(number of correct answers)* _____

Section 4: Math Test Answers (with Calculator)

1. D	11. A	21. B	31. 24
2. D	12. C	22. D	32. 12
3. C	13. A	23. D	33. 11
4. D	14. D	24. C	34. 81
5. A	15. B	25. E	35. 25
6. C	16. A	26. C	36. 36.2
7. C	17. A	27. A	37. 18
8. C	18. B	28. B	38. 10.9
9. D	19. C	29. A	
10. B	20. B	30. D	

Math Test (Calculator) Raw Score *(number of correct answers)* _____

RAW SCORE CONVERSION TABLE: SECTION AND TEST SCORES

Raw Score (# of correct answers)	Math Test Score	Reading Test Score	Writing and Language Test Score
0	200	10	10
1	200	10	10
2	210	10	10
3	230	11	10
4	240	12	11
5	260	13	12
6	280	14	13
7	290	15	13
8	310	15	14
9	320	16	15
10	330	17	16
11	340	17	16
12	360	18	17
13	370	19	18
14	380	19	19
15	390	20	19
16	410	20	20
17	420	21	21
18	430	21	21
19	440	22	22
20	450	22	23
21	460	23	23
22	470	23	24
23	480	24	25
24	480	24	25
25	490	25	26
26	500	25	26
27	510	26	27
28	520	26	28
29	520	27	28

Raw Score (# of correct answers)	Math Test Score	Reading Test Score	Writing and Language Test Score
30	530	28	29
31	540	28	30
32	550	29	30
33	560	29	31
34	560	30	32
35	570	30	32
36	580	31	33
37	590	31	34
38	600	32	34
39	600	32	35
40	610	33	36
41	620	33	37
42	630	34	38
43	640	35	39
44	650	35	40
45	660	36	
46	670	37	
47	670	37	
48	680	38	
49	690	38	
50	700	39	
51	710	40	
52	730	40	
53	740		
54	750		
55	760		
56	780		
57	790		
58	800		

CONVERSION EQUATION: SECTION AND TEST SCORES

Step 1. Using the table on the previous page, convert raw scores for reading and for writing and language.

Reading Test Raw Score → Reading Test Score
        (0–52)   (10–40)

_____ = _____

Writing and Language → Writing and Language
   Test Raw Score   Test Score
       (0–44)   (10–40)

_____ = _____

Step 2. Add Reading Test Score (10–40) and Writing and Language Test Score (10–40).

Reading Test Score _____

+ Writing and Language Test Score _____

= Reading and Writing Test Score _____

Step 3. Multiply combined Reading and Writing Test Score by 10 to get your Evidence-Based Reading and Writing Section Score (200–800).

Reading and Writing Test Score _____

× 10 _____

= Reading and Writing Section Score _____*

Step 4. Add the two Math Scores.

Math Test Raw Score (No Calculator) (0–20) _____

+ Math Test Raw Score (Calculator) (0–38) _____

= Math Test Raw Score _____

Step 5. Using the table on the previous page, convert Math Test Raw Score to get your Math Section Score.

Math Test Raw Score → Math Section Score
      (0–58)   (200–800)

_____ = _____*

Step 6. Add the Evidence-Based Reading and Writing Section Score (200–800) and the Math Section Score (as marked by asterisks) to get your Total SAT Score.

Reading and Writing Section Score _____

+ Math Section Score _____

= **TOTAL SAT SCORE** _____

EXPLANATORY ANSWERS

Section 1: Reading

As you read these Explanatory Answers, you are advised to refer to "13 Verbal Strategies" (beginning on page 123) whenever a specific strategy is referred to in the answer. Of particular importance is the Reading Comprehension Strategy 2 (page 135).

Note: All Reading questions use Reading Comprehension Strategies 1, 2, and 3 (pages 132–137) as well as other strategies indicated.

The Sussex Place Answers

1. Choice B is correct. The description shows that Alton perceived that the other boy felt "resentment" because of his father's status working for Alton's father. In his memory, Alton believes the valet's son must have hated him as a result (consequence) of their difference in status.

2. Choice A is correct. Alton enjoys believing that others at the club thought that he was behaving inappropriately. He, in fact "relished the idea that he was attracting attention in the hushed room, was encouraging the viewpoint that he was insufficiently appreciative of his standing at the Brookshire." Behaving as he did (making noises, for instance) was not the custom at the club.

3. Choice A is correct. The explanation to question 2 includes a reference to this line.

4. Choice D is correct. Alton at first jokes in a friendly manner with Smetana about whether he should have another drink. However, Smetana's manner, including whispering and squatting down by the chair, clearly makes Alton uncomfortable. He interrupts Smetana before he finishes a sentence and, at the end of the story, asks for his drink with some annoyance.

5. Choice C is correct. The visit to the hospital was awkward, but Dearing's wife could not reduce the "stuffy discomfort." To *alleviate* means to make a bad situation better.

6. Choice A is correct. Bowles ridicules Smetana's English ("He has experience in . . .") and doesn't appear to care that he may have gotten the waiter in trouble and cost him his job. He clearly looks down on Smetana, which is to say that he has a condescending attitude.

7. Choice B is correct. The situation is already somewhat tense, since Alton is uneasy talking to Smetana about the position of valet, especially in the presence of Bowles. The headwaiter watching closely and then approaching the scene makes the situation more tense; he may not approve of Smetana talking to the members.

8. Choice C is correct. The passage makes clear that Alton is moving to a smaller home, in the words of Bowles—"Just a cozy cottage for two in the country?" This may be an exaggeration, since Alton is still going to have a valet, a cook, etc., but Alton also thinks that "He did not want a house full of *servants*." He wants to drive his own car—even, as he says, learn to fix it. Clearly, he wishes to live with fewer luxuries than he had growing up.

9. Choice C is correct. The explanation to question 8 includes a reference to this line.

10. Choice A is correct. Alton wishes to appear less concerned with social status than others at the club. This is clear from his behavior in the first paragraph and from the way that he at first jokes with Smetana. This is also made clear from his attitude regarding the terms used to refer to a

valet, such as "manservant." Despite this, he is uncomfortable being too familiar with Smetana and he tells him that he would not be able to do the job of valet because he's a waiter, he's foreign-born, and he doesn't know the same people that Alton knows.

11. Choice D is correct. Alton responds to Smetana's bending down to whisper in his ear by smiling, *but* he withdraws a few inches. This implies that though he appears to be fine with the waiter's behavior, he feels uncomfortable enough to pull back a few inches from the man's face.

Advanced Technological Institutions **Answers**

12. Choice D is correct. See paragraph 2: "Formerly, technical rationality had been employed only to organize the production of rather simple physical objects. . . . Now technical rationality is increasingly employed to organize all of the processes necessary to the utilization of physical objects. . . ."

13. Choice B is correct. See paragraph 1: "The absence of direct controls or of coercion should not serve to obscure from our view the . . . social controls which are employed (such as . . . advertising, selective service channeling, and so on)."

14. Choice A is correct. It can be seen from the context of the sentence: ". . . there would be frequent errors. . . ." Choice A is correct. See also **Reading Comprehension Strategy 5** (pages 139–140).

15. Choice C is correct. See paragraph 5: ". . . the workforce must be relatively over-trained. . . ."

16. Choice B is correct. See paragraph 4: "The assembly line also introduced standardization in work skills and thus makes for a high degree of interchangeability among the workforce. . . . If each operation taxed the workers still there would be frequent errors. . . ."

17. Choice D is correct. See paragraph 6: ". . . the workforce within technologically advanced organizations is asked to work not less hard but more so."

18. Choice D is correct. See paragraph 3: ". . . there are very profound social antagonisms or contradictions. . . ." This article is one of skepticism. It frequently points out the contradictions, irrationality, and coercive tactics exhibited by advanced technological institutions.

19. Choice C is correct. See paragraph 6: "Salary and wage increases . . . lose their . . . importance . . . once . . . an ample supply of luxuries are assured."

20. Choice D is correct. We link "technical specialists" with "such retraining only for a managing elite." Therefore Choice D is correct. See also **Reading Comprehension Strategy 5** (pages 139–140).

21. Choice D is correct. See paragraph 5: ". . . technological progress requires a continuous increase in the skill levels of its workforce, skill levels which frequently embody a fairly rich scientific and technical training. . . . [T]hose skills will be less and less fully used."

22. Choice B is correct. See paragraph 6: ". . . among young people one can already observe a radical weakening in the power of such incentives as money, status, and authority."

Large Hadron Collider **Answers**

23. Choice C is correct. In the first paragraph, the author states, "These purposes can seem quite specific, even trivial." In other words, some people might say that the reasons for the LHC are precise (specific) but not significant (they are trivial).

24. Choice D is correct. The author states that in string theory, "the traditional idea of point-like particles is replaced by one-dimensional objects known a *strings*." Furthermore, string theory "depends on the existence of more dimensions than the four we know of." Later in the same paragraph, the author states that the ATLAS detector "could provide observational data confirming the validity of extra dimensions," therefore supporting a key idea in string theory.

25. Choice A is correct. It has been suggested that dark matter consists of WIMPs, which barely affect matter at all. The LHC could *indirectly* support the theory, not through directly observing a WIMP but through the detection of "large amounts of energy [that] go missing."

26. Choice B is correct. The author emphasizes the huge amount of data that must be analyzed. It is a finite amount (not unlimited), not thrilling (not the data itself) or incomprehensible (Why bother if it can't be understood?). *Daunting* can mean "almost overwhelming" or "highly challenging." Something of this nature can be seen as intimidating.

27. Choice A is correct. The author states that the Standard Model does not "resolve questions regarding gravity and general relativity." Later in the passage, the author describes gravity as "by far the weakest" of the forces.

28. Choice D is correct. The author states that the LHC's ATLAS detector "could provide observational data confirming the validity of extra dimensions." Earlier the author states that string theory "depends on the existence of more dimensions than the four we know of."

29. Choice C is correct. The author states that "if the symmetry is 'broken,' the sparticles may have masses thousands of times greater than their partners, and producing them, even in an energy powerhouse like the LHC, will prove difficult."

30. Choice C is correct. The explanation to question 7 includes this line.

31. Choice A is correct. The author states that the Standard Model "predicts that the decay width of the Higgs particle depends on the value of its mass." This is clearly what the graph shows. As one value changes, so does the other.

32. Choice B is correct. The higher the line in the graph rises, the greater is its decay width. Between the approximate mass values (along the horizontal axis) of 140 and 180, the line rises at its fastest rate, showing a large increase in decay width.

33. Choice D is correct. A value of 1,500 is beyond the graph, but a clear trend can be seen. At a mass of 500, the decay width is about 100, and at a mass of 1,000, the decay width is close to 1,000. In other words, an increase in mass of 500 (from 500 to 1,000) yielded a decay width 10 times greater (from 100 to 1,000). If the mass is 1,500, again an increase of 500, the decay width would again increase by a factor of (about) 10. It would increase from 1,000 to about 10,000.

Double Passage Answers

34. Choice D is correct. The author is stressing the point that the true artist—the person with rare creative ability and keen perception, or high intelligence—fails to communicate well with those about him—"differs from the rest of us" (lines 4–5). He is likely to be considered a "nut" by many with whom he comes in contact. "Great wits" in the Choice D quotation refers to the true artist. The quotation states, in effect, that there is a thin line between the true artist and the "nut." Choices A, B, and C are incorrect because they have little, if anything, to do with the main idea of the passage.

    Note: Choices B and D were composed by John Dryden (1631–1700), and Choices A and C by Alexander Pope (1688–1744).

35. Choice C is correct. See lines 9–10. The artist creates because he is "less fitted to prosper and enjoy himself under the conditions of life which he and we must face alike." Choice A is incorrect. Although they may be true, they are never mentioned in the passage. Choice B is incorrect because, although the artist may be a threat to the social order, he is by no means an unnecessary one. The author, throughout the passage, is siding with the artist against the social order. Choice D is incorrect. See lines 10–12: "Therefore he takes . . . attempt to escape from life." A person who is attempting to escape from life hardly knows how to enjoy life.

36. Choice B is correct. The author ridicules Samuel Johnson, saying that he is as much a true artist as a kazoo player is a musician. The author then says that if Johnson were alive today, he would be a senator or a university president. The author thus implies that these positions do not merit high respect. Choice A is the opposite of Choice B. Therefore, Choice A is incorrect. Choice C is incorrect because, although the statement may be true, the author neither states nor implies that senators and university presidents are generally appreciative of the great literary classics. Choice D is incorrect. The fact that the author lumps Johnson, senators, and university presidents together as nonartistic people indicates that the author believes that senators and university presidents do not have native writing ability.

37. Choice C is correct. Although a love of beauty is a quality we usually associate with artists, that idea about artists is never mentioned in the passage. All of the other characteristics are expressly mentioned in the first two paragraphs of the passage.

38. Choice C is correct. From the context in Passage 2, we see that "world's eye" and "world's heart" refer to culture and wisdom, respectively. See lines 61–65: ". . . public and illustrious thoughts . . . resist the vulgar prosperity . . . by preserving and communicating . . . noble biographies . . . melodious verse. . . ." This is all about *culture* and *wisdom*.

39. Choice D is correct. See the first sentence in Passage 2: ". . . the self-accusation, the faint heart, the frequent uncertainty and loss of time, which are the nettles and tangling vines . . ." Here "nettles and tangling vines" refers to "self-accusation" and "uncertainty." Nettles are plants covered with stinging hairs. Tangling vines give the impression of weaving all around in no particular or certain direction. So nettles can be thought of as "self-accusation"—something "stinging." And "tangling vines" can be thought of as "uncertainty." See also **Reading Comprehension Strategy 5** (pages 139–140).

40. Choice C is correct. See Passage 2: The most appropriate groups are the hardships of the scholar, the scholar's functions, and the scholar's justifications for disregarding the world's business, as can be seen from the structure and content of the passage.

41. Choice C is correct. So far the tone of the passage is sympathetic toward the difficulties of the artist, so by placing "seems to be" in the context of the "virtual hostility" the artist feels from society, it is clear that the author is contrasting what the artist is and what he is perceived to be. The words "false impression" in Choice C fit best. See also **Reading Comprehension Strategy 5** (pages 139–140).

42. Choice A is correct. See lines 100–107 and 59–61 in Passage 2 and lines 14–18 and 27–37 in Passage 1.

43. Choice D is correct. The statements in I can be seen to be associated with the artist in Passage 2 from lines 92–94 and 62–63, respectively. The statements in II can be seen to be associated with the artist in Passage 1 from lines 29–35 and 5–6, respectively. The statements in III can be seen to be associated with the artist in Passage 2 from lines 57–59 and 49–57, respectively.

How Brilliant People Think Answers

44. Choice D is correct. See lines 22–23: "All human beings have at least four types of intelligence." Choice A is incorrect. The passage simply states: "The idea for a self-starting electric motor came to Nikola Tesla one evening as he was reciting a poem by Goethe and watching a sunset" (lines 32–35). Choice B is incorrect. The author indicates a span of time when he states: "The discoveries made by scientific geniuses, from Archimedes through Einstein. . . ." (lines 1–2). Archimedes was an ancient Greek mathematician, physicist, and inventor (287–212 BC), whereas Einstein was, of course, a modern scientist (1879–1955). Choice C is incorrect. The passage states: ". . . while an IQ above a certain point—about 120—is very helpful for a scientist, . . . [it] is not crucial for producing a work of genius" (lines 19–22). The passage does not specifically say that most scientists have IQ scores above 120.

45. Choice D is correct. See lines 45–47: "The scientist solves a problem by shifting from one intelligence to another, although the logical-mathematical intelligence is dominant." Accordingly, Choices A, B, and C are incorrect.

46. Choice B is correct. When the author describes the work experiences of Einstein and Tesla, he refers to their use of one or more of the four types of intelligence. Moreover, lines 28–30 state: "Some corroboration of these [four intelligence] categories comes from the reports of scientists who describe thought processes centered on images, sensations, or words." Choices A, C, and D are incorrect because the author does not refer to these choices in the passage.

47. Choice C is correct. The author indicates that great scientists use to advantage four intelligences—logical-mathematical, spatial, linguistic, and bodily-kinesthetic. See lines 23–27: "The great scientist possesses the ability to move back and forth among

them—the logical-mathematical, the spatial, which includes visual perception, the linguistic, and the bodily kinesthetic." Choices B and D are brought out in the passage but not at any length. Therefore, Choices B and D are incorrect. Choice A is incorrect because the author nowhere compares the thinking of the average individual and that of the great scientist.

48. Choice D is correct. As a football star, he would certainly have to have a high level of (a) spatial intelligence [II], which involves space sensitivity as well as visual perception, and (b) bodily kinesthetic intelligence [IV], which involves the movement of muscles, tendons, and joints. As a literature major, he would certainly have to have a high level of linguistic intelligence [III], which involves the ability to read, write, speak, and listen. Whether he would have logical-mathematical intelligence to a high degree is questionable. It follows that Choices A, B, and C are incorrect.

49. Choice D is correct. According to what is stated in lines 51–57, persistence is an important characteristic of the scientist. Thus the author would probably not agree with the statement in Choice D. The author would agree with the statement in Choice A. See lines 32–35 and lines 62–65. The author would agree with the statement in Choice B. See lines 45–50 in the context of the rest of the passage. The author would probably not disagree with the statement in Choice C since the author does not appear to distinguish artists from scientists in their thinking process even though the passage is primarily about the scientists: See lines 10–15.

50. Choice C is correct. See lines 57–59. Note that although persistence is mentioned in lines 51–57, the passage states that fluid thinking may be connected to persistence, not defined as persistence. Thus Choice A is incorrect. See also **Reading Comprehension Strategy 5** (pages 139–140).

51. Choice B is correct. Given the context in lines 45–50, the word *paradoxically* means "seemingly contradictorily." See also **Reading Comprehension Strategy 5** (pages 139–140).

52. Choice A is correct. It can be seen in the passage that the author is intrigued by and interested in the way the scientist thinks but at the same time feels that the scientist reports the findings very objectively.

EXPLANATORY ANSWERS

Section 2: Writing and Language

For further practice and information, refer to the Grammar and Usage Refresher starting on page 325.

Art as Destruction Answers

1. Choice D is correct. There is no reason for making this comparison at this point in the passage. The sentence does not provide information that follows the previous sentence or that leads into the following paragraph. Choice A is incorrect because the comparison is not relevant to the surrounding text. Choice B is wrong because the comparison to the post-modern movement is not expanded on in the following paragraph. Choice C is wrong because the issue is not whether the statement needs evidence but whether it is relevant.

2. Choice A is correct. The choice correctly places the phrase "especially those who first gathered at the Cabaret Voltaire in Switzerland in 1916" between a pair of commas. Choice B incorrectly says that the artists "were gathered" as if they were gathered *by* someone or something. Choice C uses a dash and the a comma, rather than a pair of dashes or a pair of commas. Choice D, by placing the second comma after "Switzerland," makes it sound as though "in 1916 French artist Marcel Duchamp and others were engaged in something very similar a year or so earlier in New York." The comma belongs after "1916."

3. Choice B is correct. The correct phrase to use in this context is to say that *x* is opposed to *y*. The artists were opposed to the traditional process. Choice A incorrectly implies that the artists were opposed *by* tradition. Choice C uses the meaningless phrase "in opposition from." Choice D uses the phrase "opposite from," which has no clear meaning in this context.

4. Choice B is correct. This choice clearly describes a "creation to be consumed by elitists." Choice A incorrectly uses a contraction for "that is" without using an apostrophe (that's). Choice C incorrectly uses the plural form "are," though "creation" is singular. Choice D confusingly uses the conjunction "and" though there are no two things to connect.

5. Choice D is correct. This sentence leads logically to the quote at the end of the paragraph. Choice A makes unclear who the "they" of the following sentence refers to. Choices B and D place the sentence in locations that make the "therefore" in the sentence illogical. Also, the sentence should lead into the quote at the end of the paragraph.

6. Choice C is correct. To "rail against" is to speak out (or write) forcefully against something. Choice A redundantly states that the artists created papers and manifestoes that "protested against." To protest already implies "against," so the word "against" is not needed. "Choice B states that the artists wrote materials that "dictated against," which has no clear meaning. Choice D illogically implies that the contents of the papers and manifestoes somehow "demonstrated against," as if what was written could perform this action.

7. Choice A is correct. This choice makes clear that the theater-goers were scandalized by certain kinds of plays. Choice B makes it sound as though people went to the theater "with plays." Choice C confusingly uses the pronoun "them" without making clear what "them" refers to. Choice D confusingly states that "Plays . . . made people scandalized."

8. Choice A is correct. The semicolon correctly joins two independent clauses. Choice B incorrectly uses a comma to join two independent clauses. Choice

C incorrectly uses a comma to join two independent clauses and also incorrectly uses a colon after a dependent clause. Choice D would be somewhat better if a comma were used after "meaning," though the word "while" serves no clear purpose in the sentence.

9. Choice B is correct. This choice clearly states that surrealism and social realism were notable art forms that Dadaism "blurred into." The word "notably" means something like "most famously." Choice A needlessly uses "including" so that it sounds as if "*notably surrealism* and social realism" were included. A pair of commas to separate "notably" from the surrounding text would improve this choice. Choices C and D use the word "of," which has no clear meaning in this context.

10. Choice C is correct. The preceding sentence claims that "the spirit of Dada lives on," and this choice gives an example of that. Choice A describes punk rock as a rejection of the impulse to question authority, the opposite of the anti-authoritarian nature of Dada (and punk rock). Choice B emphasizes that punk rockers established their own traditions, a claim that does not follow from the preceding sentence. Choice D describes the international origins of punk rock, a statement that does not follow from the preceding sentence.

11. Choice D is correct. This idiom (expression) makes it clear that "the belief . . . will . . . find voice . . . many times more." It is another way to express "many more times." Choices A and B make it sound as though "the belief" will happen "more times" than something else will happen. Choice C uses a phrase—"many times again"—that is not used in standard English.

Racial Tension in New York Answers

12. Choice B is correct. This choice correctly uses the subjective form "who," because it precedes the verb phrase "would be drafted." Choice A incorrectly uses the objective form "whom." Choice C incorrectly uses the phrase "for determining." Choice D incorrectly uses "which" instead of "who."

13. Choice A is correct. This idiom (expression) is correctly linked to "resentment." Choice B incorrectly uses the phrase "amounts of resentment." Choice C incorrectly forms the phrase "much of resentment." Choice D incorrectly forms the phrase "a big deal of resentment."

14. Choice D is correct. This choice correctly uses "where" after a location. Choice A incorrectly uses "when" after a location and awkwardly places the word "there" at the end of the phrase. Choices B and C are awkwardly lengthy; the phrases "in the place" and "in the location" are not needed.

15. Choice D is correct. This sentence merely restates information found in the preceding sentence. To "hamper communication between different areas" is to "keep the other parts of the city from knowing what was going on." Choices A, B, and C are incorrect because they inaccurately describe the sentence.

16. Choice B is correct. The statement after "Usually" describes what would have happened "usually." Choice A implies that whatever follows "As usual" actually *did* take place. Choice C implies that calling in the "state militia" was *more* typical than something preceding this phrase. Choice D incorrectly implies a frequent or common occurrence.

17. Choice C is correct. This choice makes clear that "Kennedy . . . was recognized" despite not being in uniform. Choice A unnecessarily uses a comma after "though." Choice B incorrectly omits a comma after "uniform." Choice D incorrectly omits a comma after "Kennedy."

18. Choice A is correct. The two sentences are independent clauses that do not need to be joined. Choices B and C incorrectly use a semicolon to connect an independent clause to a dependent clause. Choice D uses the word "also," which has no clear meaning here.

19. Choice C is correct. "New York governor" correctly and restrictively modifies Horatio Seymour. Choice D is incorrect because it places a comma after "Governor of New York"—a restrictive modifier.

Choice A incorrectly uses "spoke" instead of the participle "speaking," which is necessary to connect to the clause that begins with "claimed."

20. Choice B is correct. This choice correctly uses the parallel phrases "Troops were brought in" and "militia forces ordered." Choice A incorrectly states that "Troops brought in" as if the troops brought (something) in. Choice C uses the pronoun "them" without making clear who this would be. Choice D needlessly puts a pair of commas around "from surrounding areas" and after "forces."

21. Choice C is correct. A "turn of events" implies a change in events, as is the case here: The draft was delayed. Choice A uses a word that is more properly used to describe a physical altering. There is no "experience," as implied by Choice B. There is no clear "condition," as implied by Choice D.

22. Choice C is correct. Though the Draft Riots took place because of the Civil War, this sentence does not connect the war to the riots, and the wording about "still feeling the effects" goes beyond the scope of the passage. Choice A is wrong because the sentence does not summarize the main events, which are all about the riots. Choice B is incorrect because the sentence, though it does, like the first sentence, refer to the Civil War, does not function as a conclusion to the passage, which focuses on the riots. Choice D is incorrect because the tone is not more personal than the tone of the rest of the passage.

Modern Nursing Answers

23. Choice C is correct. The plural "patients" matches the plural pronoun "their." Choices A and B incorrectly use the singular "patient," which does not match the pronoun "their." Choice D incorrectly uses "The patients," as if a particular group of patients is being discussed.

24. Choice D is correct. The conjunction "and" is needed to add the final item to a list. Choice A confusingly uses "still" as if nurses perform many other important functions *even though* they also diagnose health problems and prescribe medicine.

Choice B confusingly uses "or even," to set off "perform many other important functions" from the other items in this list. Choice C does not connect the final item in the list to the previous two.

25. Choice A is correct. The phrase "an individual going into nursing will first pursue . . ." is clear. Nothing else is needed to link "an individual" to "going into nursing." Choice B incorrectly uses the possessive form of "who." (The contraction "who's" would have been acceptable.) Choice C incorrectly forms the phrase "an individual goes into nursing will first pursue." Choice D confusingly uses "will go," which implies that the individual has not yet gone into nursing.

26. Choice B is correct. The introductory phrase "While pursuing an ADN" clearly refers to the word "students," which comes immediately after the comma. Choice A follows the introductory phrase "While pursuing an ADN" with anatomy, as if "anatomy" were (impossibly) pursuing the degree. Choice C needlessly states that "students study" subjects that "are studied." Choice D inconsistently uses the pronoun "one" and then "you." Both pronouns should be the same.

27. Choice B is correct. This choice makes the comparison clear: the four-year BSN program places more emphasis on research and theory than the ADN does. Choice A compares the BSN program to "taking the ADN program." This is not the correct comparison. Choice C confuses the comparison. It seems to compare the ADN program to "some people." Choice D says that the BSN degree "is opted," a phrase with no clear meaning.

28. Choice D is correct. The shortage of nurses is not discussed elsewhere in the paragraph. Choices A, B, and C are incorrect because they inaccurately describe the sentence.

29. Choice D is correct. The meaning is clear: a nurse can *perform a procedure*. Choice A incorrectly states that a nurse can perform material. Choice B states that a nurse performs a decision, but decisions are not performed. Choice C states that a nurse can perform an advanced action, but one does not *perform actions*.

30. Choice B is correct. The semicolon correctly joins two independent clauses. In Choice A an independent clause is incorrectly connected to a dependent clause with a semicolon rather than a comma. In Choice C, the word "yet" indicates a contrast or surprising situation where none exists. Choice D incorrectly joins two independent clauses with a comma.

31. Choice A is correct. The list of workplaces is relevant to the statement that nurses can work outside of a hospital setting. Choice B is incorrect because the sentence does not *explain* anything. Choice C is incorrect because the information in the sentence is not unnecessary—it does help the reader understand the kind of work that nurses do outside of a hospital. Choice D is incorrect because the information is specific and relevant to the paragraph.

32. Choice D is correct. No connecting word or phrase is needed at this point. Choice A incorrectly implies that the sentence describes something that needs to be joined to the previous sentence, as if it were part of a list or series. Choice B incorrectly implies that the sentence is the final item in a list. Choice C incorrectly implies that the sentence is somehow surprising or in contrast to the previous sentence.

33. Choice B is correct. This sentence summarizes the wide range of job possibilities within nursing, as described throughout the passage. It also emphasizes the positive aspects of nursing that are found in the previous sentence. Choice A brings in the subject of personal growth, never mentioned in the passage. Choice C emphasizes the number of people helped by nurses; this is not the main topic of the passage. Choice D emphasizes the relationship between training and the practice of nursing; this is not the main topic of the passage. Education is not mentioned in the first paragraph or the final two.

The Power of the Wind Answers

34. Choice B is correct. A venture is an activity, frequently a risky one, that is done for gain of some sort. A new business can be described as a venture. In this context, it makes sense to describe traveling by sailboat long ago as a venture. Choice A confusingly refers to travel itself as an investigation. Choice B calls travel a chance, and choice C calls it a plan. Travel involves chances and plans (and investigations, perhaps), but travel itself is not any of these things.

35. Choice B is correct. There is no reason that the two sentences have to be joined. Choice A uses "yet," though this word is not used to connect two contrasting statements. Choice C uses "and also" but does not clearly connect two parts that require connecting. This choice also creates the confusing phrase "flooded areas and also as early as 1987. . . ." Choice D creates a comma splice—two independent clauses joined by a comma.

36. Choice A is correct. The paragraph discusses the advantages of placing wind farms offshore. The parenthetical comment brings to the reader's attention, through the use of the phrase "It should be noted," one drawback of the offshore farms. Choice B illogically implies that the higher cost of offshore wind farms is *because* of the advantages of locating then offshore. Choice C implies the same thing. Choice D uses "Additionally" but does not give the sense that the parenthetical comment, which mentions a *disadvantage* to offshore farms, is in contrast to the earlier part of the paragraph, which discusses *advantages* to offshore wind farms.

37. Choice D is correct. A colon can be used after an independent clause that introduces a list, and that is the case here. Choice A incorrectly implies that the advantages of using wind power are obvious *because* wind is easily available, etc. Choice B uses a semicolon, but the second part of the sentence is not an independent clause.

38. Choice B is correct. The phrase between the commas could be taken out of the sentence and the grammar and basic meaning would be intact. Choice A incorrectly states that "the strength and frequency of wind . . . is." The plural subject (strength and frequency) does not agree with the singular form of the verb (is). Choice C incorrectly connects the plural subject (strength and frequency) to "varies" instead of "vary." Choice D confusingly uses the singular pronouns "this" and "it."

39. Choice C is correct. This choice clearly states that a day without strong winds is likely to be a sunny day. Choice A says that a day without strong winds is more likely than a sunny day, but the context does not support this comparison. The point the author is making is that the sun is more likely to be shining on a day without wind. Choice B redundantly uses "most likely" and "probably." Choice D redundantly uses "could" and "potentially."

40. Choice A is correct. This choice makes clear that forecasting (predicting) wind strength is helpful *but* hard to do (success is low). This then leads into the next sentence, which says that *consequently* here is what can be done to compensate for any unexpected loss of power. Choices B and D do not lead into the next sentence, which says that *consequently* here is what can be done to compensate for any unexpected loss of power. The idea that there is a problem with forecasting wind conditions needs to be in the first sentence. Choice C confuses the meaning of the sentence by stating that the unpredictability of wind conditions is *avoidable*.

41. Choice A is correct. This choice correctly states that "the benefits . . . are so exciting that. . . ." Choice B incorrectly states that "the benefits . . . are going to excite so much," implying that the benefits will excite (who?). Choice C misplaces "eventually." It would be somewhat better to state that "the benefits . . . will eventually be exciting." Choice D incorrectly uses the singular "is," which does not agree with "benefits."

42. Choice C is correct. The sentence begins with "For example," so it must introduce an example of something mentioned in the previous sentence. The first sentence refers to "Other challenges," and sentence 3 refers to the challenge of carrying the wind power over great distances. Choices A, B, and D do not place sentence 3, which begins with "For example," so that it clearly introduces an example of something mentioned in the previous sentence.

43. Choice B is correct. The graph increases exponentially, meaning that it does not rise in a straight line but instead rises at a faster and faster rate. The difference in cumulative capacity between consecutive years keeps increasing. This means that the cumulative capacity during the later span, 2006–2010, increased more rapidly than it did during the earlier span, 2000–2005. Choice A is wrong because the increase was continuous but not steady (straight line). Choice C is wrong because the more likely value for 2015 would be greater than 400. Choice D goes beyond the scope of the given information since we have no way of knowing what happened before 1996.

44. Choice D is correct. None of the other choices can be concluded. Choices A and B refer to hydroelectricity, but the graph does not provide any information about this type of energy. Choice C refers to the number of windy days, but that goes beyond the scope of the graph.

EXPLANATORY ANSWERS

Section 3: Mathematics, *No Calculator*

As you read these solutions, you are advised to do two things if you answered a math question incorrectly:

1. *When a specific Math Strategy is referred to in the solution, study that strategy, which you will find in "19 Math Strategies" (beginning on page 72).*

2. *When the solution directs you to the "Complete SAT Math Refresher" (beginning on page 163)—for example, Math Refresher #305—study the math principle to get a clear idea of the math operation that you needed to know in order to answer the question correctly.*

1. Choice D is correct.

   Given: $\dfrac{3x}{4} = 9$ `1`

   (Use Strategy 13: Find unknowns by multiplying.)
   Multiplying `1` by 4, we get
   $$4\left(\frac{3x}{4}\right) = (9)4$$
   $$3x = 36 \qquad `2`$$
   Multiply `2` by 2. We have
   $$2(3x) = 2(36)$$
   $$6x = 72$$

   (Math Refresher #406)

2. Choice B is correct.

   (Use Strategy 2: Translate from words into algebra.)
   We are told:
   $$A + 8 + A + 1 + A + 2$$
   $$= A + A + 1 + A + 2 + A + 3 \qquad `1`$$

   (Use Strategy 1: Cancel expressions that appear on both sides of an equation.)
   Each side contains an A, $A + 1$, and $A + 2$.

Canceling each of these from each side, we get,
$$\cancel{A} + 8 + \cancel{A} + \cancel{1} + \cancel{A} + \cancel{2}$$
$$= \cancel{A} + \cancel{A} + \cancel{1} + \cancel{A} + \cancel{2} + A + 3$$
$$\text{Thus, } 8 = A + 3$$
$$5 = A$$

(Math Refresher #406)

3. Choice D is correct.

   Given: $500w = 3 \times 700$ `1`

   (Use Strategy 13: Find an unknown by dividing.)
   Divide `1` by 500, giving
   $$\frac{500w}{500} = \frac{3 \times 700}{500}$$

   (Use Strategy 19: Factor and reduce first. Then multiply.)
   $$w = \frac{3 \times 7 \times \cancel{100}}{5 \times \cancel{100}}$$
   $$w = \frac{21}{5}$$

   (Math Refresher #406)

4. Choice B is correct.

   (Use Strategy 17: Use the given information effectively.)
   The circle graph tells you that 19% of this mixture is carbon. Since the total mixture weighs 24 pounds, 19% of that will be the amount of carbon in the mixture (in pounds). We would multiply 24 lbs $\times$ 0.19. But since the choices are not that close and since we are looking for the *closest* number of pounds, make the problem simpler by multiplying $24 \times 0.20 = 4.8$, which is close to 4.6.

   (Math Refresher #705)

5. Choice A is correct.

    (Use Strategy 14: Label unknown quantities to help solve the problem.)

    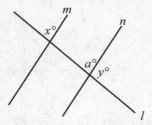

    Know the properties of parallel lines. If 2 parallel lines are crossed by a transversal, the pairs of corresponding angles are equal. Thus,

    $$x = a \qquad \boxed{1}$$

    From the diagram, $a + y = 180$ $\boxed{2}$

    Substituting $\boxed{1}$ into $\boxed{2}$, we get

    $$x + y = 180$$

    (Math Refresher #504)

6. Choice D is correct.

    (Use Strategy 11: Use new definitions carefully.)

    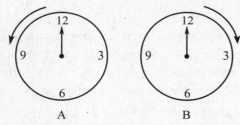

    By the definition of a move, every 4 moves brings each hand back to 12.

    Thus, after 4, 8, 12, and 16 moves, respectively, each hand is at 12.

    Hand A, moving counterclockwise, moves to 9 on its 17th move.

    Hand B, moving clockwise, moves to 3 on its 17th move.

7. Choice B is correct.

    (Use Strategy 11: Use new definitions carefully.)

    After 6 hours $\frac{x}{2}$ grams remain.

    After 12 hours, $\frac{1}{2}\left(\frac{x}{2}\right)$ grams remain.

After 18 hours, $\frac{1}{2}\left(\frac{1}{2}\right)\left(\frac{x}{2}\right)$ grams remain.

After 24 hours, $\frac{1}{2}\left(\frac{1}{2}\right)\left(\frac{1}{2}\right)\left(\frac{x}{2}\right) = \frac{x}{16}$ grams remain.

(Math Refresher #431)

8. Choice D is correct.

    I. Slope is defined as $\frac{y_2 - y_1}{x_2 - x_1}$ where (x_1, y_1) and (x_2, y_2) are points on the line. Thus here $0 = x_1$, $a = y_1$, $a = x_2$, and $0 = y_2$.

    (Use Strategy 18: Know and use facts about triangles.)

    II. The triangle created is an isosceles right triangle with sides $a, a, a\sqrt{2}$. Thus II is true.

    III. In an isosceles right triangle, the interior angles of the triangle are 90-45-45 degrees. Thus III is true.

    (Math Refreshers #416, #411, and #509)

9. Choice B is correct.

    (Use Strategy 3: Know how to find unknown quantities from known quantities.)

    To find the midpoint of two points, all you need to do is find the average of the x-coordinates and the average of the y-coordinates. In this case, the average of the x-coordinates is $\frac{-1 + 5}{2} = 2$. This is the x-coordinate of the midpoint. For the y-coordinates, the average is $\frac{-1 + 1}{2} = 0$. This is the y-coordinate of the midpoint. The midpoint's coordinates are therefore (2, 0).

10. Choice D is correct.

    (Use Strategy 8: When all choices must be tested, start with the last choice and work backward.)

    Choice A is false because if $b < -2$, the absolute value of b (denoted as $|b|$) must be greater than 2. Choice B is false: c is positive ($c > +3 > 0$) so $c \neq -|c|$, since $-|c|$ is negative. Choice C is false: Since a and b are negative numbers and since $a < b$, $|a| > |b|$. Choice D is correct and Choice C is correct.

    (Math Refreshers #419, #615, and #410)

11. Choice D is correct.

    (Use Strategy 17: Use the given information effectively.)

    Given: $w = 7r + 6r + 5r + 4r + 3r$

    Then, $w = 25r$ **1**

    We are told we must add something to w so that the resulting sum will be divisible by 7 for every positive integer r.

    Check the choices.

    (Use Strategy 8: Start with the last choice.)

    Add $3r$ to **1**

    $$25r + 3r = 28r = 7(4r)$$

    will always be divisible by 7. Thus, Choice D is correct.

    (Math Refresher #431)

12. Choice D is correct.

    (Use Strategy 17: Use the given information effectively.)

    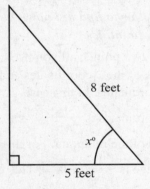

    8 feet

    $x°$

    5 feet

    Since you've been given the lengths of the adjacent side and the hypotenuse, first check the functions that involve those two values.

    $$\cos x° = \frac{adjacent}{hypotenuse} = \frac{5}{8}$$

    $$\sec x° = \frac{1}{\cos x°} = \frac{8}{5}$$

    (Math Refresher #901)

13. Choice A is correct.

    $$(3 + 4i)(6i - 1) = 3(6i) + 4i(6i) + 3(-1) + 4i(-1)$$
    $$= 18i + 24i^2 - 3 - 4i$$
    $$= 24i^2 + 14i - 3$$

    Since $i^2 = -1$:

    $$(3 + 4i)(6i - 1) = 24(-1) + 14i - 3 = 14i - 27.$$

    (Math Refresher #618)

14. Choice C is correct.

    (Use Strategy 2: Translate English words into mathematical expressions.)

    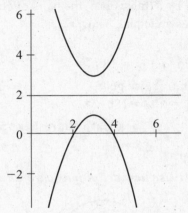

    The given equation describes a parabola, one that opens upward, has a minimum value (vertex) at 3 and has been shifted 3 units over to the right from $(0, 0)$. The line $y = 2$ is parallel to the x-axis.

    If the parabola is reflected over the line, the new parabola will face downward and will be as far from the line as the original parabola was, as seen in the figure above.

    The new parabola can be described by the equation $y = -(x - 3)^2 + 1$. To find the zeros, substitute zero for y. This will give you the x-values of the points at which the reflected parabola crosses the x-axis (and therefore has a y-value of zero).

    $$0 = -(x - 3)^2 + 1$$

    To solve, you could try out the choices, or work it out algebraically. To do so efficiently, you could realize that the equation will work out only if $(x - 3)^2$ equals 1. This means that x must equal 4 or 2.

15. Choice B is correct.

(Use Strategy 17: Use the given information effectively.)

Any circle with radius r in the xy plane whose center is (a,b) can be represented as

$(x - a)^2 + (y - b)^2 = r^2$

$x^2 + y^2 - 8y + 4 = 0$ can be factored:

$(x - 0)^2 + (y - 4)^2 = 12$

Thus $a = 0$, $b = 4$, and $r^2 = 12$

$r = \sqrt{12} = \sqrt{4 \times 3} = 2\sqrt{3}$

(Math Refreshers #410b and #524)

16. 50

(Use Strategy 2: Translate English words into mathematical expressions.)

The estimated ratio of people who came into the office to clients is $\frac{p}{c}$. This estimate would have been accurate if 30 fewer people had become clients, and since 240 *did* become clients, we can say that:

$$\frac{p}{c} = \frac{350}{240 - 30} = \frac{350}{210} = \frac{5}{3}$$

The estimated ratio was therefore 5 : 3. If we keep the number of clients the same (as it actually was) and change the number of people who came into the office by x, we get:

$$\frac{5}{3} = \frac{350 + x}{240}$$

You could solve this by cross-multiplying or by realizing the following: Since 3 times 80 equals 240, if you multiply 5 by 80, you'll get the correct numerator. Since $5 \times 80 = 400$, we can say that $350 + x = 400$ and that $x = 50$.

17. 3.81

(Use Strategy 13: Know how to find unknown expressions by adding, subtracting, multiplying, or dividing equations or expressions.)

Since the company charges $2,535,000 for less than 15,000 square feet, we can plug this information into the first equation to find x, the number of square feet:

$$2,535,000 = 200x + 135,000$$

If you subtract 135,000 from each side and then divide by 200, you'll get:

$$x = 12,000$$

If the footage had been two times greater, it would have been 24,000 square feet, which means that we should use the other equation to determine the charge:

$$g(x) = 150(24,000) + 210,000 = 3,810,000$$

This value, 3,810,000 can be expressed as 3.81×10^6, which means that $a = 3.81$.

18. 4

(Use Strategy 17: Use the given information effectively.)

By trial and error, it can be seen that 4 is the answer. A second way of approaching this problem is as follows:

Let $\square = x$. Then we have

$$x\ 1$$
$$6\ x$$
$$x\ 9$$
$$\overline{15\ x}$$

We get $1 + x + 9 = 10 + x$. So we carry the 1 and get $1 + x + 6 + x = 15$. So $7 + 2x = 15$; $2x = 8$; $x = 4$.

A third way to approach this problem (and the most sophisticated way) is: Let $\square = x$. Then $\square 1$ is $x\ 1$, which is $10x + 1$ since $\square$ is in the tens column. (Any number XY is $10X + Y$; any number XYZ is $100X + 10Y + Z$.) $6\ \square = 6\ x = 60 + x$. $\square 9 = x\ 9 = 10x + 9$. So adding, we get

$$10x + 1 + 60 + x + 10x + 9 = 21x + 70.$$

This must equal $15\square = 15\ x$
$$= 100 + 50 + x = 150 + x.$$

So $21x + 70 = 150 + x$ and $20x = 80$; $x = 4$.

(Math Refresher #406)

19. 20

(Use Strategy 17: Use the given information effectively.)

You can begin this problem by squaring both sides of the first equation. This gives you:

$$\left(\frac{x}{y}\right)^{-20} = \left(\frac{w}{z}\right)^{5}$$

A negative exponent inverts the base, so that

$$\left(\frac{x}{y}\right)^{-20} = \left(\frac{y}{x}\right)^{20}$$

You now have $\left(\frac{y}{x}\right)^{20} = \left(\frac{w}{z}\right)^{5}$, which means that $p = 20$.

20. 14

(Use Strategy 13: Know how to find unknown expressions by adding, subtracting, multiplying, or dividing equations or expressions.)

Since $f(a) = a$, we can plug a in for x in the function equation and get:

$$f(a) = a^3 + a^2 + a = a$$

We can take the "non-function notation" part of the equation and solve:

$$a^3 + a^2 + a = a$$
$$a^3 + a^2 = 0$$
$$a(a^2 + a) = 0$$

This means that a could be 0 or $a^2 + a = 0$. We are told that $a \neq 0$, so it must be that $a^2 + a = 0$. If we factor this, we get:

$$a(a + 1) = 0$$

This means that $a = -1$. If we plug this information into the question, we get:

$f[-2(-1)]$, which simplifies to $f(2)$

Using the original function equation, we get:

$$f(2) - 2^3 + 2^2 + 2 = 14$$

EXPLANATORY ANSWERS

Section 4: Mathematics, *with Calculator*

As you read these solutions, you are advised to do two things if you answered a math question incorrectly:

1. *When a specific Math Strategy is referred to in the solution, study that strategy, which you will find in "19 Math Strategies" (beginning on page 72).*

2. *When the solution directs you to the "Complete SAT Math Refresher" (beginning on page 163)—for example, Math Refresher #305—study the math principle to get a clear idea of the math operation that you needed to know in order to answer the question correctly.*

1. Choice D is correct.

$$Given: \frac{3 + y}{y} = 7 \qquad \boxed{1}$$

(Use Strategy 13: Know how to find unknown expressions by multiplying.)

Multiply $\boxed{1}$ by y, to get

$$y\left(\frac{3 + y}{y}\right) = (7)y$$
$$3 + y = 7y$$
$$3 = 6y$$
$$\frac{3}{6} = y$$
$$\frac{1}{2} = y$$

(Math Refresher #406)

2. Choice D is correct.

Given: 8 people divide a cash prize equally $\qquad \boxed{1}$

(Use Strategy 2: Translate from words into algebra.)

From $\boxed{1}$ we get:

Each person receives $\frac{1}{8}$ of the total prize $\qquad \boxed{2}$

2 people receive $\frac{2}{8} = \frac{1}{4}$ of the prize $\qquad \boxed{3}$

To change $\boxed{3}$ to a percent we multiply by 100.

$$100\left(\frac{1}{4}\right) = \frac{100}{4}$$
$$= 25\%$$

(Math Refreshers #200 and #106)

3. Choice C is correct.

(Use Strategy 10: Know how to use units.)

We are given his rate is $\dfrac{90 \text{ laps}}{6 \text{ hours}}$

$$\frac{90 \text{ laps}}{6 \text{ hours}} \times \frac{1 \text{ hour}}{60 \text{ minutes}} = \frac{90 \text{ laps}}{360 \text{ minutes}}$$

$\frac{1}{4}$ lap per minute

(Math Refresher #121)

4. Choice D is correct.

(Use Strategy 15: Know how to eliminate certain choices.)

The graph $y = 2x - 4$ is a straight line such that when $x = 0$, $y = -4$ and when $y = 0$, $2x - 4 = 0$ and thus $x = 2$. So we look for a line that cuts the y-axis (vertical axis where $x = 0$) at $y = -4$, and cuts the x-axis (horizontal axis where $y = 0$) at $x = 2$.

(Math Refreshers #413, #414, and #415)

5. Choice A is correct.

(Use Strategy 11: Use new definitions carefully.)

$$Given: \quad x \boxdot y = 3 + xy \qquad \boxed{1}$$
$$y \neq 0 \qquad \boxed{2}$$
$$x \boxdot y = 3 \qquad \boxed{3}$$

Substituting $\boxed{3}$ into $\boxed{1}$, we get

$$3 = 3 + xy$$
$$0 = xy \qquad \boxed{4}$$

Noting $\boxed{2}$, we divide $\boxed{4}$ by y

$$\frac{0}{y} = \frac{xy}{y}$$
$$0 = x$$

(Math Refreshers #431 and #406)

6. Choice C is correct.

(Use Strategy 13: Know how to find unknown expressions by adding, subtracting, multiplying, or dividing equations or expressions.)

This problem can be simply solved by adding the given equations.

$$
\begin{aligned}
r - 3s &= 9 \\
+\ 2r + 4s &= -2 \\
\hline
3r + s &= 7
\end{aligned}
$$

7. Choice C is correct.

(Use Strategy 2: Translate from words into algebra.)

In $\frac{1}{2}$ year, 600 pounds of feed were used at a rate of $1.25 per pound. Thus (600 pounds) $\times$ ($1.25 per pound), or $750, was spent. Hence,

$$
\text{Feed cost per egg} = \frac{\text{total cost for feed}}{\text{number of eggs}}
$$

$$
= \frac{\$750}{5{,}000 \text{ eggs}}
$$

(Use Strategy 19: Factor and reduce.)

$$
= \frac{\$75 \times 10}{500 \times 10 \text{ eggs}}
$$

$$
= \frac{\$25 \times 3}{25 \times 20 \text{ eggs}}
$$

$$
= \frac{\$3}{20} \text{ per egg}
$$

$$
= \$0.15 \text{ per egg}
$$

(Math Refresher #200)

8. Choice C is correct.

(Use Strategy 2: Translate from words into algebra.)
(Use Strategy 17: Use the given information effectively.)

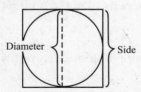

Given the perimeter of the square = 40

$$\text{Thus, } 4(\text{side}) = 40$$
$$\text{side} = 10 \quad \boxed{1}$$

A side of the square = length of diameter of circle.

$$\text{Thus, diameter} = 10 \text{ from } \boxed{1}$$
$$\text{Since diameter} = 2(\text{radius})$$
$$10 = 2(\text{radius})$$
$$5 = \text{radius} \quad \boxed{2}$$

Area of a circle = πr^2 $\qquad \boxed{3}$

Substituting $\boxed{2}$ into $\boxed{3}$, we have

$$\text{Area of circle} = \pi 5^2$$
$$\text{Area of circle} = 25\pi$$

(Math Refreshers #303 and #310)

9. Choice D is correct.

(Use Strategy 8: When all choices must be tested, start with the last choice and work backward.)

$$\text{Choice D is } x^2 + x + 2$$

(Use Strategy 7: Use specific numerical examples.)

Let $x = 3$ (an odd positive integer)

$$
\begin{aligned}
\text{Then} \quad x^2 + x + 2 &= 3^2 + 3 + 2 \\
&= 9 + 3 + 2 \\
&= 14 \text{ (an even result)}
\end{aligned}
$$

Now let $x = 2$ (an even positive integer)

$$
\begin{aligned}
\text{Then} \quad x^2 + x + 2 &= 2^2 + 2 + 2 \\
&= 4 + 2 + 2 \\
&= 8 \text{ (an even result)}
\end{aligned}
$$

Whether x is odd or even, Choice D is even.

(Math Refresher #431)

10. Choice B is correct.

(Use Strategy 11: Use new definitions carefully.)

By definition 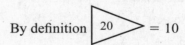 $= 10$

(Math Refreshers #603 and #607)

11. Choice A is correct.

(Use Strategy 14: Draw lines to help solve the problem.)

Before the rotation, we have

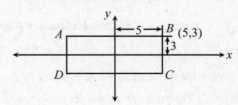

After the rotation, we have

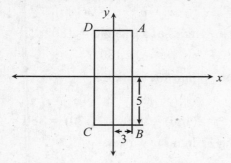

Note that the new y-coordinate of B is negative because B is below the x-axis. Since B is to the right of the y-axis, its x-coordinate is positive. By looking at the second diagram, we see that the coordinates of B are:

$$(3, -5)$$

(Math Refresher #410b)

12. Choice C is correct.

(Use Strategy 17: Use the given information effectively and ignore irrelevant information.)

To find the total cost of all uniforms in *child* sizes at *School B*, we would multiply the number of uniforms at School B of Type A with the Child's Type A cost, multiply the number of uniforms at School B of Type B with the Child's Type B cost, and multiply the number of uniforms at School B of Type C with the Child's Type C cost, and add those three quantities. That is:

$$30 \times \$9 + 60 \times \$10 + 50 \times \$11 = \$1,420$$

(Math Refresher #702)

13. Choice A is correct.

(Use Strategy 2: Translate English words into mathematical expressions.)

We can translate the first sentence into

$$d = 5c - 8$$

The second sentence becomes:

$$b = (d + c) + 20$$

The question asks for b in terms of c, so we can combine the equations, substituting $5c - 8$ in for d in the second equation.

$$b = [(5c - 8) + c] + 20$$

This simplifies to $b = 4c + 12$, which is the same as Choice A.

14. Choice D is correct.

(Use Strategy 17: Use the given information effectively.)

Two-fifths, or 40%, of the applicants fail on the examination. Of the 60% remaining, three-fourths fail to get into the program. $\frac{3}{4} \times 60\% = 45\%$.

Thus, the total number of failures is equal to 40% + 45%, or 85%.

Or, to solve it algebraically:

Let x be the number of applicants.

$\frac{3}{5}x$ = applicants who passed the exam

$\frac{\frac{3}{5}x}{4} = \frac{3}{20}x$ = applicants who passed the exam and were accepted

$\frac{\frac{3}{20}x}{x} = \frac{3}{20}$ = % of all applicants who gain admission

$1 - \frac{3}{20} = \frac{17}{20} = 85\%$ = % who *fail* to gain admission

(Math Refresher #106)

15. Choice B is correct.

Method I (shortest method):

$$a + b + c = 180 \quad \boxed{1}$$
$$g + d = 180 \quad \boxed{2}$$
$$e + i = 180 \quad \boxed{3}$$
$$f + h = 180 \quad \boxed{4}$$

(Use Strategy 13: Find unknowns by adding equations.)

Adding $\boxed{1} + \boxed{2} + \boxed{3} + \boxed{4}$, we get

$$a + b + c + g + d + e + i + f + h = 720$$

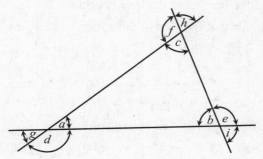

Method II:

From the diagram, we get

$$a + d = 180 \qquad 1$$
$$b + e = 180 \qquad 2$$
$$c + f = 180 \qquad 3$$

(Use Strategy 13: Find unknowns by adding equations.)

Adding 1 + 2 + 3, we get

$$a + b + c + d + e + f = 540 \qquad 4$$

(Use Strategy 3: The whole equals the sum of its parts.)

The sum of the angles of a $\Delta = 180$

Thus, $a + b + c = 180 \qquad 5$

From the diagram (vertical angles), we have

$$a = g, b = i, c = h \qquad 6$$

Substituting 6 into 5, we get

$$g + i + h = 180 \qquad 7$$

Adding 4 + 7, we get

$$a + b + c + d + e + f + g + i + h = 720$$

Method III:

Let X be the value of $a + b + c + d + e + f + g + h + i$.

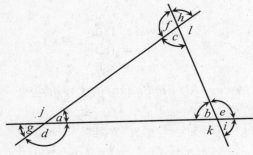

Label the unmarked angles j, k, and l.

We know that the sum of the angles in a circle is 360°. So we get:

$$a + d + g + j = 360 \qquad 8$$
$$b + e + i + k = 360 \qquad 9$$
$$c + f + h + l = 360 \qquad 10$$

(Use Strategy 13: Add equations.)

$$X + j + k + l = 3(360) \qquad 11$$

We know that the sum of angles in a straight line is 180°. So we get:

$$j + a = 180 \qquad 12$$
$$k + b = 180 \qquad 13$$
$$l + c = 180 \qquad 14$$

By adding equations 12, 13, and 14 together, we get:

$$j + k + l + a + b + c = 3(180) \qquad 15$$

And since the angles of a triangle = 180°

$$a + b + c = 180 \qquad 16$$

Substituting 16 into 15, we get:

$$j + k + l + 180 = 3(180)$$
$$j + k + l = 3(180) - 180 = 2(180) = 360 \qquad 17$$

Substituting 17 into 11, we get:

$$X + 360 = 3(360)$$
$$X = 3(360) - 360 = 2(360) = 720$$

(Math Refreshers #501, #505, and #406)

16. Choice A is correct.

(Use Strategy 12: Try not to make tedious calculations, since there is usually an easier way.)

To determine how many ways there are of combining 8 waiters with 3 hosts, you simply multiply these numbers, giving you 24 possible waiter/host combinations.

16 more combinations would give us 40 possibilities. Only A is correct because that would give us 10 waiters and 4 hosts, yielding 40 (10 × 4) possibilities.

17. Choice A is correct.

(Use Strategy 5:
$$Average = \frac{sum\ of\ values}{total\ number\ of\ values}.)$$

$$p = \frac{x + y}{2} \qquad 1$$
$$q = \frac{y + z}{2} \qquad 2$$
$$r = \frac{x + z}{2} \qquad 3$$

(Use Strategy 13: Find unknown expressions by adding equations.)

Adding 1, 2, and 3, we get

$$p + q + r = \frac{x + y}{2} + \frac{y + z}{2} + \frac{x + z}{2}$$
$$= \frac{2x + 2y + 2z}{2}$$
$$p + q + r = x + y + z \qquad 4$$

The average of x, y, and $z = \dfrac{x + y + z}{3} \qquad 5$

Substitute 4 into 5. We have

The average of x, y, and $z = \dfrac{p + q + r}{3}$

(Math Refreshers #601 and #109)

18. Choice B is correct.

    (Use Strategy 14: Label unknown quantities.)

    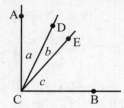

    Label angles as above with *a, b, c.*

    You are given that

    $$a + b + c = 90 \qquad \boxed{1}$$
    $$b + c = 62 \qquad \boxed{2}$$
    $$a + b = 37 \qquad \boxed{3}$$

    You want to find $\angle DCE = b$

    (Use Strategy 13: Find unknown expressions by adding or subtracting.)

    First add $\boxed{2}$ and $\boxed{2}$:

    We get:

    $$a + 2b + c = 62 + 37 = 99 \qquad \boxed{4}$$

    Now subtract $\boxed{1}$ from $\boxed{4}$:

    $$a + 2b + c = 99$$
    $$\underline{a +\ \ b + c = 90}$$
    $$b\ \ \ \ \ \ = 9$$

    (Math Refresher #509)

19. Choice C is correct.

    (Use Strategy 2: Translate from words into algebra.)

    Let the 3 consecutive even integers be

    $$x, x + 2, x + 4 \qquad \boxed{1}$$

    where *x* is even. We are told that

    $$x + x + 2 + x + 4 = K$$
    $$\text{or} \quad 3x + 6 = K \qquad \boxed{2}$$

    From $\boxed{1}$, we know that

    $$x - 5, x - 3, x - 1$$

    must be the 3 consecutive odd integers immediately preceding *x*. We are told that

    $$x - 5 + x - 3 + x - 1 = y$$
    $$\text{or} \quad 3x - 9 = y \qquad \boxed{3}$$

    (Use Strategy 13: Find unknown expressions by subtraction.)

    Subtracting $\boxed{3}$ from $\boxed{2}$, we get

    $$15 = K - y$$
    $$\text{or} \quad y = K - 15$$

    (Math Refreshers #200 and #406)

20. Choice B is correct.

    (Use Strategy 2: Translate from words into algebra.)

    Let the capacity of container *B* be *x*. Then the capacity of container *A* will be 2*x*, and that of container *C* will be 3*x*. The amount poured into container *C* is equal to half of 2*x* plus one-third of *x*, or $\frac{2x}{2} + \frac{x}{3} = x + \frac{x}{3} = \frac{4x}{3}$. Dividing this amount by the total capacity of container C, we find the fraction that was filled:

    $$\frac{\left(\frac{4x}{3}\right)}{3x} = \frac{4}{9}$$

    (Math Refresher #406)

21. Choice B is correct.

    (Use Strategy 17: Use the given information effectively.)

    By looking at the diagram, we have

    $$P_1 = -2$$
    $$P_2 = -1$$

    We can approximate the other numbers by looking at their positions on the number line:

    $$P_3 \approx \frac{1}{3}$$
    $$P_4 \approx \frac{2}{3}$$
    $$P_5 \approx \frac{3}{2}$$

    Thus,

    $$P_1\, P_2\, P_3\, P_4\, P_5 \approx (-2)(-1)\left(\frac{1}{3}\right)\left(\frac{2}{3}\right)\left(\frac{3}{2}\right)$$
    $$P_1\, P_2\, P_3\, P_4\, P_5 \approx \frac{2}{3}$$

    (Math Refresher #410)

22. Choice D is correct.

    Since vertical angles are equal, then

    $$m\angle AOC = m\angle DOB = 108 \qquad \boxed{1}$$

    Thus, from $\boxed{1}$, we get length of

    $$\text{minor } \widehat{AC} = \text{length of minor } \widehat{DB} \qquad \boxed{2}$$

    From geometry we know length of

    $$\text{minor } \widehat{AC} = \frac{108}{360} \times \text{circumference of circle}$$
    $$= \frac{108}{360} \times \pi(\text{diameter})$$
    $$= \frac{108}{360} \times \pi(20)$$

(Use Strategy 19: Factor and reduce.)

$$\text{length of minor } \widehat{AC} = \frac{\cancel{18} \times 6}{\cancel{18} \times 20} \times \pi(20)$$

$$\text{length of minor } \widehat{AC} = 6\pi \qquad \boxed{3}$$

length $\widehat{AC}$ + length $\widehat{DB}$ can be found using $\boxed{2}$ and $\boxed{3}$

$$\text{length } \widehat{AC} + \text{length } \widehat{DB} = 6\pi + 6\pi$$

$$\text{length } \widehat{AC} + \text{length } \widehat{DB} = 12\pi$$

(Math Refreshers #503 and #310)

23. Choice D is correct.

(Use Strategy 17: Use the given information effectively.)

Of the N French students, P are in both programs, so only $(N - P)$ are in the French program alone; similarly, $(M - P)$ students are in the Spanish program alone. Thus, the number of students in only one language program is equal to $(N - P) +$ $(M - P)$, which equals $N + M - 2P$.

Note: The following diagram may help you to visualize the answer better.

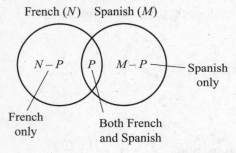

French (*N*)   Spanish (*M*)

$N - P$ P $M - P$ — Spanish only

French only

Both French and Spanish

(Math Refresher #613)

24. Choice C is correct.

(Use Strategy 17: Use the given information effectively.)

In 12 seconds, the wheel travels through 2 revolutions (since 12 seconds is $\frac{1}{5}$ of the minute it would take for ten revolutions). Since this distance is equal to 16 feet, the wheel travels 8 feet per revolution; thus, 8 feet must be the circumference of the wheel. To find the diameter, we divide this figure by π (because the circumference of a circle is π times its diameter). Thus, the diameter is $\frac{8}{\pi}$ feet.

(Math Refresher #310)

25. Choice E is correct.

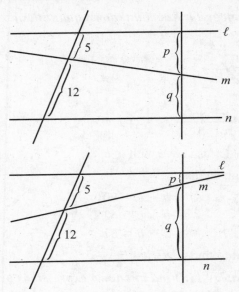

Since we know only that $\overleftrightarrow{m}$ is not parallel to either $\overleftrightarrow{\ell}$ or $\overleftrightarrow{n}$, both of the following situations could be true.

(Use Strategy 17: Use the given information effectively.)

Note: $p + q = 13$ is still true in both cases in the drawings above.

Clearly, the value of $\frac{p}{q}$ is different for each case. Hence, $\frac{p}{q}$ cannot be determined unless we know more about $\overleftrightarrow{m}$.

26. Choice C is correct.

	First Place (6 points)	Second Place (4 points)	Third Place (2 points)
Game 1			
Game 2		Arisa	
Game 3			Arisa

(Use Strategy 17: Use the given information effectively.)

Dylan can attain the *minimum* possible score by placing third in Game 1 and Game 2 and second in Game 3.

From the chart he would have 2, 2, and 4 points for each of these finishes.

Thus, minimum score = 2 + 2 + 4

    minimum score = 8 points

(Math Refreshers #701 and #702)

27. Choice A is correct.

(Use Strategy 3: The whole equals the sum of its parts.)

The area between the curved path and the dodecagon is simply the sum of the areas of the 12 semicircles.

Since area of circle = πr^2

then area of semicircle = $\frac{1}{2}\pi r^2$

where r is the radius of the circle.

Thus, the area of the shaded region = $12\left(\frac{1}{2}\pi r^2\right)$

$$= 6\pi r^2 \qquad \boxed{1}$$

We are told that the diameter of a semicircle
= the side of the dodecagon. $\qquad \boxed{2}$

Since each side of a regular dodecagon has the same length, then

length of a side of dodecagon

$= \dfrac{\text{perimeter of dodecagon}}{12}$

$= \dfrac{24}{12}$

$= 2$

From $\boxed{2}$, we know that

diameter of semicircle = 2

Thus, radius of semicircle = 1 $\qquad \boxed{3}$

Substituting $\boxed{3}$ into $\boxed{1}$,

area of shaded region = 6π

(Math Refreshers #310, #311, and #522)

28. Choice D is correct.

Given: $x^9 = 4$ $\qquad\qquad \boxed{1}$

$x^7 = \dfrac{9}{y^2}$ $\qquad\qquad \boxed{2}$

$x > 0$ and $y > 0$

(Use Strategy 13: Know how to find unknown expressions by dividing equations.)

Divide $\boxed{1}$ by $\boxed{2}$. We get

$$\frac{x^9}{x^7} = \frac{4}{\frac{9}{y^2}}$$

$$x^2 = 4 \times \frac{y^2}{9}$$

$$x^2 = \frac{4}{9}y^2$$

$$\sqrt{x^2} = \sqrt{\frac{4}{9}y^2}$$

$$x = \frac{2}{3}y$$

Note: This is the only solution because $x > 0$ and $y > 0$.

(Math Refreshers #310 and #524)

29. Choice A is correct.

$$\text{volume of cube} = (\text{side})^3$$

Thus, volume of each small cube = r^3 $\quad \boxed{1}$

volume of larger cube = s^3 $\quad \boxed{2}$

and sum of the volumes of the 27 cubes = $27r^3$ $\quad \boxed{3}$

(Use Strategy 3: The whole equals the sum of its parts.)

We are told that the sum of the volumes of the 27 cubes = the volume of the larger cube

$$= 81 \qquad \boxed{4}$$

From $\boxed{2}$, $\boxed{3}$, and $\boxed{4}$ together, we have

$$27r^3 = 81 \qquad \boxed{5}$$
$$s^3 = 81 \qquad \boxed{6}$$

(Use Strategy 13: Know how to find unknown expressions by dividing.)

Dividing $\boxed{5}$ by $\boxed{6}$, we get

$$27\frac{r^3}{s^3} = 1 \qquad \boxed{7}$$

Multiplying $\boxed{7}$ by $\frac{1}{27}$, we get

$$\frac{r^3}{s^3} = \frac{1}{27}$$

$$\text{or} \quad \frac{r}{s} = \frac{1}{3}$$

(Math Refreshers #313 and #429)

30. Choice D is correct.

(Use Strategy 3: The whole equals the sum of its parts.)

The perimeter of the shaded region

$$= PM + PN + \text{length of } \overset{\frown}{MN} \qquad \boxed{1}$$

From basic geometry, we know that if two tangents to a circle meet at a point, the lengths of the tangents from that point to where they touch the circle are equal. If a radius is drawn from the center of a circle to the point where the tangent touches the circle, the angle of the radius line is perpendicular to the tangent. Thus,

$$PM = PN \qquad m\angle PMO = 90 \qquad \boxed{2}$$

and OP bisects $\angle MON$.

(Use Strategy 14: Draw additional lines.)

Thus, we can redraw the diagram.

(Use Strategy 18: Remember facts about right triangles.)

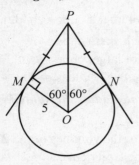

ΔPMO is similar to one of the standard triangles previously discussed.

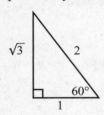

Corresponding sides of similar triangles are *in proportion*, so that

$$\frac{\sqrt{3}}{1} = \frac{PM}{5}$$

or $PM = 5\sqrt{3} = PN$ 3

It is always true that the length of $\widehat{MN}$

$$= \frac{m \angle MON}{360} \times \text{circumference of the circle}$$

$$= \frac{m \angle MON}{360} \times 2\pi(5)$$

$$= \frac{120}{360} \times 2\pi(5)$$

(Use Strategy 19: Factor and reduce.)

$$= \frac{12 \times \cancel{10}}{36 \times \cancel{10}} \times 2\pi(5)$$

$$= \frac{\cancel{12}}{\cancel{12} \times 3} \times 2\pi(5)$$

$$= \frac{10\pi}{3} \quad 4$$

Substituting 4 and 3 into 1, we get the perimeter of shaded region

$$= 10\sqrt{3} + \frac{10\pi}{3}$$

(Math Refreshers #310, #509, #510, and #529)

31. 24

(Use Strategy 2: Translate from words into algebra.)

Let $n =$ the number

We are given:

$$\frac{5}{8}n = \frac{3}{4}n - 3 \quad 1$$

(Use Strategy 13: Find unknowns by multiplication.)

Multiply 1 by 8. We get

$$8\left(\frac{5}{8}n\right) = 8\left(\frac{3}{4}n - 3\right)$$

$$5n = \frac{24}{4}n - 24$$

$$5n = 6n - 24$$

$$24 = n$$

(Math Refreshers #200 and #406)

32. 12

(Use Strategy 17: Use the given information effectively.)

In order to use the least number of rooms, you must use as many of the larger rooms as possible. These are the rooms that can fit 52 people. If all 9 of these rooms are used, that would be enough to accommodate 468 people ($52 \times 9 = 468$).

There are 510 people, so we still need rooms for 42 people ($510 - 468 = 42$).

There are no more of the larger rooms, so if we use 3 of the rooms that fit 15 people, we can accommodate the remaining 42 people ($15 \times 3 = 45$).

That's 9 of the big rooms and 3 of the smaller rooms, giving us a total of 12 rooms.

33. 11

Since lines are drawn every 10 yards after the first one, $\frac{100}{10}$ lines, or 10 additional lines, are drawn.

(Use Strategy 2: Translate from words into algebra.)

The total number of lines on the field = the original line + the number of additional lines

$$= 1 + 10 = 11$$

(Math Refresher #200)

34. 81

(Use Strategy 18: Know and use facts about triangles.)

It's important to realize that this problem presents us with two similar triangles. We know that they are similar because they both have a right angle and both share the angle at *B*. This means that the ratio between each pair of corresponding sides is the same.

Sides *DE* and *AC* are corresponding sides, we know that the ratio between them is 0.9 : 1, which is the same as 9 : 10. If these are the heights of the triangles, then the bases (sides *EB* and *CB*) have the same ratio.

It doesn't matter what the *actual* lengths of the bases and heights are when finding the ratio of the areas. You could go ahead and choose to make both the base and height of the smaller triangle 9, and make the base and height of the larger triangle 10 (though it doesn't look this way in the figure). This way you definitely have a 9 : 10 ratio. The area of the triangle is one-half (base × height), so the area of the smaller triangle is $\frac{9 \times 9}{2} = \frac{81}{2}$ and the area of the larger triangle is $\frac{10 \times 10}{2} = \frac{100}{2}$.

The ratio of the areas is therefore 81 : 100, which is the same as saying that the smaller area is $\frac{81}{100}$ of the larger triangle, and *this* is the same as saying that it is 81% of the area of the larger one.

Another approach is simply to realize that if the ratio of the sides is 9 : 10, the ratio of the areas is this ratio *squared*, which is 81 : 100.

35. 25

(Use Strategy 5:

$Average = \dfrac{sum\ of\ values}{total\ number\ of\ values}.)$

Average age of students in a class

$= \dfrac{\text{sum of the ages of students in the class}}{\text{number of students in the class}}$ 　1

Thus,

Average age of all 80 students

$= \dfrac{\text{sum of the ages of the 80 students}}{80}$ 　2

Using 1, we know that

$20 = \dfrac{\text{sum of the ages of the 60 students}}{60}$

and

$40 = \dfrac{\text{sum of the ages of the 20 students}}{20}.$

Thus, the sum of the ages of the 60 students

$= (60)(20) = 1,200$

and the sum of the ages of the 20 students

$= (40)(20) = 800$

Hence, the sum of the ages of the 80 students

$=$ sum of the ages of the 60 students

$+$ sum of the ages of the 20 students

$= 1,200 + 800 = 2,000$ 　3

Substituting 3 into 2, we get

$$\frac{2,000}{80} = 25$$

Average age of all 80 students $= 25$

(Math Refreshers #601 and #406)

36. 36.2

(Use Strategy 2: Translate from words into algebra.)

Fraction mowed during evening 1 $= \dfrac{2}{9}$ 　1

Fraction mowed during evening 2 $= 2\left(\dfrac{2}{9}\right) = \dfrac{4}{9}$ 　2

Adding 1 and 2, we get

Total fraction mowed during first two evenings

$$= \frac{2}{9} + \frac{4}{9}$$

$$= \frac{6}{9}$$

$$= \frac{2}{3}$$

(Use Strategy 3: The whole equals the sum of its parts.)

Amount left for evening 3

$= 1$ whole lawn $- \dfrac{2}{3}$ already mowed

$= \dfrac{1}{3}$ 　3

Given: Lawn area $= 108.6$ square feet 　4

Multiplying 3 by 4, we get

Amount left for evening 3

$= \dfrac{1}{3} \times 108.6$ square feet

$= 36.2$ square feet

(Math Refreshers #200 and #109)

37. 18

Method I:

(Use Strategy 14: Draw lines to help solve the problem.)

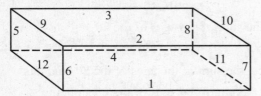

Above is a rectangular solid with each of its edges numbered 1 through 12, respectively. There are 3 groups of 4 parallel edges each.

> 1, 2, 3, and 4 are parallel.
> 5, 6, 7, and 8 are parallel.
> 9, 10, 11, and 12 are parallel.

Within each group of 4 parallel edges, there are 6 pairs of parallel edges. For example, within the first group listed above, 1 and 2 are parallel, 1 and 3 are parallel, etc. Because there are 3 groups and each group has 6 pairs of parallel edges, there are $3 \times 6 = 18$ different pairs of parallel edges in all. Below is a listing of all the pairs:

1–2	2–3	5–6	6–7	9–10	10–11
1–3	2–4	5–7	6–8	9–11	10–12
1–4	3–4	5–8	7–8	9–12	11–12

Method II:

A rectangular solid exists in three dimensions; within each dimension, there are four edges that run parallel to each other. Therefore the combinations of parallel edges for *one* dimension, taken two at a time, is:

$$_4C_2 = \frac{(4 \times 3)}{(2 \times 1)} = 6$$

Since there are three dimensions, the total number of combinations is:

$$3(_4C_2) = 3(6) = 18$$

(Math Refresher #613)

38. 10.9

(Use Strategy 18: Know and use facts about triangles.)

(Use Strategy 3: Know how to find unknown quantities [areas, lengths, arc and angle measurements] from known quantities.)

Since the triangle is inscribed in the circle, we know that $\angle ACB$ is a right angle. This is the angle that "creates" arc AB, which is a semicircle. A semicircle has 180°, and the angle that forms it along the circumference must be half of that, or 90°. Using this same principle, we know that the degree measure of $\angle CAB$ must be half of the degree measure of arc BC, the thing we're looking for. We'll come back to that later.

You are told that $126\cos85° = x$ and that leg BC is equal to x. Knowing that the cosine of an angle to its adjacent side over the hypotenuse, we can divide each side of this equation by 126, giving us:

$$\cos85° \times \frac{x}{126}$$

Since leg BC is **equal to** x, and this side is adjacent to $\angle CBA$, it must be that this angle is 85°, and BA (the hypotenuse) is equal to 126. Note that this side is also the diameter of the circle.

Since all triangles have angles that sum to 180, we can now say that $\angle CAB$ must equal 5°. Remember that we said that this is half of the degree measure of arc BC, which is therefore 10°. And since the entire circle is 360°, the *length* of minor arc BC must equal $\frac{10}{360}$ of the entire circumference. This can be simplified to $\frac{1}{36}$ of the circumference.

We know that the diameter is 126, so the circumference is 126π. The arc length we want is $\frac{1}{36}$ of this, so it's equal to $\frac{126\pi}{36}$. You can now use your calculator, using 3.1 for π, as instructed or you could simplify the fraction first to $\frac{7\pi}{2}$. Either way, youll get 10.85 which, to the nearest tenth, rounds up to 10.9.

SECTION 5: TEST 2 ESSAY SCORING

SAT Essay responses are scored using a carefully designed process:

- Two different people will read and score your essay.
- Each scorer awards 1–4 points for each dimension: reading, analysis, and writing.
- The two scores for each dimension are added.
- You'll receive three scores for the SAT Essay—one for each dimension—ranging from 2 to 8 points.

Essay Scoring Rubric

Score Point 4: Advanced

Reading

- The response demonstrates thorough comprehension of the source text.
- The response shows an understanding of the text's central idea(s) and of most important details and how they interrelate, demonstrating a comprehensive understanding of the text.
- The response is free of errors of fact or interpretation with regard to the text.
- The response makes skillful use of textual evidence (quotations, paraphrases, or both), demonstrating a complete understanding of the source text.

Analysis

- The response offers an insightful analysis of the source text and demonstrates a sophisticated understanding of the analytical task.
- The response offers a thorough, well-considered evaluation of the author's use of evidence, reasoning, stylistic and persuasive elements, and/or feature(s) of the student's own choosing.

- The response contains relevant, sufficient, and strategically chosen support for claim(s) or point(s) made.
- The response focuses consistently on those features of the text that are most relevant to addressing the task.

Writing

- The response is cohesive and demonstrates a highly effective use and command of language.
- The response includes a precise central claim.
- The response includes a skillful introduction and conclusion. The response demonstrates a deliberate and highly effective progression of ideas both within paragraphs and throughout the esssay.
- The response has a wide variety in sentence structures. The response demonstrates a consistent use of precise word choice. The response maintains a formal style and objective tone.
- The response shows a strong command of the conventions of standard written English and is free or virtually free of errors.

Score Point 3: Proficient

Reading

- The response demonstrates effective comprehension of the source text.
- The response shows an understanding of the text's central idea(s) and important details.
- The response is free of substantive errors of fact and interpretation with regard to the text.
- The response makes appropriate use of textual evidence (quotations, paraphrases, or both), demonstrating an understanding of the source text.

Analysis

- The response offers an effective analysis of the source text and demonstrates an understanding of the analytical task.

- The response competently evaluates the author's use of evidence, reasoning, and/or stylistic and persuasive elements, and/or feature(s) of the student's own choosing.

- The response contains relevant and sufficient support for claim(s) or point(s) made.

- The response focuses primarily on those features of the text that are most relevant to addressing the task.

Writing

- The response is mostly cohesive and demonstrates effective use and control of language.

- The response includes a central claim or implicit controlling idea.

- The response includes an effective introduction and conclusion. The response demonstrates a clear progression of ideas both within paragraphs and throughout the essay.

- The response has variety in sentence structures. The response demonstrates some precise word choice. The response maintains a formal style and objective tone.

- The response shows a good control of the conventions of standard written English and is free of significant errors that detract from the quality of writing.

Score Point 2: Partial

Reading

- The response demonstrates some comprehension of the source text.

- The response shows an understanding of the text's central idea(s) but not of important details.

- The response may contain errors of fact and/or interpretation with regard to the text.

- The response makes limited and/or haphazard use of textual evidence (quotations, paraphrases, or both), demonstrating some understanding of the source text.

Analysis

- The response offers limited analysis of the source text and demonstrates only partial understanding of the analytical task.

- The response identifies and attempts to describe the author's use of evidence, reasoning, and/or stylistic and persuasive elements, and/or feature(s) of the student's own choosing, but merely asserts rather than explains their importance, or one or more aspects of the response's analysis are unwarranted based on the text.

- The response contains little or no support for claim(s) or point(s) made.

- The response may lack a clear focus on those features of the text that are most relevant to addressing the task.

Writing

- The response demonstrates little or no cohesion and limited skill in the use and control of language.

- The response may lack a clear central claim or controlling idea or may deviate from the claim or idea over the course of the response.

- The response may include an ineffective introduction and/or conclusion. The response may demonstrate some progression of ideas within paragraphs but not throughout the response.

- The response has limited variety in sentence structures; sentence structures may be repetitive.

- The response demonstrates general or vague word choice; word choice may be repetitive. The response may deviate noticeably from a formal style and objective tone.

- The response shows a limited control of the conventions of standard written English and contains errors that detract from the quality of writing and may impede understanding.

Score Point 1: Inadequate

Reading

- The response demonstrates little or no comprehension of the source text.
- The response fails to show an understanding of the text's central idea(s), and may include only details without reference to central idea(s).
- The response may contain numerous errors of fact and/or interpretation with regard to the text.
- The response makes little or no use of textual evidence (quotations, paraphrases, or both), demonstrating little or no understanding of the source text.

Analysis

- The response offers little or no analysis or ineffective analysis of the source text and demonstrates little or no understanding of the analytic task.
- The response identifies without explanation some aspects of the author's use of evidence, reasoning, and/or stylistic and persuasive elements, and/or feature(s) of the student's choosing, or numerous aspects of the response's analysis are unwarranted based on the text.
- The response contains little or no support for claim(s) or point(s) made, or support is largely irrelevant.
- The response may not focus on features of the text that are relevant to addressing the task, or the response offers no discernible analysis (e.g., is largely or exclusively summary).

Writing

- The response demonstrates little or no cohesion and inadequate skill in the use and control of language.
- The response may lack a clear central claim or controlling idea.
- The response lacks a recognizable introduction and conclusion. The response does not have a discernible progression of ideas.
- The response lacks variety in sentence structures; sentence structures may be repetitive. The response demonstrates general and vague word choice; word choice may be poor or inaccurate. Th response may lack a formal style and objective tone.
- The response shows a weak control of the conventions of standard written English and may contain numerous errors that undermine the quality of writing.

WHAT YOU MUST DO
NOW TO RAISE YOUR SAT SCORE

1. Follow the directions on page 559 to determine your score for the SAT test you've just taken. These results will give you a good idea of how hard you'll need to study in order to achieve a certain score on the actual SAT.

2. Eliminate your weaknesses in each of the SAT test areas by taking the following Giant Steps toward SAT success:

Reading Part

Giant Step 1

Take advantage of the Verbal Strategies that begin on page 123. Read again the Explanatory Answer for each of the Reading questions that you got wrong. Refer to the reading comprehension strategy that applies to each of your incorrect answers. Learn each of these Reading Strategies thoroughly. These strategies are crucial if you want to raise your SAT Verbal score substantially.

Giant Step 2

You can improve your vocabulary by doing the following:

1. Study the Gruber Prefix-Root-Suffix List beginning on page 309.

2. Learn the Hot Prefixes and Roots beginning on page 627.

3. Read through 250 Most Common SAT Vocabulary Words on page 315.

4. Look through The Most Important/Frequently Used SAT Words and Their Opposites beginning on page 319.

5. Learn the 3 Vocabulary Strategies beginning on page 148.

6. Read as widely as possible—not only novels. Non-fiction is important too—and don't forget to read newspapers and magazines.

7. Listen to people who speak well. Tune in to worth-while TV programs.

8. Use the dictionary frequently and extensively—at home, on the bus, at work, etc.

9. Play word games—for example, crossword puzzles, anagrams, and Scrabble.

Math Part

Giant Step 3

Make good use of the 19 Math Strategies that begin on page 72. Read again the solutions for each Math question that you answered incorrectly. Refer to the Math Strategy that applies to each of your incorrect answers. Learn each of these Math Strategies thoroughly. I repeat that these strategies are crucial if you want to raise your SAT Math score substantially.

Giant Step 4

You may want to take "The 101 Most Important Math Questions You Need to Know How to Solve" test beginning on page 35 and follow the directions after the test for a basic math skills diagnosis.

For each math question that you got wrong in the test, note the reference to the Complete SAT Math Refresher section beginning on page 163. This reference will explain clearly the mathematical principle involved in the solution of the question you answered incorrectly. Learn that particular mathematical principle thoroughly.

For Both the Math and Reading Parts

Giant Step 5

You may want to take the Strategy Diagnostic Test for the New SAT beginning on page 1 to assess whether you're using the best strategies for the questions.

Writing and Language Part

Giant Step 6

Make use of the Grammar and Usage Refresher—Part 8, page 325.

Remember:

I am the master of my fate:
I am the captain of my soul.

—From the poem "Invictus"
by William Ernest Henley

PART 11

Brainteasers!

If You Can Answer These Questions,
You Will Increase Your Thinking Skills,
Which Will Help You on the SAT or
on Any Other Standardized Test

Note: These are not actual SAT-type questions. Nevertheless, these
are fun brainteasers which will get your brain in motion!

GOOD LUCK!

LEVEL 1: EASIEST BRAINTEASERS

1. If you didn't know the meaning of the word *pre-cursory* could you figure out what the meaning of its opposite is?

   (A) flamboyant
   (B) succeeding
   (C) cautious
   (D) simple
   (E) not planned

2. The following characteristics apply to a group of people in a room: 14 are blonds, 8 are blue-eyed, and 2 are neither blond nor blue-eyed. If 5 of the people are blue-eyed blonds, how many people are in the room?

   (A) 3
   (B) 17
   (C) 19
   (D) 24
   (E) 29

3. A rectangle is inscribed in a quarter-circle as shown below. The radius of the circle is 5 inches. Find the diagonal of the rectangle as shown in the diagram.

4. How could you figure out the meaning of the word *inextricable*?

5. Which has a greater surface area, one-half the surface area of a ball with radius 3 inches or the area of a circle with radius 3 inches?

6. In the following subtraction problem, each letter uniquely represents one digit from 0 to 9. Find the values of A, B, and C and at least one digit is not 0.

$$\begin{array}{r} A\,B\,A \\ -\quad C\,A \\ \hline A\,B \end{array}$$

7. What is the value of *x* in the diagram below?

   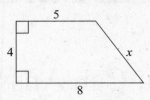

8. If A = 250 percent of B, what percent of A is B?

   (A) $\frac{1}{250}$ percent
   (B) 25 percent
   (C) 40 percent
   (D) 50 percent
   (E) 125 percent

9. In 20 seconds or less, determine which is greater:

$$\frac{410}{963} - \frac{208}{962}$$

   or

$$\frac{202}{962}$$

10. Solve this in 30 seconds or less: The following are dimensions of 5 rectangular boxes. Which box has a volume different from the other 4?

    (A) 5 by 8 by 12
    (B) 15 by 16 by 2
    (C) 3 by 32 by 5
    (D) 3 by 4 by 40
    (E) 2 by 6 by 36

11. A clothing store offers successive discounts of 30% and 10% on a sweater. The equivalent single discount would be:

    (A) 34 percent
    (B) 36 percent
    (C) 37 percent
    (D) 38 percent
    (E) 40 percent

12. Shown below, angle *AED* is 90°, angle *BED* is 40°, and angle *AEC* is 75°. What measure is angle *BEC*?

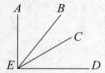

13. In 10 seconds and without a calculator, determine whether 999 × 1,001 is greater than, less than, or equal to 1,000 × 1,000.

14. If there are 24 people at a party and each person shakes another person's hand, how many hand-shakes are there?

    Better question:

    If there are 24 people at a party and they all shake hands, how many handshakes are there?

15. What is the three-digit number that can be made from the digits 2, 3, 5, and 7, where no two digits in the three-digit number are alike and where the three-digit number is a multiple of each of the digits chosen?

16. *ABCD* is a parallelogram (*AB* is parallel to *DC*, and *AD* is parallel to *BC*). A perpendicular line of length *h* is drawn from *A* to *DC*, and angle *D* is 60°. Which is greater: *h* times *AB* or *AD* times *CD*?

17. Anne has 3 blouses, 4 skirts, and 2 pairs of shoes. How many different outfits can she wear if an outfit consists of any blouse worn with any skirt and either pair of shoes?

18. What is the length of the line *x* in the diagram? (*Note*: Diagram is not drawn to scale.)

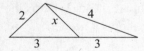

    Note: If you prefer not to use diagram above, you can use the following rewording of the question:

    Given a figure *ABC* where *AB* = 2, *AC* = 4, and *BC* = 6, and line *AD* cuts *BC* such that *BD* = *DC* = 3, what is the length of *AD*?

19. In ten seconds or less, express 1,111 divided by 25 as a percent.

20. Using root meanings to help you, define the meaning of the word MANUMIT.

    (A) to manufacture
    (B) to be masculine
    (C) to set free

21. How many different committees can be formed from a pool of 3 people, where a committee can consist of 1 to 3 people.

    (A) 3
    (B) 4
    (C) 5
    (D) 6
    (E) 7

22. If *a*, *b*, and *c* are odd consecutive integers whose sum is 57, what is *c*?

23. A man with a number of bookshelves has distributed his book collection evenly on the shelves, putting 80 books on each shelf. If he adds 3 shelves and redistributes his collection evenly on all the shelves, each shelf will have 50 books. How many books are in his collection?

24. If everyone working at a car wash works at the same speed and eight people can wash 50 cars in 60 hours, then four people can wash 100 cars in how many hours?

    (A) 30
    (B) 60
    (C) 120
    (D) 240
    (E) 360

25. Matt is the 50th fastest and the 50th slowest runner in his school. Assuming no two runners run at the same speed, how many runners are in Matt's school?

    (A) 50
    (B) 51
    (C) 99
    (D) 100
    (E) 101

26. Peter is taller than Nancy and Dan is shorter than Peter. Which of the following is true?
    (A) Dan is taller than Nancy.
    (B) Dan is shorter than Nancy.
    (C) Dan is as tall as Nancy.
    (D) none of the above

27. Together Harry and Sam caught 32 fish. Harry caught three times as many fish as Sam. How many fish did Harry catch?

    (A) 6
    (B) 8
    (C) 16
    (D) 24
    (E) 28

28. Two runners start at the same point facing in opposite directions. Each runner then runs 3 straight miles, takes a right turn, and runs straight for another 4 miles. What is the distance in miles between the two runners at that point?

    (A) 5
    (B) 8
    (C) 10
    (D) 12
    (D) 14

29. If a doctor gives you three pills, telling you to take one every half hour, how many minutes will pass between when you take the first pill and when you take the last pill?

30. Suppose a car goes uphill a distance of 1 mile, then immediately turns around and goes downhill the same distance, and suppose the average rate of the car for the whole trip is 20 miles per hour. What is the total time spent going uphill and downhill in minutes?

    (A) 6
    (B) 8
    (C) 10
    (D) cannot be determined unless the time going downhill is given
    (E) cannot be determined unless the speed going uphill is given

31. In five seconds or less, which is greater, 1 or $\frac{77}{99}$ divided by $\frac{99}{77}$?

32. Mary must get up at 7:00 AM to get to work on time. Her clock gains 9 minutes every 3 days. If she set it correctly at 11:00 PM on Sunday night, what time should she get up, according to her clock, on Tuesday morning?

33. Phil is taking a 100-mile trip. If he averages 25 miles per hour during the first 50 miles, what must he average during the second 50 miles to make his average speed for the whole trip 50 miles per hour?

34. In 10 seconds, with or without a calculator, what is the value of

    $$\frac{2}{3} \times \frac{3}{4} \times \frac{4}{5} \times \frac{5}{6} \times \frac{6}{7}?$$

35. Suppose you have three Scrabble tiles—N, T and O. What is the probability that when you randomly place the three tiles upright in a row, they will spell an English word?

36. Which two words do not belong with the others?

    (A) fallible
    (B) congruous
    (C) flammable
    (D) famous
    (E) exact

37. I throw a 5-cent coin and a 10-cent coin in the air. If at least one of them lands as a head, what is the probability that the 5-cent coin will land as a head?

    (A) $\frac{1}{3}$
    (B) $\frac{1}{2}$
    (C) $\frac{2}{3}$
    (D) $\frac{3}{4}$
    (E) $\frac{7}{8}$

Question 37 Alternate 1:

I toss two coins into the air and catch them on my palm. At least one of them is a head. What is the probability that the other shows a head?

    (A) $\frac{3}{4}$
    (B) $\frac{1}{2}$
    (C) $\frac{1}{3}$
    (D) $\frac{1}{4}$
    (E) none of these

Question 37 Alternate 2:

I toss two coins into the air and catch them on my palm. I know that one of them is a head. What is the probability that the other shows a head?

(A) $\frac{3}{4}$

(B) $\frac{1}{2}$

(C) $\frac{1}{3}$

(D) $\frac{1}{4}$

(E) none of these

Question 37 Alternate 3:

I toss two coins in the air and catch both of them on my palm. I look at one of them and see that it is a head. I then tell you that one of the coins on my palm is a head without telling you which one. What is the probability that the coin nearest you is a head?

(A) $\frac{2}{3}$

(B) $\frac{1}{2}$

(C) $\frac{1}{3}$

(D) $\frac{1}{4}$

(E) none of these

38. Find a four-digit number where the first digit is one-third the second, the third is the sum of the first and second, and the last is three times the second.

39. A bus can hold *x* people. It is half full and *y* people now get off. How many people could now get on the bus?

Questions 40 and 41 are based on the following passage.

Sometimes the meaning of glowing water is ominous. Off the Pacific Coast of North America, it may mean that the sea is filled with a minute plant that contains a poison of strange and terrible virulence. About four days after this minute plant comes to dominate the coastal plankton, some of the fish and shellfish in the vicinity become toxic. This is because in their normal feeding, they have strained the poisonous plankton out of the water.

40. Fish and shellfish become toxic when they:

(A) swim in poisonous water
(B) feed on poisonous plants
(C) change their feeding habits
(D) give off a strange glow
(E) take strychnine into their systems

41. If there was a paragraph preceding the one in the passage, it most probably discussed

(A) phenomena of the Pacific coastline
(B) poisons that affect humans
(C) toxic plants in the sea
(D) characteristics of plankton
(E) phenomena of the sea

42. A four-sided figure *ABCD* contains interior right angle *C*. *AB* equals 12, *BC* equals 3, *CD* equals 4, and *AD* equals 13. What is the area of the figure *ABCD*?

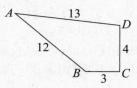

(A) 36
(B) 108
(C) 156
(D) 1,872
(E) It cannot be determined.

43. A four-sided figure has sides of lengths *a*, *b*, *c*, and *d*. Sides of lengths *c* and *d* meet at a right angle (90°). Sides of lengths *a* and *d* meet at a 140° angle. Sides of lengths *b* and *c* meet at a 40° angle.

Is "$(a \times a) - (c \times c)$" >, =, or < "$(d \times d) - (b \times b)$"?

44. In the diagram, where a circle is inscribed in a square and another square is inscribed in the circle, if a side of the larger square is 10, what is the area of the smaller square?

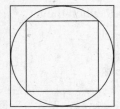

45. What is the opposite of EBULLIENT?

   (A) aggressive
   (B) subdued
   (C) compliant

46. A survey of 50 people who can write showed that 20 could write only with their left hand and 10 could write with either hand. How many could write with their right hand?

   (A) 30
   (B) 20
   (C) 25
   (D) 10
   (E) 40

47. The average of the number 10 and some unknown number, x, is divided by the sum of 10 and x. The result is $\frac{1}{2}$. What is the value of x?

48. A typist increased her speed from 60 words per minute to 80 words per minute. Her speed increased by what percent?

49. If a sheet of cardboard has an area of 186 square inches, and two rectangles each measuring 6 inches by 3 inches are cut out, what is the area of the remaining cardboard?

50. A certain orchestra has exactly 3 times as many string musicians as musicians playing wind instruments. Which of the following can be the combined number of string and wind musicians in this orchestra?

   (A) 27
   (B) 28
   (C) 29
   (D) 30
   (E) 31

51. Carl has 4 times as many quarters as Steve and 3 times as many quarters as William. If Carl, Steve, and William have less than a total of 200 quarters, what is the greatest number of quarters that Carl could have?

52. Jane is 3 times as old as Ann; three years ago, Ann was a year younger than Joyce is now. If Ellen is twice as old as Ann, list the four girls in descending age order.

53. A girl has exactly enough money to buy 3 sweaters and 2 skirts, or 3 skirts and no sweaters. All sweaters are the same price and all skirts are the same price. What is the maximum number of sweaters can she buy if she buys only one of the skirts?

54. Beads are strung onto a necklace in this order: red, white, green. A design that begins on red and ends on white could be composed of the following number of beads:

   I. 17
   II. 29
   III. 35

   (A) I only
   (B) III only
   (C) II and III only
   (D) I and III only
   (E) I, II, and III

55. The perimeter of the figure below is

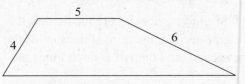

   (A) a whole number
   (B) less than 30
   (C) greater than 40
   (D) 22
   (E) 20

56. Which fraction is greater or are they equal?

   the area of a circle circumscribed about a square
   ───
   the area of the circle inscribed in the same square

   or

   the area of a square circumscribed about a circle
   ───
   the area of the square inscribed in the same circle

57. On a street there are 25 houses. 10 of the houses have fewer than 6 rooms. 10 of the houses have more than 7 rooms. 4 houses have more than 8 rooms. What is the total number of houses that have 6, 7, or 8 rooms?

(A) 5
(B) 9
(C) 11
(D) 14
(E) 15

58. What percent of 5 is 20? (Only 6% of California students got the correct answer to this question!)

(A) 25
(B) 40
(C) 100
(D) 200
(E) 400

59. Find a three-letter word such that when you place one letter at the beginning of the word you get a second word, when you place a letter at the beginning of the second word you get a third word, when you place a letter at the beginning of the third word you get a fourth word, and when you place a letter at the beginning of the fourth word you get a fifth word.

Explanatory Answers for Level 1 Brainteasers

1. Choice B is correct.

   The Gruber Prefix-Root-Suffix list (page 309) can give you the meanings of over 150,000 words. *Pre* means "before", and *curs* means "to run." So *precursory* means "to run (or go) before." The opposite is running or going after or *succeeding*.

2. Choice C is correct.

   (Use a Venn diagram or write down all the possibilities.)

   Total number of people are:

   Blonds *without* blue eyes
   $$14 - 5 = 9 \qquad \boxed{1}$$

   Blue-eyed people who are *not* blond
   $$8 - 5 = 3 \qquad \boxed{2}$$

   Blue-eyed blonds
   $$5 \qquad \boxed{3}$$

   People with neither blue eyes nor blond hair
   $$2 \qquad \boxed{4}$$

   Adding $\boxed{1}$, $\boxed{2}$, $\boxed{3}$, and $\boxed{4}$, we get
   $$9 + 3 + 5 + 2 = 19$$

3. 0.5 inch.

   (Use Strategy 14: Draw extra lines to get more information.)

   Draw the radius. The radius of circle is the same as the diagonal of the rectangle!

4. The prefix *in* means "not." Then associate *extric* with another word, *extract*. So *inextricable* means "not to extract," "cannot extract," or "inseparable." Association is a powerful strategy for getting the meanings of words.

5. *One-half the surface area of a ball is greater.* Blow up the circle like a balloon to get the ball. One half the surface area of the ball is greater than the area of the circle because the circle is being expanded as the ball is blown up.

6. From the units column, $A - A = 0$ so $B = 0$.

   We have then
   $$\begin{array}{r} A\,0\,A \\ -\ \ C\,A \\ \hline A\,0 \end{array}$$

   From the tens column, we have $A + C = 10$, so we have to borrow 1 from the A in the hundreds column. So now in the hundreds column we have $A - 1 - 0 = 0$, so $A = 1$. Since from before we had $A + C = 10$, we get $C = 9$.

   More general solution:

   Write a three-digit number with h for the hundreds digit, t for the tens digit, and u for the units digit as:
   $$100h + 10t + u$$

   You will find that $A = 1$, $B = 0$, and $C = 9$.

   We have
   $$100A + 10B + A - 10C - A = 10A + B$$

   This gives us
   $$90A + 9B = 10C \text{ or } 10A + B = \left(\frac{10}{9}\right)C$$

   The only way A and B can be integers is if $C = 9$. That makes
   $$10A + B = 10$$

   The only way this is possible with A and B integers (from 0 to 9) is if $A = 1$ and $B = 0$.

7. 5.

Draw a perpendicular line to make a rectangle in the figure and you will also have a 3-4-5 triangle.

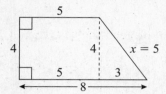

A powerful strategy in drawings or in geometry is to draw extra lines to get more information for solving the problem. You probably don't remember this, but when you first took geometry, one of the first proofs that the teacher described was "if two sides of a triangle are equal, then the base angles are equal." The teacher drew a perpendicular line to start the proof. Unfortunately the teacher probably did not tell the students that the reason she did this was to get more information to start solving the problem. A natural phenomenon! So in this problem, draw a line to make a rectangle in the figure and you will find that you will have a 3-4-5 triangle: $x = 5$.

8. Choice C is correct.

(Use Strategy 2: Translate English words into mathematical expressions.)

Translate *percent* into $\frac{1}{100}$, *of* into $\times$, *what* into x, and *is* into $=$.

$$A = \left[\frac{250}{100}\right] (B)$$

$$\frac{x}{100} (A) = B$$

Substitute:

$$\frac{x}{100}\left[\frac{250}{100}\right] B = B$$

Cancel B:

$$\frac{x}{100}\left[\frac{250}{100}\right] = 1$$

$$\frac{250x}{10,000} = 1$$

$$\text{so} \quad x = \frac{10,000}{250}$$

$$= 40$$

9. $\frac{202}{962}$ is greater.

Add $\frac{208}{962}$ to both quantities and compare.

10. Choice E is correct.

When you have to choose something different from the rest of the other choices, look for either something all the other choices have that the correct one doesn't or something that the correct choice has that the other choices don't have. So don't multiply: Notice that all choices are divisible by 5 except Choice E. Also E is the only choice that is divisible by 9.

11. Choice C is correct.

The equivalent single discount is less than the sum of the discounts.

Start with $100. A 30% discount gives you a $70 price. A 10% discount on $70 gives you a price of $63. $100 − $63 = $37, a discount that is equivalent to a 37% discount on $100.

12. 25°.

Label all the angles with angle $BEC = x$.

Let $\angle AEB = y$, $\angle BEC = x$, and $\angle CED = z$.

Since $\angle AED = 90$, $x + y + z = 90$.   1

Since $\angle BED = 40$, $x + z = 40$.   2

Since $\angle AEC = 75$, $y + x = 75$.   3

Subtracting Equation 2 from Equation 1 we get:
$$y = 50$$

Substituting $y = 50$ in Equation 3 we get:
$$x = 25$$

13. $999 \times 1,001$ is just 1 less than $1,000 \times 1,000$.

One of the key strategies in mathematics is to write what is presented in a different form: Write $999 \times 1,001$ as $(1,000 - 1) \times (1,000 + 1)$ and you'll find that's equal to $1,000 \times 1,000 - 1$, since $(a - 1) \times (a + 1) = a \times a - 1$.

14. 276.

Taking 24 combinations 2 at a time—e.g., from a, b, c, d, e, . . . ab, ac, bc, etc.—we get:

$$\frac{(24 \times 23)}{2}$$

This is how we get this: Each person can shake hands with 23 other people, so we have 24 × 23 possible combinations. But because it takes two people to make a handshake, we must divide this product by 2, so we get:

$$\frac{(24 \times 23)}{2} \quad \text{or} \quad 276$$

15. The only number that meets these requirements is 735.

16. $AD \times CD$ is greater than $h \times AB$.

Label sides with letters like a and b, then *cancel* like quantities.

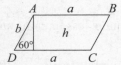

$h \times AB = h \times a$; $AD \times CD = b \times a$. We are then comparing $h \times a$ with $b \times a$. Since the a is the same, we are really comparing h with b and h is less than b because b is the largest side (the hypotenuse) of a right triangle. Thus the original $h \times AB$ is less than $AD \times CD$.

17. 24.

$(3 \times 4 \times 2)$

18. The triangle shown has a base of 6 and sides 2 and 4. Since $2 + 4 = 6$, the triangle has collapsed into a straight line. On this line, the line segment labeled x must be 1.

19. Sometimes you can get more information or simplify a problem when you multiply the numerator by a number and the denominator by the same number, and note, this process will not change the value of the original fraction. So multiply both numerator and denominator by 4: You get 4,444 divided by 100, which is 4,444 percent.

20. Choice C is correct.

Roots are a powerful tool in figuring out the meanings of words. The root *man* means "hand." The root *mit* means "to send." So *manumit* means "to send by hand" or "set free."

21. Choice E is correct.

If people are denoted by a, b, and c you have committees a, b, c, ab, ac, bc, and abc for a total of 7.

22. 21.

Represent $b = a + 2$, $c = a + 4$, so $a + b + c = 3a + 6 = 57$. $3a = 51$, $a = 17$ so $c = a + 4 = 21$.

23. 400.

Let n be the number of original shelves. Then

$$80n = 50(n + 3)$$
$$30n = 150$$
$$n = 5$$
$$80 \times 5 = 400$$

24. Choice D is correct.

Do this in steps: If 8 people can wash 50 cars in 60 hours, then 4 people can wash 50 cars in 120 hours, since it would take twice as much time to wash the cars because there are half as many people to do the washing. Thus it would take 4 people to wash 100 cars in 240 hours since there are twice as many cars now.

25. Choice C is correct.

This is tricky. If Matt is the 50th fastest runner, he would be 1, 2, 3, . . . 50. To be 50th slowest, he'd have to be 50, 51, 52, . . . 99 since there are 50 numbers from 50 to 99 inclusive.

26. Choice D is correct.

Write $P > N$ and $D < P$. This is the same as $P > N$ and $P > D$. You cannot determine the relationship of D and N. For example, if P is 6 feet, N can be 5 feet and D can be 5.5 feet or N can be 5.5 feet and D can be 5 feet or N can be 5.5 feet and D can be 5.5 feet.

27. Choice D is correct.

Write the number of fish Harry caught as H and the number of fish Sam caught as S. Then translate into math:

$$H = 3S \qquad \boxed{1}$$
$$\text{So} \quad H + S = 32 \qquad \boxed{2}$$

Substitute:

$H = 3S$ in $\boxed{2}$ and we get

$$3S + S = 32$$
$$4S = 32$$
$$S = 8$$
$$\text{So} \quad H = 3S$$
$$= 24$$

28. Choice C is correct.

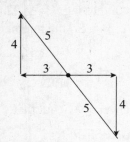

Draw a diagram. The distance between them, finally, is 10.

29. 60 minutes.

Many of you probably think that I should multiply 3 pills by 30 minutes to give me 90 minutes. But think of how you take the pills. I take the first pill and in a half-hour I take the second pill and then in the next half-hour I take the third pill. So the number of minutes that pass from the first to the third pill is *60 minutes*.

30. Choice A is correct.

You need to use the formula Rate × Time = Distance, or $R \times T = D$.

For the uphill trip, R(uphill) × T(uphill) = 1 mile. For the downhill trip, R(downhill) × T(downhill) = 1 mile.

The average rate of the car is the total distance traveled (2 miles) divided by the total time traveled, T(uphill) + T(downhill).

Since the average rate was given as 20 mph, 20 = 2 divided by [T(uphill) + T(downhill)]. Thus we get 10 = T(uphill) + T(downhill).

31. 1 is greater. Multiply 1 by $\frac{99}{77}$ and compare that with $\frac{77}{99}$.

32. 7:04 AM.

The clock gains 3 minutes every day or 1 minute every 8 hours. Between 11:00 PM Sunday night and 7:00 AM Tuesday morning is 24 + 8 hours. So the clock gains 4 minutes.

33. Average speed is total distance divided by total time. So for the first half,

$$25 = \frac{50}{\text{time of first half}}$$

Thus the time for the first half is 2 hours. For Phil to average 50 miles per hour for the whole trip we would get

$$50 = \frac{100}{\text{time for the whole trip}}$$

Time for the whole trip then is 2 hours. That would mean that Phil must go an infinite speed the second half of the trip to go 50 miles in 0 hours.

34. $\frac{2}{7}$.

Cross out all the common numerators and denominators: the 3s, 4s, 5s, and 6s. We are left with $\frac{2}{7}$.

Note: This is one of the problems that could be done faster without a calculator!

35. The favorable ways (of spelling an English word) are 2: *NOT* and *TON*. The total number of ways of arranging the three letters in a row is 6: NTO, NOT, TON, TNO, OTN, and ONT. Thus the probability is 2 in 6, or:

$$\frac{2}{6} = \frac{1}{3}$$

36. Choices C and D are correct.

If we put a prefix *in-* in front of each word, the meaning of the new word is the opposite of the old word, except for *flammable* (*inflammable* has the same meaning as *flammable*) and *famous* (*infamous* has the same denotation as *famous*, although *infamous* has the connotation of being famous in a bad way).

37. Choice C is correct.

Probability is defined as the favorable number of ways divided by the total number of ways. Since one of the coins lands as a head, the total number of ways this is possible is the following:

5-cent head; 10-cent tail
5-cent head; 10-cent head
5-cent tail; 10-cent head

There couldn't be a possibility of 10-cent tail and 10-cent tail, because we are told that one of the coins must be a head. So there are only three possibilities.

Now the favorable ways that the 5-cent coin will land as a head are two:

5-cent head; 10-cent tail

5-cent head; 10-cent head

Thus the probability is $\frac{2}{3}$.

Question 37 Alternate 1:

Choice C is correct.

Probability is defined as the favorable number of ways divided by the total number of ways. The total number of ways is

HT

TH

HH

The favorable number of ways is HH.

Thus the probability is $\frac{1}{3}$.

Question 37 Alternate 2:

Choice B is correct.

The probability that the other coin shows a head is the number of favorable ways divided by the total number of ways. The favorable number of ways is 1 (a head). The total number of ways is 2 (a head and a tail). So the probability is $\frac{1}{2}$. It does not matter that you know that the other coin is a head.

Question 37 Alternate 3:

Choice A is correct.

Probability is defined as the number of favorable ways divided by the total number of ways. The total number of ways where H is a head and T is a tail is HH, HT, and TH, three ways. The favorable number of ways is HH and HT, two ways.

Therefore the probability is $\frac{2}{3}$.

38. 1,349.

Represent digits as a, b, c, d.

So $a = \frac{1}{3}b$ 1

$c = a + b$ 2

$d = 3b$ 3

From 1 we get $3a = b$.   4

From 3 and 4 we get $d = 9a$.   5

The only way 5 can be true is if $a = 1$, since d is a single digit and not equal to 0, making $d = 9$. Thus from 1 $b = 3$, and from 2 $c = 4$. So the number *abcd* is 1,349.

39. $\frac{x}{2} + y$.

You may have gotten the answer $\frac{x}{2} - y$ but that's how many people are *left* on the bus!

$x - \left(\frac{x}{2} - y\right)$ which is $\frac{x}{2} + y$, the answer.

40. Choice B is correct.

Try to get clues from the rest of passage using inferences. Since the fish and shellfish become toxic, it can be inferred that they must eat the plankton, which could only be small animals or plants. Choice A is incorrect because "coastal plankton" is distinguished in the sentence from "fishes and shellfish." Choice D is incorrect because nowhere does it mention that the fish give off a "strange glow." Choices C and E are incorrect because it is unlikely that fish and shellfish would eat sand deposits or glacier or rock formations—they would eat plants or smaller animals.

41. Choice C is correct.

Pay attention to the three parts of a passage: The opening sentence leads into what is going to be discussed, the middle tells us about the passage, and the last sentence or paragraph usually summarizes or wraps up the passage. Look at the opening phrase, which introduces the passage. The fact that glowing water is mentioned indicates that the paragraph preceding the sentence probably talks about the sea.

42. Choice A is correct.

Draw the figure with angle C as a right angle. Now the key strategy is to draw an extra line *BD*.

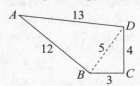

Triangle *BCD* is then a right triangle and is a 3-4-5 right triangle. Now you have triangle *BAD* as a 5-12-13 triangle. This is also a right triangle. In high school you prove these things by using the Pythagorean theorem, but usually we tell students to remember certain right triangles like the popular 3-4-5 and 5-12-13 ones. So if triangle BAD is a right triangle (where angle ABD is a right angle), you can calculate the area:

$$\frac{(5 \times 12)}{2} = 30$$

The area of triangle BCD is

$$\frac{(3 \times 4)}{2} = 6$$

so the total area of the figure is 36.

43. equal to.

Draw the figure and notice that there are two right angles because the sum of the angles of the four sided figure is 360°.

Since there are then two right triangles, with the use of the Pythagorean theorem we get:

$$(a \times a) + (b \times b) = (c \times c) + (d \times d)$$

Thus we find that:

$$(a \times a) - (c \times c) = (d \times d) - (b \times b)$$

44. 50.

(Use Strategy 14: Draw lines to get additional information.)

45. Choice B is correct.

One strategy is when the word sounds "big" like *effervescent*, *magnanimous*, or *scintillating*, it probably will mean something *big* or *flashy*. Think of *ebullient* as a big-sounding word. The opposite would be *subdued*.

46. Choice A is correct.

The total number of people = the number who can write with both hands + the number who can write with only the left hand + the number who can write with only the right hand = 50 = 10 + 20 + x. Thus x = 20 can write with only the right hand. But 10 can write with both the left and right hands, so 30 can write with the right hand.

47. **(Use Strategy 2: Translate English words into math.)**

We have $\frac{(10 + x)}{2}$ divided by $(10 + x) = \frac{1}{2}$. We get:

$$\frac{(10 + x)}{[2(10 + x)]} = \frac{1}{2}$$

Canceling the $(10 + x)$, we get:

$$\frac{1}{2} = \frac{1}{2}$$

Thus x cannot be determined.

48. $33\frac{1}{3}$ percent.

$$\frac{80 - 60}{60} \times 100 = 33\frac{1}{3} \text{ percent}$$

49. 150 square inches.

$$186 - 2 \times (6 \times 3) = 150$$

50. Choice B is correct.

Using symbols, let $S = 3W$.

$S + W$ = the number of string and wind musicians. Thus $3W + W = 4W$ is the number of string and wind musicians. The only choice where W is a whole number is where

$$4W = 28$$
$$W = 7$$

51. 120.

Write a relation:

$$C = 4S, \quad \text{or} \quad \frac{C}{4} = S \qquad \boxed{1}$$

$$C = 3W, \quad \text{or} \quad \frac{C}{3} = W \qquad \boxed{2}$$

$$C + S + W < 200 \qquad \boxed{3}$$

Substituting from $\boxed{1}$, $\frac{C}{4} = S$, from $\boxed{2}$, $\frac{C}{3} = W$ in $\boxed{3}$ we get:

$$C + \frac{C}{4} + \frac{C}{3} < 200 \qquad \boxed{4}$$

Thus $\frac{12C}{12} + \frac{3C}{12} + \frac{4C}{12} < 200$

and so $\quad 19C < 2,400$

and so $\quad C < 120$

52. Jane, Ellen, Ann, Joyce.

(Use Strategy 2: Translate English words into math.)

$$Ja = 3A, A - 3 = Jo - 1, E = 2A$$
$$\text{so} \quad Ja = 3A, A = Jo + 2, E = 2A$$
$$\text{so} \quad Ja > E > A > Jo$$

53. Six.

Let the cost of a sweater be w and the cost of a skirt be k. Let the money she has be x. Then:

$$3w + 2k = x \qquad \boxed{1}$$
$$3k = x \qquad \boxed{2}$$
$$k + yw = x \qquad \boxed{3}$$

where y is the maximum number of sweaters the girl can buy.

From $\boxed{1}$ and $\boxed{2}$, $3w + 2k = 3k$ so we get:

$$3w = k \qquad \boxed{4}$$

From $\boxed{2}$ and $\boxed{3}$ we get:

$$3k = k + yw$$
$$\text{or} \quad 2k = yw \qquad \boxed{5}$$

and from $\boxed{4}$ and $\boxed{5}$

$$2(3w) = yw$$
$$6w = yw$$
$$\text{and so} \quad 6 = y$$

54. Choice E is correct.

Where x is a whole number, the number of beads is $3x + 2$ since you are left with only a red and a white and all the rest are red, white, and green. Thus see if x is a whole number where

$$3x + 2 = 17, 29, \text{ and } 35$$

Alternate solution:

If the order is red, white, green, . . . , then the number of beads you have ending in white is

$$r, w = 2$$
$$r, w, g, r, w = 5$$
$$r, w, g, r, w, g, r, w = 8$$

so the sequence is

$$2, 5, 8, 11, 14, 17, 20, 23, 26, 29, 32, 35$$

55. Choice B is correct.

Solution 1:

The shortest distance between two points is a straight line. So $4 + 5 + 6$ must be greater than the baseline of the figure. Thus 15 is greater than the baseline. Since the perimeter = $4 + 5 + 6 +$ the baseline, the perimeter is less than $15 + 15$ or less than 30.

Solution 2:

Draw a line that makes the third side of the triangle with sides 4 and 5.

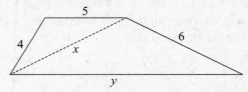

The sum of the lengths of two sides of a triangle must be greater than the third side. So

$$4 + 5 > x$$
$$x + 6 > y$$

Thus since $9 > x$, adding 6 to both sides,

$$15 > x + 6$$

But $x + 6 > y$

$$\text{so} \quad 15 > x + 6 > y$$
$$\text{and so} \quad 15 > y$$

The perimeter of the figure is

$$4 + 5 + 6 + y = 15 + y$$

Since $15 > y$, $15 + y$ (the perimeter) is less than 30.

56. The fractions are equal. They are both equal to $\frac{2}{1}$.

57. Choice C is correct.

Houses that have fewer than 6 rooms are 10 (given). Houses that have 6, 7, or 8 rooms are x (unknown). Houses that have more than 8 rooms are 4 (given). The total is 25. 10 plus x plus 4 must equal 25, so x must be 11.

58. Choice E is correct.

(Use Strategy 2: Translate English words into mathematical expressions.)

In a verbal math problem, always translate

what to x

percent to $\frac{}{100}$

of to $\times$ (times)

is to $=$

In the problem above, you would get:

What percent of 5 is 20?

$$\downarrow \qquad \downarrow \qquad \downarrow \downarrow \downarrow$$

$$x \qquad \frac{}{100} \qquad \times 5 = 20$$

This becomes: $\left(\dfrac{x}{100}\right) \times 5 = 20$.

Now use another strategy: ***Get rid of the fractions!***

Multiply both sides of the equation above by 100. You get

$$\frac{(x)(5)\ 100}{100} = 20 \times 100$$

and you find

$$(x)(5) = 20 \times 100 = 2{,}000$$

Divide both sides of the equation by 5:

$$x = 400$$

Comment:

Standardized tests would be useful if a student learned the specific strategies for testing (such as general testing strategies) and learned strategies for the specific material tested, such as Math Strategies and Reading Comprehension Strategies, *before* taking the test. Many of these strategies are not taught in schools, so it is unfair to give a student a grade on a standardized test when the student hasn't been armed with the proper strategies. When the student is aware and can use the strategies, the tests can correctly measure the student's abilities.

For example, for the above

65% of California students got the *wrong answer* of (A) 25%, 6% left out the answer, 4% answered Choice (B), 12% answered Choice (C), 7% answered Choice (D), and 6% got the answer right (Choice E).

In a study thereafter, a group of 100 students were taught the powerful but simple Math Strategy:

Translate English words into mathematical expressions.

In a verbal math problem, always translate

> **what** to x
>
> **percent** to $\overline{}\,100$
>
> **of** to $\times$ (times)
>
> **is** to $=$

Of the 100 students who were exposed to this translation from verbal to math strategy, 90% of them chose the correct answer, (E) 400.

59. ape; tape; etape (a place where troops camp after a day's march); retape (tape again); pretape (tape before).

LEVEL 2: MEDIUM-HARD BRAINTEASERS

1. I have only nickels, dimes, and quarters and have at least one of each type of coin. The total number of coins I have is 15 and the total value of all the coins is $1.00. How many of each coin do I have?

Alternate Question 1:

Now let's see if you can solve this version of the problem where there are also pennies in the mix.

Suppose I now have pennies, nickels, dimes, and quarters and at least one of each coin, but different quantities of each coin. The total number of coins I have is 15 and the total value of the coins is $1.00. How many of each coin do I now have?

2. In miles per hour, what is the average rate of a car going 20 mph and traveling back the same distance at 60 mph?

(A) 30
(B) 40
(C) 50
(D) 60
(E) cannot be determined unless the distance is given

3. Terry is half as old as Alice was when Alice was 5 years older than Terry is now. How old is Terry now?

4. The price of a watch at a department store has been discounted 20 percent and then an additional 30 percent after the first discount was applied. Would the final discounted price have been lower if there had been a single discount of 50 percent? Why or why not?

5. Suppose a four-digit number is an exact multiple of 9 and three of the four digits are 1, 2, and 3. What is the fourth digit?

6. Which is greater, the average rate of a car going uphill a certain distance at a rate of A miles per hour and downhill the same distance at a different rate, B miles per hour, or the average of the rates A and B? Assume A is not equal to B.

Alternate wording:

Suppose a car goes uphill a certain distance at the rate of A miles per hour. Then the car travels downhill the same distance at a rate of B miles per hour. Which is greater, the average of the rates A and B or the average rate of the car for the whole trip (uphill and downhill)? Assume that the value of A is not the same as the value of B.

7. Harry owes Sam $30. Sam owes Phil $20. Phil owes Harry $50. Which of the following will settle the debts?

(A) Harry could give Phil $50.
(B) Sam could give Phil $20 and Harry could give Sam $40.
(C) Harry could give Phil $20 and Sam could give Phil $10.
(D) Sam and Phil could give Harry $50 total.
(E) Phil could give Harry $20 and could give Sam $10.

8. Given a triangle ABC, draw the altitude BD to side AC and draw the altitude CE to side AB. If AC is greater than AB, what can you say about the relationship between the lengths of BD and CE. That is, is BD greater than CE, less than CE, or equal to CE, or is it impossible to make a definite comparison?

9. A test was taken by 60 students and was scored from 0 to 100. Only 21 students scored higher than or equal to 80. What is the smallest possible average score of all 60 students?

10. Choose a two-digit number. Add the digits. Then subtract that result from the original number to get a final result. (Example: Start with 13. Then add $1 + 3 = 4$. $13 - 4 = 9$, so 9 is your final result in this example.) Question: Which of the following numbers could be your final result?

(A) 31
(B) 32

(C) 33

(D) 34

(E) 35

(F) 36

11. How many ways can 4 people be seated at one table for 4 with 2 people facing the other 2 people?

12. Refrigerators come in cartons 40 inches deep $\times$ 48 inches wide $\times$ 60 inches high. They must stand upright when stored. If Jones has a storage room 45 feet across, 60 feet deep, and 8 feet high, what is the greatest number of refrigerators he can store there?

(A) 180

(B) 195

(C) 198

(D) 201

(E) 396

13. Given:

Quantity A: The average rate of a car traveling uphill at a rate of a miles per hour and downhill the same distance at a rate of b miles per hour

Quantity B: The average of the rates of a miles per hour and b miles per hour

If a does not equal b and both a and b are greater than 0, then which is greater, Quantity A or Quantity B—or are they equal?

14. Three items in a department store are sold with successive discounts: the first with successive discounts of 60% and 40%, the second with successive discounts of 50% and 50%, and the third with successive discounts of 30% and 70%. Which of the following is true?

(A) The equivalent single discount of all three items is the same, but not 100%.

(B) The equivalent discount of each of the three items is between 70% and 80%.

(C) The equivalent discount of each of the three items is between 80% and 90%.

(D) The equivalent discount of each of the three items is 100%.

(E) None of the above statements is true.

15. If you add the age of a man to the age of his wife, the result is 91. He is now twice as old as she was when he was as old as she is now. How old is the man and how old is his wife?

16. Bill bought four times as many apples as Harry, and this amount also happened to be three times as many as Martin bought. If Bill, Harry, and Martin purchased less than a total of 190 apples, what is the greatest number of apples that Bill could have purchased?

(A) 168

(B) 120

(C) 119

(D) 117

(E) 108

(F) 90

17. If I have 3 dimes, 3 nickels, and 3 quarters, how many ways can I make change for $1.00?

(A) 1

(B) 2

(C) 3

(D) 4

(E) 5

18. If $x + y = 7$ and $xy = 4$, then find the value of $(x \text{ times } x) + (y \text{ times } y)$.
Note: x and y may not be integers.

19. If a does not equal b and $a + b$ is greater than 0, is $2ab$ divided by $(a + b)$ greater than, equal to, or less than $(a + b)$ divided by 2?

20. Out of 3 females and 3 males, 3 people at random enter a previously empty room. What is the probability that with any different combination there are exactly 2 males and 1 female in the room now?

21. How many three-digit whole numbers are exactly divisible by 9?

22. Find a fraction that has a value between $\frac{1}{4}$ and $\frac{1}{3}$.

23. Suppose we have a number like 465,465 or 963,963. In general let's say we have a number *abc,abc*. Which one or more of the following choices is the number of this form divisible by?

 I. 143

 II. 91

 III. 77

24. What is a really fast way of getting the result of the multiplication of two of the same two-digit numbers with 5 as the units digit? Like 85×85?

Explanatory Answers for Level 2 Brainteasers

1. One dime, one quarter, and 13 nickels.

   Math logic way:

   The cleverest way to do this problem is to try to reduce the number of possibilities to a minimum and then figure out all the possibilities. The greatest number of quarters I can have is 3, since if I have at least 1 of every coin, I can't have 4 quarters (and I can't have more than 4 quarters because the total would be more than $1). So if I have 3 quarters, I am left with 12 dimes/nickels, which must add up to 25 cents. That's impossible, so suppose I have 2 quarters. That leaves 50 cents for the dimes/nickels. I am left with 13 dimes/nickels. I can't get 13 dimes/nickels that add up to 50 cents. So try 1 quarter. I have 75 cents left. I am left with 14 dimes/nickels. I can get 13 nickels and 1 dime to get 75 cents. So I get 13 nickels, 1 dime, and 1 quarter.

   Algebraic way:

   Let's say I have n nickels, d dimes, and q quarters. The total number of coins can be represented as:

   $$n + d + q = 15 \qquad \boxed{1}$$

   The value of all the coins is:

   $$5n + 10d + 25q = 100 \qquad \boxed{2}$$

   since a nickel is worth 5 cents, a dime is worth 10 cents, and a quarter is worth 25 cents.

   Let's divide the second equation by 5. We get:

   $$n + 2d + 5q = 20 \qquad \boxed{3}$$

   Multiply Equation $\boxed{1}$ by 2:

   $$2n + 2d + 2q = 30 \qquad \boxed{4}$$

   Subtract Equation $\boxed{3}$ from Equation $\boxed{4}$. We get:

   $$n - 3q = 10 \qquad \boxed{5}$$

   This can be rewritten as:

   $$n = 10 + 3q \qquad \boxed{6}$$

Now q (an integer) cannot be greater than 1 because if it were then n would be greater than 15, which would contradict $\boxed{1}$.

So let $q = 1$. Then according to $\boxed{6}$, $n = 13$ and according to $\boxed{1}$, $d = 1$. So I have 1 quarter, 1 dime, and 13 nickels.

Answer to Alternate Question 1:

1 dime, 2 quarters, 7 nickels, and 5 pennies.

Math logic way:

One way to do this problem as before is to try to reduce the number of possibilities to a minimum and then figure out all the possibilities. The most number of quarters I can have is 3, since if I have at least 1 of every coin, I can't have 4 quarters (and I can't have more than 4 quarters because the total would be more than $1). Suppose I have 3 quarters. Then the total value of the dimes, nickels and pennies is 25 cents. I have then 12 dimes/nickels/pennies. There is no way I can have a total of 12 nickels/dimes/pennies where I have different quantities of each coin and at least 1 of each coin. So let's say there are 2 quarters. That leaves 13 nickels/dimes/pennies valued at a total of 50 cents. I have to have less than 5 dimes in order to have at least 1 of each coin. I can't have 4 dimes because I must have at least 1 of each coin and different quantities of the coins. By the same token I can't have 3 dimes or 2 dimes. Therefore I must have 1 dime, which would give me 1 dime, 2 quarters, 7 nickels, and 5 pennies.

Note: If I had 1 quarter, I'd have 14 nickels/dimes/pennies valued at a total of 75 cents. There is no way I can have this where there are different quantities of each coin and at least 1 of each coin.

However, unlike the solution to the previous problem that had only nickels, dimes, and quarters, the better way to solve this one is the algebraic way.

Algebraic way:

Let the total number of coins

$$15 = p + n + d + q \qquad \boxed{1}$$

where p = pennies, n = nickels, d = dimes, and q = quarters.

The total amount of the coins can be represented as:

$$100 = p + 5n + 10d + 25q \qquad \boxed{2}$$

Subtracting equations, we get:

$$85 = 4n + 9d + 24q \qquad \boxed{3}$$

Now we can see that q must be less than 4. So suppose $q = 3$. Then from Equation $\boxed{3}$,

$$13 = 4n + 9d$$

There is no way that this can be if the value of n is different from the value of d. So let $q = 2$.

Then from $\boxed{3}$,

$$37 = 4n + 9d$$

The only way this is possible is if $d = 1$. Then $n = 7$.

Since $q = 2$, from $\boxed{1}$, $p = 5$.

So I have 5 pennies, 7 nickels, 1 dime, and 2 quarters.

Note: If $q = 1$, I would get from $\boxed{3}$,

$$61 = 4n + 9d \qquad \boxed{4}$$

There is no way that this equation would be satisfied with n, p, d, and q being different integers.

2. Choice A is correct.

Average rate is not the average of the rates and the answer is not 40. Also the distance does not need to be known. Where a and b are the two rates above, the average rate can be shown to be

$$\frac{2ab}{(a + b)}$$

so $\dfrac{2(20)(60)}{(20 + 60)} = 30$

Detailed explanation:

Average rate $= \dfrac{\text{total distance}}{\text{total time}}$

Let's say the distance is D one way. Then the total distance is $2D$.

Let's say the time the car travels 20 mph is t and the time the car travels 60 mph is T.

Then from the formula Rate × Time = Distance, $20 \times t = D$ and $60 - T = D$. This gives you

$$t = \frac{D}{20} \quad \text{and} \quad T = \frac{D}{60}$$

So the total time is

$$t + T = \frac{D}{20} + \frac{D}{60}$$

This is equal to

$$t + T = \frac{80D}{1200} = \frac{D}{15}$$

So the average rate is

$$\frac{2D}{(t + T)} = \frac{2D}{\left(\dfrac{D}{15}\right)} = 30$$

3. 5.

(Use Strategy 2: Translate English words into mathematical expressions.)

Translate:

Alice was five years older than Terry is now:

$$a = 5 + T$$

where a is the age that Alice was.

Now translate:

Terry is half as old as Alice was:

$$T = \left(\frac{1}{2}\right)a$$

Substitute for a:

$$T = \left(\frac{1}{2}\right)(5 + T)$$
$$2T = 5 + T$$
$$T = 5$$

So Terry is 5 years old.

Strategy/answer:

Terry is 5 years old. This is a classic SAT problem. And the key strategy is to translate from words to math so that you don't rack your brain.

Translate:

Translate Alice to A, Terry to T, *was* or *is* to =, and *older than* to +.

Now translate:

Terry is half as old as Alice was:

$$T = \left(\frac{1}{2}\right)A \qquad \boxed{1}$$

Translate:

Alice was five years older than Terry is now:

$$A = 5 + T \qquad \boxed{2}$$

Substitute for $5 + T = A$ $\boxed{2}$ in $\boxed{1}$. We get:

$$T = \left(\frac{1}{2}\right)(5 + T)$$

Simplifying we get :

$$2T = 5 + T$$
$$\text{and thus} \quad T = 5$$

So Terry is 5 years old.

4. A single 50 percent discount is better.

   Strategy/answer:

   It is better to get a single discount of 50%. Do not get lured into a process that sounds superficial or that you wouldn't bet on. In fact, it is always better to get a single discount of the sums of the successive discounts than it is to get the discounts computed successively. For example, suppose the item were originally $100. A single discount of 50% would give you the item at $50. Now if I had successive discounts of 20 and 30 percent, the first 20% discount would give me $80. The second 30% discount on $80 would give me $56.

5. If a number is an exact multiple of 9, the sum of the digits of that number is also a multiple of 9. So $1 + 2 + 3 + x = 9$ and $x = 3$.

6. The average rate is less than the average of the rates.

   $$\text{Average rate} = \frac{2AB}{(A + B)}$$

   $$\text{Average of the rates} = \frac{(A + B)}{2}$$

   Detailed solution:

   From the formula of Rate × Time = Distance, calling the time for the car to go uphill t, and the time for the car to go downhill T, with D being the distance downhill and uphill:

   $$A \times t = D \qquad \boxed{1}$$

   and

   $$B \times T = D \qquad \boxed{2}$$

   Now average rate $= \dfrac{\text{total distance}}{\text{total time}}$

   So

   $$\text{average rate} = \frac{2D}{(t + T)} \qquad \boxed{3}$$

From $\boxed{1}$ we have

$$t = \frac{D}{A} \qquad \boxed{4}$$

and from $\boxed{2}$ we have

$$T = \frac{D}{B} \qquad \boxed{5}$$

Substituting from $\boxed{4}$ and $\boxed{5}$ in $\boxed{3}$, we get

$$\text{Average rate} = \frac{2D}{\left(\dfrac{D}{A} + \dfrac{D}{B}\right)} \qquad \boxed{6}$$

This becomes

$$\text{Average rate} = \frac{2AB}{(A + B)} \qquad \boxed{7}$$

But the average of the rates is just $\dfrac{(A + B)}{2}$.

So we ask is $\dfrac{2AB}{(A + B)}$ greater, equal to, or less than $\dfrac{(A + B)}{2}$?

So we compare

$$\frac{2AB}{(A + B)} \quad \text{with} \quad \frac{(A + B)}{2}$$

Put $\dfrac{2AB}{(A + B)}$ under a Column A and $\dfrac{(A + B)}{2}$ under a Column B and let's compare the columns:

Column A	Column B
$\dfrac{2AB}{(A + B)}$	$\dfrac{(A + B)}{2}$

Now multiply both columns by 2 and then by $(A + B)$. We get

Column A	Column B
$4AB$	$(A + B)(A + B)$

This becomes

Column A	Column B
$4AB$	$A \times A + 2AB + B \times B$

Now subtract $4AB$ from both columns. We get

Column A	Column B
0	$A \times A - 2AB + B \times B$

But $A \times A - 2AB + B \times B = (A - B)(A - B)$ so we get

Column A	Column B
0	$(A - B)(A - B)$

Since we are told that A and B are *different* rates, $A - B$ cannot be 0, and so $(A - B)(A - B)$ is always greater than 0 whether A is greater than B or less than B. So Column B is greater than Column A and so the original quantity in Column B, the average of the rates is greater than the original quantity in Column A, the average rate.

7. Choice E is correct.

   This could really give you a headache if you don't represent what's given in a table.

	Harry	Sam	Phil
Harry owes Sam $30:	+$30	−$30	
(Harry is ahead $30 and Sam is behind $30.)			
Sam owes Phil $20:		+$20	−$20
(Sam is ahead $20 and Phil is behind $20.)			
Phil owes Harry $50:	−$50		+$50
(Phil is ahead $50 and Harry is behind $50.)			
Total:	−$20	−$10	+$30

   (Phil must give Harry $20 and Sam $10 to make totals 0.)

8. I know that you probably were trying to figure out the sides and the relationship of all the lengths AC, AB, BD, and CE. But what you probably didn't think of is that the *area* of triangle ABC is represented as

$$CE \times \frac{AB}{2}$$

   but also as

$$BD \times \frac{AC}{2}$$

$$\text{So} \quad CE \times AB = BD \times AC \qquad \boxed{1}$$

   Now if AC is greater than AB (given), in order for $\boxed{1}$ to be true, CE must be greater than BD!

9. 28.

   Lowest average score
$$= \frac{[21 \times 80 + (60 - 21) \times 0]}{60} = 28$$

10. Choice F is correct.

    The final result must be divisible by 9.

    It is very interesting that when you add the digits of a number and subtract that from the original number you get a number that is a perfect multiple of 9.

Here's the proof:

Represent the two-digit number as $10t + u$ where t is the tens digit and u is the units digit. Adding the digits we get $t + u$. Subtracting from the original number, we get $10t + u - t - u = 9t$. Since t is an integer, the only choice that fits is Choice F. What's more interesting is that any number that is a multiple of 9 has digits that add up to a multiple of 9.

Here's a great parlor trick:

Have someone choose a number. Then have that person add the digits. Then have the person subtract that result from the original number to get a final result. Have the person now cross out one of the digits in the final answer. You will be able to tell the person what digit he crossed out if he tells you the remaining digit. (Example: He starts with 23. $2 + 3 = 5$. $23 - 5 = 18$. He crosses off the 8. He is left with 1.) You will be able to tell the digit crossed out.

Why?

Any number that is a multiple of 9 has digits that add up to a multiple of 9. So whatever number you crossed out, the crossed out number must be 9 minus the number left!

Here's the proof:

Let's say we have a three-digit number:

$$100h + 10t + u$$

which is equal to a number that is a multiple of 9. Then:

$$100h + 10t + u = 9x \qquad \boxed{1}$$

where x is an integer.

We'd like to prove that

$$h + t + u = 9p$$

where p is an integer.

Let's say $h + t + u = R$.

Then $\boxed{1}$

$$100h + 10t + u = 9x \qquad \boxed{1}$$
$$h + t + u = R \qquad \boxed{2}$$

Subtract $\boxed{2}$ from $\boxed{1}$:

$$99h + 9t = 9x - R \qquad \boxed{3}$$
$$R = 9x - 9t - 99h$$

and so R is exactly divisible by 9. Therefore R is a multiple of 9.

11. 24.

Two people facing two other people would look something like this:

$$ab \quad ab \quad ac \quad ac$$
$$cd \quad dc \quad bd \quad db \quad \text{etc.}$$

The number of permutations (P) from people a, b, c, d on one side of the table are ab, ac, ad, ba, bc, bd, ca, cb, cd, da, db, dc—12 permutations.

(This is written as 4 permutations taken 2 at a time or 4P2, which comes out to 4×3.)

On the other side of the table facing the two people, for each permutation like ab you can have cd or dc. For ac you can have bd or db.

So for each of the 12 permutations ab, ac, ad, etc. on one side of the table, you have two possibilities on the other side. Thus you have a total of 12×2 possibilities.

Alternate variations of solutions:

Start with the first person (a) at the left side in a corner position. Then figure out the combinations you can have (ab-cd or ac-bd, etc.). Now account for the fact that b, c, or d can be at the left corner also.

Longer form for 2:

Start with the first person (a) at the left side in a corner position. Then figure out the combinations you can have (ab-cd or ac-bd, etc.). Since you can play around with combinations (permutations) of bcd, there are $3 \times 2 = 6$ of them. Now b, c, or d can be at the left corner also, so there are $6 + 6 + 6$ more combinations (permutations). That gives us 24 in total.

12. Choice D is correct.

Place 11 cartons with the 40″ side along the back of the room, and repeat in front of these so you have 15 rows deep of 11 cartons wide (165 cartons). In the remaining space place two cartons with their 48″ sides against the back, and make 18 rows of these (36 cartons). This gives $165 + 36 = 201$ refrigerators stored. You can also get 201 fridges in by changing the numbers so you have 15 rows of 5 cartons and 18 rows of 7 cartons.

13. Choice B is correct.

Understand the difference between "average rate" and the "average of the rates." Then *cross multiply*, then *subtract* $4ab$ from both quantities.

Detailed explanation:

The average rate of a car going uphill at a miles per hour and downhill at b miles per hour the same distance is $\dfrac{2ab}{(a + b)}$.

Proof:

Call the distance d. Call the time it takes for the car to go uphill t. The time it takes for the car to go downhill the same distance (d) is T. Remembering that rate $\times$ time = distance,

$$a \times t = d \qquad \boxed{1}$$
$$b \times T = d \qquad \boxed{2}$$

The average rate is the *total* distance divided by the *total* time. That is

$$\frac{2d}{(t + T)}$$

Using $\boxed{1}$, we get

$$t = \frac{d}{a}$$

and $\boxed{2}$,

$$T = \frac{d}{b}$$

So

$$\frac{2d}{(t + T)} = \frac{2d}{\left(\dfrac{d}{a} + \dfrac{d}{b}\right)}$$

which can be seen to be

$$\frac{2ab}{(a + b)}$$

The average of the rates a and b is

$$\frac{(a + b)}{2}$$

So Quantity A is

$$\frac{2ab}{(a + b)}$$

and

Quantity B is

$$\frac{(a + b)}{2}$$

Multiply both quantities by 2. You get:

Quantity A: $\dfrac{4ab}{(a + b)}$

Quantity B: $a + b$

Now multiply both quantities by $(a + b)$. You get:

Quantity A: $4ab$

Quantity B: $(a + b) \times (a + b) = a^2 + b^2 + 2ba$

Now subtract $4ab$ from both quantities. You get:

Quantity A: 0

Quantity B: $a^2 - 2ba + b^2 = (a - b) \times (a - b)$

Since a is not equal to b, $(a - b) \times (a - b)$ is always greater than 0.

Thus Quantity A is less than Quantity B and so the original quantity, A, or

$$\left[\frac{2ab}{(a + b)}\right]$$

is less than the original quantity, B, or

$$\left[\frac{(a + b)}{2}\right]$$

Thus the average rate of the car going uphill at a miles per hour and downhill at b miles per hour is less than the average of the rates a and b.

14. **Choice B is correct.**

Suppose we start with a price of $100 for each item. After the first discount the first item will be $40. After the second discount the item will be $24. This would represent an equivalent discount of 76%. Use the same process for the second and third items. For the second item we would find that the price after the second discount to be $25, which would represent an equivalent discount of 75%. For the third item we would find the equivalent discount to be 79%. Thus Choice B is correct.

15. The man is 52 and his wife is 39.

Denote the man's age now as M, the wife's age now as W, the man's age when he was as old as the wife is now as m, the wife's age when the man was as old as she is now as w.

Then we get

$$M + W = 91 \qquad \boxed{1}$$

$$m = W \qquad \boxed{1}$$

(since the man was then as old as the wife is now).

$$M = 2w \qquad \boxed{2}$$

(since the man is twice as old as the wife was).

Now the key thing to realize is that the difference in ages between the man and his wife now is the same difference then or at any other time.

That is,

$$M - W = m - w \qquad \boxed{3}$$

So substituting $\boxed{2}$ and $\boxed{3}$ into $\boxed{4}$, we get

$$M - W = \frac{W - M}{2}$$

$$\text{or} \quad M - W = \frac{(2W - M)}{2}$$

which gives us

$$2M - 2W = 2W - M$$

so we get

$$3M = 4W \quad \text{or} \quad M = \frac{4W}{3} \qquad \boxed{4}$$

We substitute $\boxed{4}$ into $\boxed{1}$ and we get

$$\frac{4W}{3} + W = 91$$

$$\frac{7W}{3} = 91$$

and

$$W = \frac{273}{7} = 39$$

From $\boxed{1}$ we get

$$M + 39 = 91$$

and so $\quad M = 52$.

16. **Choice E is correct.**

Translate:

The number of apples that Bill bought $= B$, that Harry bought $= H$, and that Martin bought $= M$. "Bill bought 4 times as many apples as Harry" translates into $B = 4H$. Similarly $B = 3M$. "Bill, Harry, and Martin purchased less than a total of 190 apples" translates into $B + H + M < 190$. You will find that manipulating these equations, we get $B < 120$. However, because H and M are integers, $B = 108$ and not 119!

Here's the complete solution:

Translate:

The number of apples that Bill bought $= B$, that Harry bought $= H$, and that Martin bought $= M$.

"Bill bought 4 times as many apples as Harry" translates into

$$B = 4H \quad \text{or} \quad H = \frac{B}{4} \qquad \boxed{1}$$

As stated in the problem, this amount also $= 3M$. So

$$B = 3M \quad \text{or} \quad M = \frac{B}{3} \qquad \boxed{2}$$

"Bill, Harry, and Martin purchased less than a total of 190 apples" translates into

$$B + H + M < 190 \qquad \boxed{3}$$

Substituting $\boxed{1}$ and $\boxed{2}$ into $\boxed{3}$ we get

$$B + \frac{B}{4} + \frac{B}{3} < 190 \qquad \boxed{4}$$

This becomes

$$\frac{19B}{12} < 190 \qquad \boxed{5}$$

and we get

$$\frac{B}{12} < 10 \qquad \boxed{6}$$

and

$$B < 120 \qquad \boxed{7}$$

So you'd think that the greatest number B could be is 119. Wrong! If $B = 119$, according to $\boxed{1}$ and $\boxed{2}$ H and M would not be whole numbers. The greatest number of apples B can be is 108 since this is the greatest integer less than 120 that lets H and M be whole numbers.

Now let's say the problem was worded as follows:

"Bill bought four times as many apples as Harry and three times as many apples as Martin. If Bill, Harry, and Martin purchased less than a total of 190 apples, what is the greatest number of apples that Bill could have purchased?"

Note that "and" really means "plus."

Using simple algebra, let B, H, and M represent the number of apples purchased by Bill, Harry, and Martin.

$$B = 4H + 3M$$
$$\text{Total} = B + H + M$$
$$\text{Total} < 190$$

To maximize B you need to maximize H.

If $H = 38$ and $M = 0$ then $B = 152$ and $T = 190$, so H is too big.

If $H = 37$ and $M = 1$ then $B = 148 + 3 = 151$ and total $= 151 + 37 + 1 = 189$.

So Bill can purchase as many as 151 apples.

17. Choice B is correct.

Write an equation:

Where n is the number of nickels, d is the number of dimes, and q is the number of quarters:

$$5n + 10d + 25q = 100$$

Start with the smallest numbers for n, d, and q that satisfy the equation. Start with $n = 0$, $d = 0$, then $q = 4$, which is not true since the most q can be is 3. Then try $n = 0$, $d = 1$. Then we get $25q = 90$, which doesn't give us a whole number for q. You will find that if $n = 1$, $d = 2$, and $q = 3$ and if $n = 3$, $d = 1$, and $q = 3$, you will satisfy the equation. So there are two ways to make change.

18. 41.

$(x + y)^2 = 7^2$. You get

$$x^2 + y^2 + 2xy = 49$$

Now substitute $xy = 4$. You get

$$x^2 + y^2 + 2(4) = 49$$

So $x^2 + y^2 + 8 = 49$

and so $x^2 + y^2 = 41$

19. less than.

Compare $2ab$ divided by $(a + b)$ with $(a + b)$ divided by 2 by manipulating the inequality or equality: Multiply both sides by 2 and then by $(a + b)$. Then multiply out

$$(a + b) \times (a + b)$$

and subtract the $4ab$ on the left side from both sides. You will get 0 as compared with

$$(a - b) \times (a - b)$$

Since a is not equal to b (given), 0 is always less than

$$(a - b) \times (a - b)$$

20. $\frac{9}{20}$.

Call females F1, F2, F3 and males M1, M2, M3. The total number of combinations of three people like F1, F2, M1 and F1, M2, M3, etc. is 6 combinations taken 3 at a time or 6C3, which is equal to

$$\frac{(6 \times 5 \times 4)}{(3 \times 2 \times 1)} = 20$$

The favorable number of combinations is

M1, M2, F1	M1, M2, F2	M1, M2, F3
M1, M3, F1	M1, M3, F2	M1, M3, F3
M2, M3, F1	M2, M3, F2	M2, M3, F3

the number of which is 9. Thus the probability of only two males in the room is

$$\frac{\text{favorable ways}}{\text{total ways}} = \frac{9}{20}$$

21. 100.

Easiest solution:

In the 100s the first number exactly divisible by 9 is 12 × 9. The next numbers exactly divisible by 9 are 13 × 9, 14 × 9, etc. up to 111 × 9. Thus from 100 to 999 (inclusive), there are 111 − 12 + 1 numbers exactly divisible by 9.

This is 100 numbers.

More difficult solution:

You of course would not want to tediously figure out all the numbers by dividing by 9. You have to realize that any number whose digits add up to a multiple of 9 is exactly divisible by 9. So let's figure out all the numbers from 100 to 999 whose digits add up to a multiple of 9. For the 100s we have 108, 117, 126, 135, . . . 190. But we also have 189—11 numbers altogether.

For the 200s we get 207, 216, 225, 234, 243, 252, 261, 270, 279, 288, 297—11 numbers in all.

Similarly we will get 11 numbers for sets of the 300s, 400s, 500s, 600s, 700s, and 800s. For the 900s we have 900, 909, 918, 927, 936, 945, 954, 963, 972, 981, 990, and 999—12 numbers.

Thus for the 100s through the 800s we have 11 × 8 = 88 numbers. For the 900s we have 12 numbers. The total is 100 numbers.

22. This can be a hard problem if you don't use a strategy for somehow relating $\frac{1}{4}$ to $\frac{1}{3}$.

For $\frac{1}{4}$ multiply both numerator and denominator by 3. You get $\frac{3}{12}$. Now for $\frac{1}{3}$ similarly multiply both numerator and denominator by 4 to get $\frac{4}{12}$. So $\frac{1}{4} = \frac{3}{12}$ and $\frac{1}{3} = \frac{4}{12}$.

But there is no obvious fraction between $\frac{3}{12}$ and $\frac{4}{12}$. So multiply both the numerators and the denominators of the fractions $\frac{3}{12}$ and $\frac{4}{12}$ by 2. We get:

$\frac{1}{4} = \frac{3}{12} = \frac{6}{24}$ and $\frac{1}{3} = \frac{4}{12} = \frac{8}{24}$. You can see that $\frac{7}{24}$ is in between the two fractions $\frac{1}{4}$ and $\frac{1}{3}$.

Here's how to get some more fractions that fit the bill:

For $\frac{1}{4}$ multiply both numerator and denominator by 12. You get $\frac{12}{48}$. Now for $\frac{1}{3}$ similarly multiply both numerator and denominator by 16 to get $\frac{16}{48}$. So $\frac{1}{4} = \frac{12}{48}$ and $\frac{1}{3} = \frac{16}{48}$. So fractions in between are also $\frac{13}{48}$ and $\frac{15}{48}$.

Even more fractions are $\frac{2}{7}, \frac{3}{10}$, and $\frac{3}{11}$.

23. All of these.

You can see that a number like 465,465 = 1,001 × 465 or 963,963 = 1,001 × 963. In general a number like *abc,abc* = 1,001 × *abc*. But 1,001 = 7 × 11 × 13.

Since 7 × 11 = 77, 13 × 7 = 91, and 11 × 13 = 143, the number *abc,abc* is exactly divisible by 143, by 91, and by 77.

24. For 85 × 85, multiply the tens digit 8 × (8 + 1) = 72. Then multiply the 5s and you get 25. Your answer will be 7,225.

Here's the general proof:

Let the two-digit number be represented as
$$10t + 5$$
where *t* is the tens digit and 5 the units digit. We have
$$(10t + 5)(10t + 5) = 100t^2 + 100t + 25$$
Factoring, this is equal to
$$100(t^2 + t) + 25 = 100(t)(t + 1) + 25$$
Thus
$$\begin{aligned} 85 \times 85 &= 100(8)(8 + 1) + 25 \\ &= 100(8 \times 9) + 25 \\ &= 7,200 + 25 \\ &= 7,225 \end{aligned}$$

So in general, you would multiply the tens digit by one more than the tens digit. Then multiply that result by 100 and add that to 25.

LEVEL 3: HARDER BRAINTEASERS

1. One segment of the game show *Let's Make a Deal* has three doors, behind one of which is a new car and behind each of the other two is a goat. The contestant will win whatever is behind the door he or she chooses. The contestant chooses one of the three doors, but before it is opened, the host opens up a different door that has a goat behind it. In order to have the greatest chance of winning the car should the contestant open the door that is his or her original choice or open the remaining door?

Alternate question 1:

Suppose in Las Vegas, a table has 10 cards randomly distributed from ace to 10 facing down on a table. The contestant has to find which card is an ace. He is asked to touch the face-down card that he thinks is an ace. Then the dealer takes away 8 of the cards that are *not* aces. Although only 2 cards remain, the ace and another card, the dealer bets the contestant $5 for his $1 that the card he touched is *not* an ace. Should the contestant take the bet? *At dull parties, I used this card game to fire up the guests.*

2. What is the value of the sum of the first 99 consecutive integers, that is,

$$1 + 2 + 3 + 4 + \ldots + 99?$$

3. In an isosceles triangle, ABC, $AB = AC$, and angle $A = 20°$. Point P is on side AC such that

$$AP = BC. \text{ Find angle } PBC.$$

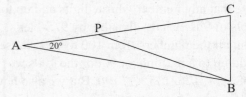

4. P is a point inside a square $ABCD$ such that $PA = 1$, $PB = 2$, and $PC = 3$. What is the measure of $\angle APB$?

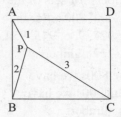

5. Suppose you have fifty American coins with at least one quarter, totaling exactly $1.00. If you drop a coin at random, what is the probability that it is a penny?

Alternate question 5:

Suppose you have fifty American coins totaling exactly $1.00. If you drop a coin at random, what is the probability that it is a penny?

6. Put the numbers 1 through 9 on the lines below so that the numbers on the four lines on each side add up to 17.

   Note: you can't use a number more than once.

   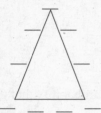

7. *Given*:　$\angle BAC = 20°$
   $\angle ABC = \angle ACB$
   $\angle ABE = 20°$
   $\angle DCA = 30°$
   $\angle BED = ?$

   And do it without trigonometry!

   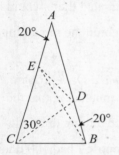

8. Suppose there are two buckets, one that contains a gallon of water and another that contains a gallon of alcohol. A cup of alcohol from the second bucket is poured into the bucket of water. A cup of the resulting mixture is then poured back into the bucket of alcohol. Which is now true?

   (A) There is more water in the bucket of alcohol than alcohol in the bucket of water.

   (B) There is more alcohol in the bucket of water than water in the bucket of alcohol.

   (C) There is the same amount of water in the bucket of alcohol as alcohol in the bucket of water.

9. You divide a figure into two squares by drawing one straight line. The original figure could have been a (an):

   (A) non-rectangular trapezoid
   (B) triangle
   (C) square
   (D) circle
   (E) octagon

10. Here's a similar problem that was posed in a famous movie as a test for someone to get something that person really wanted—I can't say "what" because of censorship. From the shovel below, how would you get the ♦ out of the shovel by moving two of the rectangles (A, B, C, and D) and creating a new shovel with the same shape?

    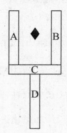

11. Find the next letter in the series.

    　　　　s　t　n　o　j　k　g　h

    (A) g
    (B) c
    (C) d
    (D) e
    (E) f

Explanatory Answers for Level 3 Brainteasers

1. He or she should open the remaining door. The probability would be $\frac{2}{3}$, not $\frac{1}{2}$!

   Note: Many people have thought that there is a $\frac{1}{2}$ chance of having the car behind the door the contestant chose since there are two doors. However because you have chosen a door first, out of 3, there is a $\frac{1}{3}$ probability there is a car behind it, and there would be a $\frac{2}{3}$ probability any other door has the car behind it. So if you chose 2 of the other doors, you would have a $\frac{2}{3}$ probability of getting the car. And if 1 door was eliminated by the host, since that door had the goat, if you switched doors, then it would be in effect as if you were choosing 2 doors, which would give you the $\frac{2}{3}$ probability that the car was behind the remaining door.

   Another explanation:

   Interestingly enough, the answer is that the contestant should switch doors because there is actually a $\frac{2}{3}$ chance of winning the car by switching, while there is only a $\frac{1}{3}$ chance of winning the car if the contestant opens his or her original door!

   This is how most people's minds approach the problem: The host eliminates 1 door with the goat, so there is a goat or a car behind the contestant's door. So the probability is $\frac{1}{2}$. And it doesn't matter whether the contestant opens his or her original door or changes doors.

   But let's see what is really happening: The probability of having a car behind the contestant's door when he or she originally chooses the door is $\frac{1}{3}$ since there are 3 doors and only 1 door that has a car behind it. And there is a $\frac{2}{3}$ probability that the car is behind 1 of the other 2 doors (since there are 2 ways a car can be behind 1 of the remaining doors [car-goat; goat-car] for a total of 3 ways: car-goat; goat-car; goat-goat). Now if the host eliminates a door there would still be the $\frac{1}{3}$ probability that the car was behind the original contestant's door—so once a door is eliminated there would be a $\frac{2}{3}$ probability the car was behind the remaining door.

   I have pondered the *Let's Make a Deal* problem for some time. I came to the conclusion that the answer is $\frac{2}{3}$ when I considered a more dramatic variation of the problem. Suppose I had 100 doors and 1 of them had a car behind it. The rest had goats. If I chose 1 door there would no doubt be a $\frac{1}{100}$ chance that there was a car behind it. So the remaining doors combined would have a $\frac{99}{100}$ chance of hiding the car. Now no matter what was done to the other doors, there would still be a $\frac{1}{100}$ chance that the car was behind the door that was chosen. So if the host knew that 98 of the doors did not have the car, and then eliminated those doors, the remaining door then must have a $\frac{99}{100}$ chance that there was a car behind it.

   Suppose you had 100 doors. The chance of the car being behind the contestant chosen door is $\frac{1}{100}$, obviously a very slim chance. That *won't change* even when the host eliminates 98 doors. When the doors are eliminated and all but 2 are left, the contestant still has chosen a door with a very slim chance that the car is behind it, namely $\frac{1}{100}$.

Because the host knows where the car is (and where the goats are), and because 98 of the goats were eliminated, the remaining door has a $\frac{(98 + 1)}{100}$ chance that there is a car behind it.

Note that initial reasoning may indicate that when there is only one door left since 98 doors that hide goats have been eliminated, the total number of options for what's behind the contestant's door is 2, a car or a goat. The favorable number of ways is 1—the car. So by strict definition of probability, the probability is $\frac{1}{2}$ no matter what the host knows or did. But according to the paragraph above that is not the case.

I think probability has a somewhat ambiguous definition especially if there is "conditional" probability, but it seems that if you tried the 100 doors you would in fact find you'd have a $\frac{1}{100}$ chance of getting the car.

Alternate question 1 answer:

You'd think that the probability that the card the contestant touched is an ace is $\frac{1}{2}$. But the probability that the card the contestant touched is an ace is $\frac{1}{10}$! The probability that the rest of any of 9 cards is an ace is $\frac{9}{10}$. So if the dealer takes away 8 cards that are not aces, the probability that the remaining card is an ace is $\frac{9}{10}$. The dealer should have bet the contestant \$10 to \$1 to be fair. So the contestant should not take the original bet since there is only a 1 in 10 chance that the touched card is an ace.

This is erroneous reasoning we are tempted to use: It seems that when the contestant has only two cards to choose from and one of them is an ace and the other is not an ace (the other 8 cards that are not aces were eliminated), the total number of ways for what is the contestant's card is 2, an ace or not an ace. The favorable number of ways is 1—the ace. So by strict definition of probability the probability is $\frac{1}{2}$ no matter what the host knows or did.

2. 4,950.

This is extremely tricky. Write the numbers as:
$$1 + 2 + 3 + 4 + \ldots + 99 = N$$
and then write the numbers below that in reverse:
$$99 + 98 + 97 + 96 + \ldots + 1 = N$$
Adding both sums we get $100 + 100 + 100 + \ldots$ (99 times)

This is just 99×100 which is just $2N$. So
$$N = 50 \times 99 = 99 \times \frac{100}{2} = 4,950$$

3. 70°.

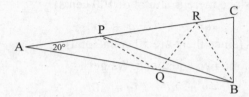

Make isosceles triangles. Where R is on AC, draw $BR = BC$, and where Q is on AB, draw $RQ = RB$. Where M is on AC, draw $MQ = RQ$. We have $\angle BAC = 20°$, $\angle ABC = 80°$, $\angle ACB = 80°$.

You can find that:

$\angle BRC = 80°$, $\angle RBC = 20°$, $\angle QBR = 60°$, $\angle RQB = 60°$, $\angle QRB = 60°$, $\angle QRM = 40°$, $\angle QMR = 40°$, and $\angle MQR = 100°$.

Note: $\angle MQA = 20°$ and $\angle A = 20°$, so $AM = MQ$. But $MQ = AP$ since $BC = AP$ and $BC = MQ$. Thus $AM = MQ$ and so point M coincides with point P, making $M = P$. Now since triangle QRB is equilateral, $QB = PQ$ so $\angle QBP = \angle QPB = 10°$. Since $\angle B = 80°$, $\angle PBC = 70°$.

4. 135°.

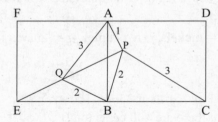

Detailed solution:

Rotate the points A, P, and D 90° anticlockwise about B to give the points E, Q, and F, respectively. Clearly, $\angle PBQ = 90°$ and $QA = PC = 3$. By the Pythagorean theorem in triangle PBQ, $PQ^2 = PB^2 + BQ^2 = 2^2 + 2^2 = 8 = QA^2 - AP^2$.

Hence by the converse of the Pythagorean theorem in triangle PQA, we know that $\angle APQ = 90°$. However, as triangle PBQ is right-angled and isosceles, $\angle BPQ = 45°$.

Therefore, $\angle APB = \angle APQ + \angle BPQ = 90° + 45° = 135°$.

5. 90%.

Represent n = nickels, p = pennies, q = quarters, d = dimes.

We have
$$5n + p + 10d + 25q = 100$$
(since there is a total of 100 cents)
$$n + p + d + q = 50$$
(since there are 50 coins total)

Subtract the two equations. We get
$$4n + 9d + 24q = 50$$

Suppose $q = 1$. Then
$$4n + 9d + 24 = 50$$
$$\text{and so}\quad 4n + 9d = 26$$

The only way this is possible is if $d = 2$ and $n = 2$.

Suppose $q = 2$. Then
$$4n + 9d + 48 = 50$$

and we get $4n + 9d = 2$, which is impossible.

So have 1 quarter, 2 dimes, and 2 nickels, which leaves 45 pennies, since the total number of coins is 50.

If I drop 1 penny we have the probability as $\frac{45}{50}$ or 90%.

Alternate question 5 answer:

The answer is 80% if I have no quarters, 90% if I have 1 quarter.

Represent n = nickels, p = pennies, q = quarters, d = dimes.

We have
$$5n + p + 10d + 25q = 100$$
(since there are 100 cents total)
$$n + p + d + q = 50$$
(since there are 50 coins total)

Subtract the two equations. We get
$$4n + 9d + 24q = 50$$

Suppose $q = 0$. Then
$$4n + 9d = 50 \qquad \boxed{1}$$

The only way this can be possible is if $d = 2$ and $n = 8$.

Suppose $q = 1$. Then
$$4n + 9d + 24 = 50$$
$$\text{and so}\quad 4n + 9d = 26 \qquad \boxed{2}$$

The only way this is possible is if $d = 2$ and $n = 2$.

Suppose $q = 2$. Then
$$4n + 9d + 48 = 50$$

and we get $4n + 9d = 2$, which is impossible.

So either we have 0 quarters, 2 dimes, and 8 nickels, which leaves 40 pennies (since the total number of coins is 50) $\qquad \boxed{1}$

or we have 1 quarter, 2 dimes, and 2 nickels, which leaves 45 pennies, since the total number of coins is 50. $\qquad \boxed{2}$

If I drop 1 penny we have the probability in $\boxed{1}$ as
$$\frac{40}{50} = 80\%$$

If I drop 1 penny we have the probability in $\boxed{2}$ as
$$\frac{45}{50} = 90\%$$

So if I have no quarters in my pile of coins the probability is 80%, and if I have 1 quarter in my pile the probability is 90%.

6. Solution:

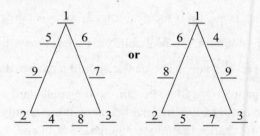

or

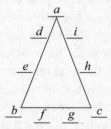

Let's see what numbers would be on the vertices of the triangle. Represent those numbers by a, b, and c. Let the numbers 1–9 be represented by a, b, c, d, e, f, g, h, i. Then we have
$$a + e + d + b = 17 \qquad \boxed{1}$$
$$b + f + g + c = 17 \qquad \boxed{2}$$

$c + h + i + a = 17$ **3**

$a + b + c + d + e + f + g + h + i = 45$

(since all the numbers $1 + 2 + 3 \ldots$ etc. add up to 45)   **4**

Adding **1**, **2**, and **3** we get

$2a + 2b + 2c + d + e + f + g + h + i = 51$ **5**

Subtracting **4** from **5** we get $a + b + c = 6$. The only way this can be possible is if the numbers for a, b, and c are 1, 2, and 3.

So start with the numbers 1, 2, and 3 at the vertices of the triangle. For the left side, since the numbers must add up to 17, the other two numbers on the left side must add up to 14. The only possibilities are 6 and 8 or 5 and 9. If it is 5 and 9, then the remaining numbers are 4, 6, 7, and 8. For the bottom side, two of these numbers (of 4, 6, 7, 8) must add up to $17 - 5 = 12$. The only numbers that work are 4 and 8. So then we'd have 6 and 7 left. For the right side, $1 + 3 + 6 + 7$ add up to 16. Similarly you can see that for the left side 6 and 8 also work and we get the triangle on the right.

7. **(Use Strategy 14: Draw and extend lines to make a problem easier.)**

   Draw the triangle as close to scale as possible.

   Draw BG at 20° to BC, cutting CA in G.

   Then $\angle GBD = 60°$ and $\angle BGC$ and $\angle BCG$ are 80°. So $BC = BG$.

   Also $\angle BCD = \angle BDC = 50°$ so $BD = BC = BG$ and triangle BDG is equilateral.

   But $\angle GBE = 40° = \angle BEG$ so $BG = GE = GD$.

   And $\angle DGE = 40°$. Since $DG = EG$, $\angle GDE = \angle DEG = 70°$, and since $\angle BEG = 40°$, $\angle BED = 30°$.

   This is considered the *second hardest* geometry problem as compared to number 3 in the Hardest Brainteasers.

8. Choice C is correct.

   Let's say the cup of alcohol you pour in the water bucket contains c gallons (c could be $\frac{1}{10}$ for example). Now the water bucket has a mixture of alcohol and water. Now you pour 1 cup of that mixture back into the alcohol bucket. Let's say there are a gallons of alcohol and w gallons of water in that cup.

   So $a + w = c$ **1**

   Now the amount of water poured into the alcohol bucket is w. The amount of alcohol in the water bucket is $c - a$ since we poured a gallons of alcohol into the alcohol bucket from the water bucket. From **1** we get

   $$c - a = w$$

   so Choice C is true.

9. Choice E is correct.

   You might have thought the figure was a rectangle. But unfortunately there's no choice that's a rectangle. Here's the figure:

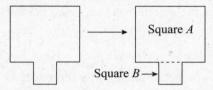

   Square A

   Square $B \rightarrow$

10. Very few people would think of moving a rectangle only halfway to the left. You move rectangle C halfway to the left and move rectangle B as shown. The ♦ is now outside the shovel.

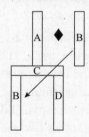

11. The sequence is arranged in pairs

    st no jk gh

    Note that we have a pattern

    gh (i) jk (lm) no (pqr) st

    where the letters in parens increase by one letter in the sequence.

    Thus the next two letters in the original sequence must be ef, since the pattern will be preserved.

    ef (no letters) gh (i) jk (lm) no (pqr) st

LEVEL 4: THE HARDEST BRAINTEASERS

1. *This problem has baffled three Nobel Physics laureates—and it doesn't seem that hard!*

   Twelve balls are identical in all ways, except that one has a different weight. Three weighings on a balance scale will not only identify the odd ball but also tell whether it is heavier or lighter. How many balls must be put on each side of the scale in the first weighing, the second weighing, and the third weighing?

   A harder problem would read:

   "How would you determine in only three weighings the odd ball and whether it is heavier or lighter than the others?"

2. *On* The Tonight Show Starring Johnny Carson, *Carson spent 15 minutes trying to solve this problem and no one, including Carson, could do it!*

   A teacher shows three very bright students of a logic class three red hats and two white ones. The students are then blindfolded and the teacher puts one hat on each of their heads and the remaining hats in a closed bag. The first student removes his blindfold and is able to see only the other two students' hats. He says he cannot say for certain what the color of his own hat is.

   After hearing the first student, the second student removes her blindfold, sees the other two students' hats, and says that she cannot say for certain what the color of her own hat is. After thinking and without removing his blindfold, the last student says he knows the color of his hat. Which is false?

   Note: Any combination of A, B, C, D, and E may be the correct answer.

   (A) The third student has enough information to determine the color of his hat without removing his blindfold.

   (B) The third student's hat can be white.

   (C) The three students' hats can be the same color.

   (D) Both remaining hats in the bag can be red.

   (E) There are exactly four possible combinations of hat colors on the students' heads.

3. *This is one of most difficult geometry problems. It also "looks" easy to solve.*

   A triangle *ABC* has sides *AB* and *AC* whose lengths are equal. Suppose there is a line from *C* to side *AB* called *CD* and a line from *B* to side *AC* called *BE*. Now draw a line, *ED*. If angle *EBC* equals 60°, angle *BCD* equals 70°, angle *ABE* equals 20°, and angle *DCE* equals 10°, how many degrees is angle *EDC*? (Do this problem geometrically to get an exact answer.)

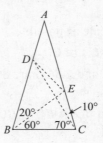

4. *This can be a real brain racker unless you know some important math strategies.*

   A ship is twice as old as the ship's boiler was when the ship was as old as the boiler is. The ratio of the boiler's age now to the ship's age now is what?

5. Suppose you can purchase donuts in boxes of 6, 9, and 20. What is the *greatest* number of donuts you *cannot* purchase?

Explanatory Answers for Level 4 Brainteasers

1. *First weighing*—four against four
   Second weighing—two against two
   Third weighing—one against one

   Try to find a set of balls as "reference" balls, none of which is the heavy or light ball.

   Note: Even though the scale may tip downward in one direction, the heavy ball may not be on the "downward" part of the scale. It may be that the lighter ball is on the upward side.

   Solution:

   Identify balls by number 1, 2, 3, 4, 5, 6, 7, 8, 9, 10, 11, 12.

   (1, 2, 3) ? (4, 5, 6) means you weigh 1, 2, 3 vs. 4, 5, 6.

   If the result of weighing is (1, 2, 3) < (4, 5, 6) it means the first group (1, 2, 3) is lighter than the second (4, 5, 6).

   If (1, 2, 3) > (4, 5, 6) it means the first group (1, 2, 3) is heavier.

   If (1, 2, 3) = (4, 5, 6) it means both groups (1, 2, 3) and (4, 5, 6) weigh the same and so all of the balls in that group are normal.

   N represents a Normal ball.

   Divide 12 balls into 3 groups (1, 2, 3, 4), (5, 6, 7, 8), (9, 10, 11, 12).

   First Weighing—Weigh (1, 2, 3, 4) ? (5, 6, 7, 8).

   Case 1:

   If after the *First Weighing* (1, 2, 3, 4) = (5, 6, 7, 8), it means that the odd ball is in (9, 10, 11, 12) and that 1, 2, 3, 4, 5, 6, 7, 8 are normal (*N*).

   Second Weighing—Weigh (*N*, 9) ? (10, 11).

   If (*N*, 9) = (10, 11) this means the odd ball is 12.

   Third Weighing—Weigh (12) ? *N*.

   If (12) > (*N*) then 12 is the heavy ball; if (12) < (*N*), then 12 is light.

   If in the *Second Weighing*, (*N*, 9) > (10, 11), then either 9 is heavy or 10 or 11 is light.

   Third Weighing—Weigh (10) ? (11).

   If (10) > (11), then (11) is light and 9 is normal. If (10) < (11), then 10 is light.

   When weighing (10) ? (11), if (10) = (11), then 9 must be heavy.

   If in the *Second Weighing*, (*N*, 9) < (10, 11), you can similarly reason that 9 is light or 10 or 11 is heavy.

   Third Weighing—Weigh (10) ? (11).

   If (10) > (11), then 10 is heavy. If (10) < (11), then 11 is heavy. If (10) = (11), then 9 is light.

   Case 2:

   If after the *First Weighing* (1, 2, 3, 4) > (5, 6, 7, 8), then you know that 9, 10, 11, 12 are normal (*N*), and one of the balls 1, 2, 3, 4 is heavy or one of the balls 5, 6, 7, 8 is light.

   Second Weighing—Weigh (*N*, 1, 2) ? (3, 4, 5).

   If (*N*, 1, 2) = (3, 4, 5) then the odd ball is in (6, 7, 8) and is lighter.

   Third Weighing—Weigh (6) ? (7).

   Pick the lightest. If (6) = (7) then 8 is light.

   If in the *Second Weighing* (*N*, 1, 2) > (3, 4, 5), (3, 4) are normal, so odd is in (1, 2, 5).

   Third Weighing—Weigh (1) ? (2).

   If (1) > (2) then 1 is heavy, if (1) < (2), then 2 is heavy, if (1) = (2), then 5 is light.

   If in the *Second Weighing* (*N*, 1, 2) < (3, 4, 5), the odd ball is in (3, 4) and is heavy, since 5 can't be heavy and (1, 2) which were in the heavy group originally, are not the heavy ones, now.

   Third Weighing—Weigh (3) ? (4). If (3) > (4), 3 is heavy. If (3) < (4), then 4 is heavy.

Case 3:

After the *First Weighing*, (1, 2, 3, 4) < (5, 6, 7, 8).

Second Weighing—Weigh (N, 1, 2) ? (3, 4, 5).

If (N, 1, 2) = (3, 4, 5), the odd ball is in (6, 7, 8) and is heavier.

Third Weighing—Weigh (6) ? (7).

Pick the heaviest. If (6) = (7) then 8 is heavy.

If in the *Second Weighing,* (N, 1, 2) > (3, 4, 5), the odd ball is in (3, 4) and is light, since according to first weighing, (5) can't be light and (1, 2) cannot be heavy.

Third Weighing—So weigh (3) ? (4). If (3) > (4), then 4 is light. If (3) < (4), then 3 is light.

If in the *Second Weighing*, (N, 1, 2) < (3, 4, 5), then either (1, 2) is light or 5 is heavy because of first weighing.

Third Weighing—So weigh (1) ? (2). If (1) > (2) then 2 is light. If (1) < (2), then 1 is light. If (1) = (2), then 5 is heavy.

2. Choice B is correct.

Think of what information you get by knowing that both the first and second students cannot figure out the color of their hats.

Detailed solution:

The color is red. The third student who is last to try his luck reasons, "If I can prove it's impossible that I have a white hat, then I must have a red hat." There are only three scenarios in which the last student could have a white hat: (1) if the first student has a red hat and the second student has a white hat, (2) if the first student has a white hat and the second student has a red hat, and (3) if both the first and second students have red hats. Scenario (1) is ruled out because the first student would have known his hat was red if the other two students had white hats, since there were only two white hats in the original bag. Scenario (2) is ruled out because the second student would have made the same deduction. Scenario (3) is ruled out because the second student would have known she was wearing a red hat if the third student was wearing a white hat, because otherwise the first student would have seen that they were both wearing white hats. But

because the second student did not know or figure out that she was wearing a red hat, the third student could not be wearing a white hat. Thus the only combinations are (where A, B, C denote first, second, and third student, respectively):

A, white; B, white; C, red

A, white; B, red; C, red

A, red; B, white; C, red

A, red; B, red; C, red

Thus Choice B is correct.

3. Choice C is correct.

Only 6 people in the nation have gotten the correct answer to this problem!

(Use Strategy 14: Draw and extend lines to make a problem easier.)

Draw the triangle as close to scale as possible.

Detailed solution:

Begin with triangle *ABC*. Label angles using the fact that the sum of the interior angles of a triangle is 180°.

(1) Draw *EF* parallel to *BC*. Then angle *DFE* = 80° because of equal corresponding angles of parallel lines.

(2) Drop a perpendicular line to *BC* from *A* hitting *BC* at *G*. Because of congruent triangles *ABG* and *AGC*, angle *BAG* = angle *CAG* = 10°.

(3) Now draw line *FC*, calling *H* the point where line *FC* intersects line *BE*. Line *AG* passes through point *H*, because of symmetry.

(4) Angle *BHC* = 60° since the rest of the angles of the triangle *BHC* are both 60°.

(5) *BE* = *FC* (because of corresponding sides of congruent triangles *FBC* and *EBC*. *BH* = *HC* (call *BH* = *b*) because triangle *BHC* is isosceles. So by subtraction, *FH* = *HE*.

(6) Since angle *FHE* = 60° (vertical angle to *BHC*), and because *FH* = *HE* from 5, angle *FHE* = angle *HEF* = 60°, so triangle *FHE* is equilateral. Thus *FE* = *FH* = *HE*. Call each of those sides *a*.

(7) Now *AF* = *AE* (because *AB* = *AC* and *FB* = *EC*, by subtraction *AF* = *AE*).

(8) Because triangle AEB is isosceles, $AE = BE = b + a$. Thus $AF = BE = b + a$ (since $AF = AE$ from 7).

(9) $BE = FC$ (congruent triangles BEC and BFC), so $AF = FC$, since $AF = BE$ from 8.

(10) Now watch this: Triangle AFH is congruent to triangle CFD because $AF = FC$; angle $AFH = 140° =$ angle CFD; angle $DCF = 10° =$ angle FAH. Thus corresponding sides of the congruent triangles AFH and triangle CFD are equal, so $FH = FD$. But $FH = FE$ from 6, so $FE = FD$.

(11) Since $FE = FD$, angle $FDE =$ angle FED and since angle $DFE = 80°$ from 1, angle $FDE = 50° =$ angle FED.

(12) But angle $FDC = 30°$, so by subtraction, angle $EDC = 20°$!

4. $3 : 4$.

(Use Strategy 2: Translate English words into math.)

Let S be the ship's age now; B is the boiler's age now; s is the ship's age then; and b is the boiler's age then. You would get:

$$S = 2b \qquad \boxed{1}$$
$$s = B \qquad \boxed{2}$$
$$\frac{B}{S} \text{ unknown} \qquad \boxed{3}$$

$B - b = S - s$, because $B - b$ and $S - s$ represent the same passage of time. $\boxed{4}$

Substituting $\boxed{1}$ in the left side of $\boxed{4}$ and $\boxed{2}$ in the right side of $\boxed{4}$, we get:

$$B - \frac{S}{2} = S - B \qquad \boxed{5}$$

Thus we get:

$$2B = \frac{3S}{2} \qquad \boxed{6}$$
$$\text{or} \quad \frac{B}{S} = \frac{3}{4} \qquad \boxed{7}$$

5. 43.

Call x the number of boxes with 6 donuts, y the number of boxes with 9 donuts, and z the number of boxes with 20 donuts. Then the total number of donuts, N, for x, y, z boxes is represented by

$$N = 6x + 9y + 20z$$
$$\text{or} \quad N = 3(2x + 3y) + 20z$$

Now $x = 0, 1, 2, 3,$ etc.; $y = 0, 1, 2, 3,$ etc.; $z = 0, 1, 2, 3,$ etc. $20z$ can be 20, 40, 60, etc.

$3(2x + 3y)$ can be 0, 6, 9, 12, 15, 18, 21, 24, 27, and any multiple of 3 thereafter.

So all the combinations become: 0, 6, 9, 12, 15, 18, 21, 24, 26, 27, 29, 30, 32, 33, 35, 36, 38, 39, 40, 41, 42, 44 (which is 20 + 24), 45, 46 (which is 40 + 6), 47 (which is 20 + 27), 48, 49 (which is 40 + 9), 50 (which is 20 + 30), 51, etc., and all consecutive numbers thereafter. The greatest number that you cannot make is 43.

Hot Prefixes and Roots

Here is a list of the most important prefixes and roots that impart a certain meaning or feeling. They can be instant clues to the meanings of more than 110,000 words.

PREFIXES

PREFIXES THAT MEAN "TO," "WITH," "BETWEEN," OR "AMONG"

Prefix	Meaning	Examples
ad, ac, af, an, ap, as, at	to, toward	adapt—to fit into adhere—to stick to attract—to draw near
com, con, co, col	with, together	combine—to bring together contact—to touch together collect—to bring together coworker—one who works together with another worker
in, il, ir, im	into	inject—to put into impose—to force into illustrate—to put into example irritate—to put into discomfort
inter	between, among	international—among nations interact—to act among the people
pro	forward, going ahead	proceed—to go forward promote—to move forward

PREFIXES THAT MEAN "BAD"

Prefix	Meaning	Examples
mal	wrong, bad	malady—illness malevolent—evil malfunction—poor function
mis	wrong, badly	mistreat—to treat badly mistake—to get wrong

PREFIXES THAT MEAN "AWAY FROM," "NOT," OR "AGAINST"

Prefix	Meaning	Examples
ab	away from	absent—not present, away abscond—to run away
de, dis	away from, down, the opposite of, apart, not	depart—to go away from decline—to turn down dislike—not to like dishonest—not honest distant—apart
ex, e, ef	out, from	exit—to go out eject—to throw out efface—to rub out, erase
in, il, ir, im	not	inactive—not active impossible—not possible illiterate—not literate irreversible—not reversible
non	not	nonsense—no sense nonstop—having no stops
un	not	unhelpful—not helpful uninterested—not interested
anti	against	antifreeze—a substance used to prevent freezing antisocial—someone who is not social
ob	against, in front of	obstacle—something that stands in the way of obstinate—inflexible

PREFIXES THAT DENOTE DISTANCE

Prefix	Meaning	Examples
circum	around	circumscribe—to write or inscribe in a circle circumspect—very careful
equ, equi	equal, the same	equalize—to make equal equitable—fair, equal
post	after	postpone—to do after postmortem—after death
pre	before	preview—a viewing that goes before another viewing prehistorical—before written history
re	back, again	retell—to tell again recall—to call back, to remember
sub	under, behind, less than	subordinate—under something else subconscious—under the consciousness
super	over, above	superimpose—to put something over something else superstar—a star greater than other stars
trans	across	transcontinental—across the continent transit—act of going across
un, uni	one	unity—oneness unanimous—sharing one view unidirectional—having one direction

ROOTS

Root	Meaning	Examples
cap, capt, cept, ceive	to take, to hold	captive—one who is held capable—to be able to take hold of things concept—an idea or thought held in mind receive—to take
cred	to believe	credible—believable credit—belief, trust
curr, curs, cours	to run	current—now in progress, running cursor—a movable indicator recourse—running for help
dic, dict	to say	indicate—to say by demonstrating diction—verbal saying
duc, duct	to lead	induce—to lead to action aquaduct—a pipe or waterway that leads water somewhere
fac, fic, fect, fy	to make, to do	facile—easy to do fiction—something that has been made up satisfy—to make happy or to fulfill affect—to have an influence on effect—to make happen or bring about
jec, ject	to throw	project—to put forward trajectory—a path of an object that has been thrown
mit, mis	to send	admit—to send in missile—something that gets sent through the air
pon, pos	to place	transpose—to place across compose—to put in place from pieces or parts deposit—to place in something
scrib, script	to write	describe—to write or tell about scripture—a written tablet
spec, spic	to look	specimen—an example to look at inspect—to look over
ten, tain	to hold	maintain—to keep up retain—to hold on to, keep (back)
ven, vent	to come	advent—a coming to, an arrival convene—to come together

APPENDIX B

Words Commonly Mistaken for Each Other

Review the following lists of words quickly and use a pencil to mark the pairs that you have trouble remembering.

Aggravate to make worse	**Irritate** to annoy
Allusion reference	**Illusion** error in vision
Arbiter a supposedly unprejudiced judge	**Arbitrary** prejudiced
Ascent upward movement	**Assent** agreement; to agree
Ascetic self-denying	**Aesthetic** pertaining to the beautiful
Ban prohibit	**Bane** woe
Canvas coarse cloth	**Canvass** examine; solicit

Capital
excellent; chief town; money;
   pertaining to death or the
   death sentence
	Capitol
	state house

Censure find fault	**Censor** purge or remove offensive passages
Complacent self-satisfied; smug	**Complaisant** kindly; submissive
Complement that which completes	**Compliment** praise
Consul diplomatic representative	**Council** group of advisors	**Counsel** advice
Contemptible despicable	**Contemptuous** scornful
Cosmopolitan sophisticated	**Metropolitan** pertaining to the city
Credible believable	**Creditable** worthy of praise
Demure pretending modesty	**Demur** hesitate; raise objection
Deprecate disapprove regretfully	**Depreciate** decline in value

Discreet	**Discrete**
judicious; prudent	separate and distinct
Disinterested	**Uninterested**
unprejudiced	not interested
Divers	**Diverse**
several	varied
Elicit	**Illicit**
extract	unlawful
Emend	**Amend**
correct a text or manuscript	improve by making slight changes
Eminent	**Imminent**
high in rank	threatening; at hand
Equable	**Equitable**
even-tempered	just
Exult	**Exalt**
rejoice	raise; praise highly
Formally	**Formerly**
in a formal manner	at a previous time
Gorilla	**Guerrilla**
large ape	mercenary
Gourmet	**Gourmand**
lover of good food	glutton
Hail	**Hale**
frozen pellets; to call; originate	strong, healthy
Healthy	**Healthful**
possessing health	bringing about health
Imply	**Infer**
indicate or suggest	draw a conclusion from
Incredible	**Incredulous**
unbelievable	unbelieving
Indigent	**Indigenous**
poor	native
Ingenious	**Ingenuous**
skillful; clever; resourceful	frank; naïve
Internment	**Interment**
imprisonment	burial
Maize	**Maze**
corn	confusing network
Martial	**Marital**
warlike	pertaining to marriage

Mendacious lying	**Meritorious** possessing merit; praiseworthy	
Personal private	**Personable** pleasant in appearance and manner	
Perspicacious shrewd; acute	**Perspicuous** clear; lucid	
Practical sensible; useful	**Practicable** timely; capable of being accomplished	
Prodigal wastefully lavish	**Prodigious** extraordinarily large	
Prophecy prediction	**Prophesy** to predict	
Provided on condition that	**Providing** furnishing; giving	
Regal royal	**Regale** entertain lavishly	
Respectfully with respect	**Respectively** in the order already suggested	
Sanction authorize	**Sanctity** holiness	
Social pertaining to human society	**Sociable** companionable; friendly	
Statue piece of sculpture	**Stature** height	**Statute** a law
Urban pertaining to the city	**Urbane** polished; suave	
Venal corrupt, mercenary	**Venial** pardonable	